Edited and Compiled by Colin Larkin

GUINNESS PUBLISHING

Dedicated to the three Steves: Winwood, Stills and Miller

First published in 1993 by
GUINNESS PUBLISHING LTD
33 London Road, Enfield, Middlesex EN2 6DJ, England

GUINNESS is a registered trademark of Guinness Publishing Ltd

British Library Cataloguing-in-Publication data
A catalogue record for this book is available from the British Library

ISBN 0-85112-727-4

Conceived, designed, edited and produced by
SQUARE ONE BOOKS LTD
Iron Bridge House, 3 Bridge Approach, Chalk Farm, London NW1 8BD
Editor and Designer: Colin Larkin
Picture Editors: Colin Larkin and John Martland
Editorial and production assistant: Susan Pipe
Special thanks to Donald McFarlan and David Roberts of Guinness Publishing
and to Guy at L&S, Peter Doggett, David Japp, John Reiss and John Eley
Logo concept: Darren Perry

This book has been produced on Apple Macintosh computers
using Quark Xpress and Microsoft Word
Image set by L & S Communications Ltd

Printed and bound in Great Britain by The Bath Press

EDITORS NOTE

The Guinness Who's Who Of Seventies Music forms a part of the multi-volume *Guinness Encyclopedia Of Popular Music*. A further 16 specialist single volumes are planned in the near future.

Already available:
The Guinness Who's Who Of Indie And New Wave Music.
The Guinness Who's Who Of Heavy Metal.
The Guinness Who's Who Of Sixties Music.
The Guinness Who's Who Of Jazz.
The Guinness Who's Who Of Country Music.
The Guinnness Who's Who Of Blues.

Having to follow a decade like the 60s was a formidable task. For many years the 70s were written off as a musically barren time as too much attention was paid to the glam/glitter rock scene of the early part of the decade. In recent years this has been redressed, now that it is clearly understood that many of the late 60s artists and bands 'came of age' in the 70s. Similarly the punk/new wave explosion of 1977, rightly shook up the industry which was becoming complacent and top heavy with too much cocaine and not enough creativity. Many of the entries selected are from 60s artists whose careers are maintained throughout the 70s and 80s. Any choice is subjective but we feel we have captured the essence of what is now seen as a vintage decade. In selecting entries for this single volume we have attempted to include as many artists as space would allow. Further suggestions and additions for the next edition will be considered by writing to the Editor. Any final list will have omissions, but I have tried to convey the spirit of the 70s with this selection. Much debate took place as to whether or not an artist like Cat Stevens should be in the 70s book in addition to the 60s volume. I felt on balance it was best not to repeat his entry, even though he was

hugely successful during the 70s. I welcome readers comments.

In the preparation of this work contributions were received from Bruce Crowther, Peter Doggett, Brian Hogg, Ian Kenyon, Colin Larkin, Spencer Leigh, John Martland, Johnny Rogan, Jeff Tamarkin, Hugh T. Wilson, Tony Burke, Rick Christian, Alan Clayson, Noel Hawks, Dave Laing, Graham Lock, Chris May, Alex Ogg, Robert Pruter, Steve Smith, John Tobler. Further contributions were received from: Mike Atherton, Alan Balfour, Michael Barnett, Lol Bell-Brown, Chris Blackford, Pamela Boniface, Keith Briggs, Michael Ian Burgess, Linton Chiswick, Paul Cross, Norman Darwin, Roy Davenport, Kevin Eden, John Eley, Per Gardin, Ian Garlinge, Mike Gavin, Andy Hamilton, Mark Hodkinson, Mark Jones, Steve Lake, Paul Lewis, Dave McAleer, Ian McCann, Toru Mitsui, Ambrose Mogg, Greg Moffitt, Nick Morgan, Michael Newman, Zbigniew Nowara, James Nye, Ian Peel, Dave Penny, John Reed, Emma Rees, Lionel Robinson, Alan Rowett, Jean Scrivener, Dave Sissons, Neil Slaven, Chris Smith, Mitch Solomons, Christopher Spencer, Jon Staines, Ray Templeton, Gerard Tierney, Pete Wadeson, Ben Watson, Pete Watson, Simon Williams and Dave Wilson.

Photographic acknowledgements: To Tony Gale of Pictorial Press, who has a fine archive of many original photographs. He supplied every picture inside this book.

I would like to warmly thank John Martland who bailed us out at a very difficult time and took to the task with care and enthusiasm and good humour. To Susan Pipe for her now familiar super-calm efficiency in putting it all together at the end. To June McLachlan and John Burton for continuing to send cuttings and obituarys. Messrs Brian Hogg, Dave

Laing, Fred Dellar, Alex Ogg and Peter Doggett for usually coming up with the right answers. To everybody at Carlin Music for making us so welcome and to Amos Biegun and Dave Carroll for their additional help. To David Japp for his professional advice and wicked practical jokes. To John Reiss for becoming so involved. To David Roberts, and the art department at Guinness, Sallie Collins and Sarah Silvé for their production work and for Donald McFarlan's receptive eardrum. To Mark Cohen, the continuing vital link in the chain and Suite Judy and Ian 'Guitar' Slater whose free services include pointing out omissions, errors and supplying Glenmorangie and Laphroaig. To Ben Larkin for work on the database and encouragement from the other Ben and Trevor. Finally to Laura, Tom, Dan, Overseen, Ed, Ariel and Goldie, who can begin to see the real possibility of a holiday together.

Colin Larkin, February 1993

A Foot In Coldwater

This prolific rock band produced four albums during their five-year career. Canadian in origin, they comprised Alex Machin (vocals), Paul Naumann (guitar), Bob Horne (keyboards), Hugh Leggat (bass) and Danny Taylor (drums). Concentrating on a traditional approach to songwriting, their work was characterized by Machin's expressive vocals and Naumann's melodic guitar lines. Leggat went on to form the Rolling Stones-influenced Private Eye, and later a progressive outfit under his own surname.
Albums: *A Foot In Coldwater* (1972), *Second Foot In Coldwater* (1973), *All Around Us* (1974), *Breaking Through* (1977).

A Taste Of Honey

A popular disco/R&B group of the late 70s and early 80s, A Taste Of Honey was formed in Los Angeles, California, USA in 1972 when an earlier band featuring Janice Marie Johnson (vocals/guitar/bass) and Perry Kimble (keyboards) disbanded. After numerous personnel changes the group solidified as a quartet featuring Johnson, Kimble, Hazel Payne (guitar/vocals) and Donald Johnson (drums). The group was signed to Capitol Records and in 1978 recorded the US number 1 and UK number 3 dance single, 'Boogie Oogie Oogie'. The self-titled album from which the single was drawn reached the US Top 10 and was certified platinum. They became the first black group to win a Best New Artist Grammy at the 1979 awards. In 1980 they were reduced to a duo of Johnson and Payne. A remake of the 1963 Kyu Sakamoto hit 'Sukiyaki', with new English words completely unrelated to the original Japanese lyric, became their only other major US chart hit, reaching number 3 in 1981. The pair split up in 1984, although they did briefly revisit the UK charts in 1985 with a remix version of their initial hit.
Albums: *A Taste Of Honey* (1978), *Another Taste* (1979), *Twice As Sweet* (1980), *Ladies Of The Eighties* (1982).

Abba

The acronym Abba, coined in 1973, represented the coming together of four leading figures in Swedish pop. Agnetha Falkstog (b. 5 April 1950) had achieved pop success in her country with the 1968 hit 'I Was So In Love'; Bjorn Ulvaeus (b. 25 April 1945) had appeared with several groups, most notably the folk-influenced Hootenanny Singers, before teaming up with Benny Andersson (b. 16 December 1946) in the popular beat group, the Hep Stars. The one non-Swede in the line-up, Anni-Frid Lyngstad had also achieved some success as pop chanteuse Frida. Under the guidance of Scandinavian svengali Stig Andersson, Bjorn and Benny left the Hep Stars and joined forces for one album, *Lycka*. The marriage of Bjorn and Agnetha, followed later by that of Benny and Anni-Frid, had laid the romantic and musical foundations of the Abba concept. The Eurovision Song Contest served as a backdrop to their international ambitions and after Anni-Frid's tentative entry as a soloist in 1971, the newly-named quartet represented their country with the infectious 'Ring Ring' in 1973. They returned the following year with the more polished and bouncy 'Waterloo', which not only won the contest, but topped the UK charts and, amazingly, for a Eurovision entry, infiltrated the US Top 10.

The middling success of the re-released 'Ring Ring' and singalong 'I Do I Do I Do' provided little indication of the chart domination that was to follow. For in September 1975, Abba returned with the worldwide hit 'SOS', a powerhouse pop production highlighted by immaculately-executed counter harmonies and an infectiously melodic arrangement. These classic ingredients of the Abba sound were ably evinced on their first trilogy of consecutive chart-toppers, 'Mamma Mia', 'Fernando' and 'Dancing Queen'. The last also brought them their only US number 1 and precipitated their rise to pop superstardom with sales unmatched since the golden age of the Beatles. Firmly in control of their destinies, both on the artistic and commercial front, the group undertook a world tour in 1977 most remarkable for its extravagant use of costume, sets and orchestration. That same year they celebrated a second trilogy of UK chart-toppers ('Knowing Me Knowing You', 'The Name Of The Game' and 'Take A Chance On Me') whose haunting grace was enhanced by some of the finest promotional videos of the period. Although their foray into film - *Abba: The Movie* - proved less memorable, there was no doubting their commercial acumen. With international stardom assured, they began the 80s with two more UK number 1s, 'The Winner Takes It All' and 'Super Trouper', taking their

Abba

chart-topping tally to an impressive nine in under six years. Although the dissolution of both marriages in the group threatened their unity, they maintained a high profile, not least on the international business circuit where they eclipsed the car manufacturers Volvo as Sweden's largest earners of foreign currency during 1982. With little left to achieve within their chosen genre, they elected to dissolve the group that same year. Agnetha Faltskog and Anni-Frid (Frida) subsequently went solo, but found chart success elusive. Bjorn and Benny, meanwhile, concentrated on composing, and enjoyed a productive relationship with Tim Rice, culminating in London's West End musical *Chess*.
Albums: *Waterloo* (1974), *Abba* (1975), *Arrival* (1976), *The Album* (1978), *Voulez-Vous* (1979), *Super Trouper* (1980), *The Visitors* (1981), *Gracias Por La Musica* (1981), *Thank You For The Music* (1983), *Abba Live* (1986). Compilations: *Greatest Hits* (1976), *Greatest Hits, Volume 2* (1979), *The Magic Of Abba* (1980), *The Singles - The First Ten Years* (1982), *The Abba Special* (1983), *I Love Abba* (1984), *Absolute Music* (1988), *Gold: The Greatest Hits* (1992). Solo: Agnetha Faltskog, *Wrap Your Arms Around Me* (1983), *I Stand Alone* (1988). Frida, *Something's Going On* (1982).
Further reading: *Abba In Their Own Words*, Rosemary York.

Abrahams, Mick

b. 7 April 1943, Luton, Bedfordshire, England. Following a musical apprenticeship in the early 60s with Neil Christian, Dickie Pride and the Toggery Five, guitarist Abrahams made a career breakthrough with Jethro Tull and Blodwyn Pig. He embarked on a largely unsuccessful solo career in 1971. His *Mick Abrahams* and *At Last* as the Mick Abrahams Band included Walt Monahan (bass), Bob Sergeant (keyboards/vocals) and Ritchie Dharma (drums). Abrahams subsequently made a guitar tuition album that eventually outsold his previous catalogue, although he left the music business in 1975. An outstanding player, Abrahams contributed (albeit briefly) to the blues boom of the late 60s. Sadly his career has not matched his undoubted potential. In 1989 it was announced that Abrahams was reforming Blodwyn Pig, and he now continues to perform with the band and as a solo acoustic blues performer. *All Said And Done* demonstrated a mature musician playing his blend of anglo-blues music with ease.
Albums: *Mick Abrahams* (1971), *At Last* (1972), *A Musical Evening With Mick Abrahams* (1971), *All*

Said And Done (1991).

AC/DC

This theatrical Australian hard rock band was formed in 1973 by Malcolm Young (b. 6 January 1953, Glasgow, Scotland; rhythm guitar) after the demise of his previous outfit, the Velvet Underground (no relation to the US group). Young, whose elder brother George had already achieved stardom in Australia as a member of the Easybeats, also enlisted his younger brother Angus Young (b. 31 March 1959, Glasgow, Scotland; guitar). Their sister suggested that Angus wear his school uniform on stage, a gimmick that rapidly became a trademark. The two brothers made their debut appearance in a bar in Sydney, along with Dave Evans (vocals), Larry Van Knedt (bass) and Colin Burgess (drums). In 1974, the Young brothers and Evans moved to Melbourne, where Mark Evans (bass) and Phil Rudd (drums) joined the band. Another immigrant from the UK, Bon Scott (b. Ronald Scott, 9 July 1946, Kirriemuir, Scotland, d. 20 February 1980; vocals), graduated from being the band's chauffeur to becoming their vocalist when Dave Evans refused to go on stage one night. Scott had previously recorded - originally as a drummer - with two Australian pop bands, the Valentines and Fraternity. AC/DC's first two albums, *High Voltage* and *TNT*, were produced by George Young and his writing partner, former Easybeat, Harry Vanda. Neither of them was issued outside Australia, though Atlantic in Britain did issue a selection of material from both records under the title *High Voltage* in 1976 - by which time bassist Mark Evans had been replaced by Cliff Williams. Once AC/DC began to tour outside Australia, the band quickly amassed a cult following, as much for the unashamed gimmickry of its live show as for its furious, frequently risque brand of hard rock. *Let There Be Rock* broke them as a chart act in the UK, but it was *Highway To Hell* in 1979 which established them as international stars. The band's first album with producer Mutt Lange, also proved to be their last with Bon Scott. On 20 February 1980, after a night of heavy drinking, he was left unconscious in a friend's car, and was later found to be dead, having choked on his own vomit. The coroner recorded a verdict of death by misadventure.
Scott's death threatened the band's future, but his replacement, former Geordie lead singer Brian Johnson (b. 5 October 1947, Newcastle, England), proved more than equal to the task. His first album with the band, *Back In Black*, reached number 1 in

the UK and Australia, and spawned the hit single 'Rock 'n' Roll Ain't Noise Pollution'. 1981 saw the release of *For Those About To Rock*, plus the band's first headlining appearance at the Castle Donington festival and two Top 20 UK singles. After *Flick Of The Switch* in 1983, drummer Phil Rudd left the band, to be replaced by Simon Wright - who in turn departed to join Dio in 1990. His replacement was Chris Slade (ex-Firm and Gary Moore). In keeping with their superstar status, AC/DC maintained an increasingly relaxed schedule through the 80s, touring to support each carefully-spaced album release. *The Razor's Edge* in 1990 proved to be one of their most successful albums, producing a Top 20 UK hit, 'Thunderstruck'. With Brian Johnson long having buried the ghost of Bon Scott, the band shows no signs of varying its winning musical formula.
Albums: *High Voltage* (1974 - Australia only), *TNT* (1975 - Australia only), *High Voltage* (1976), *Dirty Deeds Done Dirt Cheap* (1976), *Let There Be Rock* (1977), *Powerage* (1978), *If You Want Blood* (1978), *Highway To Hell* (1979), *Back In Black* (1980), *For Those About To Rock* (1981), *Flick Of The Switch* (1983), *Fly On The Wall* (1985), *Who Made Who* (1986), *Blow Up Your Video* (1988), *The Razor's Edge* (1990), *Live* (1992).

Ace

Formed in the UK during December 1972 and originally called Ace Flash And The Dynamos - quickly abbreviated after a couple of gigs - Ace comprised of Paul Carrack (b. 22 April 1951, Sheffield, Yorkshire, England; keyboards/vocals), Alan 'Bam' King (b. Kentish Town, London, England; guitar/vocals), Phil Harris (b. Muswell Hill, London, England; guitar/vocals), Terry 'Tex' Comer (b. 23 February 1949, Burnley, Lancashire, England; bass) and Steve Witherington (b. 26 December 1953, Enfield, Middlesex, England; drums). All members were assembled from known bands and were all solid musicians. Carrack, Witherington and Comer came from Warm Dust and King and Harris arrived via Mighty Baby, whose antecedents were the highly regarded 60s group, the Action. Ace became one of the darlings of the UK pub-rock circuit with their polished funky pop music. Before the recording of their first album, ex-Bees Make Honey drummer Fran Byrne had replaced Witherington. The album, *Five-A-Side*, was a credible debut. The single 'How Long', culled from this record, gave them an enormous hit that they were never able to emulate. It was a perfectly crafted song with a hypnotic bass introduction followed by Carrack's sweet electric piano. The simple tale of infidelity captured people's attention and it became a Top 20 hit in the UK and reached the Top 3 in the USA. They eventually moved to America but disbanded in July 1977 when most of the remaining members joined Frankie Miller's band.
Albums: *Five-A-Side* (1974), *Time For Another* (1975), *No Strings* (1977). Compilation: *The Best Of Ace* (1988).

Ackerman, William

b. November 1949, Germany. He moved to California at the age of nine when he was adopted by a Stanford professor and his wife. Ackerman started playing the acoustic guitar at 12, shunning the electric guitar and preferring open, modal tunings. He was influenced by John Fahey, Leo Kottke and Robbie Basho. Following a home-made recording, the entrepreneurial Ackerman started the low-key Windham Hill Records in 1976, together with his friend and future wife Anne Robinson. As he built up the label's roster he released several relaxing and sparse new-age albums of guitar music. Tracks like 'The Bricklayer's Beautiful Daughter' from *Passage* and 'Visiting' from *Past Light* are examples of evocative melodic excursions. Occasionally Ackerman's guitar is accompanied by cello, piano or violin, but the music remains hauntingly uncluttered. Alongside his own productions he simultaneously acted as producer to his other artists and led numerous tours as he spread the word about the innovative Windham Hill. His early signings and successes were with George Winston, Michael Hedges and Alex de Grassi. As the label has grown Ackerman's own musical output has slowed as he takes more time being father to the Windham Hill family, which has developed into one of the world's leading new-age record labels.
Albums: *In Search Of The Turtle's Navel* (1976), *It Takes A Year* (1977), *Childhood And Memory* (c.1979), *Passage* (1981), *Past Light* (1983), *Conferring With The Moon* (1986), *Imaginary Roads* (1990).

Addrisi Brothers

Don b. 1939, California, USA and Dick Addrisi were a Californian-based pop duo who recorded for over two decades, but are best remembered as songwriters for their composition, the gentle ballad, 'Never My Love', which was a US number 2 in 1967 for the Association. As singers, they first charted in the US in 1959 with 'Cherrystone' on

Del-Fi, the west coast label that also recorded Ritchie Valens. They later recorded without success for various labels, and it was not until 1972, signed to Columbia, that they re-appeared in the US chart and had their first Top 30 hit with 'We've Got To Get It On Again'. Five years later, at the height of the disco craze, they scored their third and biggest hit with 'Slow Dancin' Don't Turn Me On' on Buddah Records, the label on which they also had a minor hit with their own version of their classic composition 'Never My Love'. They also recorded less successfully on Bell, Private Stock, Elektra and Scotti Brothers. Many of their singles were released in the UK but none achieved chart status. Don Addrisi died from cancer in 1984 aged 45.
Albums: *We've Got To Get It On Again* (1972), *Addrisi Brothers* (1977).

Adverts

The Adverts first came to prominence in 1976 at the celebrated London punk venue, the Roxy Club. Fronted by vocalist Tim 'TV' Smith and Gaye Advert (vocals/bass), the line-up was completed with Howard Pickup (guitar) and Laurie Driver (drums). Damned guitarist Brian James was so impressed by their performance that he offered them a support slot, as well as introducing them to the hip new wave label, Stiff. On tour they were initially promoted with the witty poster: 'The Adverts can play one chord, the Damned can play three. Come and see all four at . . .' Their debut single, the self-effacingly titled 'One Chord Wonders' was well received, but it was their second outing that attracted controversy and chart fame. 'Gary Gilmore's Eyes', a song based on the death-row criminal who had requested permission to donate his eyes to science, was a macabre but euphoric slice of punk/pop which catapulted the Adverts into the UK Top 20. One of the first punk groups to enjoy commercial success, the quartet also boasted the first female punk star in Gaye Advert. Despite some tabloid newspaper publicity, the next single, 'Safety In Numbers' failed to chart, though its successor 'No Time To Be 21' reached number 34. The group barely had time to record their debut album, *Crossing The Red Sea With The Adverts* (1978) before Laurie Driver was ousted and replaced by former Chelsea/Generation X drummer John Towe, who himself left shortly afterwards, succeeded by Rod Latter. Changing record labels, personnel problems and unsuitable production dogged their progress while *Cast Of Thousands* (1979) was largely ignored. On 27

October 1979, with a line-up comprising Smith, Dave Sinclair, (drums), Mel Weston (keyboards), Eric Russell (guitar) and former Doctors Of Madness bassist, Colin Stoner, the Adverts gave their last performance at Slough College of Art. The group spawned one notable offshoot: TV Smith's Explorers.
Albums: *Crossing The Red Sea With The Adverts* (1978), *Cast Of Thousands* (1979).

Aerosmith

One of the USA's most popular hard-rock acts, Aerosmith was formed in 1970 when vocalist Steven Tyler (b. Steven Victor Tallarico, 26 March 1948, New York, USA; vocals) joined Joe Perry (b. 10 September 1950, Boston, Massachusetts, USA; guitar) and Tom Hamilton (b. 31 December 1951, Colorado Springs, Colorado, USA; bass) in Chain Reaction, an aspiring New Hampshire-based group. Joey Kramer (b. 21 June 1950, New York, USA; drums) and Ray Tabano (guitar) completed the original line-up, but the latter was quickly replaced by Brad Whitford (b. 23 February 1952, Winchester, Massachusetts, USA). Their popularity throughout the Boston area led to a recording deal with Columbia/CBS Records, and in 1973 Aerosmith secured a minor chart place with their self-named debut album. Although its attendant single, 'Dream On', initially peaked at number 59, it became a Top 10 hit when reissued in 1976. *Get Your Wings* introduced a fruitful working relationship with producer Jack Douglas. Nationwide tours established the quintet as a major attraction, a position consolidated by the highly successful *Toys In The Attic*, which has sold in excess of six million copies. A fourth album, *Rocks*, achieved platinum status within months of its release. Aerosmith maintained their pre-eminent position with *Draw The Line* and the powerful *Live! Bootleg*, but despite popular acclaim, failed to gain the approbation of many critics who dubbed the group 'derivative' particularly of Led Zeppelin. Tyler's physical resemblance to Mick Jagger, and his foil-like relationship with guitarist Perry, also inspired comparisons with the Rolling Stones, with whom they shared musical reference points.
In 1978 Aerosmith undertook a US tour of smaller, more intimate venues in an attempt to decelerate their rigorous schedule. They appeared in the ill-fated film of *Sgt. Pepper's Lonely Hearts Club Band*, and although their rousing version of 'Come Together' reached the US Top 30, tension between Tyler and Perry proved irreconcilable. The guitarist left the group following the release of

the disappointing *Night In The Ruts* and subsequently founded the Joe Perry Project. Jimmy Crespo joined Aerosmith in 1980, but the following year Brad Whitford left to pursue a new career with former Ted Nugent band member, Derek St Holmes. Newcomer Rick Dufay debuted on *Rock In A Hard Place*, but this lacklustre set failed to capture the fire of the group's classic recordings.

Contact between the group and Perry and Whitford was re-established during a 1984 tour. Antagonisms were set aside, and the following year, the quintet's most enduring line-up was performing together again. *Done With Mirrors* was a tentative re-embarkation, after which Tyler and Perry underwent a successful rehabilitation programme to rid themselves of drug and alcohol dependencies, synonymous with the group's hedonistic lifestyle. In 1986 they accompanied rappers Run DMC on 'Walk This Way', an Aerosmith song from *Toys In The Attic* and a former US Top 10 entry in its own right. The collaboration was an international hit, rekindling interest in Aerosmith's career. *Permanent Vacation* became one of their best-selling albums, and the first to enter the UK chart, while the highly-acclaimed *Pump*, emphasized their revitalization. Feted by a new generation of acts, including Guns N' Roses, the quintet are now seen as elder statesmen, but recent recordings show them leading by example.

Albums: *Aerosmith* (1973), *Get Your Wings* (1974), *Toys In The Attic* (1975), *Rocks* (1976), *Draw The Line* (1977), *Live! Bootleg* (1978), *Night In The Ruts* (1979), *Rock In A Hard Place* (1982), *Done With Mirrors* (1985), *Permanent Vacation* (1987), *Pump* (1989). Compilations: *Greatest Hits* (1980), *Classics Live* (1986), *Anthology* (1988).

Airforce

Formed in 1970 by drummer Ginger Baker, this capacious ensemble included Steve Winwood (keyboards) and Ric Grech (bass), ex-colleagues from the 'supergroup' Blind Faith. The initial Airforce line-up also featured two of Baker's early mentors, the mighty Graham Bond (saxophone/keyboards/vocals) and Phil Seaman (drums), as well as Denny Laine (guitar/vocals), Chris Wood (saxophone), Harold McNair (flute), Bud Beadle (horns), Remi Kabaka (percussion) and Diane Stewart (Bond's wife) (backing vocals). Although *Airforce* included the unit's promising, if ragged, interpretation of the Peter Yarrow and Paul Stookey song, 'Man Of Constant Sorrow', the set

was marked by the leader's predilection for lengthy percussive interludes. Bond's guttural jazz-rock was another influential factor in a largely self-indulgent approach which precluded commercial success. The departures of Winwood, Wood, McNair, Kabaka and Seaman undermined an already unstable act and although the remains were augmented by eight new members, *Airforce 2* was a largely undistinguished collection. Having dissolved the band, Baker moved to Lagos to study African drumming, while Bond and Stewart pursued elements of the Airforce sound in a new venture, Holy Magick.

Albums: *Airforce* (1970), *Airforce 2* (1970).

Akkerman, Jan

b. 24 December 1946, Amsterdam, The Netherlands. When Akkerman surfaced in 1973 as Best Guitarist in a *Melody Maker* poll, it was the public zenith of a professional career that started in Amsterdam in 1958 as one of Johnny And The Cellar Rockers. Their drummer, Pierre Van Der Linden, later played with Akkerman in the Hunters - who owed much to the Shadows artistically - during the guitarist's five years of study at the city's Music Lyceum from which he graduated with a catholic taste that embraced mainstream pop, Latin, medieval and the music of Frank Zappa among leading preferences. With Van Der Linden, Bert Ruiter (bass) and Kaz Lux (vocals) he formed Brainbox, a hard rock outfit whose only album (featuring the single, 'Down Man') was issued on Parlophone in 1969. For his keen participation in rehearsals with the nascent Focus, Brainbox dismissed Akkerman who, after 1971's *In And Out Of Focus*, asked Van Der Linden to join him in a new group for which it made sense to retain the name Focus on recruiting that outfit's Thijs Van Leer and Cyril Havermans. Among the major factors in the band's success over the next few years were Akkerman's powers of improvisation on his trademark Les Paul guitar and his skill as an arranger. Gilding it too was critical acclaim for his solo albums - although the first, *Profile*, was simply an accumulation of tracks taped during the interval between Brainbox and Focus. Orchestrated by Columbia University professor of music, George Flynn, *Tabernakel* was a more ambitious affair, containing Jan's developing dexterity on the lute, and guest appearances by Tim Bogart and Carmine Appice.

Suddenly unhappy with their overall musical drift and tired of the treadmill of the road, Akkerman left Focus in March 1976 to begin sessions with

Lux for what would become *Eli*. Several more jazz fusion collections would follow including the lushly orchestrated *Arunjuez* and a 1979 live set. During the 80s, many Akkerman albums reached only Dutch shops until re-released by Charly for the UK market. Although his periodic reunions with Focus have attracted most attention, he also recorded the albums *The Talisman* (1988) and *To Oz And Back* (1989) as part of Forcefield with Ray Fenwick (ex-Spencer Davis Group) and Cozy Powell before retracing a solo path with *The Noise Of Art* for Miles Copeland's IRS label.
Albums: *Profile* (1973), *Tabernakel* (1974), *Eli* (1977), *Jan Akkerman* (1978), *Arunjuez* (1978), *Live* (1979), *3* (1980), *It Could Happen To You* (1985), *Can't Stand Noise* (1986), *Pleasure Point* (1987), *The Noise Of Art* (1990).

Albert, Morris

b. Morris Albert Kaisermann. Although Albert was born in Brazil, most listeners to his one and only hit assumed that he was French. The musically gifted Morris wrote 'Feelings', a slow ballad in the romantic style of Sacha Distel and Julio Iglesias which became a major worldwide hit in 1975. The song was later used as the theme music to an Italian tragi-romantic film. The subsequent album found similar success, but since then he has joined the one-hit-wonder club. A decade after the song was first released, Albert found himself losing a case of plagiarism. This now notorious song was taken from 'Pour Toi' by French composer Louis Gaste. Not only did Morris lose the case, but he parted with £250,000 as a settlement. He is still actively performing in Brazil, but is understandably reticent about releasing any new songs.
Albums: *Feelings* (1975), *Morris Albert* (1976).

Alberto Y Lost Trios Paranoias

This Manchester-based rock comedy troupe in the vein of the Bonzo Dog Doo-Dah Band and National Lampoon, was formed in 1973 by two former members of Greasy Bear; Chris 'C.P.' Lee (vocals/guitar) and Bruce Mitchell (drums) with Les Prior (vocals), Jimmy Hibbert (vocals/bass), Bob Harding (vocals/guitar/bass), Simon White (steel guitar/guitar), Tony Bowers (bass/guitar) and Ray 'Mighty Mongo' Hughes (second drummer). The group mercilessly parodied the major rock names of the 70s - 'Anadin' was a reworking of Lou Reed's 'Heroin'/'Sweet Jane'. As with most comedy ensembles, the Albertos belied their comic aspirations by their exemplary musicianship, but by the time it came to committing to record their finely-honed act, the artists they had pilloried had ceased to become valid targets and the album flopped. The follow-up in 1977, *Italians From Outer Space*, went some way to re-establishing the Albertos' reputation, but once more the majority of songs were more miss than hit. That same year, the easy targets of the early 70s were put aside with the ascent of punk rock and the Albertos' highly acclaimed stage performance of C.P. Lee's rock play, *Sleak* at London's Royal Court Theatre, presented the story of the manipulation of an innocent Norman Sleak into giving the ultimate in rock performance - onstage suicide, giving birth to 'Snuff Rock'. The play's performances were punctuated by the comic disc jockey role by Les Prior, quite possibly his finest performance. The accompanying EP *Snuff Rock*, released on Stiff, poked fun at the punk rock phenomenon, targeting the Sex Pistols ('Gobbing On Life'), the Damned ('Kill') and the Clash ('Snuffin' Like That') as well as the myriad of reggae bands in 'Snuffin' In A Babylon'. For once the Albertos act was successfully transferred to vinyl. They hit the UK Top 50 with the Status Quo spoof, 'Heads Down No Nonsense Mindless Boogie' in 1978. Chas Jankel and Roger Ruskin Spear assisted the Albertos on their last album, *Skite*. The group soldiered on into the 80s taking *Sleak* to Broadway as well as producing a less successful stage production entitled, *Never Mind The Bullocks*. The death of Les Prior on 31 January 1980 from leukaemia left a large gap in the group, and although his illness had limited him to rare performances in his final years, his comic inspirations were sorely missed. On folding, Mitchell joined Vini Reilly in Durutti Column. Hibbert made an unsuccessful attempt to launch a heavy metal career with *Heavy Duty* (1980), but later found success as the writer and voice character to the children's television cartoon, *Count Duckula*. Lee made a successful stage appearance portraying the hip-beat poet Lord Buckley as well as releasing on cassette only, under the name of the C.P. Lee Mystery Guild, *Radio Sweat* (1981) a spoof on commercial radio stations. Bowers joined Durutti Column, and later Simply Red. There was a brief, but unsuccessful re-formation, as the Mothmen.
Albums: *Alberto Y Lost Trios Paranoias* (1976), *Italians From Outer Space* (1977), *Skite* (1978). Compilation: *The Best Of The Albertos* (1991).

Alessi

Formerly members of Barnaby Bye along with ex-Blues Magoos singer Peppy Castro, American

Alessi Brothers

brothers Billy and Bobby Alessi sprang to fame in 1977 with the UK Top 10 single, 'Oh Lori'. This sumptuous slice of harmony pop evoked the carefree, summertime atmosphere of a more innocent era. Although subsequent releases continued in a similar vein, they lacked the charm of that initial success. The duo were signed to producer Quincy Jones' Qwest label in 1982, but this made little difference to Alessi's subsequent commercial fortunes.
Albums: *Alessi* (1977), *All For A Reason* (1978), *Driftin'* (1978), *Words And Music* (1979), *Long Time Friends* (1982).

Alternative TV
Formed in 1977, ATV was the brainchild of Mark Perry, the editor of Britain's seminal punk fanzine, *Sniffin' Glue*. The original line-up featured Perry (vocals), Alex Fergusson (b. 16 December 1952, Glasgow, Scotland; guitar), Micky Smith (bass) and John Towe (ex-Generation X, drums), but this unstable group later underwent several changes. Although ATV completed several albums throughout their career, they are best remembered for a series of uncompromising singles, including their self-effacing debut, 'Love Lies Limp' (free with *Sniffin' Glue*) and the declamatory 'How Much Longer?'. A disillusioned Perry abandoned the group in 1979 in favour of the Good Missionaries and subsequent projects, namely the

Door And The Window and the Reflections. He returned to recording under the ATV banner in 1981 and continued to do so sporadically throughout the 80s. Fergusson went on to join Psychic TV, up until 1986, subsequently turning his hand to producing for the Gaye Bykers On Acid and the Popguns.
Albums: *The Image Has Cracked* (1978), with Here And Now *What You See Is What You Are* (1978), *Vibing Up The Senile Man* (1979), *Live At The Rat Club '77* (1979), *Strange Kicks* (1981), *Peep Show* (1987), *Dragon Love* (1990). Compilations: *Action Time Vision* (1980), *Splitting In Two* (1989).

Althia And Donna
Jamaican schoolgirls Althia Forest and Donna Reid were 17 and 18 years old, respectively, when their catchy, novelty hit 'Uptown Top Ranking' on the independent Lightning label, hit the top of the charts in their home country. Their producer Joe Gibson had supplied the tune and the girls were responsible for the patois lyrics, complete with girlish yelps in the background. The infectious tune and puzzling lyrics caught the attention of the British record buying public in 1978 and the record went to number 1. Without the backing of a major record company, the duo found it impossible to produce an equally effective follow-up and went into the annals of pop history as chart-topping one-hit wonders.

Album: *Uptown Top Ranking* (1978).

Amazing Blondel

Formed in 1969 by John Gladwin (vocals/guitar/woodwind) and Terry Wincott (vocals/guitar/percussion), former members of Lincolnshire rock group, Methuselah. The duo completed their debut album with the assistance of session guitarist 'Big' Jim Sullivan, before switching labels from Bell Records to Island. Edward Baird (guitar/lute) joined the group in April 1970 as they honed a peculiarly English direction, embracing the music of the Elizabethan and Tudor periods. *Evensong* and *Fantasia Lindum* reflected this interest, although the trio also acquired an unsavoury reputation for a stage act that offset their scholarly music with 'off-colour' jokes. Gladwin left the group following the release of *England 72*, and the 'Amazing' prefix was then dropped from their name. Wincott and Baird continued to record throughout the 70s, augmented by a series of well-known musicians including Steve Winwood, Mick Ralphs and several members of Free, a group that had proved instrumental in introducing Blondel to Island. William Murray (drums) and Mick Feat (guitar) joined the duo for *Mulgrave Street*, their first release for DJM Records, but the unit's popularity withered in the wake of this rockier perspective. Wincott was the sole remaining original member to appear on *Live In Tokyo*, after which Blondel was dissolved.
Albums: *The Amazing Blondel And A Few Faces* (1970), *Evensong* (1970), *Fantasia Lindum* (1971), *England 72* (1972), *Blondel* (1973), *Mulgrave Street* (1974), *Inspiration* (1975), *Bad Dreams* (1976), *Live In Tokyo* (1977). Compilation: *Mulgrave Street/Inspiration* (c.70s).

Amboy Dukes

Originally from Detroit, Michigan, USA, the Amboy Dukes - John Drake (vocals), Ted Nugent (lead guitar), Steve Farmer (rhythm guitar), Rick Lober (keyboards), Bill White (bass) and Dave Palmer (drums) - achieved notoriety for their rendition of 'Baby Please Don't Go', which took Them's classic version as its inspiration, but added Ted Nugent's snarling guitar. A US Top 20 hit, its brashness set the tone for the group's subsequent albums on which Farmer's rather pretentious lyrics often undermined the music on offer. Frequent changes in personnel (Drake, Lorber and White were replaced, in turn, by Rusty Day, Andy Solomon and Greg Arama), made little difference to the Amboy Dukes' development as the group increasingly became an outlet for Nugent's pyrotechnics. He unveiled a new line-up in 1974 with *Call Of The Wild*, the first of two albums recorded for Frank Zappa's Discreet label. The guitarist then abandoned the band's name altogether and embarked on a solo career.
Albums: *The Amboy Dukes* (1968), *Journey To The Centre Of The Mind* (1968), *Migration* (1969), *Marriage On The Rocks* (1970), *Survival Of The Fittest* (c.70s), *Call Of The Wild* (1974), *Tooth, Fang And Claw* (1975).

Ambrosia

Formed in Los Angeles, California, USA in 1970, this group consisted of David Pack (guitar/vocals), Joe Puerta (bass/vocals), Burleigh Drummond (drums) and Christopher North (keyboards). The group was discovered by Zubin Mehta, conductor of the Los Angeles Philharmonic Orchestra, which included them as part of an 'All-American Dream Concert' in 1971. The group was signed to 20th Century Records in 1975 and charted that summer with the single 'Holdin' On To Yesterday' and a self-titled album. A second 1975 chart single, 'Nice, Nice, Very Nice', was inspired by a book by Kurt Vonnegut, Jr. Ambrosia were featured in the film *All This And World War II* in 1977, performing the Beatles' 'Magical Mystery Tour', which as a single reached the US Top 40. Despite the departure of North from the line-up, their real breakthrough came in 1978 when they switched to Warner Brothers Records, with a US number 3 single, 'How Much I Feel'. They matched that chart position in 1980 with 'Biggest Part Of Me'. After two lesser hits and another album, Ambrosia faded, but individual members remain active as session musicians, notably as harmony vocalists and in production.
Albums: *Ambrosia* (1975), *Somewhere I've Never Travelled* (1976), *Life Beyond LA* (1978), *One Eighty* (1980), *Road Island* (1982).

Anderson, Moira

b. 5 June 1940, Kirkintilloch, Scotland. Soprano vocalist Anderson rose to prominence in Scottish entertainment circles as an interpreter of the country's traditional music. Although drawing material from folk, the singer's work was the subject of MOR arrangements, as evinced on *Moira Anderson's Scotland*, in which she was accompanied by an orchestra conducted by Peter Knight. Later recordings encompassed popular standards and light opera, notably those of Gilbert And Sullivan, but the artist's forte remained the songs of her homeland. A popular figure on British television, Moira Anderson has made regular appearances on religious programmes and was later awarded an OBE for her services to the music industry.

Albums: *Moira Anderson's Scotland, Moira Anderson Sings, These Are My Songs* (1970), *This Is Moira Anderson* (1971), *A Rosebud By My Early Walk* (1973), *At The End Of The Day* (1974), *The Auld Scotch Songs* (1975), *Moira Anderson Sings The Ivor Novello Songbook* (1976), *Someone Wonderful* (1978), *A Star For Sunday* (1979), *Favourite Scottish Songs* (1980), *Golden Memories* (1981), *Moira Anderson Sings Operetta* (1985), *The Love Of God* (1986), *Moira - In Love* (1987), *A Land For All Seasons* (1988). Compilations: *The World Of Moira Anderson Volume 1* (1974), *The World Of Moira Anderson Volume 2* (1974), *The World Of Moira Anderson Volume 3* (1975), *The World Of Moira Anderson Volume 4* (1976), *The World Of Moira Anderson Volume 5* (1976), *Focus On Moira Anderson* (1978), *Sunday Songs* (1978).

April Wine

Formed in 1969 in Montreal, Quebec, Canada, this hard-rock group became an immediate success. After fluctuating line-ups, they arrived at steady membership by the late 70s, including original lead singer Myles Goodwyn (b. 23 June 1948, Halifax, Nova Scotia, Canada), Brian Greenway (b. 1 October 1951; guitar), Gary Moffet (b. 22 June 1949; guitar), Steve Lang (b. 24 March 1949; bass) and Jerry Mercer (b. 27 April 1939; drums). Among their first admirers were former Rascals members Dino Dinelli and Gene Cornish, who produced some early material for the group. The ensemble began achieving success in the USA after it had already established itself as a platinum act in Canada. Eventually, April Wine placed three Top 40 singles and five albums in the US charts. Their greatest commercial successes were the gold album *Harder...Faster* and the platinum *The Nature Of The Beast*.

Albums: *April Wine* (1972), *Electric Jewels* (1973), *On Record* (1974), *Live* (1974), *Stand Back* (1975), *The Whole World's Goin' Crazy* (1976), *Live At The El Macambo* (1977), *First Glance* (1978), *Harder...Faster* (1979), *The Nature Of The Beast* (1981), *Power Play* (1982), *Animal Grace* (1984), *Walking Through Fire* (1988).

Armageddon

This short-lived, mid-70s supergroup specialized in psychedelia-based melodic rock. The band comprised ex-Yardbirds and Renaissance vocalist Keith Relf, guitarist Martin Pugh formerly of Steamhammer, bassist Louis Cennamo and ex-Johnny Winter drummer Bobby Caldwell. Their self-titled debut, released in 1975, graced the US album charts. It featured long esoteric compositions that fused rock, jazz, blues and symphonic influences. This album is now much sought-after by collectors. Relf was fatally electrocuted not long after the album was released, so ending a still promising career. Jeff Fenholt was recruited as the new vocalist, but things did not work out as planned; the band split up after recording tracks for a second album. These have yet to be released.

Album: *Armageddon* (1975).

Argent

When the 60s pop group the Zombies finally disintegrated, keyboardist Rod Argent (b. 14 June 1945, St Albans, Hertfordshire, England) wasted no time in forming a band that would enable his dexterity as pianist and songwriter to flourish. The assembled unit also included Russ Ballard (b. 31 October 1947, Waltham Cross, Hertfordshire, England; guitar/vocals), Bob Henrit (b. 2 May 1944, Broxbourne, Hertfordshire, England; drums) and Jim Rodford (b. 7 July 1941, St. Albans, Hertfordshire, England; bass). Their critically acclaimed debut contained Ballard's 'Liar'; a song that became one of their concert regulars and was also a US Top 10 hit for Three Dog Night in 1971. *All Together Now* contained the exhilarating 'Hold Your Head Up' which became a Top 5 hit on both sides of the Atlantic. Likewise *In Deep* produced another memorable hit, 'God Gave Rock 'N' Roll To You' (a hit in 1992 for Kiss). Ballard, who by now had developed into an outstanding pop songwriter, left in 1974 to pursue a solo career and his place within the group was taken by two new members, John Verity (b. 3 July 1949, Bradford, Yorkshire, England; guitar/bass/vocals) and John Grimaldi (b. 25 May 1955, St. Albans, Hertfordshire, England; cello/mandolin/violin). From this point on the band became lost in an atrophy of improvisational solos. Argent disbanded in 1976, Rodford eventually joined the Kinks while Argent opened keyboard shops and continued as a successful record producer and session player. He explored his jazz roots working with Barbara Thompson showing an ability he had first demonstrated almost 30 years before, during the piano solo on the Zombies' superlative 'She's Not There'. He has now become established as a respected record producer, with recent major success with Tanita

Argent

Tikaram.
Albums: *Argent* (1970), *Ring Of Hands* (1971), *All Together Now* (1972), *In Deep* (1973), *Nexus* (1974), *Encore - Live In Concert* (1974), *Circus* (1975), *Counterpoint* (1975). Compilations: *Rock Giants* (1982), *Anthology* (1982), *Music From The Spheres* (1991).

Argent, Rod

b. 14 June 1945, St. Alban's, Hertfordshire, England. At this ancient town's fee-paying Abbey School, he studied clarinet, violin and, crucially, keyboards to scholarship level. Although his preferences lay in jazz and the classics, he was broadminded enough to consider a career in pop. In 1962, he was a founder member of the Zombies, and became the quintet's principal composer - notably of the 1964 million-seller 'She's Not There'. Argent himself invested in a Worcester musical equipment shop and conducted session work for the Who, the Hollies, John Williams, Andrew Lloyd Webber and Cleo Laine and John Dankworth, before releasing *Moving Home* and its attendant single, 'Light Fantastic'. This was his first essay as a soloist (albeit with aid from famous friends). After collaborating with

Lloyd Webber and Don Black on singer Marti Webb's *Tell Me On A Sunday* concept album in 1980, Argent penned *Masquerade*, an ambitious musical based on the Kit Williams book, which opened at the Young Vic in 1982. That same year, he was also seen on the boards in person with John Hiseman and Barbara Thompson with whom he recorded the jazzy *Siren Songs*. Argent's portfolio since has embraced incidental music for films and new age ventures epitomized by 1988's *Red House* (named after his Chiswick studio) - which hedged its bets with vocal items. More lucrative, however, were his production (with drummer Peter Van Hooke) of Tanita Tikaram's first two albums - and the use of sturdy old 'She's Not There' (sung by former Zombie Colin Blunstone) in a 1990 British Telecom television advertisement.
Albums: *Argent* (1969), *Ring Of Hands* (1971), *All Together Now* (1972), *In Deep* (1973), *Nexus* (1974), *Encore* (1974), *Circus* (1975), *Counterpoint* (1976), *Moving Home* (1979), *Masquerade* (1982), *Siren Songs* (1983), *Red House* (1988). Compilation: *The Best Of Argent* (1976).

Armatrading, Joan

b. 9 December 1950, Basseterre, St Kitts, West

Indies. Joan Armatrading was the first black woman singer/songwriter based in Britain to compete on equal terms with white women. While Madeleine Bell and P.P. Arnold pre-dated Armatrading's success, the latter has remained consistent for 20 years. Although she has been inaccurately compared with Tracy Chapman, the two women have little in common other than the colour of their skin and the fact that they are both guitar playing singer/songwriters. The Armatrading family moved to Birmingham, England, in 1958, and Joan taught herself to play piano and guitar, before meeting Pam Nestor, also a West Indian immigrant (b. Berbice, Guyana, 28 April, 1948). Both were working in a touring cast of the celebrated hippie musical, *Hair*. Armatrading and Nestor worked as a team, writing songs together, but Armatrading was given the major role on *Whatever's For Us*, her 1972 debut album produced by Gus Dudgeon (who was also working with Elton John at the time, hence the participation of musicians such as guitarist Davey Johnstone and percussionist Ray Cooper). Released in the UK on Cube Records, the album was a greater critical than commercial success, and was licensed for North America by A&M Records. Armatrading and Nestor dissolved their partnership after the album; Nestor made an excellent one-off single for Chrysalis in the late 70s, but seems not to have recorded since.

By 1975, Armatrading was signed to A&M worldwide, working with producer Pete Gage, (husband of Elkie Brooks). The album which resulted, *Back To The Night*, featured instrumentalists such as Andy Summers (later of the Police) and keyboard player Jean Roussal, but again failed to trouble the chart compilers. 1976 brought the album which first thrust Armatrading into the limelight. The first of four consecutive albums produced by Glyn Johns, *Joan Armatrading* made the Top 20 of the UK album chart, and includes her only UK Top 10 hit (and her best known song) 'Love And Affection'. 1977's *Show Some Emotion* became the first album to reach the UK Top 10 and 1978's *To The Limit* made the UK Top 20, although neither album included a hit single. 1979 saw the end of her partnership with Johns in *Steppin' Out*, a live album recorded in the USA, which did not chart on either side of the Atlantic. 1980 brought a change of producer for her seventh album, after a brief working alliance with Henry Dewy had provided a minor hit single 'Rosie', which was included on a mini album, *How Cruel*, released in the USA and continental Europe but strangely not

in the UK. Richard Gottehrer (once part of the Strangeloves and the producer of Blondie's first album) was obviously a good choice, as *Me Myself I*, released in 1980, became Armatrading's first album to reach the US Top 40 and returned her to the UK Top 10, while it included two minor UK hit singles, in the title track and 'All The Way From America'. *Walk Under Ladders*, Armatrading's 1981 album, was produced by Steve Lillywhite, and among the musicians who contributed to it were the celebrated Jamaican rhythm section of Sly Dunbar and Robbie Shakespeare, plus Andy Partridge of XTC and Thomas Dolby. The album, which reached the UK Top 10, but peaked somewhat lower in the US chart, included two more minor UK chart singles, 'I'm Lucky' and 'No Love'. Her 1983 album, *The Key*, was mainly produced by Lillywhite again, but with two tracks, 'Drop The Pilot' (which was her second biggest UK hit single, almost reaching the Top 10) and 'What Do Boys Dream', produced by Val Garay. The album largely restored Armatrading to international commercial prominence, peaking just outside the US Top 30 and reaching the UK Top 10. Later that year, a 'Best Of' album, *Track Record*, made the UK Top 20. By this point in her career, Armatrading appeared to have a solid core of fans who would buy every album, but who were too few to provide first division status. 1985's *Secret Secrets* was produced by Mike Howlett with musicians including bass player Pino Palladino (of Paul Young fame) and Joe Jackson, who was the only other musician involved on the track 'Love By You'. 'Temptation', another track from the album, was a minor UK hit single, and while the album once again made the Top 20 of the UK chart, it was not a major US success, despite a sleeve shot taken by celebrated New York photographer Robert Mapplethorpe. *Sleight Of Hand*, was Armatrading's first self-produced album, which she recorded in her own quaintly named Bumpkin studio, and which was remixed by Steve Lillywhite. This was her least successful album in commercial terms since her debut, stalling outside the Top 30 of the UK chart and considerably lower in the USA, even despite the fact that this time the sleeve photographer was Lord Snowdon. 1988's *The Shouting Stage* was arguably her most impressive album in some time but failed to reach the height achieved by many of its predecessors despite featuring Mark Knopfler of Dire Straits and Mark Brzezicks of Big Country as guests. *Hearts And Flowers* again demonstrated that even though the quality of Armatrading's output was seldom less than exemplary, it rarely achieved its commercial desserts. 1991 brought a further compilation album, *The Very Best Of Joan Armatrading*, which largely updated the earlier *Track Record*, and included a remix (by Hugh Padgham) of 'Love And Affection' which was released as a single. Armatrading seems to have reached a plateau in her career which is slightly below the top echelon in commercial terms, but which will enable her to continue recording with reasonable success (especially in critical terms) for as long as she desires. She has also contributed her services to a number of charitable concerts, such as the Prince's Trust, the 1988 Nelson Mandela Concert and Amnesty International. She is equally at home reading through her considerable collection of comics. She is to be applauded for remaining unpretentious, and is also in the enviable position of being able to choose her own touring and recording timetable.

Albums: *Whatever's For Us* (1972), *Back To The Night* (1975), *Joan Armatrading* (1976), *Show Some Emotion* (1977), *To The Limit* (1978), *Steppin' Out* (1978), *Me Myself I* (1980), *Walk Under Ladders* (1981), *The Key* (1983), *Secret Secrets* (1985), *Sleight Of Hand* (1986), *Shouting Stage* (1988), *Hearts And Flowers* (1990). Compilations: *Track Record* (1983), *The Very Best Of Joan Armatrading* (1991).

Arrival

This late 60s Liverpool group came together when former NEMS employee Dyan Birch (b. 25 January 1949), teamed up with Paddy McHugh (b. 28 August 1946) and Frank Collins (b. 25 October 1947) of local group the Excels. A second Merseyside girl, vocalist Carroll Carter (b. 10 June 1948) was added, along with Lloyd Courtney (b. 20 December 1947, Cheshire, England), Don Hume (b. 31 March 1950, Watford, Hertfordshire, England) and Tony O'Malley (b. 15 July 1948). The septet sent a tape to Decca Records' A&R representative Tony Hall, who was so impressed by the group's sound that he decided to record and manage them. Their early 70s Top 20 UK hits, 'Friends' and 'I Will Survive' were urgent performances with some excellent vocal work. Although their professed ambition was for 'Arrival to become a household name', the seven-piece band proved unwieldy and eventually split, with Birch, Collins and McHugh re-emerging in Kokomo.

Album: *Arrival* (1970).

Arrows

Formed in 1973, the Arrows - Jake Hooker (b. 3 May 1952, New York City, New York, USA; guitar/saxophone), Alan Merrill (b. 19 February 1951, New York City, New York, USA; bass/piano/harmonica) and Paul Varley (b. 24 May 1952, Preston, Lancashire, England; drums/piano) - was one of several groups associated with the glam-rock/bubblegum team of songwriters Chinn And Chapman. Merrill interrupted his solo career in Japan at the behest of old friend Hooker to form the Arrows along with Varley. Their debut release, 'A Touch Too Much', was a UK Top 10 hit in May 1974, but despite securing their own television series, the group's only other success came the following year with 'My Last Night With You', which peaked at number 25. This 50s styled performance contrasted the perky pop of its predecessors, but the Arrows were unable to shake off the teenybop tag which they had once studiously courted. The trio split up when their mentor's own commercial grasp faltered. Hooker and Merrill's song, 'I Love Rock 'N' Roll' would later provide Joan Jett And The Blackhearts with a US number 1 in 1982.

Albums: *First Hit* (1976), *Stand Back* (1984).

Ashford And Simpson

Nickolas 'Nick' Ashford (b. 4 May 1942, Fairfield, South Carolina, USA) and Valerie Simpson (b. 26 August 1946, The Bronx, New York, New York City, USA). This performing and songwriting team met in the choir of Harlem's White Rock Baptist Church. Having recorded, unsuccessfully, as a duo, they joined another aspirant, Jo 'Joshie' Armstead, at the Scepter/Wand label where their compositions were recorded by Ronnie Milsap 'Never Had It So Good', Maxine Brown 'One Step At A Time', the Shirelles and Chuck Jackson. Another of the trio's songs, 'Let's Go Get Stoned', gave Ray Charles a number 1 US R&B hit in 1966. Ashford and Simpson then joined Holland/Dozier/Holland at Motown where their best-known songs included 'Ain't No Mountain High Enough', 'You're All I Need To Get By', 'Reach Out And Touch Somebody's Hand' and 'Remember Me'. Simpson also began 'ghosting' for Tammi Terrell when the latter became too ill to continue her partnership with Marvin Gaye, and she sang on part of the duo's *Easy* album. In 1971 Simpson embarked on a solo career, but two years later she and Nickolas were recording together for Warner Brothers. A series of critically welcomed, if sentimental, releases followed, but despite appearing on the soul chart, few crossed over into pop. However, by the end of the decade, the couple achieved their commercial reward with the success of 'It Seems To Hang On' (1978) and 'Found A Cure' (1979). At the same time their production work for Diana Ross (*The Boss*) and Gladys Knight (*The Touch*) enhanced their reputation. Their status as imaginative performers and songwriters was further assured in 1984 when 'Solid' became an international hit single. Ashford and Simpson, who were married in 1974, remain one of soul's quintessential partnerships.

Albums: Valerie Simpson solo *Exposed!* (1971), *Valerie Simpson* (1972); Ashford And Simpson *Keep It Comin'* (1973), *Gimme Something Real* (1973), *I Wanna Be Selfish* (1974), *Come As You Are* (1976), *So, So Satisfied* (1977), *Send It* (1977), *Is It Still Good To Ya?* (1978), *Stay Free* (1979), *A Musical Affair* (1980), *Performance* (1981), *Street Opera* (1982), *High-Rise* (1983), *Solid* (1984), *Real Love* (1986), *Love Or Physical* (1989).

Ashton, Gardner And Dyke

This short-lived but popular UK rock group consisted of two ex-members of the Remo Four, Tony Ashton (b. 1 March 1946, Blackburn, Lancashire, England; vocals/keyboards) and Roy Dyke (drums), plus bassist Kim Gardner (b. 27 January 1946, Dulwich, London, England), formerly of Creation. Having served briefly in one of singer P.P. Arnold's backing groups, alongside Steve Howe, the trio embarked on an independent career in 1968. Their albums emphasized an instrumental prowess, honing a light, jazz-rock direction similar to that of the Brian Auger Trinity. The three-piece proved equally adept at pop and scored a UK Top 3 hit in 1971 with the light-hearted 'Resurrection Shuffle', in which Ashton's throaty delivery was matched by a rasping brass section comprising Dave Caswell (trumpet) and Lyle Jenkins (saxophone) with additional guitarwork from Mick Lieber. Its success, however, was not sustained and the group broke up in 1972 without fulfilling its obvious potential. Dyke later became a founder member of Badger, where he was latterly joined by Gardner, while Ashton replaced 'Poli' Palmer in Family.

Albums: *Ashton, Gardner And Dyke* (1969), *The Worst Of Ashton, Gardner And Dyke* (1971), *What A Bloody Long Day It's Been* (1972).

Asylum Records

Asylum Records was the brainchild of David Geffen (b. 1944, USA) whose start in the entertainment business came with the William Morris Agency where he booked comedians for television. He set up his own agency with Elliott Roberts and they became the managers of the singer-songwriter Laura Nyro. They also helped run the burgeoning careers of Joni Mitchell and Crosby, Stills, Nash And Young. In the summer of 1971 Geffen formed Asylum with the promise that only bands he liked would be signed, and artists would be free to create work without pressure.

Ashton, Gardner And Dyke

The first signing was Jackson Browne (formerly in a very early version of the Nitty Gritty Dirt Band) followed by David Blue, the Eagles, Judee Sill, Joni Mitchell, Linda Ronstadt, and Jo Jo Gunne who provided the label with its first hit, 'Run Run Run'. Geffen also managed to pull off several coups by enticing Bob Dylan away from CBS (although only for two albums), and by persuading the original line-up of the Byrds to reform for one album, released in 1973. In 1974 Asylum linked up with Jac Holzman's Elektra label. As time went on, Geffen's original policy was compromised in a bid to attract a wider range of acts to the label, and in 1976 he left. Asylum then became home for artists including Dictators. Geffen meanwhile formed his own label - called simply Geffen - in 1980, and signed John and Yoko Lennon for John's comeback album *Double Fantasy*, plus Elton John (US only), and Donna Summer.

Atlanta Rhythm Section

The cream of Atlanta, Georgia, USA's studio musicians, the Atlanta Rhythm Section (actually from nearby Doraville, Georgia) came together in 1970 after working at a Roy Orbison recording session. Dean Daughtry (b. 8 September 1946, Kinston, Alabama, USA; keyboards) and drummer Robert Nix had been members of Orbison's backing group, the Candymen, and both Daughtry and J.R. Cobb (b. 5 February 1944, Birmingham, Alabama, USA; guitar) had been members of the Top 40 hitmakers Classic IV. Rounding out the line-up were vocalist Rodney Justo (replaced after the first album by Ronnie Hammond), Barry Bailey (b. 12 June 1948, Decatur, Georgia, USA; guitar), and Paul Goddard (b. 23 June 1945, Rome, Georgia, USA; bass). The group recorded two albums for Decca Records in 1972, neither of which made an impact, before signing to Polydor Records in 1974. Their first album for that company, *Third Annual Pipe Dream*, only reached number 74 in the US and the next two albums fared worse. Finally, in 1977, the single 'So In To You' became the band's breakthrough, reaching the US Top 10, as did the album from which it came, *A Rock And Roll Alternative*. Their follow-up album, *Champagne Jam*, went to the Top 10 in 1978, together with the single 'Imaginary Lover', after which Nix left, to be replaced by Roy Yeager (b. 4 February 1946, Greenwood, Mississippi, USA). The group's last hit on Polydor was a 1979 remake of 'Spooky', a song Cobb and Daughtry had been involved with when they were with Classics IV. A switch to Columbia Records in

1981 gave the group one last chart album, *Quinella*, and a US Top 30 single, 'Alien', after which they faded from the national scene.
Albums: *The Atlanta Rhythm Section* (1972), *Back Up Against The Wall* (1973), *Third Annual Pipe Dream* (1974), *Dog Days* (1975), *Red Tape* (1976), *A Rock And Roll Alternative* (1977), *Champagne Jam* (1978), *Underdog* (1979), *Are You Ready!* (1979), *The Boys From Doraville* (1980), *Quinella* (1981). Compilation: *The Best Of The Atlanta Rhythm Section* (1982).

Atomic Rooster

Formed in 1969 at the height of the UK progressive rock boom, the original Rooster line-up comprised Vincent Crane (b. 1945, d. February 1989; organ), Nick Graham (bass) and Carl Palmer (b. 20 March 1951, Birmingham, England; drums). Crane and Palmer had just departed from the chart-topping Crazy World Of Arthur Brown and it was assumed that their new group would achieve sustained success. After only one album, however, the unit fragmented with Graham joining Skin Alley and Palmer founding Emerson, Lake And Palmer. Crane soldiered on with new members John Cann (guitar/vocals) and Paul Hammond (drums) who were featured on the album *Death Walks Behind You*. Their excursions into hard rock produced two riff-laden yet catchy UK hit singles in 1971: 'Tomorrow Night' and 'The Devil's Answer'. With assistance from Pete French of Cactus the trio recorded their third album *In Hearing Of*, but just when they seemed settled, they split. The irrepressible Crane refused to concede defeat and recruited new members, guitarist Steve Bolton, bassist Bill Smith and drummer Rick Parnell (son of the orchestra leader, Jack Parnell). The new line-up was completed by the famed singer Chris Farlowe. A dramatic musical shift towards blue-eyed soul won few new fans, however, and Crane finally dissolved the band in 1974. Thereafter, he collaborated with former colleague Arthur Brown, but could not resist reviving the fossilised Rooster in 1979. Two anti-climactic albums later, Crane finally killed off his creation. In 1983, he accepted an invitation to record and tour with Dexys Midnight Runners and appeared on their album *Don't Stand Me Down*. For some time he had been suffering from depression and he took his own life in 1989.
Albums: *Atomic Rooster* (1970), *Death Walks Behind You* (1970), *In Hearing Of* (1971), *Made In England* (1972), *Nice 'N' Greasy* (1973), *Home To Roost* (1977), *Atomic Rooster* (1980), *Headline News*

(1983). Compilations: *Assortment* (1973), *This Is Atomic Rooster* (1977), *The Devil Hits Back* (1990).

Audience

This London-based act - Howard Werth (vocals, guitar), Keith Gemmell (saxophone), Trevor Williams (bass, vocals) and Tony Connor (drums) - made its recording debut in 1969 with *Audience*. A commercial flop, the album has since become one of the era's most sought-after artefacts of the art rock genre. The quartet was then signed by the fledgling Charisma label, where *Friends Friends Friends* and *House On The Hill* both produced by Gus Dudgeon, confirmed their quirky, quintessentially English, style of rock. A US tour in support of the Faces followed, but internal friction resulted in Gemmell's departure. Patrick Neubergh (saxophone) and Nick Judd (keyboards) joined for *Lunch*, on which Bobby Keyes (saxophone) and Jim Price (trumpet) also participated, but the group was dissolved following its release. Werth later forged an intermittently successful solo career.

Albums: *Audience* (1969), *Friends Friends Friends* (1970), *Bronco Bullfrog* (soundtrack 1970), *House On The Hill* (1971), *Lunch* (1972). Compilation - *You Can't Beat Them* (1973).

Average White Band

This sextet was the natural culmination of several soul-influenced Scottish beat groups. The unit featured Alan Gorrie (b. 19 July 1946, Perth, Scotland; bass/vocals), Mike Rosen (trumpet/guitar - ex-Eclection), replaced by Hamish Stuart (b. 8 October 1949, Glasgow, Scotland; guitar/vocals), Owen 'Onnie' McIntyre (b. 25 September 1945, Lennoxtown, Scotland; guitar), Malcolm 'Mollie' Duncan (b. 24 August 1945, Montrose, Scotland; saxophone), Roger Ball (b. 4 June 1944, Broughty Ferry, Scotland; saxophone/keyboards) and Robbie McIntosh (b. 6 May 1950, Dundee, Scotland, d. 23 September 1974, Hollywood, USA; drums). Although their 1973 debut album, *Show Your Hand*, showed promise, it was not until the band was signed to Atlantic Records that its true potential blossomed. *AWB*, also known as the 'White Album' in deference to its cover art, was a superb collection and paired the group's dynamism with Arif Mardin's complementary production. The highlights included a spellbinding version of the Isley Brothers' 'Work To Do', and the rhythmic original instrumental, 'Pick Up The Pieces', a worthy US number 1/UK Top 10 single. *AWB* also topped the US album charts but this euphoric period was abruptly punctured in 1974 by the tragic death of Robbie McIntosh following a fatal ingestion of heroin at a Hollywood party. He was replaced by Steve Ferrone (b. 25 April 1950, Brighton, England), a former member of Bloodstone. The group secured further success

Average White Band

with 'Cut The Cake', the title song to a third album, but subsequent releases, despite an obvious quality, betrayed a creeping reliance on a proven formula. However a pairing with singer Ben E. King (*Benny And Us*) seemed to galvanize a newfound confidence and two later recordings, 'Walk On By' and 'Let's Go Round Again', reclaimed the group's erstwhile inventiveness. The Average White Band retired during much of the 80s as the members pursued individual projects, the most surprising of which was Ferrone's work with Duran Duran. Hamish Stuart later surfaced in Paul McCartney's *Flowers In The Dirt* touring group, and was sadly unavailable when the AWB reformed in 1989. The resultant album, *After Shock*, featured original members Gorrie, Ball and McIntyre alongside Alex Ligertwood, a fellow-Scot and former vocalist with Santana.

Albums: *Show Your Hand* (1973), *AWB* (1974), *Cut The Cake* (1975), *Soul Searchin'* (1976), *Person To Person* (1977), with Ben E. King *Benny And Us* (1977), *Warmer Communications* (1978), *Volume VIII* (1979), *Feel No Fret* (1979), *Shine* (1980), *Cupid's In Fashion* (1982), *After Shock* (1989). Solo album: Alan Gorrie *Sleepless Nights* (1985). Compilation: *Best Of The Average White Band* (1984).

Ayers, Kevin

b. 16 August 1945, Herne Bay, Kent, England. Ayers spent much of his childhood in Malaya. A founder member of Soft Machine, this talented singer and songwriter abandoned the group in 1968 following an arduous US tour. Ayers' debut album, *Joy Of A Toy*, nonetheless bore a debt to his former colleagues, all of whom contributed to this innovative collection. Its charm and eccentricity set a pattern for much of the artist's later work, while the haunting, languid ballads, including 'Lady Rachel' and 'Girl On A Swing', stand among his finest compositions. In 1970 Ayers formed the Whole World, a unit that featured saxophonist Lol Coxhill, guitarist Mike Oldfield and pianist/arranger David Bedford. This impressive group was featured on *Shooting At The Moon*, a radical, experimental release which offered moments of rare beauty ('May I') and others of enchanting outlandishness ('Pisser Dans Un Violin', 'Colores Para Dolores'). The results were breathtaking and this ambitious collection is a landmark in British progressive rock. Coxhill left the Whole World soon after the album's completion and his departure precipitated their ultimate demise. Oldfield and Bedford did, however, contribute to *Whatevershebringswesing*,

wherein Ayers withdrew from explicit experimentation, although the lugubrious 'Song From The Bottom Of A Well' maintained his ability to challenge. However, the artist never quite fulfilled his undoubted potential and while a fourth collection, *Bananamour*, offered moments of inspiration, an ambivalent attitude towards commercial practices undermined Ayer's career. A high profile appearance at London's Rainbow Theatre resulted in *June 1 1974*, on which Ayers was joined by John Cale, Nico and Brian Eno (as ACNE). Unfortunately, later inconsistent albums such as, *Sweet Deceiver*, *Yes We Have No Mañanas* and *Rainbow Takeaway*, were interspersed by prolonged holidays in the singer's beloved Ibiza. Despite this reduced public profile, Kevin Ayers retains a committed cult following and continued to follow his highly personal path throughout the 80s and into the 90s with a well-received album.

Albums: *Joy Of A Toy* (1969), *Shooting At The Moon* (1970), *Whatevershebringswesing* (1971), *Bananamour* (1973), *The Confessions Of Doctor Dream* (1974), with John Cale, Brian Eno and Nico *June 1 1974* (1974), *Sweet Deceiver* (1975), *Yes We Have No Mañanas* (1976), *Rainbow Takeaway* (1978), *Diamond Jack And The Queen Of Pain* (1983), *As Close As You Think* (1986), *Falling Up* (1988), *Still Life With Guitar* (1992). Compilations: *Odd Ditties* (1976), *The Kevin Ayers Collection* (1983), *Banana Productions - The Best Of Kevin Ayers* (1989).

Aznavour, Charles

b. 22 May 1924, Paris, France. Premier vocalist/songwriter Aznavour's parents fled from Armenia after the Turkish massacre, and his composition, 'They Fell', shows the bewilderment felt by all Armenians. He declares, 'I am Armenian. Everybody figures out that I am a Frenchman because I sing in French, I act like a Frenchman and I have all the symptoms of a Frenchman.' Aznavour's father had a small restaurant but he was preoccupied with music. When aged only 15, he wrote his one-man show. In 1942 Aznavour formed a partnership with Pierre Roche and they had success in Canada between 1948 and 1950. Aznavour's first hit song was 'J'ai Bu' for Charles Ulmer in 1950, the year he also became a solo performer. He comments, 'I was small and undistinguished, so I had to become rich and famous.' Aznavour often opened for Edith Piaf, who recorded several of his songs, including 'Il Pleut', 'Le Feutre Tropez', as well as a translation of 'Jezebel'. 'When I gave "Je Hais Les

Charles Aznavour

Dimanches" to her, she laughed in my face and told me to give it to an existentialist singer,' he recalled. 'I took her at her word and gave it Juliette Greco. She said, "You idiot! You've given my song to that girl. Now I'll have to record it to show her how to sing it."' Aznavour has written numerous songs about ageing, notably 'Hier Encore', which was translated into English by Herbert Kretzmer as 'Yesterday When I Was Young'. 'I wrote my first song about being old when I was 18. The songs I wrote many years ago haven't dated at all, although my way of singing them, my interpretation, has become sweeter.' 'The Old-Fashioned Way' was an antidote to rock 'n' roll, but ironically in the film *And Then There Was None*, the character he played was poisoned after singing it. His film appearances have included the title role in François Truffaut's meritorious *Shoot The Piano Player* (1960), and he has been featured in popular films, including *Candy, The Adventurers* and *The Games*. Matt Monro made the UK charts with the maudlin 'For Mama', while Jack Jones recorded a tribute album, *Write Me A Love Song, Charlie*. In 1974 Aznavour had a UK number 1 with 'She', the theme for the ITV television series, *The Seven Faces Of Woman*. Although small (3feet 3inches), slight and with battered, world-weary features, he is nonetheless an imposing concert performer, acting his songs with the ability of a leading mime artist. Aznavour starred in the 1975 Royal Command Performance, and he has been parodied by the Goodies as Charles Aznovoice. He rarely records anything other than his own songs and his inventive compositions have included 'You've Let Yourself Go' in which his woman is overweight and argumentative, 'What Makes A Man' about a transvestite, 'Pretty Shitty Days' about an English word that amused him, and the hilarious account of a disastrous wedding anniversary in 'Happy Anniversary'. He says, 'Songs mature inside of me and then take their life on paper. A song may take me five minutes to write but it also takes 40 years of living'.

Selected albums (UK releases): *Charles Aznavour Sings* (1963), *Qui?* (1964), *Et Voici* (1964), *Aznavour Sings His Love Songs In English* (1965), *Charles Aznavour '65* (1965), *Encore* (1966), *De T'avoir Aimée* (1966), *Aznavour Sings Aznavour, Volume 1* (1970), *Aznavour Sings Aznavour, Volume 2* (1971), *Désormais* (1972), *Aznavour Sings Aznavour, Volume 3* (1973), *Chez Lui A Paris* (1973), *A Tapestry Of Dreams* (1974), *I Sing For...You* (1975), *Charles Aznavour Esquire* (1978), *A Private Christmas* (1978), *In Times To Be* (1983). (French releases): *Guichets Fermés* (1978, 2 album), *Comme Ils Disent, Aimez Moi, Face Au Public, Hier Encore, Il Faut Savoir, Je M'Voyais Déjà, Je N'Ai Pas Vu Le Temps Passé, La Bohème, La Mama, Le Temps, Non, Je N'Ai Rien Oublié, Paris Au Mois D'Aôut, Plein Feu Sur Aznavour, Reste, Une Première Dance, 1980...A L'Olympia*.

Further reading: *Yesterday When I Was Young*, Charles Aznavour.

B

Babe Ruth

Formed in Hatfield, Hertfordshire, England in 1971, this engaging hard rock group was originally named Shacklock after founding guitarist Alan Shacklock. Janita 'Jenny' Haan (vocals), Dave Punshon (keyboards), Dave Hewitt (bass) and Dick Powell (drums) completed the initial line-up, which took its new name from the legendary American baseball player. *First Base*, which included 'Wells Fargo', a popular stage-favourite, enhanced the quintet's growing reputation, much of which rested on Haan's raw delivery. However, despite enjoying commercial success in the USA and Canada, where *Amar Cabalero* achieved a gold disc, the group was plagued by personnel problems. Ed Spevock (drums) and Steve Gurl (piano, ex-Wild Turkey) replaced Powell and Punshon, but the departure of Shacklock following the release of *Babe Ruth* proved pivotal. A second Wild Turkey refugee, Bernie Marsden, was added for *Stealin' Home*, but in 1976 the line-up was again undermined by the loss of Haan and Hewitt. Ellie Hope (vocals) and Ray Knott (bass) joined for *Kid's Stuff*, but the group was now bereft of direction and split up. Marsden later surfaced in Paice, Ashton And Lord and Whitesnake while Spevock switched to Pete Brown's Piblokto!

Albums: *First Base* (1972), *Amar Cabalero* (1973), *Babe Ruth* (1975), *Stealin' Home* (1975), *Kid's Stuff* (1976). Compilation: *The Best Of Babe Ruth* (1977).

Babys

Considerable attention attended the launch of this much-touted British rock group. John Waite (b. 4 July 1955, London, England; vocals/bass), Mike Corby (b. 3 July 1955, London, England; guitar/keyboards), Walter 'Wally' Stocker (b. 27 March 1954, London, England; guitar) and former Spontaneous Combustion and Strider member Tony Brock (b. 31 March 1954, Bournemouth, Dorset, England; drums) were promoted as the most promising newcomers of 1976, but while *The Babys* offered a competent blend of pop and rock, similar to that of the Raspberries, it lacked an identifiable sound and image. Obscured by the punk explosion, the quartet looked to the USA for commercial succour over the ensuing years. Jonathan Cain replaced Corby following the release of *Head First*, but although the Babys did achieve considerable US success, including two Top 20 singles with 'Isn't It Time' and 'Every Time I Think Of You', they remained in the shadow of AOR stalwarts Fleetwood Mac, Foreigner and Journey. Waite subsequently embarked on a high-profile solo career.

Albums: *The Babys* (1976), *Broken Heart* (1977), *Head First* (1978), *Union Jacks* (1980), *On The Edge* (1980). Compilation: *Anthology* (1981).

Bachman-Turner Overdrive

25**

Baccara

This Spanish girl duo had a UK number 1 in 1978 with the disco orientated 'Yes Sir, I Can Boogie'. Sung by Maria Mendiola and Mayte Mateus, it was written and produced by the Dutch team of Frank Dostal and Rolf Soja, backed by studio musicians. There was a UK Top 10 follow-up 'Sorry I'm A Lady', but after this the group faded from view as times and fashions changed.
Album: *Baccara* (1978).

Bachman-Turner Overdrive

Formed in Vancouver, British Columbia, Canada in 1972, Bachman-Turner Overdrive was a hard-rock group featuring former Guess Who member Randy Bachman (b. 27 September 1943, Winnipeg, Manitoba, Canada; guitar/lead vocals). Randy Bachman had left the Guess Who in 1970, recorded a solo album *Axe* and, due to a bout of illness, had to cancel a projected collaboration with former Nice keyboardist Keith Emerson. Bachman subsequently formed Brave Belt with his brother Robbie Bachman (b. 18 February 1943, Winnipeg, Manitoba, Canada; drums), C.F. 'Fred' Turner (b. 16 October 1943, Winnipeg, Manitoba, Canada; bass/vocals) and Chad Allan, who had been a member of an early incarnation of Guess Who called Chad Allan and the Expressions. Brave Belt recorded two unsuccessful albums for Reprise Records in 1971-72, after which Allan was replaced by another Bachman brother, Tim. In 1972 the new band took its new name, the word Overdrive being borrowed from a trade magazine for truck drivers. They signed to Mercury Records in 1973 and released a self-titled first album which made a minor impact in the USA and at home in Canada. Tim Bachman departed at that point, replaced by Blair Thornton (b. 23 July 1950). After constant touring in the USA, BTO's second album, *Bachman-Turner Overdrive II*, provided their breakthrough, reaching number 4 in the US and yielding the number 12 hit 'Takin' Care Of Business'. The third album, *Not Fragile*, released in the summer of 1974, topped the US album charts and provided the US number 1/UK number 2 hit single 'You Ain't Seen Nothing Yet', sung with a dramatized stutter by Randy Bachman. *Four Wheel Drive*, the group's 1975 album, was its last Top 10 recording, although the group continued to release singles and albums until the end of the 70s. Randy Bachman departed from the group in 1977 and formed a band called Ironhorse as well as recording solo. He was replaced by Jim Clench, who appeared on the album *Freeways*. The following year the band officially changed its name to BTO but could not revive its earlier fortunes. In 1984, Randy Bachman, Tim Bachman and C.F. Turner regrouped and released a second self-titled album, this time for Compleat Records, which barely dented the US charts. The group was still touring in the early 90s but had not released any further albums.
Albums: as Brave Belt *Brave Belt* (1971), *Brave Belt II* (1972); as Bachman-Turner Overdrive *Bachman-Turner Overdrive* (1973), *Bachman-Turner Overdrive II* (1974), *Not Fragile* (1974), *Four Wheel Drive* (1975), *Head On* (1975), *Freeways* (1977), *Street Action* (1978), *Rock 'N' Roll Nights* (1979), *Bachman-Turner Overdrive* (1984). Compilation: *Best Of BTO (So Far)* (1976).

Back Door

This jazz-rock trio from Blakey, Yorkshire, comprised Colin Hodgkinson (bass/vocals), Ron Aspery (saxophone/keyboards/flute/clarinet) and Tony Hicks (drums). This trio attracted much interest due to Hodgkinson's unique, adept full-chording bass technique. Their critically acclaimed first album recorded in 1972 was initially released on the independent Blakey label. The praise and attention generated by the album resulted in the band signing to Warner Brothers which later re-issued the set. Subsequent releases, which included production work from Felix Pappalardi and Carl Palmer of Emerson, Lake And Palmer, failed to capture the spirit of the debut set or the fire of their live performances. By the time of the fourth album, *Activate* in 1976, Hicks had departed to be replaced by Adrian Tilbrook before the group split the following year. Aspery went on to work with the Icelandic jazz rock group Mezzoforte, while Hodgkinson guested with various artists including, Alexis Korner, Jan Hammer and Brian Auger.
Albums: *Back Door* (1972), *8th Street Blues* (1974), *Another Mine Mess* (1975), *Activate* (1976).

Back Street Crawler

Formed in England during 1975, Back Street Crawler took its name from founder Paul Kossoff's solo album. The ex-Free guitarist was joined by Terry Wilson-Slessor (vocals), Michael Montgomery (keyboards), Terry Wilson (bass) and Tony Braunagel (drums), but concerts in support of *The Band Played On*, were cancelled when the group's leader was hospitalized after a drugs-related seizure. An American tour offered newfound hope, but such optimism was shattered on 19 March 1976 when Kossoff died in his sleep. The band truncated its name to Crawler following the release of *2nd Avenue*. Geoff Whitehorn, formerly of If and Maggie Bell's group, was added on guitar, while John 'Rabbit' Bundrick, another ex-member of Free, replaced Montgomery. Despite minor US chart success, the quintet was unable to escape the heritage of its founder and split up following *Snake, Rattle And Roll*.

Albums: as Back Street Crawler *The Band Plays On* (1975), *2nd Avenue* (1976); as Crawler *Crawler* (1977), *Snake, Rattle And Roll* (1978).

Bacon Fat

One of the less-renowned groups signed to Mike Vernon's respected UK Blue Horizon label, Bacon Fat are best recalled for the exemplary harmonica work of Rod 'Gingerman' Piazza. A former member of a Californian unit, the Dirty Blues Band, this accomplished musician rivalled Paul Butterfield and Charlie Musselwhite as a leading exponent of the instrument. Buddy Reed (guitar/vocals), Gregg Schaefer (guitar), J.D. Nicholson (vocals/piano), Jerry Smith (bass) and Dick Innes Jnr. (drums) completed Bacon Fat's debut album, *Grease One For Me*. Although they were subsequently augmented by vocalist George Smith, this promising group broke up following the release of their second album.

Albums: *Grease One For Me* (1970), *Tough Dude* (1971).

Bad Boy

The origin of this US rock band date back to the mid-70s, when Steve Grimm (guitar/vocals) teamed up with John Marcelli (bass). The first incarnation of Bad Boy, included Lars Hanson (drums) and Joe Lavie (guitar). The band chemistry was wrong however, and their debut album was a disappointing, half-hearted affair. Things improved with the subsequent release, as the band moved in a heavier direction and made greater use of an up-front guitar sound. Following a period of inactivity between 1978-82, the band hit back with a revamped line-up that saw Xeno (keyboards) and Billy Johnson (drums) alongside Grimm and Marcelli. Unfortunately, they switched back to a melodic pop-rock style once more. Both albums sold poorly and the band split up as a result.

Albums: *The Band That Made Milwaukee Famous* (1977), *Back To Back* (1978), *Private Party* (1982), *Electric Eyes* (1984).

Bad Company

This solid, highly acclaimed UK heavy rock group

formed in 1973 with a line-up comprising, Paul Rodgers (b. 12 December 1949, Middlesbrough, England; vocals), Simon Kirke (b. 27 August 1949, Wales; vocals/drums), Mick Ralphs (b. 31 May 1944, Hertfordshire, England; vocals/guitar) and Boz Burrell (b. Raymond Burrell, 1946, Lincolnshire, England; bass guitar). With Ralphs (ex-Mott The Hoople) and Rodgers and Kirke (both ex-Free), Bad Company were akin to a blues-based supergroup. Much of their style was owed to Free, both musically and because of Paul Rodgers' distinct vocals. Their internationally best-selling self-titled debut album established their style - strong vocals placed beside hard, distinctive riffing. A string of albums through the mid/late 70s brought them chart success on both sides of the Atlantic and a series of arduous, stadium tours maintained their reputation as an exemplary live act. They achieved singles success with a number of powerful songs, well produced and faultlessly played, although lyrically they were often quite pedestrian: 'Well I take whatever I want, and baby I want you' ('Can't Get Enough Of Your Love'), and 'Baby, when I think about you I think about love' ('Feel Like Makin' Love'). A three year hiatus ended with the release of *Rough Diamonds*, which provided another UK Top 20 album success (US number 26). After nearly a decade of extensive gigging and regularly released albums, the group finally dissolved in 1983. A new version of the group with former Ted Nugent vocalist Brian Howe replacing Rodgers came together in 1986 for the reunion album, *Fame And Fortune*. The band's subsequent releases have been mediocre, and are but a pale shadow of their first two albums.

Albums: *Bad Company* (1974), *Straight Shooter* (1975), *Run With The Pack* (1978), *Burning Sky* (1977), *Desolation Angels* (1979), *Rough Diamonds* (1984), *Fame And Fortune* (1986), *Dangerous Age* (1988), *Holy Water* (1990), *Here Comes Trouble* (1992). Compilation: *10 From 6* (1986).

Badfinger

Originally an all-Welsh group, they played the legendary Cavern in the mid-60s with a line-up comprising Pete Ham (b. 27 April 1947; vocals), Mike Gibbons (b. 1949; drums), David Jenkins (guitar) and Ron Griffiths (bass) using the name the Iveys. Not surprisingly for a group who had taken their name in imitation of the Hollies, they were vocally tight and very melodic. During 1967, they became backing group to operatic pop singer David Garrick before leaving him to try their luck on the Beatles' enterprising new label Apple. By

Badfinger

this time, Jenkins had been replaced by Liverpudlian Tom Evans, who wrote their debut for the label, 'Maybe Tomorrow', produced by Tony Visconti. The single passed unnoticed, as did the UK follow-up 'Walls Ice Cream', so the group decided to bury the Iveys and re-invent themselves as Badfinger. By the time their next record was completed their original bassist left and was replaced by Joey Molland. The new line-up enjoyed an immediate hit on both sides of the Atlantic with 'Come And Get It', written by their label boss Paul McCartney. In order to increase their public profile, the group were invited to contribute to the soundtrack of the movie *The Magic Christian*, which starred Peter Sellers and Ringo Starr. The Beatles patronage, which the press were quick to latch on to, was reinforced by the group's sound, which had strong traces of the Fab Four influence, particularly on the vocals. 'No Matter What', another transatlantic Top 10 hit, compounded the Beatles comparisons, though it was a fine pop record in its own right. By the beginning of the 70s, Badfinger were something of an Apple houseband and even appeared on three solo Beatle recordings (*All Things Must Pass*, 'It Don't Come Easy' and *Imagine*) as well as appearing at George Harrison's Bangla Desh benefit concert.

The obvious songwriting talent that existed in the group was not fully revealed until 1972 when Nilsson enjoyed a huge transatlantic chart topper with the Ham/Evans neurotic ballad, 'Without You'. From that point onwards, however, the group failed to exploit their potential to the fullest. By the time of their final Apple recording *Ass*, Molland was writing over half of their songs, but he chose to leave soon after, clearly weary of the financial and business wranglings that were now dominating proceedings. Worse was to follow the next year when Pete Ham took his own life, after a long period of personal and professional worries. At that point the band split. Nearly four years later, Joey Molland and Tom Evans reformed the group, changing the subsidiary members frequently over the next few years. Commercial success proved elusive and in November 1983, history repeated itself in the most bizarre scenario possible when Tom Evans committed suicide at his Surrey home. Like Pete Ham he had been suffering from depression and financial worries. The Badfinger story is uniquely tragic and among its greater ironies is the now morbid chorus of the song with which Pete Ham and Tom Evans are best associated: 'I can't live, I can't live anymore' ('Without You').

Albums: *Magic Christian Music* (1970), *No Dice* (1970), *The Magic Christian* (1970, film soundtrack), *Straight Up* (1972), *Ass* (1974), *Badfinger* (1974), *Wish You Were Here* (1974), *Airwaves* (1979).

Baker, George, Selection

Led by vocalist George Bouens – who assumed the stage surname 'Baker' – this MOR Dutch quintet scaled charts throughout Europe and then North America in 1970 with a debut single 'Little Green Bag' – composed by Bouens and group member, Jan Visser. Bouens alone wrote his Selection's next major hit, 'Una Paloma Blanca', which caught a holiday mood during the summer of 1975. Despite a cover by Jonathan King, it reached the UK and Australasian Top 10 charts and sold a million in Germany alone. There were no further international smashes but, despite a brisk turnover of personnel, the band continued as domestic chart contenders until the 80s.

Albums: *Little Green Bag* (1970), *Summer Melody* (1977), *Paloma Blanca* (1975), *River Song* (1976). Compilation: *The Best Of Baker* (1978).

Baker Gurvitz Army

Former Gun and Three Man Army members, Paul and Adrian Gurvitz joined forces with ex-Cream and Airforce drummer Ginger Baker to form this tempestuous trio. Their self-titled debut featured a powerful blend of heavy rock laced with Baker's unmistakable drumming. The lengthy 'Mad Jack' was the album's outstanding track. This autobiographical tale masquerading as a novelty lyric from Baker, told the story of his exploits through the African desert in his Land-Rover. The band enlisted the help of Snips from Sharks and ex-Seventh Wave member, Peter Lemer. The two following albums contained similar material, but the combination of a lack of success in America and personality clashes between the members, led them to retreat back to solo careers.

Albums: *Baker Gurvitz Army* (1974), *Elysian Encounter* (1975), *Hearts On Fire* (1976).

Ballard, Russ

b. 31 October 1945, Waltham Cross, Hertfordshire, England. Ballard attended the same secondary modern school as Cliff Richard before joining the Daybreakers, the backing group to Buster Meakle, another local singer (and future mainstay of Unit 4 + 2). By 1963, with Daybreaker drummer Robert Henrit, Ballard was a member of Adam Faith's Roulettes in which he played keyboards before transferring to guitar. Among tracks recorded by the quartet alone were a handful of Ballard numbers - including its last a-side, 1967's 'Help Me Help Myself'. While briefly one of the latter-day Unit 4 + 2 members, Ballard also co-wrote that outfit's final single, 1969's psychedelic '3.30', before he and Henrit joined Argent. Ballard's compositions complemented those of leader Rod Argent and his confidence was boosted when his 'God Gave Rock And Roll To You' was among the group's hits. Three Dog Night reached the US Top 10 with a version of Ballad's 'Liar' in 1972.

After this lucrative syndication, Ballard remained with Argent for a further two years before showing his hand as a soloist. However, as neither *Russ Ballard* nor *Winning* attracted sufficient attention, he elected to concentrate on writing adult-orientated material. He was especially favoured by America who he serviced well into the 80s with accessible catchy compositions. Other notable beneficiaries of his efforts were Hot Chocolate ('So You Win Again') UK number 1 and Rainbow ('Since You've Been Gone' and 'I Surrender'). Ringo Starr recorded another Ballard composition 'As Far As You Go' on his 1983 album, *Old Wave*. Ballard was also active as a session player for both old associates such as Faith (and his protege Leo Sayer) and Rainbow's Graham Bonnet as well as newer acquaintances such as Lea Nicholson, Starry Eyed And Laughing and Phoenix.

By 1979, he returned to the fray as a recording artist with *On The Third Stroke* (with its 'You Can Do Voodoo' single) which, like its *Barnet Dogs* and *Into The Fire* follow-ups, was a likeable collection. The second album entitled *Russ Ballard* was issued in 1984. Its singles and those on its successor, *Fire Still Burns*, were promoted on video with the artist still wearing the sunglasses that have been his visual trademark since treading the boards with Meakle's Daybreakers. A belated rise to a qualified prominence in his own right is not out of the question but Ballard's fame in the early 90s rests still on interpretations of his material by others. In recent times, the Little Angels, Magnum and Kiss have recorded his songs. Kiss had a hit in 1992 with 'God Gave Rock And Roll To You' after Ballard had been commissioned to pen the soundtrack to the 1991 movie, *Bill And Ted's Bogus Journey*.

Albums: *Russ Ballard* (1975), *Winning* (1976), *At The Third Stroke* (1979), *Barnet Dogs* (1980), *Into The Fire* (1981), *Russ Ballard* (1984), *Fire Still Burns* (1986).

Band

When the Band emerged in 1968 with *Music From Big Pink*, they were already a seasoned and cohesive unit. Four of the group, Robbie Robertson (b. Jaime Robbie Robertson, 5 July 1943, Toronto, Ontario, Canada; guitar/vocals), Richard Manuel (b. 3 April 1943, Stratford, Canada, d. 7 March 1986; piano/drums/vocals), Garth Hudson (b. Eric Hudson, 2 August 1937, London, Ontario, Canada; organ) and Rick Danko (b. 9 December 1943, Simcoe, Canada; bass/vocals), had embraced rock 'n' roll during its first flush of success. One by one they joined the Hawks, a backing group fashioned by rockabilly singer Ronnie Hawkins, which included Levon Helm (b. Mark Levon Helm, 26 May 1942, Marvell, Arkansas, USA; drums/vocals). A minor figure in America, by the late 50s Hawkins had moved to Toronto where he pursued a career largely shaped around rabble-house cover versions. 'Bo Diddley' (1963) was a major hit in Canada, but the musicians flexed their independence during sessions for the subsequent *Mojo Man*, recording 'She's 19' and 'Farther Up The Road' with Helm taking the vocal. The quintet left Hawkins later that year and criss-crossed America's small town bars, performing for 'pimps, whores, rounders and flakeouts', as Hudson later recalled! Billed as the Canadian Squires or Levon And The Hawks, they developed a loud, brash repertoire, drawn from R&B, soul and gospel styles, while the rural life they encountered left a trail of impressions and images. The group completed a single, 'Leave Me Alone', under the former appellation, before settling in New York where 'Go Go Liza Jane' and 'The Stones I Throw' were recorded as Levon And The Hawks.

The quintet enjoyed the approbation of the city's famed Red Bird label. Robertson, Helm and Hudson supported blues singer John Hammond Jnr. on his debut single, 'I Wish You Would' (1964), while Levon's pacey composition, 'You Cheated, You Lied', was recorded by the Shangri-Las. The trio maintained their link with Hammond on the latter's fiery *So Many Roads* (1965), through which they were introduced to Bob Dylan. In August 1965 Robertson and Helm accompanied the singer for his Forest Hills concert and although the drummer reneged on further involvement, within months the remaining Hawks were at the fulcrum of Dylan's most impassioned music. They supported him on his 'electric' 1966 world tour and followed him to his Woodstock retreat where, reunited with Helm, they recorded the famous

Basement Tapes whose lyrical, pastoral performances anticipated the style the quintet would soon adopt. *Music From Big Pink* restated traditional American music in an environment of acid-rock and psychedelia. Natural in the face of technocratic artifice, its woven, wailing harmonies suggested the fervour of sanctified soul, while the instrumental pulse drew inspiration from carnivals, country and R&B. The Band's deceptive simplicity was their very strength, binding lyrics of historical and biblical metaphor to sinuous, memorable melodies. The set included three Dylan songs, but is best recalled for 'The Weight' which, if lyrically obtuse, was the subject of several cover versions, notably from Jackie DeShannon and Spooky Tooth.

The Band confirmed the quintet's unique qualities. Robertson had emerged as their principle songwriter, yet the panoramic view remained intact, and by invoking Americana past and present, the group reflected the pastoral desires of a restless generation. It contained several telling compositions - 'Across The Great Divide', 'The Unfaithful Servant' and 'The Night They Drove Old Dixie Down' - as well as 'Rag Mama Rag', an ebullient UK Top 20 hit. The Band then resumed touring, the perils of which were chronicled on *Stage Fright*. By openly embracing contemporary concerns, the quintet lacked their erstwhile perspective, but in 'The Rumour' they created one of the era's most telling portraits. Yet the group's once seamless sound had grown increasingly formal, a dilemma increased on *Cahoots*. Melodramatic rather than emotional, the set offered few highlights, although Van Morrison's cameo on '4% Pantomime' suggested a *bonhomie* distinctly absent elsewhere. It was followed by a warm in-concert set, *Rock Of Ages*, arranged by Allan Toussaint, and *Moondog Matinee*, a wonderful selection of favourite oldies. It served as a spotlight for Richard Manuel, whose emotional, haunting voice wrought new meaning from 'Share Your Love', 'The Great Pretender' and 'A Change Is Gonna Come'.

In 1974 the Band backed Bob Dylan on his acclaimed *Planet Waves* album and undertook the extensive tour documented on *Before The Flood*. The experience inspired a renewed creativity and *Northern Lights Southern Cross*, their strongest set since *The Band*, included 'Arcadian Driftwood', one of Robertson's most evocative compositions. However, the individual members had decided to dissolve the group and their partnership was sundered the following year with a gala performance at San Francisco's Winterland ballroom. The event, *The Last Waltz*, featured many guest contributions, including those by Dylan, Eric Clapton, Muddy Waters, Van Morrison, Neil Young, Joni Mitchell and Paul Butterfield, and was the subject of Martin Scorsese's film of the same name and a commemorative triple album. The Band also completed their contractual obligations with *Islands*, a somewhat tepid set notable only for 'Knockin' Lost John', which featured a rare lead vocal from Robertson. Levon Helm then pursued a dual career as a performer and actor, Rick Danko recorded an intermittently interesting solo album, while Hudson saved his talent for session appearances. Robbie Robertson scored soundtracks to several more Scorsese films, but kept a relatively low profile, refusing to join the ill-fated Band reunions of 1984 and 1985. A third tour ended in tragedy when, on 7 March 1986, Richard Manuel hanged himself in a motel room. His death inspired 'Fallen Angel' on Robertson's outstanding 'comeback' album, but despite the presence of Hudson and Danko elsewhere on the record, the guitarist refused to join his colleagues when they regrouped again in 1991.

Albums: *Music From Big Pink* (1968), *The Band* (1969), *Stage Fright* (1970), *Cahoots* (1971), *Rock Of Ages* (1972), *Moondog Matinee* (1973), *Northern Lights - Southern Cross* (1975), *Islands* (1977), with various artists *The Last Waltz* (1977). Compilations: *The Best Of The Band* (1976), *Anthology Volume 1* (1978), *Anthology Volume 2* (1980), *To Kingdom Come* (1989).

Barclay James Harvest

Formed in Oldham, England, the band comprised: Stewart 'Woolly' Wolstenholme (b. 15 April 1947, Oldham, Lancashire, England; keyboards/vocals), John Lees (b. 13 January 1947, Oldham, Lancashire, England; guitar/vocals), Les Holroyd (b. 12 March 1948, Bolton, Lancashire, England; bass/vocals) and Mel Pritchard (b. 20 January 1948, Oldham, Lancashire, England; drums). This quartet was made up of musicians from two Lancashire bands, the Keepers, and the Wickeds. As members of the former, Wolstenholme and Lees were invited to join the rival Wickeds, briefly making a sextet. After two original members departed this left them with the unit that was to become Barclay James Harvest. Following their inauspicious debut on EMI's Parlophone label the band became one of the first signings to the aptly named Harvest outlet. The band were perfectly suited to the marketing aims of that label; progressive, symphonic and

Barclay James Harvest

occasionally improvisational. Their blend of melodic 'underground' music was initially acclaimed, although commercial success in the charts eluded them for many years. Their early albums heavily featured the mellotron, although they were able to combine earthy guitar with superb harmony vocals. 'Mockingbird' from *Once Again* became their unwanted 'Damocles' sword', the orchestrated classical style left them wide open to sniping critics. The unfair press they often received was itself perplexing. Here was a musically excellent band, writing material that was perfect for the time, yet they failed to increase their following. Fortunes looked set to change when they left Harvest and signed with Polydor in 1974. The release of their finest album to date, *Everyone Is Everybody Else*. Why it failed to chart is one of rock's minor mysteries, yet it contained many outstanding songs. The beautiful harmonies of 'Poor Boy Blues' set against their *tour de force*, 'For No One', featuring a blistering example of wah-wah guitar, were two reasons alone why the album

should have been a major success. It was in 1976 that their first chart success came, with the excellent *Octoberon*. The intricate and expensive, embossed album sleeve became a financially viable record. 'Rock 'n' Roll Star'and 'Suicide' were two of the outstanding tracks. Although they were unable to make any impression in the USA, their appeal in Europe kept them busy. *Gone To Earth*, again with a special sleeve, this time a cut-out, was a massive selling record in Germany. Their own subtle 'Poor Man's Moody Blues' sniped back at critics, while the beautiful Christian anthem 'Hymn' became a regular encore. Their live *Concert For The People*, recorded in Berlin, became their most commercially successful record in the UK. In Germany the band are major artists, while in Britain their loyal followers are able to view, with a degree of satisfaction, that Barclay James Harvest rode out the criticism, stayed on their chosen musical path without compromise and produced some of the finest 'Art rock' music of all time.

Albums: *Barclay James Harvest* (1970), *Once Again*

(1971), *Short Stories* (1971), *Early Morning Onwards* (1972), *Baby James Harvest* (1972), *Everyone Is Everybody Else* (1974), *Barclay James Harvest Live* (1974), *Time Honoured Ghosts* (1975), *Octoberon* (1976), *Gone To Earth* (1977), *XII* (1978), *Eyes Of The Universe* (1979), *A Concert For The People (Berlin)* (1982), *Turn Of The Tide* (1981), *Ring Of Changes* (1983), *Victims Of Circumstance* (1984), *Face To Face* (1987), *Glasnost* (1988), *Welcome To The Show* (1990). Compilation: *Alone We Fly* (1990), *The Harvest Years* (1991). Solo albums: John Lees *A Major Fancy* (1977); Woolly Wolstenholme *Maestro* (1980).

Bay City Rollers

Originally formed during 1967 in Edinburgh, the Rollers were a Beatles cover group based round two brothers Derek Longmuir (b. 19 March 1955, Edinburgh, Scotland; drums) and Alan Longmuir (b. 20 June 1953, Edinburgh, Scotland; bass). After falling into the hands of entrepreneur Tam Paton, they played consistently on the Scottish circuit until their big break in 1971. A posse of record company talent spotters, including Bell Records' president Dick Leahy, producer Tony Calder and agent David Apps witnessed their live performance and within months the group were in the UK Top 10. The hit, a revival of the Gentrys' 'Keep On Dancing', produced by Jonathan King, proved a one-off and for the next couple of years the group struggled. Names like Nobby Clark and John Devine came and went until they finally found a relatively stable line-up with the Edinburgh born trio of Les McKeown (b. 12 November 1955; vocals), Stuart 'Woody' Wood (b. 25 February 1957; guitar) and Eric Faulkner (b. 21 October 1955; guitar). With the songwriting assistance of Phil Coulter and Bill Martin, they enjoyed a steady run of teen-orientated hits, including 'Remember (Sha La La)', 'Shang-A-Lang', 'Summerlove Sensation' and 'All Of Me Loves All Of You'. Paton remained firmly in control of their visual image (all fresh faces clad in tartan scarves and trousers) which struck a chord with young teenagers and pre-pubescent fans in search of pin-up pop stars. 1975 proved the watershed year with two consecutive UK number 1 hits, 'Bye Bye Baby' (a Four Seasons cover) and 'Give A Little Love'. That same year they topped the US charts with 'Saturday Night'. Further line-up changes followed with the arrival of Ian Mitchell and Billy Lyall but these did not detract from the group's following. Rollermania was triumphant. Inevitably, there was a backlash as the press determined to expose the group's virginal, teetotal image. During the next three years, disaster was heaped upon disaster. McKeown was charged with reckless driving after hitting and killing a 75-year-old widow, Eric Faulkner and Alan Longmuir attempted suicide, Paton was jailed for committing indecent acts with underage teenagers, Ian Mitchell starred in a pornographic movie and Billy Lyal died from an AIDS-related illness in 1989. It was a tawdry conclusion for one of the most famous teenybop acts in British pop history.
Albums: *Rollin'* (1974), *Once Upon A Star* (1975), *Wouldn't You Like It* (1975), *Dedication* (1976), *It's A Game* (1977), *Strangers In The Wind* (1978), as the Rollers *Richocet* (1981).

B.B. Blunder

Formed in 1971, the innovative UK rock group B.B. Blunder comprised of Brian Godding (vocals/guitar/keyboards), Brian Belshaw (bass/vocals) and Kevin Westlake (drums/vocals), all ex-members of Blossom Toes. The trio's sole album, *Workers' Playtime*, displayed an appreciably heavy sound, but this power was combined with a penchant for quirky melody, notably on the loose 'Rocky Ragbag' the choral 'New Day' and the gritty 'Put Your Money Where Your Mouth Is'. The set featured sterling support from Brian Auger, Julie Driscoll and Mick Taylor, but is equally renowned for an imaginative sleeve design which was a typographical spoof copy of the BBC publication *Radio Times*, both on the front and inner. B.B. Blunder also supported ex-Action singer Reg King during his brief solo career but, unable to translate its cult appeal into wider success, the group was dissolved in 1972. Godding subsequently joined Centipede, a jazz-rock collective, which included Julie Driscoll and Keith Tippett.
Album: *Workers' Playtime* (1971).

Beaver And Krause

Paul Beaver (b. 1925, d. 16 January 1975) and Bernie Krause (b. Detroit, Michigan, USA) were early exponents of electronic music. Beaver played in several jazz groups prior to exploring synthesized instrumentation, and later contributed sound effects to various film soundtracks (*Rosemary's Baby* (1968), *Catch 22* (1970), *Performance* (1970)). Krause came from a folk background, as a member of the Weavers and was later employed at Motown in studio production. Moving on to Elektra, it was as a staff producer that he met Paul Beaver. Working together, their use of spoken word,

Bay City Rollers

acoustic instruments, tape loops and improvisation to push back the boundaries of rock and, as session men, their work graced albums by the Beatles, Beach Boys, Rolling Stones, Simon And Garfunkel, Neil Young and many more. *Gandharva*, recorded live in San Francisco's Grace Cathedral, proved the most popular of their own releases, and featured additional contributions from guitarist Mike Bloomfield and saxophonist Gerry Mulligan. Paul Beaver completed a solo album, *Perchance To Dream*, prior to his death from a heart attack in January 1975. Krause has meanwhile continued to forge a career in electronic music.
Albums: *Ragnarock* (1969), *In A Wild Sanctuary* (1970), *Gandharva* (1971), *All Good Men* (1972), *A Guide To Electronic Music* (1975).

Be-Bop Deluxe

During the comparatively barren times for progressive music during the early 70s, guitarist Bill Nelson (b. 18 December 1948, Wakefield, Yorkshire, England) recorded the limited edition *Northern Dream*. Tapes of this collector's item, were played by the pioneering disc jockey John Peel on his legendary BBC radio programme *Top Gear*. The line-up of Nelson, Nick Chatterton-Dew (drums), Robert Bryan (bass) and Ian Parkin (guitar) recorded *Axe Victim* as Be-Bop Deluxe. Nelson soon disbanded the group, and following a tour supporting Cockney Rebel he formed a new band, taking members from that fragmented unit. This short-lived combo also broke up. With the addition of New Zealander Charlie Tumahai and Simon Fox, Nelson released *Futurama* and *Sunburst Finish*. The latter contained a surprise hit single 'Ships In The Night'. Nelson's undeniable talent as a guitarist began to dominate the band and as his technical virtuosity grew, the songs became weaker. Nelson abandoned the name in 1978 for the more radical Red Noise, retaining Andrew Clarke from the old band, although he now records under his own name. During their peak, Be-Bop Deluxe were an exciting and refreshing group who were ultimately unable to find a musical niche that suited their varied styles.
Albums: *Axe Victim* (1974), *Futurama* (1975), *Sunburst Finish* (1976), *Modern Music* (1976), *Live! In The Air Age* (1977), *Drastic Plastic* (1978). Compilation: *Raiding The Divine Archive: The Best Of Be-Bop Deluxe* (1990).

Beck, Bogert And Appice

The plan for guitar virtuoso Jeff Beck (b. 24 June 1944, Surrey, England), to form a power trio with the ex-Vanilla Fudge rhythm section was mooted in 1969. Both drummer, Carmine Appice (b. 15 December 1946, New York, USA), and bassist Tim Bogert (b. 27 August 1944, Richfield, New Jersey, USA), were dissatisfied with their present band. The plans were spoiled when Beck was involved in a serious car crash that put him out of action. Meanwhile, Bogert and Appice formed the heavy rock band Cactus, until in 1972 their paths crossed again with Beck and they put together the heavy rock unit Beck, Bogert And Appice. The self-titled commercially successful debut was instrumentally superb, heavy and loud, but suffered from a lack of any songwriting ability and strained vocals. Twenty years later the album sounds ponderous, clumsy and is justifiably disowned by its members.
Albums: *Beck, Bogert And Appice* (1973), *Live In Japan* (1974).

Beck, Jeff

b. 24 June 1944, Wallington, Surrey, England. As a former choir boy the young Beck was interested in music from an early age, becoming a competent pianist and guitarist by the age of 11. His first main band was the Tridents, who made a name for themselves locally. After leaving them Beck took on the seemingly awesome task of stepping into the shoes of Eric Clapton, who had recently departed from the 60s R&B pioneers, the Yardbirds. Clapton had a fiercely loyal following, but Beck soon had them gasping with his amazing guitar pyrotechnics, utilizing feedback and distortion. Beck stayed with the Yardbirds adding colour and excitement to all their hits until October 1966. The tension between Beck and the joint lead guitarist Jimmy Page was resolved during a US tour. Beck walked out and never returned. His solo career was launched in March 1967 with a different sounding Beck on a pop single 'Hi-Ho Silver Lining'. Jeff's unremarkable voice was heard on a sing-along number which was saved by his trademark guitar solo. The record was a sizeable hit and has subsequently demonstrated its perennial appeal to party-goers by re-entering the charts twice in 1972 and 1982. The follow-up, 'Tallyman' was also a minor hit, but by now Jeff's ambitions were in other directions. He retired from being a singing, guitar-playing, pop star and started a career that led him to become one of the world's leading rock guitarists. The Jeff Beck Group, formed in 1968, consisted of Beck, Rod Stewart (vocals), Ron Wood (bass), Nicky Hopkins (piano) and Mickey Waller (drums). This powerhouse

Jeff Beck

quartet released *Truth*, which became a major success in the USA, resulting in the band undertaking a number of arduous tours. The second album *Cosa Nostra Beck-Ola* had similar success, although Stewart and Wood had now departed for the Faces. Beck also contributed some sparkling guitar and received equal billing with Donovan on the hit 'Goo Goo Barabajagal (Love Is Hot)'. In 1968 Jeff's serious accident with one of his hot-rod cars put him out of action for almost 18 months. A recovered Beck formed another group with Cozy Powell, Max Middleton and Bob Tench, and recorded two further albums, *Rough And Ready* and *Jeff Beck Group*. The latter became a sizeable hit. Beck was now fully accepted as a serious musician, and figured highly in various guitarist polls. In 1973 the erratic Beck musical style changed once again and he formed the trio Beck, Bogert And Appice with the two former members of Vanilla Fudge. Only one official album was released and Beck introduced yet another facet, this time forming an instrumental band. The result was the excellent *Blow By Blow*, thought by many to be his best work. His guitar work showed extraordinary technique combining rock, jazz and blues styles. It was a million seller and the follow-up, *Wired* had similar success. Having allied himself with some of the jazz/rock fraternity Beck teamed up with Jan Hammer for a frantic live album. Following its release Beck effectively retired for three years. He returned in 1980 with *There And Back*. His loyal fans had not deserted him, and, now rejuvenated, he found himself riding the album charts. During the 80s, Beck's appearances have been sporadic. He has appeared at charity functions and has spent much of his leisure time with automobiles. In one interview Beck stated that he could just as easily have been a car restorer. In the mid-80s he toured with Rod Stewart and was present on his version of 'People Get Ready'. The album *Flash* came in 1985, but proved his least successful to date. Jeff Beck has already ensured his place in the history book of guitarists and his no-nonsense approach to the music industry has earned him considerable respect. The release of a box-set in 1992, chronicling his career, was a fitting tribute to this accomplished guitarist.
Albums: *Truth* (1968), *Cosa Nostra Beck-Ola* (1969), *Rough And Ready* (1971), *Jeff Beck Group* (1972), *Blow By Blow* (1975), *Wired* (1976), *Jeff Beck With The Jan Hammer Group Live* (1977), *There And Back* (1980), *Flash* (1985), with Terry Bozzio, Tony Hymas *Jeff Beck's Guitar Shop* (1989).
Compilations: with Rod Stewart *The Late '60s*

(1988), CD box set *Beckology* (1992).

Bedford, David

A graduate from London's Royal Academy of Music in London, this accomplished musician achieved considerable acclaim for his striking arrangements on Kevin Ayers's debut, *Joy Of A Toy* in 1969. Their working relationship was maintained on several subsequent releases and Bedford was also a member of the singer's backing group, the Whole World, prior to embarking on an independent recording career. The artist's first solo offering, *Nurses Song With Elephants*, was released in 1972. This eclectic, experimental collection featured former Whole World guitarist, Mike Oldfield, one of several fruitful collaborations that Bedford would enjoy. Roy Harper was another artist to benefit from the arranger's intuitive talent, exemplified in such stellar achievements as 'Me And My Woman' (*Stormcock*) and 'When An Old Cricketer Leaves The Crease (*HQ*). Bedford's 1974 release, *Star's End*, featured a composition commissioned by the Royal Philharmonic Orchestra, while the following year he completed *The Orchestral Tubular Bells*, a classical interpretation of Oldfield's multi-million-selling album, and *The Rime Of The Ancient Mariner*, a musical portrayal of the famous Samuel Taylor Coleridge poem. Literature also provided the inspiration for *The Odyssey*, but such ambitious projects lacked the humility the artist bestowed on his external work. Bedford's grandiose performances fell from favour in the late 70s, but he remains a respected, and imaginative figure arranging studio orchestration for various musicians and groups.
Albums: *Nurses Song With Elephants* (1972), *Star's End* (1974), *The Orchestral Tubular Bells* (1975), *The Rime Of The Ancient Mariner* (1975), *The Odyssey* (1976), *Instructions For Angels* (1977), *Rigel 9* (1988).

Bedlam

Formed in 1972 and originally known as Beast, Bedlam comprised of former Truth singer Frank Aiello (vocals), Dave Ball (guitar), Dennis Ball (bass) and Cozy Powell (drums). Each of the group, barring Aiello, were previously members of the Ace Kefford Stand and Big Bertha, but this new act was convened following Powell's tenure with Jeff Beck and Dave Ball's spell in Procol Harum. Despite early optimism, *Bedlam* failed to establish the UK quartet as a commercial proposition and they split in 1974. Powell and

Aiello then formed Cozy Powell's Hammer, while their ex-colleagues left music altogether.
Album: *Bedlam* (1973).

Bee Gees

This hugely successful Anglo/Australian trio comprised of the twins Maurice and Robin Gibb (b. 22 December 1949, Isle Of Man, British Isles) and their elder brother Barry Gibb (b. 1 September 1946, Isle Of Man, British Isles). Hailing from a showbusiness family based in Manchester, England, they played as a child act in several of the city's cinemas. In 1958, the Gibb family emigrated to Australia and the boys performed regularly as a harmony trio in Brisbane, Queensland. Christened the Bee Gees, an abbreviation of Brothers Gibb, they signed to the Australian label Festival Records and released a series of singles written by the elder brother. While their single 'Spicks And Specks' was topping the Australian charts, the brothers were already on their way to London for a fateful audition before Robert Stigwood, a director of NEMS Enterprises, the company owned by Beatles svengali Brian Epstein. This, in turn, led to a record contract with Polydor and the swift release of 'New York Mining Disaster, 1941'. The quality of the single with its evocative, intriguing lyrics and striking harmony provoked premature comparison with the Beatles and gained the group a sizeable UK hit. During this period the trio were supplemented by Australian friends Colin Peterson (drums) and Vince Melouney (guitar). The second UK single, 'To Love Somebody', departed from the narrative power of their previous offering towards a more straightforward ballad style. Although the disc failed to reach the Top 40, the enduring quality of the song was evinced by a number of striking cover versions, most notably by Nina Simone, Eric Burdon And The Animals and Janis Joplin. The Beatlesque songs on their outstanding acclaimed UK debut, *The Bee Gees First* garnered further comparisons. Every track was a winner from the delightfully naive 'Cucumber Castle' to the sublime 'Please Read Me', while 'Holiday' had the beautiful stark quality of McCartney's 'Yesterday'. The 14 tracks, were all composed by the twins and Barry, still aged only 17 and 19 respectively. By October 1967, the group had registered their first UK number 1 with the moving 'Massachusetts', which showed off their ability as arrangers to particular effect. Aware of the changes occurring in the pop firmament, the group bravely experimented with different musical styles and briefly followed the Beatles and the Rolling Stones along the psychedelic road. Their progressive forays confused their audience, however, and the double album *Odessa* failed to match the work of their major rivals. Their singles remained adventurous and strangely eclectic with the unusual tempo of 'World' followed by the neurotic romanticism of 'Words'. Both singles hit the Top 10 in the UK but signs of commercial fallibility followed with the relatively unsuccessful double a-side 'Jumbo'/'The Singer Not The Song'. Masters of the chart come-back, the group next turned to a heart-rending ballad about the final hour of a condemned prisoner. 'I've Gotta Get A Message To You' gave them their second UK number 1 and sixth consecutive US Top 20 hit. The stark but startling 'First Of May' followed, again revealing the Bee Gees willingness to tackle a mood piece in favour of an easily accessible melodic ballad. To complete their well-rounded image, the group showed their talent as composers, penning the Marbles' Top 10 UK hit 'Only One Woman'.

Without question, the Bee Gees were one of the most accomplished groups of the late 60s' but as the decade ended they fell victim to internal bickering and various pressures wrought by international stardom. Maurice Gibb married pop star Lulu and the group joined the celebrity showbusiness elite with all its attendant trappings of drink and drugs. Dissent among the brotherhood saw Robin Gibb embark on a solo career with brief success while the twins retained the group name. Remarkably, they ended the 60s with another change of style emerging with an authentic country standard in 'Don't Forget To Remember'. With Colin Peterson still in tow, Maurice and Barry worked on a much-publicized but ultimately insubstantial film, *Cucumber Castle*. This fractious period ended with a ludicrous series of law suits in which the drummer had the audacity to claim rights to the Bee Gees name. A year of chaos and missed opportunities ensued during which the group lost much of their impetus and following. Maurice and Barry both released one single each as soloists, but their efforts were virtually ignored. Their career in the UK was in tatters but after reuniting with Robin in late 1970 they went on to score two major US hits with 'Lonely Days' and the chart-topping 'How Can You Mend A Broken Heart'.

After a brief flurry of transatlantic hits in 1972 with 'My World' and 'Run To Me', the group's appeal diminished to an all-time low. Three hitless years saw them reduced to playing in cabaret at such inauspicious venues as the Batley Variety Club in Yorkshire. A switch from Polydor Records to Robert Stigwood's new label RSO encouraged the group to adopt a more American sound with the album *Life In A Tin Can*. Determined to explore a more distinctive style, the group were teamed with famed producer Arif Mardin. *Mr. Natural*, recorded in London, indicated a noticeable R&B/soul influence which was extended on 1975's *Main Course*. Now ensconced in Miami, the group gathered together a formidable backing unit featuring Alan Kendall (guitar), Dennis Bryon (drums) and Blue Weaver (keyboards). 'Jive Talkin'', a pilot single from the album, zoomed to number 1 in the US and brought the trio back to the Top 10 in Britain. Meanwhile, fellow RSO artist Olivia Newton-John enjoyed a US hit with the group's country ballad 'Come On Over'. The Bee Gees were well and truly back.

The changes in their sound during the mid-70s was nothing short of remarkable. They had virtually re-invented themselves, with Mardin encouraging them to explore their R&B roots and experiment with falsetto vocals. The effect was particularly noticeable on their next US Top 10 hit 'Nights On Broadway' (later a hit for Candi Staton). The group were perfectly placed to promote and take advantage of the underground dance scene in the US, and their next album *Children Of The World* went platinum. The attendant single 'You Should Be Dancing' reached number 1 in the US, while the follow-up 'Love So Right' hit number 3. Not content to revitalize their own career the trio's soundtrack contributions also provided massive hits for Yvonne Elliman ('If I Can't Have You') and Tavares ('More Than A Woman'). The Bee Gees' reputation as the new gods of the discotheque was consummated on the soundtrack of the movie *Saturday Night Fever*, which sold in excess of 30 million copies. In their most successful phase to date, the group achieved a quite staggering run of six consecutive chart toppers: 'How Deep Is Your Love', 'Stayin' Alive', 'Night Fever', 'Too Much Heaven', 'Tragedy' and 'Love You Inside Out'. Their grand flurry continued with the movie *Grease*, for which they produced the chart-topping title track by Frankie Valli. Having already received Beatles comparisons during their early career, it was ill-advised of the group to take the starring role in the movie *Sgt. Pepper's Lonely Hearts Club Band*. The film proved an embarrassing detour for both the brothers and their co-star Peter Frampton.

As the 70s ended the Bee Gees increasingly switched their interests towards production.

Although they released two further albums, *Spirits Having Flown* (1979) and *Living Eyes* (1981), far greater attention was being focused on their chart-topping younger brother Andy Gibb. A multi-million dollar dispute with their mentor Robert Stigwood was settled out of court following which the group contributed towards another movie soundtrack *Stayin' Alive*. With the group's activities put on hold, it was Barry who emerged as the most prolific producer and songwriter. He duetted with Barbra Streisand on the chart-topping 'Guilty' and composed and sang on 'Heartbreaker' with Dionne Warwick. The brothers, meanwhile, also wrote the Kenny Rogers and Dolly Parton US chart topper 'Islands In The Stream' and Diana Ross's excellent Motown pastiche 'Chain Reaction'. Seemingly content to stay in the background masterminding platinum discs for others, they eventually reunited in 1987 for the hugely successful *ESP*. The indisputable masters of melody, their 'come-back' single 'You Win Again' was warmly received by usually hostile critics who applauded its undoubted craftsmanship. The single gave the group their fifth UK number 1, a full eight years after their last chart topper, 'Tragedy'. Sadly, the death of younger brother Andy the following year added a tragic note to the proceedings. In deference to their brother's death they declined to attend an Ivor Novello Awards ceremony in which they were honoured for their Outstanding Contribution to British Music.

Looking back over the Bee Gees' career, one cannot fail to be impressed by the sheer diversification of their talents and their remarkable ability to continually re-invent themselves again and again. Like that other great family group the Beach Boys they have survived family feuds, dissension, tragic death, harsh criticism, changes in musical fashion and much else to become one of pop's ineffable institutions. Throughout all the musical changes they have undergone, the one constant has been their vocal dexterity, strength and an innate ability to arrange some wondrous pop melodies. The legacy of their performing, songwriting and production activities represents one of the richest tapestries in the entire history of modern popular music.

Albums: *Barry Gibb And The Bee Gees Sing And Play 14 Barry Gibb Songs* (1965), *Spicks And Specks* (1966), *The Bee Gees First* (1967), *Horizontal* (1968), *Idea* (1968), *Odessa* (1969), *Cucumber Castle* (1970), *Two Years On* (1970), *Trafalgar* (1971), *To Whom It May Concern* (1972), *Life In A Tin Can* (1973), *Mr Natural* (1974), *Main Course* (1975),

Children Of The World (1976), *Here At Last . . . Bee Gees Live* (1977), *Saturday Night Fever* (1977), *Sgt. Pepper's Lonely Hearts Club Band* (1978), *Spirits Having Flown* (1979), *Living Eyes* (1981), *Stayin' Alive* (1983), *ESP* (1987), *High Civilisation* (1991). Compilations: *Rare Precious And Beautiful* (1968), *Rare Precious And Beautiful Vol. 2* (1968), *Rare Precious And Beautiful Vol. 3* (1969), *Best Of The Bee Gees* (1969), *Best Of The Bee Gees Vol. 2* (1973), *Bee Gees Gold Volume One* (1976), *Bee Gees Greatest* (1979), *The Early Days Vol. 1* (1979), *The Early Days Vol. 2* (1979), *The Early Days Vol. 3* (1979).

Bell, Maggie

b. 12 January 1945, Glasgow, Scotland. Bell's career began in the mid-60s as the featured singer in several resident dance-hall bands. She made her recording debut in 1966, completing two singles, with Bobby Kerr, under the name Frankie And Johnny. Bell then joined guitarist Leslie Harvey, another veteran of the same circuit, in Power, a hard-rock group which evolved into Stone The Crows. This earthy, soul-based band, memorable for Harvey's imaginative playing and Maggie's gutsy, heart-felt vocals, became a highly popular live attraction and helped the singer win several accolades. The group split up in 1973, still rocked by Leslie's tragic death the previous year. Bell embarked on a solo career with *Queen Of The Night*, which was produced in New York by Jerry Wexler and featured the cream of the city's session musicians. The anticipated success did not materialize and further releases failed to reverse this trend. The singer did score a minor UK hit with 'Hazell' (1978), the theme tune to a popular television series, but 'Hold Me', a tongue-in-cheek duet with B.A. Robertson, remains her only other chart entry. Bell subsequently fronted a new group, Midnight Flyer, but this tough, underrated singer, at times redolent of Janis Joplin, has been unable to secure a distinctive career.
Albums: *Queen Of The Night* (1974), *Suicide Sal* (1975). Compilation: *Great Rock Sensation* (1977).

Bell And Arc

Formed in 1970 by songwriters John Turnbull (guitar/vocals) and Mickey Gallagher (keyboards/vocals), one-time colleagues in Skip Bifferty. Their new venture, originally known simply as Arc, was completed by Tommy Duffy (bass) and Dave Trudex (drums), although the latter was replaced by Rob Tait (ex-Battered Ornaments) prior to the recording of *Arc At This*. The quartet was then invited to back singer Graham Bell, another Skip Bifferty acolyte, on a projected album. This in turn inspired a new epithet, Bell And Arc, but their sole release sadly failed to capture the live sparkle displayed on tours supporting Genesis and the Who. Drummer Alan White, later of Yes, replaced Tait late in 1971, but the quintet broke up the following year. Bell then resumed his solo career while Gallagher and Turnbull pursued separate paths with among others, Glencoe and Peter Frampton, before reuniting in Ian Dury's Blockheads.
Albums: as Arc *Arc At This* (1971), as Bell And Arc *Bell And Arc* (1971).

Benno, Marc

b. Benny Darron, 1 July 1947, Dallas, Texas, USA. Benno initially played guitar in several Austin-based garage-bands, including the Outcasts and White Tornadoes, before fronting the Nightcrawlers between 1967 and 1968. He then moved to Los Angeles and having befriended Leon Russell, joined this talented multi-instrumentalist in the Asylum Choir. However, the duo's psychedelic debut was not a commercial success, and they split up when a second set was denied a release. Benno then provided bass guitar on *L.A. Woman*, the final Doors' album to feature singer Jim Morrison, before returning to Texas. Here he completed four competent, if unexceptional, releases for the A&M label, of which the first, *Marc Benno*, was the strongest. The artist worked on a session basis with Georgie Fame, before forming a new band with Bonnie Bramlett in 1975. Although commanding a certain respect, Benno enjoys a reputation as a dependable sideman, rather than leader.
Albums: *Marc Benno* (1970), *Window* (1971), *Ambush* (1972), *Lost In Austin* (1979).

Bethnal

Formed in London in 1972, Bethnal found themselves caught up in the 'new wave' of 1977 and were automatically re-defined as punk so as not to be ignored. They quickly severed their connection with the movement in 1978, when the press and media abandoned punk, describing it as 'dead'. Composed of George Csapo (vocals/keyboards/violin), Pete Dowling (drums), Nick Michaels (guitar) and Everton Williams (bass), they built up a large following through intense live gigging, and the end of 1977 saw them sign to Vertigo Records. Their debut came with 'The Fiddler', a live recording given away throughout their December UK tour. It was quickly followed by the release of 'We Gotta Get Out Of This Place', a cover of the classic Animals track. After a further single 'Don't Do It', they participated in the Reading Festival and continued a heavy gig schedule in preparation for the release of *Crash Landing*. It was recorded at Abbey Road Studios under the guidance of Pete Townshend as 'musical director'. Gaining much critical acclaim, the album marked a very creative period for Bethnal, displaying great originality and proficiency. Even so, the anticipated success did not arrive and in 1979 they left Vertigo and looked for a new contract. For almost a year they remained unsigned until tension within the band caused the final split in 1980.

Albums: *Dangerous Times* (1978), *Crash Landing* (1978).

Betts, Richard 'Dickie'

b. 12 December 1943, Jacksonville, Florida, USA. Formerly with Tommy Roe's Romans, this exceptional guitarist was also a member of the Second Coming, a Jacksonville group which featured bassist Berry Oakley. Both musicians joined the Allman Brothers Band at its inception in 1969 and Richard's melodic lines provided the foil and support for leader Duane Allman's inventive slide soloing. Allman's tragic death in 1971 allowed Betts to come forward, a responsibility he shouldered admirably on the group's excellent *Brothers And Sisters* album. The country flavour prevalent on several of the tracks, most notably 'Ramblin' Man', set the tone for Dickie's solo career. *Highway Call* was released in 1974 but its promise was overshadowed by the parent group's own recordings. Betts formed a new group, Great Southern, in 1976, but their progress faltered when the guitarist was drawn into the resurrected Allman's fold. In 1971, Betts formed BHLT with Jimmy Hall (from Wet Willie), Chuck Leavell, Butch Trucks and David Goldflies, but they too were doomed to a premature collapse and the guitarist withdrew from active work. However, in the late 80s Betts was signed to Epic, the outlet for whom Gregg Allman was recording, prompting rumours of a reunion.

Albums: *Highway Call* (1974), *Dickie Betts And The Great Southern* (1977), *Atlanta Burning Down* (1978).

Big Star

Formed in Memphis, Tennessee, USA in 1971, Big Star evolved when ex-Box Tops' singer Alex Chilton joined a local group, Ice Water - Chris Bell (guitar/vocals), Andy Hummel (bass) and Jody Stephens (drums). The realigned quartet made an impressive debut with *#1 Record*, which skilfully synthesized British pop and 60s-styled Los Angeles harmonies into a taut, resonant sound. Its commercial potential was marred by poor distribution while internal friction led to Bell's departure late in 1972. This talented artist was killed in December 1979 as a result of a car crash. Although the remaining trio dissolved Big Star in 1973, they reconvened later in the year for a rock writer's convention where the resultant reaction inspired a more permanent reunion. *Radio City* lacked the polish of its predecessor, but a sense of urgency and spontaneity generated a second excellent set, of which the anthemic 'September Gurls' proved an undoubted highlight. Corporate disinterest once again doomed the project and an embittered Big Star retreated to Memphis following a brief, ill-starred, tour on which John Lightman had replaced a disinclined Hummel. Chilton and Stephens then began work on a projected third album with the assistance of Steve Cropper (guitar), Jim Dickinson (piano) and Tommy McLure (bass), but sessions proved more fractured than ever and the group broke up without officially completing the set. *3rd* has subsequently appeared in various guises and mixes, yet each betray Chilton's vulnerability as a series of bare-nerved compositions show his grasp of structure slipping away and providing a template for the singer's equally erratic solo career.

Albums: *#1 Record* (1972), *Radio City* (1974), *3rd* (1978), *3rd/Sister Lovers* (1992), *Live* (recorded 1974)1992.

Billion Dollar Babies

This short-lived group revolved around Michael Bruce (b. 21 November 1948, California, USA; guitar/vocals), Dennis Dunaway (b. 15 March 1946, California, USA; bass) and Neal Smith (b. 10 January 1946, Washington, USA; drums). Founder members of Alice Cooper, the trio were summarily fired in 1974 by lead singer Vince Furnier, who was known as 'Alice Cooper'. Protracted legal entanglements delayed this riposte, which took its name from one of their former group's best-selling albums. Sessionmen Bob Dolin (keyboards) and Mike Marconi (guitar) completed the line-up, but the resultant album, *Battle Axe* was a major disappointment. Its uncomfortable mix of technology and heavy metal did not prove popular and the quintet was then dissolved. Bruce embarked on a solo career and thereafter teamed up with ex-Angel drummer Barry Brandt to pursue

a jazz-orientated path. Dunaway and Smith formed the Flying Tigers while Dolin and Marconi reverted to studio work.
Album: *Battle Axe* (1977).

Birtha

Birtha were one of the first USA all-female bands to try and penetrate the exclusively male bastion of heavy rock. Comprising Rosemary Butler (bass/vocals), Sherry Hagler (keyboards), Liver Favela (drums) and Shele Pinizzotto (guitar/vocals), they released two excellent hard-rock albums during the early 70s. They specialized in tight harmonies and a style not dissimilar to that of early Uriah Heep. They were regarded as a novelty at the time, which on reflection is a little unjust. Their tasteless publicity handout during their early 70s UK tour with the Kinks stated 'Birtha has balls'. Along with Fanny they undoubtedly helped to pave the way for future female rockers such as the Runaways.
Albums: *Birtha* (1972), *Can't Stop The Madness* (1973).

Bishop, Elvin

b. 21 October 1942, Tulsa, Oklahoma, USA. Bishop moved to Chicago in his teens to study at university. An aspiring guitarist, he became one of several young, white musicians to frequent the city's blues clubs and in 1965 he joined the houseband at one such establishment, Big John's. This group subsequently became known as the Paul Butterfield Blues Band, and although initially overshadowed by guitarist Michael Bloomfield, it was here Bishop evolved a distinctive, if composite style. Elvin was featured on four Butterfield albums, but he left the group in 1968 following the release of *In My Own Dream*. By the following year he was domiciled in San Francisco, where his own group became a popular live fixture. Bishop was initially signed to Bill Graham's Fillmore label, but these and other early recordings achieved only local success.
In 1974, Dickie Betts of the Allman Brothers Band introduced the guitarist to Capricorn Records which favoured the hippie/hillbilly image Elvin had fostered and understood his melange of R&B, soul and country influences. Six albums followed, including *Let It Flow*, *Juke Joint Jump* and a live album set, *Live! Raisin' Hell*, but it was a 1975 release, *Struttin' My Stuff*, which proved most popular. It included the memorable 'Fooled Around And Fell In Love' which, when issued as a single, reached number 3 in the US chart. The featured voice was that of Mickey Thomas, who later left the group for a solo career and subsequently became frontman of Jefferson Starship. The loss of this powerful singer undermined Bishop's momentum and his new-found ascendancy proved short-lived. Elvin's career suffered a further setback in 1979 when Capricorn filed for bankruptcy. Although he remains a much-loved figure in the Bay Area live circuit, the guitarist's recorded output has been thin on the ground during the last ten years, most recently on the Alligator label, with Dr. John on *Big Fun*.
Albums: *The Elvin Bishop Group* (1969), *Feel It* (1970), *Rock My Soul* (1972), *Let It Flow* (1974), *Juke Joint Jump* (1975), *Struttin' My Stuff* (1975), *Hometown Boy Makes Good!* (1976), *Live! Raisin' Hell* (1977), *Hog Heaven* (1978), *Is You Is Or Is You Ain't My Baby* (1982), *Big Fun* (1988).

Bishop, Stephen

b. San Diego, California, USA. While he had mastered both piano and trombone, it was an older brother's gift of an electric guitar that launched a vocational flight whereby an unprepossessing, bespectacled 14-year-old became a highly popular songwriter of US pop. In 1967, he formed his first group, the Weeds, who taped some Beatles'-inspired demos in Los Angeles before disbanding. During a consequent seven-year search for a solo recording contract, Bishop worked as a tunesmith for a publishing house before landing a contract in 1976 via the patronage of Art Garfunkel. Indeed, his debut album for ABC Records, *Careless*, was much in the style of his champion. It also employed the cream of Los Angeles session players. Fortunately for ABC, it was nominated for a Grammy and, like the succeeding *Bish,* hovered in the lower reaches of the national Top 40 for several months. The spin-off singles (particularly 'On And On' from *Careless)* also fared well. The Four Tops, Chaka Khan and Barbra Streisand covered his compositions and Bishop gained studio assistance from Khan, Garfunkel, Gary Brooker, Steve Cropper, Phil Collins and other stars. He returned these favours by contributing to Collins' *Face Value* (1981), and composing 'Separate Lives'. the Englishman's duet with Marilyn Martin from the movie *White Nights*.
Bishop's own performances on film included the theme songs to *National Lampoon's Animal House* ('Dream Girl'), *Roadie* ('Your Precious Love' with Yvonne Elliman), 1982's *Tootsie* 'It Might Be You, a non-original) and *China Syndrome*. In common with the ubiquitous Garfunkel, he also tried his

band as a supporting actor - notably in 1980's *The Blues Brothers* and *Kentucky Fried Movie* - but his musicianship remains Bishop's calling card. Although his 80s albums have been commercially erratic, he has extended his stylistic range - as exemplified by *Red Cab To Manhattan*, which embraced both a stab at big band jazz ('This Is The Night', and 'Don't You Worry', a tribute to the Beatles.

Albums: *Careless* (1976), *Bish* (1978), *Red Cab To Manhattan* (1980).

Blackfeather

The controversy that embroiled this Australian band, formed in Sydney in 1970, seemed to ensure it's longevity. The group disbanded and reformed numerous times with as many as 30 musicians having passed through the ranks. On two occasions during the 70s, there were two entirely different line-ups claiming to have rights to the name. However, there are two distinct periods when Blackfeather had Australian chart success and considerable live popularity, the only link being Neale Johns (vocals). The first in 1970-71 was as a progressive rock band, featuring John Robinson (guitar), which produced the excellent 'Seasons Of Change' and *Mountains Of Madness*. The second period was based around the thumping piano of Paul Wylde and Johns, who in 1972 scored hit singles with 'Boppin' The Blues' (an Australian number 1) and its follow-up 'Slippin' And Slidin''. This enhanced the band's live reputation, attracting large crowds wherever they played. A live album was released in 1974, by which time some confusion was compounded by the fact that Johns and previous Blackfeather members were gigging under the name of Flake, another Sydney band that had undergone many changes. Several Blackfeather incarnations later Johns went to the UK to form Fingerprint and record an album with ex-Marc Bolan band members. The remaining members took on John Swan as vocalist and shortened their name to Feather. Johns returned to Australia and fronted several more Blackfeathers, but by 1980 both Blackfeather and Feather were finally laid to rest.

Albums: *Mountains Of Madness* (1971), *Boppin' The Blues* (1972), *Live At Sunbury* (1974).

Blackfoot

Southern USA rock practitioners Blackfoot initially comprised of Rick Medlocke (guitar/vocals), Charlie Hargrett (guitar), Greg Walker (bass) and Jakson Spires (drums/vocals). The quartet shared common origins with Lynyrd Skynyrd and in turn offered a similar blues/rock-based sound, centred on Medlocke's confident playing. Session pianist Jimmy Johnson produced Blackfoot's early work at the revered Muscle Shoals studio, but despite this impressive pedigree, the group was unable to translate an in-concert popularity into record sales. *Strikes*, the unit's first release for Atlantic/Atco, offered a heavier perspective, while the cream of their early work was captured live on *Highway Song*. Ken Hensley, formerly of Uriah Heep, joined the line-up for *Siogo* and *Vertical Smiles*, but Blackfoot was disbanded following the latter's release.

Albums: *No Reservations* (1975), *Flying High* (1976), *Blackfoot Strikes* (1979), *Tomcattin'* (1980), *Maurauder* (1981), *Highway Song* (1982), *Siogo* (1983), *Vertical Smiles* (1984).

Blackfoot Sue

Previously known as Gift and led by twin brothers Tom (bass/keyboards/vocals) and Dave Farmer (both b. 2 March 1952, Birmingham, England; drums), this group was completed by Eddie Galga (b. 4 September 1951, Birmingham, England; lead guitar/keyboards) and Alan Jones (b. 5 January 1950, Birmingham, England; guitar/vocals). The quartet scored a UK Top 5 hit in 1972 with 'Standing In The Road', but although its rhythmic performance appealed successfully to pop and rock audiences, Blackfoot Sue proved unable to retain such a deft balance. They scored a minor hit the same year with 'Sing Don't Speak', but heavier elements displayed on subsequent albums were derided by commentators viewing the group as a purely 'teeny-bop' attraction. Blackfoot Sue broke up following the release of *Strangers* which appeared in the midst of the punk boom.

Albums: *Nothing To Hide* (1973), *Gun Running* (1975), *Strangers* (1977).

Black Oak Arkansas

A sextet formed in the late 60s, Black Oak Arkansas took its name from the USA town and state where singer Jim 'Dandy' Mangrum (b. 30 March 1948) was born. The other members of the group were born and lived in nearby towns: Ricky Reynolds (b. 28 October 1948, Manilan, Arkansas, USA; guitar), Stanley Knight (b. 12 February 1949, Little Rock, Arkansas, USA; guitar), Harvey Jett (b. Marion, Arkansas, USA; guitar), Pat Daugherty (b. 11 November 1947, Jonesboro, Arkansas, USA; bass) and drummer Wayne Evans, replaced on the third album by Thomas Aldrich (b. 15 August,

1950, Jackson, Mississippi, USA). Before forming the band, the future members were a gang that shared a house. At first calling themselves the Knowbody Else, the group recorded an unsuccessful album for Stax Records in 1969. Two years later they changed their name and signed with Atco Records, for which they recorded a self-titled album that fared moderately on US charts. Touring steadily, the hard-rock/southern boogie band built a core following, yet its records never matched its concert appeal. Of their 10 charting albums between 1971 and 1976, *High On The Hog*, proved the best-selling at number 52. It featured the best-selling 1974 Top 30 single, 'Jim Dandy' (sung by female vocalist Ruby Starr, who reappeared on the 1976 *Live! Mutha* album). In 1975, guitarist Jett was replaced by James Henderson (b. 20 May 1954, Jackson, Mississippi, USA) and the following year, after switching to MCA Records, Black Oak Arkansas had only one further minor chart single, 'Strong Enough To Be Gentle'. By 1977 only Mangrum remained from the original band and although they signed to Capricorn Records, there was no further record success. Mangrum did, however, keep variations of the group on the road during the 80s as well as recording a solo album in 1984.

Albums: as the Knowbody Else *The Knowbody Else* (1969); as Black Oak Arkansas *Black Oak Arkansas* (1971), *Keep The Faith* (1972), *If An Angel Came To See You, Would You Make Her Feel At Home?* (1972), *Raunch 'N' Roll/Live* (1973), *High On The Hog* (1973), *Street Party* (1974), *Ain't Life Grand* (1975), *X-Rated* (1975), *Live! Mutha* (1976), *Balls of Fire* (1976), *10 Year Overnight Success* (1976), *Race With The Devil* (1977), *I'd Rather Be Sailing* (1978), *Black Attack Is Back* (1986). Compilation: *The Best Of Black Oak Arkansas* (1977). Solo album: Jim Dandy *Randy As Hell* (1984).

Black Sabbath

Group members Terry 'Geezer' Butler (b. 17 July 1949, Birmingham, England; bass), Tony Iommi (b. 19 February 1948, Birmingham, England; guitar), Bill Ward (b. 5 May 1948, Birmingham, England; drums) and 'Ozzy' Osbourne (b. 3 December 1948, Birmingham, England; vocals) were originally known as Earth, a name they changed to Black Sabbath in 1969. The members of this band grew up together in the musically fertile English midlands, and their name hints at the heavy, doom-laden and yet ingenious music they produced. The name comes from a book by the occult writer Denis Wheatley, and many of their songs deal with alternative beliefs and ways of life. The title track of *Paranoid* confronts mental instability, and other songs are concerned with the effects of narcotic substances such as cocaine and marijuana. The line-up remained unchanged until 1973 when Rick Wakeman, keyboard player for Yes was drafted in to play on *Sabbath Bloody Sabbath*. By 1977, personnel difficulties within the band were beginning to take their toll, and the music was losing some of its earlier orchestral, heavy metal feel, and in 1978 Ozzy Osbourne left to pursue a solo career. He was replaced by Ronnie James Dio. Dio had been a central figure in the early 70s band Elf, and spent three years with Ritchie Blackmore's Rainbow. Dio's experience with the band was to be short-lived, and he left in 1982. For a while Vinnie Appice, brother of Carmine Appice, had been Sabbath's drummer The replacement vocalist was Ian Gillan. It is this Sabbath incarnation which is commonly regarded as the most disastrous for band and fans alike, *Born Again* failing to capture any of the original vitality of the group. In 1986, the entire line-up was rethought. Iommi was the only original member of the band, which now consisted of Geoff Nichols (b. Birmingham, England; keyboards), Glenn Hughes (b. England; vocals), Dave Spitz (b. New York City, New York, USA; bass), and Eric Singer (b. Cleveland, Ohio, USA; drums).This was an accomplished combination, Singer having been a member of the Lita Ford Band, and Glenn Hughes having worked with such legendary bands as Misunderstood, Trapeze and Deep Purple. In 1986, the surprisingly blues-sounding *Seventh Star* was released, the lyrics and music for which had been written by Iommi. In the first of a succession of personnel changes, Hughes left the band to be replaced by Ray Gillen, an American singer who failed to record anything with them. Vandenburg is the vocalist on the powerful 1987 the *Eternal Idol* and on *Headless Cross,* the album which skilled and renowned drummer Cozy Powell produced and appeared on. By late 1991, Sabbath was suffering from flagging record sales and declining credibility so Iommi recruited their original bassist, Butler, and attempted to persuade drummer Bill Ward to rejoin too. Ward, however, was not interested, Cozy Powell was still recuperating after being crushed by his horse, and so Vinnie Appice became Sabbath's new drummer. After much speculation, a return to the band by Ronnie Dio completed the 1982/3 line-up.

Albums: *Black Sabbath* (1970), *Paranoid* (1970),

Master Of Reality (1971), *Black Sabbath Vol. 4* (1972), *Sabbath Bloody Sabbath* (1974), *Sabotage* (1975), *Technical Ecstasy* (1976), *We Sold Our Soul For Rock And Roll* (1976), *Never Say Die* (1978), *Heaven And Hell* (1980), *Live At Last* (1980), *Mob Rules* (1981), *Live Evil* (1982), *Born Again* (1983), *Seventh Star* (1986), *The Eternal Idol* (1987), *Headless Cross* (1989), *Tyr* (1990). Compilations: *Greatest Hits* (1980), *Collection: Black Sabbath* (1985), *The Ozzy Osbourne Years* (1991).

Black Sheep

This group was formed in New York in 1974, by vocalist Louis Grammatico and guitarist Donald Mancuso. Recruiting Larry Crozier (keyboards), Bruce Turgon (bass), and Ron Rocco (drums), they signed with Capitol Records the following year. Influenced by Bad Company, Free and Led Zeppelin, they recorded two excellent hard-rock albums, characterized by Grammatico's powerful, yet soulful vocal style. Unable to make an impact, the band split up, with Grammatico changing his name to Lou Gramm and found considerable success with Foreigner. Turgon, after a spell with Warrior, later helped co-write Gramm's first solo album.
Albums: *Black Sheep* (1975), *Encouraging Words* (1976).

Black Widow

A progressive rock band from Leicester, England, the group was formed as soul band Pesky Gee in 1966 by Jim Gannon (vocals/guitar/vibraphone) with Kay Garrett (vocals), Kip Trevor (vocals/guitar/harmonica), Zoot Taylor (keyboards), Clive Jones (woodwind), Bob Bond (bass) and Clive Box (drums). Pesky Gee made one album for Pye before re-forming without Garrett as Black Widow.
The band's first album and its elaborate stage act (choreographed by members of Leicester's Phoenix Theatre company) were based by Gannon on research into black magic rituals. Black Widow's 'Come To The Sabbat' appeared on the CBS sampler, *The Rock Machine Turns You On* which was a Top 20 hit in 1969. The group toured throughout Europe and appeared at the Isle of Wight Festivals of 1969 and 1970.
The debut album reached the Top 40 in the UK and after its release Romeo Challenger and Geoff Griffiths replaced Box and Bond. Later albums abandoned the witchcraft theme and were unmemorable. On *Three*, John Culley from Cressida replaced Gannon who later worked with

Trevor on an abortive project to turn the *Black Widow* stage show into a Broadway musical.
Gannon went on to play with songwriter Kenny Young in Fox and Yellow Dog before joining Sherbet and moving to Australia where he leads a club band called Bop Till You Drop. Trevor worked as a session singer and music publisher while Challenger plays drums for Showaddywaddy.
Albums: *Sacrifice* (1970), *Black Widow* (1971), *Three* (1971).

Blakley, Ronee

b. Idaho, USA. Blakely emerged from the Los Angeles-based singer/songwriter milieu of the early 70s. *Ronee Blakely*, an accomplished country-rock collection, drew considerable critical acclaim and in turn inspired film director Robert Altman to cast the artist in his film *Nashville* (1975). *Welcome*, which featured the crack Muscle Shoals houseband, was another crafted selection, but the singer is best recalled for her participation in Bob Dylan's informal touring ensemble, the Rolling Thunder Revue (1976). Blakely's subsequent ambition to form a new wave-influenced unit floundered, and she has latterly pursued an acting career.
Albums: *Ronee Blakely* (1972), *Welcome* (1975).

Blondie

Blondie was formed in New York City in 1974 when Debbie Harry (b. 1 July 1945, Miami, Florida, USA; vocals), Chris Stein (b. 5 January 1950, Brooklyn, New York, USA; guitar), Fred Smith (bass) and Bill O'Connor (drums) abandoned the revivalist Stilettos for an independent musical direction. Backing vocalists Julie and Jackie, then Tish and Snookie, augmented the new group's early line-up, but progress was undermined by the departure of Smith for Television and the loss of O'Connor. Newcomers James Destri (b. 13 April 1954; keyboards), Gary Valentine (bass) and Clement Burke (b. 24 November 1955, New York, USA; drums) joined Harry and Stein in a reshaped unit which secured a recording deal through the aegis of producer Richard Gottehrer. Originally released on the Private Stock label, *Blondie* was indebted to both contemporary punk and 60s' girl groups, adeptly combining melody with purpose. Although not a runaway commercial success, the album did engender interest, particularly in the UK, where the group became highly popular. Internal disputes resulted in the departure of Gary Valentine, but the arrival of Frank Infante (guitar) and Nigel Harrison (b. Princes Risborough, Buckinghamshire,

Blondie

England; bass) triggered the group's most consistant period. Having freed themselves from the restrictions of Private Stock and signed to Chrysalis Records, *Plastic Letters* contained two UK Top 10 hits in 'Denis' and '(I'm Always Touched By Your) Presence Dear' while *Parallel Lines*, produced by pop svengali Mike Chapman, included the chart-topping 'Heart Of Glass' and 'Sunday Girl' (both 1979). Although creatively uneven, *Eat To The Beat* signalled Blondie's dalliance with disco and the set spawned three highly-successful singles in 'Union City Blue', 'Atomic' and 'Call Me'. The last-named, culled from the soundtrack of *American Gigolo* and produced by Giorgio Moroder, reached number 1 in both the UK and US. *Autoamerican* provided two further US chart toppers in 'The Tide Is High' and 'Rapture' while the former song, originally recorded by reggae group the Paragons, reached the same position in Britain. However, despite this commercial ascendancy, Blondie was beset by internal difficulties as the media increasingly focused on their photogenic lead singer. The distinction between the group's name and Harry's persona became increasingly blurred, although a sense of distance between the two was created with the release of her solo album, *Koo Koo. The Hunter*, a generally disappointing set

which Debbie completed under duress, became Blondie's final recording, their tenure ending when Stein's ill-health brought an attendant tour to a premature end. The guitarist was suffering from the genetic disease pemphigus and between 1983-85, both he and Debbie Harry absented themselves from full-time performing. The latter then resumed her solo career, while former colleague Burke joined the Eurythmics.
Albums: *Blondie* (1977), *Plastic Letters* (1978), *Parallel Lines* (1978), *Eat To The Beat* (1979), *Autoamerican* (1980), *The Hunter* (1982). Compilations: *The Best Of Blondie* (1981), *Once More Into The Bleach* (1988, contains remixes and rare cuts), *The Complete Picture - The Very Best Of Deborah Harry And Blondie* (1991).

Blood, Sweat And Tears

The jazz/rock excursions by one of the genre's leading pioneers came as a refreshing change to late 60s guitar dominated rock music. The many impressive line-ups of the band comprised (amongst others) David Clayton-Thomas (b. David Thomsett, 13 September 1941, Surrey, England; vocals), Al Kooper (b. 5 February 1944, New York, USA; keyboards/vocals), Steve Katz (b. 9 May 1945, New York, USA; guitar), Dick

Blood Sweat And Tears

Halligan (b. 29 August 1943, New York, USA; trombone/flute/keyboards), Fred Lipsius (b. 19 November 1944, New York, USA; alto saxophone/piano), Bobby Colomby (b. 20 December 1944, New York, USA; drums), Jim Fielder (b. 4 October 1947, Denton, Texas, USA; bass), Lew Soloff (b. 20 February 1944, Brooklyn, New York, USA; trumpet), Chuck Winfield (b. 5 February 1943, Monessen, Pennsylvania, USA; trumpet), Jerry Hyman (b. 19 May 1947, Brooklyn, New York, USA; Trumpet) and Dave Bargeron (b. 6 September 1942, Athol, Massachusetts, USA; trumpet). The band was the idea of Al Kooper, who together with Katz, both from the Blues Project, created a monster that would soon outgrow them. Kooper departed soon after the debut *Child Is Father To The Man*, which contained two of his finest songs, 'I Can't Quit Her' and 'My Days Are Numbered'. The record was ultimately flawed by less than perfect vocals. *Blood Sweat And Tears* with Clayton-Thomas taking over the vocal chores was their finest work, which stands up today as a brilliantly scored and fresh-sounding record. Kooper, although working on the arrangements, missed out on the extraordinary success this record achieved. It topped the US album charts for many weeks during its two-year stay, sold millions of copies, won a Grammy award and spawned three major worldwide hits; 'You've Made Me So Very Happy', 'Spinning Wheel' and 'And When I Die'. The following two albums were both considerable successes, although basically more of the same, gutsy brass arrangements, occasional biting guitar solos and most of all Clayton-Thomas's growling effortless vocal delivery. Following *BS&T4*, Clayton-Thomas departed for a solo career, resulting in a succession of lead vocalists, including the former member of Edgar Winter's White Trash, Jerry LaCroix (b. 10 October 1943, Alexandria, Lousiana, USA). The fortunes of the band never returned to their former glory; even when Clayton-Thomas returned, their magic had gone. *New City* made a respectable showing in the album charts in the USA but the supper-club circuit ultimately beckoned. The band reformed briefly in 1988 to play a back catalogue; they deserve a place in rock history as both innovators and brave exponents of jazz/rock.
Albums: *Child Is Father To The Man* (1968), *Blood, Sweat And Tears* (1969), *Blood, Sweat And Tears 3* (1970), *BS&T4* (1971), *New Blood* (1972), *No Sweat* (1973), *Mirror Image* (1974), *New City* (1975), *More Than Ever* (1976), *Brand New Day* (1977),

Nuclear Blues (1980). Compilation: *Greatest Hits* (1972).

Blue

This Glasgow-based group made its debut in 1973 when Timmy Donald (b. 29 September 1946, Bristol, Avon, England; drums, ex-White Trash) joined two former members of the Poets, Hugh Nicholson (b. 30 July 1949, Rutherglen, Strathclyde, Scotland; guitar/vocals) and Ian MacMillan (b. 16 October 1947, Paisley, Strathclyde, Scotland; bass/vocals). Their debut album showcased an engaging, melodic rock and continued the style forged by Nicholson during his brief spell in the Marmalade. *Life In The Navy* introduced a new addition to the line-up, Robert 'Smiggy' Smith (b. 30 March 1946, Kiel, Germany; guitar), but this second set lacked the charm of its predecessor. The unit was briefly disbanded, but re-emerged in 1977 with a Top 20 single, 'Gonna Capture Your Heart'. Charlie Smith (drums) and David Nicholson (guitar) had replaced Donald and 'Smiggy', but despite completing two further albums, Blue was unable to repeat this success and latterly broke up.
Albums: *Blue* (1973), *Life In The Navy* (1974), *Another Night Time Flight* (1977), *Fool's Party* (1979).

Blue, Barry

b. Barry Green, 4 December 1950, London, England. During the early 70s singing in public was secondary to his composing skills - which peaked commercially with an international smash in 1972's 'Sugar Me' (co-written and recorded byLynsey de Paul). His confidence boosted by this syndication, Blue sought more prestigious customers. As it turned out, the act that derived most benefit from his songwriting talents was himself, 1973 was his richest period was '(Dancing) On A Saturday Night' and 'Do You Wanna Dance' reaching the UKTop 10. The following year brought smaller entries with 'School Love' and 'Miss Hit And Run' - and after 'Hot Shot' completed a five-week chart run, Blue began a successful career as a writer and producer. His many credits include producing for Heatwave, Bananarama, Brotherhood Of Man and Diana Ross

Blue Mink

When four UK session men, a leading songwriter and an in-demand girl singer pooled their resources in 1969, the result was a new hit group, Blue Mink. The original line-up comprised: Madeline

Blue

Bell (vocals), Roger Cook (vocals), Roger Coulam (organ), Herbie Flowers (bass) and Barry Morgan (drums). With Cook And (Roger) Greenaway (alias David And Jonathan) providing the material, the group enjoyed a run of hits from 1969-73 beginning with the catchy anti-racist plea 'Melting Pot' and continuing with 'Good Morning Freedom', 'Our World', 'Banner Man', 'Stay With Me', 'By The Devil' and 'Randy'. With so much talent and experience in the group it seemed inevitable that they would drift off into extra-curricular projects and when the hits stopped they enjoyed continued success as session musicians, writers and soloists.
Album: *Blue Mink* (1969), *A Time Of Change* (1972), *Live At The Talk Of The Town* (1972), *Only When I Laugh* (1973), *Fruity* (1974), *Attention* (1975). Compilation: *Collection: Blue Mink* (1987).

Blue Ridge Rangers
The Blue Ridge Rangers was the brainchild of John Fogerty (b. 28 May 1945, Berkeley, California, USA) and followed the break-up of his highly successful group Creedence Clearwater Revival. One album, *The Blue Ridge Rangers*, on which Fogerty was the sole musician, resulted from this new departure. Purely country in content, it featured excellent versions of 'Jambalaya', 'Hearts Of Stone' and 'Today I Started Loving You Again' on which this accomplished artist's arranging and production skills were also to the fore. Although cloaked in an air of seeming mystery, this fine collection was the platform from which Fogerty launched his solo career in earnest.
Album: *The Blue Ridge Rangers* (1973).

Barry Blue

Blue Mink

Blues Image

Known mainly for their 1970 US number 4 hit 'Ride Captain Ride', Blues Image was a quintet from Tampa, Florida, USA. Formed in the mid-60s, the group began as a trio featuring Mike Pinera (b. 29 September 1948, Tampa, Florida, USA, guitar/vocals), Joe Lala (b. Tampa, Florida, USA; drums) and Manuel Bertematti (b. 1946, Tampa, Florida, USA; percussion). In 1966 bassist Malcolm Jones, (b. Cardiff, Wales), joined and the group took the name Blues Image. Frank 'Skip' Konte, originally from Canyon City, California, was enlisted in 1968 at which time the group relocated to New York City. The band opened their own club, The Image, where besides booking some of the top acts of the day they were able to provide themselves with a ready-made venue for the Blues Image's performances. Signed to Atco Records in 1969, they recorded their self-titled debut album, which landed at number 112 on the US album charts. The following year, the band released *Open*, which did not fare as well as the first despite the inclusion of the band's hit single. A third album was issued in 1970, minus Pinera (who briefly joined Iron Butterfly), but proved unsuccessful. The group disbanded upon that record's release, and although Atco issued two more singles, neither charted. Some members of the group started a new band called Manna. Konte joined Three Dog Night in 1974. Lala became renowned as a session drummer and percussionist, working with among others, Crosby, Stills, Nash And Young, Manassas, Joe Walsh and Harry Chapin. Pinera joined Ramatam in 1972, then he and Bertematti formed the New Cactus Band in 1973, which recorded one album for Atlantic Records. Pinera started a short-lived band called Thee Image in 1975 and recorded two solo albums for Capricorn Records and Spector Records in 1978-79. He took to the 60s revival circuit in the 80s and in 1990 was linked somewhat ironically with a new recording by Tiny Tim.
Albums: *Blues Image* (1969), *Open* (1970), *Red White And Blues Image* (1970).

Blunstone, Colin

b. 24 June 1945, St Albans, Hertfordshire, England. The former lead vocalist of 60s pop group the Zombies possessed a unique creamy-breathy voice that contributed greatly to their success. Two of his performances, 'She's Not There' and 'Time Of The Season' have since become pop classics. He started a promising solo career initially as Neil MacArthur and then reverting to his own name with *One Year* in 1971. This Rod Argent-produced record included sensitive arrangements and exquisite vocals to Tim Hardin's 'Misty Roses' and Denny Laine's 'Say You Don't Mind', the latter become a UK Top 20 hit. *Ennismore* in 1972 was his finest work, a faultless, almost continuous suite of songs which included two further UK chart hits 'How Could We Dare To Be Wrong' and 'I Don't Believe In Miracles'. After two further albums Blunstone kept a low profile. He surfaced in 1981 as vocalist on the Dave Stewart hit remake of Jimmy Ruffin's 'What Becomes Of The Broken Hearted', and the following year had a minor hit with Smokey Robinson's 'Tracks Of My Tears'. During the 80s he attempted further commercial success with Kipps, but the conglomeration folded shortly after the debut album. His 1991 album, *Sings His Greatest Hits*, was a collection of his most popular songs, re-recorded with his former colleagues, including Rod Argent and Russ Ballard. The shy and nervous Blunstone has never become part of the rock cognoscenti and consequently this exemplary singer has never reached his full potential.
Albums: *One Year* (1971), *Ennismore* (1972), *Journey* (1974), *Planes* (1977), *Sings His Greatest Hits* (1991).

Bob And Marcia

Bob Andy and Marcia Griffiths had two UK chart entries at the turn of the 70s - the first a version of Nina Simone's 'Young, Gifted And Black', was a UK Top 5 hit in 1970 on reggae producer Harry J's self-titled label and the follow-up, 'Pied Piper', which reached number 11 a year later on the Trojan label. Both Andy and Griffiths were hugely popular artists in Jamaica in their own right before and after their pop crossover success, but neither felt that this particular interlude was successful for them, especially in financial terms. It is sad that these two hits have become all that they are known for outside of reggae music circles. Sadder still, that their best duet of the period, the timeless 'Always Together', which they recorded for Coxsone Dodd, failed to make any impression outside Jamaica.
Album: *Young, Gifted And Black* (1976).

Bolan, Marc

b. Mark Feld, 30 July 1947, London, England, d. 16 September 1977. A former model in the halcyon 'Mod' era, Bolan began his singing career during the mid-60s folk boom. Initially dubbed 'Toby Tyler', he completed several unsuccessful demo discs before reportedly adopting his new

Colin Blunstone

surname from (Bo)b Dy(lan). The artist's debut single, 'The Wizard' (1965), revealed an early penchant for pop mysticism whereas its follow-up, 'The Third Degree', was indebted to R&B. Its b-side, 'San Francisco Poet', gave first airing to the distinctive, tremulous vocal warble for which Bolan became renowned and which flourished freely on his third single, 'Hippy Gumbo'. This slow, highly-stylized performance, produced by new manager Simon Napier-Bell, made no commercial impression, but was latterly picked up by the pirate station Radio London, whose disc jockey John Peel became a pivotal figure in Bolan's history. A series of demos was also undertaken at this point, several of which surfaced on *The Beginning Of Doves* (1974) and, with overdubs, on *You Scare Me To Death* (1981), but plans for a fourth single were postponed following the failure of its predecessor. Frustrated at his commercial impasse, the artist then opted to join Napier-Bell proteges John's Children in 1967. He composed their best-known single, 'Desdemona', but left the line-up after a matter of months to form Tyrannosaurus Rex. Here Bolan gave full rant to the 'underground' poetic folk-mysticism, redolent of author J.R.R. Tolkien, which 'Hippy Gumbo' had suggested. Such pretensions gave way to unabashed pop when the unit evolved into T. Rex three years later. Between 1970-73 this highly popular attraction enjoyed a run of 10 consecutive Top 5 singles, but Marc's refusal to alter the formula of his compositions resulted in an equally spectacular decline. Bolan was, nonetheless, one of the few established musicians to embrace punk and a contemporary television series, *Marc*, revived a flagging public profile. This ascendancy ended abruptly in September 1977 when the artist, as a passenger in a car driven by singer Gloria Jones, was killed when they crashed into a tree on Barnes Common, London.

Albums: *The Beginning Of Doves* (1974), *You Scare Me To Death* (1981), *Beyond The Rising Sun* (1984), *Love And Death* (1985), *The Marc Shows* (1989, television recordings). Compilation: *20th Century Boy* (1985 - provides an overview of the artist's entire career).

Bolin, Tommy

b. 1 August, 1951, Sioux City, Iowa, USA, d. 4 December 1976, Miami, Florida, USA. Tommy Bolin was a highly versatile progressive rock guitarist who successfully branched into fusion with considerable success and respect. Bolin became interested in music after seeing Elvis Presley in concert in 1956. He quickly learned to play Elvis songs on guitar and won local amateur contests. His first groups, Denny and the Triumphs and American Standard, found little or no success, and Bolin took work backing blues guitarist Lonnie Mack. In 1968 he formed Ethereal Zephyr, later shortened to Zephyr. Signed to Probe Records, their debut release was a US Top 50 album in 1969. Following the failure of their follow-up Bolin departed and formed the jazz/fusion group Energy with flautist Jeremy Steig, based in Colorado. Bolin also worked on an unreleased Steig album that also featured Jan Hammer and Billy Cobham. The latter then asked Bolin to play guitar on his *Spectrum* album in 1973 (which reputedly inspired Jeff Beck to try his hand at fusion). Having become a 'name' guitarist he was asked to replace Domenic Troiano (who had replaced Joe Walsh) in the James Gang. Bolin performed on their 1973 *Bang* album and the following year's *Miami*. After contributing to sessions for jazz drummer Alphonse Mouzon's *Mind Transplant* album, he was hired in 1975 by Deep Purple, to replace the departed Ritchie Blackmore. He wrote and co-wrote many songs for the English hard-rock group's *Come Taste The Band*. During the early stages of that band's dissolution in late 1975 Bolin went solo, recording the critically-acclaimed *Teaser* for Nemperor Records and, the following year, *Private Eyes* for Columbia. He toured with the Tommy Bolin Band to promote the albums. In December 1976, Bolin was found dead in a Miami hotel room, the victim of a drug overdose.

Albums: with Zephyr *Zephyr* (1969), *Going Back To Colorado* (1971); with Billy Cobham *Spectrum* (1973); with James Gang *Bang* (1973), *Miami* (1974); with Alphonse Mouzon *Mind Transplant* (1975); with Deep Purple *Come Taste The Band* (1975); solo *Teaser* (1975), *Private Eyes* (1976). Compilation: *The Ultimate...Tommy Bolin* (1989).

Boney M

In 1976, German-based producer/composer Frank Farian invented a group to front a single he had already recorded, 'Baby Do You Wanna Bump?', which sold well in Belgium and Holland. The line-up was Marcia Barrett (b. 14 October 1948, Jamaica; vocals), Bobby Farrell (b. 6 October 1949, Aruba, West Indies; vocals), Liz Mitchell (b. 12 July 1952, Clarendon, Jamaica; vocals) and Maisie Williams (b. 25 March 1951, Monserrat, West Indies; vocals). Between 1976 and 1977, the group enjoyed four UK Top 10 hits with 'Daddy Cool',

Marc Bolan

'Sunny', 'Ma Baker' and 'Belfast'. Their peak period, however, was 1978 when the chart-topping 'Rivers Of Babylon'/'Brown Girl In The Ring' spent 40 weeks on the UK chart, becoming the third best-selling UK single in history. Its follow-up, 'Rasputin' climbed to number 2 and Boney M ended 1978 with the festive chart-topper 'Mary Boy's Child - Oh My Lord'. They experienced similarly phenomenal success in Europe (over 50 million total sales). Their unusual choice of material was emphasized the following year with a revival of Creation's 'Painter Man', which reached the Top 10. The singalong 'Hooray Hooray It's A Holi-Holiday' and 'Gotta Go Home'/'El Lute' were their last Top 20 hits, after which their appeal declined. However, the commercial power of their catalogue is emphasized by their third number 1 album, *The Magic Of Boney M*, which neatly punctuated their extraordinary hit career in 1980.

Albums: *Take The Heat Off Me* (1977), *Love For Sale* (1977), *Night Flight To Venus* (1978), *Oceans Of Fantasy* (1979). Compilations: *The Magic of Boney M* (1980), *The Best Of 10 Years* (1986).

Boomtown Rats

One of the first new wave groups to emerge during the musical shake-ups of 1977, Boomtown Rats were also significant for spearheading an interest in young Irish rock. Originally formed in 1975, the group comprised Bob Geldof (b. Robert Frederick Zenon Geldof, 5 October 1954, Dun Laoghaire, Eire; vocals), Gerry Roberts (vocals/guitar), Johnny Fingers (keyboards), Pete Briquette (bass) and Simon Crowe (drums). Before moving to London, they signed to the recently established Ensign Records, which saw commercial possibilities in their high energy yet melodic work. Their self-titled debut album was a UK chart success and included two memorable singles, 'Looking After No. 1' and 'Mary Of The Fourth Form', which both reached the UK Top 20. The following summer, their *A Tonic For The Troops* was released to critical acclaim. Among its attendant hit singles were the biting 'She's So Modern' and quirky 'Like Clockwork'. By November 1978, a third hit from the album, the acerbic, urban protest 'Rat Trap', secured them their first UK number 1. In spite of their R&B leanings, the group were initially considered in some quarters as part of the punk upsurge and were banned in their home country. Unduly concerned they received considerable press thanks to the irrepressible loquaciousness of their lead singer.

A third album, *The Fine Art Of Surfacing* coincided with their finest moment, 'I Don't Like Mondays', the harrowing true-life story of an American teenage girl who wounded eight children and killed her school janitor and headmaster. The weirdest aspect of the tale was her explanation on being confronted with the deed: 'I don't like Mondays, this livens up the day'. Geldof adapted those words to produce one of pop's most dramatic moments in years, with some startlingly effective piano-work from the appropriately named Johnny Fingers. A massive UK number 1, the single proved almost impossible to match, as the energetic but average follow-up 'Someone's Looking At You' proved. Nevertheless, the Rats were still hitting the Top 5 in the UK and even released an understated but effective comment on Northern Ireland in 'Banana Republic'. By 1982, however, the group had fallen from critical and commercial grace and their subsequent recordings seemed passe. For Geldof, more important work lay ahead with the founding of Band Aid and much-needed world publicity on the devastating famine in Ethiopia. The Rats performed at the Live Aid concert on 13 July 1985 before bowing out the following year at Dublin's Self Aid benefit.

Albums: *The Boomtown Rats* (1977), *A Tonic For The Troops* (1978), *The Fine Art Of Surfacing* (1979), *Modo Bongo* (1981), *V Deep* (1982), *In The Long Grass* (1984). Compilation: *Ratrospective* (1983).

Boston

As a result of home-made demos recorded by the enterprising Tom Scholz (b. 10 March 1947, Toledo, Ohio, USA) one of the finest AOR albums of all time was unwittingly created. The tapes impressed Epic Records and Scholz joined with friends, Fran Sheehan (b. 26 March 1949, Boston, Massachusetts, USA; bass), Brad Delp (b. 12 June 1951, Boston, Massachusetts, USA; guitar/vocals), Barry Goudreau (b. 29 November 1951, Boston, Massachusetts, USA; guitar) and Sib Hashian (b. 17 August 1949, Boston, Massachusetts, USA; drums). The name Boston was adopted and their first release was a US Top 3 album which eventually sold 10 million copies worldwide and spent two years in the US charts. The memorable single 'More Than A Feeling' is a classic, containing all the ingredients of adult-orientated rock; upfront guitar, powerful lead vocal with immaculate harmonies and heavy bass and drums. Two years later they repeated the formula virtually note for note with *Don't Look Back* (featuring the same futuristic space-craft masquerading as guitars on the cover) which also topped the US charts. During this time Scholz, formerly a product designer for the Polaroid Company, invented a mini-amplifier marketed as the Rockman. Never a prolific band, Boston in the guise of Scholz and Delp returned seven years later with *The Third Stage* which spawned two further US hit singles, the number 1 'Amanda' and 'We're Ready'. Those fans wanting to replace worn copies of the previous albums merely had to purchase this one. It too went straight to the top spot giving Boston a unique record in rock history, the highest selling debut album and three number 1 albums with total sales of over 20 million copies.

Albums: *Boston* (1976), *Don't Look Back* (1978), *Third Stage* (1986). Solo album: Barry Goudreau *Barry Goudreau* (1980).

Bothy Band

Formed in 1975, this Irish folk-rock group featured Donal Lunny (synthesizer/dulcimer), who had formerly been with Planxty, Michael O'Domhnaill (guitar/vocals), Triona Ni Domhnaill (clarinet/harpsichord), Paddyn Glackin (fiddle), and Matt Molloy (b. Ballaghaderreen, Co. Roscommon, Eire; flute/whistle). Tommy Peoples (fiddle) and Paddy Keenan (pipes), had also played in the group during its relatively short lifespan, which lasted till only 1979. Despite their traditional background, and playing largely traditional tunes, the group, in comparison to the Chieftains, pursued more of a rock orientated style, akin to Planxty. After five albums the individual members went their separate ways. Triona Ni Domhnaill moved to North Carolina, USA, forming Touchstone, while her brother Michael, along with fiddle player Kevin Burke, based themselves in Portland, Oregon, where they released albums from their own studio, as well as appearing on numerous recordings by other artists. After the break up of the Bothy Band, Planxty reformed.

Albums: *1975* (1975), *Old Hag You Have Killed Me* (1976), *The Bothy Band* (1976), *Out Of The Wind Into The Sun* (1977), *After Hours-Live In Paris* (1978) Compilation: *The Best Of The Bothy Band* (1980).

Bowie, David

b. David Robert Jones, 8 April 1947, Brixton, London, England. One of the great enigmas of popular music and certainly the most mercurial, Bowie underwent a veritable odyssey of career moves and minor crises before establishing himself as a major performer. He began playing saxophone during his teens, initially with various school groups. School also contributed to his future pop star career in a more bizarre way as a result of a playground fight, which left the singer with a paralysed pupil (being stabbed in the eye with a school compass). Consequently, he had eyes of a different colour, an accident that would later enhance his otherworldly image. In the early 60s, however, his style was decidedly orthodox, all mod clothes and R&B riffs. Over the next few years, he went through a succession of backing groups including the King Bees, the Manish Boys, the Lower Third and the Buzz. In late 1966, he changed his surname owing to the imminent emergence of Davy Jones of the Monkees. During that same period, he came under the wing of manager Kenneth Pitt, who would nurture his career for the remainder of the decade. A contract with the fashionable Decca subsidiary Deram saw Bowie achieve some high-profile publicity but subsequent singles and a well-promoted debut album failed to sell. Bowie even attempted a cash-in novelty number 'The Laughing Gnome', but the charts remained resilient to his every move. Bowie persisted with mime classes while Pitt financed a television film, *Love You Till Tuesday*, but it was never shown on a major network. For a time, the star-elect performed in cabaret and retained vocal inflexions that betrayed a strong debt to his idol Anthony Newley.

As the 60s wound to a close Bowie seemed one of the least likely pop idols of the new decade. He was known only because of numerous advertisements in the British music press, as an artist who had released many records for many labels without success. The possibility of re-inventing himself as a 70s pop star seemed remote at best, but in the autumn of 1969 he finally broke through with 'Space Oddity', released to coincide with the American moon launch. The novel tale of Major Tom, whose sojourn in space disorientates him to such a degree that he chooses to remain adrift rather than return to Earth, was a worthy UK Top 10 hit. Unfortunately, Bowie seemed unable to follow up the single with anything similarly clever and when 'The Prettiest Star' flopped, most critics understandably dismissed him as a one-hit-wonder. Only weeks before, the American duo Zager And Evans had scored a far bigger hit with the transatlantic chart topper 'In The Year 2525', the theme of which bore superficial similarities to Bowie's tale, each dealing with possible future events and containing a pat moral. The fate of Zager And Evans (instant obscurity) weighed heavily over Bowie's fragile pop career while an

David Bowie

interesting yet patchy album named after his hit provided little clues to his future.

1970 saw a remarkable series of changes in Bowie's life, both personal and professional. His brother Terry had been committed to a mental institution; his father died and, soon after, David married art student Angela Barnett and finally he dispensed with the services of his loyal manager Kenneth Pitt, who was replaced by the more strident Tony De Fries. Amid this period of flux, Bowie completed his first major work, an extraordinary album, titled *The Man Who Sold The World*. With musical assistance from guitarist Mick Ronson, drummer Mick Woodmansey and producer Tony Visconti on bass, Bowie employed an arrestingly heavy sound, aided by the eerie synthesizer work of Ralph Mace to embellish his chillingly dramatic vocals. Lyrically, the album brilliantly complemented the instrumentation and Bowie worked through a variety of themes including sexual perversion ('The Width Of A Circle'), mental illness ('All The Madmen'), dystopianism ('Saviour Machine') and Nietzschean nihilism ('The Supermen'). All these leitmotifs would be reiterated on later albums. The package was completed with a striking cover revealing Bowie lounging seductively in a flowing dress. The transvesticism again provided a clue to the future in which Bowie would habitually disguise his gender and even publicize his bisexuality.

With the svengali-like De Fries aggressively promoting his career, Bowie was signed to RCA for a reportedly large advance and completed *Hunky Dory* in 1971. The album was lighter in tone than its predecessor with Bowie reverting to acoustic guitar on some tracks and exploring a more commercial, yet still intriguing, direction. There was the catchy 'Changes', the futuristic 'Life On Mars', tributes to Bob Dylan and the Velvet Underground, and the contrastingly celebratory 'Kooks' and sombre 'The Bewlay Brothers'. *Hunky Dory* was an excellent album yet modest seller. Bowie took full advantage of his increasingly hip media profile by embarking on a UK tour in which his outrageous costume, striking vocals and treasure trove of new material revealed the artist in full flow. Up until this point, Bowie had experimented with diverse ideas, themes and images that coalesced effectively, though not necessarily coherently. The complete fusion was revealed in June 1972 on the album *The Rise And Fall Of Ziggy Stardust And The Spiders From Mars*. Here, Bowie embraced the persona of an apocalyptic rock star whose rise and fall coincides with the end of the

world. In addition to the doom-laden breeziness of 'Five Years', there were the now familiar space-age themes ('Starman', 'Lady Stardust', 'Moonage Daydream') and the instant encore ('Rock 'N' Roll Suicide').

By this point, Bowie was deemed to have the Midas touch and his production talents brought rewards for his old hero Lou Reed (*Transformer* and the single 'Walk On The Wild Side') and a resurrected Mott The Hoople who scored their first hit with 'All The Young Dudes'. The track 'Oh You Pretty Things' (from *Hunky Dory*) had already provided a hit for Peter Noone and an equally unlikely artist, Lulu, enjoyed a Top 10 smash courtesy of 'The Man Who Sold The World'. Meanwhile, Bowie had undertaken a world tour and scored a UK number 1 album with *Aladdin Sane*, another concept work which centred on global destruction as its main plot. While still at his peak, Bowie shocked the rock world on 4 July 1974 by announcing his retirement from the stage of London's Hammersmith Odeon. It later transpired that it was not Bowie who was retiring, but his now overused persona, Ziggy Stardust. Taking stock, Bowie took an unlikely detour by recording an album of his favourite mid-60s songs. *Pin Ups* proved a patchy collection though there were some memorable moments including a hit reworking of the Merseys' 'Sorrow', a frantic reading of the Rolling Stones' 'Let's Spend The Night Together' and an interesting cover of the Kinks' neglected song 'Where Have All The Good Times Gone'.

After recording a US broadcast television special at London's Marquee club titled 'The 1980 Floor Show', Bowie produced his next work *Diamond Dogs*. Having failed to receive permission to use the title *1984*, he nevertheless adapted George Orwell's famous novel as the basis for his favourite forays into dystopianism, sexuality and doomed love. There were even some delightful flashes from the novel neatly translated into rock by Bowie. Julia, described as 'a rebel from the waist downwards' by the book's anti-hero Winston Smith, becomes the hot tramp of 'Rebel Rebel' (itself a hit single). What the album lacked was the familiar sound of the Spiders From Mars and especially the cutting guitar work of Mick Ronson. A massive tour of USA and Canada saw the 'Diamond Dogs' spectacle at its most excessive and expansive, but the whole project was hampered by the production budget. Beneath the spectacle, the music tended to be somewhat forgotten, a view reinforced by the release of the critically-panned

David Live in 1974.

Bowie's popularity was as great as ever in the mid-70s when he effectively righted the wrongs of history by taking 'Space Oddity' to number 1, six years after its initial UK chart entry. That same year, he also enjoyed his first US number 1, 'Fame', which featured the voice and co-composing skills of John Lennon. The song appeared on his next album, *Young Americans*, which saw the emergence of a new Bowie, successfully tackling Philadelphia soul. Meanwhile, there were significant changes in his business life with Tony De Fries finally falling from favour amid an acrimonious lawsuit. During the same period, Bowie's often stormy marriage to Angie was about to be dissolved. As ever in Bowie's life, personal upheavals coincided with creative endeavour and he was busy working on Nicholas Roeg's film *The Man Who Fell To Earth*, in which he was given the leading role of the displaced alien marooned on Earth. The movie received mixed reviews. Returning to London, Bowie was reprimanded in the liberal music press for allegedly displaying a Nazi salute and suggesting that his home country needed a 'new Hitler'. His fascist flirtation was partly provocative and perhaps related to the self-grandeur stemming from his heavy use of cocaine during the period. The image was crystallized in the persona of the Thin White Duke, the icy character who came to life on his next album, *Station To Station*. An austere yet opaque production, the album anticipated the next phase of his career when he would work with Brian Eno. The duo relocated to Berlin for a cycle of albums which displayed Bowie at his least commercial and most ambitious. *Low* and *'Heroes'*, both released in 1977, were predominantly instrumental works whose mood was strongly influenced by Eno's minimalist electronics. Surprisingly, segments from each album found their way on to a live album *Stage,* a considerable improvement upon its predecessor, *David Live*. Following a best-forgotten appearance in the movie *Just A Gigolo*, Bowie concluded his collaborative work with Eno on 1979's *Lodger*. Generally regarded as the least impressive of the Eno triology, it nevertheless contained some strong songs, including 'Boys Keep Swinging' and 'Repetition'. Bowie's thespian pursuits continued with a critically acclaimed starring role in the Broadway production of *The Elephant Man*. During the show's run in Chicago, Bowie released an album of new material which leaned closer to the rock mainstream. *Scary Monsters (And Super Creeps)* was adventurous, with its modern electro-pop and distorted electric guitar, provided by former King Crimson helmsman Robert Fripp. The album contained the reflective 'Ashes To Ashes', a fascinating track, which included references to one of Bowie's earlier creations, Major Tom. Coincidentally, the Major brought Bowie his first UK number 1 since 'Space Oddity'.

The early 80s saw Bowie taking on a series of diverse projects including an appearance in Bertolt Brecht's *Baal*, surprise chart collaborations with Queen ('Under Pressure') and Bing Crosby ('Peace On Earth/Little Drummer Boy') and two more starring roles in the films *The Hunger* and the critically acclaimed *Merry Christmas Mr Lawrence*. A switch of record label from RCA to EMI saw Bowie release his most commercial work since the early 70s with *Let's Dance,* produced by Nile Rodgers of Chic. In striking contrast to his recent excursions with Eno and previous doom-laden imagery, the work showed Bowie embracing a new positivism with upbeat, uplifting songs that were both slick and exciting. Even his interviews revealed a more open, contented figure intent upon stressing the positive aspects of life, seemingly without ambiguity. The title track of the album gave Bowie his third solo UK number 1 and effectively revitalized his recording career in the process. The 'Serious Moonlight' tour which accompanied the album, played to over two million people and garnered excellent reviews. That same year (1983) he had two further hits both narrowly missing the top spot in the UK charts with 'China Girl' and 'Modern Love'. In the meantime, Bowie's influence could be detected in the work of a number of younger artists who had fallen under the spell of his various aliases. Gary Numan, the Human League, Japan and Bauhaus each displayed aspects of his music and imagery with varying results. Similarly the New Romantics from Visage, Ultravox and Spandau Ballet to the New Pop of Culture Club were all descendants of the one time glam rocker and Thin White Duke.

Bowie followed up *Let's Dance* quickly with the anti-climactic *Tonight* which attracted universally bad reviews, but managed to spawn a hit single with 'Blue Jean'. During 1985, Bowie was chiefly in demand as a collaborator, first with the Pat Metheny Group on 'This Is Not America' (from the film *The Falcon And The Snowman*) and next with Mick Jagger on a reworking of Martha And The Vandellas' 'Dancing In The Street' for Live Aid. The following year was dominated by Bowie's various acting pursuits. The much publicised movie

Absolute Beginners divided the critics, but the strong title track provided Bowie with a major hit. He also starred in the fantasy film *Labyrinth* and sang the theme of the anti-nuclear war cartoon film *Where The Wind Blows*. 1987 saw Bowie return to his roots by teaming up with former classmate Peter Frampton for the 'Glass Spider' tour. The attendant album, *Never Let Me Down* was again poorly received, as speculation grew that Bowie was at last running dry of musical ideas and convincing new personae. Never predictable, Bowie decided to put a group together in 1989 and called upon the services of Reeves Gabrels (guitar), Tony Sales (bass) and Hunt Sales (drums) - the two brothers having previously worked with Iggy Pop and Todd Rundgren. The unit took their name from the title song of their new album, *Tin Machine*, a set that displayed some good, old-fashioned guitar work, occasionally bordering on heavy metal. Bowie also took his band on the road with a tour of purposely 'low-key' venues, Bowie expressing a desire to play in 'sweaty' clubs and get back to his roots. It was an interesting experiment but neither the album nor the tour did much to increase Bowie's critical standing in the late 80s. Ironically, it was the re-release of his back catalogue on CD that brought a more positive response from his followers and in order to promote the campaign Bowie set out on an acoustic 'greatest hits' tour. At the beginning of the 90s it served as a milestone and worthwhile tribute to a career that had encapsulated a staggering number of musical and image changes, spanning nearly 25 years.

Albums: *David Bowie* (1967, later re-issued as *The World Of David Bowie*), *David Bowie* aka *Man Of Words, Man Of Music* (1969, later re-issued as *Space Oddity*), *The Man Who Sold The World* (1971), *Hunky Dory* (1972), *The Rise And Fall Of Ziggy Stardust And The Spiders From Mars* (1972), *Aladdin Sane* (1973), *Pin Ups* (1973), *Diamond Dogs* (1974), *David Live* (1974), *Young Americans* (1975), *Station To Station* (1976), *Low* (1977), *'Heroes'* (1977), *Stage* (1978), *Lodger* (1979), *Scary Monsters (And Super Creeps)* (1980), *Christiane F.* (1982, film soundtrack), *Rare* (1983), *Let's Dance* (1983), *Ziggy Stardust - The Motion Picture* (1983, film soundtrack), *Tonight* (1984), *Never Let Me Down* (1987), *Tin Machine* (1989), *Tin Machine II* (1991). Compilations: *Images 1966-67* (1973), *Changesonebowie* (1976), *Very Best Of David Bowie* (1981), *Changestwobowie* (1981), *Golden Years* (1983), *Fame And Fashion (All Time Greatest Hits)* (1984), *Love You Til Tuesday* (1984, Decca

recordings).
Further reading: *Alias*, Gilman.

Boxer

Formed in 1975, Boxer featured two former members of Patto, Mike Patrick McCarthy/Mike Patto (b. 22 September 1942, Glasgow, Scotland, d. 4 March 1979; vocals) and Ollie Halsall (b. 14 March 1949, Southport, Merseyside, England; guitars). The line-up was completed by two experienced musicians, Keith Ellis (bass, ex-Koobas, Juicy Lucy and Van Der Graaf Generator) and Tony Newman (drums, ex-Sounds Incorporated, Jeff Beck and May Blitz). *Below The Belt* is better recalled for the controversy surrounding its tasteless 'nude' cover rather than the hard rock unveiled within. The original Boxer broke up when a second album, *Bloodletting*, was withdrawn and not released until 1979. The singer re-established the group in 1977 with Chris Stainton (keyboards, ex-Grease Band), Adrian Fisher (guitar, ex-Sparks), Tim Bogert (bass, ex-Vanilla Fudge) and Eddie Tuduri (drums). Boxer was dissolved following the release of the disappointing *Absolutely*. Mike Patto resumed work with the *ad hoc* unit, Hinkley's Heroes, but died in 1979 following a long battle with throat cancer.
Albums: *Below The Belt* (1975), *Absolutely* (1977), *Bloodletting* (1979).

Boyzz

Influenced by Steppenwolf, Black Oak Arkansas and Lynyrd Skynyrd, the US-based Boyzz combined hard-driving rock 'n' roll, with southern-style boogie. With a strong leather-clad, biker image, their sole album *Too Wild To Tame*, featured Dirty Dan Buck (vocals), Anatole Halinkovitch (keyboards), Gil Pini (guitar), Mike Tafoya (guitar), David Angel (bass) and Kent Cooper (drums). Unable to transform media interest into record sales, the band disintegrated soon after the album's release. Halinkovitch, Tafoya and Angel later went on to form B'zz.
Album: *Too Wild To Tame* (1978).

Brand X

Brand X was one of the most commercially successful of the British jazz rock groups of the late 70s and early 80s. Their *Moroccan Roll* reached number 37 in the UK album chart in May 1977 while *Is There Anything About* crept in at number 93 in September 1982. The original line-up of the band was John Goodsall (guitar), Robin Lumley (keyboards), Percy Jones (bass) (ex-Liverpool

Scene), Phil Collins (drums) and Maurice Pert (percussion). This was the band that Collins thought second only to Weather Report. There were similarities, especially in that each group of musicians had great technical ability and a desire to play popular music; but Brand X's individuality came through in their compositions. They produced sharp arrangements of appealing melodies, often with a gangling counterpoint provided by Jones's slurred fretless bass lines. Collins and Pert could contribute anything from the lightest colouring to a furiously propulsive rhythm and both Goodsall and Lumley were exciting soloists. All the musicians were also busy with studio work and Collins had been expanding his role with Genesis after Peter Gabriel's departure. He had also released a solo album and, as his second career as a solo artist took off, he decided to leave Brand X. He was replaced by Chuck Bergi, and then by Mike Clarke. A little later Percy Jones left and was replaced by John Gilbin.

Albums: *Unorthodox Behaviour* (1976), *Livestock* (1977), *Moroccan Roll* (1977), *Masques* (1978), *Product* (1979), *Do They Hurt* (1980), *Is There Anything About* (1982).

Brass Construction

Led by keyboards player and singer Randy Muller (b. Guyana), Brass Construction was a leading group in the disco movement of the 70s. Muller originally formed the band in Brooklyn, New York as Dynamic Soul, mixing funk, salsa and reggae rhythms with a more orthodox jazz line-up to create a highly danceable sound. Renamed Brass Construction, the nine-piece group was signed by United Artists in 1975. The members included Michael Grudge (b. Jamaica) and Jesse Ward Jnr. (saxophones), Wayne Parris (b. Jamaica) and Morris Price (trumpets), Joseph Arthur Wong (b. Trinidad; guitar), Wade Williamson (bass), Larry Payton (drums) and percussionist Sandy Billups. With infectious polyrhythms and minimal, chanted vocals, the group's first release 'Movin'' topped the R&B charts and was a pop Top 20 hit. It was followed by 'Changin'', 'Ha Cha Cha' and 'L-O-V-E-U', all best-sellers. Later singles were less successful although successive Brass Construction albums rode the disco boom. Muller also wrote for and produced New York disco group Skyy and B.T. Express. The group's popularity dwindled in the 80s, although the remix craze brought numerous versions of its early hits into the clubs in 1988 including 'Ha Cha Cha (Acieed Mix)'.

Albums: *Brass Construction* (1975), *II* (1976), *III* (1977), *IV* (1978), *V* (1979), *VI* (1980), *Attitudes* (1982), *Conversations* (1983), *Renegades* (1984), *Conquest* (1985). Compilation: *Movin' - The Best Of Brass Construction* (1988).

Brave Belt

This Canadian quartet was formed in 1970 by ex-Guess Who duo, Randy Bachman (guitar/vocals) and Chad Allen (keyboards). With the addition of drummer Rob Bachman and bassist C.F. Turner, they made one album of blues/country influenced rock. In 1972, Tim Bachman replaced Chad Allen and Brave Belt became known as Bachman Turner Overdrive. The band then pursued a much more aggressive style of hard-rock boogie.
Album: *Brave Belt* (1971).

Bread

Bread was formed in 1969 when David Gates (b. 11 December 1940, Tulsa, Oklahoma, USA), a leading Los Angeles session musician, produced an album for the Pleasure Faire, a group which included vocalist/guitarist Rob Royer. Songwriter James Griffin (b. Memphis, Tennessee, USA) contributed several compositions to the set and the three aspirants then decided to pool resources. All were assured multi-instrumentalists, and although not a commercial success, their debut album established a penchant for melodious soft-rock. Mike Botts (b. Sacramento, California, USA; drums) augmented the group for *On The Water*, which included the million-selling 'Make It With You', while *Manna* spawned a further gold disc with 'If', later successfully revived by actor/singer Telly Savalas. Royer was then replaced by keyboard veteran Larry Knechtel (b. Bell, California, USA), but Bread's smooth approach was left unruffled as they scored further international success with immaculate pop songs, 'Baby I'm-A Want You' (1971), 'Everything I Own' and 'Guitar Man' (both 1972). However, increasing friction between Gates and Griffin led to the group's collapse later that year. The combatants embarked on solo careers while Botts joined the Linda Ronstadt Band, but the late period quartet re-convened in 1976 for *Lost Without Your Love*, the title track of which reached the US Top 10. Guitarist Dean Parks augmented the line-up when Griffin resumed his independent direction, but *The Goodbye Girl* failed to emulate its predecessors and Bread was again disbanded.
Albums: *Bread* (1969), *On The Waters* (1970), *Manna* (1971), *Baby I'm-A Want You* (1972), *Guitar*

Bread

Man (1972), Lost Without Your Love (1977), The Goodbye Girl (1978). Compilations: The Best Of Bread (1972), The Best Of Bread Volume 2 (1974), The Sound Of Bread (1977), The Very Best Of Bread (1987).

Brett, Paul

A former guitarist with Elmer Gantry's Velvet Opera, Brett left that particular group to join Fire, a cultishly popular combo which featured Dave Lambert, a future member of the Strawbs. Fire's original bassist, Dick Dufall and drummer, Bob Voice, then broke off to join Brett in his own group, Paul Brett Sage. This respected musician recorded prolifically throughout the 70s, honing a tasteful yet accomplished style. A 1974 collection, Clocks, is arguably his best remembered album, but as the decade progressed so his work became increasingly less exciting.

Albums: Paul Brett Sage (1970), Jubilation Foundry (1971), Schizophrenia (1972), Paul Brett (1973), Clocks (1974), Phoenix Future (1975), Earthbirth (1977), Interlife (1978), Eclipse (1979), Guitar Trek (1980), Romantic Guitar (1980).

Brewer's Droop

From High Wycombe, England, Ron Watts (vocals), Steve Darrington (keyboards), John McKay (guitar), Malcolm Barrett (bass) and Bob Walker (drums) constituted perhaps the most alarming blues revivalist act of the early 70s. They specialized in an Anglicized form of cajun with more than a dash of the hilarious smut that got them banned from many venues. With his foam-rubber phallus and wobbling beer gut, Watts was their sex symbol but Birmingham's Big Bear Records still saw much star potential in the group's beer-sodden outrage. Augmented with horns, the aptly-titled Opening Time was a diverting encapsulation of their bawdy humour and stylistic motivation but it struck the populous with, shrugged Ron, 'the impact of a feather hitting concrete'. It seemed that the moment for a UK equivalent of Canned Heat had passed. Produced by Dave Edmunds, a second album was released posthumously when it was discovered that Droop's line-up for this venture had included Pick Withers and Mark Knopfler, later of the more marketable Dire Straits.

Albums: Opening Time (1972), Booze Brothers (1989).

Brinsley Schwarz

The roots of this enduringly-popular attraction lay in Kippington Lodge, a Tunbridge Wells-based pop group. Formed in 1965, they completed five varied, if lightweight, singles under the direction of producer Mark Wirtz. The initial line-up - Brinsley Schwarz (guitar/vocals), Barry Landerman (organ/vocals), Nick Lowe (b. 25 March 1949, Woodbridge, Suffolk, England; bass/vocals) and Pete Whale (drums) - remained intact until 1968 when Bob Andrews replaced Landerman, who had joined Vanity Fare. Dissatisfied with their conservative image, the group began emphasizing original material. In October 1969 they emerged with a new drummer, Bill Rankin, and had re-named themselves in deference to their lead guitarist. The quartet secured a management deal with the ambitious Famepushers agency, but were engulfed by controversy when British journalists were flown to witness the Brinsleys' debut appearance, bottom-of-the-bill at New York's Fillmore East. The plan failed in the wake of a shaky performance and the group was perceived as a hype. Their debut album *Brinsley Schwarz*, was pleasant but undemanding, and did little to dispel suspicions. However a second collection, ironically entitled *Despite It All*, showed more promise as the group began shedding its derivative side and emerged with a distinctive style.

A second guitarist, Ian Gomm (b. 17 March 1947, Ealing, London, England), was added prior to *Silver Pistol*, arguably the group's most unified and satisfying release. It preceded a period when the Brinsleys popularized 'pub rock', a back-to-basics genre which reviled the pomposity perceived in more commercial contemporaries. Having enjoyed a resident slot at the Tally Ho pub in Kentish Town, north London, the group then performed extensively throughout the country. Their extended sets featured a plethora of different influences, be it the Band, reggae, rock 'n' roll or soul and this melting pot, in turn, inspired some of Nick Lowe's finest songs. *Nervous On The Road* featured the exquisite 'Don't Lose Your Grip On Love', while '(What's So Funny 'Bout) Peace, Love and Understanding', later revived by Elvis Costello, made its debut on *The New Favourites Of Brinsley Schwarz*. This exceptional selection was produced by Dave Edmunds, but despite critical plaudits, it failed to sell. The group was now tiring and broke up in March 1975, unable to escape the 'good-time' niche they had ploughed. Schwarz and Andrews later joined Graham Parker And The Rumour while Ian Gomm and Nick Lowe

embarked on solo careers.
Albums: *Brinsley Schwarz* (1970), *Despite It All* (1970), *Silver Pistol* (1972), *Nervous On The Road* (1972), *Please Don't Ever Change* (1973), *The New Favourites Of Brinsley Schwarz* (1974). Compilations: *Original Golden Greats* (1974), *The Fifteen Thoughts Of Brinsley Schwarz* (1978).

British Lions

A spin-off group from Mott The Hoople, the British Lions formed after Ian Hunter left that group in December 1974. Keyboards player Morgan Fisher, bassist Pete 'Overend' Watts (b. 13 May 1947, Birmingham, West Midlands, England), and drummer Dale 'Buffin' Griffin (b. 24 October 1948, Ross On Wye, Worcestershire, England) formed Mott with Hackensack guitarist Ray Major and vocalist Nigel Benjamin. They lasted until November 1976 recording two albums after which all except Benjamin (who walked out and joined the English Assassins in Southend, Essex) became the British Lions with Medicine Head vocalist John Fiddler coming in. At first, they moved to Vertigo Records and released two albums before drowning under the 'new wave'. Fisher went on to found his own Pipe label, while Griffin and Watts put together Grimstone Productions, producing Department S and Slaughter And The Dogs amongst others. Griffin would progress to the BBC where he was in charge of various radio sessions, notably for the John Peel programme. Morgan Fisher went on to make solo albums for the Cherry Red and Strike Back labels.
Albums: *British Lions* (1978), *Trouble With Women* (1982).

Bromberg, David

b. 19 September 1945, Philadelphia, Pennsylvania, USA. Bromberg was a session musician who later recorded a series of albums under his own name. Proficient on guitar (primarily acoustic), violin, mandolin and banjo, Bromberg's music took in elements of folk, blues, bluegrass, rock, comedy and lengthy narrative stories often stuck in between choruses. His career began in New York's Greenwich Village in the 60s, where he performed on sessions for diverse artists such as Jay And The Americans, Rick Derringer, Blood, Sweat And Tears, Jerry Jeff Walker, Chubby Checker and Bob Dylan - he performed on the latter's *Self Portrait* and *New Morning* albums in 1970 and 1971. He signed a recording contract with Columbia Records and released a self-titled album in 1971. His next two albums, *Demon In Disguise* and

Wanted Dead Or Alive, included guest appearances by members of the Grateful Dead. *Midnight On The Water* featured appearances including Emmylou Harris, Linda Ronstadt, Dr. John, Jesse Ed Davis, Bonnie Raitt and Ricky Skaggs. In 1976 Bromberg signed to Fantasy Records and released a further five albums, including the live *How Late'll Ya Play 'Til?* In 1977 he appeared with other acoustic musicians, including Vassar Clements and D.J. Fontana, on the critically acclaimed albums *Hillbilly Jazz*. Bromberg gave up performing and recording throughout much of the 80s and undertook making and repairing violins and other instruments. He occasionally performed one-off gigs, including an annual appearance at New York club the Bottom Line. In 1990, Bromberg resurfaced on Rounder Records with a new album, *Sideman Serenade*. Never a large commercial success, Bromberg retains a devoted following into the 90s, despite his relaxed work schedule.

Albums: *David Bromberg* (1971), *Demons In Disguise* (1972), *Wanted Dead Or Alive* (1974), *Midnight On The Water* (1975), *How Late'll Ya Play 'Til?* (1976), *Reckless Abandon* (1977), *Bandit In A Bathing Suit* (1978), *My Own House* (1978), *You Should See The Rest Of The Band* (1980), *Sideman Serenade* (1990). Compilations: (various artists) *Hillbilly Jazz, Vol. 1* (1977), *Hillbilly Jazz, Vol. 2* (1977).

Bronco

Vocalist Jess Roden, formerly of the Alan Bown Set, instigated this excellent group in 1970. Kevin Hammond (guitar/vocals), John Pasternak (bass) - both ex-Band Of Joy, Robbie Blunt (guitar) and Pete Robinson (drums) completed the line-up which made its debut that year with *Country Home*. The quintet offered a relaxed, sympathetic setting for the singer's soulful delivery, best exemplified on *Ace Of Sunlight*, which featured support from Ian Hunter and Mick Ralphs from Mott The Hoople and Fotheringay's Trevor Lucas. Despite their promise, Bronco was unable to secure a sound commercial footing and the departure of Roden for a solo career effectively killed the group. Blunt subsequently joined Silverhead and appeared in several short-lived aggregations before securing widespread recognition with his work for Robert Plant.

Albums: *Country Home* (1970), *Ace Of Sunlight* (1971), *Smokin' Mixture* (1973).

Brotherhood Of Man

This pop vocal group was formed in London in 1969 by songwriter Tony Hiller. The lead singer was Tony Burrows, veteran of such groups as the Ivy League, the Flower Pot Men and Edison Lighthouse. The group's first success was Hiller's 'United We Stand', a UK Top 10 hit in 1970. With a changing personnel, the group continued to record for Deram and Dawn in the early 70s but its career only revived when it was chosen to represent the UK in the 1976 Eurovision Song Contest. Appearing as an Abba-inspired male/female quartet led by Martin Lee and Lee Sheridan, Brotherhood Of Man's breezy rendition of 'Save Your Kisses For Me' won the competition and became an international hit, even reaching the Top 30 in America. The group followed with a series of UK successes including the number 1 hits, 'Angelo' and 'Figaro', co-written by Hiller with Lee and Sheridan. Thereafter, their popularity dwindled and by the 80s Brotherhood Of Man was relegated to the lucrative though uninspiring scampi-and-chips nightclub circuit, although 'Lightning Flash' in 1982 was a minor hit.

Albums: *Love & Kisses From The Brotherhood Of Man* (1976), *B For Brotherhood* (1978), *Sing 20 Number One Hits* (1980), *Lightning Flash* (1983). Compilation: *The Best Of The Brotherhood Of Man* (1983).

Brothers Johnson

This duo featured George Johnson (b. 17 May 1953, Los Angeles, California, USA; guitar/vocals) and Louis Johnson (b. 13 April 1955, Los Angeles, California, USA; bass). Having previously worked with Billy Preston and appeared on Quincy Jones's 1975 US Top 20 album, *Mellow Madness*, the duo signed to A&M Records. This hard-funk duo scored three notable disco and US Top 10 hits with 'I'll Be Good To You' (1976), 'Strawberry Letter 23' (1977) and 'Stomp!' (1980). A brief hiatus involving the duo in studio production and session work came to an end with the recording of the not altogether successful *Kickin'*.

Albums: *Look Out For Number One* (1976), *Right On Time* (1977), *Blam!!* (1978), *Light Up The Night* (1980), *Winners* (1981), *Out Of Control* (1984), *Kickin'* (1988). Compilation: *Blast! (The Latest And The Greatest)* (1983).

Broughton, Edgar, Band

The London 'underground' scene welcomed the anarchic, revolutionary and irreverent Broughtons, into an active fraternity during the early days of 1969. The band comprised of Edgar Broughton (b. 24 October 1947, Warwick, Warwickshire, England; guitar/vocals), Steve Broughton (b. 20

Brotherhood Of Man

May 1950, Warwick, Warwickshire, England; drums/vocals) and Arthur Grant (bass/guitar/vocals). Edgar's growling voice was similar to that of Captain Beefheart and they regularly featured his 'Dropout Boogie' in their act. Following their arrival in London they played at a number of small club gigs arranged by Blackhill Enterprises. They were given a wider audience by playing at the famous Blind Faith free concert in Hyde Park, where the Broughtons incited the crowd to a frenzy with exhaustive rendition of the favourite, 'Out Demons, Out'. Despite the exposure that disc jockey John Peel gave the band on his pioneering UK radio show, *Top Gear*, the political and sexual themes of their songs had dated by the early 70s, although the band soldiered on for a number of years, maintaining a defiant political stance that gained acceptance with a loyal core of British and West German rock fans. Into the early 90s Broughton could still be found performing part-time as part of a late 60s revival show and on the London pub circuit.

Albums: *Wasa Wasa* (1969) *Sing Brother Sing* (1970), *The Edgar Broughton Band* (1971), *In Side Out* (1972), *Oora* (1973), *Bandages* (1975), *Parlez-Vous English* (1979), *Live Hits Harder* (1979). Compilations: *A Bunch Of 45s* (1975), *As Was* (1988).

Brown, Peter

b. 11 July 1953, Blue Island, Illinois, USA. Brown was a dance music vocalist, producer and keyboardist who made a brief impact in the late 70s. Brown taught himself to play the drums when he was aged 13. He then progressed to a four-track tape recorder and began composing and overdubbing in his bedroom. In 1977 he was in the midst of selling one of his paintings when he presented a demo recording to producer Cory Wade. Wade got Brown a recording contract with the small Drive label, distributed by Florida's TK Records and his first single, 'Do You Wanna Get Funky With Me?', became a hit at discos, reportedly becoming the first 12-inch single to sell a million copies, despite only reaching number 18 on the US pop charts and just missing the Top 40 in the UK. Brown's follow-up, 'Dance With Me', which featured Betty Wright on vocals, became a US Top 10 hit the following year and he charted with two more minor US hits 'Crank It Up (Funk Town) Pt. 1' and 'Stargazer'. His chart career came to a halt in early 1980.

Album: *A Fantasy Love Affair* (1978).

Browne, Jackson

b. 9 October 1948, Heidelberg, Germany, but resident of Los Angeles, California from the age of three. Introduced to folk music while in his teens, Browne began writing songs at the instigation of two high school friends, Greg Copeland and Steve Noonan. The youngsters frequented the Paradox club, a favoured haunt of traditional musicians, where Jackson was introduced to the Nitty Gritty Dirt Band. He joined the group in February 1966, only to leave within six months, but some of his early compositions appeared on their subsequent albums. An ensuing deal with Nina Music, the publishing arm of Elektra Records, resulted in several of Browne's songs being recorded by the label's acts, including Tom Rush and the aforementioned Noonan. Jackson had meanwhile ventured to New York, where he accompanied singer Nico during her engagement at the Dom, a club owned by Andy Warhol. The singer's *Chelsea Girl* set featured three Browne originals, but their relationship quickly soured and the young musician retreated to California. In 1968 Jackson began work on a solo album, but both it and a projected 'supergroup', revolving around the artist, Ned Doheny and Jack Wilce, were later abandoned. Undeterred, Browne continued to frequent the Los Angeles clubs and music fraternity until a demo tape resulted in a recording deal with the newly-established Asylum Records. *Jackson Browne/Saturate Before Using* confirmed that the artist's potential had not withered during earlier prevarications. David Crosby added sterling support to a set including the composer's own readings of 'Jamaica Say You Will' and 'Rock Me On The Water', previously covered by the Byrds and Brewer And Shipley respectively, and 'Doctor My Eyes', an up-tempo performance which reached the US Top 10, but became an even bigger hit in the hands of the Jackson Five. Browne also drew plaudits for 'Take It Easy', which he wrote with Glenn Frey during a spell when they shared an apartment and penury. The song was a major success for the latter's group, the Eagles, and in turn inspired several subsequent collaborations including 'Nightingale', 'Doolin' Dalton' and 'James Dean'. Jackson's own version of 'Take It Easy' appeared on *For Everyman*, which also featured 'These Days', one of the singer's most popular early songs. The album introduced a long-standing relationship with multi-instrumentalist David Lindley, but although the punchy 'Redneck Friend' became a regional hit, the set was not a commercial success. *Late For The Sky* was an altogether stronger collection, on which Browne ceased relying on older material and in its place offered a more contemporary perspective. Extensive touring helped bring the artist a much wider audience and in 1975 he produced Warren Zevon's debut album for Asylum, infusing a measure of consistency to the performer's jaundiced wit and delivery. These facets contrasted Browne's own, rather languid approach which he attempted to reverse by employing producer Jon Landau for *The Pretender*. The resultant sense of contrast enhanced much of the material, including 'Here Come Those Tears Again' and the anthemic title track. One of the benchmarks of 70s American rock, this homage to blue-collar values became a staple part of AOR radio, while its poignancy was enhanced by the suicide of Jackson's wife, Phyllis, in March 1976. *The Pretender* earned a gold disc and the singer's newfound commercial appeal was emphasized with *Running On Empty*. However, Browne did not meekly repeat the formula of its predecessor and in place of its homogeneous sheen was a set recorded at different locations during a tour. The album included material written by Danny O'Keefe and Danny Kortchmar, as well as an affectionate reading of 'Stay', originally recorded by Maurice Williams And The Zodiacs. This performance reached number 20 in the US, but fared better in the UK, climbing to number 12 and providing the singer with his only British hit to date. Despite its rough edges, *Running On Empty* became the singer's most popular release, closing a particular chapter in his career. During the late 70s Jackson pursued a heightened political profile through his efforts on behalf of the anti-nuclear lobby. In partnership with Graham Nash he organized several cross-country benefits culminating in a series of all-star concerts at New York's Madison Square Garden. The best of these were later compiled on *No Nukes*.

It was 1980 before Browne completed a new studio album, but although *Hold On* was undeniably well-crafted, it lacked the depth of earlier work. Nonetheless two of its tracks, 'Boulevard' and 'That Girl Could Sing', became Top 20 hits in America while in 1982 the singer reached number 7 with 'Somebody's Baby', a song taken from the soundtrack of *Fast Times At Ridgemont High*. Commitments to social causes and his personal life only increased Browne's artistic impasse and *Lawyers In Love* was a major disappointment. It did, however, contain 'Tender Is The Night', which combined the strength of early work to a memorable hookline. *Lives In The Balance*, which addressed the Reagan presidential era, showed a greater sense of accomplishment, a feature continued on *World In Motion*. Jackson Browne remains a highly-regarded singer/songwriter, as testified by the numerous acts who have turned to his work over the years. The craftsmanship of his work assures him a devoted audience.

Albums: *Jackson Browne* aka *Saturate Before Using* (1972), *For Everyman* (1973), *Late For The Sky* (1974), *The Pretender* (1976), *Running On Empty* (1977), *Hold Out* (1980), *Lawyers In Love* (1983), *Lives In The Balance* (1986), *Worlds In Motion* (1989).

Brownsville Station

This Detroit-based quartet - Cub Koda (guitar/harmonica), Michael Lutz (guitar/vocals), Bruce Nazarian (guitar/synthesiser) and Henry Week (drums/vocals) - forged its early reputation as a superior 'oldies' group. Their attention to 'roots' music was later fused to an understanding of pop's dynamics, exemplified in 'Smokin' In The Boys' Room' (1973), which reached number 3 in the US charts and the UK Top 30 the following year. Subsequent releases lacked the quartet's early sense of purpose and the band was latterly folded. Koda later fronted several 'revival' styled units while proclaiming his love of R&B and blues through columns in USA collectors' magazines.

Albums: *Brownsville Station* (1970), *No B.S.* (1970), *A Night On The Town* (1972), *Yeah!* (1973), *School Punks* aka *Smokin' In The Boys' Room* (1974), *Motor City Connection* (70s), *Air Special* (1980).

Budgie

This hard-rock group was formed in Cardiff, Wales by John Burke Shelley (b. 10 April 1947, Cardiff, South Glamorgan, Wales; bass/acoustic guitar/lead vocals) and Ray Phillips (drums) in 1968. Joined by Tony Bourge (b. 23 November 1948, Cardiff, South Glamorgan, Wales; lead guitar/vocals) the trio established a substantial following in the south Wales college and club circuit and were subsequently signed to MCA Records. Plying their trade in a basic, heavy riffing style, the standard was set with the first single, charmingly entitled 'Crash Course To Brain Surgery'. The vagaries of early 70s British album artwork were typified by the treatment given to Budgie's releases and promotional material, depicting a ludicrous image of a budgerigar variously posed dressed as a fighter pilot (staring nobly out into the far horizon), a Nazi Gestapo officer, or as a squadron of fighter budgies flying in formation, tearing into combat! Founder member Phillips quit in 1974 before the recording of their fourth album and was replaced by Pete Boot (b. 30 September 1950, West Bromwich, Staffordshire, England), who in turn, departed that year before Steve Williams took over. With the success of *In For The Kill*, Budgie won over a wider audience, although they were held in higher esteem in Europe during this time. Their sixth album, *If I Was Brittania I'd Waive The Rules*, on A&M Records was the last to feature Bouge, who left in 1978, forming Tredegar with Ray Phillips, and was replaced by former George Hatcher Band guitarist John Thomas. The group's popularity grew in the USA resulting in Budgie concentrating on touring there for two years. Returning to Britain, and now signed to RCA, Budgie found themselves fitting in well with the new heavy rock scene, and despite being labelless for much of the mid-80s, their reputation and influence on a younger generation of musicians brought them consistent work until Shelley wound up the group in 1987. He subsequently worked with a new trio, Superclarkes.

Albums: *Budgie* (1971), *Squawk* (1972), *Never Turn Your Back On A Friend* (1973), *In For The Kill* (1974), *Bandolier* (1975), *If I Was Brittania I'd Waive The Rules* (1976), *Impeckable* (1978), *Power Supply* (1980), *Nightflight* (1981), *Deliver Us From Evil* (1982). Compilations: *Best Of (71-72)* (1981), *Best Of Budgie* (1982).

Buffalo

Buffalo emerged in Sydney, Australia in 1970 and soon picked up a healthy following of heavy rock fans. Signed by the prestigious Vertigo label, the band's albums sold slowly but steadily enough to retain the interest of the label. The group received bad press owing to the overtly sexist nature of the covers of their first three albums and also for some of the song lyrics (eg 'Skirt Lifter'), which perhaps limited their appeal. Buffalo were an anomaly among bands in Australia during the 70s in that they were as popular in Europe, particularly France, as they were in their homeland. The outfit were musically akin to the likes of Black Sabbath and Deep Purple while retaining their own rock sound, enhanced by Norm Roue's slide guitar playing and the powerful performances of vocalist Dave Tice. Eventually the dearth of original members lead the band to split, after recording five albums. Interestingly the first album went gold three years after initial release. Bassist Pete Wells, played slide guitar in Rose Tattoo with Angry

Anderson, while Tice joined original drummer, Paul Balbi, in the Count Bishops in the UK.

Albums: *Dead Forever* (1972), *Volcanic Rock* (1973), *Only Want You For Your Body* (1974), *Mother's Choice* (1976), *Average Rock And Roller* (1977). Compilation: *Best Of* (1980).

Bundrick, John 'Rabbit'

A popular journeyman keyboardist, Bundrick made his mark in Johnny Nash's backing band. He later joined erstwhile Free members Paul Kossoff and Simon Kirke in the 1971 amalgamation, Kossoff, Kirke, Tetsu And Rabbit, resulting in one album. Bundrick subsequently joined Free when the group reformed. Between recording two albums, Bundrick had been heavily employed as a session musician for many of the leading names on the British music scene, including; Joan Armatrading, Mallard, Russ Ballard, Sandy Denny, Pete Townshend, Bob Marley And The Wailers, Richard And Linda Thompson, Ralph McTell, Donovan, Frankie Miller, Jim Capaldi, the Only Ones, Eric Burdon, the Sutherland Brothers and John Martyn.

Albums: *Broken Arrows* (1973), *Dark Saloon* (1974).

Burland, Dave

b. 12 July 1941, Barnsley, South Yorkshire, England. A respected, and long established performer, Burland has a wide repertoire of material ranging from traditional and contemporary, including songs that often are not classified as 'folk'. Having turned professional in 1968, Burland has continued to perform and record, at folk festivals, in clubs, and has toured much of Europe, Hong Kong and Australia during his career. His first release, *A Dalesman's Litany*, an album of traditional songs, was voted *Melody Maker* Folk Album Of The Year in 1971. There followed the equally well-received *Dave Burland*, again on Trailer. *Songs And Buttered Haycocks*, featured songs by writers such as Richard Thompson, David Ackles and Mike Waterson of the Watersons. In 1978, Burland joined the folk rock band Hedgehog Pie, the combination of guitars, flute, uillean pipes, cittern and piccolo, resulting in the release of *Just Act Normal*. This was to be the group's last album, before splitting up in 1981. During this time, Burland released *Songs Of Ewan MacColl*, which again showed his ability to interpret different styles of writing. After the split, Dave, again solo, put out *You Can't Fool The Fat Man*, which displayed his wide taste in quality songs. The album featured songs from the pens of diverse names such as

Randy Newman and Cyril Tawney. Dave's other commitments included hosting folk shows on BBC and independent local radio, as well as organizing folk festivals in Leeds, with Andy Kershaw. *Rollin'*, an album of modern material, was released on the Moonraker label, and since then Burland has been touring and performing at festivals and clubs. He has also appeared as session player on albums by Mike Harding, and Nic Jones among others. *Willin'* was a live recording, and included some of Dave's earlier material alongside previously unrecorded works. He has recently released an album of Richard Thompson songs, *His Master's Choice*, and in 1992 joined the Lost Nation Band with Sara Grey and Roger Wilson.

Albums: *A Dalesman's Litany* (1971), *Dave Burland* (1972), *Songs And Buttered Haycocks* (1975), *Songs Of Ewan MacColl* (1978), with Hedgehog Pie *Just Act Normal* (1978), *You Can't Fool The Fat Man* (1978), *Rollin'* (1983), *Willin'* (1989), *His Master's Choice* (1992).

Butts Band

Formed in 1974, the Butts Band included two former members of the Doors, Robbie Krieger (b. 8 January 1946, Los Angeles, California, USA; guitar) and John Densmore (b. 1 December 1945, Los Angeles, California, USA; drums). After the 1973 dissolution of the Doors, the two musicians teamed up with vocalist Jess Roden, formerly of Bronco. Roy Davies (keyboards) and Philip Chen (bass) filled out the original line-up. One of the first white American groups to specialize in reggae music, the group signed to Blue Thumb Records. The first album was a self-titled affair which did not chart. For the second and final album, 1975's *Hear And Now*, Krieger and Densmore fired the rest of the band and formed a completely new line-up, featuring Michael Stull (guitar/keyboards), Alex Richman (keyboards/vocals), Karl Ruckner (bass) and Mike Berkowitz (drums). It too failed to chart and the group disbanded in 1975. Krieger and Densmore returned to their solo careers and the other members have returned to obscurity, with the exception of Roden, who recorded a number of solo albums for Island Records.

Albums: *The Butts Band* (1974), *Hear And Now* (1975).

Byron, David

b. David Garrick, 29 January 1947, Essex, England, d. 28 February 1985. Byron began his music career as vocalist with the Stalkers, an Essex-based act which, by 1969, had evolved into Uriah Heep.

Although subjected to critical denigration, the group became one of the 70s leading hard rock/heavy metal attractions, thanks in part to the singer's powerful delivery. In 1975, Byron completed a solo album, *Take No Prisoners*, as excessive alcohol consumption put his position within the line-up under increasing pressure. He was fired the following year, but hopes of an artistic rebirth with Rough Diamond proved ill-founded and this highly-touted attraction featuring Dave Clempson broke apart within a year. Bereft of a regular group, he completed *Baby Faced Killer*, but the set appeared during the height of the punk boom, and was not a commercial success. A similar fate befell the ensuing Byron Band whose ill-focused *On The Rocks* did little to further the leader's progress. They folded soon after its release after which the disconsolate vocalist attempted to maintain his career. He died in 1985 as a result of a heart attack.

Albums: *Take No Prisoners* (1975), *Baby Faced Killer* (1977), *This Day And Age* (1980); as the Byron Band *On The Rocks* (1981), *Bad Widow* (1984).

C

Cactus

Formed in 1969, the original Cactus consisted of Rusty Day (vocals), Jim McCarty (guitar, ex-Mitch Ryder and Buddy Miles' Express), and two former members of Vanilla Fudge, Tim Bogert (bass) and Carmine Appice (drums). Their exciting, uncompromising brand of hard rock was best displayed on *One Way Or Another*, but internal disputes hampered their progress. Day and McCarty left to join Detroit in 1971, but although a reshaped line-up completed *Restrictions*, the initial rhythm section abandoned their creation to form Beck, Bogert And Appice. Recent arrival Duane Hitchins (keyboards) then instigated the New Cactus Band with Mike Pinera (guitar, ex-Iron Butterfly), Roland Robinson (bass) and Jerry Norris (drums), but the group disintegrated in 1973.

Albums: *Cactus* (1970), *One Way...Or Another* (1971), *Restrictions* (1971), *'Ot 'N' Sweaty* (1972), *Son Of Cactus* (1973).

Cale, J.J.

b. Jean Jacques Cale, 5 December 1938, Tulsa, Oklahoma, USA. This mercurial artist began performing professionally in the 50s as guitarist in a western swing group. With the advent of rock 'n' roll he led his own group, Johnnie Cale And The Valentines, before moving to Nashville late in the decade for an unsuccessful career in country music. He subsequently settled in Los Angeles, thereby joining fellow Tulsa ex-patriots Leon Russell, Carl Radle and Chuck Blackwell. Cale played in bar-bands, worked as a studio engineer and recorded several low-key singles before collaborating with songwriter Roger Tillison on a psychedelic album, *A Trip Down Sunset Strip*. Credited to the Leathercoated Minds, this tongue-in-cheek selection has since become a cult favourite.

An impoverished Cale returned to Tulsa in 1967. He remained an obscure, local talent for three years but his fortunes changed dramatically when Eric Clapton recorded 'After Midnight', a song Cale had written and released as a single in 1965. 'It was like discovering oil in your own backyard', he later commented. Producer Audie Ashworth then invited him to Nashville where he completed the excellent *Naturally*. The completed tape was then forwarded to Leon Russell, who released it on his fledgling Shelter label. The concise, self-confident album, arguably Cale's best, featured a re-recording of 'After Midnight', as well as several equally enchanting compositions, including 'Call Me The Breeze', 'Magnolia' and 'Crazy Mama', which became a US Top 30 hit. His laconic, almost lachrymose delivery quickly became a trademark, while the sympathetically light instrumental support from veterans David Briggs (keyboards), Norbert Putnam (bass) and Tim Drummond (drums), previously members of Area Code 615, enhanced its intimate atmosphere. *Naturally* created a style from which Cale has rarely strayed and while some critics detected a paucity of ideas, others enthuse over its hypnotic charm.

Really confirmed the high quality of the artist's compositions. Marginally tougher than its predecessor, it included the R&B-flavoured 'Lies' and featured contributions from the Muscle Shoals team of Barry Beckett (keyboards), David Hood (bass) and Roger Hawkins (drums). While *Okie* and *Troubadour* lacked its immediacy, the latter contained the singer's own version of 'Cocaine', another song popularized by Clapton, who also recorded 'I'll Make Love To You Anytime' from *Five*. Although Cale has remained a somewhat shy and reticent figure, his influence on other musicians has been considerable. Mark Knopfler of Dire Straits appropriated much of his delivery from Cale's self-effacing style, yet while such devotees enjoyed massive commercial success, the originator entered a period of semi-retirement following an ill-fated dalliance with a major label. Despite the inclusion of the popular 'Money Talks' and the acquisition of Cale's back-catalogue, Cale's two albums for Phonogram, *Grasshopper* and *8*, failed to sell in the quantities anticipated and he asked to be released from his contract. The artist re-emerged in 1989 with *Travel Log*, which was issued on Silvertone, a British independent label. Devotees were relieved to hear little had changed, the songs were still largely based on 12-bar structures, his guitar style retained its rhythmic, yet relaxed pulse while Cale's warm, growling voice was as distinctive as ever.

Albums: *Naturally* (1971), *Really* (1972), *Okie* (1974), *Troubadour* (1976), *Five* (1979), *Shades* (1981), *Grasshopper* (1982), *8* (1983), *Travel Log* (1989). Compilations: *Special Edition* (1984), *La Femme De Mon Pote* (1984), *Nightriding* (1988).

Cale, John

b. 5 December 1940, Crynant, West Glamorgan,

Wales. Cale was a student of viola and keyboards at London's Goldsmith's college when introduced to electronic music. In 1963 he won a Leonard Bernstein scholarship to study modern composition at the Eastman Conservatory in Massachusetts, but later moved to New York where he joined the Dream Syndicate, an *avant garde* ensemble founded by LaMonte Young. It was during this period that Cale began playing rock and the following year he met Lou Reed through a mutual association with Pickwick Records. Sceptical of the company's desire for exploitative releases, the duo left to form a group which would evolve into the Velvet Underground. Cale remained with this highly influential act until 1968 during which time his experimental predisposition combined with Reed's grasp of pop's traditions to create a truly exciting lexicon, embodied to perfection in 'Sister Ray' from *White Light/White Heat*. Cale's contribution to the group should not be under-emphasized, a fact enhanced by the shift in style which followed his summary dismissal from the line-up. He produced *The Marble Index* for Nico, the first of several collaborations with the former Velvet's *chanteuse*, and the Stooges, before embarking on a solo career with *Vintage Violence*. Those anticipating a radical set were pleasantly surprised by the melodic flair which marked its content. However, *Church Of Anthrax*, a rather unsatisfactory pairing with Terry Riley, and the imaginative *The Academy In Peril*, re-affirmed his experimental reputation. Whilst working for the Warner Brothers label in studio production and A&R, he assembled a backing band which included the services of Little Feat members Lowell George and Richard Hayward. Together they recorded the haunting *Paris 1919*, which continued the popular style of Cale's debut and remains, for many, the artist's finest work. Cameos on albums by Nick Drake and Mike Heron preceded a spell with UK-based Island Records. Cale's first album for the label, *Fear*, featured and included a selection of compositions both overpoweringly dense and also light-hearted. It also featured Brian Eno, who also contributed to the follow-up *Slow Dazzle* and appeared with Cale, Nico and Kevin Ayers (as ACNE) on *June 1 1974*. Such a punishing schedule undermined Cale's creativity, a fact exemplified in the disappointing *Helen Of Troy*, but his production on Patti Smith's *Horses* (1976) nonetheless enhanced the urgency of this exemplary work. Now fêted by the punk audience, Cale's own recordings increasingly borrowed ideas rather than introducing them and he reached an artistic torpor

with the onstage beheading of a chicken, resulting in his band walking out on him. However, *Music For A New Society* marked a renewed sense of adventure, adeptly combining the popular and cerebral. The personal tribulations of the 70s now behind him, Cale continued to offer innovative music and *Words For The Dying* matched his initial work for purpose and imagination. *Songs For 'Drella*, a 1990 collaboration with Lou Reed as a tribute to their recently deceased former mentor, Andy Warhol, was rightly lauded by critics and audiences alike.

Albums: *Vintage Violence* (1970), with Terry Riley *Church Of Anthrax* (1971), *The Academy In Peril* (1972), *Paris 1919* (1973), *Fear* (1974), as ACNE *June 1 1974* (1974), *Slow Dazzle* (1975), *Helen Of Troy* (1975), *Sabotage/Live* (1979), *Honi Soit* (1981), *Music For A New Society* (1982), *Caribbean Sunset* (1984), *John Cale Comes Alive* (1984), *Black Rose* (1985), *Artificial Intelligence* (1985), *Land* (1989), *Words For The Dying* (1989), with Lou Reed *Songs For 'Drella* (1990), *Even Cowgirls Get The Blues* (1991, a live recording during the late-70s from New York's CBGB's), *Paris S'Eveille, Suivi D'Autres* (1992). Compilation: *Guts* (1977).

California, Randy

b. Randy Wolfe, 20 February 1951, Los Angeles, California, USA. California is better known for his often lustrous rock guitar work and fine songwriting ability with the west coast band Spirit. He has kept the band name alive for over 25 years with numerous line-ups. His solo career started in 1972 during one of Spirit's many break-ups, with the perplexing *Captain Kopter And The Fabulous Twirlybirds*. This Jimi Hendrix-inspired outing featured versions of the Beatle's 'Day Tripper' and 'Rain', and Paul Simon's 'Mother And Child Reunion'. The accompanying band featured Ed Cassidy from Spirit and Clit McTorious (alias Noel Redding) on bass. California has since made a further two albums bearing his name, but neither has appealed to a market outside the loyal cult of kindred spirits.

Albums: *Captain Kopter And The Fabulous Twirlybirds* (1972), *Euro American* (1982), *Restless* (1985).

Calvert, Robert

b. c.1945, Pretoria, South Africa, d. 14 August 1988. Domiciled in London's bohemian Ladbroke Grove/Portobello Road area, Calvert became acquainted with Hawkwind, one of the area's atypical 'underground' attractions. His poetry readings became part of the group's act during the early 70s and in 1972 he joined the line-up as an official member. Calvert wrote, and originally sang, 'Silver Machine', their Top 3 hit, although by that point his vocal had been overdubbed. He left Hawkwind the following year but three of the group - Dave Brock (guitar), Lemmy (bass) and Simon King (drums) - joined ex-Pink Fairies Twink (drums) and Paul Rudolph (guitar) on *Captain Lockheed And The Starfighters*, the artist's highly praised solo debut. His second set, *Lucky Leif And The Longships*, which featured science-fiction writer Michael Moorcock, was produced by Brian Eno, but it proved less popular than its predecessor. Calvert returned to the Hawkwind fold in 1977, but left again at the end of the decade. Two more solo albums, blending science fiction with rock ensued, before this respected performer succumbed to a heart attack on 14 August 1988.

Albums: *Captain Lockheed And The Starfighters* (1974), *Lucky Leif And The Longships* (1975), *Hype* (1980), *Freq* (1984), *Test Tube Conceived* (1986).

Camel

Formed in the spring of 1972 by former members of Philip Goodhand-Tait's backing band, Camel comprised Doug Ferguson (b. 4 April 1947, Carlisle, Cumbria, England; bass), Andy Ward (b. 28 September 1952, Epsom, Surrey, England; drums) and Andy Latimer (b. 17 May 1947, Guildford, Surrey, England; guitar/flute/vocals) and Peter Bardens (b. 19 June 1945, Westminster, London, England; keyboards). Bardens, whose pedigree included stints with Them and Shotgun Express, would dominate the group's sound to the extent that they would come to be known as Peter Barden's Camel in deference to Peter Frampton's Camel. As regular performers on the UK college circuit, it took an adaptation of the Paul Gallico children's story, *The Snow Goose*, to put this foremost progressive band into the UK Top 30 album chart. After the release of *Moonmadness*, Ferguson departed, to be replaced by ex-Caravan member Richard Sinclair. They consolidated their position with the Top 30 albums *Rain Dances* and *Breathless*. Although their success preceded the rise of the punk/new wave movement, the band's image as out-dated progressive rockers threatened their future. However, they survived, but not without some changes to the line-up and consequently, the style of music. Peter Barden's replacement by Jan Schelhaas (another ex-Caravan member) made the biggest impact, leaving room

for lighter song structures typified on *The Single Factor*. The group continued to record and perform well into the 80s when the final line-up, now led by the only remaining original member Latimer and comprising Tom Scherpenzeel (keyboards), Christopher Rainbow (vocals), Paul Burgess (drums) and Paul Bass (bass), closed proceedings with the live set, *Pressure Points*.

Albums: *Camel* (1973), *Mirage* (1974), *The Snow Goose* (1975), *Moonmadness* (1976), *Rain Dances* (1977), *A Live Record* (1978), *Breathless* (1978), *I Can See Your House From Here* (1979), *Nude* (1981), *The Single Factor* (1982), *Stationary Traveller* (1984), *Pressure Points* (1984). Compilation: *The Camel Collection* (1986).

Campbell, Junior

b. William Campbell, 31 May 1947, Glasgow, Scotland. The former lead singer of Marmalade began a promising solo career in 1972 with the stirring 'Hallelujah Freedom'. Combining much of the melody of Marmalade, this soul-influenced single made the UK Top 10. The following year similar success came with 'Sweet Illusion'. The chart singles stopped and Campbell's direction moved towards back-room production. In the early 80s he wrote the theme music to award-winning UK television children's programmes, notably *Thomas The Tank Engine* (narrated by Ringo Starr) and *Tugs*.

Album: *Second Time Around* (1977).

Can

Formed in Cologne, Germany and originally known as Inner Space, this experimental unit was founded by two students of modern classical music, Irmin Schmidt (b. 29 May 1937, Berlin, Germany; keyboards) and Holger Czukay (b. 24 March 1938, Danzig, Germany; bass). The group embraced a rock-based perspective with the addition of Michael Karoli (b. 29 April 1948, Straubing, Lower Bavaria, Germany; guitar), Jaki Leibezeit (b. 26 May 1938, Dresden, Germany; drums) and the inclusion in this early line-up of David Johnson (flute).

The arrival of black American vocalist Malcolm Mooney coincided with the adoption of a new name, Can. Johnson left the group in December 1968 as the unit began work on their official debut album. *Monster Movie* introduced many of Can's subsequent trademarks: Schmidt's choppy, percussive keyboard style, Karoli's incisive guitar and the relentless, hypnotic pulse of its rhythm section. At times reminiscent of a Teutonic Velvet

Underground, the set's highlight was the propulsive 'You Doo Right', a 20-minute excerpt from a 12-hour improvisatory session. The group completed several other masters, later to appear on *Soundtracks* and *Delay 1968*, prior to the departure of Mooney. He was replaced by Kenji 'Damo' Suzuki (b. 16 January 1950, Japan), whom Liebezeit and Czukay had discovered busking outside a Munich cafe. *Tago Mago*, a sprawling, experimental double set, then followed, the highlight of which was the compulsive 'Hallelujah'. However, despite retaining a penchant for extended compositions, Can also began exploring a more precise, even ambient direction on *Ege Bamyasi* and *Future Days*.

Suzuki left the group in 1973, and although they flirted with other featured vocalists, Can remained a quartet for some time. In 1976 the group scored an unlikely UK Top 30 hit with 'I Want More', a song written by Pink Floyd guitarist David Gilmour, who also guested on several tracks from the attendant album, *Flow Motion*. Can was later augmented by two former members of Traffic, Rosko Gee (bass) and Reebop Kwaku Baah (percussion), but the departure of Czukay signalled their demise. The group completed *Out Of Reach* without him, but the bassist returned to edit their next release, *Can*. These largely disappointing releases made little impact and the unit split up at the end of 1978.

Holger Czukay then pursued a successful solo career with a series of excellent solo albums and fruitful partnerships with David Sylvian and the Eurythmics. Irmin Schmidt completed several film soundtracks, Jaki Liebezeit formed his own group, the Phantom Band, and worked with systems musician Michael Rother, while Karoli recorded an excellent solo set. The four musicians remained in close contact and a reformed Can, complete with Malcolm Mooney, returned to the studio in 1987. The fruits of their renewed relationship appeared two years later in the shape of the excellent *Rite Time*.

Albums: *Monster Movie* (1969), *Deep End* (1970, film soundtrack), *Tago Mago* (1971), *Ege Bamyasi* (1972), *Future Days* (1973), *Soon Over Babaluma* (1974), *Landed* (1975), *Flow Motion* (1976), *Saw Delight* (1977), *Out Of Reach* (1978), *Can* (1979 - later released as *Inner Space*), *Rite Time* (1989). Compilations: *Limited Edition* (1974), *Unlimited Edition* (1976), *Opener* (1976), *Cannibalism* (1978), *Incandescence* (1981), *Delay 1968* (1981), *Onlyou* (1982), *Prehistoric Future* (1985).

Candlewick Green

This pop group from Liverpool, England, had one hit in 1974 with 'Who Do You Think You Are'. Consisting of Jimmy Nunnen, Tony Webb, Alan Leyland, Lennie Coswell and Andy Bell, they started their career in 1973 with the Decca single 'Doggie'. This was followed by 'Sunday Kinda Monday', before the aforementioned hit. Subsequent releases 'Leave A Little Love', and 'Everyday Of My Life' rapidly disappeared with their authors following their fate soon after.

Capaldi, Jim

b. 24 August 1944, Evesham, Worcestershire, England. The son of a music teacher, Capaldi studied piano and sang from an early age but it was drums that ultimately attracted his attention. Following his membership of the Hellions (with Dave Mason) and Deep Feeling (with Chris Wood), he befriended Steve Winwood, who was still with the Spencer Davis Group. Traffic was formally launched in 1967, and during its turbulent stop-go eight year history, became one of the leading progressive bands. Capaldi made his name during this time as the perfect lyricist for Winwood's innovative musical ideas. During Winwood's enforced absence through peritonitis in 1972, Capaldi released a solo album, *Oh How We Danced*. Its respectable showing in the US charts enabled him to continue to record albums at regular intervals. *Short Cut Draw Blood* in 1974 proved to be his finest work, containing two hit singles: 'Its All Up To You' and a lively version of Boudleaux Bryant's 'Love Hurts'. He toured with his band the Space Cadets in 1976 to average response. He eventually moved to Brazil, effectively ending his lucrative songwriting partnership with Steve Winwood. Often known as 'Gentleman' Jim Capaldi, he has an affectionate rather than important place in musical history. He returned in 1989 with the album *Some Came Running* and contributed to Winwood's multi-million selling *Roll With It* the same year. In 1990 he again collaborated with Winwood on the album *Refugees Of The Heart* and co-wrote the US hit ' One And Only Man'.

Albums: *Oh How We Danced* (1972), *Whale Meat Again* (1974), *Short Cut Draw Blood* (1975), *Play It By Ear* (1977), *The Contender* (1978), *Electric Nights* (1979), *The Sweet Smell Of Success* (1980), *Let The Thunder Cry* (1981), *Fierce Heart* (1983), *One Man Mission* (1984), *Some Come Running* (1989). Further reading: *Keep On Running: The Steve Winwood Story*, Chris Welch. *Back In The High Life:*

A Biography Of Steve Winwood, Alan Clayson.

Capstick, Tony

A Sheffield-born folk singer and comic songwriter, Capstick was one of a spate of 'folk comedians' who emerged on the UK folk scene during the 70s. Among the others were Fred Wedlock, Mike Harding, Richard Digance and most successfully Jasper Carrott and Billy Connolly. Capstick first recorded for the Newcastle-based Rubber Records. After he provided tracks for a comedy compilation, *There Was This Bloke* (with Harding, Derek Brimstone and Bill Barclay), his first solo album had an accompaniment from folk-rock band Hedgehog Pie and was an eclectic mixture of skiffle ('Goodnight Irene'), Bob Dylan ('To Ramona') and creditable versions of traditional songs such as 'The Foggy Dew' and 'Arthur McBride'. Capstick came to national prominence when he recorded a parody of a popular television commercial for Hovis bread. 'Capstick Comes Home', with accompaniment by the Carlton Main And Frickley Colliery Band, was a surprise Top 10 hit in 1981 on the small Dingles label. Chrysalis released the album of the same name which included German and Chinese versions of the hit song, but neither that nor a seasonal follow-up, 'Christams Cracker' were successful. Capstick remains active as a local performer and radio personality in South Yorkshire.

Albums: *His Round* (1972), *Punch And Judy Man* (1974), *Capstick Comes Home* (1981), *Tony Capstick Does A Turn* (1982).

Captain And Tennille

Toni Tennille (b. 8 May 1943, Montgomery, Alabama, USA) co-wrote the 1972 rock musical *Mother Earth*. When it was staged in Los Angeles, the house band included keyboards player Daryl Dragon, (b. 27 August 1942, Los Angeles, California, USA), the son of conductor Carmen Dragon. The duo teamed up and toured as part of the Beach Boys' backing group before writing and producing 'The Way I Want To Touch You', their first recording as Captain And Tennille. The first hit was the jaunty 'Love Will Keep Us Together' (1975) a Neil Sedaka composition which established the group as a close-harmony favourite of Top 40 radio programmers. That song sold a million copies as did 'Lonely Night (Angel Face)' and 'Muskrat Love'. 'You Never Done It Like That' (1978) was their last Top 10 record before they moved from A&M to the Casablanca label. The sensual slow ballad 'Do That To Me One

More Time' reached number 1 in 1979 but afterwards the hits tailed off. By now, however, Captain And Tennille were established in television, with their own primetime series which was followed in the 80s by a daytime show hosted by Tennille with Dragon as musical director. Toni Tennille later made solo albums of standard ballads. Albums: *Love Will Keep Us Together* (1975), *Por Amor Viviremos* (1975), *Song Of Joy* (1976), *Come In From The Rain* (1977), *Dream* (1988), *Make Your Move* (1979), *Keeping Our Love Warm* (1980). Toni Tennille solo: *Moonglow* (1986), *All Of Me* (1987), *Do It Again* (1990).

Captain Beefheart

b. Don Van Vliet, 15 January 1941, Glendale, California, USA. As a child he achieved some fame as a talented sculptor but for more than three decades the enigmatic and charismatic 'Captain', together with his various Magic Bands has been one of rock music's more interesting subjects. During his teens he met Frank Zappa, who shared the same interest in R&B, and while an attempt to form a band together fell through, Zappa (and members of the Mothers Of Invention, would crop up every now and again during Beefheart's career. The first Magic Band was formed in 1964, although it was not until 1966 that they secured a record contract. The unit comprised, in addition to Beefheart, Alex St. Clair Snouffer (guitar), Doug Moon (guitar), Paul Blakely (drums) and Jerry Handley (bass). The ensuing singles, including 'Diddy Wah Diddy', were a commercial disaster and he was dropped by the record label A&M. Beefheart reappeared with the pioneering *Safe As Milk* in April 1967, and was immediately adopted by the underground scene as a mentor. The album was helped by Ry Cooder's unmistakable guitar and it was a critical success throughout the 'summer of love'. Beefheart found that Europe was more receptive to his wonderfully alliterated lyrics, full of nonsensical juxtaposition that defied the listener to decode. The follow-up, *Strictly Personal* has fallen from grace as a critics' favourite, but at the time it was one of the most advanced albums of the 60s. It is now regarded as more of a blues-based album, with a heavily phased recording that was at times hard to listen to. Titles such as 'Beatle Bones And Smokin' Stones' and 'Ah Feel Like Ahcid' were astonishing hallucinogenic voyages. It was with the remarkable *Trout Mask Replica* that Beefheart reached his peak. The double album, crudely recorded by Frank Zappa, contained a wealth of bizarre pieces, including 'Old Fart At

Captain And Tennille

Play', 'Veterans Day Poppy', 'Hair Pie Bake One' and 'Neon Meat Dream Of A Octofish'. Beefheart used his incredible octave range to great effect as he narrated and sang a wealth of lyrical 'malarkey'. The definitive Magic Band were present on this record, consisting of the Mascara Snake (unidentified, reputedly Beefheart's cousin), Antennae Jimmy Semens (Jeff Cotton), Drumbo (John French), Zoot Horn Rollo (Bill Harkelroad) and Rockette Morton (Mark Boston). It was reliably reported that the band recorded and played most of the tracks in one studio, while Beefheart added his lyrics in another (out of ear-shot). The structure and sound of many of the pieces was reminiscent of Ornette Coleman. At one stage on the record, Beefheart is heard laconically stating; 'Shit, how did the harmony get in there?' The listener required a high tolerance level, and while Beefheart and Zappa may have intended to inflict one of the greatest musical jokes of our time, the album is cherished as one of the classic albums from the psychedelic era of the 60s.

A similar theme was adopted for *Lick My Decals Off, Baby* and *Spotlight Kid*, although the latter had a more structured musical format. This album contained the delightfully perceptive 'Blabber And Smoke', written by Jan Van Vliet commenting on her husband. Beefheart sings her lyrics, 'Why don't you stop acting like a silly dope, all you ever do is blabber and smoke'. Beefheart also received considerable attention by contributing the vocals to 'Willie The Pimp' on Zappa's *Hot Rats* in 1969. Following the release of the overtly commercial (by Beefheart standards) *Clear Spot* and a heavy touring schedule, the Magic Band split from Beefheart to form Mallard. The Captain signed to the UK Virgin Records label, releasing two albums, including the critically acclaimed *Unconditionally Guaranteed*. In 1975 Beefheart and Frank Zappa released *Bongo Fury*, a superb live set recorded in Austin, Texas. However, the release of the album resulted in protracted litigation with Virgin Records, which won an injunction over Warner Brothers on the sale of the album in the UK. Beefheart began to spend more time with his other interest, painting. His colourful oils were in the style of Francis Bacon, and it eventually became his main interest. Beefheart has toured and recorded only occasionally and seemed destined to be an important cult figure until the release of *Ice Cream For Crow* in 1982. This excellent return to form saw him writing and performing with renewed fervour. The album glanced the UK charts but was ignored in his homeland. Since that time there have been no new recordings and Don Van Vliet, as he is now known, is a respected artist, exhibiting regularly. His paintings are now fetching considerable prices.

Albums: *Safe As Milk* (1967), *Strictly Personal* (1968), *Trout Mask Replica* (1969), *Lick My Decals Off, Baby* (1970), *The Spotlight Kid* (1972), *Clear Spot* (1972), *Mirror Man* (1973), *Unconditionally Guaranteed* (1974), *Bluejeans And Moonbeams* (1974), with Frank Zappa *Bongo Fury* (1975), *Shiny Beast (Bat Chain Puller)* (1978), *Doc At The Radar Station* (1980), *Ice Cream For Crow* (1982). Further reading: *Captain Beefheart: The Man And His Music*, C.D. Webb.

Captain Beyond

Based in Los Angeles, this Anglo-American 'supergroup' was formed in 1972 around Rod Evans (b. 19 January 1947, Slough, Berkshire, England; vocals, ex-Deep Purple), Bobby Caldwell (drums, ex-Johnny Winter) and two former members of Iron Butterfly, Larry 'Rhino' Rhinehardt (b. 7 July 1948, Florida, USA; guitar) and Lee Dorman (b. 15 September 1945, St. Louis, Missouri, USA; bass). Although *Captain Beyond* established the unit's hard-rock style, this initial line-up proved incompatible and Caldwell was replaced by Marty Rodriguez for *Sufficiently Breathless*. The departure of Evans precipitated a lengthy period of inactivity but in 1976 the remaining trio was joined by Willy Daffern (vocals), Reese Wynanas (keyboards) and Guille Garcia (percussion). This final version broke up following the release of *Dawn Explosion*.
Albums: *Captain Beyond* (1972), *Sufficiently Breathless* (1973), *Dawn Explosion* (1977).

Caravan

Formed in Canterbury, England in 1968, Caravan evolved from the Wilde Flowers, a seminal local attraction which had included Robert Wyatt, Kevin Ayers and Hugh Hopper, each later of the Soft Machine. Pye Hastings (b. 21 January 1947, Tominavoulin, Bamffshire, Scotland; guitar/vocals), David Sinclair (b. 24 November 1947, Herne Bay, Kent, England; keyboards), Richard Sinclair (b. 6 June 1948, Canterbury, Kent, England; bass/vocals) and Richard Coughlan (b. 2 September 1947, Herne Bay, Kent, England; drums) forged the original Caravan line-up whose gift for melody and imaginative improvisation was made apparent on an excellent debut album. The haunting 'Place Of My Own' and 'Love Song With Flute' were particularly impressive and set the

tone for much of the quartet's early work. *If I Could Do It All Over Again, I'd Do It All Over You* continued their blend of wistfulness and the *avant garde*, but it was not until *In The Land Of Grey And Pink* that the quartet achieved due commercial plaudits. Its extended title track contrasted the quirky economy of 'Golf Girl' and the set remains, for many, Caravan's finest album. Dave Sinclair then joined Matching Mole, but the unit was reshaped around Steve Miller, formerly of Delivery, for *Waterloo Lily*. However, a period of frantic activity saw Richard Sinclair leave for Hatfield And The North, before the prodigal David returned to augment a line-up of Hastings, Coughlan, John Perry (b. 19 January 1947, Auburn, New York, USA; guitar) and Geoff Richardson (b. 15 July 1950, Hinckley, Leicestershire, England; viola/violin). An ensuing rigorous touring schedule was punctuated by *For Girls Who Go Plump In The Night* and *Symphonia*, but further personnel changes undermined the group's early charm. Although *Cunning Stunts* provided a surprise US chart entry, Caravan were blighted by their concern for technical perfection. Although increasingly confined to a post-progressive rock backwater inhabited by fellow distinctly-English acts National Health and Anthony Phillips, the irrepressible Hastings continued to lead the group into the 80s. The original quartet was reunited for *Back To Front*, Caravan's last new recording to date, although live appearances have since been made. A flurry of activity in 1991 saw Caravan performing once more, with the addition of Richard Sinclair's amalgamation of former Caravan and Camel members undertaking a series of low-key London club dates under the name of Caravan Of Dreams.
Albums: *Caravan* (1968), *If I Could Do It All Over Again, I'd Do It All Over You* (1970), *In The Land Of Grey And Pink* (1971), *Waterloo Lily* (1972), *For Girls Who Grow Plump In The Night* (1973), *Caravan And The New Symphonia* (1974), *Cunning Stunts* (1975), *Blind Dog At St. Dunsta's* (1976), *The Show Of Our Lives* (1981), *The Album* (1983), *Back To Front* (1983), *Live At The Paris Theatre, 1975* (1991). Compilations: *The Canterbury Tales* (1976), *Collection: Caravan* (1984), *And I Wish I Weren't Stoned Don't Worry* (1985), *The Best Of Caravan* (1987), *Canterbury Collection* (1987). Richard Sinclair solo: *Caravan Of Dreams* (1992).

Carlos, Wendy (Walter)
b. Walter Carlos, 1941. A former physicist, Carlos entered music by composing commercials and, having befriended electronics expert Dr. Robert A. Moog, later took up the latter's pivotal 60s' invention, the Moog synthesizer. He recorded *Switched On Bach* with the assistance of musicologist Benjamin Folkman and, despite the objection of purists, their unlikely transcription proved highly popular, topping the US classical chart for 94 weeks and remaining on its best-selling list throughout 1969-71. The blend of Bach's best-known fugues and movements to 20th-century technology sold in excess of 1 million copies and garnered three Grammy Awards for Best Classical Album, Best Engineered Recording and Best Performance by Instrumental Soloist. Similarly-styled follow-ups failed to match such success, and although Carlos was highly praised for *Sonic Seasonings*, a suite of four original, evocative compositions, her work is now confined to the experimental fringes. The artist's sex change incurred disproportionate publicity. On the 25th anniversary of Switched On Bach she recorded a second volume using today's state-of-the art technology.
Albums: *Switched On Bach* (1968), *The Well-Tempered Synthesizer* (1969), *A Clockwork Orange* (1972, film soundtrack), *Walter Carlos' Clockwork Orange* (1972), *Switched On Bach Volume 2* (1974), *Sonic Seasonings* (1972), *Brandenburg Concertos 3-5* (1976), *The Shining* (1980, film soundtrack), *Tron* (1982, film soundtrack), *Beauty And The Beast* (1986), *Switched On Bach II* (1992). Compilations: *Walter Carlos...By Request* (1977), *Best Of Carlos* (1983).

Carmen, Eric
b. 11 August 1949, Cleveland, Ohio, USA. A veteran of several aspiring mid-west groups, Carmen first achieved success with the Raspberries. This melodious quartet drew inspiration from British 60s' pop and scored notable US hits with 'Go All The Way', 'I Wanna Be With You' and 'Let's Pretend'. Carmen wrote and sang lead on each of these releases and was the sole member to prosper commercially when the group was dissolved in 1975. The following year Carmen scored an international hit with a dramatic ballad, 'All By Myself'. Although he enjoyed two further US Top 20 entries with 'Never Gonna Fall In Love Again' (1976) and 'Change Of Heart' (1978), the artist was unable to sustain a consistent momentum. He returned to the US Top 10 in 1987 with the single, 'Hungry Eyes' (from the film *Dirty Dancing*) and the following year reached number 3 with 'Make Me Lose Control'. Carmen

remains a cultured and versatile performer, although his recent work lacks the panache of his early releases.

Albums: *Eric Carmen* (1975), *Boats Against The Current* (1977), *Change Of Heart* (1978), *Tonight You're Mine* (1980), *Eric Carmen* (1985). Compilations: *The Best Of Eric Carmen* (1988), *Greatest Hits - Eric Carmen* (1988).

Carpenters

This brother-and-sister duo featured Richard Carpenter (b. 15 October 1946, New Haven, Connecticut, USA; piano) and Karen Carpenter (b. 2 March 1950, New Haven, Connecticut, USA, d. 4 February 1983; vocals/drums). During 1963, Richard appeared at various New Haven clubs and bars in an instrumental trio. After his family relocated to Los Angeles, he studied piano and backed his sister, who was signed to the small local label Magic Lamp in 1965. With assistance from Wes Jacobs (bass/tuba) and session bassist Joe Osborn, Karen recorded one single 'I'll Be Yours'. Retaining Jacobs, the brother and sister team next formed a predominantly jazz/instrumental unit known as the Richard Carpenter Trio. After winning a battle of the bands contest at the Hollywood Bowl they were duly signed to RCA Records, but no material was issued. In 1967, Jacobs left the group to study music and Richard and Karen teamed up with a friend, John Bettis, in the short-lived Spectrum. The following year, A&M Records president Herb Alpert heard some demos that they had recorded and signed the brother-and-sister duo, now called the Carpenters. In late 1969, their debut album *Offering* was issued, but failed to chart. A harmonic version of the Beatles 'Ticket To Ride' subsequently climbed to number 54 in the US singles charts early the following year, and this set their hit career in motion. A wonderful reading of Burt Bacharach and Hal David's 'Close To You', complete with a superbly understated piano arrangement, took them to number 1 in the USA. The song was a massive hit all over the world and ushered in an era of chart domination by the wholesome duo. Towards the end of 1970, they were back at number 2 in the US singles chart with the Paul Williams/Roger Nichols composition, 'We've Only Just Begun'. Once more, the track highlighted Karen's crystal-clear diction, overladen with intricated harmonies and a faultless production. Throughout 1971, the duo consolidated their success with such Top 3 US hits as 'For All We Know', 'Rainy Days And Mondays'

and 'Superstar'/'Bless The Beasts And Children'. They also enjoyed Grammy Awards for Best New Artist and Best Vocal Performance, as well as launching their own television series, *Make Your Own Kind Of Music*.

Between 1972-73, the group's run of hits was unrelenting with 'Goodbye To Love', 'Sing' and 'Yesterday Once More' all reaching the US Top 10, while the irresistibly melodic 'Top Of The World' climbed to number 1. All of these songs (with the exception of 'Sing' were composed by Richard Carpenter and his former bassist John Bettis). A cover of the Marvelettes/Beatles 'Please Mr Postman' brought the Carpenters back to number 1 in the summer of 1974, and that same year they played before President Richard Nixon at the White House. Although they continued to chart regularly with such smashes as 'Only Yesterday', there was a noticeable decline in their Top 40 performance during the second half of the 70s. Personal and health problems were also taking their toll. Richard became addicted to prescription drugs and eventually entered a clinic in 1978 to overcome his addiction. Karen, meanwhile, was suffering from the slimmers' disease anorexia nervosa, a condition from which she never recovered.

The latter part of the 70s saw the duo tackle some unlikely material, including covers of Herman's Hermits' 'There's A Kind Of Hush' and Klaatu's 'Calling Occupants Of Interplanetary Craft'. The latter fared particularly well in the UK, reaching number 10 and convincing many that the duo could adapt any song to their distinctive style. Anxious to improve her own standing as a singer, Karen subsequently completed a solo album during 1979 but it was destined to remain unreleased. Thereafter, she reunited with Richard for another Carpenters album, *Made In America* and that same year the duo registered their final US Top 20 hit with 'Touch Me When We're Dancing'. The group's low profile during the early 80s coincided with Karen's increasingly poor health and weak state. On 4 February 1983 she was discovered unconscious at her parents' home in New Haven and died in hospital that morning of a cardiac arrest. The coroner's report revealed the cause of death as 'heartbeat irregularities brought on by chemical imbalances associated with anorexia nervosa'.

Following his sister's death, Richard moved into production. In the meantime, various Carpenters' compilations were issued as well as a posthumous studio album, *Voice Of The Heart*. Richard returned

Carpenters

to recording with 1987's *Time*, on which he sang lead, with guest appearances by such notable female vocalists as Dusty Springfield and Dionne Warwick. In late 1989, he supervised the remixing and release of an ambitious 12-CD anthology of the Carpenters' recordings. During their heyday they were passed over by many critics as being too bland and 'nice' following a surprise reappraisal in the early 90s their standing in popular music today, is high.

Albums: *Offering* (1969, later reissued as *Ticket To Ride*), *Close To You* (1970), *The Carpenters* (1971), *A Song For You* (1972), *Now And Then* (1973), *Horizon* (1975), *Live In Japan* (1975), *A Kind Of Hush* (1976), *Live At The Palladium* (1976), *Passage* (1977), *Christmas Portrait* (1978), *Made In America* (1981), *Voice Of The Heart* (1983), *An Old Fashioned Christmas* (1984). Compilations: *The Singles 1969-73* (1973), *Collection* (1976), *The Singles 1974-78* (1978), *Silver Double Disc Of The Carpenters* (1979), *The Best Of The Carpenters* (1981), *The Carpenters Collection - The Very Best Of The Carpenters* (1984), *Loveline* (1989), *The Compact Disc Collection* (1989, CD boxed set), *From The Top (1965-82)* (1992, CD release). Solo album: Richard Carpenter *Time* (1987).

Carradine, Keith

b. 8 August 1949, San Mateo, California, USA, Keith Carradine is the son of actor John Carradine and the brother of actor David Carradine. An actor himself, he appeared in such films as *The Duellists* (1977), *Welcome To L.A.* (1977), *Pretty Baby* (1978), *The Long Riders* (1980) and *Southern Comfort* (1981). His 1975 appearance in the film *Nashville*, as a rock star, featured Carradine singing 'I'm Easy'. The song was released on ABC Records the following year and reached number 17 in the US charts, eventually winning an Oscar for Best Song. An album of the same title, on Asylum Records, reached number 61. Although Carradine continued to record sporadically he never again had any success in the field of music.

Album: *I'm Easy* (1976).

Cassidy, David

b. 12 April 1950, New York, New York, USA. The son of actor Jack Cassidy, David pursued a show-business career and received his big break after being cast in *The Partridge Family*. The television series was inspired by the life of another hit group, the Cowsills and it was not long before the Partridge Family began registering hits in their own right. Cassidy appeared as lead vocalist on their earnest 1970 US chart-topper, 'I Think I Love You'. Further hits followed and, in October 1971, Cassidy was launched as a solo artist. One month later he was number 1 in the US with a revival of the Association's 'Cherish'. Cassidy was classic teen-idol material but was ambivalent about the superficiality of his image and attempted to create a more adult sexual persona by appearing semi-naked in the pages of *Rolling Stone*. The publicity did not help his career at home, but by mid-1972 he was finding even greater success as a soloist in the UK, where teen-idols were suddenly in the ascendant. That year, he climbed to number 2 in Britain with 'Could It Be Forever' and enjoyed a solo chart-topper with a revival of the Young Rascals' 'How Can I Be Sure?' The more R&B-style 'Rock Me Baby' just failed to reach the Top 10 in the UK and peaked at number 38 in the USA. It was to be his last hit in his home country. By 1973, Cassidy was concentrating on the UK market and his efforts were rewarded with the Top 3 'I Am A Clown' and the double-sided 'Daydreamer'/'The Puppy Song' gave him his second UK number 1. His ability to raid old catalogues and recycle well-known songs to teenage audiences was reflected through further successful covers, including the Beatles' 'Please Please Me' and the Beach Boys' 'Darlin''. By the mid-70s, it was clear that his teen-idol days were reaching their close, so he switched to serious acting, appearing in Tim Rice and Andrew Lloyd Webber's *Joseph And The Amazing Technicolour Dreamcoat*. In 1985, he made a surprise return to the UK Top 10 with the self-penned 'The Last Kiss', which featured backing vocals from George Michael. Two years later, he took over from Cliff Richard in the lead role of Dave Clark's musical *Time*. His teen-idol mantle was meanwhile passed on to his younger brother Shaun Cassidy.

Albums: *Cherish* (1972), *Could It Be Forever* (1972), *Rock Me Baby* (1972), *Dreams Are Nothin' More* (1973), *Cassidy Live* (1974), *The Higher They Climb* (1975), *Romance* (1985), *His Greatest Hits, Live* (1986). Compilation: *Greatest Hits* (1977).

Cassidy, Shaun

b. 27 September 1959, Los Angeles, California, USA. This vocalist was the son of actress/singer Shirley Jones and half-brother of David Cassidy. Shaun signed to Warner Brothers/Curb in 1975 and first tasted chart success in Europe when his debut single 'Morning Girl' reached the Top 10 in Holland and the follow-up 'That's Rock And Roll' did likewise in Germany and Australia.

David Cassidy

Shortly after recording his debut self-titled album, he landed the role of Joe Hardy in the US television series *The Hardy Boys*. This exposure helped the album, released in the US in 1977, climb into the Top 10. It contained mainly updated versions of early 60s hits, including 'Take Good Care Of My Baby', 'Da Doo Ron Ron' - the latter topping the singles charts in July - and a reissue of 'That's Rock And Roll' which went to the Top 3 in October. His follow-up *Born Late* featured the Top 10 smash 'Hey Deanie' in late 1977 and a cover of the Lovin' Spoonful's 'Do You Believe In Magic' which reached number 31, thus ending a run of three consecutive Top 10 hits. After *Under Wraps* failed to make the Top 30 in 1978 he returned to acting and in 1987 joined the cast of the US television series *General Hospital*.
Albums: *Shaun Cassidy* (1977), *Born Late* (1977), *Under Wraps* (1978).

Cate Brothers

A duo composed of twin brothers Ernie and Earl Cate (b. 26 December 1942, Fayetteville, Arkansas, USA), the Cate Brothers specialized in southern soul music and enjoyed brief popularity in the late 70s. Ernie (piano/vocals) and Earl (guitar/vocals) signed to Asylum Records in 1975 and released their first album, a self-titled effort, using numerous studio musicians, among them Memphis legends Steve Cropper and Donald 'Duck' Dunn, Timothy B Schmit (ex Poco and the Eagles), Nigel Olsson of Elton John's band, Klaus Voormann and Levon Helm of the Band. The album charted in 1976 and the single 'Union Man' reached number 24. The brothers' second album, *In One Eye And Out The Other*, also charted in 1976, as did one other single, 'Can't Change My Heart'. Although there were no other commercial successes, two further albums were recorded, 1977's *The Cate Brothers Band* and *Fire On The Tracks*, the last for Atlantic in 1979. In the early 80s the two brothers and members of the current edition of their group joined Levon Helm and three other original members of the Band in a reformation of the latter group, the entire quartet replacing guitarist Robbie Robertson. No further recordings have emerged since the 70s.
Albums: *The Cate Brothers* (1975), *In One Eye And Out The Other* (1976), *The Cate Brothers Band* (1977), *Fire On The Tracks* (1979).

Cavaliere, Felix

b. 29 November 1944, Pelham, New York, USA. Formerly keyboard player/vocalist with the (Young) Rascals, Cavaliere is one of rock's definitive blue-eyed soul performers. By the 70s his group was embracing a cool jazz-rock and this crafted, smooth approach also marks the singer's solo releases. His debut album, *Felix Cavaliere* was a promising affair, but the follow-up, *Destiny*, was even more accomplished, and featured contributions from former Rascals Dino Danelli and Buzz Feiten, and singer Laura Nyro. A third collection followed in 1979, from which 'Only A Lonely Heart Sees' was a US hit single at the start of the new decade. However, Cavaliere has since been unable to fulfil his undoubted potential and in 1988 he, Danelli and Gene Cornish were reunited for a national Rascals' tour.
Albums: *Felix Cavaliere* (1974), *Destiny* (1975), *Castles In The Air* (1979). Compilation: *A Rascal Alone* (1988).

CCS

CCS - Collective Consciousness Society - was an unlikely collaboration between blues traditionalist Alexis Korner (b. 19 April 1928, Paris, France. d. January 1984; vocals/guitar), producer Mickie Most and arranger John Cameron. Formed in 1970, the group revolved around Korner and longtime associate Peter Thorup (vocals), plus several of Britain's leading jazz musicians, including Harry Beckett, Henry Lowther, Kenny Wheeler, Les Condon (trumpets), Johnnie Watson, Don Lusher (trombones), Ronnie Ross, Danny Moss (saxophones), Ray Warleigh (flute), Herbie Flowers, Spike Heatley (basses), Barry Morgan and Tony Carr (drums), and Bill Le Sage (tuned percussion). Although the exact line-up was determined by availability, the unit's commercial, brass-laden sound remained intact over three albums. CCS enjoyed several hit singles, each of which was marked by Korner's distinctive growl. Their version of Led Zeppelin's 'Whole Lotta Love', which served as the theme to BBC television's *Top Of The Pops*, reached number 13 in 1970, and the following year the group enjoyed two UK Top 10 entries with 'Walkin'' and 'Tap Turns On The Water'. CCS was dissolved in 1973 when Korner and Thorup formed Snape with Boz Burrell (bass) and Ian Wallace (drums), two former members of King Crimson.
Albums: *CCS* aka *Whole Lotta Love* (1970), *CCS (2)* (1972), *The Best Band In The Land* (1973). Compilation: *The Best Of CCS* (1977).

Celebration

This informal Californian group served as an alternate, if short-lived, outlet for Beach Boys'

vocalist Mike Love. Formed in 1978, Celebration also featured jazz saxophonist Charles Lloyd, as well as several of the singer's associates from the region's music fraternity. The title track from *Almost Summer* reached the US Top 40 in 1978, a success which inspired a second album, released on former Monkees' guitarist Mike Nesmith's Pacific Arts label. However, Celebration was dropped as Love's commitment to the Beach Boys took precedence and Lloyd returned to his first love, jazz.
Albums: *Almost Summer* (1978), *Celebration* (1979).

Centaurus

This US, blues-based rock quartet was formed in 1977 by guitar virtuoso Nick Paine. Enlisting the services of Nick Costello (bass), Louis Merlino (vocals) and Joey Belfiore (drums), they took their musical lead primarily from Led Zeppelin and Aerosmith. Paine's guitar work was structured on the style made famous by Jimmy Page. Their sole release is noticeably derivative, but the excellent production and rawness of the band's delivery makes it more than worthwhile. They split soon after the album hit the racks, with Costello going on to join Toronto.
Album: *Centaurus* (1978).

Champion

When David Byron quit Rough Diamond in 1977, the remaining band members recruited US vocalist Garry Bell as replacement and subsequently changed their name to Champion. With former Humble Pie guitarist Dave Clempson, ex-Wings drummer Geoff Britton plus Damon Butcher (keyboards) and Willy Bath (bass) completing their line-up, Champion's music never lived up to the promise suggested by their impressive pedigree. Picked up by Epic Records, they released a self-titled album in 1978 of blues-based rock. Failing to attract media attention, they disbanded shortly after the disc was released.
Album: *Champion* (1978).

Chapin, Harry

b. 7 December 1942, New York, USA, d. 16 July 1980. The son of a big band drummer, Chapin played in the Brooklyn Heights Boys' Choir and during his teens formed a group with his brothers, Tom and Stephen. Immensely talented as a writer and film-maker, he directed the Oscar-nominated *Legendary Champions* in 1968, after which he returned to music. In 1971, he formed a group with John Wallace (bass), Ron Palmer (guitar) and

Tim Scott (cello) and played in various clubs in New York. The following year, he was signed to Elektra Records and his debut *Heads And Tales* and the six-minute single 'Taxi' enjoyed minor success in the US charts. Chapin's strength as a writer was already emerging in the form of fascinating narrative songs, which often had a twist in the tale. 'W-O-L-D', an acute observation of the life of a local disc jockey, went on to become something of an FM radio classic. In 1974, Chapin secured the US Christmas number 1 single with the evocative 'Cat's In The Cradle', a moral warning on the dangers of placing careerism above family life. In the song, the neglectful father realizes too late that he has no relationship with his son, who abandons him in his old age. Despite the quality of the recording, it made surprisingly little headway in the UK, failing even to reach the Top 40. With a series of albums, strongly narrative in tone, it was clear that Chapin was capable of extending himself and in 1975 he wrote the Broadway musical revue, *The Night That Made America Famous*. That same year, he also won an Emmy award for his musical work on the children's television series, *Make A Wish*. By 1976, Chapin was still enjoying immense success in his homeland and his double live album *Greatest Stories - Live* received a gold record award. During the late 70s, he became increasingly involved in politics and was a delegate at the 1976 Democratic Convention. He also played many benefit concerts, raising millions of dollars in the process. In 1980, he switched labels to the small Boardwalk. The title track to his album *Sequel*, which was a story sequel to his first hit 'Taxi', gave him his final US Top 30 entry. On 16 July, while travelling to a benefit concert, his car was hit by a truck in Jericho, New York and the singer was killed. A Harry Chapin Memorial Fund was subsequently launched in honour of his memory.
Albums: *Heads And Tails* (1972), *Sniper And Other Love* (1972), *Short Stories* (1974), *Verities And Balderdash* (1974), *Portrait Gallery* (1975), *Greatest Stories - Live* (1976), *On The Road To Kingdom Come* (1976), *Dance Band On The Titanic* (1977), *Living Room Suite* (1978), *Legends Of The Lost And Found - New Greatest Stories Live* (1979), *Sequel* (1980), *The Last Protest Singer* (1989).

Charisma Records

Formed in 1969 by ex-sports journalist and pop manager Tony Stratton-Smith, the label showcased much of the best in British progressive rock during the 70s. Stratton-Smith had entered management with the Koobas, Paddy, Klaus And Gibson, Beryl

Marsden and Creation in the 60s. Frustrated with conventional record labels, he decided to found a new record company for his groups (which included the Nice and Van Der Graaf Generator) and for new talent. The distribution was through reggae company B&C, Island and EMI. Initial hits came from the Nice (soon to split and be replaced by Emerson, Lake And Palmer) and Rare Bird. But the greatest successes for the label came from group and solo albums by Genesis and the folk-rock group Lindisfarne, signed in 1970. Among the other artists recording for Charisma in the 70s were Bell 'N Arc, Audience, Rick Wakeman, String Driven Thing, Clifford T. Ward and Swedish instrumentalist Bo Hansson, composer of a suite based on *Lord Of The Rings*. Away from progressive rock, Stratton-Smith released three comedy albums by Monty Python's Flying Circus and four of poetry and music featuring Sir John Betjeman reading his own work. His sporting interests were reflected in releases by broadcasters John Arlott and Peter O'Sullivan. Charisma also briefly had a book publishing division and for several years was the publisher of the rock magazine *ZigZag*. By the 80s, ELPhad split and Phil Collins had left the label. However, it still signed diverse acts such as Patrick Moraz, Brand X, Hawkwind, Malcolm McLaren, Julian Lennon and the opposition. Charisma was losing market share and after Stratton-Smith's death the label was sold to Virgin in 1984. There, it was used mainly for reissues and in 1990 was revived in the USA as an outlet for artists signed on the west coast.

Compilation: *Repeat Performances* (1980).

Cheap Trick

Formed in Chicago, Illinois, USA in 1973. Rick Neilsen (b. 22 December 1946, Rockford, Illinois, USA; guitar/vocals) and Tom Petersson (b. Peterson, 9 May 1950, Rockford, Illinois, USA; bass/vocals) began their careers in various high-school bands, before securing a recording deal as members of Fuse. This short-lived attraction folded on completing a debut album, and the duo subsequently formed a new group with Thom Mooney and Robert 'Stewkey' Antoni from the recently disbanded Nazz. Mooney was subsequently replaced by drummer Brad Carlson aka Bun E. Carlos (b. 12 June 1951, Rockford, Illinois, USA), and with the departure of 'Stewkey', the initial Cheap Trick line-up was completed by vocalist Randy 'Xeno' Hogan. He in turn was replaced by Robin Zander (b. 23 January 1952, Loves Park, Illinois, USA; guitar/vocals), a former colleague of Carlson in the short-lived Toons. Relocated to America's mid-west, the quartet followed the gruelling bar-band circuit before a series of demonstration tapes secured a recording deal. Although *Cheap Trick* is generally regarded as a disappointment, it introduced the group's inventive flair and striking visual image. The heart-throb good-looks of Zander and Petersson contrasted Carlos' seedy garb, while Neilsen's odd-ball costume - baseball cap, bow-tie and monogrammed sweater - compounded this unlikely combination. Having spent a frenetic period supporting Queen, Journey and Kiss, Cheap Trick completed a second collection within months of their debut. *In Color* offered a smoother sound in which a grasp of melody was allowed to flourish and established the group's ability to satisfy visceral and cerebral demands. It contained several engaging performances, including 'I Want You To Want Me', 'Hello There' and 'Clock Strikes Ten', each of which became in-concert favourites. *Heaven Tonight* consolidated the group's unique approach while 'Surrender' contained the consummate Cheap Trick performance, blending the British pop of the Move with the urgent riffing of the best of America's hard rock. *At Budokan* followed a highly-successful tour of Japan, and this explosive live set became the quartet's first platinum disc, confirming them as a headline act in their own right. However, *Dream Police* added little to the sound extolled on the previous two studio releases, and indeed the title song was originally recorded for the Trick's debut album. Producer George Martin did little to deflect this sterility on *All Shook Up*, while *Found All The Parts*, a mini-album culled from out-takes, suggested internal problems. A disaffected Petersson left the group in 1982, but although Pete Comita initially took his place, the latter quickly made way for Jon Brandt. Neither *One On One*, nor the Todd Rundgren produced *Next Position Please*, halted Cheap Trick's commercial slide, but *Standing On The Edge* offered hopes of a renaissance. A 1986 recording, 'Mighty Wings', was used on the soundtrack of the successful *Top Gun* film, while the return of Petersson the same year re-established the group's successful line-up. *Lap Of Luxury* achieved multi-platinum status when an attendant single, 'The Flame', topped the US chart in 1988 while *Busted* scaled similar heights, confirming Cheap Trick's dramatic resurrection as a major US act.

Albums: *Cheap Trick* (1977), *In Color* (1977), *Heaven Tonight* (1978), *Cheap Trick At Budokan* (1979), *Dream Police* (1979), *Found All The Parts*

(1980), *All Shook Up* (1980), *One On One* (1982), *Next Position Please* (1983), *Standing On The Edge* (1985), *The Doctor* (1986), *Lap Of Luxury* (1988), *Busted* (1990). Compilation: *Greatest Hits* (1992).

Cheech And Chong

Richard 'Cheech' Marin (b. 1946, Watts, Los Angeles, California, USA) became acquainted with Tommy Chong (b. 24 May 1940, Edmonton, Alberta, Canada) while fleeing to escape induction into the US Army. The latter was a noted musician, having performed in Bobby Taylor And The Vancouvers, but the duo's plans for a rock group were sidelined on discovering an aptitude for comedy. A residency at the famed Los Angeles Troubador venue resulted in a recording deal through which a succession of albums established their unique humour. Drawing upon their rock backgrounds, Cheech And Chong pursued subjects apposite to hippie culture - long hair, drugs, sex and police harassment - in a manner indebted to comedian Lenny Bruce and the San Francisco-based *avant garde* troupe, the Committee. Initially fêted by those whose lifestyles provided their subject matter, the duo won a Best Comedy Album Grammy for *Los Cochinos*, and later enjoyed three US hit singles with 'Basketball Jones Featuring Tyrone Shoelaces', 'Sister Mary Elephant (Shudd-Up!)' and 'Earache My Eye Featuring Alice Bowie'. In 1979 they began a film career with *Up In Smoke*, the first of several such ventures, while under the influence of MTV and a concurrent video boom, began placing a greater emphasis on music. *Get Out Of My Room* included 'Born In East LA', a satirical reworking of Bruce Springsteen's 'Born In The USA'. The duo's song referred to a true-life incident wherein a Latin-American, legally domiciled in the USA, was deported to Mexico when he was unable to prove his citizenship during an immigration raid. 'Born In East LA' became a hit single and inspired a film of the same title.
Albums: *Cheech And Chong* (1971), *Big Bambu* (1972), *Los Cochinos* (1973), *Wedding Album* (1974), *Sleeping Beauty* (1976), *Six* (1977), *Up In Smoke* (1978, film soundtrack), *Let's Make A New Dope Deal* (1980), *Get Out Of My Room* (1986).

Chicago

Formed in 1966 in Chicago, Illinois, USA, Chicago was a consistent hit-making group throughout the 70s and 80s. The band was initially called the Missing Links, next becoming the Big Thing and then, the same year, Chicago Transit Authority, at the suggestion of manager Jim Guercio. The original line-up was Terry Kath (b. 31 January 1946, Chicago, USA, d. 23 January 1987; guitar/vocals), Peter Cetera (b. 13 September 1944, Chicago, USA; bass/vocals), Robert Lamm (b. 13 October 1944, Brooklyn, New York, USA; keyboards/vocals), Walter Parazaider (b. 14 March 1945, Chicago, USA; saxophone), Danny Seraphine (b. 28 August 1948, Chicago, USA; drums), Walt Perry (b. 1945, Chicago, USA; brass), James Pankow (b. 20 August 1947, Chicago, USA; trombone) and Lee Loughnane (b. 21 October 1941, Chicago, USA; trumpet). The horn section set the group apart from other mid-60s rock bands, although *Chicago Transit Authority* was preceded on record by similar sounding groups such as Blood, Sweat And Tears and the Electric Flag. During 1967 and 1968 Guercio built the band's reputation, particularly in the Los Angeles area, where they played clubs such as the Whisky A-Go-Go. In January 1969 Guercio landed the group a contract with Columbia Records, largely through his reputation as producer of Blood, Sweat and Tears and the Buckinghams. With jazz influences the group released its self-titled album in 1969. Although it never made the Top 10 the album stayed on the charts for 171 weeks. The group also enjoyed singles hits with 'Does Anybody Really Know What Time It Is' and 'Beginnings'. In 1970 the group shortened its name to Chicago. Still working in the jazz-rock idiom they released *Chicago II*. Henceforth each of the group's albums would receive a number as its title, up to *Chicago 21* by 1991, with the sole exceptions of their fourth album, the four-record boxed set *Chicago At Carnegie Hall*, their twelfth, titled *Hot Streets*, and their fifteenth and twentieth, greatest hits volumes. By the early 70s Chicago began breaking away from its jazz sound toward more mainstream pop, resulting in such light-rock staples as 'Colour My World', the 1976 transatlantic number 1 'If You Leave Me Now' and the 1982 number 1 'Hard To Say I'm Sorry'. Five consecutive Chicago albums topped the charts between 1972 and 1975, however the group experienced a sales slump in the late 70s only to rebound in the early 80s.
In 1974 Lamm recorded a poor-selling solo album. That same year the group added Brazilian percussionist Laudir de Oliveira to the line-up. The following year the group toured with the Guercio-managed Beach Boys. In 1977, after *Chicago X* was awarded a Best Album Grammy, Guercio and the group parted ways. On 23 January

Chicago

1978 founding member Kath was killed by a self-inflicted accidental gunshot wound. The group continued, with Donnie Dacus (ex-Stephen Stills sideman) joining on guitar (he left the following year and was replaced by Chris Pinnick; Pinnick left in 1981, when Bill Champlin, ex-Sons Of Champlin, joined on keyboards). In 1981, Chicago was dropped by Columbia and signed to Full Moon Records, distributed by Warner Brothers. Also that year, Cetera released a solo album, which was a mild success. After leaving the group in 1985 (his replacement was Jason Scheff, son of Elvis Presley bassist Jerry Scheff), he released two further solo albums, the first of which yielded two number 1 singles, 'Glory Of Love' and 'The Next Time I Fall', the latter a duet with Amy Grant. Switching to Reprise Records in 1988, Chicago was still considered a major commercial force by 1991, despite having long abandoned their original jazz-rock roots.

Albums: *Chicago Transit Authority* (1969), *Chicago II* (1970), *Chicago III* (1971), *Chicago At Carnegie Hall* (1971), *Chicago V* (1972), *Chicago VI* (1973), *Chicago VII* (1974), *Chicago VIII* (1975), *Chicago X* (1976), *Chicago XI* (1977), *Hot Streets* (1978), *Chicago 13* (1979), *Chicago XIV* (1980), *Chicago 16* (1982), *Chicago 17* (1984), *Chicago 18* (1987), *Chicago 19* (1988), *Chicago 21* (1991). Compilations: *Chicago IX - Chicago's Greatest Hits* (1975), *Chicago - Greatest Hits, Volume II* (1981), *Greatest Hits 1982-1989* (1989), *The Heart Of Chicago* (1989).

Chicory Tip

Hailing from Maidstone, Kent in England, this pop quartet was formed in 1968 by singer Peter Hewson (b. 1 September 1950, Gillingham, Kent, England). The rest of the group comprised Barry Mayger (b. 1 June 1950, Maidstone, Kent, England; bass), Brian Shearer (b. 4 May 1951, Lewisham, London, England; drums) and Dick Foster (guitar). Foster was replaced in October 1972 by Rod Cloutt (b. 26 January 1949, Gillingham, Kent, England; lead guitar/synthesizer/organ). Chicory Tip's main claim to fame was a gnawingly infectious piece of pop ephemera titled 'Son Of My Father' which topped the UK charts for three weeks in early 1972. The record was something of a combined star effort having been written by the soon-to-be-famous disco producer Giorgio Moroder. The distinctive synthesizer backing on the disc was played by another producer-elect, Chris Thomas. Finally, the man who actually produced the record was Roger Easterby, manager of another seasoned pop outfit, Vanity Fare. Although Chicory Tip had a low-key image, they rode the glam rock wagon long enough to enjoy two further UK Top 20 hits

with 'What's Your Name?' (1972) and 'Good Grief Christina' (1973).
Album: *Son Of My Father* (1972).

Child

This British teen band from the late 70s comprised of Timothy Atack (b. 5 April 1959, Wakefield, Yorkshire, England; drums), Graham Robert Bilbrough (b. 23 March 1958, Fairburn, Yorkshire, England; lead vocals/rhythm guitar), Keith Atack (b. 5 April 1959, Wakefield, Yorkshire, England; lead guitar), Mike McKenzie (b. 20 August 1955, Edinburgh, Scotland; bass guitar). They charted in the UK with three uninspired cover versions of 'When You Walk In The Room', 'It's Only Make Believe' (both 1978) and 'Only You (And You Alone)' (1979). Two albums were also released of non-original material. Sold entirely as a visual band and aimed at the young female teenage market, the group worked for 18 months.
Albums: *Child: The First Album* (1978), *Total Recall* (1979).

Child, Desmond, And Rouge

This US, commercially minded and chart-oriented soft-rock outfit was formed in 1975 by keyboardist Desmond Child, backed by an array of musicians. With college friends Maria Vidal, Myriam Naomi Vaille and Diana Graselli completing the line-up as vocalists, they attracted the interest of Kiss guitarist Paul Stanley. Signing to Capitol Records, their debut album released in 1978 was a pot-pourri of styles, that included elements of pop, rock, funk, blues and soul. The follow-up, *Runners In The Night*, adopted a more hard-rock stance, but was also met with indifference. The band became redundant as Child decided to concentrate on writing and production, rather than actually playing. He has composed for Cher, Michael Bolton, Bon Jovi, Alice Cooper, Kiss and Jimmy Barnes among others. 'You Give Love A Bad Name' and 'Livin' On A Prayer' co-written with Bon Jovi and the Kiss million-seller 'I Was Made For Loving You' have been his greatest successes to date. Child made a return to recording in 1991 for Elektra Records, which despite the competent performance failed to set the charts alight.
Albums: *Desmond Child And Rouge* (1978), *Runners In The Night* (1979), as Desmond Child *Discipline* (1991).

Chilliwack

This was the third version of a Canadian, Vancouver-based group previously known as the Classics and the Collectors. Claire Lawrence (woodwind, harmonica, vocals), Bill Henderson (guitar, recorder, vocals), Glenn Miller (bass/vocals) and Ross Turney (drums) abandoned the latter name in 1971 and embarked on a new direction. Chilliwack's eponymous debut album acknowledged this transition by including a restructured version of 'Seventeeth Summer', a track previously associated with the Collectors. Their third release, *All Over You*, provided a major Canadian hit single in 'Ground Hog', and Chilliwack subsequently became one of the country's most popular home-grown talents. Their often melodious hard-rock was best heard on *Dreams Dreams Dreams*, but inconsistant material and an unstable personnel (Henderson would become the lone original member), hampered a wider success.
Albums: *Chilliwack* i (1971), *All Over You* (1972), *Chilliwack* ii (1972), *Chilliwack* iii (1974), *Rockerbox* (1975), *Dreams Dreams Dreams* (1977), *Lights From The Valley* (1978), *Breakdown In Paradise* (1980), *Wanna Be A Star* (1981), *Opus X* (1982).

Chilli Willi And The Red Hot Peppers

Although fondly recalled as a leading 'pub rock' attraction, Chilli Willi began life as a folksy-cum-country duo comprising of Martin Stone (b. 11 December 1946, Woking, Surrey, England; guitar/mandolin/vocals) and Phil 'Snakefinger' Lithman (b. 17 June 1949, Tooting, London, England; guitar/lap steel/fiddle/piano/vocals). Both were former members of Junior's Blues Band, an aspiring early 60s group, but while Lithman moved to San Francisco, Stone found a measure of notoriety with the Savoy Brown Blues Band and Mighty Baby. The friends were reunited on *Kings Of The Robot Rhythm*, an informal, enchanting collection which featured assistance from singer Jo-Ann Kelly and several members of Brinsley Schwarz. In December 1972 the duo added Paul 'Dice Man' Bailey (b. 6 July 1947, Weston-super-Mare, Somerset, England; guitar/saxophone/banjo), Paul Riley (b. 3 October 1951, Islington, London, England; bass) and Pete Thomas (b. 9 August 1954, Sheffield, Yorkshire, England; drums) and over the ensuing two years, the quintet became one of Britain's most compulsive live attractions. Despite its charm, incorporating many diverse American styles such as blues, country, swing, rock and R&B, *Bongos Over Balham* failed to capture the group's in-concert passion and a disillusioned Chilli Willi split up in February 1975. Pete Thomas later joined the

Attractions, Paul Riley played with Graham Parker's band, while Bailey helped form Bontemps Roulez. Martin Stone joined the Pink Fairies prior to leaving music altogether, while Lithman returned to San Francisco where, as Snakefinger, he resumed his earlier association with the Residents.

Albums: *Kings Of The Robot Rhythm* (1972), *Bongos Over Balham* (1974).

Chinn And Chapman

Mike Chapman (b. 15 April 1947, Queensland, Australia) and Nicky Chinn (b. 16 May 1945, London, England) teamed up to form a songwriting partnership while the former was a member of the group Tangerine Peel and the latter a garage owner. With the encouragement of the Rak label boss, Mickie Most, they were to later to compose a string of hits in the early 70s for such acts as New World, Sweet, Gary Glitter, Mud, Suzi Quatro and Smokie. The duo became one of the most successful songwriting teams of the era and obtained a reputation in the UK that was only to be matched in the 80s by the team of Stock, Aitken And Waterman. Mike Chapman emerged as an influential force in moulding Blondie for the pop market, providing production credit on such hits as 'Heart Of Glass', 'The Tide Is High', 'Sunday Girl', 'Atomic' and 'Rapture'. Chinn and Chapman inaugurated the Dreamland label in 1979 which folded two years later. Chapman later worked with Pat Benatar, Exile ('Kiss You All Over', a US number 1 - a Chinn/Chapman composition), Nick Gilder ('Hot Child In The City', a US number 1), the Knack ('My Sharona' a US number 1), Patti Smith and Lita Ford. During this time the duo's songwriting skills later earned them a US number 1 in 1982 with 'Mickey' for Toni Basil.

Christie

This UK pop-based trio was formed around vocalist/bassist/songwriter Jeff Christie, a veteran of several groups, including the Outer Limits and the Epics. Vic Elmes (guitar) and Mike Blakely (drums), members of the latter attraction, completed the line-up which enjoyed a UK number 1 hit in May 1970 with the ebullient 'Yellow River'. The song was initially intended for the Tremeloes, who featured Mike's brother Alan Blakely, but when they prevaricated Christie decided to record it himself. However, although a follow-up, 'San Bernadino' reached the UK Top 10, the trio, by now featuring Paul Fenton on

Mike Chapman And Nicky Chinn

drums, was unable to sustain a lasting career and a 1972 release, 'Iron Horse', was their final chart entry.

Album: *Yellow River* (1970).

Christie, Tony

b. Anthony Fitzgerald, 25 April 1944, Conisborough, Yorkshire, England. Christie was a self-taught guitarist who became a professional singer in 1964. By the time he made his BBC radio debut three year later, he had acquired vocal mannerisms similar to those of Tom Jones, and this attracted the interest of songwriters Mitch Murray and Peter Callender, who provided Christie with his first UK Top 30 entry in 1970 with 'Las Vegas'. Next came the title track to *I Did What I Did For Maria*, a number 2 UK hit which cleared the way for the million-selling 'Is This The Way To Amarillo' (written by Howard Greenfield and Neil Sedaka), which topped charts throughout Europe while managing only to break into the UK Top 20. Touring Australasia and South Africa for much of 1972, Christie's chart placings tailed off until a minor hit with 'Avenues And Alleyways' sparked off robust sales for 1973's *With Loving Feeling*. To a lesser degree, he did it again in 1975 with 'Drive Safely Darlin'' and an in-concert offering. A 'best of' selection the following year rounded off his career as a serious chart contender - though he was heard on the *Evita* studio cast album in 1978. However, his refusal of a part in the London stage production led to a schism with his manager, Harvey Lisberg, resulting in Christie continuing to earn his living on the cabaret/supper club circuit.

Albums: *I Did What I Did For Maria* (1971), *With Loving Feeling* (1973), *Live* (1975), *Ladies Man* (1983). Compilations: *The Best Of Tony Christie* (1976), *Golden Greats* (1985), *Baby I'm A Want You* (1986).

Christmas, Keith

b. 13 October 1946, Wivenhoe, Essex, England. A popular figure on the British folk circuit, Christmas emerged with a rock-oriented style on his 1969 debut, *Stimulus*. Reminiscent, in places, of Al Stewart, the album featured support from Mighty Baby as well as Southern Comfort's pedal-steel guitarist, Gordon Huntley. *Fable Of The Wings* and *Pigmy* continued this direction, during which time Christmas toured as support act for many of the top bands of the day, including: the Who, Ten Years After, King Crimson and Roxy Music. A brief liaison as vocalist with the Esperanto Rock Orchestra led to an appearance on their 1974

album, *Danse Macabre*. That same year, a return to solo work produced *Brighter Day*, which was recorded on Emerson, Lake And Palmer's Manticore label. This release offered a tougher perspective than previous albums while *Stories From A Human Zoo*, recorded in Los Angeles, featured assistance from several stellar American musicians, including Steve Cropper and Donald 'Duck' Dunn. However, Christmas was unable to transform his obvious potential into commercial success, and subsequently spent the last years of the 70s performing low-key dates in London and at summer festivals. Disenchanted with the music business, he retired from the scene in 1981 only to re-emerge in the late 80s with a fresh outlook, playing on the folk club circuit performing solo and occasionally with a backing band.

Albums: *Stimulus* (1969), *Fable Of The Wings* (1970), *Pigmy* (1971), *Brighter Day* (1974), *Stories From The Human Zoo* (1976), *Dead Line Blues* (1991).

City Boy

This Birmingham based group started out as a four piece acoustic folk band playing in the pubs and clubs of the English Midlands in the early 70s. The original line-up was Lol Mason (vocals), Steve Broughton (guitar), Mike Slamer (guitar) and Max Thomas (guitar). They turned professional in 1975 and started writing their own songs, mainly through Broughton. Thomas took up keyboards in addition to guitar, and after being signed to Phonogram they recruited Chris Dunn (bass) and Roy Ward (drums). They had released several albums without success, before they made a breakthrough in 1978 when their single '5-7-0-5' made the UK Top 10. Subsequently they scored two more hits, including the title track of their 1979 album. A further single emerged on the band's own City Boy label in 1982, after which the band split. Mason went on to form the Maisonettes, who had their own hit single with 'Heartache Avenue'

Albums: *City Boys* (1975), *Dinner At The Ritz* (1976), *Young Men Gone West* (1978), *The Day The Earth Caught Fire* (1979), *Heads Are Rolling* (1980).

Clark, Gene

b. 17 November 1941, Tipton, Missouri, USA, d. 24 May 1991. After playing in various teenage groups, Clark was offered a place in the sprawling New Christy Minstrels in late 1963. He stayed long enough to contribute to two albums, *Merry Christmas* and *Land Of Giants* before returning to

Los Angeles, where he teamed up with Jim (Roger) McGuinn and David Crosby in the Jet Set. This fledgling trio evolved into the Byrds and during 1965-66 achieved international acclaim with a series of hits. At that point Clark was the leading songwriter in the group and contributed significantly to their first two albums. Following the release of 'Eight Miles High' in March 1966, he dramatically left the group, citing fear of flying as the major cause.

Under the auspices of producer Jim Dickson, Clark recorded a solo album, *Echoes (With The Gosdin Brothers)*, which remains one of the best 'singer/songwriter' albums of its era. Surprisingly, it failed to sell, effectively putting Clark's solo career in jeopardy. At the end of 1968, following Crosby's dismissal from the Byrds, Clark was re-enlisted but left within weeks due to his long standing aerophobia. Revitalizing his career in 1971 with *White Light*, Clark seemed a prime candidate for singer-songwriter success, but middling sales and a lack of touring forestalled his progress. A recorded reunion with the original Byrds in late 1973 temporarily refocused attention on Gene, who dominated the album with lead vocals on over one-third of the tracks. Soon, he was back in the studio recording a solo album for Asylum Records with producer Thomas Jefferson Kaye. *No Other* (1974) was a highly acclaimed work, brilliantly fusing Clark's lyrical power with an ethereal mix of choral beauty and rich musicianship provided by some of the finest session players in Hollywood. Sales again proved disappointing prompting Clark to record a less complex album for RSO, which was reasonably publicized but fared no better.

The irresistible lure of the original Byrds brought Gene back together with two of his former colleagues in the late 70s. McGuinn, Clark And Hillman enjoyed brief success, but during the recording of their second album *City* (1980), history repeated itself and Clark left amid some acrimony. Since then, he has mainly recorded for small labels, occasionally touring with other ex-Byrds as well as solo. His most recent collaborator has been Carla Olson, formerly of the Textones. After years of ill health Gene died in 1991 making any possible Byrds reunion no longer achievable.

Albums: *Echoes (With The Gosdin Brothers)* (1967), *White Light* (1972), *Roadmaster* (1972), *No Other* (1974), *Two Sides To Every Story* (1977) *Firebyrd* (1984), with Carla Olson *So Rebellious A Lover* (1987).

Clash

The Clash at first tucked in snugly behind punk's loudest noise, the Sex Pistols (whom they supported on 'the Anarchy tour'), and later became a much more consistent and intriguing force. Guitarist Mick Jones (b. 26 June 1953, London, England) had formed London SS in 1975, whose members at one time included bassist Paul Simonon (b. 15 December 1956, London, England) and drummer Nicky 'Topper' Headon (b. 30 May 1955, Bromley, Kent, England). Joe Strummer (b. John Graham Mellor, 21 August 1952, Ankara, Turkey) had spent the mid-70s fronting a pub-rock group called the 101ers, playing early rock 'n' roll style numbers like 'Keys To Your Heart'. The early line-up of the Clash was completed by guitarist Keith Levine but he left early in 1976 with another original member, drummer Terry Chimes, whose services were called upon intermittently during the following years. They signed to CBS Records and during three weekends they recorded *The Clash* in London with sound engineer, Mickey Foote, taking on the producer's role. In 1977 *Rolling Stone* magazine called it the 'definitive punk album' and elsewhere it was recognized that they had brilliantly distilled the anger, depression and energy of mid-70s England. More importantly, they had infused the message and sloganeering with strong tunes and pop hooks, as on 'I'm So Bored With The USA' and 'Career Opportunities'. The album reached number 12 in the UK charts and garnered almost universal praise. CBS was keen to infiltrate the American market and Blue Oyster Cult's founder/lyricist Sandy Pearlman was brought in to produce *Give 'Em Enough Rope*. The label's manipulative approach failed and it had very poor sales in the USA but in the UK it reached number 2, despite pertinent claims that its more rounded edges amounted to a sell out of the band's earlier much flaunted punk ethics. They increasingly embraced reggae elements, seemingly a natural progression of their anti-racist stance, and had a minor UK hit with '(White Man) In Hammersmith Palais' in July 1978 and followed it up with the frothy punk-pop of 'Tommy Gun' - their first Top 20 hit. Their debut album was finally released in the USA as a double set including tracks from their singles and it sold healthily before *London Calling*, produced by the volatile Guy Stevens, marked a return to almost top form. They played to packed houses across the USA early in 1980 and were cover stars on many prestigious rock magazines. Typically, their next

move was over-ambitious and the triple set *Sandinista!* was leaden and too sprawling after the acute concentration of earlier records. It scraped into the UK Top 20 and sales were disappointing despite CBS making it available at a special cut-price. The experienced rock producer, Glyn Johns, was brought in to instigate a tightening-up and *Combat Rock* was as snappy as anticipated. It was recorded with Terry Chimes on drums after Headon had abruptly left the group. Chimes was later replaced by Pete Howard. 'Rock The Casbah', a jaunty, humorous song written by Headon, became a Top 10 hit in the USA and reached number 30 in the UK, aided by a sardonic video. During 1982, they toured the USA supporting the Who at their stadium concerts. Many observers were critical of a band that had once ridiculed superstar status, for becoming part of the same legend. A simmering tension between Jones and Strummer eventually led to bitterness and Jones left in 1983 after Strummer accused him of becoming lazy and he told the press: 'He wasn't with us any more'. Strummer later apologised for lambasting Jones and admitted he was mainly to blame for the break-up of a successful songwriting partnership: 'I stabbed him in the back' was his own honest account of proceedings. The Clash struggled without Jones's input although the toothless *Cut The Crap* reached number 16 in the the UK charts in 1985. Mick Jones formed Big Audio Dynamite with another product of the 70s London scene, Don Letts, and for several years became a relevant force merging dance with powerful, spikey pop choruses. Strummer finally disbanded the Clash in 1986 and after a brief tour with Latino Rockabilly War and a period playing rhythm guitar with the Pogues, he turned almost full time to acting and production. He supervised the soundtrack to the film, *Sid And Nancy*, about the former Sex Pistols bassist Sid Vicious and his girlfriend Nancy Spungen. In 1988, the Clash's most furious but tuneful songs were gathered together on the excellent compilation, *The Story Of The Clash*. They made a dramatic and unexpected return to the charts in 1991 when 'Should I Stay Or Should I Go?', originally a UK number 17 hit in October 1982, was re-released by CBS after the song appeared in a Levi's jeans advertisement. Incredibly, the song reached number 1, thereby prompting more reissues of Clash material and fuelling widespread rumours of a band reunion.
Albums: *The Clash* (1977), *Give 'Em Enough Rope* (1978), *London's Calling* (1979), *Sandinista!* (1980), *Combat Rock* (1982), *Cut The Crap* (1985).

Compilations: *The Story Of The Clash* (1988), *The Singles Collection* (1991).

Clayton-Thomas, David

b. 13 September 1941, Surrey, England. This British born, naturalized Canadian vocalist made his name with the US jazz rock outfit, Blood, Sweat And Tears. After singing on such worldwide hits as 'You've Made Me So Very Happy' and 'Spinning Wheel', he departed to forge a solo career, briefly returning to the group in 1975.
Albums: *David Clayton-Thomas!* (1969, pre-BS&T recordings), *David Clayton-Thomas* (1972), *Tequila Sunrise* (1972), *Harmony Junction* (1973).

Clifford, Linda

b. c.1944, Brooklyn, New York, USA. Clifford was singing professionally at the age of seven and appeared on television variety programmes in 1950-51. At the age of 17 she had won the Miss New York state beauty pageant and by the mid-60s was singing in nightclubs, performing show music, jazz, standards and R&B material. In 1974 Clifford recorded a single, 'A Long, Long Winter', for Paramount Records, which made the R&B charts. That was followed by another the next year for the small Gemigo label, a division of Curtis Mayfield's Curtom label. She switched over to Curtom itself in 1977 and recorded in the disco genre. An album, *Linda*, and the single 'From Now On' were critically favoured but not commercially successful. However, 'Runaway Love' (1978), reached number 3 in the US R&B charts. Her album, *If My Friends Could See Me Now* was also a success that year and the title song reached the Top 50 in the UK. Clifford transferred to the Robert Stigwood-owned RSO Records in 1979 and continued to have moderate R&B hits, including a disco-styled remake of Simon And Garfunkel's 'Bridge Over Troubled Water' (a UK Top 30 hit) and two duets with Mayfield. Clifford continued to appear in the US R&B charts with Capitol Records and the small Red label, but by the mid-80s was no longer a factor on the charts.
Albums: *Linda* (1977), *If My Friends Could See Me Now* (1978), *Here's My Love* (1979), with Curtis Mayfield *The Right Combination* (1980), *I'm Yours* (1980).

Climax

Formed in 1971 in Los Angeles, California, Climax was the idea of vocalist Sonny Geraci (b. 1947, Cleveland, Ohio, USA), formerly of the US chart-topping group the Outsiders. Their guitarist Walter

Nims, who was also a member of the Outsiders. Completing the group were session man Steve York (bass) - formerly of East Of Eden and Manfred Mann's Chapter Three, Virgil Weber (keyboards) and Robert Neilson (drums). Climax was a considerably softer group than the Outsiders. The group was signed to the small Carousel label and recorded a Nims ballad, 'Precious And Few', which became a US number 3 hit in early 1972. A second chart single, 'Life And Breath', this time for Rocky Road Records, marked the end of Climax's stay on the US charts. The group recorded one self-titled album in 1972, which was a minor success. Geraci has maintained the group as a part-time venture, while Steve York went on to join Vinegar Joe and has continued his career as an in-demand session player, recording with, amongst others, Joan Armatrading, Marianne Faithfull and Charlie Musselwhite as well as recording a solo album, *Manor Live* in 1973, under the name of Steve York's Camelo Pardalis.
Album: *Climax* (1972).

Climax Blues Band

Originally known as the Climax Chicago Blues Band, this long-enduring group comprised of Colin Cooper (b. 7 October 1939, Stafford, England; vocals/saxophone), Peter Haycock (b. 4 April 1952, Stafford, England; vocals/guitar), Richard Jones (keyboards), Arthur Wood (keyboards), Derek Holt (b. 26 January 1949, Stafford, England; bass) and George Newsome (b. 14 August 1947, Stafford, England; drums). They made their recording debut in 1969 with *The Climax Chicago Blues Band* which evoked the early work of John Mayall and Savoy Brown. Its somewhat anachronistic approach gave little indication of a potentially long career. Jones departed for university prior to the release of *Plays On*, which displayed a new-found, and indeed sudden, sense of maturity. A restrictive adherence to 12-bar tempos was replaced by a freer, flowing pulse, while the use of wind instruments, in particular on 'Flight', inferred an affiliation with jazz-rock groups like Colosseum and Blodwyn Pig. In 1970 CCBB switched labels to Harvest. Conscious of stereotyping in the wake of the blues' receding popularity, the group began emphasizing rock-based elements in their work. *A Lot Of Bottle* and *Tightly Knit* reflected a transitional period where the group began wooing the affections of an American audience responsive to the unfettered styles of Foghat or ZZ Top. Climax then embarked on a fruitful relationship with producer

Richard Gottehrer who honed the group's live sound into an economic, but purposeful, studio counterpart. *Rich Man*, their final album for Harvest, and *Sense Of Direction* were the best examples of their collaboration. Richard Jones rejoined the band in 1975 having been a member of the Principal Edwards Magic Theatre since leaving university. The band enjoyed a surprise UK hit single when 'Couldn't Get It Right' reached number 10 in 1976, but the success proved temporary. Although they have pursued a career into the 90s, the Climax Blues Band have engendered a sense of predictability and consequently lost their eminent position as a fixture of America's lucrative FM rock circuit.
Albums: *Climax Chicago Blues Band* (1969), *Plays On* (1969), *A Lot Of Bottle* (1970), *Tightly Knit* (1971), *Rich Man* (1972), *FM/Live* (1973), *Sense Of Direction* (1974), *Stamp Album* (1975), *Gold Plated* (1976), *Shine On* (1978), *Real To Reel* (1979), *Flying The Flag* (1980), *Lucky For Some* (1981), *Sample And Hold* (1983), *Total Climax* (1985), *Drastic Steps* (1988). Compilations: *1969-1972* (1975), *Best Of The Climax Blues Band* (1983), *Loosen Up (1974-1976)* (1984), *Couldn't Get It Right* (1987).

Clover

Formed in Mill Valley, California when bassist Johnny Ciambotti joined John McFee (b. 18 November 1953, Santa Cruz, California, USA; guitar/pedal steel guitar/vocals), Alex Call (guitar/vocals) and Mitch Howie (drums) in the Tiny Hearing Aid Company. Having decided on a less-cumbersome name, the quartet made its debut as Clover in July 1967 and soon became a popular attraction in the region's thriving dancehalls. *Clover* consolidated their reputation as a feisty bar-band, although a primitive production undermined its charm. *Forty-Niner* was a marked improvement, but although its informality was both varied and infectious, the group was unable to break out of its now stifling good-time niche. A dispirited Howie left the line-up which was then bolstered by the addition of Huey (Louis) Lewis (vocals/harmonica), Sean Hopper (keyboards/vocals) and Mickey Shine (drums) but fortunes remained unchanged until 1976 when the group came to the UK at the urging of Nick Lowe. Clover quickly became a popular attraction in their adopted homeland, during which time they accompanied Elvis Costello on *My Aim Is True*. However, despite completing two promising albums, Clover were unable to make a significant breakthrough and returned to the USA in 1978 where they folded. McFee subsequently joined the Doobie Brothers while Lewis and Hooper eventually achieved considerable commercial success as Huey Lewis And The News.

Albums: *Clover* (1970), *Forty-Niner* (1971), *Unavailable* (1977), *Love On The Wire* (1977). Compilations: *Clover Chronicle - The Best Of The Fantasy Years* (1979), *The Best Of Clover* (1986).

Cochise

This melodic British country-rock group - Stewart Brown (vocals), Mick Grabham (guitar, ex-Plastic Penny), B.J. Cole (b. 17 June 1946, London, England; pedal steel), Rick Wills (bass) and Willie Wilson (drums) - made its recording debut in 1970. The confidence displayed on *Cochise* continued on its successor, *Swallow Tales*, where a grasp of contemporary Americana was enhanced by several supporting musicians, including Tim Renwick and Cal Batchelor. Their rapport with drummer Wilson resurfaced in a subsequent group, Quiver. Cochise broke up in 1972 following the release of *So Far*. Cole and Wills became respected session musicians; the latter was also a member of several bands including (Peter) Frampton's Camel, Roxy Music and later versions of the Small Faces, while Grabham joined Procol Harum where he remained until their break-up in 1977.

Albums: *Cochise* (1970), *Swallow Tales* (1971), *So Far* (1972).

Cockney Rebel

Formed in 1973 by the strongly opinionated ex-journalist Steve Harley (b. Steven Nice, 27 February 1951, South London, England). Following his advertisement in a music paper he recruited Jean-Paul Crocker, Paul Avron Jeffreys (b. 13 February 1952, d. 21 December 1988 in the Lockerbie air disaster), Milton Reame-James and Stuart Elliott. Visually they looked like early Roxy Music with a strong David Bowie influence. Their debut hit 'Judy Teen' was a confident start, but one that was spoilt by the self-destructive Harley. He antagonized the music press and shortly afterwards disbanded his group. The most stable line-up was with Jim Cregan (guitar, ex-Family), George Ford (keyboards), Lindsay Elliott (percussion), Duncan McKay (keyboards) and Stuart Elliott, the drummer from the original band. Their first two albums remain their best and most satisfying works with Harley venturing into dangerous fields with his Dylanesque lyrics, winning him few critical friends. They reached the UK number 1 position

with the sparkling 'Make Me Smile (Come Up And See Me)' now billed as Steve Harley And Cockney Rebel. Harley's limited but interesting vocal range was put to the test on George Harrison's 'Here Comes the Sun', which made the UK Top 10 in 1976. Harley spent much of the next few years living in America and returned to the lower echelons of the charts in 1983 with 'Ballerina (Prima Donna)'. Ironically this was the second time he had visited the charts with a song containing the word Prima Donna (in 1976 'Love's A Prima Donna' had similar success). Harley returned to the best sellers in 1986 duetting with Sarah Brightman in the title song from *The Phantom Of The Opera*, a part that Harley was originally scheduled to play. That year he attempted a comeback after being signed by Mickie Most. Little was heard until 1988 when a UK television commercial used one of his early hits 'Mr Soft'. This prompted a compilation album of the same name. In 1992 Harley returned to the UK top 50 with the re-released 'Make Me Smile (Come Up And See Me)' and embarked on a major tour.

Albums: *The Human Menagerie* (1973), *Psychomodo* (1974), *The Best Years Of Our Lives* (1975), *Love's A Prima Donna* (1976), *Face To Face - A Live Recording* (1977), *Hobo With A Grin* (1980). Compilations: *Timeless Flight* (1976), *The Best Of Steve Harley And Cockney Rebel* (1980), *Mr Soft - Greatest Hits* (1988), *Make Me Smile, The Best Of Steve Harley And Cockney Rebel* (1992).

Cold Blood

A popular live attraction in their native San Francisco, Cold Blood featured the powerful, bluesy voice of Lydia Pense and echoed the hard, brassy sound of Tower Of Power. Formed in 1968, the group - Larry Field (guitar), Paul Matute (keyboards), Danny Hull (saxophone), Jerry Jonutz (saxophone), David Padron (trumpet), Larry Jonutz (trumpet), Paul Ellicot (bass), Frank J. David (drums), plus Pense - was signed to impresario Bill Graham's San Francisco label the following year. Two albums resulted from this relationship before the group moved to Reprise. Later releases failed to recapture the gritty quality of those early records, although their final album was produced by guitarist Steve Cropper. Most of the group then dropped out from active performing, but a late-period drummer, Gaylord Birch, later worked with Santana, the Pointers Sisters and Graham Central Station.

Albums: *Cold Blood* (1969), *Sysiphus* (1970), *First*

Cockney Rebel

Taste Of Sin (1972), *Thriller!* (1973), *Lydia* (1974), *Lydia Pense And Cold Blood* (1976).

Collins, Bootsy

b. William Collins, 26 October 1951, Cincinnati, Ohio, USA. This exceptional showman was an integral part of the JBs, the backing group fashioned by James Brown to replace the Famous Flames. Between 1969 and 1971, the distinctive Bootsy basswork propelled some of the era's definitive funk anthems. Collins was later part of the large-scale defection in which several of Brown's most valued musicians switched to George Clinton's Parliament/Funkadelic organization. The bassist's popularity inspired the formation of Bootsy's Rubber Band, a spin-off group featuring such Brown/Clinton associates as Fred Wesley, Maceo Parker and Bernie Worrell. Bootsy's outrageous image - part space cadet, part psychedelic warlord - emphasized a mix of funk and fun encapsulated in 'Psychoticbumpschool' (1976), 'The Pinocchio Theory' (1977) and 'Bootzilla' (1978), a US R&B chart-topper. The internal problems plaguing the Clinton camp during the early 80s temporarily hampered Collins' career although subsequent releases reveal some of his erstwhile charm. Collins and the Bootzilla Orchestra were employed for the production of Malcolm McLaren's 1989 album *Waltz Darling* and by the early 90s the Rubber Band had started full-time touring again.
Albums: *Stretchin' Out* (1976), *Aah...The Name Is Bootsy, Baby* (1977), *Player Of The Year* (1978), *This Boot Is Made For Fonkin'* (1979), *What's Bootsy Doin'* (1988).

Collins, Dave And Ansil

This Jamaican duo topped the UK charts in 1971 with 'Double Barrel', which was written and produced by Winston Riley. It was also one of the first reggae hits to appear in national US charts. The follow-up, that same year, 'Monkey Spanner', was a UK Top 10 hit. Ansil had previously recorded solo for Trojan Records in the late 60s and has continued to record for small reggae labels throughout the 80s.
Albums: *Double Barrell* (1971), *In The Ghetto* (1976).

Colosseum

The commercial acceptance of jazz/rock in the UK was mainly due to Colosseum. The band was formed in 1968 from the nucleus of the musicians who accompanied John Mayall on his influential album *Bare Wires*. Colosseum comprised: Jon Hiseman (b. 21 June 1944, London, England; drums), Dick Heckstall-Smith (b. 26 September 1934, Ludlow, Shropshire, England; saxophone), Dave Greenslade (b. 18 January 1943, Woking, Surrey, England; keyboards), Tony Reeves (b. 18 April 1943, London, England; bass), James Litherland (b. 6 September 1949, Manchester, England; guitar/vocals). Ex-Graham Bond Organisation members Heckstall-Smith and Hiseman took their former boss's pivotal work and made a success of it. From the opening track of their strong debut, *Those Who Are About To Die Salute You* (1969), with Bond's 'Walkin' In The Park', the band embarked on a brief excursion that would showcase each member as a strong musical talent. Heckstall-Smith, already a seasoned jazz professional, combined with 19-year-old Litherland and integrated furious wah-wah guitar with bursting saxophone. Greenslade's booming Hammond organ intertwined with Reeve's melodically inventive bass patterns. This sparkling cocktail was held together by the masterful pyrotechnics of Hiseman, whose solos, featuring his dual bass drum pedal technique, were awesome. *Valentyne Suite* the same year maintained the momentum notably with the outstanding Heckstall-Smith composition 'The Grass Is Greener'. As with many great things, the end came quite soon, although the departing member Litherland was replaced with a worthy successor in Dave 'Clem' Clempson (b. 5 September 1949, England). In order to accommodate Clempson's wish to concentrate on guitar they further enlisted Greenslade's former boss in the Thunderbirds, Chris Farlowe. His strong vocals gave a harder edge to their work. Following the departure of Reeves and the recruitment of Mark Clarke, their work took on a more rock-orientated approach. The end came in 1971 with their last studio album *Daughter Of Time*, although their record company posthumously issued a double-live album. Hiseman and Clarke formed Tempest, but after two mediocre albums he resurrected the name in the shape of Colosseum II in 1975. The new version was a great deal heavier in sound and featured ex-Thin Lizzy guitarist Gary Moore, future Whitesnake bassist Neil Murray and future Rainbow keyboard player Don Airey. Vocalist Mike Starrs completed the line-up and they progressed through the mid-70s with three albums before Colosseum II finally collapsed through Hiseman's exhaustion, who wished to return to his jazz roots. He would eventually join his wife

Colosseum

Barbara Thompson playing jazz with her band Paraphernalia. Colosseum will be remembered for their initial pioneering work in making jazz-rock accessible to a wider market.

Albums: *Those Who Are About To Die Salute You* (1969), *Valentyne Suite* (1969), *The Daughter Of Time Is Truth* (1970), *Live* (1971), *Strange New Flesh* (1976), *Electric Savage* (1977), *Wardance* (1977). Compilations: *The Grass Is Greener* (1969), *Collector's Colosseum* (1971), *Pop Chronik* (1974). Further reading: *The Smallest Place In The World*, Dick Heckstall-Smith.

Coloured Balls

A product of the working-class area of the western suburbs of Melbourne, Australia, the Coloured Balls had a ready-made, predominantly male audience. This consisted of fans of the cult movie *A Clockwork Orange*, who also adopted the aggressive 'skinhead' style of closely-shaven heads and thick boots and braces. The band reflected this in their music and image. Led by Lobby Loyde (b. Barry Lyde), a product of the R&B/rock scene of the 60s (the Wild Cherries, Purple Hearts), the Coloured Balls comprised Trevor Young (drums), John Miglans (bass) and Bobsy Miller (guitar). The group covered Chuck Berry songs and wrote others around this rock 'n' roll rhythm complete with Loyde's lead guitar work, all played at an eardrum-shattering volume. The band had success mainly in Melbourne; it was short-lived (1972-74) and waned as fashions invariably do. Loyde went solo, then relocated to the UK, releasing an album of guitar experimentation, learnt to produce and, since his return, has been producing underground and alternative bands.

Albums: *Ball Power* (1974), *Heavy Metal Kid* (1974), *First Supper Last* (1976).

Company Caine

Formed in Melbourne, Australia in 1970, this psychedelic/blues group centred around lyricist and vocalist Gulliver Smith (b. Kevin Smith) who had previously worked with such outfits as Dr Kandy's Third Eye and Time And The Forest Flower. Along with Smith, Company Caine (often referred to as Co Caine), the band comprised; Russell Smith (b. Russell Kinross-Smith; guitar), John McInerney (drums), Arthur Eisenberg (bass) and Dave Kane (guitar). In hindsight, the band had several excellent songs, some ordinary, but with obscure lyrics - most evident in their debut single 'Trixie Stonewells Wayward Home For Young Women' (1971) - but whether the group fully

deserves its later cult status is debatable. The band were originally championed by a national magazine, *Go Set*, and its columnist 'Dr Pepper'. Company Caine emerged from the late 60s' psychedelic era of concerts and drug-taking (organized both in Melbourne and Sydney by US band Nutwood Rug). The band suffered from frequent changes and additions to the line-up which, although not seeming to adversely affect their high-energy white blues live performances, ultimately took their toll with the result of the band dissolving in 1973. Gulliver went on to form the Bad Companions and Gulliver Smith And The Dead End Kids, while Russell worked with Mighty Kong. The two Smiths reformed in 1975 under the name of Metropolis before briefly returning to the Company Caine monicker. The reformed band was a much steadier, solid affair but did not attract the attention of the earlier incarnation and soon gave way to Gulliver's next project, Little Gulliver.

Albums: *A Product Of A Broken Reality* (1972), *Dr Chop* (1975).

Congregation

This British mixed choir and accompanying orchestra was a one-shot studio creation of composers Roger Cook and Roger Greenaway. It was fronted by veteran session vocalist Brian Keith (ex-Plastic Penny) who was ideal for 'Softly Whispering I Love You' which, hinged on an eminently hummable melody, climbed to number 4 in the UK chart and exhaled from many a late-night stereo during the festive build-up to 1972. Too cumbersome for concert tours, Congregation was laid to rest after the single's television promotions but the song itself proved sufficiently durable to be revived successfully by Paul Young in 1989.

Cooder, Ry

b. Ryland Peter Cooder, 15 March 1947, Los Angeles, California, USA. One of rock's premier talents, Cooder mastered the rudiments of guitar while still a child. He learned the techniques of traditional music from Rev. Gary Davis and by the age of 17 was part of a blues act with singer Jackie DeShannon. In 1965 he formed the Rising Sons with Taj Mahal and veteran Spirit drummer Ed Cassidy, but this promising group broke up when the release of a completed album was cancelled. However the sessions brought Ry into contact with producer Terry Melcher, who in turn employed the guitarist on several sessions, notably with Paul Revere And The Raiders. Cooder enjoyed a brief, but fruitful, association with Captain Beefheart And His Magic Band. His distinctive slide work is apparent on the group's debut album, *Safe As Milk*, but the artist declined an offer to join on a permanent basis. Instead he continued his studio work, guesting on sessions for Randy Newman, Little Feat and Van Dyke Parks, as well as to the soundtracks of *Candy* and *Performance*. Cooder also contributed to the Rolling Stones' album *Let It Bleed*, and was tipped as a likely replacement for Brian Jones until clashes with Keith Richard, primarily over authorship of the riff to 'Honky Tonk Woman', precluded further involvement.

Cooder's impressive debut album included material by Leadbelly, Sleepy John Estes and Blind Willie Johnson, and offered a patchwork of Americana which became his trademark. A second collection, *Into The Purple Valley*, established his vision more fully and introduced a tight but sympathetic band, which included long-standing collaborators, Jim Keltner and Jim Dickinson. By contrast, several selections employed the barest instrumentation, resulting in one of the artist's finest releases. The rather desolate *Boomer's Story* completed Cooder's early trilogy and in 1974 he released the buoyant *Paradise And Lunch*. His confidence is immediately apparent on the reggae interpretation of 'It's All Over Now' and the silky 'Ditty Wa Ditty', and it was this acclaimed collection that established him as a major talent. A fascination with 30s topical songs was now muted in favour of a greater eclecticism, which in turn anticipated Cooder's subsequent direction. *Chicken Skin Music* was marked by two distinct preoccupations. Contributions from Flaco Jiminez and Gabby Pahuini enhanced its mixture of Tex-Mex and Hawaiian styles, while Cooder's seamless playing and inspired arrangements created a sympathetic setting. The guitarist's relationship with Jiminez was maintained on a fine in-concert set, *Showtime*, but Cooder then abandoned this direction with the reverential *Jazz*. This curiously unsatisfying album paid homage to the dixieland era, but a crafted-meticulousness denied the project life and its creator has since disowned it.

Cooder then embraced a more mainstream approach with *Bop Till You Drop*, an ebullient, rhythmic, yet rock-based collection, reminiscent of Little Feat. The album, which included cameo-performances from soul singer Chaka Khan, comprised of several urban R&B standards, including 'Little Sister', 'Go Home Girl' and 'Don't Mess Up A Good Thing'. Its successor, *Borderline*, offered similar fare, but when the style was continued on a third release, *The Slide Area*, a sense of weariness became apparent. Such overtly commercial selections contrasted with Cooder's soundtrack work. *The Long Riders*, plus *Paris, Texas* and *Crossroads* owed much to the spirit of adventure prevalent in his early work, while the expansive tapestry of these films allowed a greater scope for his undoubted imagination. It was five years before Cooder released an official follow-up to *The Slide Area* and although *Get Rhythm* offered little not already displayed, it re-established purpose to his rock-based work. This inventive, thoughtful individual has embraced both commercial and ethnic styles with equal dexterity, but has yet to achieve the widespread success that his undoubted talent deserves. In 1992, Cooder had joined up with Nick Lowe, Jim Keltner and John Hiatt to record and perform under the name of Little Village.

Albums: *Ry Cooder* (1970), *Into The Purple Valley* (1971), *Boomer's Story* (1972), *Paradise And Lunch* (1974), *Chicken Skin Music* (1976), *Showtime* (1976), *Jazz* (1978), *Bop Till You Drop* (1979), *Borderline* (1980), *The Long Riders* (1980, film soundtrack), *The Border* (1980, film soundtrack), *Ry Cooder Live* (1982), *The Slide Area* (1982), *Paris, Texas* (1985, film soundtrack), *Bay* (1985, film soundtrack), *Blue City* (1987, film soundtrack), *Crossroads* (1987, film soundtrack), *Get Rhythm* (1987), *Johnny Handsome* (1989, film soundtrack), with Little Village *Little Village* (1992). Compilation: *Why Don't You Try Me Tonight* (1985).

Coolidge, Rita

b. 1 May 1944, Nashville, Tennessee, USA, from mixed white and Cherokee Indian parentage. Coolidge's father was a baptist minister and she first sang radio jingles in Memphis with her sister Priscilla. Coolidge recorded briefly for local label Pepper before moving to Los Angeles in the mid-60s. There she became a highly-regarded session singer, working with Eric Clapton, Stephen Stills and many others. She had a relationship with Stills and he wrote a number of songs about her including 'Cherokee', 'The Raven' and 'Sugar Babe' In 1969-70, Coolidge toured with the Delaney And Bonnie and Leon Russell (*Mad Dogs & Englishmen*) troupes. Russell's 'Delta Lady' was supposedly inspired by Coolidge. Returning to Los Angeles, she was signed to a solo recording contract by A&M. Her debut album included the cream of LA session musicians (among them Booker T. Jones, by now her brother-in-law) and it was followed by almost annual releases during the 70s. Coolidge also made several albums with Kris Kristofferson to whom she was married between 1973 and 1979. The quality of her work was uneven since the purity of her natural voice was not always matched by subtlety of interpretation. Her first hit singles were a revival of the Jackie Wilson hit 'Higher And Higher' and 'We're All Alone', produced by Booker T. in 1977. The following year a version of the Temptations' 'The Way You Do The Things You Do' reached the Top 20. Coolidge was less active in the 80s although in 1983 she recorded a James Bond movie theme, 'All Time High' from *Octopussy*.

Albums: *Rita Coolidge* (1971), *Nice Feelin'* (1971), *Lady's Not For Sale* (1972), *Full Moon* (1973), *Fall Into Spring* (1974), *It's Only Love* (1975), *Anytime Anywhere* (1977), *Love Me Again* (1978), *Satisfied* (1979), *Heartbreak Radio* (1981), *Never Let You Go* (1983), *Inside The Fire* (1988).

Cooper, Alice

b. Vincent Damon Furnier, 4 February 1948, Detroit, Michigan, USA. Alice Cooper became known as the 'master of shock rock' during the 70s and remained a popular hard-rock artist into the 90s. The Furnier family moved to Phoenix, Arizona where Vincent began writing songs while in junior high school. Inspired by a dream to become famous by bands such as the Beatles and Rolling Stones, Furnier formed a group in the early 60s called the Earwigs. By 1965 their name had changed to the Spiders and then the Nazz (no relation to Todd Rundgren's band of the same name). Both the Spiders and Nazz played at local dances and recorded singles that were moderately popular regionally. In 1968, the Nazz, which also included Mike Bruce (lead guitar), Dennis Dunaway (bass), Glen Buxton (guitar) and Neal Smith (drums), changed its name to Alice Cooper, reportedly due to Furnier's belief that he was the reincarnation of a 17th century witch by that name. The name Alice Cooper was also attached to Furnier, who invented an androgynous, outrageously attired character to attract attention. The band played deliberately abrasive rock music with the intention of shocking and even alienating those attending its concerts.

In 1969 the Alice Cooper band found a kindred spirit in Frank Zappa, who signed them to his new Straight Records label. The group recorded two albums, *Pretties For You* and *Easy Action*, before switching to Warner Brothers Records in 1970. By that time Cooper had taken on more extreme tactics in his live performances, using a guillotine and electric chair as stage props and a live snake as part of his wardrobe. Cooper wore thick black eye make-up which dripped down his face, giving him a demonic appearance.

As the group and its singer built a reputation as a bizarre live act, their records began to sell in greater quantities. In 1971, the single 'Eighteen' was the first to reach the US charts, at number 21. Cooper's commercial breakthrough came the following year with the rebellious 'School's Out' single and album, both of which made the US Top 10 as well as topping the UK chart. A streak of best-selling albums followed: the number 1 *Billion Dollar Babies*, then *Muscle Of Love*, *Alice Cooper's Greatest Hits* and *Welcome To My Nightmare*, all of which reached the US Top 10. The last was his first true solo album, as during this period, the band fractured and Cooper officially adopted the Alice Cooper name as his own. In contrast to his professional image, the offstage Cooper became a Hollywood celebrity, playing golf and appearing on television talk shows. In the late 70s, Cooper began appearing in films such as *Sextette* and *Sgt. Pepper's Lonely Hearts Club Band*.

In 1978 Cooper admitted chronic alcoholism and entered a New York hospital for treatment. *From The Inside*, with songs co-written by Bernie Taupin, reflected on the experience. Cooper continued recording into the early 80s with diminishing results. In 1986, after a four-year recording absence, he signed to MCA Records, but none of his albums for that label reached the US charts. A 1989 album, *Trash*, his first on Epic Records, returned him to the Top 40 and yielded a Top 10 single, 'Poison', his first in 12 years. A tour during 1990 found Cooper drawing a new, younger audience which considered him a heavy metal pioneer. *Hey Stoopid* found him accompanied by Joe Satriani, Steve Vai and Slash and Axl from Guns N' Roses. This collection showed Cooper singing with as much energy as his work of more than 20 years ago.

Albums: *Pretties For You* (1969), *Easy Action* (1970), *Love It To Death* (1971), *Killer* (1971), *School's Out* (1972), *Billion Dollar Babies* (1973), *Muscle Of Love* (1973), *Welcome To My Nightmare* (1975), *Alice Cooper Goes To Hell* (1976), *Lace And Whiskey* (1977), *The Alice Cooper Show* (1977), *From The Inside* (1978), *Flush The Fashion* (1980), *Special Forces* (1981), *Zipper Catches Skin* (1982), *Dada* (1982), *Constrictor* (1986), *Raise Your Fist And Yell* (1987), *Trash* (1989), *Hey Stoopid* (1991).

Alice Cooper

Compilation: *Alice Cooper's Greatest Hits* (1974).

Copperhead

This San Francisco-based act centred on rock guitarist John Cipollina (b. 24 August 1943, Berkeley, California, USA, d. 29 May 1989), formerly of Quicksilver Messenger Service. Established on an informal basis in 1970, the new group achieved a degree of stability two years later upon securing a prestigious recording deal with Columbia/CBS. Gary Phillipet (ex-Freedom Highway; guitar, vocals/keyboards), Jim McPherson (ex-Stained Glass; guitar/keyboards), Hutch Hutchinson (bass) and David Weber (drums) joined Cipollina for *Copperhead*, which married the guitarist's distinctive style with an urgent, driving rock. The quintet was a highly popular live attraction, but their fortunes stalled when Columbia managing director Clive Davis was fired within weeks of the album's release. Copperhead was dropped from the label in the rancorous aftermath, and their brief tenure was effectively ended. Phillipet subsequently joined Earthquake while the remaining ex-members participated in several of Cipollina's later projects, notably Terry And The Pirates and Raven.
Album: *Copperhead* (1973).

Cosmotheka

Brothers Dave Sealey (b. 20 February 1946, Redditch, Worcestershire, England) and Al Sealey (b. Alan Sealey, 18 May 1940, Redditch, Worcestershire, England), formed their modern day 'music hall act' in 1971, making their debut at a folk club in Stratford-upon-Avon. Both had previously sung, Al singing with a Midlands-based folk group, while Dave had released a number of singles in his own right. The stage name, Cosmotheka, was taken from an old time 'hall' located in Paddington, London. During the mid-70s, the pair were invited to appear on *Saturday Night At The Mill*, on BBC television, with Sandy Powell. This in turn led to a number of appearances on BBC's lunch-time show *Pebble Mill At One*. It also resulted in them being given their first radio series, on BBC Radio 4, and their own mini-series *A Postcard From Cosmotheka*. They have since guested on numerous television shows where their verbal dexterity and a wealth of *double entendres* proved popular. They have produced a number of albums recalling the heyday of the music hall, keeping alive the songs of singers such as Harry Champion. The duo have appeared at folk festivals, arts festivals and arts centres throughout the British Isles, and overseas. In addition to their music hall show, 'These Are The Days', Dave and Al have written and performed *The Black Sheep Of The Family*, a show chronicling the life and songs of singer Fred Barnes. The show was debuted at the Purcell Room, on London's South Bank and has since been presented on national radio. For BBC Radio 2, Dave and Al wrote and performed *Wot A Mouth*, a 'definitive life story' of singer Harry Champion. Yet another diversion from their usual act is the tribute to variety artists of the 30s and 40s, called *In The Box*. The pair continue to promote and praise the history of the music hall and have plans to present a show charting the rise of ragtime from its beginnings through to its absorption into the popular music culture.
Albums: *A Little Bit Off The Top* (1974), *Wines And Spirits* (1977), *A Good Turn Out* (1981), *Cosmotheka* (1986), *Keep Smiling Through* (1989).

Costello, Elvis

b. Declan McManus, 25 August 1955, Paddington, London, England, but brought up in Liverpool. The son of singer and bandleader Ross McManus first came to prominence during the UK punk era of 1977. The former computer programmer toured A&R offices giving impromptu performances. While appealing to the new wave market, the sensitive issues he wrote about, combined with the structure of the way he composed them, indicated a major talent that would survive and outgrow this comparatively narrow field. Following a tenure in Flip City he was signed to Jake Riviera's pioneering Stiff Records, Costello failed to chart with his early releases, which included the anti-fascist 'Less Than Zero' and the sublime ballad of a broken relationship, 'Alison'. His Nick Lowe-produced debut *My Aim Is True* featured members of the west-coast cult band Clover, who in turn had Huey Lewis as their vocalist. The album is a classic of lyrical brilliance. Costello spat, shouted and crooned a cornucopia of radical issues and was hailed by the critics. His debut hit single 'Watching The Detectives' contained scathing verses about wife-beating over a beautifully simple reggae beat. His new band, the Attractions, gave Costello a solid and tight sound that put them into rock's first division. The combination of Bruce Thomas (b. Stockton-on-Tees, Cleveland, England; bass), ex-Chilli Willi And The Red Hot Peppers' Pete Thomas (b. 9 August 1954, Sheffield, Yorkshire, England; drums) and Steve Nieve (b. Steven Nason; keyboards), became an integral part of the Costello sound. The Attractions provided the

Elvis Costello

backing for the strong *This Year's Model* and further magnificent singles ensued prior to the release of another landmark, *Armed Forces* in 1979. This vitriolic collection narrowly missed the coveted number 1 position in the UK and reached the Top 10 in the USA. Costello's standing in the USA was seriously dented by his regrettably flippant dismissal of Ray Charles as 'an ignorant, blind nigger', an opinion which he later recanted. 'Oliver's Army', a major hit taken from the album, was a bitter attack on the mercenary soldier, sung in a happy-go-lucky fashion. By the end of the 70s Costello was firmly established as both performer and songwriter with Linda Ronstadt and Dave Edmunds having success with his compositions. During 1981 Elvis spent time in Nashville recording a country album *Almost Blue* with the legendary producer Billy Sherrill. An honest UK television documentary showed work in progress, with Sherrill unable to be totally complimentary to Costello. George Jones's 'Good Year For The Roses' became the album's major hit, although a superb reading of Patsy Cline's 'Sweet Dreams' was a comparative failure. The following year with seven albums already behind him, the prolific Elvis released another outstanding collection, *Imperial Bedroom*, many of the songs are romantic excursions into mistrust and deceit, including 'Man Out Of Time', 'I'm Your Toy'. The fast paced 'Beyond Belief' is a perfect example of vintage Costello lyricism: 'History repeats the old conceits, the glib replies the same defeats, keep your finger on important issues with crocodile tears and a pocketful of tissues'. That year Robert Wyatt recorded the best-ever interpretation of an Elvis song. The superlative 'Shipbuilding' was a wickedly subtle indictment of the Falklands War. Wyatt's high strained voice gave true depth to the lines 'Is it worth it, a new winter coat and shoes for the wife, and a bicycle on the boy's birthday' while later on the listener is awakened to the reality of the irony with: 'diving for dear life, when we should be diving for pearls'. The next year Costello as the Imposter released 'Pills And Soap', a similar theme cleverly masking a bellicose attack on Thatcherism. Both *Punch The Clock* and *Goodbye Cruel World* maintained the high standards that Costello had already set and astonishingly he had found the time to produce albums by the Specials, Squeeze, the Bluebells and the Pogues (where he met his future wife Cait O'Riordan). During 1984 he played a retarded brother on BBC television in Alan Bleasdale's *Scully*. The following year he bravely took the stage at Live Aid and in front of millions,

he poignantly and unselfishly sang Lennon's 'All You Need Is Love' accompanied by his solo guitar. His version of the Animals' 'Don't Let Me Be Misunderstood' was a minor hit in 1986 and during another punishing year he released two albums; the rock 'n' roll influenced *King Of America*, yet another success with notable production from T-Bone Burnett and guitar contributions from the legendary James Burton and, reunited with the Attractions and producer Nick Lowe, Costello stalled with the less than perfect *Blood And Chocolate*. Towards the end of the 80s he collaborated with Paul McCartney and co-wrote a number of songs for *Flowers In The Dirt*, and returned after a brief hiatus (by Costello standards) with the excellent *Spike* in 1989. During 1990 he wrote and sang with Roger McGuinn for his 1991 comeback *Back To Rio*. During that year a heavily bearded and long-haired Elvis co-wrote the soundtrack to the highly controversial television series *GBH*, (written by Bleasdale) and delivered another success, *Mighty Like A Rose*. With lyrics as sharp as any of his previous work, this introspective and reflective album had Costello denying he was ever cynical - merely realistic. Costello is without doubt one of the finest songwriters and lyricists Britain has ever produced, his left-of-centre political views have not clouded his horizon; he remains a critics' favourite with his credibility as high as ever.

Albums: *My Aim Is True* (1977), *This Year's Model* (1978), *Armed Forces* (1979), *Get Happy* (1980), *Trust* (1981), *Almost Blue* (1981), *Imperial Bedroom* (1982), *Punch The Clock* (1983), *Goodbye Cruel World* (1984), *King Of America* (1986), *Blood And Chocolate* (1986), *Spike* (1989), *Mighty Like A Rose* (1991). Compilations: *Ten Bloody Marys And Ten Hows Your Fathers* (1984), *The Best Of Elvis Costello - The Man* (1985), *Girls Girls Girls* (1989), *Out Of Our Idiot* (1987).

Covington, Julie

b. c.1950, England. An actress and singer, Covington had the original hit version of 'Don't Cry For Me Argentina' from Andrew Lloyd Webber and Tim Rice's *Evita*. A student at Cambridge University, her performance in the 1967 Footlights Revue led to an appearance on David Frost's UK television show, singing a song by Pete Atkin and Clive James. Covington was subsequently signed to EMI's Columbia label, recording *Beautiful Changes*. During the 70s, she pursued a career in the theatre and in 1976 was cast with Rula Lenska and Charlotte Cornwell as a vocal group in the television series *Rock Follies*. With music by Sue Lloyd-Jones and Roxy Music's Andy Mackay, the group had a hit album on Island and a Top 10 single, 'O.K.?' in 1977. Covington's performance in *Rock Follies* won her the role of Evita Peron in the studio version of the musical and she had a number 1 hit with 'Don't Cry For Me Argentina' (1977), the big ballad from the show. Covington now signed to Virgin to make a solo album with all-star sidemen like Richard Thompson, John Cale and Steve Winwood. It included a version of Alice Cooper's 'Only Women Bleed' which reached the Top 20 in 1977. The next year she was guest vocalist on the Albion Band's *Rise Up Like The Sun*, and also sang on Richard And Linda Thompson's *First Light* album. Her only later recording was 'When Housewives Had The Choice' (1989), the theme for a selection of ballads featured on a 50s BBC Radio show. She continues to work in the theatre and as an occasional broadcaster.

Albums: *Beautiful Changes* (1970), *Julie Covington* (1978).

Coxhill, Lol

b. Lowen Coxhill, 19 September 1932, Portsmouth, Hampshire, England. Coxhill first attracted attention in the early 60s playing soprano saxophone with a startlingly wide variety of bands. In his early career, he was at home playing with R&B singers, rock groups, free jazz ensembles and was especially adept playing unaccompanied solos. On occasion, he would also happily sit in with traditional bands, making no attempt to adapt his forthright and contemporary style and yet improbably making the results work. In the 70s and 80s Coxhill was involved with such musicians as Chris McGregor's Brotherhood Of Breath, Bobby Wellins, Evan Parker, Derek Bailey and Tony Coe; he worked frequently with pianist Steve Miller, was co-leader of the now-defunct Johnny Rondo Trio, and is now a member of two regular groups - the Recedents (with Mike Cooper and Roger Turner) and the Melody Four (actually trio, with Tony Coe and Steve Beresford). For a while in the early 80s, he was a guest member of the punk group, the Damned. In the 70s he also began to develop a sideline career as an actor, and has appeared in a number of plays in the theatre and on television: he was also the subject of documentary film, *Frog Dance*. A strikingly original player, Coxhill's fiercely independent approach to his music has always been leavened by his droll sense of humour and a broad-minded eclecticism -

in the early 90s he was playing early jazz with bassist Dave Green, singing Marx Brothers songs with the Melody Four and continuing his total improvisations both solo and with the Recedents.

Albums: *Ear Of The Beholder* (1971), *Toverbal Sweet* (1971), with Steve Miller *Coxhill/Miller* (1973), *The Story So Far...Oh Really, One Side?* (1974), *Lol Coxhill And The Welfare State* (1975), *Fleas In The Custard* (1975), *Diverse* (1977), *Lid* (1978), *The Joy Of Paranoia* (1978), *Moot* (1978), with Morgan Fisher *Slow Music* (1978), *Chantenay '80* (1980), *The Dunois Solos* (1981), *Instant Replay* (1982), with Eyeless In Gaza *Home Produce* (1982), *Cou$ Cou$* (1983), *Frog Dance* (1986), with Daniel Deshays *10:02* (1986), *Café De La Place* (1986), *Before My Time* (1987), *Looking Back Forwards* (1990), *Lol Coxhill* (1990).

Further reading: *The Bald Soprano*, Jeff Nuttall.

Coyne, Kevin

b. 27 January 1944, Derby, England. A former art student, psychiatric therapist and social worker, Coyne also pursued a singing career in local pubs and clubs. His fortunes flourished on moving to London where he joined Siren, a group later signed to disc jockey John Peel's Dandelion label. Coyne left the band in 1972, and having completed the promising *Case History*, switched outlets to Virgin the following year. *Marjory Razor Blade* emphasized his idiosyncratic talent in which the artist's guttural delivery highlighted his lyrically raw compositions. Taking inspiration from country blues, Coyne successfully constructed a set of invective power and his obstinate quest for self-effacement was confirmed on *Blame It On The Night*. Although showing a greater sophistication, this enthralling set was equally purposeful and introduced a period marked by punishing concert schedules. Coyne formed a group around Zoot Money (keyboards), Andy Summers (guitar), Steve Thompson (bass) and Peter Wolf (drums) to promote *Matching Head And Feet* and this line-up later recorded *Heartburn*. This period was captured to perfection on the live *In Living Black And White*, but escalating costs forced the singer to abandon the band in 1976. His work was not out of place in the angst-ridden punk era, while a 1979 collaboration with former Slapp Happy vocalist Dagmar Krause, *Babble*, was an artistic triumph. Coyne parted company with Virgin during the early 80s, but recordings for Cherry Red Records, including *Pointing The Finger* and *Politicz* showed an undiminished fire. *Peel Sessions*, a compendium of radio broadcasts from between 1974 and 1990, is a testament to the artist's divergent styles and moods. Albums: *Case History* (1972), *Marjory Razor Blade* (1973), *Blame It On The Night* (1974), *Matching Head And Feet* (1975), *Heartburn* (1976), *In Living Black And White* (1977), *Dynamite Daze* (1978), *Millionaires And Teddy Bears* (1978), *Beautiful Extremes* (1978), with Dagmar Krause *Babble* (1979), *Bursting Bubbles* (1980), *Pointing The Finger* (1981), *Politicz* (1982), *Beautiful Extremes Etcetera* (1983), *Legless In Manila* (1984), *Peel Sessions* (1991). Compilation: *Dandelion Years* (1982).

Crabby Appleton

This promising US rock group was formed in 1970, when singer/guitarist Michael Fennelly (b. New Jersey, USA), an ex-member of Sagittarius and the Millennium, joined forces with Stonehenge, a struggling Los Angeles bar band. Casey Foutz (b. Iowa, USA; keyboards), Hank Harvey (b. California, USA; bass), Phil Jones (b. Iowa, USA; drums) and Felix 'Falco' Falcon (b. Cuba; percussion) completed the line-up, which took its name from a cartoon character. Signed to the Elektra label, their excellent debut album included 'Go Back', which reached the US Top 40, but despite completing a well-received tour, sustained success eluded the quintet. Their second set, *Rotten To The Core*, lacked the cohesion of its predecessor and the group disbanded in 1972 when Fennelly embarked on a solo career.
Albums: *Crabby Appleton* (1970), *Rotten To The Core* (1971).

Crawler

This UK heavy rock group was an off-shoot of Back Street Crawler, the band that had featured the late and legendary Paul Kossoff. Crawler comprised Terry Wilson Slesser (vocals), Geoff Whitehorn (guitar), John 'Rabbit' Bundrick (keyboards and ex-Free), Terry Wilson (bass) and Tony Braunagel (drums). They released two blues-rock albums during the late 70s, which were ignored amid the punk rock explosion at the time. The group disbanded in 1978, with Whitehorn going back to session work and Slesser reappearing later in Charlie.
Albums: *Crawler* (1977), *Snake, Rattle And Roll* (1978).

Crazy Horse

Crazy Horse evolved in 1969 when singer Neil Young invited Danny Whitten (guitar), Billy Talbot (b. New York, New York, USA; bass) and Ralph Molina (b. Puerto Rico; drums) - all

formerly of struggling local attraction the Rockets - to accompany him on his second album, *Everybody Knows This Is Nowhere*. The impressive results inspired an attendant tour, but although the group also contributed to Young's *After The Goldrush*, their relationship was sundered in the light of Whitten's growing drug dependency. *Crazy Horse*, completed with the assistance of Jack Nitzsche and Nils Lofgren, featured several notable performances, including the emotional 'I Don't Want To Talk About It', later revived by Rod Stewart and Everything But The Girl. Whitten succumbed to a heroin overdose in November 1972, but although Talbot and Molina kept the group afloat with various different members, neither *Loose* or *At Crooked Lake* scaled the heights of their excellent debut. Reunited with Young for *Tonight's The Night* and *Zuma*, and buoyed by the arrival of guitarist Frank Stampedro (b. West Virginia, USA), the group reclaimed its independence with the excellent *Crazy Moon*. Although Crazy Horse has since abandoned its own career, their role as the ideal foil to Young's ambitions was amply proved on the blistering *Ragged Glory* (1991).
Albums: *Crazy Horse* (1970), *Loose* (1971), *Crazy Horse At Crooked Lake* (1973), *Crazy Moon* (1978).

Creach, 'Papa' John

b. 8 May 1917, USA. John Creach began his career as a fiddle player upon his family's move to Chicago in 1935. He later toured the midwest of the USA as a member of cabaret attraction the Chocolate Music Bars, but settled in California in 1945. Creach played in the resident band at Palm Springs' Chi Chi Restaurant, undertook session work and entertained tourists on a luxury liner before securing a spot at the Parisian Room in Los Angeles. He was 'discovered' at this venue by Joey Covington, drummer in Hot Tuna and Jefferson Airplane, and by October 1970 Creach was a member of both groups. His tenure was not without controversy, many aficionados resented this intrusion, but although he left the former group two years later, 'Papa' John remained with the latter act until 1975, surviving their transformation into Jefferson Starship. *Papa John Creach* featured support from many bay area acolytes, including Jerry Garcia, Carlos Santana and John Cipollina, while *Filthy* was notable for 'Walking The Tou Tou', effectively a Hot Tuna master. *Zulu (Playing My Fiddle For You)* marked Creach's growing estrangement from the 'Airplane' family and was his final release on their in-house

Grunt label. Successive releases failed to achieve the profile of those early recordings, but Creach remained an enduring live attraction in Los Angeles throughout the 70s.

Albums: *Papa John Creach* (1971), *Filthy* (1972), *Zulu (Playing My Fiddle For You)* (1974), *I'm The Fiddle Man* (1975), *Rock Father* (1976), *The Cat And The Fiddle* (1977), *Inphasion* (1978).

Creed

This US blues-based boogie outfit was formed in 1977 by vocalist Steve Ingle and guitarist Luther Maben. Enlisting the services of Hal Butler (keyboards), James Flynn (bass) and Chip Thomas (drums) they were soon signed by Asylum Records. Their self-titled debut appeared in 1978 and was notable for 'Time And Time Again', an epic southern-style guitar work-out, comparable in stature to Lynyrd Skynyrd's 'Freebird'. Unable to attract enough media attention, the band split up soon after the album's release.

Album: *Creed* (1978).

Croce, Jim

b. 10 January 1943, Philadelphia, Pennsylvania, USA, d. 20 September 1973. Originally a university disc jockey, Croce played in various rock bands before moving to New York in 1967 where he performed in folk clubs. By 1969, he and his wife Ingrid (b. 27 April 1947, Philadelphia, Pennsylvania, USA) were signed to Capitol Records for *Approaching Day*. The album's failure led to Croce returning to Pennsylvania and taking on work as a truck driver and telephone engineer. Meanwhile, he continued with songwriting and, after sending demo tapes to former college friend and New York record producer Tommy West, Croce secured a new deal with the ABC label. Croce's second album, *You Don't Mess Around With Jim*, provides him with a US Top 10 hit in the title track and, along with 'Operator (That's Not The Way It Feels)' helped establish Croce as a songwriter of distinction. In July 1973, he topped the US charts with the narrative 'Bad Boy Leroy Brown'. Exactly two months later, he died in a plane crash at Natchitoches, Louisiana. In the wake of his death he registered a Top 10 hit with 'I Got A Name', which was featured in the film *The Last American Hero*. The contemplative 'Time In A Bottle' was released in late 1973 and became the final US number 1 of the year. It was a fitting valediction. During 1974, further releases kept Croce's name in the US charts, including 'I'll Have To Say I Love You In A Song' and 'Workin' At The Car Wash Blues'.

Albums: *Approaching Day* (1969), *You Don't Mess Around With Jim* (1972), *Life And Times* (1973), *I Got A Name* (1973). Compilation: *Photographs And Memories - His Greatest Hits* (1974), *The Faces I've Been* (1975, early recording from 1961-71), *Time In A Bottle - Jim Croce's Greatest Love Songs* (1977).

Cronshaw, Andrew

b. 18 April 1949, Lytham St. Annes, Lancashire, England. Cronshaw undertook his debut performances at Edinburgh University, where he gained a degree in psychology, and where he was involved in running the University Folksong Society. He gave up singing in favour of playing guitar, tin whistle, zither, and later, the concertina and dulcimer. *A Is For Andrew, Z Is For Zither*, released on Transatlantic's Xtra subsidiary, showcased his potential. Turning his busy hand to production, Cronshaw produced the single 'Casey's Last Ride'/'Nostradamus' by Suzie Adams, and later albums by June Tabor (*Abyssinians* and *Aqaba*) and the second release by Tabor and Maddy Prior as Silly Sisters, *No More To The Dance*. Cronshaw went on to produce *The Wild West Show* by Bill Caddick, and *Wolf At Your Door* by Zumzeaux. During this time, Cronshaw continued to record for a variety of labels, producing music that could be defined as a cross between new age and folk. Although concentrating latterly on production and writing, he also writes regular articles for *Folk Roots* and a number of other UK magazines. In 1991, Cronshaw made two tours of selected village churches in England, under the banner of the 'Splendid Venues Tour', partly in an attempt to get people out of thinking of folk music as only being performed in the dingy backrooms of public houses. He has performed for many years, with a host of 'names' from the folk scene, in duos and groups, including Ric Sanders, Martin Simpson, and June Tabor, as well as undertaking solo performances.

Albums: *A Is For Andrew, Z Is For Zither* (1974), *Earthed In Cloud Valley* (1977), *Wade In The Flood* (1978), *The Great Dark Water* (1982), *Till The Beasts Returning* (1988). Compilation: *The Andrew Cronshaw CD* (1989).

Cummings, Burton

b. 31 December 1947, Winnipeg, Manitoba, Canada. Burton Cummings was the lead vocalist on the majority of the recordings by the Guess Who during that Canadian group's reign during the 60s. Upon leaving the group for a solo career

in the mid-70s, three years after the group's guitarist Randy Bachman had left to form Bachman-Turner Overdrive, Cummings signed a solo deal with Portrait Records, a new CBS subsidiary. Cummings' first single for the label, 'Stand Tall', was also his greatest solo success, a US Top 10 hit in late 1976. He continued to record for that label until 1978 and charted three more times before being dropped. He emerged on the small Alfa label for one last US chart single 'You Saved My Soul'. Cummings recorded three solo albums for Portrait, two of which sold reasonably well in 1976 and 1977, and he cut one for Alfa in 1981, which saw little action. Still considered a major talent in Canada by the end of the 80s, Cummings and Bachman briefly regrouped for a Guess Who reunion tour and live video release.
Albums: *Burton Cummings* (1976), *My Own Way To Rock* (1977), *Dream Of A Child* (1978), *Sweet, Sweet* (1981).

Curved Air

Originally emerging from the classically-influenced progressive band Sisyphus, Curved Air formed in early 1970 with a line-up comprising Sonja Kristina (b. 14 April 1949, Brentwood, Essex, England; vocals), Darryl Way (b. 17 December 1948, Taunton, Somerset, England; violin), Florian Pilkington Miksa (b. 3 June 1950, Roehampton, London, England), Francis Monkman (b. 9 June 1949, Hampstead, London, England; keyboards) and Ian Erye (bass). After establishing themselves on the UK club circuit, the group were signed by Warner Brothers for a much-publicized advance of £100,000. Their debut album *Air Conditioning* was heavily promoted and enjoyed a particular curiosity value as one of rock's first picture disc albums. In the summer of 1971, the group enjoyed their sole UK Top 5 hit with 'Back Street Luv', while their *Second Album* cleverly fused electronic rock and classical elements to win favour with the progressive music audience. By the time of *Phantasmagoria*, Erye had made way for Mike Wedgewood (b. 19 May 1956, Derby, England) and Monkman and Way were in disagreement over musical direction and presentation. By October 1972, both had left the group and Kristina was the sole original member and the line-up consistently changed thereafter. One new member, teenager Eddie Jobson (b. 28 April 1955) would later leave to join Roxy Music to replace Brian Eno. Following a two-year hiatus during which Kristina rejoined the cast of the musical *Hair* the group was reactivated, with Way returning, for

touring purposes. Two further albums followed before the unit dissolved in 1977. Kristina pursued a largely unsuccessful solo career in music and acting - although her 1991 album *Songs From The Acid Folk* augers well for the future. Monkman went on to form Sky, while latter-day drummer Stewart Copeland joined the immensely successful Police.
Albums: *Air Conditioning* (1970), *Second Album* (1971), *Phantasmagoria* (1972), *Air Cut* (1973), *Curved Air Live* (1975), *Midnight Wire* (1975), *Airborne* (1976). Compilation: *The Best Of Curved Air* (1976). Solo albums: Sonja Kristina *Sonja Kristina* (1980), *Songs From The Acid Folk* (1991).

Cymarron

A soft-rock group which placed one single in the US Top 20 in 1971, 'Rings', Cymarron consisted of Rick Yancey (b. 1948), Sherrill Parks (b. 1948, Jackson, Tennessee, USA; guitar/saxophone) and Richard Mainegra (b. 1948, New Orleans, Louisiana, USA). The trio was formed after Yancey was hired as a studio musician and songwriter by Chips Moman for the latter's American Recording Studios in Memphis, Tennessee. Yancey met Parks, they decided to work together, and Parks brought in Mainegra. They named the group Cymarron after a television western called *Cimarron Strip*. 'Rings', released on Entrance Records, was not written by the group but by outside writers, Eddie Reeves and Alex Harvey, and it became Cymarron's only success, despite a handful of subsequent singles and an album.
Album: *Rings* (1971).

D

Dactyl, Terry, And The Dinosaurs

This UK jugband-cum-skiffle group enjoyed a concurrent career as Brett Marvin And The Thunderbolts. Little effort was spared to hide this fact, even though each 'act' was signed to different recording companies. The Dinosaurs enjoyed the patronage of producer/entrepreneur Jonathan King, who signed them to his UK label. Their debut single, 'Seaside Shuffle', reached number 2 in 1972, while the following year the group scored a minor chart entry with 'On A Saturday Night'. The 'Brett Marvin' appellation was fully resurrected when further releases proved unsuccessful, while vocalist/keyboard player Jona Lewie later embarked on a solo career.

Daddy Cool

At a time when Australian audiences were non-participatory, preferring to sit cross-legged and stoned, Daddy Cool was a fresh, startling, danceable pop band. Led by Ross Wilson (vocals/guitar), the band comprised Ross Hunnaford (guitar), Gary Young (drums), Wayne Duncan (bass), Jerry Noone (saxophone/piano) and Ian Winter (guitar). Daddy Cool was designed as a good-time, fun band, utilizing the 50s doo-wop and basic rock 'n' roll approach, as played by Frank Zappa's Ruben And The Jets earlier in America. Formed in 1970 the band soon took the country by storm, each member wearing strange, zany headgear - Mickey Mouse ears, propeller hats etc. Their initial hits were covers but Wilson was able to write in the style that mirrored the band's image for later hits. Torch ballads like 'I'll Never Smile Again' were also prominent. The band toured the USA three times during 1971-72, without making much impact, and broke up. They reformed in 1974, for a year. The band's masterpiece, 'Eagle Rock' is re-released every few years in Australia, and charts each time, keeping the Daddy Cool legend alive.
Albums: *Daddy Who Daddy Cool* (1971), *Sex, Dope And Rock 'N' Roll* (1972), *Last Drive-In Movie* (1973), *Missing Masters* (1980). Compilations: *Daddy's Coolest* (1982), *Daddy's Coolest Volume 2* (1984), *The Daddy Cool Collection* (1984).

Damned

Formed in 1976, this UK punk group comprised Captain Sensible (b. Ray Burns, 23 April 1955, England; bass), Rat Scabies (b. Chris Miller, 30 July 1957, Surrey, England; drums), Brian James (b. Brian Robertson, England; guitar) and Dave Vanian (b. David Letts, England; vocals). Scabies and James had previously played in the unwieldy punk ensemble London SS and, joined by Sensible, they backed Nick Kent's Subterraneans. The Damned emerged in May 1976 and two months later they were supporting the Sex Pistols at the 100 Club. After appearing at the celebrated Mont de Marsan punk festival in August, they were signed to Stiff Records one month later. In October, they released what is generally regarded as the first UK punk single, 'New Rose', which was backed by a frantic version of the Beatles' 'Help!' Apart from being dismissed as support act during the Sex Pistols' ill-fated Anarchy tour, they released UK punk's first album *Damned Damned Damned*, produced by Nick Lowe. The work was typical of the period, full of short, sharp songs played extremely fast, with high energy compensating for competence. During April 1977, they became the first UK punk group to tour the USA. By the summer of that year, they recruited a second guitarist, Lu Edmunds; and soon after drummer Rat Scabies quit. A temporary replacement, Dave Berk, deputized until the recruitment of London percussionist Jon Moss. In November, their second album *Music For Pleasure*, produced by Pink Floyd's Nick Mason, was mauled by the critics and worse followed when they were dropped from Stiff's roster. Increasingly dismissed for their lack of earnestness and love of pantomime, they lost heart and split in early 1978. The members went in various directions: Sensible joined the Softies, Moss and Edmunds formed the Edge, Vanian teamed-up with Doctors Of Madness and James founded Tanz Der Youth.
The second part of the Damned story reopened one year later when Sensible, Vanian and Scabies formed the Doomed. In November 1978, they were allowed to use the name Damned and opened this new phase of their career with their first Top 20 single, 'Love Song'. Some minor hits followed and the group was pleasantly surprised to find themselves a formidable concert attraction. When their recently recruited bassist Algy Ward (previously with the Saints) left to join Tank, he was replaced by Paul Gray, from Eddie And The Hot Rods. The group continued to reach the lower regions of the chart during the next year

while Captain Sensible simultaneously signed a solo deal with A&M Records. Amazingly, he zoomed to number 1 with a novel revival of 'Happy Talk', which outsold every Damned release. Although he stuck with the group for two more years, he finally left in August 1984. A third phase in the group's career ushered in new members and a more determined pop direction. In 1986, they enjoyed their biggest ever hit with a cover of Barry Ryan's 'Eloise'. Another 60s pastiche, this time a rather pedestrian reading of Love's classic 'Alone Again Or', gave them a minor UK hit. Still gigging regularly, the Damned have lasted much longer than any critic could have dreamed back in 1976.

Albums: *Damned Damned Damned* (1977), *Music For Pleasure* (1977), *Machine Gun Etiquette* (1979), *The Black Album* (1980), *Strawberries* (1982), *Phantasmagoria* (1985), *Anything* (1986), *Final Damnation* (1989, live 1988 recording), *Not The Captain's Birthday Party* (1991, live 1977 recording). Compilations: *The Best Of The Damned* (1981), *Light At The End Of The Tunnel* (1987).

Darrow, Chris

b. 1944, South Falls, Dakota, USA. A founder member of the fabled Kaleidoscope, this versatile multi-instrumentalist left the group in 1968 to join the Nitty Gritty Dirt Band. The following year Darrow helped form the Corvettes, an under-rated country-rock group who later backed Linda Ronstadt on a tour to promote her *Hand Sewn* album. Chris then began a solo career with *Artist Proof*, and also found employment as a studio musician. He contributed to releases by John Stewart, John Fahey and others as well as appearing on several Tamla/Motown sessions. A second album, *Chris Darrow*, continued his eclectic nature and featured cameos by Dolly Collins and Alan Stivell, while an equally crafted third, *Under My Own Disguise*, followed in 1974.

Darrow's subsequent profile has been more low key. He was involved in the brief Kaleidoscope reunion (1976), which in turn led to the formation of another short-term group, Rank Strangers, whose album appeared the following year. Having helped launch the career of guitarist Toulouse Engelheart, Darrow then completed another solo release, *Fretless*. By preferring to work in a small-scale circuit, this exceptional player has retained an integrity at the expense of the wider recognition his talent deserves.

Albums: *Artist Proof* (c.70s), *Chris Darrow* (1973), *Under My Own Disguise* (1974), *Fretless* (1979), *A South California Drive* (1980).

Darts

After the demise of UK's John Dummer Blues Band, Iain Thompson (bass) and drummer Dummer joined forces with Hammy Howell (keyboards), Horatio Hornblower (Nigel Trubridge; saxophone) and singers Rita Ray, Griff Fender (Ian Collier), bassist Den Hegarty and Bob Fish (ex-Mickey Jupp Band) as revivalists mining the vocal harmony seam of rock 'n' roll. Dave Kelly, an ex-Dummer guitarist, was a more transient participant. Bursting upon metropolitan clubland in the late 70s, Darts were championed by pop historian and Radio London disc jockey Charlie Gillett who helped them procure a Magnet Records contract. Their debut single - a medley of 'Daddy Cool' and Little Richard's 'The Girl Can't Help It' - ascended the UK Top 10 in 1977, kicking off three years of entries in both the singles and albums lists that mixed stylized self-compositions (eg 'It's Raining', 'Don't Let It Fade Away') with predominant revamps of such US hits as the Cardinals' 'Come Back My Love', the Ad-Libs' 'Boy From New York City', 'Get It' (Gene Vincent) and 'Duke Of Earl' (Gene Chandler). After the eventual replacement of Hegarty with Kenny Edwards in 1979, their records were less successful. Without the television commercial coverage that sent the Jackie Wilson original to number 1 a few years later, Darts' version of 'Reet Petite' struggled to number 51 while 'Let's Hang On' - also 1980 - was their last *bona fide* smash - and 'White Christmas'/'Sh-Boom' the first serious miss. With the exit of Howell (to higher education) and Dummer (to form the ribald True Life Confessions), Darts were still able to continue in a recognizable form but were no longer hit parade contenders. As leader of Rocky Sharpe And The Replays, Hegarty had hovered between 60 and 17 in the UK singles list until 1983 when his post as a children's television presenter took vocational priority. Keeping the faith longer, Ray and Collier produced a 1985 album for the Mint Juleps, an a cappella girl group who had been inspired initially by Darts.

Albums: *Darts* (1977), *Everyone Plays Darts* (1978), *Dart Attack* (1979). Compilation: *Amazing Darts* (1978).

Dawn

Formed in 1970 by singer Tony Orlando (b. 1945, New York, USA), when a demo of 'Candida', co-written by Toni Wine, arrived on his desk. Orlando elected to record it himself with support from Tamla/Motown session vocalists Telma

Darts

Hopkins and Joyce Vincent, and hired instrumentalists. On Bell Records, this single was attributed to Dawn, despite the existence of 14 other professional acts of that name – which is why, after 'Candida' and 'Knock Three Times' topped international charts, the troupe came to be billed as 'Tony Orlando and Dawn' three more million-sellers later. Though the impetus slackened with 'What Are You Doing Sunday' and a 'Happy Together'/'Runaway' medley (with Del Shannon), the irresistible 'Tie A Yellow Ribbon Round The Old Oak Tree' proved *the* hit song of 1973. With typical bouncy accompaniment and downhome libretto - about a Civil War soldier's homecoming - it was to amass hundreds of cover versions. Its 'Say Has Anybody Seen My Sweet Gypsy Rose' follow-up exuded a ragtime mood that prevailed throughout its associated album and Dawn's *New Ragtime Follies* variety season in Las Vegas which was syndicated on television spectaculars throughout the globe - though such exposure could not prevent the comparative failure of 1974's 'Who's In The Strawberry Patch With Sally'. After moving to Elektra/Asylum, the outfit scored their last US number 1 - with 'He Don't Love You', a re-write of a Jerry Butler single from 1960. Another revival - of Marvin Gaye and Tammi

Terrell's 'You're All I Need To Get By' - was among other releases during their less successful years.
Albums: *Ragtime Follies* (1973), *Golden Ribbons* (1974).

Dawson, Jim

b. 27 June 1946, Miami, Oklahoma, USA. Dawson moved to Littleton, Colorado at an early age, and lived there until 1964. After teaching himself to play piano and guitar, he played in a high school group, then joined the navy. Dawson's first two albums were recorded on Kama Sutra, but he signed with RCA in 1974, releasing *Jim Dawson*. For this recording, he had worked with producers Terry Cashman and Tommy West, known for their work with Jim Croce. Although not a true folk performer in the strictest sense of the word, his work is difficult to put into one genre.
Albums: *Songman* (1971), *You'll Never Be Lonely With Me* (1972), *Jim Dawson* (1974), *Elephants In The Rain* (1975). Compilations: *Essential Jim Dawson* (1974).

Deaf School

Art-rock band that practically started the Liverpool new wave scene single-handed. Deaf School were

formed in January 1974 by a large group of students at Liverpool Art College. The original line-up could be as big as 15 but the basic 12 were singers Bette Bright (b. Ann Martin, Whitstable, Kent, England), Ann Bright, Hazel Bartram, and Eric Shark (b. Thomas Davis), Enrico Cadillac Jnr, (b. Steve Allen), guitarists Cliff Hanger (b. Clive Langer) and Roy Holder, bassist Mr Average (b. Steve Lindsay), keyboards player the Rev. Max Ripple (b. John Wood), drummer Tim Whittaker and saxophonists Ian Ritchie and Mike Evans. Sandy Bright soon left to get married and she was quickly followed by Bartram, Evans and Holder, the last of whom was fired. The remaining eight-piece line-up developed an entertaining blend of rock music and almost vaudevillian stage theatrics. This combination helped them win a *Melody Maker* Rock Contest in which the prize was a recording contract with WEA. The debut - *Second Honeymoon* - came out in August 1976 (by which time former Stealers Wheel guitarist Paul Pilnick had been added to the line-up). Hugely popular, particularly in Liverpool, their audience contained a host of names soon to make it in their own right. Two more albums and three singles emerged before the band finally dissolved after Bette Bright appeared in the *Great Rock 'N' Roll Swindle*, recorded two singles for Radar and a third for Korova with her backing band The Illuminations (variously Glen Matlock, Rusty Egan, Henry Priestman, Clive Langer, and Paul Pilnick). In 1981 she married Suggs from Madness. Eric Shark quit music to run a shop in Liverpool, Enrico Cadillac reverted to his real name and formed the Original Mirrors. Clive Langer formed the Boxes but had more success as a producer. Steve Lindsay replaced Holly Johnson in Big In Japan, went on to the Secrets and then found limited success with the Planets. The Rev. Max Ripple became the head of the Fine Art department at Goldsmith College in London. Tim Whittaker concentrated on session work with such Liverpool luminaries as Pink Military. Ian Ritchie finished up with Jane Aire. Steve Lindsay released a solo single ('Mr Average') while still in Deaf School, and another as Steve Temple in 1981, before forming the Planets. Steve Allen later joined with Steve Nieve in Perils Of Plastic. Various ex-Deaf School kids have also turned up in the deliberately dreadful Portsmouth Sinfonia. In 1988 Cadillac, Bright, Shark, Langer, Lindsay and Ripple reformed for five sell-out shows to celebrate the 10th anniversary of their demise.
Albums: *Second Honeymoon* (1976), *Don't Stop The World* (1977), *English Boys Working Girls* (1978).

Decameron

Formed in 1968, this group comprised Dave Bell (guitar/percussion/vocals), and Johnny Coppin (b. 5 July 1946, Woodford, Essex, England; guitar/piano/vocals). The line-up grew, in September 1969, when they added Al Fenn (guitar/mandolin/vocals), and further still with the addition of Geoff March (cello/violin/vocals), in December 1969; Dik Cadbury (bass/guitar/violin/vocals) in July 1973; and finally Bob Critchley (drums/vocals), in September 1975. From 1971-74, the group were signed to the Fingamigig agency, which was then run by Jasper Carrott and John Starkey. Based in Cheltenham, Gloucester, Decameron performed contemporary folk-rock material, much of which was composed by Bell and Coppin. The group released three singles on as many labels: 'Stoats Grope' in 1973, on Vertigo; 'Breakdown Of The Song' in 1974, on Mooncrest; and 'Dancing' in 1976, on Transatlantic. Two other singles, both on Transatlantic, were released by the band, under the name of the Magnificent Mercury Brothers, in which guise they sang 60s doo-wop style. The singles were 'New Girl In School' in 1975, and a version of the classic 'Why Do Fools Fall In Love', in 1976. Neither single achieved any great commercial success, and the group split, Coppin going on to pursue a solo career.
Albums: *Say Hello To The Band* (1973), *Mammoth Special* (1974), *Third Light* (1975), *Beyond The Light* (1975), *Tomorrows Pantomime* (1976).

Dee, Kiki

b. Pauline Matthews, 6 March 1947, Bradford, England. Having begun her career in local dancebands, this popular vocalist made her recording debut in 1964 with the Mitch Murray-penned 'Early Night'. Its somewhat perfunctory pop style was quickly replaced by a series of releases modelled on US producer Phil Spector before Kiki achieved notoriety for excellent interpretations of contemporary soul hits, including Tami Lynn's 'I'm Gonna Run Away From You' and Aretha Franklin's 'Running Out Of Fools'. Her skilled interpretations secured a recording deal with Tamla/Motown, the first white British act to be so honoured. However, although lauded artistically, Kiki was unable to attain due commercial success, and the despondent singer sought cabaret work in Europe and South Africa. Her career was revitalized in 1973 on signing up

Kiki Dee

with Elton John's Rocket label. He produced her 'comeback' set, *Loving And Free*, which spawned a UK Top 20 entry in 'Amoureuse', while Kiki subsequently scored further chart success with 'I Got The Music In Me' (1974) and 'How Glad I Am' (1975) fronting the Kiki Dee Band - Jo Partridge (guitar), Bias Boshell (piano), Phil Curtis (bass) and Roger Pope (drums). Her duet with John, 'Don't Go Breaking My Heart', topped the UK and US charts in 1976, and despite further minor UK hits, the most notable of which was 'Star', which reached number 13 in 1981, this remains her best-known performance. She took a tentative step into acting by appearing in the London stage musical, *Pump Boys And Dinettes* in 1984. Kiki Dee's career underwent yet another regeneration in 1987 with *Angel Eyes*, which was co-produced by David A. Stewart of the Eurythmics. She has since appeared in Willy Russell's award-winning musical, *Blood Brothers* in London's West End.

Albums: *I'm Kiki Dee* (1968), *Great Expectations* (1971), *Loving And Free* (1973), *I've Got The Music In Me* (1974), *Kiki Dee* (1977), *Stay With Me* (1979), *Perfect Timing* (1982), *Angel Eyes* (1987). Compilations: *Patterns* (1974), *Kiki Dee's Greatest Hits* (1980).

Deep Purple

Deep Purple evolved in 1968 following sessions to form a group around former Searchers' drummer Chris Curtis (b. 26 August 1942, Liverpool, England). Jon Lord (b. 9 June 1941, Leicester, England; keyboards) and Nick Simper (bass), veterans, respectively, of the Artwoods and Johnny Kidd And The Pirates, joined guitarist Ritchie Blackmore (b. 14 April 1945, Weston-super-Mare, England) in rehearsals for this new act, initially dubbed Roundabout. Curtis dropped out within days, and when Dave Curtis (bass) and Bobby Woodman (drums) also proved incompatible, two members of Maze, Rod Evans (vocals) and Ian Paice (drums), replaced them. Having adopted the Deep Purple name following a brief Scandinavian tour, the quintet began recording their debut album, which they patterned on USA group Vanilla Fudge. *Shades Of Deep Purple* thus included dramatic rearrangements of well-known songs, including 'Hey Joe' and 'Hush', the latter of which became a US Top 5 hit when issued as a single. Lengthy tours ensued as the group, all but ignored at home, steadfastly courted the burgeoning American concert circuit. *The Book Of Taliesyn* and *Deep Purple* also featured several excellent

reworkings, notably of 'Kentucky Woman' (Neil Diamond) and 'River Deep Mountain High' (Ike And Tina Turner), but the unit also drew acclaim for its original material and the dramatic interplay between Lord and Blackmore. In July 1969 both Evans and Simper were axed from the line-up, which was then buoyed by the arrival of Ian Gillan (b. 19 August 1945, Hounslow, Middlesex, England; vocals) and Roger Glover (b. 30 November 1945, Brecon, Wales; bass) from the pop group Episode Six. Acknowledged by aficionados as the 'classic' Deep Purple line-up, the reshaped quintet made its album debut on the grandiose *Concerto For Group And Orchestra*, scored by Lord and recorded with the London Philharmonic Orchestra. Its orthodox successor, *Deep Purple In Rock*, established the group as a leading heavy-metal attraction and included such now-established favourites as 'Speed King' and 'Child In Time'. Gillan's powerful intonation brought a third dimension to their sound and this new-found popularity in the UK was enhanced when an attendant single, 'Black Night', reached number 2. 'Strange Kind Of Woman' followed it into the Top 10, while *Fireball* and *Machine Head* topped their respective chart. The latter included the riff-laden 'Smoke On The Water', now lauded as a seminal example of the hard rock oeuvre, and was the first release on the group's own Purple label. Although the platinum-selling *Made In Japan* captured their live prowess in full flight, relations within the band grew increasingly strained, and *Who Do We Think We Are?* marked the end of this highly-successful line-up. The departures of Gillan and Glover robbed Deep Purple of an expressive frontman and imaginative arranger, although Dave Coverdale (b. 22 September 1949, Saltburn, Lancashire, England; vocals) and Glenn Hughes (late of Trapeze, bass) brought a new impetus to the act. *Burn* and *Stormbringer* both reached the Top 10, but Blackmore grew increasingly dissatisfied with the group's direction and in May 1975 left to form Rainbow. USA guitarist Tommy Bolin, formerly of the James Gang, joined Deep Purple for *Come Taste The Band*, but his jazz/soul style was incompatible with the group's heavy metal sound, and a now-tiring act folded in 1976 following a farewell UK tour. Coverdale then formed Whitesnake, Paice and Lord joined Tony Ashton in Paice Ashton And Lord, while Bolin tragically died of a heroin overdose within months of Purple's demise. Judicious archive and 'best of' releases kept the group in the public eye, as did the high profile enjoyed by its several ex-members.

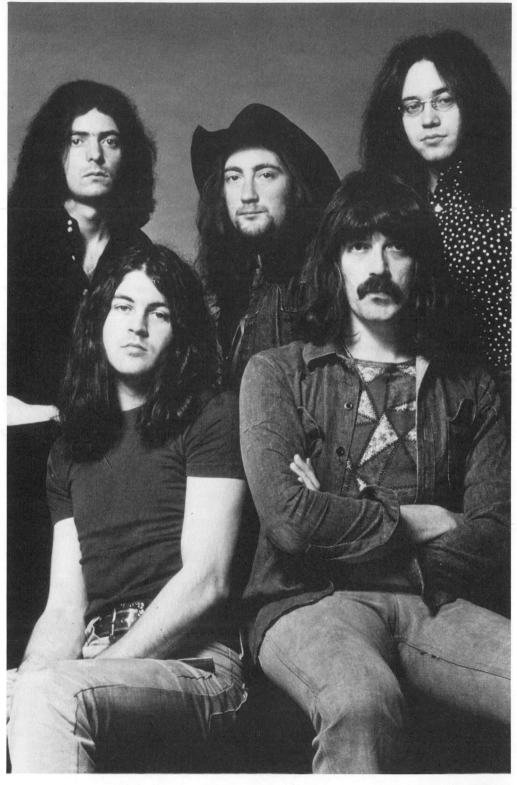

Deep Purple

Pressure for a reunion bore fruit in 1984 when Gillan, Lord, Blackmore, Glover and Paice completed *Perfect Strangers*. A second set, *House Of Blue Lights*, ensued but recurring animosity between Gillan and Blackmore resulted in the singer's departure following the in-concert *Nobody's Perfect*. Former Rainbow vocalist, Joe Lynn Turner, was brought into the line-up for *Slaves And Masters* as Purple steadfastly maintained their revitalized career.

Albums: *Shades Of Deep Purple* (1968), *The Book Of Taliesyn* (1969), *Deep Purple* (1969), *Concerto For Group And Orchestra* (1970), *Deep Purple In Rock* (1970), *Fireball* (1971), *Machine Head* (1972), *Made In Japan* (1972), *Who Do We Think We Are?* (1973), *Burn* (1974), *Stormbringer* (1974), *Come Taste The Band* (1975), *Perfect Strangers* (1985), *House Of Blue Light* (1987), *Nobody's Perfect* (1988), *Slaves And Masters* (1990). Compilations: *Purple Passages* (1972), *24 Carat Purple* (1975), *Made In Europe* (1976), *Last Concert In Japan* (1977), *Powerhouse* (1978), *Singles: As & Bs* (1978), *When We Rock We Rock When We Roll We Roll* (1978), *Deepest Purple* (1980), *Live In London: Deep Purple* (1982), *Anthology: Deep Purple* (1985), *Scandinavian Nights* (1988), *Knebworth '85* (1991).

Dees, Rick, And His Cast Of Idiots

b. Rigdon Osmond Dees III, 1950, Memphis, Tennessee, USA. While working as a disc jockey on Memphis radio in 1976, Dees decided to record a disco parody. Inspired by Jackie Lee's 1965 hit 'The Duck', he wrote a song, added a memorable disco backing overladen with a chorus that owed much to the spirit of cartoon character Donald Duck. At a time when disco records were the rage, the novelty 'Disco Duck (Part One)' insinuated its way into public consciousness and hit the top of the US charts. Dees attempted a follow-up, 'Dis-Gorilla', inspired by the movie *King Kong*, but won only minimal chart success. After a belated final hit with the comic 'Eat My Shorts'/'Get Nekked' in 1984, Dees wisely concentrated on his broadcasting activities.

Album: *The Original Disco Duck* (1977).

DeFranco Family

This teenage family pop group from Port Colborne, Ontario, Canada, comprised Tony (b. 31 August 1959), Benny (b. 11 July 1954), Nino (b. 19 October 1956), Marisa (b. 23 July 1955) and Merlina (b. 20 July 1957). At a time when acts like the Osmonds, Jackson Five and Partridge Family were popular, top teen magazine publishers Laufer Publications promoted this clean-cut Canadian quartet. They launched a massive campaign in their magazines *Tiger Beat* and *Fave* which was focussed mainly on their 14-year-old Donny Osmond look-a-like lead singer Tony DeFranco. Helped by successful record label 20th Century, they pushed the group's debut single 'Heartbeat - It's A Lovebeat' to number 3 in the US chart, selling over two million copies on the way. The follow-up 'Abra-Ca-Dabra' made the Top 40 and they returned to the Top 20 with their last hit, a revival of 'Save The Last Dance For Me'. It seemed that success came and went for the personable family in less than a heartbeat.

Albums: *Heartbeat - It's A Lovebeat* (1973), *Save The Last Dance For Me* (1974).

Delaney And Bonnie

Delaney Bramlett (b. 1 July 1939, Pontotoc, Mississippi, USA) first came to prominence as a member of the Shindogs, the houseband on US television's *Shindig*. As well as recording with the group, Delaney made several unsuccessful solo singles prior to meeting Bonnie Lynn (b. 8 November 1944, Acton, Illinois, USA) in California. His future wife had already sung with several impressive figures including Little Milton, Albert King and Ike And Tina Turner. The couple's first album, *Home*, produced by Leon Rusell and Donald 'Duck' Dunn, was only released in the wake of *Accept No Substitute* (1969). This exemplary white-soul collection featured several excellent Delaney compositions, including 'Get Ourselves Together' and 'Love Me A Little Bit Longer'. An expanded ensemble, which featured Bobby Keys (saxophone), Jim Price (trumpet), Bobby Whitlock (guitar), Carl Radle (bass) and Jim Keltner (drums) alongside the Bramletts, then toured America with Blind Faith. The Bramletts' refreshing enthusiasm inspired guitarist Eric Clapton, who guested with the revue in Britain. This period was documented on their *On Tour* (1970) collection and a powerful single, 'Comin' Home'. Lavish praise by the media and from George Harrison and Dave Mason was undermined when the backing group walked out to join Joe Cocker's *Mad Dogs And Englishmen* escapade. *To Bonnie From Delaney* (1970), recorded with the Dixie Flyers and Memphis Horns, lacked the purpose of previous albums. *Motel Shot*, an informal, documentary release, recaptured something of the duo's erstwhile charm, but it was clear that they had not survived the earlier defections. *Together* (1972) introduced their new deal with Columbia Records, but the couples' marriage was now collapsing and they broke up later that year. Delaney subsequently released several disappointing albums for MGM and Prodigal but Bonnie's three collections for Capricorn showed a greater urgency and she took to singing gospel when she become a 'born again' Christian. Overwhelmed by their brief spell in the spotlight, the duo is better recalled for the influence they had on their peers.

Albums: *Accept No Substitute - The Original Delaney & Bonnie* (1969), *Home* (1969), *Delaney & Bonnie & Friends On Tour With Eric Clapton* (1970), *To Bonnie From Delaney* (1970), *Motel Shot* (1971), *D&B Together* (1972), *Country Life* (1972). Compilation: *Best Of Delaney And Bonnie* (1972). Solo albums: Delaney Bramlett *Delaney* (1972), *Something's Coming* (1972), *Mobius Strip* (1973), *Giving Birth To A Song* (1975), *Class Reunion* (1977). Bonnie Bramlett *Sweet Bonnie Bramlett* (1973), *It's Time* (1975), *Lady's Choice* (1976), *Memories* (1978).

Denny, Sandy

b. Alexandra Elene Maclean Denny, 6 January 1947, Wimbledon, London, England, d. 21 April 1978, London, England. A former student at Kingston Art College where her contemporaries included John Renbourn and Jimmy Page, Sandy Denny forged her early reputation in such famous London folk clubs as Les Cousins, Bunjies and the Scots Hoose. Renowned for an eclectic repertoire, she featured material by Tom Paxton and her then boyfriend Jackson C. Frank as well as traditional English songs. Work from this early period was captured on two 1967 albums, *Sandy And Johnny* (with Johnny Silvo) and *Alex Campbell & His Friends*.

The following year the singer spent six months as a member of the Strawbs. Their lone album together was not released until 1973, but this melodic work contained several haunting Denny vocals and includes the original version of her famed composition, 'Who Knows Where The Time Goes'. In May 1968 Sandy joined Fairport Convention with whom she completed three excellent albums. Many of her finest performances date from this period, but when the group vowed to pursue a purist path at the expense of original material, the singer left to form Fotheringay. This accomplished quintet recorded a solitary album before internal pressures pulled it apart, but Sandy's contributions, notably 'The Sea', 'Nothing More' and 'The Pond And The Stream', rank among her finest work.

Denny's debut album, *North Star Grassman And The Ravens*, was issued in 1971. It contained several excellent songs, including 'Late November' and the expansive 'John The Gun', as well as sterling contributions from the renowned guitarist Richard Thompson, who would appear on all of the singer's releases. *Sandy* was another memorable collection, notable for the haunting 'It'll Take A Long Time' and a sympathetic version of Richard Farina's 'Quiet Joys Of Brotherhood', a staple of the early Fairport's set. Together, these albums confirmed Sandy as a major talent and a composer of accomplished, poignant songs.

Like An Old Fashioned Waltz, which included the gorgeous 'Solo', closed this particular period. Sandy married Trevor Lucas, her partner in Fotheringay, who was now a member of Fairport Convention. Despite her dislike of touring, she rejoined the group in 1974. A live set and the crafted *Rising For The Moon* followed, but Denny and Lucas then left in December 1975. A period of domesticity ensued before the singer completed *Rendezvous*, a charming selection which rekindled an interest in performing. Plans were made to record a new set in America, but following a fall down the staircase at a friend's house Sandy died from a cerebral haemorrhage on 21 April 1978. She is recalled as one of Britain's finest singer/songwriters and for work which has grown in stature over the years. Her effortless and smooth vocal delivery still sets the standard for many of today's female folk-based singers.

Albums: *The North Star Grassman And The Ravens* (1971), *Sandy* (1972), *Like An Old Fashioned Waltz* (1973), *Rendezvous* (1977). Compilations: *The Original Sandy Denny* (1984), *Who Knows Where The Time Goes* (1986), *The Best Of Sandy Denny* (1987).

Further reading: *Meet On The Ledge*, Patrick Humphries.

Denver, John

b. Henry John Deutschendorf Jnr., 31 December 1943, Roswell, New Mexico, USA. One of America's most popular performers during the 70s, Denver's rise to fame began when he was 'discovered' in a Los Angeles night club. He initially joined the Back Porch Majority, a nursery group for the renowned New Christy Minstrels but, tiring of his role there, left for the Chad Mitchell Trio where he forged a reputation as a talented songwriter.

With the departure of the last original member, the

Mitchell Trio became known as Denver, Boise and Johnson, but their brief life-span ended when John embarked on a solo career in 1969. One of his compositions, 'Leaving On A Jet Plane', provided an international hit for Peter, Paul And Mary, and this evocative song was the highlight of Denver's debut album, *Rhymes And Reasons*. Subsequent releases, *Take Me To Tomorrow* and *Whose Garden Was This*, garnered some attention, but it was not until the release of *Poems, Prayers And Promises* that the singer enjoyed popular acclaim when one of its tracks, 'Take Me Home, Country Roads', broached the US Top 3 and became a UK Top 20 hit for Olivia Newton-John in 1973. The song's undemanding homeliness established a light, almost naive style, consolidated on the albums *Aerie* and *Rocky Mountain High*. 'I'd Rather Be A Cowboy' (1973) and 'Sunshine On My Shoulders' (1974) were both gold singles, while a third million-seller, 'Annie's Song', secured Denver's international status when it topped the UK charts that same year and subsequently became an MOR standard, as well as earning the classical flautist James Galway a UK number 3 hit in 1978. Further US chart success came in 1975 with two number 1 hits, 'Thank God I'm A Country Boy' and 'I'm Sorry'. Denver's status as an all-round entertainer was enhanced by many television spectaculars, including *Rocky Mountain Christmas*, and further gold-record awards for *An Evening With John Denver* and *Windsong*, ensuring that 1975 was the artist's most successful year to date.

He continued to enjoy a high profile throughout the rest of the decade and forged a concurrent acting career with his role in the film comedy *Oh, God* with George Burns. In 1981 his songwriting talent attracted the attention of yet another classically trained artist, when opera singer Placido Domingo duetted with Denver on 'Perhaps Love'. However, although Denver became an unofficial musical ambassador with tours to Russia and China, his recording became less prolific as increasingly he devoted time to charitable work and ecological interests. Despite the attacks by music critics, who have deemed his work as bland and saccharine, Denver's cute, simplistic approach has nonetheless achieved a mass popularity which is the envy of many artists.

Albums: *Rhymes & Reasons* (1969), *Take Me To Tomorrow* (1970), *Whose Garden Was This* (1970), *Poems, Prayers And Promises* (1971), *Aerie* (1971), *Rocky Mountain High* (1972), *Farewell Andromeda* (1973), *Back Home Again* (1974), *An Evening With John Denver* (1975), *Windsong* (1975), *Rocky Mountain Christmas* (1975), *Live In London* (1976), *Spirit* (1976), *I Want To Live* (1977), *Live At The Sydney Opera House* (1978), *John Denver* (1979), with the Muppets *A Christmas Together* (1979), *Autograph* (1980), *Some Days Are Diamonds* (1981), with Placido Domingo *Perhaps Love* (1981), *Seasons Of The Heart* (1982), *It's About Time* (1983), *Dreamland Express* (1985), *One World* (1986), *Higher Ground* (1988), *Stonehaven Sunrise* (1989), *The Flower That Shattered The Stone* (1990), *Earth Songs* (1990). Compilations: *The Best Of John Denver* (1974), *The Best Of John Denver Volume 2* (1977), *The John Denver Collection* (1984), *Greatest Hits Volume 3* (1985).

Further reading: *The Man And His Music*, Leonore Fleischer. *Rocky Mountain Wonderboy*, James M. Martin.

Derek And The Dominos

Eric Clapton (b. 30 March 1945, Ripley, Surrey, England), formed this short-lived band in May 1970 following his departure from the supergroup Blind Faith and his brief involvement with the down-home loose aggregation of Delaney And Bonnie And Friends. He purloined three members of the latter; Carl Radle (bass), Bobby Whitlock (keyboards/vocals) and Jim Gordon (drums). Together with Duane Allman on guitar they recorded *Layla And Other Assorted Love Songs*, a superb double album. The band were only together for a year, during which time they toured the UK, playing small clubs, toured the USA, and imbibed copious amounts of hard and soft drugs. It was during his time with the Dominos that Eric became addicted to heroin. This however, did not detract from the quality of the music. In addition to the classic 'Layla' the album contained Clapton's co-written compositions mixed with blues classics like 'Key To The Highway' and a sympathetic reading of Jimi Hendrix's 'Little Wing'. The following live album, recorded on their USA tour, was a further demonstration of their considerable potential had they been able to hold themselves together.

Albums: *Layla And Other Assorted Love Songs* (1970), *In Concert* (1973).

Derringer, Rick

b. Richard Zehringer, 5 August 1947, Fort Recovery, Ohio, USA. Originally a member of the chart-topping McCoys, he produced two of their later albums, paving the way for his new career. Along with his brother Randy, Rick formed the nucleus of Johnny Winter's backing group. After

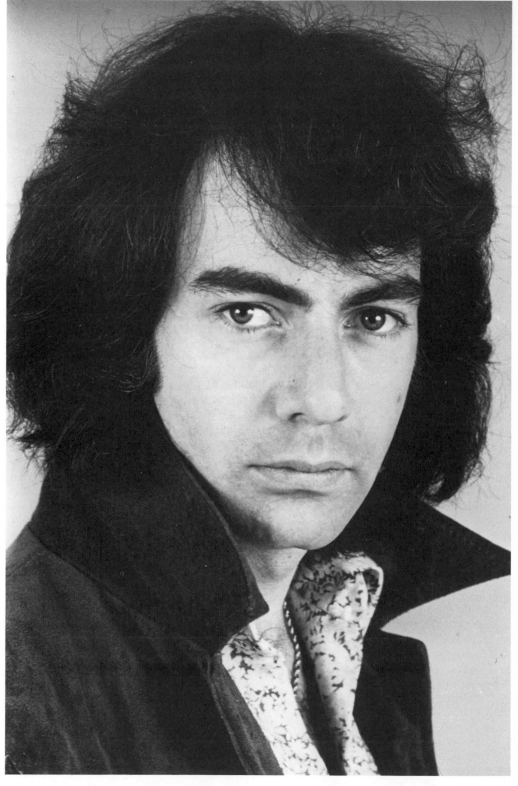

Neil Diamond

producing four of Winter's albums, Derringer joined the Edgar Winter Group and produced their best-selling 1973 album, *They Only Come Out At Night*. Meanwhile, Derringer finally recorded his first solo album, the heavy metal tinged *All American Boy* (1974). After several albums with the group Derringer, Rick reverted to solo work and appeared as guest guitarist on albums by Steely Dan, Bette Midler, Todd Rundgren, Donald Fagen and 'Weird Al' Yankovic.

Albums: *All American Boy* (1974), *Spring Fever* (1975), *Derringer* (1976), *Sweet Evil* (1977), *Live* (1977), *If You Weren't So Romantic* (1978), *Guitars And Women* (1979), *Face To Face* (1980).

Diamond, Neil

b. 24 January 1941, Brooklyn, New York, USA. With a career as a hitmaker stretching across three decades, Diamond has veered between straightforward pop, a progressive singer-songwriter style and middle-of-the-road balladry. He attended the same high school as Neil Sedaka and Bobby Feldman of the Strangeloves and began songwriting as a young teenager. He made his first records in 1960 for local label Duel with Jack Packer as Neil And Jack. After college, Diamond became a full-time songwriter in 1962, recording unsuccessfully for CBS before 'Sunday And Me' produced by Leiber And Stoller for Jay And The Americans brought his first success as a composer in 1965. The following year, Diamond made a third attempt at a recording career, joining Bert Berns' Bang label. With Jeff Barry and Ellie Greenwich as producers, he released 'Solitary Man' before the catchy 'Cherry Cherry' entered the US Top 10. In 1967 the Monkees had multi million-sellers with Diamond's memorable 'I'm A Believer' and 'A Little Bit Me, A little Bit You'. Like his own 1967 hit, 'Thank The Lord For The Night', these songs combined a gospel feel with a memorable pop melody. In the same year, Diamond also showed his mastery of the country-tinged ballad with 'Kentucky Woman'.

After a legal dispute with Bang, Diamond signed to MCA Records' Uni label, moving from New York to Los Angeles. After a failed attempt at a progressive rock album (*Velvet Gloves And Spit*) he began to record in Memphis and came up with a series of catchy, and simple hits, including 'Sweet Caroline' (1969), 'Holly Holy' and two number 1s, 'Cracklin Rosie' (1970) and 'Song Sung Blue' (1972). At the same time, Diamond was extending his range with the semi-concept album *Tap Root Manuscript* (on which Hollywood arranger Marty Paich orchestrated African themes) and the confessional ballad, 'I Am . . . I Said', a Top 10 single on both sides of the Atlantic. He was also much in demand for live shows and his dynamic act was captured on *Hot August Night*. Soon after its release, Diamond announced a temporary retirement from live appearances, and spent the next three years concentrating on writing and recording. He moved into film work, winning a Grammy award for the soundtrack of *Jonathan Livingston Seagull* to which his long-time arranger Lee Holdridge also contributed. *Beautiful Noise* (on his new label, CBS) was a tribute to the Brill Building songwriting world of the 50s and 60s. It cost nearly half a million dollars to make and was produced by Robbie Robertson. Diamond also appeared in *The Last Waltz*, the star-studded tribute movie to the Band.

In 1978, he recorded his first duet since 1960 and his biggest hit single. The wistful 'You Don't Bring Me Flowers' had previously been recorded solo by both Diamond and Barbra Streisand but after a disc jockey had spliced the tracks together, producer Bob Gaudio brought the pair together for the definitive version which headed the US chart. Now at the peak of his success, Diamond accepted his first film acting role in a re-make of *The Jazz Singer*. The film was undistinguished although Diamond's performance was credible. The soundtrack album sold a million, in part because of 'America', a rousing, patriotic Diamond composition which he later performed at the Statue Of Liberty centenary celebrations. During the 80s, he increasingly co-wrote songs with Gilbert Becaud, David Foster and above all Carole Bayer Sager and Burt Bacharach. They collaborated on the ballad 'Heartlight' (1982), inspired by the film *E.T.* The next year, UB 40 revived one of his earliest songs 'Red Red Wine' and had a UK number 1. There were also disputes with CBS, which insisted on changes to two of Diamond's proposed albums, bringing in Maurice White to produce *Headed For The Future*. However, 'The Best Years Of Our Lives', written by Diamond alone, showed a return to the form of the 70s while he worked on his 1991 album with leading contemporary producers Don Was and Peter Asher. Diamond has neither courted nor has been fully accepted by the *cognoscenti*, his track record however speaks volumes; almost 60 hits in the USA, over 30 charting albums and is one of the Top 20 most successful artists ever in the USA. His success in the UK is comparable with 26 charting albums and a fiercely loyal fan base.

Albums: *The Feel Of Neil Diamond* (1966), *Just For You* (1967), *Velvet Gloves And Spit* (1968), *Brother Love's Travelling Salvation Show* (1969), *Touching You, Touching Me* (1969), *Gold* (1970), *Shilo* (1970), *Tap Root Manuscript* (1970), *Do It* (1971), *Stones* (1971), *Moods* (1972), *Hot August Night* (1972), *Double Gold* (1973), *Rainbow* (1973), *Jonathan Livingston Seagull* (1974), *Serenade* (1974), *Beautiful Noise* (1976), *And The Singer Sings His Song* (1976), *Love At The Greek* (1977), *I'm Glad You're Here With Me Tonight* (1977), *You Don't Bring Me Flowers* (1978), *September Morn* (1980), *The Jazz Singer* (1980), *On The Way To The Sky* (1981), *Heartlight* (1982), *Primitive* (1984), *Headed For The Future* (1986), *Hot August II* (1987), *The Best Years Of Our Lives* (1989), *Lovescape* (1991). Selected compilations: *20 Golden Greats* (1978), *Diamonds* (1981), *Classics: The Early Years* (1983), *Red Red Wine* (1988), *Touching You Touching Me* (1988), *The Greatest Hits 1966-1992* (1993).

Dingoes

Working out of Melbourne's inner suburban pubs in 1973, the Dingoes soon became Australia's premier country-influenced rock band, using the popular American west coast sound of the time, but with Australian imagery in their lyrics, and featuring the fine talents of lead singer Broderick Smith and Kerryn Tolhurst and Chris Stockley on guitars. The band's initial success was due to the hard work of all the members over a long period in previous bands. After some commercial success with the first single and album in 1974, the band was keen to go overseas. Rather than tackling the American market directly, they established themselves in Canada in 1976. Despite sharing management with the Rolling Stones, under Peter Rudge the band was not able to break into the market as they had hoped. Their second album recorded in California in 1977, included several re-recordings of songs off their first album, in an attempt to appeal to the USA market. The album and subsequent singles failed to make much impact and Stockley departed early in 1978. The band took on an American as replacement and a third album was recorded amid growing despondency. The band broke up as *Orphans Of The Storm* was released, and gradually all the members returned home to Australia.
Albums: *The Dingoes* (1974), *Five Times The Sun* (1977), *Orphans Of The Storm* (1979).

Disco Tex And The Sex-O-Lettes

Led by Sir Monti Rock III (b. Joseph Montanez Jnr.) whose camp posturings in an extravagant white pimp suit made him a favourite in the gay and straight disco clubs in the USA and UK during the 70s, the group were put together by producer Bob Crewe. The outfit scored two highly influential hits on the Chelsea label in the US and UK charts with the irresistible 'Get Dancin'' (1974) hitting the US and UK Top 10 and 'I Wanna Dance Wit' Choo (Doo Dat Dance), Part One' (1975) making the UK Top 10 and US Top 30.
Album: *Disco Tex And The Sex-O-Lettes* (1975). Compilation: *Get Dancin'* (1989).

Dixie Dregs

Formed in 1973, the instrumental Dixie Dregs fused rock, jazz, classical and bluegrass with seamless musicianship, and one of their alumni, guitarist Steve Morse (b. 28 July 1954, Hamilton, Ohio, USA) is regarded as one of the most technically proficient players of that instrument. The group was formed by Morse, electric violinist Allen Sloan, bassist Andy West (b. 6 February 1954, Newport, Rhode Island, USA) and drummer Rod Morgenstein while attending the University of Miami School of Music in Florida, USA. Morse and West had played in the Augusta group Dixie Grit. They met Sloan, from Miami, and Morgenstein, from Plainview, New York, at the university and the four formed a group, adding Steve Davidowski on keyboards. For college credit, the quintet, now calling itself the Dixie Dregs, produced and recorded an album called *The Great Spectacular*, later privately issued in 1976 and long out of print. After graduating from college, the group moved to Augusta and began playing live dates. They were signed by Capricorn Records in December 1976 and moved to Atlanta, Georgia. Their debut album for the label, *Free Fall*, was released in spring 1977, and Mark Parrish replaced Davidowski that autumn. Their next two albums, *What If* and *Night Of The Living Dregs*, received critical acclaim and charted (as did the rest of their albums), the latter including one side of live performances from the Montreux Jazz Festival. After completion of that album, Tee Lavitz replaced Parrish. The group switched to Arista Records for *Dregs Of The Earth* and remained there for their last two, *Unsung Heroes* and *Industry Standard*. By the time of *Unsung Heroes*, they had shortened their name to the Dregs and for *Industry Standard*, had replaced Sloan with violinist Mark O'Connor, who stayed for about a year and later went on to record several solo albums of virtuoso bluegrass and jazz. The Dregs carried on as a

Disco Tex

quartet for several months and disbanded in 1982, and Morse's highly-acclaimed solo career began with the 1984 release of *The Introduction*. Rod Morgenstein later joined the pop-heavy metal band Winger. Some of the members of the Dixie Dregs reunited for a tour in 1988 but no albums were released.

Albums: *The Great Spectacular* (c.1976), *Free Fall* (1977), *What If* (1978), *Night Of The Living Dregs* (1979), *Dregs Of The Earth* (1980), *Unsung Heroes* (1981), *Industry Standard* (1982).

Dr. Feelgood

The most enduring act to emerge from the much touted 'pub rock' scene, Dr. Feelgood was formed in 1971. The original line-up included Lee Brilleaux (b. 1953; vocals/harmonica), Wilko Johnson (b. John Wilkinson, 1947; guitar), John B. Sparks (b. 1953; bass), John Potter (piano) and 'Bandsman' Howarth (drums). When the latter pair dropped out, the remaining trio recruited a permanent drummer in John 'The Big Figure' Martin. Initially based in Canvey Island, Essex, on the Thames estuary, Dr. Feelgood broke into the London circuit in 1974. Brilleaux's menacing personality complemented Johnson's propulsive, jerky stage manner, while the guitarist's staccato style, modelled on Mick Green of the Pirates, emphasized the group's idiosyncratic brand of rhythm and blues.

Their debut album, *Down By The Jetty*, was released in 1974, but despite critical approbation, it was not until the following year that the quartet secured due commercial success with *Stupidity*. Recorded live in concert, this raw, compulsive set topped the UK charts and the group's status seemed assured. However, internal friction led to Johnson's departure during sessions for a projected fourth album and although his replacement, John 'Gypie' Mayo, was an accomplished guitarist, he lacked the striking visual image of his predecessor. Dr. Feelgood then embarked on a more mainstream direction which was only intermittently successful. 'Milk And Alcohol' (1978) gave them their sole UK Top 10 hit, but they now seemed curiously anachronistic in the face of the punk upheaval. In 1981 Johnny Guitar replaced Mayo, while the following year both Sparks and the Big Figure decided to leave the line-up. Brilleaux has meanwhile continued undeterred, and while Dr. Feelgood can claim a loyal audience, it is an increasingly small one. However, they are a popular live attraction in the USA where their records also achieve commercial success.

Albums: *Down By The Jetty* (1975), *Malpractice* (1975), *Stupidity* (1976), *Sneakin' Suspicion* (1977), *Be Seeing You* (1977), *Private Practice* (1978), *As It Happens* (1979), *Let It Roll* (1979), *A Case Of The Shakes* (1980), *On The Job* (1981), *Fast Women And Slow Horses* (1982), *Doctor's Orders* (1986), *Brilleaux* (1986), *Classic Dr. Feelgood* (1987), *Mad Man Blues* (1988), *Live In London* (1990). Compilations: *Casebook* (1981), *Case History - The Best Of Dr. Feelgood* (1987), *Singles (The UA Years)* (1989).

Doctors Of Madness

When punk exploded on an unsuspecting UK music scene in 1976, several relatively established bands waiting in the wings were somehow dragged along with it. The Doctors Of Madness were one such group. Comprising the weird Richard 'Kid' Strange (vocals, guitar, keyboards, percussion), Stoner (bass, vocals, percussion), Peter (drums, percussion, vocals) and Urban (guitar, violin), the Doctors were already signed to Polydor Records and had already issued two rock albums verging on the theatrical by late 1976: *Late Night Movies, All Night Brainstorms* and *Figments Of Emancipation*. Much of their momentum was lost, however, when they issued only one single in 1977, 'Bulletin', and it was not until 1978 that *Sons Of Survival* appeared. By that time, the post-punk era had arrived, awash with new ideas, and the Doctors Of Madness seemed acutely out of date. They broke up soon after, their career later summarized on a compilation, *Revisionism*. Richard Strange, meanwhile, set about an erratic but fascinating solo career, which included such singles as 'International Language' (1980) on Cherry Red and the narcissistically-entitled album *The Phenomenal Rise Of Richard Strange* (1981) on Virgin Records.

Albums: *Late Night Movies, All Night Brainstorms* (1976), *Figments Of Emancipation* (1976), *Sons Of Survival* (1978). Compilation: *Revisionism (1975-78)* (1981).

Doobie Brothers

This enduring act evolved from Pud, a San Jose-based trio formed in March 1970 by Tom Johnson (b. Visalia, California, USA; guitar) and John Hartman (b. 18 March 1950, Falls Church, Virginia, USA; drums). Original bassist Greg Murphy was quickly replaced by Dave Shogren (b. San Francisco, California, USA). Patrick Simmons (b. 23 January 1950, Aberdeen, Washington, USA; guitar) then expanded the line-up, and within six

Doobie Brothers

months the group had adopted a new name, the Doobie Brothers, in deference to a slang term for a marijuana cigarette. Their muted debut album, although promising, was commercially unsuccessful and contrasted with the unit's tougher live sound. A new bassist, Tiran Porter and second drummer, Michael Hossack (b. 18 September 1950, Paterson, New York, USA), joined the group for *Toulouse Street*, which spawned the anthem-like (and successful) single, 'Listen To The Music'. This confident selection was a marked improvement on its predecessor, while the twin-guitar and twin-percussionist format inspired comparisons with the Allman Brothers Band. A third set, *The Captain And Me*, contained two infectious US hits, 'Long Train Running' and 'China Grove', while *What Were Vices...*, a largely disappointing album, did feature the Doobies' first US chart-topper, 'Black Water'. By this point the group's blend of harmonies and tight rock was proving highly popular, although critics pointed to a lack of invention and a reliance on proven formula. Michael Hossack was replaced by Keith Knudsen (b. 18 October 1952, Ames, Iowa, USA) for *Stampede*, which also introduced ex-Steely Dan guitarist, Jeff 'Skunk' Baxter (b. 13 December 1948, Washington DC, USA). In April 1975, his former colleague, Michael McDonald, (b. 2 December 1952, St Louis, Missouri, USA; keyboards/vocals) also joined the Doobies when founder member Johnson succumbed to a recurrent ulcer problem. Although the guitarist rejoined the group in 1976, he left again the following year. The arrival of McDonald heralded a new direction. He gradually assumed control of the group's sound, instilling the soul-based perspective revealed on the excellent *Minute By Minute* and its attendant US number 1 single, the ebullient 'What A Fool Believes'. Both Hartman and Baxter then left the line-up, but McDonald's impressive, distinctive voice proved a unifying factor. *Takin' It To The Streets* and its titled hit single maintained a high standard. *One Step Closer* featured newcomers John McFee (b. 18 November 1953, Santa Cruz, California, USA; guitar), Cornelius Bumpus (b. 13 January 1952; sax/keyboards) and Chet McCracken (b. 17 July 1952, Seattle, Washington, USA; drums) yet it was arguably the group's most accomplished album. Willie Weeks subsequently replaced Porter, but by 1981 the Doobies' impetus was waning. They split in October the following year, with McDonald and Simmons embarking on contrasting solo careers. Johnson released a solo album in 1979

Everything You've Heard Is True and a second in 1981, *Still Feels Good To Me*. However, a reformed unit, comprising the *Toulouse Street* line-up, plus long-time conga player Bobby Lakind, completed a 1989 release, *Cycles*, on which traces of their one-time verve are still apparent. They found a similar audience and 'The Doctor' made the US Top 10. The Doobie Brothers remain critically underrated, their track record alone making them one of the major US rock bands of the 70s.
Albums: *The Doobie Brothers* (1971), *Toulouse Street* (1972), *The Captain And Me* (1973), *What Were Once Vices Are Now Habits* (1974), *Stampede* (1975), *Takin' It To The Streets* (1976), *Livin' On The Fault Line* (1977), *Minute By Minute* (1980), *One Step Closer* (1981), *Farewell Tour* (1974), *Cycles* (1989), *Brotherhood* (1991). Compilations: *The Best Of The Doobie Brothers* (1976), *Best Of The Doobies* (1980), *The Best Of The Doobies Volume 2* (1981).

Dragon

Along with Split Enz, Dragon were considered one of New Zealand's finest rock exports. Formed in 1972 and based around the Hunter brothers (Mark and Todd), the band has been together for nearly two decades. Their early influences were English rock-based bands and they released two albums in New Zealand, but by the time the band emigrated to Australia in 1975, its leanings were towards silky-smooth, soul-inspired melodies, highlighting the songwriting of Paul Hewson. Hits such as 'April Sun In Cuba' and 'Are You Old Enough' were in the middle of a run of seven Top 10 singles and four Top 20 albums. They were highly popular with the young teenage audience, and yet the band also had a rapport with the older generation. The group were not short of publicity, with frequent newspaper stories on the excesses indulged by the band and the arrogance of its members. Despite the deaths of Hewson and early drummer Neal Storey due to drug overdoses, the band toured extensively but eventually imploded in 1979 due to friction between members. Marc Hunter released a solo album and Top 20 single 'Island Nights', which encouraged him to form his own band to tour and promote the album. 1990 saw him record an album of jazz covers. Todd Hunter collaborated with Johanne Piggott, in the bands XL Capris and Scribble, which received some attention. Dragon re-formed in 1982, releasing several hit singles (co-written with Piggot), again illustrating the talent of the band, which currently consists of the Hunter brothers, who add musicians when needed.

Albums: *Universal Radio* (1973), *Scented Gardens For The Blind* (1974), *Sunshine* (1977), *Running Free* (1977), *Ozambezi* (1978), *Powerplay* (1979), *Live* (1984), *Dreams Of Ordinary Men* (1986), *Bondi Road* (1989).

Driver 67

An alias for Paul Phillips, this act had a surprise UK hit during Christmas 1978 with the novelty record 'Car 67', concerning a mini-cab driver despatched to pick up the former love of his life. The song was performed in the manner of the cabby talking to his controller over the radio. After the follow-up single 'Headlights' flopped, Phillips went on to be a successful publisher with magazines like the highly-rated black music weekly *Echoes*, and *Video Trade Weekly*. Perhaps, not surprisingly, he does not wish to be reminded of his former career.

Ducks Deluxe

Denizens of London's 70s' 'pub rock' circuit, Ducks Deluxe was formed in 1972 by Sean Tyla (b. 3 August 1947, Barlow, Yorkshire, England; guitar/vocals) and ex-Help Yourself member Ken Whaley (bass). The line-up was completed by former Brinsley Schwarz roadie, Martin Belmont (b. 21 December 1948, Grove Park, London, England; guitar) and Tim Roper (b. 9 April 1953, Hampstead, London, England; drums), before Whaley was replaced by Nick Garvey (b. 26 April 1951, Stoke-on-Trent, Staffordshire, England). The reconstituted quartet completed *Ducks Deluxe*, an exciting, emphatic set drawn from rock's traditional sources. Andy McMaster (b. 27 July 1947, Glasgow, Scotland; keyboards) expanded the group for *Taxi To The Terminal Zone*, but dissent over Tyla's autocratic rule resulted in a split. Garvey and McMasters left in October 1974; they were later reunited in the Motors, while Mick Groom (bass) joined the now-ailing Ducks. Although popular in Europe, the band was all but ignored at home and a dispirited Roper quit the following year. Brinsley Schwarz (guitar) and Billy Rankin (drums), both from the defunct Brinsley Schwarz group, augmented Ducks Deluxe on a tour of France, but the group broke up on 1 July 1975 following a final appearance at London's 100 Club. Martin Belmont later resurfaced in Graham Parker And The Rumour, while Tyla formed the Tyla Gang with the prodigal Ken Whaley.
Albums: *Ducks Deluxe* (1974), *Taxi To The Terminal Zone* (1975). Compilations: *Don't Mind Rockin' Tonite* (1978), *Last Night Of A Pub Rock Band* (1982).

Dundas, David

b. c.1945, Oxford, England. The son of the Marquess of Zetland, Dunda's original vocation in life was as an actor, mainly playing minor roles on stage, television and film, at one point working alongside Judy Geeson and David Niven in *Prudence And The Pill* (1968). Eschewing the actor's life, Dundas' claim to fame in the music world came when, as an advertising jingle writer, his work for the Brutus jeans advert on UK television spawned the hit single 'Jeans On'. The Dundas composition was fleshed-out with help from Roger Greenaway, and released on the Air/Chrysalis label, eventually reaching number 3 in the UK charts in the summer of 1976. The tune also reached the US Top 20 in January the following year. His only other UK chart entry came in 1977 with 'Another Funny Honeymoon' which reached number 29. He released two, for the most part, unremarkable albums for Chrysalis before taking up a career as a composer. His recent credits include the scores for *Dark City*, *Withnail And I* (with Rick Wentworth) and *How To Get Ahead In Advertising*.
Albums: *David Dundas* (1977), *Vertical Hold* (1978).

Dury, Ian

b. 12 May 1942, Upminster, Essex, England. The zenith of Dury's musical career, *New Boots And Panties*, came in 1977, when youth was being celebrated amid power chords and bondage trousers - he was 35 at the time. Stricken by polio at the age of seven, he initially decided on a career in art, and until his 28th birthday taught the subject at Canterbury School of Art. He began playing pubs and clubs in London with Kilburn And The High Roads, reinterpreting R&B numbers and later adding his own wry lyrics in a semi-spoken cockney slang. The group dissolved and the remainder became a new line-up called the Blockheads. In 1975 Stiff Records signed the group and considered Dury's aggressive but honest stance the perfect summary of the contemporary mood. The Blockheads' debut and finest moment, *New Boots And Panties*, received superlative reviews and spent more than a year in the UK albums chart. His dry wit, sensitivity and brilliant lyrical caricatures were evident in songs like 'Clever Trevor', 'Wake Up And Make Love To Me' and his tribute to Gene Vincent, 'Sweet Gene Vincent'. He lampooned the excesses of the music business on 'Sex And Drugs And Rock And Roll' and briefly crossed over from critical acclaim to commercial acceptance with the UK number 1 'Hit Me With Your Rhythm Stick' in December

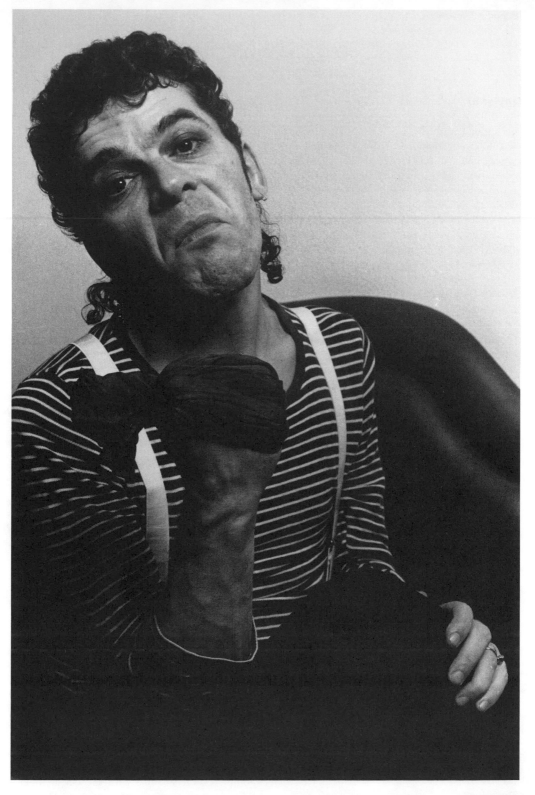

Ian Dury

1979. *Do It Yourself* and *Laughter* were similarly inspired although lacking the impact of his debut, and by his third album he had teamed up with Wilko Johnson (ex-Dr. Feelgood) and lost the co-writing services of pianist Chaz Jankel. He continued to work towards a stronger dance context and employed the masterful rhythm section of Sly Dunbar and Robbie Shakespeare on *Lord Upminster* which also featured the celebrated jazz trumpeter Don Cherry. He continued to make thoughtful, polemic records in the 80s and audaciously suggested that his excellent song, 'Spasticus Autisticus', should be adopted as the musical emblem of the Year Of The Disabled. Like many before him, he turned to acting and appeared in several television plays and films in the late 80s. In 1989 he wrote the musical *Apples* with another former member of the Blockheads, Mickey Gallagher. In the 90s Dury was seen hosting a late night UK television show *Metro*.

Albums: with the Kilburns *Handsome* (1975), *Wot A Bunch* (1978), *Kilburn And The High Roads* (1982), *Upminster Kids* (1983); solo and with the Blockheads *New Boots And Panties* (1977), *Do It Yourself* (1979), *Laughter* (1980), *Lord Upminster* (1981), *Juke Box Dury* (1981), *4,000 Weeks Holiday* (1984). Compilation: *Greatest Hits* (1981).

E

Eagles

Formed in Los Angeles, California in 1971, this highly successful unit comprised of musicians drawn from singer Linda Ronstadt's backing group. Of the original quartet Bernie Leadon (b. 19 July 1947, Minneapolis, Minnesota, USA; guitar/vocals) boasted the most prodigious pedigree, having embraced traditional country music with the Scottsville Squirrel Barkers, before bringing such experience to rock as a member of Hearts And Flowers, Dillard And Clark and the Flying Buritto Brothers. Randy Meisner (b. 8 March 1947, Scottsbluff, Nabraska, USA; bass/vocals) was formerly of Poco and Rick Nelson's Stone Canyon Band, Glenn Frey (b. 6 November 1948, Detroit, Michigan, USA; guitar/vocals) had recorded as half of Longbranch Pennywhistle, while Don Henley (b. 22 July 1947, Gilmer, Texas, USA; drums/vocals) had led Texas-based aspirants Shiloh. Such pedigrees ensured interest in the new venture, which was immediately signed to David Geffen's nascent Asylum label. *The Eagles*, recorded in London under the aegis of producer Glyn Johns, contained 'Take It Easy', co-written by Frey and Jackson Browne and 'Witchy Woman', both of which reached the US Top 20 and established the quartet's meticulous harmonies and relaxed, but purposeful country-rock sound. Critical reaction to *Desperado*, an ambitious concept album based on a western theme, firmly established the group as leaders in their field and contained several of their most enduring compositions. The follow-up, *On The Border*, reasserted the unit's commerciality. 'Best Of My Love' became their first US number 1 while new member Don Felder (b. 21 September 1947, Topanga, California, USA; guitar/vocals), drafted from David Blue's backing group in March 1974, considerably bolstered the Eagles' sound. The reshaped quintet reached superstar status with *One Of These Nights*, the title track from which also topped the US charts. This platinum-selling album included 'Lyin' Eyes', now considered a standard, and the anthemic 'Take It To The Limit'. The album also established the Eagles as an international act; each of these tracks reached the UK Top 30, but the new-found pressure proved too great for Leadon who left the line-up in December 1975.

He subsequently pursed a low-key career with the Leadon-Georgiades band. His replacement was Joe Walsh (b. 20 November 1947, Wichita, Kansas, USA), former lead guitarist with the James Gang and a successful solo artist in his own right. His somewhat surprising induction was tempered by the knowledge that he shared the same manager as his new colleagues. The choice was ratified by the powerful *Hotel California*, which topped the US album charts for eight weeks and spawned two number 1 singles in the title track and 'New Kid In Town'. The set has become the Eagles' most popular collection, selling nine million copies in its year of release alone, as well as appearing in many 'all time great' albums listings. A seasonal recording, 'Please Come Home For Christmas', was the quintet's sole recorded offering for 1978 and internal ructions the following year resulted in Meisner's departure. His replacement, Timothy B. Schmit (b. 30 October 1947, Sacramento, California, USA), was another former member of Poco, but by this point the Eagles' impetus was waning. *The Long Run* was generally regarded as disappointing, despite containing a fifth US number 1 in 'Heartache Tonight', and a temporary hiatus taken at the end of the decade became a fully-fledged break in 1982 when long-standing disagreements could not be resolved. Henley, Frey and Felder began solo careers with contrasting results, while Walsh resumed the path he had followed prior to joining the group. Although latterly denigrated as representing 70s musical conservatism and torpidity, the Eagles' quest for perfection and committed musical skills rightly led to their becoming one of the era's leading acts.

Albums: *The Eagles* (1972), *Desperado* (1973), *On The Border* (1974), *One Of These Nights* (1975), *Hotel California* (1976), *The Long Run* (1979), *Eagles - Live* (1980). Compilations: *Their Greatest Hits 1971-1975* (1976), *Greatest Hits Volume 2* (1982), *Best Of The Eagles* (1985), *The Legend Of The Eagles* (1987).

East Of Eden

Formed in 1968, this versatile UK group originally consisted of Dave Arbus (violin), Ron Gaines (alto saxophone), Geoff Nicholson (lead guitar), Andy Sneddon (bass) and Geoff Britton (drums). Their debut *Mercator Projected*, offered an imaginative brew of progressive rock, jazz and neo-eastern predilections, but this robust, *avant garde* direction contrasted with the novelty tag placed on the group in the wake of their surprise hit single, 'Jig A Jig'. This lightweight, fiddle-based instrumental

Eagles

reached number 7 in the UK in April 1971, and in the process confused prospective audiences. East Of Eden was plagued by personnel problems and by 1972 had shed every original member. Joe O'Donnell (violin), Garth Watt-Roy (guitar, ex-Greatest Show On Earth), Martin Fisher (bass) and Jeff Allen (drums, ex-Beatstalkers) then maintained the group's name before their demise later in the decade. Meanwhile, Arbus gained further acclaim for his contributions to the Who's *Who's Next* album while Geoff Britton later joined Wings.

Albums: *Mercator Projected* (1969), *Snafu* (1970), *East Of Eden* (1971), *New Leaf* (1971), *Another Eden* (1975), *Here We Go Again* (1976), *It's The Climate* (1976), *Silver Park* (1978). Compilations: *The World Of East Of Eden* (1971), *Masters Of Rock* (1975), *Things* (1976).

Eddie And The Hot Rods

Formed in 1975, this quintet from Southend, Essex, England, originally comprised Barrie Masters (vocals), Lew Lewis (harmonica), Paul Gray (bass), Dave Higgs (guitar), Steve Nicol (drums) plus 'Eddie', a short-lived dummy that Masters pummelled on stage. After one classic single, 'Writing On The Wall', Lewis left, though he appeared on the high energy 'Horseplay', the flip-side of their cover of Sam The Sham And The Pharoahs' 'Wooly Bully'. Generally regarded as a younger, more energetic version of Dr Feelgood, the Rods pursued a tricky route between the conservatism of pub rock and the radicalism of punk. During the summer of 1976, the group broke house records at the Marquee Club with a scorching series of raucous, sweat-drenched performances. Their power was well captured on a live EP which included a cover of ? And The Mysterians' '96 Tears' and a clever amalgamation of the Rolling Stones' 'Satisfaction' and Them's 'Gloria'.

The arrival of guitarist Graeme Douglas from the Kursaal Flyers gave the group a more commercial edge and a distinctive jingle-jangle sound. A guest appearance on former MC5 singer Robin Tyner's 'Till The Night Is Gone' was followed by the strident 'Do Anything You Want To Do', which provided a Top 10 hit in the UK. A fine second album, *Life On The Line* was striking enough to suggest a long term future, but the group fell victim to diminishing returns. Douglas left, followed by Gray, who joined the Damned. Masters disbanded the group for a spell but reformed the unit for pub gigs and small label appearances.

Albums: *Teenage Depression* (1976), *Life On The Line* (1977), *Thriller* (1979), *Fish 'N' Chips* (1980), *One Story Town* (1985), *The Curse Of The Rods* (1990).

Edelman, Randy

This US vocalist won his audience by writing and performing some classic love songs. He made his debut in 1972, with a self-titled album that went largely unnoticed. During the 70s, however, he slowly built up his reputation and finally reached the big time with the worldwide smash 'Uptown Uptempo Woman'. His highest chart entry in the UK came with a revival of Unit Four Plus Two's 1965 hit 'Concrete And Clay'. By 1978 his singles career had ground to a halt. During this period one of his songs 'Weekend In New England' was covered and made into a million selling record by Barry Manilow. An attempted comeback in 1982 failed, but a new career was found when he was invited to provide the music for a new animated feature *The Care Bears*. He went on to write and perform the soundtrack for a number of movies and by 1988 was in the big league writing scores for movies including *Parenthood* and *Kindergarden Cop*.

Albums: *Randy Edelman* (1972), *Laughter And Tears* (1973), *Prime Cuts* (1975), *Fairwell Fairbanks* (1976), *If Love Is Real* (1977), *You're The One* (1979), *On Time* (1982), *... And His Piano* (1984). Compilation: *Best Of* (1979).

Edmunds, Dave

b. 15 April 1944, Cardiff, Wales. The multi-talented Edmunds has sustained a career for many years by being totally in touch with modern trends while maintaining a passionate love for music of the 50s and 60s, notably rockabilly, rock 'n' roll and country music. He first came to the public eye as lead guitarist of Love Sculpture with an astonishing solo played at breakneck speed on their only hit, Khatchaturian's 'Sabre Dance'. At the end of the 60s Edmunds built his own recording studio, Rockfield. The technical capabilities of Rockfield soon became apparent, as Edmunds became a masterful producer working with Shakin' Stevens, the Flamin' Groovies and Brinsley Schwarz. The Brinsley's bass player was Nick Lowe, and they formed a musical partnership that lasted many years. Edmunds' own recordings were few, but successful. He brilliantly reproduced the sound of his rock 'n' roll heroes and had hits with Smiley Lewis's 'I Hear You Knocking', the Ronettes' 'Baby, I Love You' and the Chordettes, 'Born To

Dave Edmunds

Be With You'. The former was a worldwide hit selling several million copies and topping the UK charts. In 1975 his debut *Subtle As A Flying Mallet* was eclipsed by his credible performance in the film *Stardust* and he wrote and sang on most of the Jim McLaine (David Essex) tracks. *Get It* in 1977 featured the fast-paced Nick Lowe composition, 'I Knew the Bride' which gave Edmunds another hit. Lowe wrote many of the songs on *Tracks On Wax* in 1978, during a hectic stage in Edmund's career when he played with Emmylou Harris, Carl Perkins, with his own band Rockpile, and appeared at the Knebworth Festival and the Rock For Kampuchea concert. *Repeat When Necessary* arrived in 1979 to favourable reviews; it stands as his best album. He interpreted Elvis Costello's 'Girls Talk', giving it a full production with layers of guitars, and the record was a major hit. Other outstanding tracks were 'Crawling From The Wreckage' written by Graham Parker, 'Queen Of Hearts' and the 50s sounding 'Sweet Little Lisa'. The latter contained arguably one of the finest rockabilly/country guitar solos ever recorded, although the perpetrator is Albert Lee and not Edmunds. The fickle public ignored the song and the album barely scraped into the Top 40. The following year Edmunds succeeded with Guy Mitchell's 50s hit 'Singin' The Blues' and the road-weary Rockpile released their only album, having been previously prevented from doing so for contractual reasons. The regular band of Edmunds, Lowe, Billy Bremner and Terry Williams was already a favourite on the UK pub-rock circuit. Their *Seconds Of Pleasure* was unable to do justice to the atmosphere they created at live shows, although it was a successful album. In 1981 Edmunds charted again, teaming up with the Stray Cats and recording George Jones' 'The Race Is On', although a compilation of Edmund's work that year, failed to sell. His style changed for the Jeff Lynne- produced *Information* in 1983; not surprisingly he sounded more like Lynne's ELO. As a producer he won many friends by crafting the Everly Brothers' comeback albums *EB84* and *Born Yesterday* and he wrote much of the soundtrack for *Porky's Revenge*. He was producer of the television tribute to Carl Perkins; both Edmunds and George Harrison are long-time admirers, and Edmunds cajoled the retiring Harrison to make a rare live appearance. During the mid-80s Edmunds worked with the Fabulous Thunderbirds, Jeff Beck, Dr. Feelgood, k.d. lang and Status Quo. His own music was heard during his first tour for some years together with the live *I Hear You Rockin'*, although more attention was given to Edmunds for bringing Dion back into the centre stage with live gigs and an album. Edmunds, like his US counterpart Leon Russell, has made a major contribution to popular music, but not by stealing the limelight. He is a major figure destined to be able to work freely in his chosen area with his undiminished love for old fashioned rock 'n' roll.

Albums: *Subtle As A Flying Mallet* (1975), *Get It* (1977), *Tracks On Wax* (1978), *Repeat When Necessary* (1979), *Seconds Of Pleasure* (1980), *Twangin'* (1981), *D.E.7th* (1982), *Information* (1983), *Riff Raff* (1984), *I Hear You Rockin'* (1987), *Closer To The Flame* (1990). Compilations: *The Best Of Dave Edmunds* (1981), *The Original Rockpile Vol2* (1987), *The Complete Early Edmunds* (1991).

Egan, Walter

An accomplished singer, guitarist and songwriter, Egan first attracted attention on a UK tour, accompanying former Kaleidoscope member Chris Darrow. Their association helped introduce the younger musician to the Los Angeles-based fraternity and he achieved due recognition when one of his songs, 'Hearts On Fire', was recorded by Gram Parsons. He then formed the short-lived Southpaw, which also included Jules Shear and Stephen Hague. In 1976 Egan embarked on a solo career. *Fundamental Roll* was produced by Fleetwood Mac mainstays Lindsay Buckingham and Stevie Nicks, while the former was also responsible for overseeing a second set, *Not Shy*. This entertaining album included 'Magnet And Steel', Egan's solo hit single which reached number 8 in the US chart. His brand of pop-cum-country grew progressively less popular and after the release of the *Wild Exhibitions* in 1983, the artist released no further albums throughout the 80s.

Albums: *Fundamental Roll* (1977), *Not Shy* (1978), *Hi Fi* (1979), *The Last Stroll* (1980), *Wild Exhibitions* (1983).

Egg

Egg was formed in July 1968 by Dave Stewart (keyboards), Hugh Montgomery 'Mont' Campbell (bass/vocals) and Clive Brooks (drums). The three musicians were all previous members of Uriel, a flower-power influenced group which had featured guitarist Steve Hillage. Egg recorded two albums, *Egg* and *The Polite Force*, between 1970 and 1972. Stylistically similar to the Soft Machine, these releases featured Stewart's surging keyboard work and a complex, compositional flair, bordering on the mathematical. The group's aficionados were thus stunned when Brooks abandoned this experimental path for the more orthodox, blues-based Groundhogs, and his departure resulted in Egg's demise. Stewart rejoined former colleague Hillage in the short-lived Khan, before replacing David Sinclair in Hatfield And The North.

However, the three original members of Egg were later reunited for the final album, *The Civil Surface*, on the Virgin Records subsidiary label, Caroline, before dissolving again. Stewart and Campbell remained together in another experimental group, National Health, but then embarked on separate paths. The former has latterly enjoyed several hit singles by rearranging well-known 60s songs. 'It's My Party', a collaboration with singer Barbara Gaskin, topped the UK charts in 1981 but, for all their charm, such releases contrast the left-field explorations of his earlier trio.

Albums: *Egg* (1970), *The Polite Force* (1970), *The Civil Surface* (1974). Compilation: *Seven Is A Jolly Good Time* (1988).

801

Formed by Roxy Music guitarist Phil Manzanera in 1976 comprising, Lloyd Watson (slide guitar/vocals) Francis Monkman (keyboards) Bill MacCormick (bass) and Simon Phillips (drums), during one of Roxy's quiet periods. Manzanera's initial impetus was to form a group to perform material from his own 1975 album, *Diamond Head* and his pre-Roxy group, Quiet Sun's reunion recording *Mainstream*. The group took their name from the 'True Wheel' song on Brian Eno's *Taking Tiger Mountain (By Strategy)*. 'We are the 801/We are the central shaft'. The other members were already vastly experienced musicians; Francis Monkham had recorded three albums with Curved Air before turning to session work; Bill MacCormick who had played in Quiet Sun from 1970-71, recorded two albums as a member of Robert Wyatt's Matching Mole in 1972 and joined Gong in 1973. He also appeared on various albums by Wyatt, Eno and Manzanera among others. Simon Phillips was a session drummer who had played on albums by Roger Glover, Greenslade and Jack Bruce. With this line-up, 801 only played three gigs, culminating in a sell-out at the Queen Elizabeth Hall, London on 3 September 1976 recorded for *801 Live*. Material played that evening was drawn from Manzanera's *Diamond Head*, Quiet Sun and Eno's *Here Come The Warm Jets*, *Taking Tiger Mountain* and *Another Green World*, as well as performing covers of the Beatles 'Tomorrow Never Knows' and the Kinks 'You Really Got Me'. The group folded immediately following this gig but Manzanera issued one further 801 album *Listen Now*, in 1977 using various rock luminaries as special guests before taking revamped 801 on the road. The group finally dissolved after Roxy Music's re-activation in 1978.

Albums: *801 Live* (1976), *Listen Now* (1977)

Electric Light Orchestra The original ELO line-up comprised of Roy Wood (b. 8 November 1946, Birmingham, England; vocals/cello/woodwind/guitars), Jeff Lynne (b. 30 December 1947, Birmingham, England; vocals/piano/guitar) and Bev Bevan (b. Beverley Bevan, 25 November 1945, Birmingham, England; drums). They had all been members of pop group the Move, but viewed this new venture as a means of greater self-expression. Vowing to 'carry on where the Beatles' "I Am The Walrus" left off', they completed an experimental debut set with the aid of Bill Hunt (french horn) and Steve Woolam (violin). Despite their lofty ambitions, the group still showed traces of its earlier counterpart with Lynne's grasp of melody much in evidence, particularly on the startling '10538 Overture', a UK Top 10 single in 1972. Although Woolam departed, the remaining quartet added Hugh McDowell, Andy Craig (cellos), ex-Balls keyboardist Richard Tandy (b. 26 March 1948, Birmingham, England; bass/piano/guitar) and Wilf Gibson (b. 28 February 1945, Dilston, Northumberland, England; violin) for a series of indifferent live appearances, following which Wood took Hunt and McDowell to form Wizzard. With Craig absenting himself from either party, the remaining quartet maintained the ELO name with the addition of Mike D'Albuquerque (b. 24 June 1947, Wimbledon, London, England; bass/vocals) and cellists Mike Edwards (b. 31 May, Ealing, London, England) and Colin Walker (b. 8 July 1949, Minchinhampton, Gloucestershire, England). The reshaped line-up completed the transitional *ELO II* and scored a Top 10 single with an indulgent version of Chuck Berry's 'Roll Over Beethoven' which included quotes from Beethoven's 5th Symphony. ELO enjoyed a third hit with 'Showdown', but two ensuing singles, 'Ma Ma Ma Ma Belle' and 'Can't Get It Out Of My Head', surprisingly failed to chart. However, the latter song reached the US Top 10 which in turn helped its attendant album, *Eldorado*, achieve gold status. By this point the group's line-up had stabilized around Lynne, Bevan, Tandy and the prodigal McDowell, Kelly Groucett (bass), Mik Kaminski (violin) and Melvyn Gale (cello). They became a star attraction on America's lucrative stadium circuit and scored considerable commercial success with *A New World Record*, *Out Of The Blue* and *Discovery*. Lynne's compositions successfully steered the line between pop and rock, inspiring commentators to compare his group with the Beatles. Between 1976 and 1981 ELO scored an unbroken run of 15 UK Top 20 singles, including 'Livin' Thing' (1976), 'Telephone Line' (1977),

Electric Light Orchestra

'Mr. Blue Sky' (1978) 'Don't Bring Me Down' (1979) and 'Xanadu', a chart-topping collaboration with Olivia Newton-John, taken from the film of the same name. The line-up had now been slimmed to that of Lynne, Bevan, Tandy and Grouchett, but recurrent legal and distribution problems conspired to undermine ELO's momentum. *Time* and *Secret Messages* lacked the verve of earlier work and the group's future was put in doubt by a paucity of releases and Lynne's growing disenchantment. The guitarist's subsequent pursuance of a solo career signalled a final split, but in 1991 Bevan emerged with ELO 2. It remains doubtful that he can regain the heights scaled in the 70s when Lynne's songwriting talent seemed untenable.

Albums: *Electric Light Orchestra* aka *No Answer* (1971), *ELO II* (1973), *On The Third Day* (1973), *The Night The Lights Went On In Long Beach* (1974), *Eldorado* (1975), *Face The Music* (1975), *A New World Record* (1976), *Out Of The Blue* (1977), *Discovery* (1979), with Olivia Newton-John *Xanadu* (1980, film soundtrack), *Time* (1981), *Secret Messages* (1983), *Balance Of Power* (1986). Selected compilations: *Showdown* (1974), *Ole ELO* (1976), *The Light Shines On* (1976), *Greatest Hits* (1979), *A Box Of Their Best* (1980), *First Movement* (1986), *A Perfect World Of Music* (1988).

Elf

This UK heavy-rock unit was formed in 1970 by vocalist Ronnie James Dio (b. Ronald Padavona) with Steve Edwards (guitar), Mickey Lee Soule (keyboards), Craig Gruber (bass), Gary Driscoll (drums) and Mark Nausseef (percussion). Delivering a mixture of hard-rock, boogie and blues, they impressed Deep Purple's Roger Glover enough for him to offer them his production skills and a deal with Purple Records. They supported Deep Purple on their 1974 tour, promoting their newly released *Carolina County Ball*. This was undoubtedly their finest work and is still highly regarded by metal aficionados today. After the erratic *Trying To Burn The Sun*, Elf became redundant as Ritchie Blackmore hired Dio, Soule, Gruber and Edwards to help record his solo album *Ritchie Blackmore's Rainbow*.

Albums: *Elf* (1972), *Carolina County Ball* (1974), *Trying To Burn The Sun* (1975), *Live* (1976).

Ellington, Marc

This 70s singer and songwriter failed to achieve any great commercial success, despite recording with a number of highly respected musicians, including Richard Thompson and Simon Nicol. *Marc Time* followed more of a country direction, and for this Ellington was joined by steel guitarist and dobro player B.J. Cole. Ellington was also engaged in much session work and provided back-up on albums by Fairport Convention and Matthew's Southern Comfort.

Albums: *Marc Ellington* (1969), *Rains/Reins Of Change* (1971), *A Question Of Roads* (1972), *Restoration* (1972), *Marc Time* (1975).

England Dan And John Ford Coley

Dan Seals (b. 8 February 1950, McCamey, Texas, USA) comes from a family of performing Seals. His father played bass for many country stars (Ernest Tubb, Bob Wills) and his brother, Jimmy, was part of the Champs and then Seals And Croft. His cousins include 70s country star Johnny Duncan and songwriters Chuck Seals ('Crazy Arms') and Troy Seals. Seals formed a partnership with John Ford Coley (b. 13 October 1951) and they first worked as Southwest F.O.B., the initials representing Freight On Board. The ridiculous name did not last, but Jimmy, not wanting them to be called Seals And Coley, suggested England Dan And John Ford Coley. Their first albums for A&M sold moderately well, but they struck gold in 1976 with a move to Big Tree Records. The single, 'I'd Really Love To See You Tonight', went to number 2 in the US charts and also made the UK Top 30, although its hook owed something to James Taylor's 'Fire And Rain'. The resulting album, *Nights Are Forever*, was a big seller and the pair opted for a fuller sound which drew comparisons with the Eagles. The title track, 'Nights Are Forever Without You', was another Top 10 single. With their harmonies, acoustic-based songs and tuneful melodies, they appealed to the same market as the Eagles and, naturally, Seals And Croft. They had further US hits with 'It's Sad To Belong', 'Gone Too Far', 'We'll Never Have To Say Goodbye Again' and 'Love Is The Answer'. When the duo split, Seals, after a few setbacks, became a country star. Coley found a new partner, but their 1981 album, *Kelly Leslie And John Ford Coley*, was not a success.

Albums: as Southwest F.O.B. *Smell Of Incense* (1968), *England Dan And John Ford Coley* (1971), *Fables* (1971), *I Hear The Music* (1976), *Nights Are Forever* (1976), *Dowdy Ferry Road* (1977), *Some Things Don't Come Easy* (1978), *Dr. Heckle And Mr. Jive* (1978), *Just Tell Me If You Love Me* (1980).

Enid

Influential art-rockers, formed in 1974 at experimental school Finchden Manor by keyboardist Robert John Godfrey (b. 30 July 1947, Leeds Castle, Kent, England) with guitarists Stephen Stewart and Francis Lickerish. The Enid's leader, Godfrey was educated at Finchden Manor (other alumni included Alexis Korner, Tom Robinson) and the Royal Academy Of Music. After starting a promising career as a concert pianist, Godfrey joined Barclay James Harvest as musical director in 1969 and moved them towards large orchestral works. He left BJH in 1972, then recorded a solo album, *The Fall Of Hyperion*, for Charisma in 1973. He returned to Finchden Manor to form the Enid in 1974, taking the name from a school in-joke. Supported by dynamic live shows, a debut album, *In The Region of the Summer Stars*, appeared in 1976. The simultaneous growth of punk 'put us in a cul-de-sac' according to Godfrey but, despite an ever-changing line-up, subsequent concept albums, rock operas and tours saw them increasing their cult audience and playing large venues. A move to Pye Records just as the label went bankrupt in 1980 broke the band up. Godfrey formed his own label, distribution and studio with Stewart. They functioned uncredited as the backing band on all Kim Wilde albums up to *Cambodia*, and re-formed as the Enid in 1983. Operating as independents, their following still grew, and the fifth album, *Something Wicked This Way Comes*, was their biggest success yet. Simultaneously, Godfrey began collaboration with healer Matthew Manning on meditational music albums. In 1986, the group presented its eighth album, *Salome*, as a ballet at London's Hammersmith Odeon. By 1988, the band's popularity appeared to have peaked so, after two sold-out farewell gigs at London's Dominion Theatre, Godfrey split the band again. In 1990, based in an old house near Northampton, Godfrey re-emerged as manager of a new band, Come September, for whom he writes the material, but does not perform.

Albums: *The Fall Of Hyperion* (1973), *In The Region Of The Summer Stars* (1976), *Aerie Faerie Nonsense* (1978), *Touch Me* (1979), *Six Pieces* (1980), *Rhapsody In Rock* (1980), *Something Wicked This Way Comes* (1983), *Live At Hammersmith* (1983), *The Spell* (1984), *Fand Symphonic Tone Poem* (1985), *Salome* (1986), *Lovers And Fools* (1987), *Reverberations* (1987), *The Seed And The Sower* (1988), *Final Noise* (1988).

Eno, Brian

b. Brian Peter George St. Baptiste de la Salle Eno, 15 May 1948, Woodbridge, Suffolk, England. While studying at art schools in Ipswich and Winchester, Eno fell under the influence of *avant garde* composers Cornelius Cardew and John Cage. Although he could not play an instrument, Eno liked tinkering with multi-track tape recorders and in 1968 wrote the limited edition theoretical handbook, *Music For Non Musicians*. During the same period he established Merchant Taylor's Simultaneous Cabinet which performed works by himself and various contemporary composers, including Christian Wolff, La Monte Young, Cornelius Carden and George Brecht. This experiment was followed by the formation of a short-lived *avant garde* performance group, the Maxwell Demon. After moving to London, Eno lived in an art commune and played with Carden's Scratch Orchestra, the Portsmouth Sinfonia and his own group. As a result of his meeting with saxophonist Andy Mackay, Eno was invited to join Roxy Music in January 1971 as a 'technical adviser', but before long his powerful visual image began to rival that of group leader Bryan Ferry. It was this fact that precipitated his departure from Roxy Music on 21 June 1973. That same day, Eno began his solo career in earnest, writing the strong 'Baby's On Fire'. Shortly afterwards, he formed a temporary partnership with Robert Fripp, with whom he had previously worked on the second album by Robert Wyatt's Matching Mole, *Little Red Record*. By November 1973, their esoteric *No Pussyfooting* was released, and a tour followed. With the entire Roxy line-up, bar Ferry, Eno next completed *Here Come The Warm Jets*, which was issued less than three months later in January 1974. It was a more than expected and highlighted Eno's bizarre lyrics and quirky vocals. A one-off punk single 'Seven Deadly Finns' prompted a tour with the Phil Rambow led Winkies. On the fifth date, Eno's right lung collapsed and he was confined to hospital. During his convalescence, Eno visited America, recorded some demos with Television and worked with John Cale on *Slow Dazzle* and later *Helen Of Troy*. His fraternization with former members of the Velvet Underground reached its apogee at London's Rainbow Theatre on 1 June 1974 when he was invited to play alongside Cale, Kevin Ayers and Nico, abetted by Robert Wyatt and Mike Oldfield. An souvenir album of the event was subsequently issued.

A second album *Taking Tiger Mountain (By Strategy)* was followed by several production credits on albums by Robert Wyatt, Robert Calvert and Phil Manzanera. This, in turn, led to Eno's experiments with environment-conscious music. He duly formed the mid-price label Obscure Records whose third release was his own *Discreet Music*, an elongated synthesizer piece conceived during a period of convalescence from a road accident. During the same period, he completed *Another Green World*, a meticulously crafted work that displayed the continued influence of John Cage. A further album with Robert Fripp followed, called *Evening Star*. After performing in Phil Manzanera's group 801, Eno collaborated with painter Peter Schmidt on a concept titled 'Oblique Strategies', which was actually a series of cards designed to promote lateral thinking.

During a hectic 18-month period, Eno recorded 120 tracks, the sheer bulk of which temporarily precluded the completion of his next album. In the meantime, he began a fruitful alliance with David Bowie on a trilogy of albums: *Low*, *Heroes* and *Lodger*. Even with that workload, however, he managed to complete his next solo work, *Before And After Science*. An unusually commercial single followed with 'King's Lead Hat'. The title was an anagram of Talking Heads and Eno would later work with that group as producer on three of their albums. Eno then turned his attention to soundtrack recordings before returning to ambient music. *Music For Films* was a pot-pourri of specific soundtrack material allied to pieces suitable for playing whilst watching movies. The experiment was continued with *Music For Airports*. Throughout this period, Eno remained in demand as a producer: and/or collaborator on albums by Ultravox, Cluster, Harold Budd, Devo and Talking Heads. In 1979 Eno moved to New York where he began making a series of vertical format video installation pieces. Numerous exhibitions of his work were shown throughout the world accompanied by his ambient soundtracks.

During the same period he produced the *No New York* album by New York No Wave *avant garde* artists the Contortions, DNA, Teenage Jesus And The Jerks, and Mars. Two further Talking Heads album productions followed culminating in 1981 with a Top 30 album *My Life In The Bush Of Ghosts*, a fascinating collaboration with the Talking Heads' David Byrne that fused 'found voices' with African rhythms. In 1980 Eno forged an association with Canadian producer/engineer Daniel Lanois. Between them they produced *Voices*, by Eno's brother Roger, and a collaboration with Harold Budd, *The Plateaux Of Mirror*. This association with Lanois culminated in the highly successful U2 albums, *The Unforgettable Fire* and *The Joshua Tree*. In 1990, Eno completed a collaborative album with John Cale, *Wrong Way Up*. Eno's back-catalogue remains a testament to his love of esoteria, ever-shifting musical styles and experimentation.

Albums: with Robert Fripp *No Pussyfooting* (1973), *Here Come The Warm Jets* (1974), with John Cale, Kevin Ayers, Nico *June 1st 1974* (1974), *Taking Tiger Mountain (By Strategy)* (1974), *Another Green World* (1975), *Discreet Music* (1975), with Fripp *Evening Star* (1975), *Before And After Science* (1977), with Cluster *Cluster And Eno* (1978), *Music For Films* (1978), with Moebius And Roedelius *After The Heat* (1979), *Music For Airports* (1979), with Harold Budd *The Plateaux Of Mirror* (1980), with Jon Hassell *Fourth World Vol i: Possible Musics* (1980), with David Byrne *My Life In The Bush Of Ghosts* (1981), *On Land* (1982), with Daniel Lanois, Roger Eno *Apollo: Atmospheres And Soundtracks* (1983), with Budd, Lanois *The Pearl* (1984), with Michael Brook, Lanois *Hybrid* (1985), with Roger Eno *Voices* (1985), *Thursday Afternoon* (1985), with Cale *Wrong Way Up* (1990), *My Squelchy Life* (1991). Compilations: with Moebius, Roedelius And Plank *Begegnungen* (1984), *Begegnungen ii* (1985), with Cluster *Old Land* (1986), *More Blank Than Frank* (1986).

Further reading: *Music For Non-Musicians*, Brian Eno. *Roxy Music: Style With Substance - Roxy's First Ten Years*, Johnny Rogan. *More Dark Than Shark* Brian Eno and Russell Mills. *Brian Eno: His Music And The Vertical Colour Of Sound*, Eric Tamm.

Entwistle, John

b. John Alec Entwistle, 9 October 1944, Chiswick, London, England. As bassist (and occasional French horn player) in the Who, Entwistle provided the necessary bedrock to the group's individual sound. His immobile features and rigid stage manner provided the foil to his colleagues' impulsive pyrotechnics, yet paradoxically it was he who most enjoyed performing live. The sole member to undergo formal musical tuition, having played the French horn with the Middlesex Youth Orchestra, Entwistle quickly asserted his compositional talent, although such efforts were invariably confined to b-sides and occasional album tracks. His songs included 'Doctor Doctor', 'Someone's Coming' and 'My Wife', but he is generally recalled for such macabre offerings as 'Boris The Spider', 'Whiskey Man' and his two contributions to *Tommy*: 'Fiddle About' and 'Cousin Kevin'. These performances

enhanced a cult popularity and several were gathered on *The Ox*, titled in deference to the bassist's nickname. Entwistle released his first solo album, *Smash Your Head Against The Wall*, in 1971. It contained a new version of 'Heaven And Hell', a perennial in-concert favourite and the set attracted considerable attention in the USA. *Whistle Rymes*, a pun on his often misspelt surname, confirmed the bassist's new-found independence with what is perhaps his strongest set to date, containing within such entertaining dark tales of peeping Toms, isolation, suicide and nightmares. The following album, *Rigor Mortis Sets In*, paid homage to 50s rock 'n' roll and although an ambitious tour to support its release was set up it had to be abandoned when the whole venture proved too costly. Entwistle then compiled the Who's archive set, *Odds And Sods*, before forming a new group, Ox, but the attendant album, *Mad Dog*, was poorly received. He subsequently worked as musical director on two soundtrack sets, *Quadrophenia* and *The Kids Are Alright*, before completing his 1981 release, *Too Late The Hero*, which featured former James Gang/Eagles' guitarist, Joe Walsh. While Entwistle's solo career has since been deferred, his stature as one of rock's great bass players was enhanced by his outstanding performance on the Who's 1973 double album, *Quadrophenia*.
Albums: *Smash Your Head Against The Wall* (1971), *Whistle Rymes* (1972), *Rigor Mortis Sets In* (1973), *Mad Dog* (1975), *Too Late The Hero* (1981). Compilation: *The Ox* (1971).

Essex, David

b. David Albert Cook, 23 July 1947, London, England. Originally a drummer in the semi-professional Everons, Essex subsequently turned to singing during the mid-60s, and recorded a series of unsuccessful singles for a variety of labels. On the advice of his influential manager, Derek Bowman, he switched to acting and after a series of minor roles received his big break upon winning the lead part in *Godspell*. This was followed by a more familiar role in the authentic 50s inspired *That'll Be The Day* and its sequel *Stardust*. The former reactivated Essex's recording career and the song he composed for the film, 'Rock On' was a transatlantic Top 10 hit. It was in Britain, however, that Essex enjoyed several years as a pin-up teen idol. During the mid-70s, he registered two UK number 1s, 'Gonna Make You A Star' and 'Hold Me Close', plus the Top 10 hits 'Lamplight', 'Stardust' and 'Rollin' Stone'. After parting with producer Jeff Wayne, Essex continued to chart,

though with noticeably diminishing returns. As his teen appeal waned, his serious acting commitments increased, most notably with the role of Che Guevera in the production of *Evita*. The musical also provided another Top 5 hit with the acerbic 'Oh What A Circus'. His lead part in the film *Silver Dream Machine* resulted in a hit of the same title. Thereafter, Essex took on a straight non-singing part in *Childe Byron*. The Christmas hit, 'A Winter's Tale', kept his chart career alive, as did the equally successful 'Tahiti'. The latter anticipated his biggest project to date, an elaborate musical *Mutiny* (based on *Mutiny On The Bounty*). Despite pursuing two careers, Essex has managed to achieve consistent success on record, film and stage.
Albums: *Rock On* (1973), *David Essex* (1974), *All The Fun Of The Fair* (1975), *Out On The Street* (1976), *On Tour* (1976), *Gold And Ivory* (1977), *Hold Me Close* (1979), *Imperial Wizard* (1979), *The David Essex Album* (1979), *The David Essex Collection* (1980), *Be-Bop - The Future* (1981), *Silver Dream Racer* (1980), *Hot Love* (1980), *Stage Struck* (1982), *Mutiny!* (1983), *The Whisper* (1983), *This One's For You* (1984), *Live At The Royal Albert Hall* (1984), *Centre Stage* (1987), *Touching The Ghost* (1989). Compilation: *The Very Best Of David Essex* (1982).

Every Which Way

This short-lived act was formed by ex-Nice drummer Brian 'Blinky' Davidson in May 1970. The line-up initially comprised of Graham Bell (vocals - previously of Skip Bifferty), Geoff Peach (flute), and Alan Cartwright (bass), before being expanded to accommodate guitarist John Hedley. Bell provided much of the material featured on *Every Which Way* which combined elements of fantasy with jazz-rock. However, despite an acclaimed debut at London's Marquee club and the best efforts of manager Tony Stratton-Smith, the quintet failed to find commercial favour. In 1971 Bell left to join Arc while Cartwright switched to Procol Harum. Davidson subsequently surfaced in Refugee.
Album: *Every Which Way* (1970).

David Essex

F

Faces

Formed from the ashes of the defunct UK mod group the Small Faces, this quintet comprised Ronnie Lane (b. 1 April 1946, Plaistow, London, England; bass), Kenney Jones (b. 16 September 1948, Stepney, London, England; drums), Ian McLagan (b. 12 May 1945, London, England; organ), Rod Stewart (b. 10 January 1945, Highgate, London, England; vocals) and Ron Wood (b. 1 June 1947; guitar). The latter two members were originally part of Jeff Beck's group. The Faces 1970 debut *First Step* reflected their boozy, live appeal in which solid riffing and strong gutsy vocals were prominent. Their excellent follow-up *Long Player* enhanced their appeal with its strong mix of staunch rock songs. Throughout this period, Rod Stewart had been pursuing a simultanous solo career which took off in earnest in the summer of 1971 with the worldwide success of the chart-topping 'Maggie May'. At that point, the Faces effectively became Stewart's backing group. Although they enjoyed increasingly commercial appeal with *A Nod's As Good As A Wink . . . To A Blind Horse* and a string of memorable good-time singles, including 'Stay With Me' and 'Cindy Incidentally', there was no doubt that the focus on Stewart unbalanced the unit. Lane left in 1973 and was replaced by Tetsu Yamauchi. Despite further hits with 'Pool Hall Richard', 'You Can Make Me Dance Sing Or' and a live album to commemorate their Stateside success, the band clearly lacked unity. In 1975, Stewart became a tax exile and by the end of the year announced that he had separated from the group. Wood went on to join the Rolling Stones, while the remaining members briefly teamed up with Steve Marriott in an ill-fated reunion of the Small Faces. The Faces are fondly remembered by all, their 'sloppy' image belied a solid, impressive standard of high musicianship.
Albums: *First Step* (1970), *Long Player* (1971), *A Nod's As Good As A Wink . . . To A Blind Horse* (1971), *Ooh La La* (1973), *Coast To Coast Overture And Beginners* (1974). Compilation: *The Best Of The Faces* (1977).

Fairport Convention

The unchallenged inventors of British folk-rock have struggled through tragedy and changes, retaining the name that now represents not so much who is in the band, but what it stands for. The original group of 1967 comprised Iain Matthews (b. Ian Matthews MacDonald, 16 June 1946, Scunthorpe, Lincolnshire, England; vocals), Judy Dyble (b. 13 February 1949, London, England; vocals), Ashley 'Tyger' Hutchings (b. 26 January 1945, Muswell Hill, London, England; bass), Richard Thompson (b. 3 April 1949, London, England; guitar/vocals), Simon Nicol (b. 13 October 1950, Muswell Hill, London, England; guitar/vocals) and Martin Lamble (b. 28 August 1949, St. Johns Wood, London, England, d. 12 May 1969; drums). The band originally came to the attention of the London 'underground' club scene by sounding like a cross between the Jefferson Airplane and the Byrds. As an accessible alternative they immediately took to people's hearts. American producer Joe Boyd signed them and they released the charming 'If I Had A Ribbon Bow'. On their self-titled debut they introduced the then little-known Canadian songwriter Joni Mitchell to a wider audience. The album was a cult favourite, but like the single, it sold poorly. Judy Dyble departed and was replaced by former Strawbs vocalist, Sandy Denny (b. Alexandra Denny, 6 January 1948, Wimbledon, London, England, d. 21 April 1978). Denny brought a traditional folk-feel to their work which began to appear on the superlative *What We Did On Our Holidays*. This varied collection contained some of their finest songs: Denny's version of 'She Moved Through The Fair', her own 'Fotheringay', Matthews' lilting 'Book Song', the superb 'I'll Keep It With Mine' and Thompson's masterpiece 'Meet On The Ledge'. This joyous album was bound together by exemplary musicianship, of particular note was the guitar of the shy and wiry Thompson. Matthews left soon after its release, unhappy with the traditional direction the band were pursuing. Following the album's critical acclaim and a modest showing in the charts, they experienced tragedy a few months later when their Transit van crashed, killing Martin Lamble and their friend and noted dressmaker Jeannie Franklyn. *Unhalfbricking* was released and, although not as strong as the former, it contained two excellent readings of Bob Dylan songs, 'Percy's Song' and 'Si Tu Dois Partir' (If You Gotta Go, Go Now). Sandy contributed two songs, 'Autopsy' and the definitive, and beautiful, 'Who Knows Where The Time Goes'. More significantly, *Unhalfbricking* featured guest musician, Dave

Swarbrick, on fiddle and mandolin. The album charted, as did the second Dylan number; by now the band had opened the door for future bands like Steeleye Span, by creating a climate that allowed traditional music to be played in a rock context. The songs that went on their next album were premièred on John Peel's BBC radio show *Top Gear*. An excited Peel stated that their performance would 'sail them into uncharted waters'; his judgement proved correct. The live-set was astonishing - they played jigs and reels, and completed all 27 verses of the traditional 'Tam Lin', featuring Swarbrick, now a full-time member, plus the debut of new drummer, Dave Mattacks (b. March 1948, Edgeware, Middlesex, England). The subsequent album *Liege And Lief* was a milestone; they had created British folk-rock in spectacular style. This, however, created problems within the band and Hutchings left to form Steeleye Span and Sandy departed to form Fotheringay with ex-Eclection and future husband Trevor Lucas. Undeterred, the band recruited Dave Pegg on bass and Swarbrick became more prominent both as lead vocalist and as an outstanding fiddle player. From their communal home in Hertfordshire they wrote much of the next two album's material although Thompson left before the release of *Angel Delight*. They made the *Guinness Book Of Records* in 1970 with the longest-ever title 'Sir B. McKenzies's Daughter's Lament For The 77th Mounted Lancer's Retreat From The Straits Of Loch Knombe, In The Year Of Our Lord 1727, On The Occasion Of The Announcement Of Her Marriage To The Laird Of Kinleakie'. *Full House* was the first all-male Fairport album and was instrumentally strong with extended tracks like 'Sloth' becoming standards. The concept album *Babbacombe Lee,* although critically welcomed, failed to sell and Simon Nicol left to form the Albion Band with Ashley Hutchings. Swarbrick struggled on, battling against hearing problems. With such comings and goings of personnel it was difficult to document the exact changes. The lack of any animosity from ex-members contributed to the family atmosphere, although by this time record sales were dwindling. Sandy Denny rejoined, as did Dave Mattacks (twice), but by the end of the 70s the name was put to rest. The family tree specialist Pete Frame has documented their incredible array of line-ups. Their swan-song was at Cropredy in Oxfordshire in 1979. Since then an annual reunion has taken place and is now a major event on the folk calendar. The band have no idea which ex-members will turn up! They have continued to release albums, making the swan-song a sham. With Swarbrick's departure, his position was taken by Ric Sanders in 1985 who rapidly quietened his dissenters by stamping his own personality on the fiddler's role. Some of the recent collections have been quite superb, including *Gladys Leap*, with Simon Nicol back on lead vocals, and the instrumental *Expletive Delighted*. With the release in 1990 of *The Five Seasons*, the group had established the longest lasting line-up in their history. The Fairports are now as much a part of the folk music tradition as the music itself.

Albums: *Fairport Convention* (1968), *What We Did On Our Holidays* (1969), *Unhalfbricking* (1969), *Liege And Lief* (1969), *Full House* (1970), *Angel Delight* (1971), *Babbacombe Lee* (1971), *Rosie* (1973), *Nine* (1973), *Live Convention (A Moveable Feast)* (1974), *Rising For The Moon* (1975), *Gottle O'Geer* (1976), *Live At The LA Troubadour* (1977), *A Bonny Bunch Of Roses* (1977), *Tipplers Tales* (1978), *Farewell, Farewell* (1979), *Moat On The Ledge* (1981), *Gladys Leap* (1985), *Expletive Delighted* (1986), *House Full* (1986), *Heyday: The BBC Radio Sessions 1968-9* (1987), *'In Real Time' - Live '87* (1988), *Red And Gold* (1988), *Five Seasons* (1990). Compilations: *History Of Fairport Convention* (1972), *The Best Of Fairport Convention* (1988).

Further reading: *Meet On The Ledge*, Patrick Humphries.

Fairweather

This Welsh quintet - Andy Fairweather-Low (b. 2 August 1948, Ystrad, Mid Glamorgan, Wales; vocals/guitar), Neil Jones (guitar), Blue Weaver (keyboards), Clive Taylor (bass) and Dennis Bryon (drums) - evolved from the ashes of the pop group Amen Corner. Although the new unit was determined to plough a more progressive furrow, they reached number 6 in the UK charts with 'Natural Sinner' in July 1970. Fairweather was unable to rid itself of a 'teenybopper' tag, and split up on completing their lone album. Blue Weaver later became a respected session musician, appearing with such disparate acts as the Strawbs, the Bee Gees and the Pet Shop Boys, while Andy Fairweather-Low pursued a solo career.

Album: *Beginning From An End* (1971).

Fairweather-Low, Andy

b. 1948, Cardiff, Wales. This Welsh guitarist and singer took over Dave Edmunds' sales assistant job at the music shop Barrett's Of Cardiff in the mid-60s, which enabled him to mix with the top

Fairweather

musicians on the local scene. He recruited a number of these to form the pop/soul band Amen Corner. It was Low's intention to play guitar in the outfit but as they had too many guitarists and no vocalists, he had to take on the singing duties and became a teen idol in Britain as the band scored a run of hit singles. When the band split, Low and the brass section formed Fairweather who signed to RCA's new progressive label Neon. They immediately blew their underground 'cool' by having a big hit single with 'Natural Sinner', but after a couple of less successful singles they too broke up. Low retired to Wales to concentrate on writing and playing for his own amusement. He returned in 1975 with an album and hit single 'Reggae Tune'. Another memorable big hit with 'Wide Eyed And Legless' highlighted his characteristic voice. Low's subsequent releases, including a 1986 single on the Stiff label, failed to chart and he spent more time playing on sessions and live gigs for Pink Floyd and Roger Waters. He also sang with the all-star ARMS band during 1987 to raise money for research in to multiple sclerosis. In 1990, Low toured with Chris Rea and in December 1991 with George Harrison and Eric Clapton (Japanese tour) and is currently playing in Clapton's band and is regularly called upon for other prestigious gigs throughout the rock world.

Albums: as Fairweather *Beginning From An End* (1971), *Spider Jivin'* (1974), *La Booga Rooga* (1975), *Be Bop 'N' Holla* (1976), *Mega-Shebang* (1980).

Family

Highly respected and nostalgically revered, Family were one of Britain's leading progressive rock bands of the late 60s and early 70s. They were led by the wiry yet vocally demonic Roger Chapman (b. 8 April 1942, Leicester, England), a man whose stage presence could both transfix and terrify his audience, who would duck from the countless supply of tambourines he would destroy and hurl into the crowd. Chapman was ably supported by Rick Grech (b. 1 November 1946, Bordeaux, France, d. 17 March 1990; violin/bass), Charlie Whitney (b. 24 June 1944, Leicester, England; guitar), Rob Townsend (b. July 7 1947, Leicester, England; drums) and Jim King (b. Kettering, Northamptonshire, England; flute/saxophone). The band was formed in 1962 and known variously as the Roaring Sixties and the Farinas, finally coming together as Family in 1967 with the arrival of Chapman and Townsend. Their first album released in 1968 was given extensive exposure on John Peel's influential BBC radio programme, resulting in this Dave Mason-produced collection becoming a major cult record.

Family

Chapman's remarkable strangulated vibrato caused heads to turn. Following the release of their most successful album *Family Entertainment* they experienced an ever changing personnel of high pedigree musicians when Rick Grech departed to join Blind Faith in 1969, being replaced by John Weider, who in turn was supplanted by John Wetton in 1971, then Jim Cregan in 1972. Poli Palmer superseded Jim King in 1969 who was ultimately replaced by Tony Ashton in 1972. Throughout this turmoil they maintained a high standard of recorded work and had singles success with 'No Mules Fool', 'Strange Band', 'In My Own Time' and the infectious 'Burlesque'. Family disintegrated after their disappointing swan-song *Its Only A Movie*, Chapman and Whitney departing to form Streetwalkers. While their stage performances were erratic and unpredictable, the sight of Roger Chapman performing their anthem 'The Weaver's Answer' on a good night was unforgettable and one that rock fans who saw them will cherish.
Albums: *Music In A Doll's House* (1968), *Family Entertainment* (1969), *A Song For Me* (1970), *Anyway* (1970), *Fearless* (1971), *Bandstand* (1972), *It's Only A Movie* (1973). Compilation: *Best Of Family* (1974).

Fanny
Warner Brothers Records claimed in 1970 that their recent signing Fanny were the 'first all-female rock group'. They sustained a career for four years on that basis, throwing off all rivals to the throne, including Birtha, whose tasteless publicity handout stated 'Birtha has balls'. Formerly Wild Honey, the name Fanny was suggested by George Harrison to their producer Richard Perry. It was only later in their career that the group realized how risque their name was internationally. Comprised: Jean Millington (b. 1950, Manila, California, USA; bass/vocals), June Millington (b. 1949, Manila, California, USA; guitar/vocals), Alice de Buhr (b. 1950, Mason City, Iowa, USA; drums) and Nickey Barclay (b. 1951, Washington, DC, USA; keyboards). Their blend of driving hard rock and rock 'n' roll was exciting, although they were always a second division act. They were more popular in the UK where they toured regularly, recording albums at Apple and Olympic studios. June Millington was replaced in 1974 by Patti Quatro from the Pleasure Seekers, the sister of Suzi Quatro. None of their albums charted in the UK and their sales in the USA were minimal. Their second album, *Charity Ball* was their best work, giving them a US Top 40 hit with the title song. Ironically, their biggest hit 'Butter Boy' came as they fragmented in 1975.
Albums: *Fanny* (1970), *Charity Ball* (1971), *Fanny Hill* (1972), *Mother's Pride* (1973), *Rock 'N' Roll*

Survivors (1974). Solo album: June and Jean Millington *Millington* (1977).

Farnham, John

b 1 July 1949, Dagenham, Essex, England. Farnham has sustained a successful career in Australia for over three decades. Having initial success in 1968 with 'Sadie', a throw-away pop song, his manager pushed Farnham into the pop limelight with 13 more hit singles to follow. He was voted Australia's 'King of Pop' five years in a row, between 1969 and 1973, and was also active in a variety of stage shows and musicals. However, for the second half of the 70s his career seemed dead, and it was not until mid-80 that he re-emerged with another hit record, a unique rendition of the Beatles' 'Help'. He formed his own band and went back on the road until 1982 when he was asked to sing with the Little River Band, replacing original singer Glenn Shorrock. Despite adding some bite to its music, Farnham was unable to assist the band in repeating its earlier successes and so he resumed his solo career. For his comeback, *Whispering Jack,* Farnham sifted through hundreds of songs from local and international writers, which proved fruitful as it became the largest selling album in Australia's history. The record deserved its success as the songs were varied and strong, and it showcased Farnham's excellent singing voice. Because of his earlier successes, his fans continued to support him and, unlike other performers, he was not afraid to change and move in new directions. The single 'You're The Voice' was a Top 10 hit in the UK in 1987. While his next album, *Age Of Reason*, repeated the success formula of the first, his latest album contained mostly his own co-written songs.

Albums: *Sadie* (1968), *Looking Through A Tear* (1970), *Christmas Is John Farnham* (1970), *Everybody Oughta Sing A Song* (1971), *JF Sings The Shows* (1972), with Alison Durbin *Together* (1972), *Hits Magic And Rock 'N' Roll* (1973), *JF Sings The Hits Of 1973* (1973), *Uncovered* (1980), *Whispering Jack* (1986), *Age Of Reason* (1988), *Chain Reaction* (1990). Compilation: *Best Of John Farnham* (1981).

Fat City

Fat City formed in Washington, DC, USA and included in their line-up the husband and wife team, Bill Danoff (b. 7 May 1946, Springfield, Massachusetts, USA; guitar/vocals) and Taffy Danoff (b. Kathleen Nivert, 24 October 1944, Washington, DC, USA; vocals), plus Jim Parker (guitar/vocals). With their cheerful, summery vocals they released two albums, enlisting as guest musicians such notable artists as Bob James, Eric Weissberg, Artie Traum and Hubert Laws. After failing to achieve the predicted success, Fat City's ultimate demise led to the Danoff's forming a duo as Bill and Taffy which, in turn, led to the Starland Vocal Band and national fame. After the demise of Starland, the duo resurrected Fat City and, despite their marital split, they were still to be found performing together in the Washington, DC area during the 80s.

Albums: *Reincarnation* (1969), *Welcome To Fat City* (1971), *Blue Band* (1991), *Blue Band* (1991); as Bill And Taffy *Pass It On* (1973), *Aces* (1974).

Faust

Producer/advisor Uwe Nettelbeck formed this group in Wumme, Germany in 1971. The initial line-up - Werner Diermaier, Jean Herve Peron, Rudolf Sosna, Hans Joachim Irmler, Gunther Wusthoff and Armulf Meifert - worked from a custom-built studio, sited in a converted schoolhouse. *Faust* was a conscious attempt to forge a new western 'rock' music wherein fragments of sound were spliced together to create a radical collage. Released in a clear sleeve and clear vinyl, the album was viewed as an experimental masterpiece, or grossly self-indulgent, dependant on taste. *So Far* proved less obtuse, and the group subsequently secured a high-profile recording deal with Virgin. *The Faust Tapes*, a collection of private recordings reassembled by a fan in the UK, retailed at the price of a single (49p) and this inspired marketing ploy not unnaturally generated considerable interest. The label also issued *Outside The Dream Syndicate* on which the group accompanied Tony Conrad, a former colleague of John Cale. Faust's music remained distanced from mainstream acceptance, as evinced on *Faust 4*, and subsequent recordings, as well as items drawn from their back catalogue, were later issued by Recommended Records, specialists in *avant garde* recordings. Faust remained active throughout the 70s and 80s, albeit with a different line-up. In 1988 they reduced the price of admission to those persons arriving at live concerts with a musical instrument who were prepared to play it during the performance.

Albums: *Faust* (1972), *So Far* (1972), *The Faust Tapes* (1973), with Tony Conrad *Outside The Dream Syndicate* (1973), *Faust 4* (1973), *One* (1979). Compilation: *Munich And Elsewhere* (1986).

Ferguson, Jay

b. John Ferguson, 10 May 1947, Burbank, California, USA. The former lead singer of seminal progressive rock band Spirit and hard rock quartet Jo Jo Gunne. Jay's debut album was well received but sold poorly. However, two years later the sparkling 'Thunder Island' made the US Top 10. The accompanying album stands as his best work. His name often appeared as session singer on other albums amidst the occasional (and usually abortive) Spirit reunions.
Albums: *All Alone In The End Zone* (1976), *Thunder Island* (1978), *Real Life Ain't This Way* (1979), *White Noise* (1982).

Ferry, Bryan

b. 26 September 1945, Washington, Tyne & Wear, England. Ferry began his musical career in local group the Banshees, following which he enrolled at Newcastle-Upon-Tyne University where he formed R&B group the Gas Board, whose ranks included Graham Simpson and John Porter. After studying Fine Art under Richard Hamilton, Ferry briefly worked as a teacher before forming the celebrated Roxy Music. During their rise to fame, he plotted a parallel solo career, beginning in 1973 with *These Foolish Things*, an album of favourite cover versions. At the time, the notion of recording an album of rock standards was both innovative and nostalgic. Ferry recorded half an album of faithful imitations, leaving the other half to more adventurous arrangements. Some of the highlights included a revival of Ketty Lester's obscure 'Rivers Of Salt', a jaunty reading of Elvis Presley's 'Baby I Don't Care' and a remarkable hit version of Bob Dylan's 'A Hard Rain's A-Gonna Fall'. The album received mixed reviews but effectively paved the way for similar works including David Bowie's *Pin Ups* and John Lennon's *Rock 'N' Roll*. Ferry continued the cover game with *Another Time Another Place*, which was generally less impressive than its predecessor. Two stylish pre-rock numbers that worked well were 'Smoke Gets In Your Eyes' and 'Funny How Time Slips Away'. A gutsy revival of Dobie Gray's 'The In Crowd' brought another UK Top 20 hit. By 1976, Ferry had switched to R&B covers on *Let's Stick Together* which, in addition to the hit Wilbert Harrison title track, featured a rousing re-run of the Everly Brothers' 'The Price Of Love'. It was not until 1977 that Ferry finally wrote an album's worth of songs for a solo work. *In Your Mind* spawned a couple of minor hits with 'This Is Tomorrow' and 'Tokyo Joe'. That same spring,

Ferry appeared on the soundtrack of *All This And World War II* singing the Beatles' She's Leaving Home'. The following year, he retired to Montreux to complete the highly accomplished *The Bride Stripped Bare*. Introspective and revelatory, the album documented his sense of rejection following the loss of his jet-setting girlfriend, model Jerry Hall. The splendid 'Sign Of The Times' presented a Dadaist vision of life as total bleakness: 'We live, we die . . . we know not why'. The track 'Can't Let Go', written at a time when he considered giving up music, maintained the dark mood. It was another seven years before Ferry recorded solo again. In the meantime, he married society heiress Lucy Helmore, abandoning his lounge lizard image in the process. The 1985 comeback *Boys And Girls* was stylistically similar to his work with Roxy Music and included the hits 'Slave To Love' and 'Don't Stop The Dance'. After a further two-year break, Ferry collaborated with guitarist Johnny Marr on 'The Right Stuff' (adapted from the Smiths' instrumental, 'Money Changes Everything'). The album *Bete Noire* was a notable hit indicating that Ferry's muse was still very much alive, even though his solo work continues to be eclipsed by the best of Roxy Music.
Albums: *These Foolish Things* (1973), *Another Time Another Place* (1974), *Let's Stick Together* (1976), *In Your Mind* (1977), *The Bride Stripped Bare* (1978), *Boys And Girls* (1985), *Bete Noire* (1987).
Further reading: *Roxy Music: Style With Substance - Roxy's First Ten Years*, Johnny Rogan.

Firefall

Firefall were a second generation US country rock band in the tradition of Poco and the Eagles. Formed during the genre's heyday the initial line-up comprised of ex-Flying Burrito Brothers members Rick Roberts (b. 1950, Florida, USA; guitar/vocals) and Michael Clarke (also ex-Byrds) (b. Michael Dick. 3 June 1943, New York, USA; drums), ex-Spirit Mark Andes (b. 19 February 1948, Philadelphia, Pennsylvania, USA; bass), Jock Bartley (guitar/vocals), David Muse (keyboards/saxophone/flute) and Larry Burnett (guitar/vocals). Their debut was a refreshing though laid-back affair, and in addition to three US hit singles the album contained a version of the Stephen Stills/Chris Hillman song 'It Doesn't Matter', with alternative lyrics by Roberts. Their first three albums were all strong sellers and for a brief while Firefall were one of the biggest selling artists in their genre. *Luna Sea* contained a further

major US hit with the memorable 'Just Remember
I Love You'. Whilst their instrumental prowess was
faultless their inability to progress significantly, was
their ultimate failing, although *Elan* demonstrated a
will to change, with the sparkling hit 'Strange
Way' which featured a breathy jazz influenced flute
solo. They continued to produce sharply
engineered albums with Muse playing an
increasingly important role adding other
instruments, giving a new flavour to a guitar
dominated genre. They experienced hits even
beyond the era of mainstream country rock.
Albums: *Firefall* (1976), *Luna Sea* (1977), *Elan*
(1978), *Undertow* (1980), *Clouds Across The Sun*
(1981), *Mirror Of The World* (1983), Compilation:
Best Of (1981).

First Class

This studio group was conceived by hit-makers
John Carter and Ken Lewis in 1974. Carter And
Lewis were formerly the leaders of Carter-Lewis
And The Southerners and the Ivy League, and
were prolific songwriters, session singers and hit-
makers. They assembled some of the UK's finest
studio musicians to record the summery 'Beach
Baby' which made the UK Top 20 in the summer
of 1974. The cast included singer Tony Burrows,
previously in the Ivy League with Carter/Lewis,
and the man chosen to lead the touring version of
their 1967 studio group, the Flowerpot Men.
Burrows also sang on records by hit-makers White
Plains, Edison Lighthouse, Pipkins, the
Brotherhood Of Man and others. In 1970 he made
Top Of The Pops history by appearing on one show
with three different groups. Others on the record
included John Carter himself, Del John, and Chas
Mills completing the vocal harmonies plus Spencer
James on guitar, Clive Barrett on keyboards, Robin
Shaw on bass, and Eddie Richards on drums. The
follow-ups to 'Beach Baby' - 'Dreams Are Ten A
Penny' and the old Ivy League hit 'Funny How
Love Can Be' - were flops and the band were
dismantled in 1976. Carter went on to form
another studio group - Ice. In the early 80s the
First Class name was resurrected for a cover of
Brenton Wood's 'Gimme Little Sign' on Sunny
Records. The label suggests that the British Surf
mafia of Carter and company were involved but
personnel details are not known.

Flash

This British rock group was formed around Peter
Banks (b. 7 July 1947, Barnet, Hertfordshire,
England; guitar) and Tony Kaye (b. 11 January

1946, Leicester, England; organ), both ex-members
of Yes. Colin Carter (vocals), Ray Bennett
(bass/keyboards) and Mike Hough (drums)
completed the line-up featured on *Flash*, after
which Kaye left to join Badger. The remaining
quartet completed two further progressive rock-
styled albums, but were unable to make a
significant commercial breakthrough, although the
group did reach the US Top 30 singles chart in
1972 with 'Small Beginnings'. Following a brief
association with Jan Akkerman, guitarist with
Focus, Banks enjoyed a moderate, albeit brief, solo
career releasing *Peter Banks* and *Two Sides Of Peter
Banks* in 1973. Hough meanwhile surfaced in the
short-lived Fast Buck.
Albums: *Flash* (1972), *Flash In The Can* (1972), *Out
Of Our Hands* (1973).

Flash Cadillac And The Continental Kids

Formed in Colorado, USA in 1969, Flash Cadillac
And The Continental Kids were one of several
groups to parody 50s rock in the wake of Sha Na
Na. The original line-up - Flash Cadillac (Kenny
Moe) (vocals), Sam McFadin (guitar/vocals), Linn
Phillips (guitar/vocals), George Robinson
(saxophone), Kris Angelo (keyboards/vocals),
Warren 'Butch' Knight (bass/vocals) and Ricco
Masino (drums) - later moved to Los Angeles
where they met pop svengali Kim Fowley. The
group made a successful appearance in the film
American Graffiti before releasing a promising debut
album which contained respectable readings of
rock 'n' roll favourites. A second set, *No Face Like
Chrome*, contained material indebted to 50s, 60s
and 70s styles and was arguably reminiscent of
Britain's 'pub rock' groups. Although they enjoyed
two minor US hits with 'Dancin' On A Saturday
Night' and 'Good Times Rock 'n' Roll', Flash
Cadillac were unable to escape a revivalist tag and
broke up without realizing their full potential.
Albums: *Flash Cadillac And The Continental Kids*
(1973), *There's No Face Like Chrome* (1974), *Sons
Of Beaches* (1975).

Fleetwood Mac

The original Fleetwood Mac was formed in July
1967 by Peter Green (b. Peter Greenbaum, 29
October 1946, Bethnel Green, London, England;
guitar) and Mick Fleetwood (b. 24 June 1947,
London, England; drums), both of whom had
recently left John Mayall's Bluesbreakers. They
secured a recording deal with Blue Horizon
Records on the strength of Green's reputation as a
blues guitarist before the label's overtures

uncovered a second guitarist, Jeremy Spencer (b. 4 July 1948, Hartlepool, Cleveland, England), in a semi-professional group, the Levi Set. A temporary bassist, Bob Brunning, was recruited into the line-up, until a further Mayall acolyte, John McVie (b. 26 November 1945, London, England), was finally persuaded to join the new unit. Peter Green's Fleetwood Mac, as the group was initially billed, made its debut on August 12, 1967 at Windsor's National Jazz And Blues Festival. Their first album, *Fleetwood Mac*, released on Blue Horizon in February the following year, reached the UK Top 5 and established a distinctive balance between Green's introspective compositions and Spencer's debt to Elmore James. A handful of excellent cover versions completed an album that was seminal in the development of the British blues boom of the late 60s.

The group also enjoyed two minor hit singles with 'Black Magic Woman', a hypnotic Green composition later popularized by Santana, and a delicate reading of 'Need Your Love So Bad', first recorded by Little Willie John. Fleetwood Mac's second album, *Mr. Wonderful*, was another triumph, but while Spencer was content to repeat his established style, Green, the group's leader, extended his compositional boundaries with several haunting contributions, including the heartfelt 'Love That Burns'. His guitar playing, clean and sparse but always telling, was rarely better, while McVie and Fleetwood were already an instinctive rhythm section. *Mr. Wonderful* also featured contributions from Christine Perfect (b. 12 July 1943, Birmingham, England), pianist from Chicken Shack, and a four-piece horn section, as the group began to leave traditional blues behind. A third guitarist, Danny Kirwan, (b. 13 May 1950, London, England), was added to the line-up in September 1968. The quintet scored an immediate hit when 'Albatross', a moody instrumental reminiscent of 'Sleep Walk' by Santo And Johnny, topped the UK charts. The single, which reached number 2 when it was reissued in 1973, was the group's first million seller.

Fleetwood Mac then left Blue Horizon, although the company subsequently issued *Blues Jam At Chess*, on which the band jammed with several mentors, including Buddy Guy, Otis Spann and Shakey Horton. Following a brief interlude on Immediate Records, which furnished the hypnotic 'Man Of The World', the quintet made their debut on Reprise with 'Oh Well', their most ambitious single to date, and the superb *Then Play On*. This crafted album unveiled Kirwan's songwriting

talents and his romantic leanings offset the more worldly Green. Although pictured, Jeremy Spencer was notably absent from most of the sessions, although his eccentric vision was showcased on a self-titled solo album.

Fleetwood Mac now enjoyed an international reputation, but it was a mantle too great for its leader to bear. Peter Green left the band in May 1970 as his parting single, the awesome 'The Green Manalishi', became another Top 10 hit. He was replaced by Christine Perfect, now married to John McVie, and while his loss was an obvious blow, Kirwan's songwriting talent and Spencer's sheer exuberance maintained a measure of continuity on a fourth album, *Kiln House*. However in 1971 the group was rocked for a second time when Spencer disappeared mid-way through an American tour. It transpired he had joined a religious sect, the Children Of God and while Green deputized for the remainder of the tour, a permanent replacement was found in a Californian musician, Bob Welch (b. 31 July 1946, California, USA).

The new line-up was consolidated on two melodic albums, *Future Games* and *Bare Trees*. Neither release made much impression with UK audiences who continued to mourn the passing of the Green-led era, but in America the group began to assemble a strong following for their new-found transatlantic sound. However, further changes occurred when Kirwan's chronic stage-fright led to his dismissal. Bob Weston, a guitarist from Long John Baldry's backing band, was his immediate replacement, while the line-up was also bolstered by former Savoy Brown vocalist, Dave Walker. The group, however, was unhappy with a defined frontman and the singer left after only eight months, having barely completed work on their *Penguin* album. Although not one of the band's strongest collections, it does contain an excellent Welch composition, 'Night Watch'.

The remaining quintet completed another album, *Mystery To Me*, which was released at the time of a personal nadir within the group. Weston, who had been having an affair with Fleetwood's wife, was fired midway through a prolonged US tour and the remaining dates were cancelled. Their manager, Clifford Davis, assembled a bogus Mac to fulfil contractual obligations, thus denying the 'real' group work during the inevitable lawsuits. Yet despite the inordinate pressure, Perfect, Welch, McVie and Fleetwood returned with *Heroes Are Hard To Find*, a positive release which belied the wrangles surrounding its appearance. Nonetheless the controversy proved too strong for Welch, who left the group in December 1974. His departure robbed Fleetwood Mac of an inventive songwriter whose American perspective helped redefine the group's approach.

It was while seeking prospective recording studios that Fleetwood was introduced to Stevie Nicks and Lindsey Buckingham via the duo's self-named album. Now bereft of a guitarist, he recalled Buckingham's expertise and invited him to replace Welch. Lindsey accepted on condition that Nicks also join, thus cementing Fleetwood Mac's most successful line-up. *Fleetwood Mac*, released in 1975, was a promise fulfilled. The newcomers provided easy, yet memorable compositions with smooth harmonies while the British contingent gave the group its edge and power. A succession of stellar compositions, including 'Over My Head', 'Say You Love Me' and the dramatic 'Rhiannon', confirmed a perfect balance had been struck giving the group their first in a long line of US Top 20 singles. The quintet's next release, *Rumours*, proved more remarkable still. Despite the collapse of two relationships - the McVies were divorced, Buckingham and Nicks split up - the group completed a remarkable collection which laid bare the traumas within, but in a manner neither maudlin nor pitiful. Instead the ongoing drama was charted by several exquisite songs; 'Go Your Own Way', 'Don't Stop', 'Second Hand News' and 'Dreams', which retained both melody and purpose. An enduring release, *Rumours* has sold upwards of 25 million copies and is second to Michael Jackson's *Thriller* as the best-selling album of all time.

Having survived their emotional anguish, Fleetwood Mac was faced with the problem of following-up a phenomenon. Their response was *Tusk*, an ambitious double-set which showed a group unafraid to experiment, although many critics damned the collection as self-indulgent. The title track, a fascinating instrumental, was an international hit, although its follow-up, 'Sara', a composition recalling the style of *Rumours*, was better received in the USA than the UK. An in-concert selection, *Fleetwood Mac: Live*, was released as a stop-gap in 1980 as rumours of a complete break-up flourished. It was a further two years before a new collection, *Mirage*, appeared by which point several members were pursuing independent ventures. Buckingham and Nicks, in particular, viewed their own careers with equal importance and *Mirage*, a somewhat self-conscious attempt at creating another *Rumours*, lacked the sparkle of its illustrious predecessor. It nonetheless yielded three

successful singles in 'Hold Me', 'Gypsy' and Buckingham's irrepressible 'Oh Diane'.

Five years then passed before a new Fleetwood Mac album was issued. *Tango In The Night* was a dramatic return to form, recapturing all the group's flair and invention with a succession of heartwarming performances in 'Little Lies', 'Family Man' and 'You And I (Part 2)'. Christine McVie contributed a further high-point with the rhythmic sing-a-long 'Anyway'. The collection was, however, Lindsey Buckingham's swan-song, although his departure from the band was not officially confirmed until June 1988. By that point two replacement singer/guitarists, ex-Thunderbyrd Rick Vito (b. 1950) and Billy Burnette (b. 7 May 1953), had joined the remaining quartet. The new line-up's debut, *Behind The Mask*, ushered in a new decade and era for this tempestuous group, that gained strength from adversity and simply refused to die. Its success confirmed their status as one of the major groups in the history of popular music.

Albums: *Fleetwood Mac* (1968), *Mr. Wonderful* (1968), *English Rose* (1969), *Then Play On* (1969), *Blues Jam At Chess* aka *Fleetwood Mac In Chicago* (1969), *Kiln House* (1970), *Future Games* (1971), *Bare Trees* (1972), *Penguin* (1973), *Mystery To Me* (1973), *Heroes Are Hard To Find* (1974), *Fleetwood Mac* (1975), *Rumours* (1977), *Tusk* (1979), *Fleetwood Mac Live* (1980), *Mirage* (1982), *Live In Boston* (1985), *London Live '68* (1986), *Tango In The Night* (1988), *Behind The Mask* (1989). Compilations: *The Pious Bird Of Good Omen* (1969), *The Original Fleetwood Mac* (1971), *Fleetwood Mac's Greatest Hits* (1971), *The Vintage Years* (1975), *Albatross* (1977), *Man Of The World* (1978), *Best Of* (1978), *Cerulean* (1985), *Greatest Hits: Fleetwood Mac* (1988), *The Chain* (CD box set 1992).

Further reading: *Fleetwood: My Life And Adventures With Fleetwood Mac*, Mick Fleetwood with Stephen Davis.

Flintlock

This UK teenybop band of the mid-70s was led by heartthrob drummer Mike Holoway, introduced to television audiences via the children's science fiction programme *The Tomorrow People*. The series told the story of several teenagers who had evolved beyond the rest of humanity and acted as guardians to its fate. Holoway appeared as Mike Bell in the fourth series of the programme, a would-be pop star both on screen and off with an affected cockney accent. In one serial, 'The Heart Of Sogguth', Holoway performed with Flintlock on a musical piece with a supposedly mind controlling beat heralding the arrival of extra-terrestrials. However, Flintlock's music was as cardboard as the sets and they achieved only one hit with 'Dawn' in 1976 despite considerable exposure from children's magazines like *Look In*.

Albums: *On The Way* (1975), *Hot From The Lock* (1976), *Tears 'N' Cheers* (1977), *Stand Alone* (1979).

Flo And Eddie

Lead singers (and songwriters) of the Turtles, Marc Volman and Howard Kaylan took their name - the Phlorescent Leech and Eddie - from two of their roadies when the group split up in 1970. The Turtles' brand of innocent folk pop could not survive in the new sex-and-drug-oriented climate of rock. As if to advertise the change, they joined counter-cultural supremo Frank Zappa for tours and recordings. In his role as circus-master, Zappa had the pair perform hilarious routines about backstage groupie shenanigans (*Fillmore East June 1971*) and act desperate on-the-road popstars in the film *200 Motels* (1972). Zappa wrote suitably operatic lines for their strong voices and the results - though they dismayed fans of the 'serious' Mothers Of Invention - are undeniably effective. The sleeve of *Just Another Band From LA* (1972) - with Zappa reduced to a puppet in Kaylan's hand - seems to imply they had taken control of the group. They certainly split amidst much animosity, leaving Zappa just as his accident at the Rainbow Theatre, London had made him wheel-chair bound. The comedy albums they released subsequently - *Flo & Eddie, Immoral Illegal & Fattening, Moving Targets* - haven't the punch of their work with Zappa, nor did the pair seem capable of re-creating the catchy pop they wrote for The Turtles. However, they did enliven the rock scene with an animated satirical film, *Cheap,* and a weekly three-hour radio show, *Flo & Eddie By The Fireside,* which originated on LA's KROQ but was syndicated all over the States by 1976. They also supplied their powerful falsettos to give Marc Bolan's voice a lift on many T. Rex hits. Indelibly associated with 70s 'progressive' rock culture, their careers dived in the 80s. However, the early 90s Marc Bolan revival brought their voices back to the airwaves (albeit only as backing), and Jason Donovan brought the Turtles' evergreen 'Happy Together' back to the charts in 1991.

Albums: *Flo & Eddie* (1973), *Immoral Illegal & Fattening* (1974), *Moving Targets* (1976).

Flowers, Herbie

As as session musician, Flower's many performances have ensured his reputation as one of world's finest bass players (with the occasional demand for trumpet playing). He found fame in the late 60s session players 'supergroup', Blue Mink, enjoying success with the international hit, 'Melting Pot'. His songwriting talents brought him fame with the novelty number 1 hit for Clive Dunn, 'Grandad' in January 1971. Flower's performance on Lou Reed's UK Top 10/US Top 20 hit 'Walk On The Wild Side' (*Transformer* 1972) produced one of rock's most distinctive bass lines. His later work with the virtuoso group Sky, with John Williams, Kevin Peek, Tristan Fry and Francis Monkman, brought him worldwide fame. Flowers also performed as part of one of the later line-ups of T. Rex in the late 70s. His many studio credits throughout his career have included work for David Bowie (*Space Oddity* 1969, *Diamond Dogs* 1974 and *David Live* 1974), CCS (*CCS* 1970), Melanie (*Candles In The Rain* 1970), Elton John (*Madman Across The Water* 1971 and *A Single Man* 1978), Cat Stevens (*Foreigner* 1973), Ginger Baker (*Eleven Sides Of Baker* 1977), Roy Harper (*Bullinamingvase* 1977), Ian Gomm (*Summer Holiday* 1978), Jeff Wayne (*War Of The Worlds* 1978), Steve Harley (*Hobo With A Grin* 1978), Roger Daltry (*McVicar* 1980), George Harrison (*Gone Troppo* 1982) and Paul McCartney (*Give My Regards To Broad Street* 1984). Along the way he has also managed to release two solo albums on Philips and EMI Note.

Albums: *Plant Life* (1975), *A Little Potty* (1980).

Flying Aces

Despite having never issued a record, this hard-working band from the British rock scene of the mid-70s won many admirers. As one of the many branches of the Man family tree, the band started life as the Splendid Humans in 1973 with the core members comprising Martin Ace (bass) and his wife Georgina Ace (guitar/vocals), eventually evolving into the Flying Aces with former Help Yourself guitarist Richard Treece and ex-Badfinger member Mickey Gibbons (drums). A brief, live appearance on vinyl occurred with the group's inclusion on the 1973 compilation *Xmas At The Patti*. Appearing on the UK pub/club circuit throughout the mid-70s they performed a condensed version of the 'west coast' rock style favoured by the Welsh musicians, a feel for which was mastered by Treece. Earning critical acclaim the Flying Aces still found difficulty in securing a recording deal due to the prevalent punk trend and after a brief line-up change in 1977, with Steve

Flo And Eddie

Jordan and Clive Roberts replacing Gibbons and Treece respectively, the final split came in 1978. Gibbons later worked with Bonnie Tyler and Digby Richards, while Treece eventually relocated to the USA playing in various groups in the San Francisco Bay area. Martin Ace has throughout the early 90s been working alongside his erstwhile partners in a Man reunion.

Flying Burrito Brothers

The Flying Burrito Brothers initially referred to an informal group of Los Angeles musicians, notably Jesse Davis and Barry Tashain. The name was appropriated in 1968 by former Byrds' Gram Parsons (b. 5 November 1946, Waycross, Georgia USA, d. 19 September 1973; guitar/vocals) and Chris Hillman (b. 4 December 1944, Los Angeles, California, USA; guitar/vocals) for a new venture which would integrate rock and country styles. 'Sneaky' Pete Kleinow (pedal steel), Chris Ethridge (bass) plus various drummers completed the line-up featured on *The Gilded Palace Of Sin*, where the founding duo's vision of a pan-American music flourished freely. The material ranged from the jauntily acerbic 'Christine's Tune' to the maudlin 'Hippy Boy', but its highlights included Parson's emotional reading of two southern soul standards, 'Dark End Of The Street' and 'Do Right Woman', and his own poignant 'Hot Burrito #1' and the impassioned 'Hot Burrito #2'. The album's sense of cultural estrangement captured a late 60s restlessness and reflected the rural traditions of antecedents the Everly Brothers. This artistic triumph was never repeated. *Burrito Deluxe*, on which Bernie Leadon replaced Ethridge and Michael Clarke (b. Michael Dick, 3 June 1944, Texas, USA), formerly of the Byrds became the permanent drummer, showed a group unsure of direction as Parsons' role became increasingly questionable. He left for a solo career in April 1970 and with the arrival of songwriter Rick Roberts, the Burritos again asserted their high quality. The underrated *The Flying Burrito Brothers* was a cohesive, purposeful set, marked by the inclusion of Roberts' 'Colorado', Gene Clark's 'Tried So Hard' and Merle Haggard's 'White Line Fever', plus several other excellent Roberts originals. Unfortunately, the group was again bedevilled by defections. In 1971 Leadon joined the Eagles while Kleinow opted for a career in session work, but Hillman, Clarke and Roberts were then buoyed by the arrival of Al Perkins (pedal steel), Kenny Wertz (guitar), Roger Bush (bass) and Byron Berline (fiddle). *The Last Of The Red Hot Burritos* captured the excitement and power of the group live. The septet was sundered in 1971 with Wertz, Bush and Berline forming Country Gazette, Hillman and Perkins joining Manassas while Roberts embarked on a solo career before founding Firefall with Clarke. However, much to the consternation of Hillman, Pete Kleinow later commandeered the Burritos' name and in 1975 completed *Flying Again* with Chris Ethridge, Gene Parsons (guitar/vocals) and Gib Guilbeau (fiddle). The last-named joined Kleinow in a full-scale reactivation during the 80s. The arrival of country veteran John Bleland has provided the group with a proven songwriter worthy of the early, pioneering line-up.

Albums: *The Gilded Palace Of Sin* (1969), *Burrito DeLuxe* (1970), *The Flying Burrito Brothers* (1971), *The Last Of The Red Hot Burritos* (1972), *Flying Again* (1975), *Airborne* (1976), *Close Encounters On The West Coast* (1978), *Live In Tokyo, Japan* (1978), *Flying High* (1980), *Back To The Sweethearts Of The Rodeo* (1988), *Southern Tracks* (1990). Compilations: *Live In Amsterdam* (1972), *Bluegrass Special* (1974), *Close Up The Honky Tonks* (1974), *Honky Tonk Heaven* (1974), *Hot Burrito - 2* (1975), with Gram Parsons *Sleepless Nights* (1976), *Dim Lights, Thick Smoke And Loud, Loud Music* (1987), *Hollywood Nights 1979-1981* (1990).

Focus

A former Amsterdam Conservatory student, Thijs van Leer (keyboards/flute/vocals) with Martin Dresden (bass) and philosophy graduate Hans Cleuver (drums) backed Robin Lent, Cyril Havermans and other Dutch singers before 1969's catalytic enlistment of guitarist Jan Akkerman, veteran of the progressive unit Brainbox. The new quartet's first collective essay as recording artists was humble - accompaniment on a Dutch version of *Hair* - but, heartened by audience response to a set that included amplified arrangements of pieces by Bartok and Rodrigo, Focus released a *bona fide* album debut with a spin-off single, 'House Of The King', that sold well in continental Europe. However, aiming always at the English-speaking forum, the group engaged Mike Vernon to produce *Moving Waves* which embraced vocal items (in English) and melodic if lengthy instrumentals. The album included the startling 'Hocus Pocus', a UK Top 20 hit. After reshuffles in which only van Leer and Akkerman surfaced from the original personnel, the group stole the show at British outdoor festivals, and a slot on BBC television's *Old Grey Whistle Test* assisted the passage of the glorious 'Sylvia', into the UK Top 5,

Focus III and earlier album also reached the upper echelons of the charts. After stoking up modest interest in North America, 1973 began well with each member figuring in respective categories in the more earnest music journals' popularity polls. An in-concert album from London and *Hamburger Concerto* both marked time artistically and, following 1975's *Mother Focus*, Akkerman left to concentrate on the solo career that he had pursued parallel to that of Focus since his *Profile* in 1973. With several solo efforts, Van Leer was also well-placed to do likewise but elected instead to stick with a latter-day Focus in constant flux which engaged in a strange studio amalgamation with P.J. Proby before its final engagement in Terneuzen in 1978. Akkerman and Van Leer guided Focus through a 1985 album before the 1972 line-up reformed solely for a Dutch television special five years later.

Albums: *In And Out Of Focus* (1971), *Moving Waves* (1971), *Focus III* (1972), *At The Rainbow* (1973), *Hamburger Concerto* (1974), *Mother Focus* (1975), *Ship Of Memories* (1977), *Focus Con Proby* (1978). Compilation: *Greatest Hits* (1984).

Fogelberg, Dan

b. 13 August 1951, Peoria, Illinois, USA. Having learned piano from the age of 14, Fogelberg moved to guitar and songwriting. Leaving the University of Illinois in 1971 he relocated to California and started playing on the folk circuit, at one point touring with Van Morrison. A move to Nashville brought him to the attention of producer Norbert Putnam. Fogelberg released *Home Free* for Columbia shortly afterwards. This was a very relaxed album, notable for the backing musicians involved, including Roger McGuinn, Jackson Browne, Joe Walsh and Buffy Sainte-Marie. Despite the calibre of the other players, the album was not a success, and Fogelberg, having been dropped by Columbia, returned to session work. Producer Irv Azoff, who was managing Joe Walsh, signed Fogelberg and secured a deal with Epic. Putnam was involved in subsequent recordings by Fogelberg. In 1974, Fogelberg moved to Colorado, and a year later released *Souvenirs*. This was a more positive album, and Walsh's production was evident. From here on, Fogelberg played the majority of the instruments on record, enabling him to keep tight control of the recordings, but inevitably it took longer to finish the projects. Playing support to the Eagles in 1975 helped to establish Fogelberg. However, in 1977, due to appear with the Eagles at Wembley, he failed to

show on-stage, and it was later claimed that he had remained at home to complete recording work on *Netherlands*. Whatever the reason, the album achieved some recognition, but Fogelberg has enjoyed better chart success in the USA than in the UK. In 1980, 'Longer' reached number 2 in the US singles charts, while in the UK it did not even reach the Top 50. Two other singles, 'Same Auld Lang Syne' and 'Leader Of The Band', both from *The Innocent Age*, achieved Top 10 places in the USA. The excellent *High Country Snows* saw a return to his bluegrass influences and was in marked contrast to the harder-edged *Exiles* which followed. From plaintive ballads to rock material, Fogelberg is a versatile writer and musician who continues to produce credible records and command a loyal cult following.

Albums: *Home Free* (1973), *Souvenirs* (1975), *Captured Angel* (1975), *Netherlands* (1977), with Tim Weisberg *Twin Sons Of Different Mothers* (1978), *Phoenix* (1980), *The Innocent Age* (1981), *Windows And Walls* (1984), *High Country Snows* (1985), *Exiles* (1987), *The Wild Places* (1990), *Dan Fogelberg Live - Greetings From The West* (1991). Compilation: *Greatest Hits* (1985).

Fogerty, John

b. 28 May 1945, Berkeley, California, USA. As the vocalist and composer with Creedence Clearwater Revival, one of the most successful acts of its era, Fogerty seemed assured of a similar status when he began a solo career in 1972. However his first release, *Blue Ridge Rangers*, was a curiously understated affair, designed to suggest the work of a group. The material consisted of country and gospel songs, two tracks from which, 'Jambalaya (On The Bayou)' and 'Hearts Of Stone', became US hit singles in 1973. Despite the exclusion of original songs and its outer anonymity, the work was clearly that of Fogerty, whose voice and instrumentation were unmistakable.

The first of many problems arose when the singer charged that his label, Fantasy Records, had not promoted the record sufficiently. He demanded a release from his contract, but the company claimed the rights to a further eight albums. This situation remained at an impasse until Asylum Records secured Fogerty's North American contract, while Fantasy retained copyright for the rest of the world. *John Fogerty* was duly released in 1975 and this superb collection contained several classic tracks, notably 'Almost Saturday Night' and 'Rockin' All Over The World' which were successfully covered, respectively, by Dave Edmunds and Status

Quo. However, Fogerty's legal entanglements still persisted and although a single, 'Comin' Down The Road', was released from a prospective third album, *Hoodoo*, it was never issued. It was 1985 before the artist re-emerged with the accomplished *Centerfield*, which topped the US album charts and provided an international hit single in 'The Old Man Down The Road'. The set also included two powerful rock songs, 'Mr. Greed' and 'Zanz Kan't Danz', which Fantasy owner Saul Zaentz assumed was a personal attack. He sued Fogerty for $142 million, claiming he had been slandered by the album's lyrics, and filed for the profits from 'The Old Man Down The Road', asserting the song plagiarised CCR's 'Run Through The Jungle'. Fogerty's riposte was a fourth album, *Eye Of A Zombie* which, although failing to scale the heights of its predecessor, was the impetus for series of excellent live performances. Since then the artist has maintained a lower profile, and successfully secured a decision against Zaentz's punitive action.
Albums: *The Blue Ridge Rangers* (1973), *John Fogerty* (1975), *Centerfield* (1985), *Eye Of A Zombie* (1986).

Fogerty, Tom

b. 9 November 1941, Berkeley, California, USA, d. September 1991. A self-taught musician, this artist's career flourished upon joining a rock 'n' roll band founded by his younger brother, John Fogerty. Having completed their lone single, 'Bonita', in 1963, Tom Fogerty And The Blue Velvets secured a recording deal with Fantasy, but were persuaded to change their name to the Golliwogs in an effort to capitalize on the concurrent British beat boom. The group kept this detested appellation until 1967 when they became known as Creedence Clearwater Revival. As such they were one of the most successful groups of the era, but relationships between the siblings soured and in November 1971, Tom Fogerty left for a solo career. He initially participated in an informal group which included guitarist Jerry Garcia and organist Merle Saunders, before completing four albums which, if inconsistent, contained several excellent tracks. Fogerty then formed a new act, Ruby, around Randy Oda (guitar/keyboards), Anthony Davis (bass) and Bobby Cochran (drums). The group recorded three albums, the last of which was preceded by Tom's final solo set, *Deal It Out*. Fogerty moved to Flagstaff, Arizona during the mid-80s, voicing plans to write an account of the Creedence story. However, he died prematurely of a heart attack in 1991.
Albums: solo *Tom Fogerty* (1972), *Excalibur* (1973),

Zephyr National (1974), *Myopia* (1975), *Deal It Out* (1981); as Ruby *Ruby* (1977), *Rock And Roll Madness* (1977), *Precious Gems* (1985).

Foghat

Although British in origin, Foghat relocated to the USA, where this boogie-blues band built a sizable following during the 70s. The band originally consisted of 'Lonesome' Dave Peverett (b. 1950, London, England; guitar/vocals), Tony Stevens (b. 12 September 1949, London, England; bass), Roger Earl (b. 1949; drums) and guitarist Rod Price. Peverett and Earl had been members of Savoy Brown, the British blues band. They left and immediately settled in the USA with the new unit, where Foghat signed with Bearsville Records, owned by entrepreneurial manager Albert Grossman. Their self-titled debut album, reached the US charts, as did the single, a cover of Willie Dixon's blues standard 'I Just Want To Make Love To You'. (A live version of that song also charted, in 1977.) The group held on to its formula for another dozen albums, each on Bearsville and each a chart item in the USA. Of those, the 1977 live album was the most popular. The band underwent several personnel changes, primarily bassists, with Price being replaced by Erik Cartwright in 1981. As Foghat's brand of boogie lost favour in the 80s the group disbanded.
Albums: *Foghat* i (1972), *Foghat* ii (1973), *Energized* (1974), *Rock And Roll Outlaws* (1974), *Fool For The City* (1975), *Night Shift* (1976), *Foghat Live* (1977), *Stone Blue* (1978), *Boogie Motel* (1979), *Tight Shoes* (1980), *Girls To Chat And Boys To Bounce* (1981), *In The Mood For Something Rude* (1982), *Zig-Zag Walk* (1983).

Fotheringay

The folk rock group Fotheringay was formed in 1970 by singer Sandy Denny upon her departure from Fairport Convention, and drew its name from one of her compositions for that group. Trevor Lucas (guitar/vocals), Gerry Conway (drums - both ex-Eclection), Jerry Donahue (guitar) and Pat Donaldson (bass; both ex-Poet And The One Man Band) completed the line-up responsible for the quintet's lone album. This impressive, folk-based set included several superior Denny originals, notably 'Nothing More', 'The Sea' and 'The Pond And The Stream', as well as meticulous readings of Gordon Lightfoot's 'The Way I Feel' and Bob Dylan's 'Too Much Of Nothing'. Although criticized contemporaneously as constrained, *Fotheringay* is now rightly viewed as a confident,

accomplished work. However, the album failed to match commercial expectations and pressures on Denny to undertake a solo career - she was voted Britain's number 1 singer in *Melody Maker*'s 1970 poll - increased. Fotheringay was disbanded in 1971 during sessions for a projected second set. Some of its songs surfaced on the vocalist's debut album, *The Northstar Grassman* and whereas Donaldson and Conway began session work, Lucas and Donahue resurfaced in Fairport Convention.
Album: *Fotheringay* (1970).
Further reading: *Meet On The Ledge*, Patrick Humphries.

Fox

This UK group was formed in the mid-70s and comprised Noosha Fox (lead vocals), Herbie Armstrong (guitar/vocals, ex-duo partner to Rod Demick), Kenny Young (guitar/vocals), Jim Gannon (guitar/vocals, ex-Black Widow), plus session musicians Pete Solley (keyboards/vocals), Jim Frank (drums) and Gary Taylor (bass). They scored three UK hits on the GTO label with 'Only You Can' (number 3, 1975), 'Imagine Me, Imagine You' (number 15, 1975) and 'S-S-S-Single Bed' (number 4, 1976) - a run of hits that earned Fox a UK Top 10 album. Despite the group's musical credentials, their popularity centred mainly around the sexily-voiced Noosha Fox, who later left the group in 1977 to pursue a solo career. The only notable profit for Noosha from this move however, was the achievement of a UK Top 40 single, 'Georgina Bailey'. The group soldiered on for one more album, *Blue Hotel* which flopped, resulting in the group splitting soon afterwards. Herbie Armstrong and Kenny Young went on to form the briefly successful Yellow Dog in 1977. Armstrong later engaged in solo performances and worked with Van Morrison from 1978-82 appearing on *Wavelength, Into The Music, Common One* and *Beautiful Vision*.
Albums: *Fox* (1975), *Tales Of Illusion* (1975), *Blue Hotel* (1977).

Frampton, Peter

b. 22 April 1950, Beckenham, Kent, England. The former 'Face of 1968', with his pin-up good looks as part of the 60s' pop group the Herd, Frampton grew his hair longer and joined Humble Pie. His solo career debuted with *Wind Of Change* in 1971, although he immediately set about forming another band, Frampton's Camel, to carry out US concert dates. This formidable unit consisted of Mike Kellie (drums), Mickey Gallagher (keyboards) and Rick Wills (bass), all seasoned players from Spooky Tooth, Cochise and Bell And Arc respectively. *Frampton* in 1975 was a great success in the USA, while in the UK he was commercially ignored. The following year a double set, *Frampton Comes Alive* scaled the US chart and stayed on top for a total 10 weeks, in four visits during a record breaking two-year stay. The record became the biggest-selling live album in history and to date has sold over 12 million copies. Quite why the record was so successful has perplexed many rock critics. Like Jeff Beck, Frampton perfected the voice tube effect and used this gimmick on 'Show Me The Way'. The follow-up *I'm In You*, sold in vast quantities, although compared to the former it was a flop, selling a modest 'several million'. Again Frampton found little critical acclaim, but his records were selling in vast quantities. He continued to reach younger audiences with aplomb. In 1978 he suffered a near fatal car crash, although his fans were able to see him, in the previously filmed *Sgt Pepper's Lonely Hearts Club Band*. Frampton played Billy Shears alongside the Bee Gees in the Robert Stigwood extravaganza that was a commercial and critical disaster. When he returned in 1979 with *Where I Should Be*, his star was dwindling. The album garnered favourable reviews, but it was to be his last successful record. Even the short-haired image for *Breaking All The Rules* failed, with only America, his loyal base, nudging it into the Top 50. Following *The Art Of Control* Frampton 'disappeared' until 1986, when he was signed to Virgin Records and released the synthesizer-laced *Premonition*. He returned to session work thereafter. Later on in the decade Frampton was to be found playing guitar with his former school-friend David Bowie on his *Never Let Me Down*. In 1991 he was allegedly making plans to reform Humble Pie with Steve Marriott, but a week after their meeting in New York, Marriott was tragically burnt to death in his home.
Albums: *Wind Of Change* (1972), *Frampton's Camel* (1973), *Somethin's Happening* (1974), *Frampton* (1975), *Frampton Comes Alive!* (1976), *I'm In You* (1977), *Where I Should Be* (1979), *Breaking All The Rules* (1981), *The Art Of Control* (1982), *Premonition* (1986).

Fraser, Andy

b. 7 August 1952, London, England. Fraser was a founder member and bass player of the late 60s and early 70s UK blues/rock group, Free. He cut his musical teeth as a teenager working for John Mayall. Fraser broke from Free on two occasions,

Peter Frampton

first in 1971, going on to form the ill-fated trio, Toby, with guitarist Adrian Fisher (later to join Sparks) and drummer Stan Speake. The reformation of Free early in 1972, was short-lived, for Fraser quit in July that same year. He teamed up with Chris Spedding to form Sharks, recording two albums for Island. With the folding of Sharks and after a brief period with Frankie Miller and Henry McCullough, Fraser created the Andy Fraser Band with Nick Judd (keyboards) and Kim Turner (drums), recording two albums for CBS in 1975. Having retired from playing, Fraser still enjoys the benefits of regular royalty cheques from his most productive period with Free.

Albums: as the Andy Fraser Band *The Andy Fraser Band* (1975), *In Your Eyes* (1975).

Free

Formed in the midst of 1968's British blues boom, Free originally included Paul Rodgers (b. 12 December 1949, Middlesbrough, Cleveland, England; vocals), Paul Kossoff (b. 14 September 1950, London, England, d. 19 March 1976; guitar), Andy Fraser (b. 7 August 1952, London, England; bass) and Simon Kirke (b. 28 July 1949, Shrewsbury, Shropshire, England; drums). Despite their comparative youth, the individual musicians were seasoned performers, particularly Fraser, a former member of John Mayall's Bluesbreakers. Free gained early encouragement from Alexis Korner, but having completed an earthy debut album, *Tons Of Sobs*, the group began honing a more individual style with their second set. The injection of powerful original songs, including 'I'll Be Creeping', showed a maturing talent, while Rodgers' expressive voice and Kossoff's stinging guitar enhanced a growing reputation.

The quartet's stylish blues/rock reached its peak on *Fire And Water*. This confident collection featured moving ballads; 'Heavy Load', 'Oh I Wept' and compulsive, uptempo material, the best-known of which is 'All Right Now'. An edited version of this soulful composition reached number 2 in the UK and number 4 in the US in 1970, since when the song has become one of pop's most enduring performances making periodic appearances in the singles chart. A fourth set, *Highway*, revealed a mellower perspective enhanced by an increased use of piano at the expense of Kossoff's guitar. This was due, in part, to friction within the group, a factor exacerbated when the attendant single, 'The Stealer', failed to emulate its predecessor. Free split up in May 1971, paradoxically in the wake of another successful single, 'My Brother Jake', but regrouped in January the following year when spin-off projects faltered, although Kossoff and

Free

Kirke's amalgamation (Kossoff, Kirke, Tetsu And Rabbit) proved fruitful.

A sixth album, *Free At Last*, offered some of the unit's erstwhile fire and included another UK Top 20 entrant, 'Little Bit Of Love'. However Kossoff's increasing ill-health and Fraser's departure for the Sharks undermined any newfound confidence. A hastily convened line-up consisting of Rodgers, Kirke, John 'Rabbit' Bundrick (keyboards) and Tetsu Yamauchi (b. 1946, Fukuoka, Japan; bass) undertook a Japanese tour, but although the guitarist rejoined the quartet for several British dates, his contribution to Free's final album, *Heartbreaker*, was muted. Kossoff embarked on a solo career in October 1972; Wendel Richardson from Osibisa replaced him on a temporary basis, but by July the following year Free had ceased to function. Rodgers and Kirke subsequently formed Bad Company.

Albums: *Tons Of Sobs* (1968), *Free* (1969), *Fire And Water* (1970), *Highway* (1971), *Free Live* (1971), *Free At Last* (1972), *Heartbreaker* (1973). Compilations: *The Free Story* (1974), *Completely Free* (1982), *All Right Now* (1991).

Freedom

Formed in 1969, this progressive UK rock trio comprised: Bobby Harrison (b. 28 June 1943, East Ham, England; drums/vocals), Roger Saunders (guitar/piano/vocals) and Walt Monaham (organ/cello/bass). Harrison stepped from behind the drum-stool of Procol Harum to lead this highly-respected power unit who made an impact with audiences during late 60s British blues boom. The original members with Harrison were Steve Shirley and Robin Lumson. Together, they recorded a little known album which was the soundtrack to the Dino De Laurentis film *Black On White* (1969). The ever-restless Harrison sealed the band's fate when he decided to make a solo album in 1970. Ironically, *Funkist* eclipsed Freedom's efforts in total sales.

Albums: *Freedom* (1970), *At Last* (1970), *Through The Years* (1971), *Is More Than A Word* (1972).

Free Movement

Formed in Los Angeles, California, USA in 1970, Free Movement made the *Billboard* Top 5 in the US with 'I've Found Someone On My Own'. The group was a sextet, some of whom had gospel singing experience, including Josephine Brown, Godoy Colbert, Cheryl Conley, Jennifer Gates, Adrian Jefferson and Claude Jefferson. The group made a demo record and was signed by Decca Records in 1971. The debut single took six months to climb the charts, eventually reaching number 5. Ironically, by the time the record was a hit, the group had left Decca and signed with Columbia Records, where they released an album and two singles.

Album: *I've Found Someone On My Own* (1972).

Friedman, Dean

This New Jersey, USA born vocalist found instant success on both sides of the Atlantic with a mixture of sentimental ballads and joyful pleasant tunes about romance. He scored a US hit with 'Ariel' which made ripples in Europe, but his 1978 record 'Lucky Stars', reached the Top 3 position in the UK and made him a household name. A lack of promotion and sporadic record releases led to declining sales (due mainly to problems at the Lifesong/GTO label), although 'Lydia' gave him his last notable chart hit, reaching the UK Top 40. Although he briefly recorded for the Epic label, releasing *Rumpled Romeo* in 1982, throughout the 80s he released occasional singles on minor labels. One track though 'The Lakelands' was included on a compilation album which sold a quarter of a million units. He re-appeared in 1990 writing and performing the soundtrack to a low-budget British horror film *I Bought A Vampire Motorcycle*.

Albums: *Dean Friedman* (1977), *Well, Well, Said The Rocking Chair* (1978), *Rumpled Romeo* (1982). Compilation: *Very Best Of Dean Friedman* (1991).

Frijid Pink

Kelly Green (vocals/harmonica), Gary Ray Thompson (guitar), Thomas Beaudry (bass), Larry Zelanka (keyboards) and Rick Stevens (drums) emerged from the hard rock circuit in Detroit, USA. In 1970 they scored a surprise transatlantic hit with their powerhouse interpretation of 'The House Of The Rising Sun', based on the Animals' highly original arrangement, but to which they added a searing, guitar-strewn approach, reminiscent of contemporaries the MC5 and Stooges. The single reached number 7 in the US and number 4 in the UK, but the group's subsequent chart entries, 'Sing A Song For Freedom' and 'Heartbreak Hotel' (both 1971), were confined to the lower regions of the US chart. It confirmed a suspicion that the song, rather than the group, was responsible for that first flush of success. By the time of their final album in 1975 for Fantasy Records only Stevens remained from the original line-up.

Albums: *Frijid Pink* (1970), *Defrosted* (1970), *Earth*

Omen (1972), *All Pink Inside* (1975).

Fripp, Robert
b. 16 May 1946, Wimbourne, Dorset, England. Guitarist, composer and producer, Fripp began his diverse career in the small, but flourishing, circuit centred on Bournemouth, Dorset. He subsequently joined the League Of Gentlemen, a London-based group renowned for backing visiting American singers, and later founded Giles Giles And Fripp with brothers Pete and Mike Giles. This eccentric trio completed one album, *The Cheerful Insanity of Giles Giles And Fripp* in 1968 before evolving into King Crimson, the progressive act though which the artist forged his reputation. Between 1969-74, Fripp led several contrasting versions of this constantly challenging group, during which time he also enjoyed an artistically fruitful collaboration with Brian Eno. *No Pussyfooting* (1972) and *Evening Star* (1974) were among the era's leading *avant garde* recordings, the former of which introduced the tape loop and layered guitar technique known as 'Frippertronics', which later became an artistic trademark. During this period Fripp also produced several experimental jazz releases, notably by Centipede, and having disbanded King Crimson at a time 'all English bands in that genre should have ceased to exist', Fripp retired from music altogether. He re-emerged in 1977, contributing several excellent passages to David Bowie's *Heroes*, before playing on, and producing, Peter Gabriel's second album. Fripp provided a similar role on Daryl Hall's *Sacred Songs*, before completing *Exposure*, on which the artist acknowledged the concurrent punk movement. Simpler and more incisive than previous work, its energetic purpose contrasted the measured, sculpted approach of King Crimson, whom Fripp nonetheless surprisingly reconstituted in 1981. Three well-received albums followed, during which time the guitarist pursued a parallel, more personal, path leading a group bearing another resurrected name, the League Of Gentlemen. Both units were disbanded later in the decade, and Fripp subsequently performed and gave tutorials under a 'League Of Crafty Guitarists' banner and recorded with former Police member Andy Summers. Now married to singer/actress Toyah Wilcox, this highly talented individual has doggedly followed an uncompromising path, resulting in some highly individual, provocative music.
Albums: with Giles Giles And Fripp *The Cheerful Insanity Of Giles Giles And Fripp* (1968), with Brian Eno *No Pussyfooting* (1972), *Evening Star* (1974);

solo *Exposure* (1979), *God Save The Queen/Under Heavy Manners* (1980), *Let The Power Fall* aka *The League Of Gentlemen* (1981), *God Save The King* (1985), with Toyah *The Lady And The Tiger* (1986), *Network* (1987); with The League Of Crafty Guitarists *Robert Fripp And The League Of Crafty Guitarists Live* (1986), *Live II* (1990), *Show Of Hands* (1991), (1991), with Andy Summers *I Advance Masked* (1982), *Bewitched* (1984).
Further reading: *Robert Fripp: From King Crimson To Guitar Craft*, Eric Tamm.

Fruup
Vince McCusker (guitar/vocals) was the mainstay of this 70s outfit from Belfast, Northern Ireland. With Steve Houston (keyboards/vocals), Peter Farrelly (bass/vocals) and Martin Foye (drums), he recorded a debut album for Dawn Records, which defined the pomp-rock style with vaguely mystical overtones that sustained Fruup on a five-year career around the European college circuit. During exploratory sessions for 1974's *Seven Secrets*, Houston was replaced by John Mason, Ian McDonald played saxophone on the following year's *Modern Masquerades*. Although respected as a competent act, and the group were unable to climb to higher rungs on the progressive rock ladder before punk's levelling blow. Obliged to drastically reduce engagement fees, the inevitable cracks appeared and, by 1978, Fruup was no more.
Albums: *Future Legends* (1973), *Prince Of Heaven's Eyes* (1974), *Seven Secrets* (1974), *Modern Masquerades* (1975).

Furay, Richie
b. 9 May 1944, Yellow Springs, Ohio, USA. Originally a member of the Au Go-Go Singers, Furay first came to prominence as the crystal clear vocalist acting as a foil between the voices of Stephen Stills' soulful blues and Neil Young's Canadian folk rock in the seminal Buffalo Springfield during 1967. The short-lived Springfield fragmented and out of the ashes came Poco, one of the leaders of the country-rock movement. Much of Furay's best work appeared during his time as leader of Poco, with notably impressive contributions to *A Good Feelin' To Know* and *Crazy Eyes*. His subsequent departure was mainly out of frustration of seeing Poco unable to break out of the second division, while bands like the Eagles reaped massive fame and fortune by mining the same seam. A lucrative contract with David Geffen saw the formation of the Souther Hillman Furay Band in 1974. Touted as a country

rock supergroup, they were unable to live up to expectations and after two average albums each member resumed their respective solo careers with varying degrees of success. Furay's solo debut, *I've Got A Reason*, was a credible but laid-back album. Billed as the Richie Furay Band the record was an autobiographical journey with 'Look At The Sun' and the title track as the strongest songs. A new line-up supported him on *Dance A Little Light*, a lesser album marred by lethargy. *I Still Have Dreams* however, was a marked improvement, benefiting from the seasoned talents of musicians such as Dan Dugmore, Leland Sklar, Craig Doegre and the steady drumming of Russell Kunkel. Further vocal enhancements were added by J.D. Souther, Timothy B. Schmit, Randy Meisner and Craig Fuller. Ironically the two stand-out songs were written by band member Billy Batstone, who contributed the title track and the tear-jerking ballad 'I Was A Fool'. Furay then began to devote his life to the church. The content of *Satisfied* clearly showed this direction. He retired for many years appearing on a latter-day Poco album, and adding the occasional vocal backing to other albums. In 1990, now as a full-time pastor in Colorado, he joined with his original Poco colleagues for the excellent reunion album *Legacy*. Furay's shining voice was once again leading the only band he ever sounded in total control with.
Albums: *I've Got A Reason* (1976), *Dance A Little Light* (1978), *I Still Have Dreams* (1979), *Satisfied* (1979).

G

Gallagher And Lyle

Benny Gallagher (vocals/guitar) and Graham Lyle (vocals/guitar) were both born in Largs, Ayrshire, Scotland. Having sung with several nascent beat groups, they began a songwriting career with 'Mr. Heartbreak's Here Instead', a 1964 single for Dean Ford And The Gaylords. The duo later moved to London where they joined the Apple label as in-house composers. One of their songs, 'International', was recorded by Mary Hopkin.

In 1969 the pair joined McGuinness Flint for whom they wrote two successful singles, 'When I'm Dead And Gone' (1970) and 'Malt And Barley Blues' (1971), before leaving the group for an independent career. Several well-crafted, if low-key, albums followed, which showcased the duo's flair for folk-styled melody, but it was not until 1976 that they enjoyed a commercial breakthrough. *Breakaway* spawned two major hits in 'I Wanna Stay With You' and 'Heart On My Sleeve', both of which reached number 6 in the UK. Further recognition of their compositional talents was endorsed by Art Garfunkel taking a cover version of the album's title track into the US Top 40, but the act was curiously unable to sustain its newfound profile. Gallagher and Lyle parted following the release of *Lonesome No More* in order to pursue different projects. Graham Lyle later found a new partner, Terry Britten, with whom he composed 'What's Love Got To Do With It' and 'Just Good Friends' which were recorded, respectively, by Tina Turner and Michael Jackson.
Albums: *Gallagher And Lyle* (1972), *Willie And The Lap Dog* (1973), *Seeds* (1973), *The Last Cowboy* (1974), *Breakaway* (1976), *Love On The Airwaves* (1977), *Showdown* (1978), *Gone Crazy* (1979), *Lonesome No More* (1979). Compilations: *The Best Of Gallagher And Lyle* (1980), *Heart On My Sleeve* (1991).

Garfunkel, Art

b. 5 November 1941, New York, New York, USA. The possessor of one of the pitch-perfect voices in popular music has had a sparse recording career since the demise of Simon And Garfunkel. The break-up of one of the most successful post-war singing duos was due in part to Garfunkel's desire to go into acting and Paul Simon's understandable resentment that Art took the glory on his compositions like 'Bridge Over Troubled Water'. While Simon had the songs, Garfunkel possessed *the* voice. Garfunkel's acting career landed him substantial parts in *Catch 22*, *Carnal Knowledge*, *Bad Timing* and *Good To Go*. During this time his recording output, although sporadic, was of a consistent high quality. His debut *Angel Clare* contained the beautiful 'All I Know', which was a Top 10 US hit. In the UK two of his records

Gallagher And Lyle

Art Garfunkel

made the top spot, a luscious 'I Only Have Eyes For You' and the Mike Batt theme for *Watership Down*, 'Bright Eyes'. In 1978 '(What A) Wonderful World' featured the additional voices of James Taylor and Paul Simon, fuelling rumours of a reunion. They appeared together occasionally both on television and on record, but it was not until October 1981 that the historic Central Park concert occurred. The duo struggled through a world tour, opening up old wounds; once again they parted company. Since then Garfunkel has released *Lefty*, and although it contained some good quality Jim Webb songs, it sold poorly.
Albums: *Angel Clare* (1973), *Breakaway* (1975), *Watermark* (1978), *Fate For Breakfast* (1979), *Scissors Cut* (1981), *Lefty* (1988), *Moment Of Truth* (1988).

Garrett, Leif

b. 8 November 1961, Hollywood, California, USA. Blond teen vocalist, Garrett had already been seen in the film *Walking Tall* in 1973. He also appeared in both sequels before signing to Atlantic Records. He hit the US Top 20 with a remake of the Beach Boys' 'Surfin' USA', in the summer of 1977. His US chart career continued with updates of Dion's 'Runaround Sue' and 'The Wanderer' and Paul Anka's 'Put Your Head On My Shoulder', before he moved to the Scotti Brothers label in 1978 and achieved his biggest hit, the disco galloper, 'I Was Made For Dancing', a Top 10 smash in both the UK and US in 1979. He was instrumental in promoting the skateboard craze in the mid to late 70s in the UK.

Albums: *Leif Garrett* (1977), *Feel The Need* (1978), *Same Goes For You* (1979), *My Movie Of You* (1981).

Gates, David

b. 11 December 1940, Tulsa, Oklahoma, USA. Having played in a hometown high school band alongside Leon Russell, Gates followed his former colleague to Los Angeles. He initially pursued a career as a rockabilly singer, recording a series of locally-issued singles including 'Swinging Baby Doll' (1958), which featured Russell on piano, and 'My Baby's Gone Away' (1961). He later switched to studio work, and appearances on sessions for Duane Eddy and Pat Boone preceded a fruitful period in the budding 'girl-group' genre. Gates produced and/or composed a string of excellent releases, notably Merry Clayton's 'Usher Boy', the Murmaids' 'Popsicles And Icicles', Dorothy Berry's 'You're So Fine' (all 1963), Shelly Fabares' 'He Don't Love Me' and Connie Stevens' 'A Girl Never Knows' (both 1964). Having founded, then closed, the short-lived Planetary label in 1966, Gates switched his attentions to the emergent west coast group scene. He produced material for Captain Beefheart and the Gants, while work with a harmony act, the Pleasure Fair in 1968, led to the formation of Bread. For three years Gates led this highly popular attraction, composing many of their best-known songs including 'Make It With You', 'If', 'Baby I'm A Want You' and 'Everything I Own'. He began a solo career in 1973, but despite two albums of a similar high quality, the artist

Leif Garrett

failed to sustain this level of success. A short-lived Bread reunion was equally ill-starred, suggesting that Gates' brand of soft, melodic pop was now out of fashion. He did enjoy a US Top 20 hit in 1978 with 'Goodbye Girl' but ensuing releases were less well received and Gates has now reportedly retired from music altogether.

Albums: *First Album* (1973), *Never Let Her Go* (1975), *Goodbye Girl* (1978), *Songbook* (1979), *Falling In Love Again* (1980), *Take Me Now* (1981).

Geils Band, J.

Formed in Boston, Massachusetts, USA in 1969, the group - J. Geils (b. Jerome Geils, 20 February, 1946, New York, USA; guitar), Peter Wolf (b. 7 March 1947, Bronx, New York, USA; vocals), Magic Dick (b. Richard Salwitz, 13 May 1945, New London, Connecticut, USA; harmonica), Seth Justman (b. 27 January 1951, Washington, DC, USA; keyboards), Danny Klein (b. 13 May 1946, New York, USA; bass) and Stephan Jo Bladd (b.31 July 1942, Boston, Massachusetts; drums) - was originally known as the J. Geils Blues Band. Their first two albums established a tough, raw R&B which encouraged comparisons with the respected Butterfield Blues Band. Versions of songs by Albert Collins, Otis Rush and John Lee Hooker showed an undoubted flair, and with Wolf as an extrovert frontman, they quickly became a popular live attraction. *Bloodshot*, a gold US album release in 1973, introduced the group to a wider audience, but at the same time suggested a tardiness which marred subsequent releases. The major exception was *Monkey Island* where Wolf, Geils and Magic Dick reclaimed the fire and excitement enlivening those first two albums. The group moved from the Atlantic label to EMI at the end of the 70s and secured a massive international hit in 1982 with the leering 'Centrefold'. Now divorced from their blues roots, the J. Geils Band was unsure of its direction, a factor emphasised in 1984 when Wolf departed for a solo career, midway through a recording session. The group completed a final album, *You're Gettin' Even, While I'm Gettin' Old*, without him.

Albums: *J. Geils Band* (1970), *The Morning After* (1971), *Live - Full House* (1972), *Bloodshot* (1973), *Ladies Invited* (1973), *Nightmares...And Other Tales From The Vinyl Jungle* (1974), *Hotline* (1975), *Live - Blow Your Face Out* (1976), *Monkey Island* (1977), *Sanctuary* (1978), *Love Stinks* (1980), *Freeze Frame* (1981), *Showtime!* (1984), *You're Gettin' Even While I'm Gettin' Old* (1984). Compilation: *The Best Of The J. Geils Band* (1979).

Genesis

This leading UK band first came together at the public school Charterhouse. Peter Gabriel (b. 13 May 1950, London, England; vocals), Tony Banks (b. 27 March 1951, East Heathly, Sussex, England; keyboards) and Chris Stewart (drums) were in an ensemble named the Garden Wall, and joined forces with Anthony Philips (guitar/vocals) and Mike Rutherford (b. 2 October 1950; bass/guitar/vocals), who were in a rival group, the Anon. In January 1967, the student musicians sent a demonstration tape to another Charterhouse alumnus, Jonathan King, then at Decca Records. King financed further recordings and also christened the band Genesis. They recorded one single, 'The Silent Sun' in 1968, but it was not until the following year that their debut album *From Genesis To Revelation* was issued. Its lack of success left them without a label until the enterprising Tony Stratton-Smith signed them to his recently formed Charisma Records in 1970. The group had already lost three drummers from their line-up before finding the perfect candidate that August. Phil Collins (b. 31 January 1951, London, England) had already worked with a professional group, Flaming Youth, and his involvement would later prove crucial in helping Genesis achieve international success.

The already recorded *Trespass* was issued in October 1970, but sold poorly. Further line-up changes ensued with the arrival of new guitarist Steve Hackett (b. 12 February 1950, London, England). The group were already known for their highly theatrical stage act and costumes, but this did not help record sales. When the 1971 album *Nursery Cryme* also failed commercially, the group were again in danger of being dropped from their label. Success on the continent brought renewed faith, which was vindicated with the release of *Foxtrot*. The album reached the UK Top 20 and included the epic live favourite 'Supper's Ready'. Over the next two-and-a-half years, Genesis increased their profile with the best-selling albums *Selling England By The Pound* and *The Lamb Lies Down On Broadway*. Having reached a new peak, however, their prospects were completely undermined by the shock departure of singer Gabriel in May 1975.

Many commentators understandably wrote Genesis off at this point, particularly when it was announced that the new singer was to be their drummer Collins. The streamlined quartet proved remarkably resilient, however, and the succeeding albums *A Trick Of The Tail* and *Wind And*

Wuthering were well received. In the summer of 1977, Hackett left to pursue a solo career, after which Genesis carried on as a trio, backed by various short-term employees. Amazingly, the group appeared to grow in popularity with the successive departure of each key member. During 1978, they received their first gold disc for the appropriately titled *And Then There Were Three* and two years later enjoyed a chart-topping album with *Duke*. With various solo excursions underway, Genesis still managed to sustain its identity as a working group and reached new levels of popularity with hits in the USA. By late 1981, they were in the US Top 10 with *Abacab* and could rightly claim to be one of the most popular groups in the world. Helped by Collins' high profile as a soloist, they enjoyed their biggest UK singles hit with 'Mama' and followed with 'Thats All' and 'Illegal Alien'. Both *Genesis* and *Invisible Touch* topped the UK charts, while the latter also reached number 1 in the USA. By the mid-80s, the group format was not sufficient to contain all their various projects and Collins pursued a parallel solo career, while Rutherford formed the hit group Mike And The Mechanics. Meanwhile, Genesis soldiered on, reuniting at various intervals for tours and albums. There was no sign of decline in their popularity and in America they scored a number 1 single in 1986 with 'Invisible Touch', while the following four singles all made the US Top 5. Although their working partnership is less prolific these days, the concept of Genesis continues, amid a myriad of offshoot projects. In 1991, the group reconvened to record and issue *We Can't Dance*. Although this was their first album in over five years it immediately scaled the charts throughout the world confirming their status as one of the world's leading bands.

Albums: *From Genesis To Revelation* (1969), *Trespass* (1970), *Nursery Cryme* (1971), *Foxtrot* (1972), *Genesis Live* (1973), *Selling England By The Pound* (1973), *The Lamb Lies Down On Broadway* (1974), *A Trick Of The Tail* (1976), *Wind And Wuthering* (1977), *Seconds Out* (1977), *And Then There Were Three* (1978), *Duke* (1980), *Abacab* (1981), *3 Sides Live* (1982), *Genesis* (1983), *Invisible Touch* (1986), *We Can't Dance* (1991), *The Way We Walk - Vol 1: The Shorts* (1992), *Live The Way We Walk - Vol. 2: The Longs* (1993).

Gentle Giant

Formed in 1969 by the Shulman brothers; Derek (b. 11 February 1947, Glasgow, Scotland; vocals/guitar/bass), Ray (b. 3 December 1949, Portsmouth, Hampshire, England; vocals/bass/violin) and Phil (b. 27 August 1937, Glasgow, Scotland; saxophone), on the collapse of their previous group, Simon Dupree And The Big Sound. Kerry Minnear (b. 2 January 1948, Shaftsbury, Dorset, England; keyboards/vocals), Gary Green (b. 20 November 1950, Muswell Hill, London, England; guitar/vocals) and Martin Smith (drums) completed the first Gentle Giant line-up which eschewed the pop/soul leanings of its predecessor for an experimental, progressive style reminiscent of Yes and King Crimson. The sextet was signed to the renowned Vertigo label in 1970 and, teamed with producer Tony Visconti, completed a debut album which offered all the hallmarks of their subsequent recordings. This ambitious set blended hard rock and classics with an adventurous use of complex chord changes which, if not commercially successful, indicated a quest for both excellence and originality. Although deemed pretentious by many commentators, there was no denying the ambition and individuality this release introduced. Smith left the line-up following *Acquiring The Taste*, but although his replacement, Malcolm Mortimore, appeared on *Three Friends*, a motorcycle accident forced the newcomer's departure. John 'Pugwash' Weathers (b. 2 February 1947, Carmarthen, Glamorganshire, Wales), veteran of Eyes Of Blue, Graham Bond and Pete Brown's Piblokto!, joined Gentle Giant for *Octopus*, arguably their best-known release. However, an attendant tour ended with the departure of Phil who retired from music altogether. The group then switched outlets to WWA, but encountered problems in America when *In A Glass House* was deemed too uncommercial for release there. *The Power And The Glory* proved less daunting and in turn engendered a new recording deal with Chrysalis. The ensuing *Free Hand* became Gentle Giant's best-selling UK album, but this ascendancy faltered when *Interview* invoked the experimental style of earlier releases. A double-set, *Playing The Fool*, confirmed the quintet's in-concert dexterity, but subsequent albums unsuccessfully courted an AOR audience. *Civilian* was a conscious attempt at regaining former glories, but the departure of Minnear, by this point the band's musical director, signalled their demise. Gentle Giant split up in 1980 and several former members have pursued low-key careers. Ray Shulman has become a highly successful producer, working with such diverse acts as the Sugarcubes, the Sundays and Ian McCulloch. Brother Derek moved to New York to become director of A&R at Polygram.

Albums: *Gentle Giant* (1970), *Acquiring The Taste* (1971), *Three Friends* (1972), *Octopus* (1972), *In A Glass House* (1973), *The Power And The Glory* (1974), *Free Hand* (1975), *Interview* (1976), *The Official 'Live' Gentle Giant - Playing The Fool* (1977), *The Missing Piece* (1977), *Giant For A Day* (1978), *Civilian* (1980). Compilations: *Giant Steps (The First Five Years)* (1975), *Pretentious (For The Sake Of It)* (1977).

Geordie

Hailing from the north east of England, Tynesiders Brian Johnson (vocals), Victor Malcolm (guitar), Tom Hill (bass) and Brian Gibson (drums) started as a poor man's Slade with an unselfconsciously professional style based on the pop end of heavy metal, and a stage act that included an audience participation opus, the dialectal 'Geordie's Lost His Liggy', which involved Johnson hoisting Malcolm onto his shoulders. After one single for Regal Zonophone, 'Don't Do That', tickled the hit parade, they were signed by EMI whose faith was justified when 'All Because Of You' from 1973's *Hope You Like It* made the UK Top 20. Two lesser entries - 'Can You Do It' and 'Electric Lady' - followed, and the group's albums sold steadily if unremarkably. Geordie's power as a concert attraction outlasted this chart run, and when the going got rough in the watershed year of 1976-77, the quartet signed off with *Save The World* - a consolidation rather than development of their derivative music. They were remembered not for their hits but as the *alma mater* of Johnson (b. 5 October 1947, Dunston, England) who, after a lean period in which he was heard in a vacuum cleaner commercial, replaced the late Bon Scott in AC/DC.

Albums: *Hope You Like It* (1973), *Masters Of Rock* (1974), *Don't Be Fooled By The Name* (1974), *Save The World* (1976). Compilation: *Featuring Brian Johnson* (1981).

Gibb, Andy

b. 5 March 1958, Manchester, England, d. 10 March 1988, Oxford, England. Following the international success of his three elder brothers in the Bee Gees, Andy appeared as a star in his own right in 1977. Emerging at the beginning of the disco boom, he scored three consecutive US number 1 hits with his first three chart entries. 'I Just Want To Be Your Everything', '(Love Is) Thicker Than Water' and 'Shadow Dancing' made him one of the most commercially successful recording artists of his era and for a time he even eclipsed his illustrious brothers in popularity. Six further hits followed, including a collaboration with Olivia Newton-John ('I Can't Help It') before Gibb moved into television work. The pressure of living with the reputation of his superstar brothers, coupled with immense wealth and a hedonistic bent, brought personal problems

and he became alarming reliant upon cocaine. Within months of his brothers autumnal and highly successful reunion in the late 80s, tragedy struck when the 30-year-old singer died of an inflammatory heart virus at his home. It was the end of a career that had brought spectacular success in a remarkably short period.

Albums: *Flowing Rivers* (1977), *Shadow Dancing* (1978), *After Dark* (1980). Compilation: *Andy Gibb's Greatest Hits* (1980).

Gibbons, Steve

b. c.1942, Birmingham, England. Gibbons was the quintessential product of the English beat group era, with a powerful vocal style and a quiverful of imaginative and intelligent compositions. He started in 1958 as the vocalist with the Dominettes. After several changes of line-up this became the Uglys in 1962. With Dave Pegg (later of Fairport Convention) on bass the group recorded unsuccessfully for Pye and later for MGM. In 1969, the Uglys split and Gibbons joined Denny Laine (ex-Moody Blues) and Trevor Burton (ex-Move), in Balls, an abortive attempt by ex-Move manager Tony Secunda to create a Brum 'supergroup'. With the aid of session guitarists Albert Lee and Chris Spedding, Balls made *Short Stories* for Secunda's Wizzard label before disbanding in 1971. Gibbons next briefly joined the Idle Race which evolved into the Steve Gibbons Band, which has continued with line-up changes to this day. The early personnel included Burton (bass), Dave Carroll and Bob Wilson on guitars and Bob Lamb (drums). Their debut album appeared on Roger Daltrey's Goldhawk label in 1976 and the following year Gibbons had a Top 20 hit with Chuck Berry's 'Tulane', from *Caught In The Act* produced by Kenny Laguna. Soon afterwards Lamb quit the band to concentrate on running his own studio, where he produced the early work of UB40. In the early 80s the Steve Gibbons Band recorded two albums for RCA with Gibbons maintaining his imaginative and witty approach co-songwriting, as the titles 'Biggles Flys Undone', 'B.S.A.' and 'Somebody Stole My Synthesiser' suggest. Burton left the band around this time but Gibbons continued to be a popular live performer, especially in the Birmingham area. His later albums appeared infrequently on small UK labels.

Albums: *Any Road Up* (1976), *Rolling On* (1977), *Caught In The Act* (1977), *Down In The Bunker* (1978), *Street Parade* (1980), *Saints And Sinners* (1981), *On The Loose* (1986), *Not On The Radio* (1991).

Gilder, Nick

b. 7 November 1951, London, England. Gilder is best known for the 1978 hit 'Hot Child In The City', which reached number 1 in the US. Gilder moved to Vancouver, Canada at the age of 10 and in high school formed a band called Throm Hortis. Gilder joined the band Sweeney Todd in 1971, and they charted with 'Roxy Roller' in 1976 (a second version of that song, also by Sweeney Todd featuring Bryan Adams on vocals, charted a month after the Gilder-sung version).With band member Jim McCulloch, Gilder relocated to Los Angeles and signed as a solo artist to Chrysalis Records. 'Hot Child In The City' was his first and greatest success, followed by two lesser chart singles, 'Here Comes The Night' and 'Rock Me'. Gilder also placed two albums on the chart, *City Nights* and *Frequency* but he was unable to repeat his success after the end of the 70s, despite further albums for Casablanca Records and RCA Records.

Albums: *You Know Who You Are* (1977), *City Nights* (1978), *Frequency* (1979), *Rock America* (1980), *Nick Gilder* (1985).

Glass House

Tyrone 'Ty' Hunter (b. 1943, d. 24 February 1981), Scherrie Payne, Larry Mitchell, Pearl Jones and Eric Dunham made up this Detroit-based group. Hunter's prolific career had begun in the Voice Masters, after which he followed a solid, if unspectacular solo path. Pearl Jones, meanwhile, was a back-up singer for several acts, including Billy Stewart and Mitch Ryder. Glass House secured a US R&B hit in 1969 with 'Crumbs Off The Table', but despite minor hits between 1970 and 1972, Payne's concurrent solo releases accelerated their demise. Scherrie, sister of singer Freda, joined the Supremes in 1975 and stayed there for two years. She later returned to the R&B chart in 1987 with 'Incredible' (a duet with Phillip Ingram) and 'Testify'. Hunter had meanwhile replaced C.P. Spencer in the Originals but died, almost forgotten, in February 1981.

Albums: *Inside The Glass House* (1971), *Thanks, I Needed That* (1972).

Glitter, Gary

b. Paul Gadd, 8 May 1940, Banbury, Oxfordshire, England. The elder statesman of the 70s UK glam rock scene, Glitter began his career in a skiffle group, Paul Russell And The Rebels. He then became Paul Raven, under which name he recorded an unsuccessful debut for Decca Records, 'Alone In The Night'. His cover of 'Tower Of

Gary Glitter

Strength' lost out to Frankie Vaughan's UK chart topper, after which he spent increasingly long periods abroad, particularly in Germany. During the late 60s, having been signed to MCA Records by his former orchestral backing leader and now MCA head Mike Leander, he attempted to revitalize his career under the names Paul Raven and Monday, the latter of which was used for a version of the Beatles' 'Here Comes The Sun', which flopped. Seemingly in the autumn of his career, he relaunched himself as Gary Glitter, complete with thigh high boots and a silver costume. His debut for Bell Records, 'Rock 'N' Roll Part 2' unexpectedly reached number 2 in the UK and climbed into the US Top 10. Although he failed to establish himself in America, his career in the UK traversed the early 70s, stretching up until the punk explosion of 1977. Among his many UK Top 10 hits were three number 1 singles: 'I'm The Leader Of The Gang (I Am)', 'I Love You Love Me Love' and 'Always Yours'. An accidental drug overdose and bankruptcy each threatened to end his career, but he survived and continues to play regular concerts in the UK. In recent years the now-sober figure of Glitter is courted favourably by the media and is now a minor legend.
Albums: *Glitter* (1972), *Touch Me* (1973), *Remember Me This Way* (1974), *Always Yours* (1975), *GG* (1975), *Silver Star* (1978), *The Leader* (1980), *Boys Will Be Boys* (1984). Compilations: *Greatest Hits* (1976), *Gary Glitter's Golden Greats* (1977), *The Leader* (1980).

Glitter Band

Formed as a backing group for UK pop singer Gary Glitter, the Glitter Band also enjoyed a period of fame in their own right. The group's line-up comprised John Springate, Tony Leonard, Gerry Shephard, Pete Phipps and Harvey Ellison. Their gimmick and distinctive musical punch lay in the employment of two drummers. At the height of the glitter fad they secured a series of Top 10 UK hits, including 'Angel Face', 'Just For You', 'Let's Get Together Again', 'Goodbye My Love' and 'People Like You And People Like Me'. They split-up in February 1977, but briefly reunited in 1981 in order to tour with their former mentor.
Albums: *Hey!* (1974), *Rock 'N' Roll Dudes* (1975), *Listen To The Band* (1975), *Paris Match* (1977). Compilations: *Greatest Hits* (1976), *People Like You, People Like Me* (1977).

Glover, Roger

b. 30 November 1945, Brecon, Powys, Wales.

Bassist Glover's professional musical career began when his group, the Madisons, amalgamated with fellow aspirants the Lightnings to form Episode Six. This popular act released nine singles between 1966 and 1969, but eclectic interests - including harmony pop, MOR and progressive rock-styled instrumentals - engendered a commercial impasse. Frustrated, both Glover and vocalist Ian Gillan then accepted an offer to join Deep Purple, where they enjoyed considerable international acclaim. However, clashes with guitarist Ritchie Blackmore led to Glover's sacking in 1973, although he remained nominal head of A&R at Purple Records, the group's custom-created label. Roger later embarked on a successful career in production with Nazareth, Status Quo, Judas Priest and Rory Gallagher. In 1974 Glover was commissioned to write the music to *The Butterfly Ball*, which in turn inspired a book, illustrated by Alan Aldridge, and film. The album included the services of David Coverdale, Glenn Hughes and Ronnie James Dio. He recorded a solo album, *Elements*, which again included the assistance of vocalist Dio, but Glover surprised several commentators in 1979 by rejoining Blackmore in Rainbow. Any lingering animosity was further undermined in 1984 when both musicians were active in a rekindled Deep Purple which, although unable to recreate the halcyon days of the early 70s, remains a much in-demand attraction.
Albums: *The Butterfly Ball* (1974), *Elements* (1978), *Mask* (1984), with Ian Gillan *Accidentally On Purpose* (1988).

Gold, Andrew

b. 2 August 1951, Burbank, California, USA. This accomplished guitarist/vocalist/keyboard player was the son of two notable musicians. His father, Ernest Gold, composed several film scores, including *Exodus*, while his mother, Marni Nixon, provided the off-screen singing voice for actors Audrey Hepburn and Natalie Wood in *My Fair Lady* and *West Side Story* respectively. Andrew Gold first drew attention as a member of Los Angeles-based acts, Bryndle and the Rangers. Both groups also featured guitarist Kenny Edwards, formerly of the Stone Poneys, and the pair subsequently pursued their careers as part of Linda Ronstadt's backing group. Gold's skills as a musician and arranger contributed greatly to several of her releases, including *Prisoner In Disguise* (1975) and *Hasten Down The Wind* (1976), while sessions for Carly Simon, Art Garfunkel and Loudon Wainwright were also undertaken. Gold completed his solo debut in 1975 and the following year he enjoyed a transatlantic hit with 'Lonely Boy'. A follow-up single, 'Never Let Her Slip Away', reached number 5 in the UK, while other chart entries included 'How Can This Be Love' and 'Thank You For Being A Friend'. However the artist was unable to circumvent an increasingly sterile sound and was dropped by his label in the wake of the disappointing *Whirlwind*. Gold continued to tour with Ronstadt as part of her back-up band before forming Wax with Graham Gouldman in 1986. In 1992 Undercover had a major UK hit with a dance version of 'Never Let Her Slip Away'.

Albums: *Andrew Gold* (1975), *What's Wrong With This Picture?* (1976), *All This And Heaven Too* (1978), *Whirlwind* (1980).

Golden Earring

Formed in The Hague, Netherlands in 1961 by George Kooymans (b. 11 March 1948, The Hague, Netherlands; guitar/vocals) and Rinus Gerritsen (b. 9 August 1946, The Hague, Netherlands; bass/vocals) along with Hans Van Herwerden (guitar) and Fred Van Der Hilst (drums). The group, initially known as the Golden Earrings, subsequently underwent several changes before they secured a Dutch Top 10 hit with their debut release, 'Please Go' (1965). By this point Kooymans and Gerritsen had been joined by Frans Krassenburg (vocals), Peter De Ronde (guitar) and Jaap Eggermont (drums) and the revitalized line-up became one of the most popular 'nederbeat' attractions. Barry Hay (b. 16 August 1948, Fyzabad, India; lead vocals/flute/saxophone/guitar) replaced Krassenburg in 1966, while De Ronde also left the group as they embraced a more radical direction. The group's first Dutch number 1 hit, 'Dong-Dong-Di-Ki-Di-Gi-Dong' came in 1968 and saw them branching out from their homeland to other European countries as well as a successful tour of the USA. Eggermont left the group to become a producer and was eventually supplanted by Cesar Zuiderwijk (b. 18 July 1948, The Hague, Netherlands) in 1969 as Golden Earring began courting an international audience with their compulsive *Eight Miles High*, which featured an extended version of the famous Byrds' song.

After years of experimenting with various music styles, they settled for a straight, hard rock sound and in 1972 Golden Earring were invited to support the Who on a European tour. They were subsequently signed to Track Records and the following year scored a Dutch number 1/UK Top 10 hit with 'Radar Love' which subsequently found its way into the US Top 20 in 1974. Despite this, they were curiously unable to secure overseas success, which was not helped by a consistently unstable line-up. Robert Jan Stips augmented the quartet between 1974 and 1976 and on his departure Eelco Gelling joined as supplementary guitarist. By the end of the decade, however, the group had reverted to its basic line-up of Kooymans, Gerritsen, Hay and Zuiderwijk which continued to forge an imaginative brand of rock and their reputation as a top European live act was reinforced by *Second Live*. With the release of *Cut* in 1982, Golden Earring earned themselves a US Top 10 hit with 'Twilight Zone'. This was followed by a triumphant tour of the United States and Canada, where further chart success was secured with 'Lady Smiles'. With various members able to indulge themselves in solo projects, Golden Earring have deservedly earned themselves respect throughout Europe and America as the Netherland's longest surviving and successful rock group.

Albums: *Just Earrings* (1965), *Winter Harvest* (1967), *Miracle Mirror* (1968), *On The Double* (1969), *Eight Miles High* (1970), *Golden Earring* (1971), *Seven Tears* (1971), *Together* (1972), *Moontan* (1973), *Switch* (1975), *To The Hilt* (1975), *Rock Of The Century* (1976), *Contraband* (1976), *Mad Love* (1977), *Live* (1977), *Grab It For A Second* (1978), *No Promises . . . No Debts* (1979), *Prisoner Of The Night* (1980), *Second Live* (1981), *Cut* (1982), *N.E.W.S. (North East West South)* (1984), *Something Heavy Going Down - Live From The Twilight Zone* (1984), *The Hole* (1986). Compilations: *Greatest Hits* (1968), *Best Of Golden Earring* (1970), *Greatest Hits Volume 2* (1971), *Hearring Earring* (1973), *The Best Ten Years: Twenty Hits* (1975), *The Golden Earring Story* (1978), *Greatest Hits Volume 3* (1981). Solo albums: George Kooymans *Jojo* (1971), *Solo* (1987). Barry Hay *Only Parrots, Frogs And Angels* (1972). Rinus Gerritsen and Michel Van Dijk *De G.V.D. Band* (1979), *Labyrinth* (1985).

Goldie

b. Goldie Zelkowitz, 1943, Brooklyn, New York, USA. The one-time leader of Goldie And The Gingerbreads, an all-girl US group briefly based in Britain, Zelkowitz embarked on a solo career, as Goldie, in October 1965. She was initially signed to Andrew Loog Oldham's Immediate label but although an original Mick Jagger/Keith Richard song was touted as her debut, the singer's first

single was a version of Goffin/King's 'Goin' Back'. However the record was quickly withdrawn when the composers objected to its amended lyric, and Goldie switched outlets for her second release, 'I Do'. This expressive vocalist found it hard to attain any commercial momentum and by the late 60s she had returned to the USA. Now known as Genya Ravan, the artist joined an ambitious 10-piece jazz-rock band, Ten Wheel Drive, before continuing her solo career in 1972. *Urban Desire* and *And I Mean It* captured a performer inspired by the freedom punk had afforded, yet one whose past was equally influential on newer female artists, including Debbie Harry and Patti Smith. Ravan later produced the Dead Boys' album *Young Loud And Snotty*.
Albums: *Genya Ravan With Baby* (1972), *They Love Me/They Love Me Not* (1973), *Goldie Zelkowitz* (1974), *Urban Desire* (1978), *And I Mean It* (1979).

Gomm, Ian

b. 17 March 1947, Ealing, London, England. Former Brinsley Schwarz guitarist, Gomm went into semi-retirement from the music business after the break-up of the group in 1975. After a period working in studio production at United Artists with Martin Rushent, Gomm put together a solo album with the assistance of Herbie Flowers (bass - also of Sky), Barry De Souza (drums) and Chris Parren (keyboards). Although completely out of step with the then-current fashion of punk, the album revived memories of the golden era of pub rock in enough people to entice Gomm for a short spell back on the road. An unexpected bonus in the shape of US Top 20 single with 'Hold On' in 1979 gave optimistic portents for the future, but all efforts for a successful follow-up failed. Gomm's brief flush of stardom faded after the release of his second album, and despite continuing to issue albums into the 80s, big time success still eludes Gomm.
Albums: *Summer Holiday* aka *Gomm With The Wind* (1978), *What A Blow* (1980), *The Village Choice* (1982), *Images* (1986).

Gong

Although not officially applied to a group until 1971, the name Gong had already appeared on several projects undertaken by guitarist Daevid Allen, a founder-member of the Soft Machine. After relocating to Paris, Allen recorded two idiosyncratic albums before establishing this anarchic, experimental ensemble. Gilli Smyth aka Shanti Yoni (vocals), Didier Malherbe aka

Bloomdido Bad De Grasse (saxophone/flute), Christian Tritsch aka The Submarine Captain (bass) and Pip Pyle (drums) had assisted Allen on his solo collections *Magick Brother* (1970) and *Banana Moon* (1971), but Gong assumed a more permanent air when the musicians moved into a communal farmhouse in Sens, near Fontainbleu, France. Lauri Allen replaced Pyle as the group completed two exceptional albums, *Continental Circus* and *Camembert Electrique*. Musically, these sets expanded on the quirky, *avant garde* nature of the original Soft Machine, while the flights of fancy undertaken by their leader, involving science fiction, mysticism and 'pot-head pixies', emphasized their hippie-based surrealism. Subsequent releases included an ambitious 'Radio Gnome Invisible' trilogy; *Flying Teapot*, *Angel's Egg* and *You*. This period of the Gong story saw the band reach the peak of their commercial success with stunning, colourful live performances, plus the roles of newcomers Steve Hillage (guitar), Mike Howlett (bass) and Tim Blake (synthesizer) emphasized the group's long-ignored, adept musicianship. During this period however, Allen had became estranged from his creation with Hillage becoming increasingly perceived as the group leader, resulting in the guitarist leaving the group in July 1975. Gong subsequently abandoned his original, experimental vision in favour of a tamer style. Within months Hillage, who had enjoyed great success with his solo album, *Fish Rising*, had begun a solo career, leaving Pierre Moerlen, prodigal drummer since 1973, in control of an increasingly tepid, jazz-rock direction. Mike Howlett left soon after to pursue a successful career in studio production and was replaced by Hanny Rowe. The guitarist role was filled by former Nucleus and Tempest member Allan Holdsworth. After a period of inaction in the early 80s the Gong name was used in performances alongside anarcho space/jazz rock group Here And Now, before being swallowed whole by the latter. In doing so, it returned to its roots appearing at free festivals, new age and neo-hippie gatherings. Often billed with various appendages to the name, by the late 80s and 90s Gong was once more under the control of its original leader.
Albums: *Continental Circus* (1971), *Camembert Electrique* (1971), *Radio Gnome Invisible - The Flying Teapot* (1973), *Angel's Egg* (1973), *You* (1974), *Shamal* (1976), *Gazeuse* (1977), *Gong Est Mort* (1977), *Expresso 2* (1978), *Downwind* (1979), *Time Is The Key* (1979), *Pierre Moerlen's Gong, Live* (1980), *Leave It Open* (1981), *Breakthrough* (1987). Compilations: *Live Etc.* (1977), *A Wingful Of Eyes*

(1987), *The History And The Mystery Of The Planet G**g* (1989).

Gonzalez

Gonzalez were a very loose UK-based group of some 15-30 itinerants, (many of whom also played in Georgie Fame's Blue Flames), who formed in England during 1971 to play a blend of funky soul music. The key members were keyboardist Roy Davies (also in the Butts Band with ex-Doors Robbie Krieger and John Densmore), Mick Eve (former saxophone player with Herbie Goins' Night-Timers, and Georgie Fame's Blue Flames), Chris Mercer (former saxophone player with John Mayall, Keef Hartley, and Juicy Lucy), Steve Gregory (former saxophone player with Tony Colton's Crawdaddies, Geno Washington's Ram Jam Band, and Riff Raff), Gordon Hunte (ex-guitar with Johnny Nash), Lisle Harpe (ex-bass with the Night-Timers, Juicy Lucy, and Stealers Wheel) and Rosko Gee (later to play bass with Traffic). They released a self-titled album in 1974 but it was not a great success. In 1977 however, with the line-up now standing at Davies, Hunte, Eve, Mercer, plus Ron Carthy (trumpet), Geoffrey 'Bud' Beadle (saxophone), Colin Jacas (trombone), Alan Sharp, Godfrey McLean, and Bobby 'John' Stigmac (percussion), John Giblin (bass), Richard Bailey and Preston Heyman (drums), and Lenny Zakatek (vocals), they recorded the Gloria Jones penned 'I Haven't Stopped Dancing Yet' for EMI's soul label Sidewalk. It was not issued until 1979 when it gave the band a surprise hit. The follow-up, 'Ain't No Way To Treat A Lady', flopped. They later recorded for PRT and by the mid-80s were on the Tooti Fruiti label. Having undergone many more personnel changes the band finally disintegrated in 1986 after the death of founding member Roy Davies
Album: *Gonzalez* (1974).

Goodhand-Tait, Philip

b. 3 January 1945, Hull, England. This singing pianist is best known for his work as a composer for Love Affair who recorded his 'Gone Are the Songs Of Yesterday' as the b-side of 'Everlasting Love', their 1968 UK chart-topper. Goodhand-Tait numbers became the main track on future hits - notably 'A Day Without Love' which was included in the Sex Pistols early repertoire. Although he seemed an obvious choice, Goodhand-Tait was considered too old to apply for the post when Love Affair's singer resigned in 1969. Nevertheless, he resumed writing for Love Affair after their ill-advised bid to 'go progressive'. His own outfit, the Stormsville Shakers, had been hitless despite a prestigious stint backing Larry Williams in Europe, and a Parlophone contract for 'You Can't Take Love' and other singles. Neither did he fare any better in the 70s as an alternative to Elton John - despite the promotion of 1973's *Philip Goodhand-Tait* (on DJM) on a UK tour supporting Lou Reed. After moving to Chrysalis in 1975, he was recording for the humbler Gundog label by the 80s.
Albums: *I Think I'll Write A Song* (1971), *Rehearsal* (1972), *Philip Goodhand-Tait* (1973), *Jingle Jangle Man* (1976), *Oceans Away* (1976), *Teaching An Old Dog* (1977), *Good Old Phil* (1980).

Goodies

One of the few British television comedy acts to put together a consistent run of hit records, the Goodies were Bill Oddie (b. 7 July 1941, Rochdale, Lancashire, England), Graeme Garden (b. 18 February 1943, Aberdeen, Scotland) and Tim Brooke-Taylor (b. 17 July 1940, Buxton, Derbyshire, England). All three were educated at Cambridge University and were involved in the Footlights Revue in the early 60s, although not all at the same time. Oddie and Brooke-Taylor then joined the Cambridge Circus Show (with John Cleese) and toured world-wide. They then moved on to the BBC radio show *I'm Sorry I'll Read That Again* where they were eventually joined by Graeme Garden (who replaced Graham Chapman). Brooke-Taylor also spent time in the theatre and made films before starting to work in television on programmes such as *At Last The 1948 Show*. Oddie wrote and performed for programmes like *That Was The Week That Was* and *Twice A Fortnight* before meeting up with Brooke-Taylor again, and Garden (now a qualified doctor after medical training at Kings College Hospital, London) in the comedy programme *Broaden Your Mind*. Oddie, a prolific songwriter, also entered the recording world with three singles on Parlophone including a passable stab at pop with 'Nothing Better To Do' (a lament about Mods And Rockers fighting). The three teamed up for their own comedy show which was originally to have been called *Narrow Your Mind* but was eventually broadcast as *The Goodies* starting on the BBC on 8 November 1970. Several series were broadcast throughout the 70s and a number of spin-offs including several hit singles were created including 'The In Betweenies', 'Funky Gibbon', and 'Black Pudding Bertha', the first two of which both made the UK Top 10. In

1980 they left the BBC for Independent Television but the Goodies soon went their separate ways. Oddie, a keen ornithologist, has written several books on the subject and appears regularly on television in this guise or in general factual programmes. He also hosts a jazz programme (another of his passions) on radio. Oddie's performance, impersonating Joe Cocker's 'With A Little Help From My Friends' was a classic moment. Garden works in radio quizzes and game shows but has also used his medical background to present some light-hearted health and fitness programmes. Brooke-Taylor has worked successfully in television situation comedies.

Albums: *Goodies Sing Songs* (1973), *The New Goodies LP* (1975), *Nothing To Do With Us* (1976), *The Goodies' Beastly Record* (1978). Compilation: *The World Of The Goodies* (1975), *The Goodies' Greatest* (1976).

Gorillas

Originally known as the Hammersmith Gorillas this English trio played their own brand of punk meets rhythm and blues meets heavy rock. Initially riding on the back of the punk movement they built up a loyal fan base and released a string of excellent singles during the mid to late 70s including 'You Really Got Me' (a cover of the Kinks classic), 'Gatecrasher', 'It's My Life' and 'She's My Gal'. Bandleader Jesse Hector (vocals/guitar), ably supported by Alan Butler (bass) and Gary Anderson (drums), was influenced by several dead 'stars'. The extravagantly sideburned singer was a noted self-publicist, whose passionate belief in the importance of the Gorillas' as the 'future of rock music' was taken all in, surprisingly, good humour by the UK music press. These included Elvis Presley, Eddie Cochran, Buddy Holly, Brian Jones, Marc Bolan and Jimi Hendrix. Indeed, several of the tracks on the Gorillas album were delivered in the musical style of his heroes, most notably a superb cover of Hendrix's 'Foxy Lady' and the Marc Bolan-influenced 'Going Fishing'. After a lengthy absence, Hector was to be found working the London live circuit in 1992 with his group, the Sound.

Album: *Message To The World* (1978).

Grand Funk Railroad

Formed in 1968, Grand Funk Railroad was the first American heavy-rock 'power trio' to reach massive fame, while alienating another large segment of the rock audience and critics at the same time. The group consisted of guitarist Mark Farner (b. 28 September 1948, Flint, Michigan, USA), bassist Mel Schacher (b. 3 April 1951, Owosso, Michigan, USA) and drummer Don Brewer (3 September 1948, Flint, Michigan, USA). The group was a spin-off of Terry Knight And The Pack, a popular soul-rock group in the Michigan area in the mid-60s. Farner and Brewer had both been members of that band (Brewer had also belonged to the Jazz Masters prior to the Pack). Following a single release on the small Lucky Eleven label with, 'I (Who Have Nothin)', which reached number 46 in the US, the Pack were joined by Schacher, formerly of ? And The Mysterians. At this point Knight stopped performing to become the band's manager, renaming it Grand Funk Railroad (the name was taken from the Michigan landmark the Grand Trunk Railroad).

The new trio signed with Capitol Records in 1969 and immediately began making its name by performing at several large pop festivals. Their first singles made the charts but Grand Funk soon proved its strength in the albums market. Their first, *On Time*, reached number 27 in 1969, followed by the number 11 *Grand Funk* in 1970. By the summer of 1970 they had become a major concert attraction, and their albums routinely reached the Top 10 for the next four years. Of those, 1973's *We're An American Band* was the biggest seller, reaching number 2. The group's huge success is largely attributed to the public relations expertise of manager Knight. In 1970, for example, Knight reportedly paid $100,000 for a huge billboard in New York City's Times Square to promote the group's *Closer To Home*, which subsequently became their first Top 10 album, reaching number 6 and spawning the FM radio staple title track. That promotional campaign backfired with the press, however, which dismissed the band's efforts despite spiralling success with the public. In June 1971, for example, Grand Funk became only the second group (after the Beatles) to sell out New York's Shea Stadium. Their recordings sold in greater quantity even as many radio stations ignored their releases. The 1970 *Live Album* reached number 5 and included another concert and radio favourite in Farner's 'Mean Mistreater'. The next year saw the release of *Survival* and *E Pluribus Funk*, most notable for its round album cover.

In 1972 the group fired Knight, resulting in a series of lawsuits involving millions of dollars. (The group hired John Eastman, father of Linda

McCartney, as its new manager.) In 1973 the group shortened its name officially to Grand Funk, and added a fourth member, keyboardist Craig Frost (b. 20 April 1948, Flint, Michigan, USA). Now produced by Todd Rundgren, they finally cracked the singles market, reaching number 1 with the title track 'We're An American Band', a celebration of its times on the road. In 1974 a heavy remake of Little Eva's 'Loco-motion' also reached number 1, the first time in US chart history that a cover of a song that had previously reached number 1 also ascended to that position. In 1975, with their popularity considerably diminished, the group reverted to its original name of Grand Funk Railroad. The following year they signed with MCA Records and recorded *Good Singin', Good Playin'*, produced by Frank Zappa. When it failed to reach the Top 50, Farner left for a solo career; the others stayed together, adding guitarist Billy Elworthy and changing their name to Flint, a group which did not see any commercial success with its one album. Grand Funk, this time consisting of Farner, Brewer and bassist Dennis Bellinger, reformed for two years in 1981-83 and recorded *Grand Funk Lives* and *What's Funk?* for the Full Moon label. Failing to recapture former glories, they split again. Farner returned to his solo career and Brewer and Frost joining Bob Seger's Silver Bullet Band.

Albums: *On Time* (1969), *Grand Funk* (1970), *Closer To Home* (1970), *Live Album* (1970), *Survival* (1971), *E Pluribus Funk* (1971), *Phoenix* (1972), *We're An American Band* (1973), *Shinin' On* (1974), *All The Girls In The World Beware!!!* (1974), *Caught In The Act* (1975), *Born To Die* (1976), *Good Singin' Good Playin'* (1976), *Grand Funk Lives* (1981), *What's Funk?* (1983). Selected Compilations: *Mark, Don & Mel 1969-71* (1972), *Grand Funk Hits* (1976), *The Best Of Grand Funk Railroad* (1990), *More Of The Best Of Grand Funk Railroad* (1991).

Grateful Dead

The enigmatic and mercurial Grateful Dead evolved from Mother McCree's Uptown Jug Champions to become the Warlocks in 1965. The legendary name was chosen from a randomly opened copy of the *Oxford English Dictionary*, the juxtaposition of words evidently appealed to members of the band. The original line-up comprised: Jerry Garcia (b. Jerome John Garcia, 1 August 1942, San Francisco, California, USA; lead guitar), Bob Weir (b. Robert Hall, 16 October 1947, San Francisco, California, USA; rhythm guitar), Phil Lesh (b. Philip Chapman, 15 March 1940, Berkeley, California, USA; bass), Ron 'Pigpen' McKernan (b. 8 September 1945, San Bruno, California, USA. d. 8 March 1973; keyboards) and Bill Kreutzmann (b. 7 April 1946, Palo Alto, California, USA; drums). The Grateful Dead have been synonymous with the San Francisco/Acid Rock scene since its inception in 1965 when they took part in Ken Kesey's Acid Tests. Stanley Owsley manufactured the then legal LSD and plied the band with copious amounts. This hallucinogenic opus was duly recorded onto tape over a six-month period, and documented in Tom Wolfe's book *The Electric Kool-Aid Acid Test*. Wolfe stated that 'They were not to be psychedelic dabblers, painting pretty pictures, but true explorers'.

Their music, which started out as straightforward rock and R&B, germinated into a hybrid of styles, but has the distinction of being long, wandering and improvisational. By the time their first album was released in 1967 they were already a huge cult band. *Grateful Dead* sounds raw in the light of 90s record production, but it was a brave, early attempt to capture a live concert sound on a studio album. The follow-up *Anthem Of The Sun* was much more satisfying. On this 'live' record, 17 different concerts and four different live studios were used. The non-stop suite of ambitious segments with tantalizing titles such as 'The Faster We Go The Rounder We Get' and 'Quadlibet For Tenderfeet' was an artistic success. Their innovative and colourful album covers were amongst the finest examples of San Franciscan art, utilizing the talents of Kelley Mouse Studios (Alton Kelley and Stanley Mouse). The third album contained structured songs and was not as inaccessible as the palindrome title *Aoxomoxoa* suggested. Hints of a mellowing Grateful Dead surfaced on 'China Cat Sunflower' and the sublime 'Mountains Of The Moon', complete with medieval-sounding harpsichord. In concert, the band were playing longer and longer sets, sometimes lasting six hours with only as many songs.

Their legion of fans, now known as 'Deadheads' relished the possibility of a marathon concert. It was never ascertained who imbibed more psychedelic chemicals, the audience or the band. Nevertheless the sounds produced sometimes took them to breathtaking heights of musical achievement. The interplay between Garcia's shrill, flowing solos and Lesh's meandering bass lines complemented the adventurous chords of Weir's rhythm guitar. The band had now added a second drummer, Micky Hart and a second keyboard player Tom Constanten to accompany the unstable McKernan. It was this line-up that produced the seminal *Live Dead* in 1970. Their peak of improvisation is best demonstrated on the track 'Dark Star'. During its 23 minutes of recorded life, the music simmers, builds and explodes four times, each with a crescendo of superb playing from Garcia and his colleagues. On the two following records *Workingman's Dead* and *American Beauty*, a strong Crosby, Stills And Nash harmony influence prevailed. The short, country-feel songs brought Garcia's pedal steel guitar to the fore (he had recently guested on Crosby, Stills, Nash And Young's *Déjà Vu*). Paradoxically the 'Dead' reverted to releasing live sets by issuing a second double album closely followed by the triple, *Europe '72*. After years of ill-health through alcohol abuse, McKernan died in 1973. He was replaced by Keith Godcheaux from Dave Mason's band, who together with his wife Donna on vocals compensated for the tragic loss. *Wake Of The Flood* in 1973 showed a jazz influence and proved to be their most commercially successful album to date. With this and subsequent studio albums the band produced a mellower sound. It was not until *Terrapin Station* in 1977 that their gradual move towards lethargy was averted. Producer Keith Olsen expertly introduced a fuller, more orchestrated sound.

As a touring band the Grateful Dead continued to prosper, but their studio albums began to lose direction. For their funky *Shakedown Street* they enlisted Lowell George. Although they had been with the band for some years, Keith and Donna Godcheaux had never truly fitted in. Donna had trouble with her vocal pitch, resulting in some excruciating performances, while Keith began to use hard drugs. They were asked to leave at the end of 1979 and on 21 July 1980, Keith was killed in a car crash. *Go To Heaven* (1980) with new keyboard player Brent Mydland betrayed a hint of disco-pop. The album sleeve showed the band posing in white suits which prompted 'Deadheads' to demand: 'Have they gone soft?' Ironically, it was this disappointing record that spawned their first, albeit minor, success in the US singles chart with 'Alabama Getaway'. All of the band had experimented with drugs for many years and, unlike many of their contemporaries, had survived. Garcia, however, succumbed to heroin addiction in 1982. This retrospectively explained his somnolent playing and gradual decline as a guitarist, together with his often weak and shaky vocals. By the mid-80s, the band had become

amorphous but still commanded a massive following. Garcia eventually collapsed and came close to death when he went into a diabetic coma in 1986.

The joy and relief of his survival showed in their first studio album in seven years, *In The Dark*. It was a stunning return to form, resulting in a worldwide hit single 'Touch Of Grey', with Garcia singing his long time co-songwriter Robert Hunter's simplistic yet honest lyric: 'Oh well a touch of grey, kinda suits you anyway, that's all I've got to say, it's alright'. The band joined in for a joyous repeated chorus of 'I will survive' followed by 'We will survive'. They were even persuaded to make a video and the resulting exposure on MTV introduced them to a whole new generation of fans. The laconic Garcia humorously stated that he was 'appalled' to find they had a smash hit on their hands. While *Built To Last* (1989) was a dull affair, they continued to play to vast audiences. They have since received acclaim as the largest grossing band in musical history. In August 1990 Mydland died from a lethal combination of cocaine and morphine. Remarkably this was the third keyboard player to die in the band. Mydland's temporary replacement was Bruce Hornsby until Vince Welnick was recruited full-time. In 1990, the band's live album catalogue was increased with the release of the erratic *Without A Net*. The transcendental Grateful Dead have lasted, throughout the many difficult stages in their long career. Their progress was again halted when Garcia became seriously ill again with a lung infection. After a long spell in hospital Garcia returned, this time promising to listen to doctors advice.In 1992 they remained as one of the biggest grossing artists in the music business, their takings for 91/92 were approximately $31 million.

Albums: The *Grateful Dead* (1967), *Anthem Of The Sun* (1968), *Aoxomoxoa* (1969), *Live/Dead* (1970), *Workingman's Dead* (1970), *Vintage Dead* (1970, early live recordings), *American Beauty* (1970), *Historic Dead* (1971, early live recordings), *Grateful Dead* (1971), *Europe '72* (1972), *History Of The Grateful Dead, Volume 1 - (Bear's Choice)* (1973), *Wake Of The Flood* (1973), *From The Mars Hotel* (1974), *Blues For Allah* (1975), *Steal Your Face* (1976), *Terrapin Station* (1977), *Shakedown Street* (1978), *Go To Heaven* (1980), *Reckoning* (1981), *Dead Set* (1981), *In The Dark* (1987), *Built To Last* (1989), with Bob Dylan *Dylan And The Dead* (1990), *Without A Net* (1990). Compilations: *Skeletons From The Closet* (1974), *What A Long Strange Trip It's Been: The Best Of The Grateful Dead*

(1977),

Further reading: *Grateful Dead - The Music Never Stopped*, Blair Jackson.

Gray, Dobie

b. Leonard Victor Ainsworth, 26 July 1942, Brookshire, Texas, USA. Although Gray had already been recording for a number of years, the anthem-like 'The In Crowd' (1965) was his first major hit. This compulsive, if boastful, single was followed by 'See You At The Go-Go' (1965), but it was eight years before the singer would secure another chart entry. In the interval Gray worked as an actor, appearing in productions of *Hair* and the controversial play *The Beard*. In the early 70s Gray sang lead for a hard rock group, Pollution; they recorded three albums that were well-received, but were commercial failures. He also recorded several demos for songwriter Paul Williams, whose brother Mentor, a producer, was responsible for relaunching Dobie's singing career. The superbly-crafted 'Drift Away' (a US Top 5 in 1973), provided an artistic and commercial success which the singer followed with further examples of progressive southern rock/soul. However, despite minor successes for the Capricorn and Infinity labels, Gray was unable to find a distinctive direction and his newfound promise was left unfulfilled.

Albums: *Drift Away* (1973), *Loving Arms* (1973), *Hey Dixie* (1974), *New Ray Of Sunshine* (1975), *Dobie Gray* (1979), *Midnight Diamond* (1979). Compilation: *Sings For In Crowders That Go-Go* (1987).

Grease

Opening originally off-Broadway, on 14 February 1972, the stage musical *Grease* moved onto the Great White Way later that year. Set in the 50s world of high-school students, the show was written by Jim Jacobs and Warren Casey. Starring Barry Bostwick, Adrienne Barbeau, Timothy Meyers and Carole Demas, *Grease* was a popular success even though the critics, generally at least a generation older than the cast, target audience and musical form, were indifferent. The show ran and ran, proving that for all its apparent immediacy, rock 'n' roll was already the stuff of nostalgia. Amongst the songs in the show was 'Hopelessly Devoted To You'. The 1978 screen version starring John Travolta, Olivia Newton-John and Stockard Channing again attracted large audiences even though, the leading performances apart, it contained little of real cinematic value. Songs like

'You're The One That I Want' and the title track were hit-parade material and helped sustain the show which eventually ran for 3,388 performances.

Greatest Show On Earth

This London-based octet - Ozzie Lane (vocals), Garth Watt-Roy (guitar/vocals), Mick Deacon (keyboards), Ian Aitcheson (saxophone), Tex Philpotts (saxophone), Dick Hanson (trumpet), Norman Watt-Roy (bass) and Ron Prudence (drums) - was formed in 1968 as a soul band. New Orleans-born Lane later returned to America leaving his erstwhile colleagues to forge a more progressive direction with new singer Colin Horton-Jennings. The group completed two albums which displayed a strong compositional skill as well as an imaginative use of brass. They enjoyed a brief popularity in Europe following the success of the single, 'Real Cool World', but the Greatest Show On Earth found little favour at home and broke up in 1971. Norman Watt-Roy then formed Glencoe, and later became a member of Ian Dury's Blockheads.

Albums: *Horizons* (1970), *The Going's Easy* (1970).

Greenbaum, Norman

b. 20 November 1942, Malden, Massachusetts, USA. Greenbaum first tasted minor US chart fame as the founder of Los Angeles jug band Dr. West's Medicine Show and Junk Band, who achieved a minor hit with the novelty 'The Eggplant That Ate Chicago'. After the break-up of the group in 1967, Greenbaum effectively retired from the music business to run a dairy farm (he later recorded 'Milk Cow Blues'). In 1970 however, one of his recordings, 'Spirit In The Sky', unexpectedly scaled the US charts, finally reaching number 3 and later hitting the top in the UK. It was a startling single of its era, highlighted by a memorable fuzz guitar riff and some spirited backing vocals and handclaps. Although Greenbaum was teased out of retirement to record a couple of albums, he remained the quintessential one-hit-wonder chart-topper. In 1986, 16 years after his finest moment, the British group Doctor And The Medics revived 'Spirit In The Sky', which hit number 1 in the UK for the second occasion.

Albums: *Spirit In The Sky* (1970), *Back Home* (1971).

Greenslade

Formed in 1972 by ex-Colosseum members Dave Greenslade (b. 18 January 1943, Woking, Surrey, England; keyboards) and Tony Reeves (b. 18 April

1943, London, England). The line-up was completed by ex-Episode Six and Alan Bown Set member Dave Lawson (keyboards/vocals) and Andrew McCulloch (drums). Their four well-received albums all proved to be moderately successful - the strong emphasis on keyboard sounds with a hint of classical roots were perfect for the progressive rock market of the early 70s. Their distinctive album covers were illustrated and calligraphed by Roger Dean. Dave Clempson, another ex-Colosseum member, joined them for *Spyglass Guest* and alongside new recruit, violinist Graham Smith, the organ dominated sound became less prominent. Reeves departed and returned for the second time, to his main interest as record producer, where he would become a highly respected figure. Six months after their last album Greenslade dismantled the band as managerial and legal problems continued. He embroiled himself in television music scores, where he has found great success. His solo *Cactus Choir* in 1976 sold only moderately. Greenslade reformed briefly in 1977 with yet another ex-Colosseum member, Jon Hiseman, who together with Tony Reeves and Mick Rodgers, lasted only one tour. Their intricate and occasionally brilliant music was out of step with the burgeoning punk scene.

Albums: *Greenslade* (1973), *Bedside Manners Are Extra* (1973), *Spyglass Guest* (1974), *Time And Tide* (1975).

Greenslade, Dave

b. 18 January 1943, Woking, Surrey, England. Former member of Colosseum and founder of the progressive jazz/rock group, Greenslade. In 1979 he collaborated with fantasy artist/writer Patrick Woodroffe in an lavish and expensive concept double album, *The Pentateuch Of The Cosmogony*. Released at the 'wrong' end of the 70s, it was doomed to failure, yet in recent times it has achieved a notoriety as an valued artifact amongst collectors. Throughout the 80s and into the 90s, he has carved out a successful career composing theme music for British film and television.

Albums: *Cactus Choir* (1976), *The Pentateuch Of The Cosmogony* (1979).

Guru Guru

With Ax Genrich (guitar), Mani Neumeier (keyboards/drums) and Uli Trepte as its mainstays, this idiosyncratic German progressive rock outfit inhabited an artistic area bordered by Amon Duul and Can as heard on a prolific output of mainly instrumental albums. Some were issued by Atlantic Records after the group made headway on the college circuits of English-speaking regions. Further commercial progress was hindered, perhaps, by a too-rapid turnover of personnel. Among those passing through the ranks were future new age composer Hans-Joachim Roedelius (who played keyboards on *Mani Und Seine Freunde*), and in 1976, Roland Schaeffer (synthesizer/guitar) and Ingo Bischof (keyboards), who assumed increasing responsibility for musical direction as the unit (renamed The Guru Guru Sun Band for 1979's *Hey Du*) fell back on the domestic market before quietly disbanding.

Albums: *UFO* (1970), *Hinten* (1971), *Kan Guru* (1972), *Guru Guru* (1973), *Don't Call Us We'll Call You* (1973), *This Is* (1973), *Der Elektrolurch* (1974), *Dance Of The Flames* (1974), *Mani Und Seine Freunde* (1975), *Tango Fango* (1976), *Globetrotter* (1977), *Live* (1978), *Hey Du* (1979).

Gypsy

This Leicester-based group made its debut in 1968 under the name Legay. Having completed only one single, John Knapp (vocals/guitar/keyboards), Robin Pizer (guitar/vocals), Rod Read (guitar/vocals), David McCarthy (bass/vocals) and Moth Smith (drums), took a new name, Gypsy, and were one of the attractions featured at the 1969 Isle Of Wight festival. Their debut album showed great promise and showcased an engaging, tight-harmony style reminiscent of Moby Grape. Ray Martinez then replaced Rod Read, but the group's second album lacked the purpose of its predecessor and Gypsy broke up soon after its release.

Albums: *Gypsy* (1971), *Brenda And The Rattlesnake* (1972).

H

Hackett, Steve

b. 12 February 1950, London, England. Formerly a member of various minor groups, Canterbury Glass, Heel Pier, Sarabande and Quiet World, Hackett joined Genesis as guitarist in 1971. He replaced Anthony Phillips, and stayed with the group during their successful mid-70s progressive rock period, recording with the group from *Nursery Cryme* (1971) to the live double album, *Seconds Out* (1977). By the time the latter was released, Hackett had recently departed the group. Having previously released his first solo effort, *Voyage Of The Acolyte* two years earlier, Hackett had decided to pursue a full time solo career. He achieved modest success with a string of albums, including the UK Top 10 *Defector*, but his following remained largely static and of interest only to the die-hard Genesis fan. He joined former Yes guitarist Steve Howe and Max Bacon (vocals) in GTR in 1986, issuing a self-titled album which reached the US Top 20 ,and an accompanying single, 'When The Heart Rules The Mind' reached number 14. In the UK the album barely made the Top 40 , indicating that Hackett's reputation as 'former Genesis guitarist' overshadowed all his work.
Albums: *Voyage Of The Acolyte* (1975), *Please Don't Touch* (1978), *Spectral Mornings* (1979), *Defector* (1980), *Cured* (1981), *Highly Strung* (1983), *Bay Of Kings* (1983), *Till We Have Faces* (1984), *Momentum* (1988).

Hagar, Sammy

b. 13 October 1947, Monterey, California, USA. Hagar was a singer, guitarist and songwriter whose father was a professional boxer. Legend has it that Elvis Presley persuaded him not to follow in his father's footsteps, and instead he started out in 60s San Bernardino bands the Fabulous Castillas, Skinny, Justice Brothers and rock band Dust Cloud. He joined Montrose in 1973 (formed by ex-Edgar Winter guitarist Ronnie Montrose) and became a minor rock hero in the Bay Area of San Francisco, in particular acquiring a reputation as a potent live performer. After two albums with Montrose he left to go solo, providing a string of semi-successful albums and singles. He took with him Bill Church (bass), and added Alan Fitzgerald

(keyboards), and later Denny Carmassi (also ex-Montrose; drums). The band picked up good press on support tours with Kiss, Boston and Kansas, but by 1979 created a radically altered line-up with Gary Pihl (guitar), Chuck Ruff (drums) and Geoff Workman (keyboards) backing Hagar and Church. 1983's *Three Lock Box* became their first Top 20 entry, including 'Your Love Is Driving Me Crazy', which made number 13 in the singles chart. Hagar then took time out to tour with Journey guitarist Neal Schon, Kenny Aaronson (bass) and Mike Shrieve (ex-Santana; drums), recording a live album under the band's initials HGAS. Under this title they also cut a studio version of Procol Harum's 'Whiter Shade Of Pale'. Returning to solo work Hagar scored his biggest hit to date with *Voice Of America* out-take 'I Can't Drive 55'. However, in 1985 he surprised many by joining Van Halen from whom Dave Lee Roth had recently departed. However, he has continued to pursue a parallel, if intermittant solo career. 1987's *Sammy Hagar* had its title changed to *I Never Said Goodbye* after an MTV competition, though no copies were pressed with the new motif. His solo work continues to be characterized by a refreshing lack of bombast which is unusual for the genre.
Albums: *Nine On A Scale Of Ten* (1976), *Sammy Hagar Two* (1977), *Musical Chairs* (1978), *All Night Long - Live* (1978), *Street Machine* (1979), *Danger Zone* (1979), *Loud And Clear* (1980), *Standing Hampton* (1982), *Rematch* (1982), *Three Lock Box* (1983), *Live From London To Long Beach* (1983), *VOA* (1983), as Hagar, Schon, Aaronson and Shrieve *Through The Fire* (1984), *Voice Of America* (1984), *Looking Back* (1987), *Sammy Hagar* (1987).

Hall And Oates

Like their 60s predecessors the Righteous Brothers (and their 90s successor Michael Bolton), Hall And Oates' string of hits was proof of the perennial appeal of white soul singing. The duo achieved their success through the combination of Hall's falsetto and Oates' warm baritone. A student at Temple University, Daryl Hall (b. Daryl Franklin Hohl, 11 October 1949, Pottstown, Pennsylvania, USA) sang lead with the Temptones and recorded a single produced by Kenny Gamble in 1966. Hall subsequently made solo records and formed soft-rock band Gulliver with Tim Moore, recording one album for Elektra. In 1969 he met Oates (b. 7 April 1949, New York, USA), a former member of Philadelphia soul band the Masters. The two began to write songs together and were discovered by Tommy Mottola, then a local representative of

Hall And Oates

Chappell Music. He became their manager and negotiated a recording deal with Atlantic. Their three albums for the label had star producers (Arif Mardin on *Whole Oates* and Todd Rundgren for *War Babies*) but sold few copies. However, *Abandoned Luncheonette* included the first version of one of Hall And Oates' classic soul ballads, 'She's Gone'. The duo came to national prominence with the million-selling 'Sara Smile', their first single for RCA. It was followed by the tough 'Rich Girl' which got to number 1 in the US in the 1977. However, they failed to capitalize on this success, dabbling unimpressively in the currently fashionable disco style on *X-Static*. The turning-point came with the Hall and Oates produced *Voices*. The album spawned four hit singles, notably a remake of the Righteous Brothers' 'You've Lost That Lovin' Feelin'. It also included the haunting 'Every Time You Go Away', a big hit for Paul Young in 1985. For the next five years the pair could do no wrong, as hit followed hit. Among their best efforts were 'Maneater', the pounding 'I Can't Go For That (No Can Do)', 'Out Of Touch' (co-produced by Arthur Baker) and 'Family Man' (a Mike Oldfield composition). On *Live At The Apollo*, they were joined by Temptations members Eddie Kendricks and David Ruffin. This was the prelude to a three-year hiatus in the partnership, during which time Hall recorded his second solo album with production by Dave Stewart. Reunited in 1988, Hall And Oates had a big US hit with 'Everything Your Heart Desires' on Arista. On the 1990 hit 'So Close', producers Jon Bon Jovi and Danny Kortchmar added a strong rock flavour to their sound.

Albums: *Whole Oates* (1972), *Abandoned Luncheonette* (1973), *War Babies* (1974), *Hall & Oates* (1976), *Beauty On A Back Street* (1977), *Along The Red Edge* (1978), *X-Static* (1979), *Voices* (1980), *Private Eyes* (1981), *H2O* (1982), *Bim Bam Boom* (1984), *Live At The Apollo* (1985), *Ooh Yeah!* (1988), *Change Of Season* (1990). Daryl Hall solo: *Sacred Songs* (1980), *Three Hearts In The Happy Ending Machine* (1986).

Hamill, Claire

b. c.1955, Middlesbrough, England. This 70s singer songwriter played the folk circuit and recorded a number of relatively successful albums. Her first release included John Martyn on guitar. Her 1973 album, *October*, was produced by Paul Samwell-Smith. Her initial promise was not realized commercially, and she gradually disappeared from the folk scene. *Voices*, released under the heading of new age music, was an album made up entirely of Hammill's voice, which was multi-tracked. She has subsequently enjoyed considerable success as a new age artist.

Albums: *One House Left Standing* (1971), *October* (1973), *Stage Door Johnnies* (1974), *Abracadabra* (1975), *Touchpaper* (1984), *Voices* (1986).

Hammer, Jan

b. 17 April 1948, Prague, Czechoslovakia, he trained as a jazz pianist before winning a scholarship to Berklee College in Boston, Massachusetts, the United States in 1968. In 1970, he played with Elvin Jones and Sarah Vaughan. Hammer next joined the Mahavishnu Orchestra, as well as playing synthesisers on albums by Santana, Billy Cobham and others. After leader John McLaughlin temporarily disbanded the orchestra, Hammer and violinist Jerry Goodman made a 1974 album for Nemperor. This was followed by Hammer's own composition, *The First Seven Days*, a concept album based on the creation of the earth. During the late 70s, he was one of a loose aggregation of New York based musicians creating various types of jazz rock fusion.

Among his more important collaborations were those with Jeff Beck on *Wired* and *There And Back*. Hammer also toured with Beck. He later made a record with Journey guitarist Neil Schon and another with jazz guitarist John Abercrombie before finding a wider audience through his work in television music. Hammer was responsible for the theme to *Miami Vice*, one of the most successful police series of the 80s. Released as a single, it went to number 1 in the USA (UK number 5) in 1985. He followed it in 1987 with 'Crocketts Theme', which made number 2 in the UK yet failed completely in the USA. This new role dominated his later work - Hammer wrote the music for *Eurocops* - and in 1991 he even composed special background music for a best-selling computer game. Hammer's biggest hit was sadly tarnished during 1991 and 1992 when it was oddly used as the theme music for a major television advertising campaign for a UK bank.

Albums: *Like Children* (1974), *First Seven Days* (1975), *Oh yeah* (1976), *Live With Jeff Beck* (1977), *Timeless* (1978), *Melodies* (1979), *Black Sheep* (1979), *Neil Schon And Jan Hammer* (1981), *Untold Passion* (1982), *Night* (1984), *Escape From TV* (1987), *Snapshots* (1989).

Hammill, Peter

In the late 60s, a band was formed in Manchester,

England by university friends Peter Hammill (piano/guitar/vocals), Hugh Banton (keyboards/bass), and Guy Evans (drums). Called Van Der Graaf Generator, the band folded without making any recordings, but in 1968 it re-formed with David Jackson on saxophone. Hammill had intended to release a solo album, but the new Van Der Graaf Generator seized on his material, the result being the imaginative *Aerosole Grey Machine*. The band had more success in Europe than in the UK, splitting up for the second time in 1972. This split gave Hammill the opportunity to continue with the limited success he had found in his solo career, which he pursued until 1975 when Van Der Graaf Generator regrouped yet again, this time for just three years. In 1990 Hammill guested on vocals for Peter Gabriel's fourth album.

Albums: with Van Der Graaf Generator *Aerosole Grey Machine* (1968), *The Least We Can Do Is Wave To Each Other* (1969), *H To He Who Am The Only One* (1970), *Pawn Hearts* (1971), *Godbluff* (1975), *Still Life* (1976), *World Record* (1976). Selected solo albums: *Fool's Mate* (1971), *Chameleon In The Shadow Of Night* (1972), *The Silent Corner And The Empty Stage* (1974), *In Camera* (1974), *Nadir's Big Chance* (1975), *Sitting Targets* (1981), *Enter K* (1982), *Black Box* (1983). Peter Hammill And The K Group *The Margin*.

Hard Meat

Taking its cue from Traffic, this trio were among many outfits who, in the late 60s, 'got it together in the country' - in their case, the wilds of Cornwall. To make ends meet, guitarist Michael Dolan, his bass-plucking brother Steve - with whom he shared both vocals and a Birmingham upbringing - and drummer Mick Carless took on a summer residency as the Ebony Combo at Bude's Headland Pavilion before assuming their genital monicker in 1969. By then, they had cultivated a faintly sinister 'stoned hippie' image, and a repertoire hinged on originals of 'progressive' rock plus re-inventions of works by Bob Dylan ('Most Likely You Go Your Way') and Richie Havens. After amassing an extensive work schedule they were signed to Warner Brothers for whom they recorded a brace of albums and a single - an arrangement of the Beatles' 'Rain' - before disbanding in 1971. Two years later, Steve Dolan was among the cast on Pete Sinfield's *Under The Sky*.

Albums: *Hard Meat* (1970), *Through A Window* (1970).

Harper, Roy

b. 12 June 1941, Manchester, England. Although introduced to music through his brother's skiffle group, Harper's adolescence was marked by a harrowing spell in the Royal Air Force. Having secured a discharge by feigning insanity, he drifted between mental institutions and jail, experiences which left an indelible mark on later compositions. Harper later began busking around Europe, and secured a residency at London's famed Les Cousins club on returning to Britain. His debut album, *The Sophisticated Beggar* (1966), was recorded in primitive conditions, but contained the rudiments of the artist's later, highly personal, style. *Come Out Fighting Genghis Smith* was released as the singer began attracting the emergent underground audience, but he was unhappy with producer Shel Talmy's rather fey arrangements. *Folkjokeopus* contained the first of Harper's extended compositions, 'McGoohan's Blues', but the set as a whole was considered patchy. *Flat, Baroque And Berserk* (1970) introduced the singer's long association with the Harvest label. Although he would later castigate the outlet, they allowed him considerable artistic licence and this excellent album, considered by Harper as his first 'real work', offered contrasting material, including the uncompromising 'I Hate The White Man' and 'Tom Tiddler's Ground', as well as the jocular 'Hell's Angels', which featured support from the Nice. *Stormcock*, arguably the performer's finest work, consists of four lengthy, memorable songs which feature sterling contributions from arranger David Bedford and guitarist Jimmy Page. The latter remained a close associate, acknowledged on 'Hats Off To Harper' from *Led Zeppelin III*, and he appeared on several succeeding releases, including *Lifemask* and *Valentine*. Although marred by self-indulgence, the former was another remarkable set, while the latter reaffirmed Harper's talent with shorter compositions. An in-concert album, *Flashes From The Archives Of Oblivion* completed what was arguably the artist's most rewarding period. *HQ* (1975) introduced Trigger, Harper's short-lived backing group consisting of Chris Spedding (guitar), Dave Cochran (bass) and Bill Bruford (drums). The album included 'When An Old Cricketer Leaves The Crease',in which a colliery brass band emphasized the melancholia apparent in the song's cricketing metaphor. A second set, *Commercial Break*, was left unreleased on the group's demise. The singer's next release, *Bullinamingvase*, centred on the ambitious 'One Of Those Days In England', but it is also recalled for

Roy Harper

the controversy surrounding the flippant 'Watford Gap' and its less-than-complimentary remarks about food offered at the subject's local service station. The song was later removed. It was also during this period that Harper made a memorable cameo appearance on Pink Floyd's *Wish You Were Here*, taking lead vocals on 'Have A Cigar'. Harper's subsequent work, while notable, has lacked the passion of this period and *The Unknown Soldier*, a bleak and rather depressing set, was the prelude to a series of less compulsive recordings, although his 1990 album, *Once*, was critically acclaimed as a return to form. Roy Harper remains a wayward, eccentric talent who has steadfastly refused to compromise his art. Commercial success has thus eluded him, but he retains the respect of many peers and a committed following.

Albums: *The Sophisticated Beggar* (1966), *Come Out Fighting Genghis Smith* (1967), *Folkjokeopus* (1969), *Flat, Baroque And Berserk* (1970), *Stormcock* (1971), *Lifemask* (1973), *Valentine* (1974), *Flashes From The Archives Of Oblivion* (1974), *HQ* (1975 - retitled *When An Old Cricketer Leaves The Crease*), *Bullinamingvase* (1977), *The Unknown Soldier* (1980), *Work Of Heart* (1981), with Jimmy Page *Whatever Happened To Jugula* (1985), *Born In Captivity* (1985), *Descendants Of Smith* (1988), *Loony On The Bus* (1988), *Once* (1990), *Death Or Glory* (1992). Compilations: *Harper 1970-1975* (1978), *In Between Every Line* (1986).

Hart, Mike

Hart led the respected Liverpool R&B group, the Roadrunners, before enjoying spells in less-stellar units, the Richmond Group and Henry's Handful prior to joining the Liverpool Scene, which he abandoned in 1970. The group had been championed by influential disc jockey John Peel, who then signed this excellent singer/guitarist to his fledgling Dandelion label. *Mike Hart Bleeds* took full advantage of the company's avowed policy of artistic freedom, and the performer's sense of irony and urgency resulted in a compulsive set. He performed with his band Business, at this time. *Basher, Chalky, Pongo And Me*, invoked the mock-heroism of boys' comics and showed Hart's customary incisiveness. Sadly, neither album was a commercial success and the artist later rejoined the Liverpool Scene for a 1974 reunion.

Albums: *Mike Hart Bleeds* (1970), *Basher, Chalky, Pongo And Me* (1972).

Hartley, Keef

b. 8 March 1944, Preston, Lancashire, England.

Together with Colosseum, the Keef Hartley Band of the late 60s, forged jazz and rock music sympathetically to appeal to the UK progressive music scene. Drummer Hartley had already seen vast experience in live performances as Ringo Starr's replacement in Rory Storm And The Hurricanes. When Merseybeat died, Hartley was enlisted by the London based R&B band the Artwoods, whose line-up included future Deep Purple leader Jon Lord. Hartley was present on their only album *Art Gallery* (now a much sought-after collectors item). He joined John Mayall's Bluesbreakers and was present during one of Mayall's vintage periods. Both *Crusade* and *Diary Of A Band* highlighted Hartley's economical drumming and faultless timing. The brass-laden instrumental track on John Mayall's *Bare Wires* is titled 'Hartley Quits'. The good natured banter between Hartley and his ex-boss continued onto Hartley's strong debut *Half Breed*. The opening track 'Hearts And Flowers' has the voice of Mayall on the telephone officially sacking Hartley, albeit tongue-in-cheek, while the closing track 'Sacked' has Hartley dismissing Mayall! The music in-between features some of the best ever late 60s jazz-influenced blues, and the album remains an undiscovered classic. The band for the first album comprised: Miller Anderson, guitar and vocals, the late Gary Thain (b. New Zealand d. 19 March 1976; bass), Peter Dines (organ) and Spit James (guitar). Later members to join Hartley's fluid line-up included Mick Weaver (aka Wynder K. Frog) organ, Henry Lowther (b. 11 July 1941, Leicester, England; trumpet/violin), Jimmy Jewell (saxophone), Johnny Almond (flute), Jon Hiseman and Harry Beckett. Hartley, often dressed as an American Indian, sometimes soberly, sometimes in full head-dress and war-paint, was a popular attraction on the small club scene. His was one of the few British bands to play the Woodstock Festival, where his critics compared him favourably with Blood Sweat And Tears. *The Battle Of NW6* in 1969 further enhanced his club reputation, although chart success still eluded him. By the time of the third album both Lowther and Jewell had departed, although Hartley always maintained that his band was like a jazz band, in that musicians would come and go and be free to play with other aggregations.

Dave Caswell and Lyle Jenkins came in and made *The Time Is Near*. This album demonstrated Miller Anderson's fine songwriting ability, and long-time producer Neil Slaven's excellent production. They were justly rewarded when the album briefly nudged its way into the UK and US charts. Subsequent albums lost the fire that Hartley kindled on the first three, although the formation of his Little Big Band and the subsequent live album had some fine moments. The recording at London's Marquee club saw the largest ever band assembled on the tiny stage, almost the entire British jazz/rock fraternity seemed to be present, including Chris Mercer, Lynn Dobson, Ray Warleigh, Barbara Thompson, and Derek Wadsworth. Regrettably Hartley has been largely inactive for many years apart from the occasional tour with John Mayall and sessions with Michael Chapman.

Albums: *Halfbreed* (1969), *Battle Of NW6* (1970), *The Time Is Near* (1970), *Overdog* (1971), *Little Big Band* (1971), *Seventy Second Brave* (1972), *Lancashire Hustler* (1973), *Dog Soldier* (1975). Compilation: *The Best Of Keef Hartley* (1972).

Hartman, Dan

b. 4 November 1956, Harrisburg, Pennsylvania, USA. Hartman's multi-instrumental talents and light tenor were first heard by North America at large when he served bands led, together and separately, by Johnny Winter and Edgar Winter. Employment by the latter from 1973 to 77 brought the greatest commercial rewards - principally via Hartman's co-writing all selections on the Edgar Winter Group's *They Only Come Out At Night* which contained the million-selling single, 'Frankenstein'. He was also in demand as a session player by artists including Todd Rundgren, Ian Hunter, Rick Derringer, Stevie Wonder and Ronnie Montrose. Riding the disco bandwagon, Hartman next enjoyed international success with the title track to *Instant Replay* and another of its singles, 'This Is It' but, after the relative failure of *Relight My Fire* in 1979, he retired from stage centre to concentrate on production commissions - some carried out in his own studio in Connecticut. Among his clients have been the Average White Band, Neil Sedaka, .38 Special, James Brown (notably with the 1986 'Living In America') and Hilly Michaels. In 1985, he returned to the US Top 10 with the soul concoction 'I Can Dream About You' (for the *Streets Of Fire* film soundtrack) which he followed with two lesser hits prior to another withdrawal to the sidelines of pop.

Albums: *Images* (1976), *Instant Replay* (1978), *Relight My Fire* (1979), *I Can Dream About You* (1985), *White Boy* (1986), *New Green Clear Blue* (1989).

Harvest Records

Launched by EMI in 1969, the Harvest label was a showcase for progressive/underground rock. Although primarily interested in new talent, including the Edgar Broughton Band and Michael Chapman, it initially attracted artists signed to other outlets within the parent company. The early roster was thus bolstered by Pete Brown, the Pretty Things and Barclay James Harvest, as well as two acts destined for major success: Deep Purple and Pink Floyd. The latter was managed by Pete Jenner and Andrew King who simultaneously ran the Blackhill agency. Their influence during this formative period brought Kevin Ayers, Syd Barrett and Roy Harper to the label, which in turn instilled a sense of continuity to its growing catalogue. Other early signings ranged from the experimental Third Ear Band to the self-explanatory Panama Limited Jug Band, while Bakerloo and Chicago Climax represented the concurrent blues boom. Harvest's reputation was also enhanced by a series of exceptional fold-out sleeves emanating from the Hypgnosis design studio. Their often-surreal images complemented a sense of adventure prevalent during the label's first two years when, under the stewardship of Malcolm Jones, Harvest skilfully blended altruism with professional marketing. However, by 1971, many of its best-selling acts were perceived as mainstream rather than 'alternative', a feature confirmed when Pink Floyd's *Dark Side Of The Moon* achieved sales in excess of one million and went on to sell over 25 million copies. The Electric Light Orchestra, Be-Bop Deluxe and the late-period Soft Machine were among the label's most successful 70s' acquisitions, but a drift towards mere expediency was now apparent. Harvest releases lessened as the decade progressed, but the company was regenerated in the light of the punk explosion. Wire, the Saints and US act the Shirts were signed in 1977, but despite initial optimism, the revival failed to capture former glories. Reissues, rather than new signings, marked Harvest's 20th anniversary, yet the label nonetheless retains respect for its early, pioneering catalogue.

Compilation: *Picnic* (1972).

Hatfield And The North

Formed in 1972, Hatfield And The North comprised of musicians active in England's musically incestuous, experimental fringe. The original line-up - David Sinclair (b. 24 November 1947, Herne Bay, Kent, England; keyboards), Phil Miller (b. 22 January 1949, Barnet, Hertfordshire,

England; guitar), Richard Sinclair (b. 6 June 1948, Canterbury, Kent, England; bass/vocals) and Pip Pyle (b. 4 April 1950, Sawbridgeworth, Hertfordshire, England; drums) - was drawn from ex-members of Caravan, Matching Mole and Delivery, but within months David Sinclair left to join Caravan and was replaced by Dave Stewart (b. 30 December 1950, Waterloo, London, England), previously in Egg and Khan. Taking their name from the first signpost out of London on the A1 trunk road, the group completed two albums, influenced by Soft Machine, which adeptly combined skilled musicianship with quirky melodies. Their extended instrumental passages, particularly Stewart's deft keyboard work, were highly impressive, while their obtuse song titles, including 'Gigantic Land Crabs In Earth Takeover Bid' and '(Big) John Wayne Socks Psychology On The Jaw', emphasized an air of detached intellectualism. However, their chosen genre was losing its tenuous appeal and, unable to secure a sure commercial footing, the quartet split up in June 1975. Stewart and Miller then formed National Health, Pyle became a session drummer while Richard Sinclair abandoned professional music altogether until re-emerging in the early 90s with Caravan Of Dreams.

Albums: *Hatfield And The North* (1974), *The Rotters' Club* (1975). Compilation: *Afters* (1980).

Hawkwind

Befitting a group associated with community and benefit concerts, Hawkwind was founded in the hippie enclave centred on London's Ladbroke Grove during the late 60s. Dave Brock (b. Isleworth, Middlesex, England; guitar/vocals), Nik Turner (b. Oxford, Oxfordshire, England; saxophone/vocals), Mick Slattery (guitar), Dik Mik (b. Richmond, Surrey; electronics), John Harrison (bass) and Terry Ollis (drums) were originally known as Group X, then Hawkwind Zoo, prior to securing a recording contract. Their debut, *Hawkwind*, was produced by Dick Taylor, former guitarist with the Pretty Things, who briefly augmented his new proteges on Slattery's departure. Indeed Hawkwind underwent many personnel changes, but by 1972 had achieved a core consisting of Brock, Turner, Del Dettmar (b. Thornton Heath, Surrey, England; synthesizer), Lemmy (b. Ian Kilminster, 24 December 1945, Stoke-on-Trent, Staffordshire, England; bass), Simon King (b. Oxford, Oxfordshire, England; drums), Stacia (b. Exeter, Devon, England; dancer) and poet/writer Robert Calvert (b. c.1945, Pretoria, South Africa; vocals).

One part-time member was science fiction writer Michael Moorcock who helped organize some of Hawkwind's concert appearances and often deputized for Calvert when the latter was indisposed. This role was extended to recording credits on several albums. The group's chemically-blurred science-fiction image was made apparent in such titles as *In Search Of Space* and *Space Ritual*. They enjoyed a freak UK pop hit when the compulsive 'Silver Machine' soared to number 3, but this flirtation with a wider audience ended prematurely when a follow-up single, 'Urban Guerilla', was hastily withdrawn in the wake of a terrorist bombing campaign in London. Hawkwind continued to shed personalities; Calvert left, and rejoined, Dettmar was replaced by Simon House (ex-High Tide), but the group lost much of its impetus in 1975 when Lemmy was fired on his arrest on drugs charges during a North American tour. The bassist subsequently formed Motorhead. Although the group enjoyed a period of relative stability following the release of *Astounding Sounds And Amazing Music*, (featuring a splendid pastiche cover of an American pulp paperback) it ended in 1977 with the firing of founder member Turner and two latter additions, Paul Rudolph (ex-Deviants and Pink Fairies) and Alan Powell. The following year Simon House left to join David Bowie's band before Brock, Calvert and King assumed a new name, the Hawklords, to avoid legal and contractual complications. The group reverted to using its former appellation in 1979, by which time Calvert had resumed his solo career. An undaunted Hawkwind pursued an eccentric path throughout the 80s. Dave Brock remained at the helm of a flurry of associates, including Huw Lloyd Langton, who played guitar on the group's debut album, Tim Blake (synthesizer) and drummer Ginger Baker. Nik Turner also reappeared in the ranks of a group which has continued to enjoy a committed following, despite the bewildering array of archive releases obscuring the group's contemporary standing. A 1990 release, *Space Bandits*, was particularly well-timed in the light of the prevailing psychedelic trend.

Albums: *Hawkwind* (1970), *In Search Of Space* (1971), *Doremi Fasol Latido* (1972), *Space Ritual* (1973), *Hall Of The Mountain Grill* (1974), *Warrior On The Edge Of Time* (1975), *Astounding Sounds And Amazing Music* (1976), *Quark, Strangeness And Charm* (1977), *25 Years On* (1978), *PXR 5* (1979), *Hawkwind Live 1979* (1980), *Levitation* (1980), *Sonic Attack* (1981), *Church Of Hawkwind* (1982), *Choose*

Your Masques (1982), *The Chronicle Of The Black
Sword* (1985), *The Xenon Codex* (1988), *Night Of
The Hawk* (1989), *Space Bandits* (1990).
Compilations: *Road Hawks* (1976), *Masters Of The
Universe* (1977), *Repeat Performances* (1980), *Friends
And Relations* (1982), *Text Of The Festival* (1983),
Zones (1983), *Bring Me The Head Of Yuri Gagarin*
(1985), *In The Beginning* (1985), *Space Ritual
Volume 2* (1985), *Anthology - Hawkwind Volumes 1,
2 and 3* (all 1986), *Live 70/73* (1986), *Early
Daze/Best Of* (1987), *Out And Intake* (1987), *Angels
Of Death* (1987), *Spirit Of The Age* (1988), *Stasis*
(1990).

Heads, Hands And Feet

Formed in 1970, from Poet And The One Man
Band, a promising unit which folded on the demise
of their record label. Tony Colton (b. 11 February
1942, Tunbridge Wells, Kent, England; vocals),
Ray Smith (b. 9 July 1943, London, England;
guitar), Albert Lee (b. 21 December 1943,
Leominster, Herefordshire, England; guitar) and
Pete Gavin (b. 9 September 1946, London,
England; drums) were joined by Mike O'Neil
(keyboards) and Chas Hodges (b. 11 November
1943, London, England; bass; ex-Outlaws and Cliff
Bennett) for a debut designed to indicate the
disparate influences of such talented individuals. A
double album in America, the British version was
whittled to a single album to emphasize their
musicianship. O'Neil left the group prior to *Tracks*
which offered a greater emphasis on rock than its
country-tinged predecessor. However, relationships
within the group grew strained and Heads, Hands
And Feet split up in December 1972, prior to the
release of *Old Soldiers Never Die*. Colton and Smith
pursued successful careers as songwriters and
producers, while Gavin, Hodges and Lee were
reunited in the Albert Lee Band. The guitarist later
found fame accompanying Emmylou Harris and
Eric Clapton, while Hodges formed half of the
popular Chas And Dave duo.
Albums: *Heads, Hands And Feet* (1971), *Tracks*
(1972), *Old Soldiers Never Die* (1973).

Heavy Metal Kids

Formed in London, England in 1973 the band
consisted of Gary Holton (vocals), Mickey Waller
(guitar), Ron Thomas (bass) and Keith Boyce
(drums). Signing surprisingly quickly to Atlantic
Records the band released their self-titled debut
album in 1974. Quickly gaining popularity on the
live club circuit in and around the London area,
playing brash street metal, the band followed up

their debut album with *Anvil Chorus* in 1975.
However, Gary Holton's volatile nature got the
band into trouble at various gigs. He even broke
his leg on an ill-fated American tour. Subsequently
dropped by Atlantic Records, the band was
undeterred and released their third and last album.
Kitsch appeared on RAK Records in 1977, full of
tough street metal rockers. It still did not give the
band the break it needed and Heavy Metal Kids
folded shortly after its release. Gary Holton went
on to pursue an acting career and will best be
remembered for his role as Wayne, a streetwise
cockney jack-the-lad in the hit television series *Auf
Wiedersehen Pet*. Sadly, he died of a drugs overdose
during the filming of the series.
Albums: *Heavy Metal Kids* (1974), *Anvil Chorus*
(1975), *Kitsch* (1977).

Hell, Richard

b. Richard Myers, 2 October 1949, Lexington,
Kentucky, USA. A seminal figure on New York's
emergent punk scene, Hell was a founder member
of the Neon Boys with guitarist Tom Verlaine. He
first performed several of his best-known songs,
including 'Love Comes In Spurts', while in this
group. The Neon Boys subsequently mutated into
Television, where Hell's torn clothing, the result of
impoverishment, inspired Malcolm McLaren's
ideas for the Sex Pistols. Personality clashes resulted
in Hell's departure and he then formed the
Heartbreakers with former New York Dolls's
guitarist Johnny Thunders. He also left this group
prematurely, but reappeared fronting his own unit,
Richard Hell And The Voidoids, with Bob Quine
and Ivan Julian (guitars) and Marc Bell (drums).
Hell's debut EP was released in 1976 and its
underground popularity secured a recording deal
with Sire Records. The result was the artist's
compulsive *Blank Generation*, the title track of
which achieved anthem-like proportions. However
the quartet's progress faltered when Bell left to join
the Ramones, and although Hell retained the
services of Quine, this excellent guitarist was
eventually drawn into session work. Hell
continued to work with variations of the Voidoids
and remains an charismatic, if elusive, individual.
His sporadic recordings have been punctuated by
writing and film work, the most notable of which
was a starring role in Susan Seidelman's *Smithereens*.
Albums: *Blank Generation* (1977), *Destiny Street*
(1982), *R.I.P* (1985).

Hello

Hailing from from North London, England, Bob

Hello

Bradbury (guitar/vocals), Keith Marshall (guitar/vocals), Vic Faulkner (bass) and Jeff Allen (drums) were signed to Bell Records in 1974 by glam-rock *eminence grise*, Mike Leander. A version of Chuck Berry's 'Carol' paved the way for a second single - a revival of the Exciters/Billie Davis' 'Tell Him' - to infiltrate the UK Top 10, and they were named as 'Brightest Hope For 1975' in a *Disc* readers poll. This breakthrough was dampened by a subsequent flop in 'Games Up' (composed by the Glitter Band) but Russ Ballard's 'New York Groove' at number 12 in autumn 1975 stayed the further decline that was heralded by poor sales for 'Star-Studded Sham' from *Keep Us Off The Streets*. This collection was a poor attempt of covers and previously-issued singles.
Album: *Keep Us Off The Streets* (1975).

Help Yourself

Formed in 1969, founder members Malcolm Morley (guitar/vocals) and Dave Charles (drums/vocals) met in an embryonic version of Sam Apple Pie. Richard Treece (guitar/vocals) and Ken Whaley (bass) completed the original Help Yourself line-up which made its recording debut in 1971. This promising debut was succeeded by *Strange Affair* on which the group's penchant for extended improvisation, reminiscent of America's classic west coast tradition, flourished more freely, notably with 'American Woman'. Paul Burton had replaced Whaley for this release, the latter having joined Ducks DeLuxe, and this line-up was augmented by guitarists Ernie Graham and Jo Jo Glemser. A third Help Yourself album, *Beware The Shadow*, consolidated their impressive style, highlighted by the epic 'Reaffirmation', before the group's prodigal bassist re-joined his colleagues for the apty-titled *The Return Of Ken Whaley*. This 1973 album was, however, Help Yourself's last release. All of the group, bar Morley, later joined Deke Leonard's Iceberg, while the guitarist, who was also an accomplished keyboards player, began a spell with Man. The itinerant Whaley subsequently joined him there. Treece later joined the Flying Aces.
Albums: *Help Yourself* (1971), *Strange Affair* (1972), *Beware The Shadow* (1972), *The Return Of Ken Whaley/Happy Days* (1973).

Henry Cow

This uncompromising group was formed in 1968 at Cambridge University, England by Fred Frith (b. 17 February 1949, Heathfield, East Sussex, England; guitar/violin/piano) and Chris Cutler (b. 4 January 1947, Washington, DC, USA; drums/piano). Tim Hodgkinson (b. 1 May 1949, Salisbury, Wiltshire, England; keyboards/alto saxophone/clarinet), Geoff Leigh (saxophone) and John Greaves (b. 23 February 1950, Prestatyn, Clwyd, Wales; bass/piano) completed the initial line-up of a group committed to left-wing politics and a quest for musical excellence. A reputation for uncompromising, experimental material was forged in Britain's *avant garde* circuit and the group was an early signing to the then-adventurous Virgin Records label. *Legend* and *Unrest* confirmed Henry Cow's anti-commercial, yet enthralling style, while tours in support of Faust and Captain Beefheart expanded their once-limited audience. Former Comus member Lindsay Cooper (b. 3 March 1951, Hornsey, London, England; woodwind, flute, piano) replaced Leigh in 1974, while the following year the group embarked on an artistically satisfying merger with Slapp Happy, Peter Blegvad, Anthony Moore and Dagmar Krause. This convergence resulted in two highly engaging albums, after which Dagmar opted to remain in Henry Cow while her two former colleagues embarked on separate careers. The group subsequently continued to forge its own path, eschewing mass-market popularity in favour of determined individuality. Henry Cow was disbanded at the end of the 70s and while guitarist Frith completed several compelling solo albums, his three ex-colleagues formed the Art Bears.
Albums: *The Henry Cow Legend* (1973), *Unrest* (1974), with Slapp Happy *Desperate Straights* (1975), with Slapp Happy *In Praise Of Learning* (1975), *Concerts* (1976), *Western Culture* (1978).

Hensley, Ken

b. 24 August 1945. A founder member of the Gods, organist Hensley led this tempestuous Hertfordshire group throughout its four-year history. Mick Taylor and Greg Lake were also members at different times, although both had departed before the release of the unit's two albums, *Genesis* (1968) and *To Samuel A Son* (1970). The Gods evolved into Toe Fat with the addition of singer Cliff Bennett, before Hensley left in November 1969 to join Uriah Heep. This much-maligned act survived critical denigration to become such a popular attraction that the organist was afforded the luxury of a concurrent solo career. Although *Proud Words On A Dusty Shelf* featured fellow-Heep members Gary Thain and Lee Kerslake, it was noticeably mellow in tone which, in part, may account for its commercial failure.

Eager To Please, a collaboration with Colosseum bassist Mark Clark, proved even less successful and Hensley temporarily ceased outside activities. He remained with Uriah Heep until 1980 when he was summarily fired. Having completed the disappointing *Free Spirit*, Hensley formed the short-lived Shotgun, before joining US group Blackfoot. He appeared on two releases, *Siego* (1983) and *Vertical Smiles* (1984), but subsequently switched to session work with W.A.S.P. and Ozzy Osbourne.
Albums: *Proud Words On A Dusty Shelf* (1973), *Eager To Please* (1975), *Free Spirit* (1981).

Heron

Folk-rock attraction Heron were one of several groups signed to both the Red Bus agency and Dawn label, home of Mungo Jerry and Mike Cooper. The unit's grasp of melody was unveiled on *Heron*, released to coincide with the ambitious *Penny Concert Tour* on which the group shared a bill with progressive rock acts Comus and Titus Groan and afro-rock practitioners Demon Fuzz. Heron, whose line-up included Roy Apps (guitar/vocals), Steve Jones (keyboards), Tony Pook (vocals/percussion), Mike Finesilver (bass) and Terry Gittings (drums), then completed a second set, *Twice As Nice At Half The Price*, before disbanding.
Albums: *Heron* (1970), *Twice As Nice At Half The Price* (1972). Compilation: *Best Of Heron* (1989).

Heron, Mike

b. 12 December 1942, Scotland. This multi-instrumentalist was a founder member of the Incredible String Band. Heron's first solo outing, on Island, included such names as the Who, and John Cale in the credits. After the band split, in 1974, Heron remained in the UK and formed Mike Heron's Reputation, following a more rock-orientated path. They released only *Mike Heron's Reputation*, this time on Neighbourhood Records. Although Heron recorded a number of albums, albeit on a different label every time, none of these achieved the degree of success that his former association with Robin Williamson had brought. *The Glenrow Tapes* was a set of remastered demo recordings that had not previously been released.
Albums: *Smiling Men With Bad Reputations* (1971), *Mike Heron's Reputation* (1975), *Diamond Of Dreams* (1977), *Mike Heron* (1980), *The Glenrow Tapes, Vol. 1* (1987), *The Glenrow Tapes, Vol. 2* (1987), *The Glenrow Tapes, Vol. 3* (1987).

Hillage, Steve

b. 2 August 1951, England. Guitarist Hillage played with Uriel in December 1967 alongside Mont Campbell (bass), Clive Brooks (drums) and Dave Stewart (organ). This trio carried on as Egg when Hillage went to college. He returned to music in April 1971, forming Khan with Nick Greenwood (bass), Eric Peachey (drums) and Dick Henningham. Dave Stewart also joined but they had little success and split in October 1972. Hillage then joined Kevin Ayers' touring band Decadence, before linking up with French based hippies Gong, led by Ayer's ex-Soft Machine colleague Daevid Allen. Hillage injected much needed musicianship into the band's blend of mysticism, humour and downright weirdness. In 1975 he released his first solo album *Fish Rising*, recorded with members from Gong, which marked the start of his writing partnership with longtime girlfriend Miquette Giraudy.
On leaving Gong in 1976, Hillage developed his new age idealism on the successful *L*, produced by Todd Rundgren, and featuring Rundgren's Utopia. *Motivation Radio* utilized the synthesizer skills of Malcom Cecil, of synthesizer pioneer group Tonto's Expanding Headband, and included an inspired update of Buddy Holly's 'Not Fade Away'. *Live Herald* featured one side of new studio material which developed a funkier feel, an avenue that was explored further on *Open* in 1979. *Rainbow Dome Musick* was an instrumental experiment in ambient atmospherics. In the 80s, Hillage moved into production work, including albums by Robin Hitchcock and Simple Minds. 1991 saw Steve returning to recording and live performance as the leader of System 7, a loose aggregation of luminaries including disc jockey Paul Oakenfield, Alex Paterson of the Orb and Mick MacNeil of Simple Minds. As the line-up would suggest, System 7 produce ambient dance music, combining house beats with progressive guitar riffs and healthy bursts of soul and disco.
Albums: *Fish Rising* (1975), *L* (1976), *Motivation Radio* (1977), *Green* (1978), *Live Herald* (1979), *Open* (1979), *Rainbow Dome Musick* (1979), *For To Next/And Not Or* (1983), *System 7* (1991).

Hines, Marcia

b. 20 July 1953, Boston, Massachusetts, USA. Hines went to Australia in 1970 to work in the stage production of *Hair*, and later became the world's first black Mary Magdalene, in the stage production *Jesus Christ Superstar*. With a cover of James Taylor's 'Fire And Rain' in 1975 she had immediate success. Propelled by manager Peter Rix and producer Robie Porter, she followed this with many hit singles including 'I Just Don't Know What To Do With Myself', 'What I Did For Love' and 'You', (the last single reaching number 1 in Australia). She became an established MOR performer, winning hosts of media and pop industry awards. She also toured internationally with the acclaimed Australian jazz group, the Daly Wilson Big Band. Hines has continued a divided career in acting and music.

Albums: *Marcia Shines* (1975), *Shining* (1976), *Ladies & Gentlemen, Marcia Hines* (1977), *Live Across Australia* (1978), *Ooh Child* (1979), *Take It From The Boys* (1982). Compilation: *Greatest Hits* (1982).

Hipgnosis

This innovative UK design group was founded in 1968 by Storm Thorgerson and Aubrey Powell. Their first credited piece of artwork graced Pink Floyd's third album, *More*. Friendship with this respected act led to further collaborations, including *Ummagumma* and *Atom Heart Mother*, but the duo also provided graphics for many other releases. Their brilliantly surreal photograph of red toy balls in the desert graced the cover of *Elegy* by the Nice, while a clever photographic negative effect was used on *Doctor Dunbar's Prescription* by the Aynsley Dunbar Retaliation. Other notable works include *Technical Ecstasy* (Black Sabbath), *Jump On It* (Montrose), *On The Shore* (Trees), *House On the Hill* (Audience), *How Dare You* (10cc) and *The Madcap Laughs* (Syd Barrett). Hipgnosis specialized in visual puns best exemplified in their design for the album by Quatermass which featured flying pterodactyls super-imposed against a skyscraper. Although their work was sometimes undertaken without a particular act in mind, Thorgerson and Powell were adept at tailoring specific images. One such creation was the 'teddy boy' sleeve undertaken for *To Mum From Aynsley And The Boys*, a tongue-in-cheek release, again, by the Aynsley Dunbar Retaliation.

Peter Christopherson joined the team in 1974, but by this point Hipgnosis, which now worked for most of Britain's major labels, had lost much of its panache. Their imaginative sleeves were ideal for the expansive progressive era, but their relevance faded with the genre's passing. Their memorable photographic images however are firmly implanted in most rock fans' minds; the famous cows on the cover of the Floyd's *Atom Heart Mother* and their repeat 'mirror' shot on the cover *Ummagumma*. Their most famous icon is Pink Floyd's multi-million selling *Dark Side Of The Moon*.

Holmes, Clint

b. 9 May 1946, Bournemouth, Dorset, England. Holmes is best remembered for one major hit, 'Playground In My Mind', in 1973. He was raised in Farnham, New York, USA, and began singing and acting as a child. He led a high school rock group and also studied music in college. His professional music career began upon his discharge from the army, at clubs in the Bahamas. There he met songwriters Paul Vance and Lee Pockriss, who offered Holmes their newest composition, 'Playground In My Mind'. Holmes considered it a novelty song, likely due to the inclusion of a child's vocal (by Vance's son, Philip), but recorded it despite those reservations, and after its release on Epic Records, it reached number 2 in the US. None of Holmes's subsequent releases on Epic, Buddah, Atco or Private Stock Records charted. Holmes was still performing in clubs at the end of the 80s.

Album: *Playground In My Mind* (1973).

Holmes, Rupert

b. 24 February 1947, Northwich, Cheshire, England. This American-based singer-songwriter, and arranger was born in the UK where his father was serving in the USAF. However, Holmes was brought up in New York where he attended the Manhattan School Of Music before starting out as a songwriter. He also performed on sessions for the Cuff Links and arranged songs for Gene Pitney, the Drifters and the Platters. His first success was the song 'Timothy', recorded by the Buoys and a US hit in 1971. The song, about hungry, trapped pot-holers devouring one of their number, also featured Holmes on piano. He wrote next for the Partridge Family and the Drifters before launching his own singing career with an album in 1974. The follow-up album inspired Barbra Streisand to ask him to produce her, and he followed work on her *Lazy Afternoon* with credits on albums by Sparks, Sailor, and the Strawbs amongst others. He continued to record as well and was rewarded in 1980 when *Partners In Crime* yielded two big hits - 'Escape (The Pina Colada Song)' and 'Him' - on both sides of the Atlantic.

Albums: *Widescreen* (1974), *Rupert Holmes* (1975), *The Singles* (1977), *Pursuit Of Happiness* (1978), *Partners In Crime* (1979), *Adventure* (1980), *Full Circle* (1981).

Rupert Holmes

Hookfoot

Ian Duck (vocals/guitar), Dave Glover (bass) and
Roger Pope (drums) formed the nucleus of this
highly-proficient unit. The trio had already worked
together in the Soul Agents and Loot before
establishing their new act with guitarist Caleb
Quaye. Hookfoot became the house band for
music publisher Dick James and members
appeared, individually or collectively, on numerous
sessions, notably those for Elton John's *Empty Sky*,
Elton John and *Tumbleweed Connection*. *Hookfoot* and
Good Times A-Comin' established the quartet as a
unit in its own right, but whereas Quaye's guitar
work was always meritorious, their material was
largely unexceptional. Ex-Fairies' bassist Fred
Gandy replaced Glover for *Communication*, but the
alteration made little difference to the group's
commercial fortunes. Pope and Quaye continued
studio-based careers upon Hookfoot's
disintegration.
Albums: *Hookfoot* (1971), *Good Times A-Comin'*
(1972), *Communications* (1973), *Roaring* (1974).
Compilation: *Headlines* (1975).

Horslips

This innovative and much imitated Irish folk-rock
band comprised Barry Devlin (bass/vocals), Declan
Sinnott (lead guitar/vocals), Eamonn Carr
(drums/vocals), Charles O'Connor (violin), and
Jim Lockhart (flute/violin/keyboards). Sinnott,
later joined Moving Hearts and was replaced by
Gus Gueist and John Fean in turn. Horslips,
formed in 1970 and took the theme of Irish
legends for many of their songs. The group toured
as support to Steeleye Span and featured a
complete performance of *The Tain*, a more rock-
based recording than their previous recordings.
Feans guitar work could switch from the melodic
style of 'Aliens', to the much heavier 'Man Who
Built America'. They maintained a strong cult
following, but, only one album, *The Book Of
Invasions - A Celtic Symphony*, reached the UK Top
40. *The Man Who Built America* received a lot of
air-play when it was released in 1979, but wider
acceptance evaded them, and the group split. Fean,
O'Connor and Carr later formed Host, with Chris
Page (bass), and Peter Keen (keyboards), in order
to pursue the folk path still further.
Albums: *Happy To Meet Sorry To Part* (1973), *The
Tain* (1974), *Dancehall Sweethearts* (1974),
Unfortunate Cup Of Tea (1975), *Drive The Cold
Winter Away* (1976), *Horslips Live* (1976), *The Book
Of Invasions - A Celtic Symphony* (1977), *Aliens*
(1977), *Tour A Loor A Loor* (1977), *Tracks From The
Vaults* (1978), *The Man Who Built America* (1979),
Short Stories - Tall Tales (1980), *The Belfast Gigs*
(1980). Compilations: *The Best Of Horslips* (1982),
Folk Collection (1984), *Horslips History 1972-75*
(1983), *Horslips History 1976-80* (1984).

Hot Butter

This one-man band comprised US Moog
synthesizer player Stan Free, who had performed
on recordings by John Denver, Arlo Guthrie and
the Boston Pops Orchestra. Hot Butter made one
US Top 10 record and promptly disappeared.
Having previously recorded some unsuccessful
singles under his own name in the 60s, Free took
on the name Hot Butter and recorded the cleverly
titled 'Popcorn', an instrumental which reached the
UK Top 5 in 1972. Subsequent singles attempted
to update early rock instrumentals such as 'Pipeline'
and 'Tequila' but they did not reach the charts.

Hot Chocolate

This highly commercial UK pop group was formed
in Brixton, London by percussionist Patrick Olive
(b. 22 March 1947, Grenada), guitarist Franklyn
De Allie and drummer Ian King.
Songwriter/vocalist Errol Brown (b. 12 November
1948, Kingston, Jamaica) and bassist Tony Wilson
(b. 8 October 1947, Trinidad, Jamaica) and pianist
Larry Ferguson (b. 14 April 1948, Nassau,
Bahamas) joined later in 1969. Following the
departure of De Allie the group was signed to the
Beatles' label Apple for an enterprising reggae
version of the Plastic Ono Band's 'Give Peace A
Chance'. They also provided label-mate Mary
Hopkin with the hit 'Think About Your
Children'. The following year, Hot Chocolate
signed to Mickie Most's RAK label and again
proved their songwriting worth by composing
Herman's Hermits hit 'Bet Yer Life I Do'. In
September 1970, Hot Chocolate enjoyed the first
hit in their own right with the melodic 'Love Is
Life'. Over the next year, they brought in former
Cliff Bennett guitarist Harvey Hinsley (b. 19
January 1948, Northampton, England) and
replacment drummer Tony Connor (b. 6 April
1948, Romford, Essex, England) to bolster the
line-up. The Brown-Wilson songwriting team
enabled Hot Chocolate to enjoy a formidable run
of UK Top 10 hits including 'I Believe (In Love)',
'Brother Louie' (a US number 1 for Stories),
'Emma', 'A Child's Prayer', 'You Sexy Thing',
'Put Your Love In Me', 'No Doubt About It',
'Girl Crazy', 'It Started With A Kiss' and 'What
Kinda Boy You Looking For (Girl)'. In the

summer of 1987, they scored a number 1 UK hit with the Russ Ballard song 'So You Win Again'. Although Wilson had left in 1976, the group managed to sustain their incredible hit run. However, the departure of their shaven-headed vocalist and songwriter Errol Brown in 1987 was a much more difficult hurdle to overcome and it came as little surprise when Hot Chocolate's break-up was announced. Brown went on to register a hit with 'Personal Touch', and completed a album. Albums: *Cicero Park* (1974), *Hot Chocolate* (1975), *Man To Man* (1976), *Every 1's A Winner* (1978), *Going Through The Motions* (1979), *Class* (1980), *Mystery* (1982), *Love Shot* (1983), Compilations: *Hot Chocolate's Greatest Hits* (1976), *20 Hottest Hits* (1979), *The Very Best Of Hot Chocolate* (1987). Errol Brown solo: *That's How Love Is* (1989).

Hotlegs

This UK studio group was formed in 1970 and featured Kevin Godley (b. 7 October 1945, Manchester, England; vocals/drums), and Lol Creme b. 19 September 1947, Manchester, England; vocals/guitar) and Eric Stewart (b. 20 January 1945, Manchester, England; vocals/guitar). Godley had previously played in the Mockingbirds, while Stewart was a former member of both Wayne Fontana And The Mindbenders and the Mindbenders. While working at Stewart's Strawberry Studios, the group completed a track, which caught the attention of Philips Records managing director, Dick Leahy. The result was a highly original UK Top 10 single 'Neanderthal Man' and an album *Thinks School Stinks*. The group then returned to the studio, where they formed the nucleus of 10cc. Godley And Creme later enjoyed further success.
Album: *Thinks School Stinks* (1970).

Hot Tuna

This US group represented the combination of two members of the Jefferson Airplane, Jack Casady (b. 13 April 1944, Washington DC, USA; bass) and Jorma Kaukonen (b. 23 December 1940, Washington DC, USA; guitar/vocals). The group evolved as part-time extension of the Airplane with Kaukonen and Casady utilizing the services of colleagues, Paul Kantner (guitar) and Spencer Dryden (drums) and other guests, displaying their talents as blues musicians. Stage appearances were initially integrated within the Airplane's performances on the same bill. During one of the Airplane's rest periods, the duo began to appear in their own right, often as a rock trio with then

Airplane drummer, Joey Covington. Having the name Hot Shit rejected, they settled on Hot Tuna and released a self-titled debut as a duo, with a guest appearance from harmonica player, Will Scarlet. The set was drawn largely from traditional blues/ragtime material by Jelly Roll Morton and the Rev. Gary Davis, with Casady's booming and meandering bass lines interplaying superbly with Kaukonen's fluid acoustic guitar. By the time of their second album, another live set, they were a full-blown rock quartet with the addition of violinist Papa John Creach and Sammy Piazza on drums. This line-up displayed the perfect combination of electric and acoustic rock/blues that Casady and Kaukonen had been looking for. Creach had departed by the time *The Phosphorescent Rat* was recorded, and Piazza, who had left to join Stoneground was replaced by Bob Steeler in 1974. The music became progressively louder, so that by the time of their sixth album they sounded like a rumbling heavy rock traditional ragtime blues band. Kaukonen's limited vocal range added to this odd concoction, but throughout all this time the group maintained a hard-core following. In the late 70s the duo split, resulting in Casady embarking on an ill-advised excursion into what was perceived as 'punk' with SVT. Kaukonen continued with a solo career combining both electric and acoustic performances. At best Hot Tuna were excitingly different, at worst they were ponderous and loud. Selected stand-out tracks from their erratic repertoire were 'Mann's Fate' from *Hot Tuna*, 'Keep On Truckin'' and 'Sea Child' from *Burgers*, 'Song From The Stainless Cymbal' from *Hoppkorv*, and 'Hit Single #1' from *America's Choice*. Casady and Kaukonen reunited in 1991 with a workmanlike album which found little favour with the record buying public.
Albums: *Hot Tuna* (1970), *First Pull Up Then Pull Down* (1971), *Burgers* (1972), *The Phosphorescent Rat* (1973), *America's Choice* (1974), *Yellow Fever* (1975), *Hoppkorv* (1976), *Double Dose* (1978), *Final Vinyl* (1979), *Splashdown* (1985), *Pair A Dice Found* (1991).

Hull, Alan

b. 20 February 1945, Newcastle-Upon-Tyne, England. Alan Hull's career began as a founder member of the Chosen Few, a Tyneside beat group which also included future Ian Dury pianist, Mickey Gallagher. Hull composed the four tracks constituting their output, before leaving to become a nurse and sometime folk-singer. In 1967 Alan founded Downtown Faction, which evolved into

Lindisfarne. This popular folk-rock act scored hit singles with 'Meet Me On The Corner' and 'Lady Eleanor', both of which Hull wrote, while their first two albums were critical and commercial successes. *Pipedream*, Hull's debut album, was recorded with assistance from many members of Lindisfarne, in 1973. Its content was more introspective than that of his group and partly reflected on the singer's previous employment in a mental hospital. Although Hull continued to lead his colleagues throughout the 70s and 80s, he pursued a solo career with later releases *Squire* and *Phantoms*, plus a one-off release on the Rocket label as Radiator, a group formed with the assistance of Lindisfarne drummer Ray Laidlaw. None of these albums was able to achieve the same degree of success as *Pipedream*, the second decade proved more low-key, resulting in only one collection, *On The Other Side*.

Albums: *Pipedream* (1973), *Squire* (1975), *Phantoms* (1979), *On The Other Side* (1983), with Radiator *Isn't It Strange* (1977).

Humble Pie

An early example of the 'supergroup', Humble Pie was formed in April 1969 by Peter Frampton (guitar/vocals), Steve Marriott (guitar/vocals) and Greg Ridley (b. 23 October 1943, Carlisle, Cumbria, England; bass), ex-members, respectively, of the Herd, Small Faces and Spooky Tooth. Drummer Jerry Shirley (b. 4 February 1952) completed the original line-up which scored a UK Top 5 hit with its debut release, 'Natural Born Bugie'. The quartet's first two albums blended the single's hard-rock style with several acoustic tracks. Having failed to consolidate their early success, Humble Pie abandoned the latter, pastoral direction, precipitating Frampton's departure. He embarked on a prosperous solo career in October 1971, while his former colleagues, now bolstered by former Colosseum guitarist Dave Clempson, concentrated on wooing US audiences. This period was best captured on *Smokin'*, the group's highest ranking UK chart album. Humble Pie latterly ran out of inspiration and, unable to escape a musical rut, broke up in March 1975. Marriott then formed Steve Marriott's All Stars, which latterly included both Clempson and Ridley, while Shirley joined a new venture, Natural Gas. Tragically, Marriott died on 20 April 1991, following a fire at his Essex home.

Albums: *As Safe As Yesterday Is* (1969), *Town And Country* (1969), *Humble Pie* (1970), *Rock On* (1971), *Performance - Rockin' At The Fillmore* (1971), *Smokin'* (1972), *Eat It* (1973), *Thunderbox* (1975), *Street Rats* (1975), *On To Victory* (1980), *Go For The Throat* (1981). Compilation: *Crust Of Humble Pie* (1975).

Hunter, Ian

b. 3 June 1946, Shrewsbury, Shropshire, England. Having served a musical apprenticeship in several contrasting groups, Hunter was employed as a contract songwriter when approached to audition for a new act recently signed by Island Records. Initially known as Silence, the band took the name Mott The Hoople on his installation and Hunter's gravelly vocals and image-conscious looks - omnipresent dark glasses framed by long Dylanesque curly hair - established the vocalist/pianist as the group's focal point. He remained their driving force until 1974 when, having collapsed from physical exhaustion, he left the now-fractious line-up to begin a career as a solo artist. Late-period Mott guitarist Mick Ronson quit at the same time and the pair agreed to pool resources for particular projects. Ronson produced and played on *Ian Hunter*, which contained the singer's sole UK hit, 'Once Bitten Twice Shy'. Having toured together as Hunter/Ronson with Peter Arnesen (keyboards), Jeff Appleby (bass) and Dennis Elliott (drums), the colleagues embarked on separate paths. *All American Alien Boy* contained contributions from Aynsley Dunbar, David Sanborn and several members of Queen, but despite several promising tracks, the set lacked the artist's erstwhile passion. *Overnight Angels* continued this trend towards musical conservatism, although Hunter aligned himself with the punk movement following a period of seclusion by producing *Beyond The Valley Of The Dolls* for Generation X. *You're Never Alone With A Schizophrenic* marked his reunion with Ronson and subsequent live dates were commemorated on *Ian Hunter Live/Welcome To The Club* which drew material from their respective careers. Hunter's output during the 80s was mimimal, occasionally recording the odd song for film soundtracks and in 1990 he resumed his partnership with Mick Ronson on YUI Otra. Overall, it seems the artist's reputation rests firmly on his contributions to 70s rock. He made an appearance at the 1992 Freddy Mercury Aids benefit.

Albums: *Ian Hunter* (1975), *All American Alien Boy* (1976), *Overnight Angels* (1977), *You're Never Alone With A Schizophrenic* (1979), *Ian Hunter Live/Welcome To The Club* (1980), *Short Back And Sides* (1981), *All The Good Ones Are Taken* (1983), with Mick Ronson *YUI Orta* (1990). Compilation: *Shades Of Ian Hunter* (1979).

Further reading: *Diary Of A Rock 'N' Roll Star*, Ian Hunter.

Hutchings, Ashley

b. 26 January 1945, Southgate, Middlesex, England. Although largely remembered as the founder member of Fairport Convention, where he was often afforded the nickname 'Tyger', Hutchings also went on to form Steeleye Span, in 1970. He played on the first four Fairport Convention albums, ending with the classic *Liege And Lief*. Ashley had grown unhappy with the increase in original material that the group was playing, at the expense of more traditional works. While with Fairport Convention he contributed to their one hit record, 'Si Tu Dois Partir', in 1969. After three albums with Steeleye Span, Hutchings formed the Albion Country Band, in 1971, and has led a succession of Albion Band line-ups ever since. The first of these line-ups was on *No Roses*, which included a total of 26 musicians, including himself and his then wife Shirley Collins. Many of the personnel involved have worked with Hutchings on other occasions, such as John Kirkpatrick, Barry Dransfield, Nic Jones, and the late Royston Wood, formerly of Young Tradition. With Hutchings the Albion Band became the first electric group to appear in plays at the National Theatre, London. The group also 'electrified' Morris dancing, exemplified in *Morris On*, and *Son Of Morris On*. Hutchings has also done much work with former Fairport Convention members, Richard Thompson, and the late Sandy Denny. Hutchings has written and presented programmes on folk music for the BBC, and both he and the Albion Band were the subject of their own BBC television documentary, in 1979. More recently, Hutchings wrote and acted in his own one-man show about, song collector Cecil Sharp. The show has been performed nationwide since 1984. The presentation resulted in *An Evening With Cecil Sharp And Ashley Hutchings*. Hutchins continues to tour and record. It is not undeserved that he has been called the Father of Folk Rock in Britain.

Albums: with others *Morris On* (1972), with John Kirkpatrick *The Compleat Dancing Master* (1974), *Kicking Up The Sawdust* (1977), *An Hour With Cecil Sharp And Ashley Hutchings* (1986), *By Gloucester Docks I Sat Down And Wept* (1987), the Ashley Hutchings All Stars *As You Like It* (1989), *A Word In Your Ear* (1991). Compilations: various artists *49 Greek Street* (1970), various artists *Clogs* (1971), with Shirley Collins *A Favourite Garland* (1974), with Richard Thompson *Guitar Vocal* (1976), various artists *Buttons And Bows* (1984), various artists *Buttons And Bows 2* (1985), with Sandy Denny *Who Knows Where The Time Goes?* (1985).

I

Ian, Janis

b. Janis Eddy Fink, 7 April 1951, New York City, New York, USA. A teenage prodigy, Ian first attracted attention when her early composition, 'Hair Of Spun Gold', was published in a 1964 issue of *Broadside* magazine. Performances at New York's Village Gate and Gaslight venues inspired a recording deal which began with the controversial 'Society's Child (Baby I've Been Thinking)'. Brought to national prominence following the singer's appearance on Leonard Bernstein's television show, this chronicle of a doomed, inter-racial romance was astonishingly mature and inspired a series of equally virulent recordings attacking the perceived hypocrisy of an older generation. Ian's dissonant, almost detached delivery, enhanced the lyricism offered on a series of superior folk-rock styles albums, notably *For All The Seasons Of Your Mind*. Later relocated in California, Janis began writing songs for other artists, but re-embraced recording in 1971 with *Present Company*. *Stars* re-established her standing, reflecting a still personal, yet less embittered, perception. The title song was the subject of numerous cover versions, while 'Jesse' provided a US Top 10 hit for Roberta Flack. *Between The Lines* contained 'At Seventeen', Ian's sole US chart topper, and subsequent releases continued to reflect a growing sophistication. *Night Rains* featured two film theme songs, 'The Foxes' and 'The Bell Jar', although critics began pointing at an increasingly maudlin, self-pity. The artist's impetus noticeably waned during the 80s and Janis Ian seemed to have retired from music altogether. However, she re-emerged in 1991 giving live performances and appearing on a British concert stage for the first time in 10 years.
Albums: *Janis Ian* (1967), *For All The Seasons Of Your Mind* (1967), *The Secret Life Of J. Eddy Fink* (1968), *Present Company* (1971), *Stars* (1974), *Between The Lines* (1975), *Aftertones* (1975), *Miracle Row* (1977), *Janis Ian* (1978), *Night Rains* (1979), *Restless Eyes* (1981). Compilation: *The Best Of Janis Ian* (1980).

Ides Of March

Formed in Chicago, Illinois, USA, the Ides Of March began life as anglophiles, but quickly adopted prevailing American influences to create a series of excellent pop singles. Success eluded the group until 1970 when a brass-laden single, 'Vehicle', became an international hit in the wake of Chicago and Blood, Sweat And Tears. Despite further releases, the Ides Of March - James Peterik (vocals), Ray Herr (guitar), John Larson (trumpet), Larry Millas (guitar, flute), Bob Bergland (bass), Mike Borch (drums, vibes) and Chuck Soumar (percussion) - were unable to sustain their brief spell in the spotlight and Peterik subsequently formed the soul group, Essence.
Albums: *Vehicle* (1970), *Common Bond* (1971), *World Woven* (1972), *Midnight Oil* (1973).

If

This ambitious, multi-instrumentalist jazz-rock ensemble made its recording debut in 1970. Leader Dick Morrissey (saxophones/flute) was already a well-established figure in UK jazz circles, having led a quartet which included Phil Seaman and Harry South. Having flirted with pop and rock through an association with the Animals and Georgie Fame, Morrissey formed this new venture with guitarist Terry Smith, J.W. Hodgkinson (vocals), Dave Quincy (alto saxophone), John Mealing (keyboards), Jim Richardson (bass) and Dennis Elliott (drums) completing the initial line-up. They recorded four powerful, if commercially moribund, albums before internal pressures undermined progress. Mealing, Richardson and Elliott - the latter of whom later joined Foreigner - abandoned the group in 1972, while by the release of If's final album in 1975 only Morrissey remained from the founding septet. Although they enjoyed great popularity in Europe, the group was never able to achieve consistent commercial success, although the saxophonist subsequently enjoyed a fruitful partnership with guitarist Jim Mullen as Morrissey/Mullen.
Albums: *If* (1970), *If2* (1970), *If3* (1971), *If4* aka *Waterfall* (1972), *Double Diamond* (1973), *Not Just Another Bunch Of Pretty Faces* (1974), *Tea Break Is Over, Back On Your Heads* (1975). Compilations: *This Is If* (1973), *God Rock* (1974).

Iggy Pop

b. James Jewel Osterburg, 21 April 1947, Ypsilanti, Michigan, USA. The emaciated 'Godfather Of Punk' Iggy Pop was born just west of Detroit to an English father and raised in nearby Ann Arbor. He first joined bands while at high school, initially as a drummer, most notably with the Iguanas in 1964 where he picked up the nickname Iggy. The

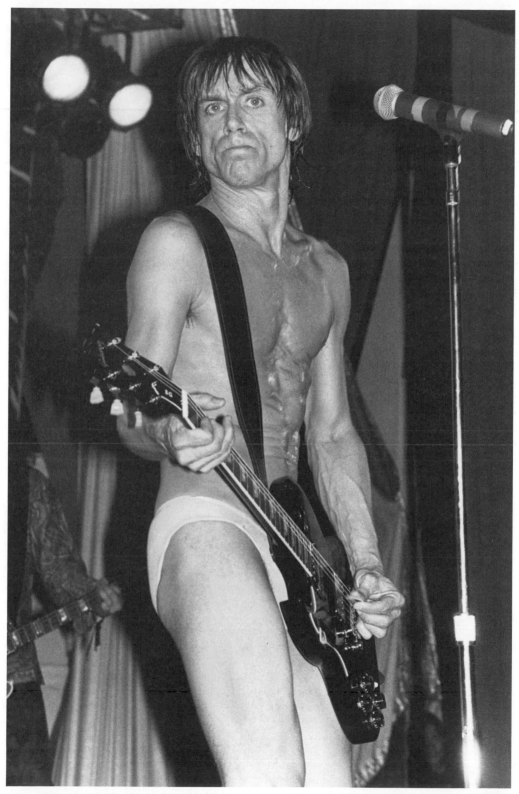

Iggy Pop

following year he joined the Denver blues-styled Prime Movers, but a year after that dropped out of the University Of Michigan to travel to Chicago and learn about the blues from former Howlin' Wolf and Paul Butterfield Blues Band drummer Sam Lay. On returning to Detroit as Iggy Stooge, and further inspired after seeing the Doors, he formed the Psychedelic Stooges with Ron Asheton of the Chosen Few. Iggy was vocalist and guitarist, Asheton initially played bass, and they later added Asheton's brother Scott on drums. Before the Chosen Few, Ron Asheton had also been in the Prime Movers with Iggy. The Psychedelic Stooges made their debut on Halloween night, 1967 in Ann Arbor. The same year Iggy also made his acting debut in a long forgotten Françoise De Monierre film that also featured Nico. Meanwhile Dave Alexander joined on bass and the word 'Psychedelic' was dropped from their name. Ron switched to guitar leaving Iggy free to concentrate on singing and showmanship. The Stooges were signed to Elektra in 1968 by A&R man Danny Fields (later manager of the Ramones). They recorded two albums (the first produced by John Cale) for the label which sold moderately at the time but later became regarded as classics, featuring such numbers as 'No Fun' and 'I Wanna Be Your Dog'. Steven MacKay joined on saxophone in 1970 in-between the first and second albums as did Bill Cheatham on second guitar. Cheatham and Alexander left in August 1970 with Zeke Zettner replacing Alexander and James Williamson replacing Cheatham but the Stooges split not long afterwards as Iggy fought a heroin problem. Stooge fan David Bowie tried to resurrect Iggy's career and helped him record *Raw Power* in London in the summer of 1972 (as Iggy and the Stooges, with Williamson on guitar, Scott Thurston on bass, and the Ashetons, who were flown in when suitable British musicians could not be found). The resultant album included the nihilistic anthem 'Search And Destroy'. Bowie's involvement continued (although his management company Mainman withdrew support because of constant drug allegations) as Iggy sailed through stormy seas (including self-admission to a mental hospital). The popular, but poor quality, live *Metallic KO* was released in France only at the time. Iggy Pop live events had long been a legend in the music industry, and it is doubtful whether any other artist has sustained such a high level of abject self destruction on stage. It was his performance on *So It Goes*, for example, that ensured the programme would never air again. After *Raw Power* there were

sessions for *Kill City*, although it was not released until 1978, credited then to Iggy Pop and James Williamson. It also featured Thurston, Hunt and Tony Sales, Brian Glascock (ex-Toe Fat and later in the Motels), and others. The Stooges had folded again in 1974 with Ron Asheton forming New Order and then Destroy All Monsters. Steve MacKay later died from a drugs overdose and Dave Alexander from alcohol abuse. Thurston also joined the Motels. Interest was stirred in Iggy with the arrival of punk, on which his influence was self evident (Television recorded the tribute 'Little Johnny Jewel'), and in 1977 Bowie produced two studio albums - *The Idiot* and *Lust For Life* - using Hunt and Tony Sales, with Bowie himself, unheralded, playing keyboards. Key tracks from these two seminal albums include 'Night Clubbin'', 'The Passenger', and 'China Girl' (co-written with and later recorded by Bowie). Iggy also returned one of the several favours he owed Bowie by guesting on backing vocals for *Low*. In the late 70s Iggy signed to Arista and released some rather average albums with occasional assistance from Glen Matlock (ex-Sex Pistols) and Ivan Kral. He went into (vinyl) exile after 1982's autobiography and the Chris-Stein produced *Zombie Birdhouse*. During his time out of the studio he cleaned up his drug problems and married. He started recording again in 1985 with Steve Jones (again ex-Sex Pistols) featuring on the next series of albums. He also developed his acting career (even taking lessons) appearing in *Sid And Nancy*, *The Color Of Money*, *Hardware*, and on television in *Miami Vice*. His big return came in 1986 with the Bowie-produced *Blah Blah Blah* and his first ever UK hit single 'Real Wild Child', a cover of Australian Johnny O'Keefe's 50s rocker. His most recent album featured Guns N' Roses guitarist Slash, who co-wrote four of the tracks, while his contribution to the *Red Hot And Blue* AIDS benefit was an endearing duet with Debbie Harry on 'Well Did You Evah?'. This was followed in 1991 by a duet with the B-52's Kate Pierson.

Albums: *The Stooges* (1969), *Fun House* (1970), *Raw Power* (1973), *Metallic KO* (1974), *The Idiot* (1977), *Lust For Life* (1977), *Kill City* (1978), *TV Eye Live* (1978), *New Values* (1979), *Soldier* (1980), *Party* (1981), *Zombie Birdhouse* (1982), *Blah Blah Blah* (1986), *Instinct* (1988), *Brick By Brick* (1990).

Further reading: *I Need More*, Iggy Pop.

Iglesias, Julio

b. 23 September 1943, Madrid, Spain. Iglesias trained as a lawyer and played football (goalkeeper)

Julio Iglesias

for Real Madrid before suffering severe injuries in a car accident. While recuperating, he learned guitar and began to write songs. After completing his studies at Cambridge University, he entered the 1968 Spanish Song Festival at Benidorm. Performing his own composition 'La Vida Sigue Igual' ('Life Continues All The Same'), he won first prize and soon afterwards signed a recording contract with the independent Discos Columbia where Ramon Arcusa became his producer. In 1970, Iglesias represented Spain in the Eurovision Song Contest, subsequently recording the song 'Gwendolyne' in French, Italian and English. During the next few years he toured widely in Europe and Latin America, scoring international hits with 'Manuela' (1975) and 'Hey' (1979). His global reach was increased in 1978 when he signed to CBS International and soon had hits in French and Italian. The first big English-language success came in 1981 when his version of 'Begin The Beguine' topped the UK charts. This was followed by the multi-language compilation album *Julio* which sold a million in America. Co-produced by Arcusa and Richard Perry, *1100 Bel Air Place* was aimed directly at American audiences and included duets with Willie Nelson ('To All The Girls I've Loved Before') and Diana Ross ('All Of You'). A later duet (and international hit) was 'My Love' with Stevie Wonder in 1988. By the end of the 80s Iglesias had sold in excess of 100 million albums in seven languages.
Albums: *Yo Canto* (1968), *Todos Los Dias Un Dia* (1969), *Soy* (1970), *Gwendolyne* (1970), *Como el Alamo al Camino* (1971), *Rio Rebelde* (1972), *Asi Nacemos* (1973), *A Flor de Piel* (1974), *El Amor* (1975), *A Mexico* (1975), *America* (1976), *En El Olympia* (1976), *A Mis 33 Anos* (1977), *Mi Vida en Canciones* (1978), *Emociones* (1979), *Hey* (1980), *Momentos* (1981), *De Nina a Mujer* (1982), *En Concierto* (1982), *Julio* (1983), *1100 Bel Air Place* (1984), *Libra* (1985), *Un Hombre Solo* (1987), *Non Stop* (1988), *Sentimental* (1988), *Raices* (1989).

Independents

This Chicago-based group consisted of Charles 'Chuck' Jackson (22 March 1945, Greenville, South Carolina, USA), Maurice Jackson - no relation (b. 12 June 1944, Chicago, Illinois, USA), Eric Thomas (b. 1951, Chicago, Illinois, USA) and Helen Curry (b. Clarksdale, Mississippi, USA). Chuck Jackson, (no relation to 'Any Day Now' artist of the same name), was at one time an art director at *Playboy* magazine and also found time to write sermons occasionally for his brother, the civil

rights leader and politician, Reverend Jesse. Fired with an ambition to put his words into song, Chuck joined Jerry Butler's writers workshop and teamed up with Marvin Yancey. The duo's talents were recognized by Butler, who recorded two of their compositions for his 1971 album, *JB Sings Assorted Songs*. Encouraged by this, the duo recorded one of their own songs, 'Just As Long As You Need Me', and discovered that they had a moderate success on their hands, enough to prompt them to form a group as a vehicle for their talents. They recruited from the Chicago club scene Maurice Jackson and Helen Curry (who had previously worked together as a duo, and prior to which Maurice had recorded with the vocal group Mark 4), and finally, Eric Thomas. Marvin preferred to stay behind the scenes to write and produce, occasionally performing live and playing keyboards. Between 1972 and 1974 they had a run of eight R&B Top 40 entries which included 'Leaving You' (1973), a million-selling single which peaked at number 21 in the US pop chart. Despite this consistency, the quartet was unable to break into the Top 20 pop chart, a factor which precipitated their demise. Yancey and Chuck Jackson continued working together and subsequently guided the early career of singer Natalie Cole.
Albums: *The First Time We Met* (1972), *Helen, Eric, Chuck, Maurice* (1973). Compilations: *Discs Of Gold* (1974), *The First Time We Met - The Greatest Hits* (1986).

Ingham, Keith

b. 5 February 1942, London, England. Ingham is a self-taught jazz pianist who turned professional in 1964. He played with artists including Sandy Brown (clarinet) and Bruce Turner (alto saxophone). In 1974 he recorded in London with Bob Wilbur and Bud Freeman and recorded two solo albums for EMI. In 1978 he moved to New York where he played with Benny Goodman and the World's Greatest Jazz Band. He became musical director and record producer for Susannah McCorkle as well as recording with Maxine Sullivan. He works with guitarist Marty Grosz in various bands including the Orphan Newsboys in which they perform some of the lesser known music of the 30s and 40s.
Albums: with Bud Freeman *Superbud* (1977), with Dick Sudhalter *Get Out And Get Under The Moon* (1989), with Marty Grosz *Unsaturated Fats* (1990), with the Orphan Newsboys *Laughing At Life* (1990).

Ingram, Luther

b. Luther Thomas Ingram, 30 November 1944, Jackson, Tennessee, USA. This singer/songwriter's professional career began in New York with work for producers Jerry Leiber and Mike Stoller. Several unsuccessful singles followed, including 'I Spy For The FBI', which failed in the wake of Jamo Thomas's 1966 hit version. Luther then moved to Koko Records, a tiny independent label later marketed by Stax. Ingram's career flourished in the wake of this arrangement. With Mack Rice he helped compose 'Respect Yourself' for the Staple Singers, while several of his own releases were R&B hits. The singer's finest moment came when his 1972 recording of the classic Homer Banks, Raymond Jackson and Carl Hampton song, '(If Loving You Is Wrong) I Don't Want To Be Right'. This tale of infidelity was later recorded by Rod Stewart, Millie Jackson and Barbara Mandrell, but neither matched the heartbreaking intimacy Luther brought to his superb original version. It went on to sell over a million copies and reached number 3 in the US pop charts. The haunting 'I'll Be Your Shelter (In Time Of Storm)' then followed as the artist proceeded to fashion a substantial body of work. His undoubted potential was undermined by Koko's financial problems, but after eight years in the commercial wilderness, Ingram returned to the R&B chart in 1986 with 'Baby Don't Go Too Far'.
Albums: *I've Been Here All The Time* (1972), *(If Loving You Is Wrong) I Don't Want To Be Right* (1972), *Luther Ingram* (1986).

Innes, Neil

Innes first attracted attention as one of the principal songwriters in the Bonzo Dog Doo-Dah Band. His affection for pop melody, evinced in the group's only hit, 'I'm The Urban Spaceman', was expanded with the World - Roger McKew (guitar), Roger Rowan (bass) and Ian Wallace (drums) - founded on the former act's collapse. Innes then embarked on a solo career with *How Sweet To Be An Idiot*, as well as fronting Grimms, an ambitious confluence of poetry, satire and rock. The artist's friendship with Eric Idle, formerly of comedy team Monty Python's Flying Circus, resulted in a short-lived though excellent BBC television series, *Rutland Weekend Television*. Its songs were later compiled on *Rutland Times*, while one of the sketches inspired the Rutles, a full-length feature which parodied the rise of the Beatles. Innes skilfully encapsulated his subject's entire oeuvre on *Meet The Rutles* (1978), while the

project was itself lampooned by maverick New York label, Shimmy Disc, on *Rutles Highway Revisited*. Innes maintained his idiosyncratic career with *Taking Off* and *The Innes Book Of Records*, and he later contributed music to television commercials and children's television programmes, including *Raggy Dolls* and *Rosie And Jim*.
Albums: with World *Lucky Planet* (1970), *How Sweet To Be An Idiot* (1973), *Rutland Times* (1976), *Taking Off* (1977), *The Innes Book Of Records* (1979), *Neil Innes A Go Go* (1981), *Off The Record* (1983).

Iommi, Tony

b. Anthony Frank Iommi, 19 February 1948, Birmingham, England. A blues/jazz influenced guitarist, Iommi was eager to escape the mundanity of industrial Birmingham and his job repairing typewriters. A number of small-time bands including Polka Tulk and Earth gradually led to the formation of Black Sabbath in 1969 with Iommi on guitar, John 'Ozzy' Osbourne (vocals), Terence 'Geezer' Butler (bass) and Bill Ward (drums). It was with Black Sabbath that Iommi was to make his international reputation as a guitarist of skill and inventiveness. The Black Sabbath sound was built on the devastatingly powerful and heavy riffing style of Iommi, delivered with a fuzzy, distorted guitar tone that was to become his trademark. He was, and still is, the godfather of the heavy metal riff. Personal differences between Iommi and Osbourne contributed to the latter's departure from Black Sabbath in 1978, to be replaced by American Ronnie James Dio. After Dio's own departure in 1982, Black Sabbath entered a highly unstable phase, and it was Iommi who held the band together and kept the Black Sabbath name alive. Iommi has a unique soloing and rhythm style, and sports an unusual set of plastic finger extensions on his right hand as a result of an accident; (Iommi is left handed.) A tall, dark, moustachioed man, he is also famed for his lack of movement on stage. The album *Seventh Star* came out under the moniker of 'Black Sabbath Featuring Tony Iommi', according to record company wishes. Iommi, however, had intended it to be a solo album and so the songs had a slightly different emphasis than any pure Black Sabbath album.
Albums with Black Sabbath: *Black Sabbath* (1970), *Paranoid* (1971), *Master of Reality* (1971), *Volume 4* (1972), *Sabbath Bloody Sabbath* (1973), *Sabotage* (1975), *Live At Last* (1976), *Technical Ecstasy* (1977), *Never Say Die* (1978), *Heaven And Hell* (1980), *Mob*

Rules (1981), *Live Evil* (1982), *Born Again* (1983), *Seventh Star* (1986), *Eternal Idol* (1987), *Headless Cross* (1989), *Tyr* (1990).

Island Records

Chris Blackwell, the son of a wealthy plantation owner and Crosse and Blackwell food family, founded this label in Jamaica in 1961. Its early, low-key singles were imported into Britain where several were subsequently issued by Starlite. Blackwell opened a UK office the following year, instigating the famed 'WI' (West Indian) prefix with Lord Creator's 'Independent Jamaica'. Island's ensuing releases included material by the Maytals, Jackie Edwards and the Skatalites and over the next four years they encompassed the shift in styles from jump R&B, through ska, to rock steady. In 1963 Island secured the UK rights to the New York-based Sue label and although the deal was later rescinded, the appellation was kept as an outlet for material licensed from a variety of sources, including VeeJay, Ace and Kent. Although most of its recordings were distributed independently, Island enjoyed a marketing deal with Fontana. Thus their first chart success - Millie's 'My Boy Lollipop' (1964) - bore the latter's imprint, a feature also prevalent on the label's first pop signing, the Spencer Davis Group. Such diversification was later shown by releases on Island by Wynder K. Frog, the V.I.Ps (later Spooky Tooth) and Kim Fowley, but the company did not undertake a fully-fledged switch to rock until 1967 and the formation of Traffic, which Blackwell also managed. The group scored three UK Top 10 hits but, more importantly, also established Island as a force within the nascent album market. Having assigned its West Indian catalogue to Trojan, the label now welcomed many of the era's best-loved 'underground' acts, including Jethro Tull, Fairport Convention and Free, and by 1970 was firmly established as one of Britain's leading labels. Judicious production deals with companies, including Chrysalis, Bronze and EG, brought further success with, among others, Roxy Music, King Crimson and Uriah Heep, but Island's eminent position was undermined later in the decade when several such enterprises themselves opted for independence. Blackwell developed a reputation for nurturing talent and persevering with his artists. John Martyn and Robert Palmer were with Island for many years, although major success eluded them. Cat Stevens by contrast became one of the most successful singer/songwriters of the 70s. By this point the company had exhumed its interest in Jamaican music with the Wailers' *Catch A Fire*. Island's relationship with group leader Bob Marley, which was maintained until his premature death, was largely responsible for introducing reggae into the rock mainstream. By the late 70s the company's diverse catalogue included the Chieftains, Inner Circle and Eddie And The Hot Rods, but a flirtation with punk act the Slits incurred the wrath of Blackwell, who returned from a recently-founded US office to take charge of UK operations. U2 became the label's most impressive signing of this period, but long-time artists Robert Palmer and Stevie Winwood also enjoyed considerable success, while Island was also responsible for transforming Grace Jones from cult act to international star. The departure of all three individuals was another major blow, but Island nonetheless boasted a roster including Tom Waits, the Christians, Julian Cope and Anthrax at the time of its 25th Anniversary celebrations in 1987. However, two years later, Blackwell sold his company to A&M, ending Island's tenure as an independent outlet.

Recommended listening: *Island Story* (1987), *Island Life* (1988).

Isotope

Led by guitarist Gary Boyle (b. 24 November 1941, Patna, India), Isotope was a highly-regarded UK jazz-rock band of the 70s. Boyle had previously played with Brian Auger, Keith Tippett, and Stomu Yamash'ta when he formed the band in 1974 with Jeff Clyne (b. 29 January 1947, London, England; bass), Brian Miller (b. 28 April 1947, St. Neots, Huntingdonshire, England; keyboards) and Nigel Norris (b. 20 June 1948, Dalston, London, England; drums). They signed to the newly-formed Gull label but after a USA tour in 1974 Clyne and Miller returned to the orthodox jazz scene. They were replaced for the second album with ex-Soft Machine stalwart Hugh Hopper (bass) and Lawrence Scott (keyboards). Vocalist Zoe Kronberger appeared on the final album and guested on *The Dancer* (1977) the first of two solo albums made by Boyle for Gull after Isotope disbanded in 1976.

Albums: *Isotope* (1974), *Illusion* (1974), *Deep End* (1976). Compilation: *The Best Of Isotope* (1979).

J

Jackson Five

The Jackson Five comprised of five brothers, Jackie (b. Sigmund Esco Jackson, 4 May 1951), Tito (b. Toriano Adaryll Jackson, 15 October 1953), Jermaine (b. 11 December 1954), Marlon (b. 12 March 1957) and Michael Jackson (b. 29 August 1958). Raised in Gary, Indiana, USA, by their father Joe, a blues guitarist, they began playing local clubs in 1962, with youthful prodigy Michael as lead vocalist. Combining dance routines influenced by the Temptations with music inspired by James Brown, they first recorded for the Indiana-based Steeltown label before auditioning for Motown Records in 1968. Bobby Taylor recommended the group to Motown, although the company gave Diana Ross public credit for their discovery. A team of Motown writers known as the Corporation composed a series of songs for the group's early releases, all accentuating their youthful enthusiasm and vocal interplay. Their debut single for Motown, 'I Want You Back', became the fastest-selling record in the company's history in 1969, and three of their next five singles also topped the American chart. Michael Jackson was groomed for a simultaneous solo recording career, which began in 1971, followed by similar excursions for Jermaine and elder brother Jackie. As the group's appeal broadened, they became the subjects of a cartoon series on American television, *The Jackson 5*, and hosted a television special, *Goin' Back To Indiana*.

After the dissolution of the Corporation in 1971, the group recorded revivals of pop and R&B hits from the 50s, and cover versions of other Motown standards, before being allowed to branch out into more diverse material, such as Jackson Browne's 'Doctor My Eyes'. They also began to record their own compositions in the early 70s, a trend which continued until 1975, by which time they were writing and producing most of the songs on their albums.

The Jackson Five reached the peak of their popularity in Britain when they toured there in 1972, but after returning to America they suffered decreasing record sales as their music grew more sophisticated. By 1973, they had dropped the teenage stylings of their early hits, concentrating on a cabaret approach to their live performances while on record they perfected a harder brand of funk. The group's recording contract with Motown expired in 1975. Feeling that the label had not been promoting their recent records, they signed to Epic Records. Jermaine Jackson, however, who was married to the daughter of Motown boss Berry Gordy, chose to leave the group and remain with the company as a solo artist. Gordy sued the Jackson Five for alleged breach of contract in 1976, and the group were forced to change their name to the Jacksons. The case was settled in 1980, with the brothers paying Gordy $600,000, and allowing Motown all rights to the 'Jackson Five' name.

Albums: *Diana Ross Presents The Jackson 5* (1969), *ABC* (1970), *Third Album* (1970), *Christmas Album* (1970), *Maybe Tomorrow* (1971), *Goin' Back To Indiana* (1971), *Lookin' Through The Windows* (1972), *Skywriter* (1973), *Get It Together* (1973), *Dancing Machine* (1974), *Moving Vibrations* (1975), *Anthology* (1976), *Joyful Jukebox Music* (1976). Compilation: *Greatest Hits* (1971).

Jackson Heights

This group was formed in 1970 by bassist/vocalist Lee Jackson (b. 8 January 1943, Newcastle-upon-Tyne, Tyne And Wear, England) on the dissolution of the Nice. His new venture pursued a more pop-orientated path than its virtuoso-based predecessor, but despite prolific live work and four well-promoted albums, an unstable line-up hampered the group's ultimate progress. Early members Charlie Harcourt (guitar), Mario Tapia (guitar) and Tommy Sloane (drums) were replaced by a series of new inductees, none of whom was able to halt Jackson's ailing fortunes. However, having decided that recent addition Patrick Moraz (b. 24 June 1948, Morges, Switzerland) played a keyboard style unsuited to the primarily melodic group, Jackson left his creation in 1974 to shape Refugee around his new discovery's dexterous technique. His former colleagues briefly continued under the truncated name Heights before breaking up.

Albums: *King's Progress* (1970), *5th Avenue Bus* (1972), *Ragmuffin's Fool* (1973), *Jackson Heights* (1973), *Bump And Grind* (1973).

Jackson, Dee D.

This UK vocalist attained instant success with a crossover dance track 'Automatic Lover', which reached the UK Top 5 as well as topping the charts all over Europe. The song had a futuristic, space theme which was continued on her second single 'Meteor Man'. An album's worth of similar

material was also released.
Album: *Cosmic Curves* (1978).

Jackson, Millie

b. 15 July 1944, Thompson, Georgia, USA. A former model, Millie Jackson's controversial singing career began professionally in 1964 at a club in Hoboken, New Jersey, USA. Her first recordings followed in 1970; over the next three years she made several excellent, if traditional, soul singles, which included two US R&B Top 10 entries, with 'Ask Me What You Want' and 'My Man A Sweet Man'. 'Hurts So Good', a song from a pseudo-feminist 'blaxploitation' film, *Cleopatra Jones*, was Jackson's biggest hit to date, but her subsequent direction was more fully shaped in 1974 with the release of *Caught Up*. Tracks, with backing from the Muscle Shoals rhythm section, included a fiery interpretation of '(If Lovin' You Is Wrong) I Don't Wanna Be Right'. The accompaniment intensified the sexual element in her work as Millie embraced either the pose of adultress or of wronged wife. A further collection, *Still Caught Up*, continued the saga, but Jackson's style later verged on self-parody as she progressed down an increasingly blind alley. The raps became longer and more explicit, and two later albums, *Feelin' Bitchy* and *Live And Uncensored*, required warning stickers for public broadcast. Despite excursions into C&W and a collaboration with Isaac Hayes, Millie seemed unable to abandon her 'bad mouth' role, exemplified in 80s titles such as 'Sexercise Pts 1 & 2' and 'Slow Tongue (Working Your Way Down)'. Despite her strong cult following, the only occasion on which Jackson has made any significant impact on the UK singles market was in 1985 when duetting with Elton John on 'Act Of War', which reached the Top 40. She possesses one of soul's outstanding voices, yet sadly chooses to limit its obvious potential.
Albums: *Millie Jackson* (1972), *It Hurts So Good* (1973), *Caught Up* (1974), *Soul Believer* (1974), *Still Caught Up* (1975), *Free And In Love* (1976), *Lovingly Yours* (1977), *Get It Out 'Cha System* (1978), *A Moment's Pleasure* (1979), with Isaac Hayes *Royal Rappings* (1979), *Live And Uncensored* (1980), *For Men Only* (1980), *Just A Lil' Bit Country* (1981), *Live And Outrageous* (1982), *Hard Times* (1982), *E.S.P. (Extra Sexual Persuasion)* (1984), *An Imitation Of Love* (1986), *The Tide Is Turning* (1988), *Back To The Sh.t* (1989). Compilation: *Best Of Millie Jackson* (1976).

Jacksons

Jackie (b. Sigmund Esco Jackson, 4 May 1951, Gary, Indiana, USA), Tito (b. Toriano Adaryll Jackson, 15 October 1953, Gary), Marlon (b. Marlon David Jackson, 12 March 1957, Gary), Michael (b. Michael Joseph Jackson, 29 August 1958, Gary) and Randy Jackson (b. Steven Randall Jackson, 20 October 1962, Gary) changed their collective name from the Jackson Five to the Jacksons in March 1976, following their departure from Motown Records. At the same time, Randy Jackson replaced his brother Jermaine, handling percussion and backing vocals. The group's new recording contract with Epic offered them a more lucrative deal than they had received from Motown, though at first they seemed to have exchanged one artistic strait-jacket for another. Their initial releases were written, arranged and produced by Gamble And Huff, whose expertise ensured that the Jacksons sounded professional, but slightly anonymous. 'Enjoy Yourself' and 'Show You The Way To Go' were both major hits in the US charts, and the latter also topped the UK sales listing. The group's second album with Gamble And Huff, *Goin' Places*, heralded a definite decline in popularity. *Destiny* saw the Jacksons reassert control over writing and production, and produced a string of worldwide hit singles. 'Blame It on The Boogie' caught the mood of the burgeoning disco market, while the group's self-composed 'Shake Your Body (Down To The Ground)' signalled Michael Jackson's growing artistic maturity.

The success of Michael's first adult solo venture, *Off The Wall* in 1979, switched his attention away from the group. On *Triumph* (1980), they merely repeated the glories of their previous album, although the commercial appeal of anything bearing Michael's voice helped singles like 'Can You Feel It?', 'Heartbreak Hotel' and 'Lovely One' achieve success on both sides of the Atlantic. The Jacksons' 1981 USA tour emphasized Michael's dominance over the group, and the resulting *Live* included many of his solo hits alongside the brothers' joint repertoire. Between 1981 and the release of *Victory* in 1984, Michael issued *Thriller*, the best-selling album of all time (total sales by 1992, 40 million units). When the Jacksons' own effort was released, it became apparent that he had made only token contributions to the record, and its commercial fortune suffered accordingly. 'State Of Shock', which paired Michael with Mick Jagger, was a US hit, but sold in smaller quantities than expected. Hysteria surrounded the group's 'Victory Tour' in the summer of 1984; adverse press comment greeted the distribution of tickets, and the Jacksons were accused of pricing themselves out of the reach of their black fans. Although they were joined onstage by their brother Jermaine for the first time since 1975, media and public attention was focused firmly on Michael. Realising that they were becoming increasingly irrelevant, the other members of the group began to voice their grievances in the press; as a result, Michael Jackson expressed that he would not be working with his brothers in future. The Jacksons struggled to come to terms with his departure, and it was five years before their next project was complete. *2300 Jackson Street* highlighted their dilemma: once the media realised that Michael was not involved, they effectively boycotted its release. :

Albums: *The Jacksons* (1976), *Goin' Places* (1977), *Destiny* (1978), *Triumph* (1980), *Live* (1981), *Victory* (1984), *2300 Jackson Street* (1989).

Jam

This highly successful late 70s group comprised Paul Weller (b. 25 May 1958, Woking, Surrey, England; vocals/bass), Bruce Foxton (b. 1 September 1955, England; guitar) and Rick Buckler (b. Paul Richard Buckler, 6 December 1955, Woking, Surrey, England; drums). After gigging consistently throughout 1976, the group were signed to Polydor Records early the following year. Although emerging at the peak of punk, the Jam seemed oddly divorced from the movement. Their leader, Paul Weller, professed to voting Conservative (although he would later switch dramatically to support the Labour Party), and the group's musical influences were firmly entrenched in the early Who-influenced mod style. Their debut, 'In The City' was a high energy outing, with Weller displaying his Rickenbacker guitar to the fore. With their next record, 'All Around The World' they infiltrated the UK Top 20 for the first time. For the next year, they registered only minor hits, including 'News Of The World' and a cover of the Kinks' 'David Watts'. A turning point in the group's critical fortunes occurred towards the end of 1978 with the release of 'Down In The Tube Station At Midnight'. This taut, dramatic anti-racist song saw them emerge as social commentators par excellence. *All Mod Cons* was widely acclaimed and thereafter the group rose to extraordinary heights. With *Setting Sons*, a quasi-concept album, Weller fused visions of British colonialism with urban decay and a satirical thrust at suburban life. The

tone and execution of the work recalled the style of the Kinks' Ray Davies, whose class-conscious vignettes of the 60s had clearly influenced the Jam. The title track of their album gave the Jam their first Top 10 single in late 1979. Early the following year, they secured their first UK number 1 with the harrowing 'Going Underground'. The fact that the song reached the top of the charts indicated the enormous strength of the group's fan base. By now, they were on their way to topping music paper polls with increasing regularity. Throughout 1982, the Jam were streets ahead of their nearest rivals but their parochial charm could not be translated into international success. While they continued to log number 1 hits with 'Start' and 'Town Called Malice', the USA market remained untapped. In late 1982, the group's recent run of UK chart-toppers was interrupted by 'The Bitterest Pill (I Ever Had To Swallow)' which peaked at number 2. Weller then announced that the group were to split, and that he intended to form a new outfit, the Style Council. It was a shock decision, as the group were still releasing some of the best music to come out of Britain and most certainly at their peak. Their final single, the exuberant, anthemic 'Beat Surrender' entered the UK chart at number 1, an extraordinary conclusion to a remarkable but brief career.

Albums: *In The City* (1977), *This Is The Modern World* (1977), *All Mod Cons* (1978), *Setting Sons* (1979), *Sound Affects* (1980), *The Gift* (1982), *Dig The New Breed* (1982). Compilations: *Snap!* (1983), *Greatest Hits* (1991).

Jefferson Starship

Formerly the Jefferson Airplane, the band evolved into the Jefferson Starship after Paul Kantner (b. 17 March 1941, San Francisco, California, USA; guitar/vocals) had previously released *Blows Against The Empire* in 1970, billed as Paul Kantner And The Jefferson Starship. His fascination with science-fiction no doubt led the Airplane to metamorphose into a Starship. The official debut was *Dragonfly* in 1974, which became an immediate success. The band played with a freshness and urgency that had been missing on recent Airplane releases. Joining Kantner on this album were Grace Slick (b. Grace Barnett Wing, 30 October 1939, Chicago, Illinois, USA; vocals), Papa John Creach (b. 28 May 1917, Beaver Falls, Pennsylvania, USA; violin), former Quicksilver Messenger Service bassist David Freiberg (b. 24 August 1938, Boston, Massachusetts, USA, vocals/keyboards), Craig Chaquico (b. 26

Jam

September 1954; lead guitar), ex-Turtles member John Barbata (drums) and Pete Sears (bass/keyboards). Among the tracks were 'Ride The Tiger', which was accompanied by an imaginatively graphic, early video and 'Hyperdrive', a Slick magnum opus featuring Chaquico's frantic screaming guitar. Old Airplane fans were delighted to hear Marty Balin guesting on one track with his own composition 'Caroline', and further cheered when he joined the band at the beginning of 1975. *Red Octopus* later that year became their most successful album and ended up selling several million copies and spending a month at the top of the US charts. The flagship track was Balin's beautiful and seemingly innocent 'Miracles'. This was the first known pop lyric to feature reference to cunnilingus with Balin singing 'I had a taste of the real world, when I went down on you' and Slick innocently responding in the background with 'Mmm, don't waste a drop of it, don't ever stop it'.

Soon after Kantner and Slick separated; she moved in with Skip Johnson, the band's lighting engineer, and eventually married him. Later that year Slick was regularly in the news when her drinking problems got out of control. *Spitfire* and *Earth* continued their success, although the band had now become a hard rock outfit. Balin's lighter 'Count On Me' was a US Top 10 hit in 1978. That year, Grace was asked to leave the band, to be allowed to return when she dried out. She was eventually dismissed in 1978, closely followed by Balin, who left towards the end of a turbulent year. He was replaced by Mickey Thomas and further changes were afoot when stalwart drummer Aynsley Dunbar (b. 1946, Liverpool, England) joined in place of Barbata. *Freedom From Point Zero* and the US Top 20 hit 'Jane', at the end of 1979, bore no resemblance to the musical style that remaining original member Kantner had attempted to steer them towards. He suffered a stroke during 1980, but returned the following spring together with a sober Grace Slick. Both *Modern Times* (1981) and *Winds Of Change* (1982), continued the success, although by now the formula was wearing thin. Kantner found his role had diminished and released a solo album later that year. He continued with them throughout the following year, although he was openly very unsettled. Towards the end of 1984 Kantner performed a nostalgic set of old Airplane songs with Balin's band, amid rumours of a Jefferson Airplane reunion.

The tension broke in 1985 when, following much acrimony over ownership of the band's name,

Jefferson Starship

Kantner was paid off and took with him half of the group's monicker. Kantner claimed the rights to the name, although he no longer wanted to use the title, as his reunion with Balin and Casady in the KBC Band demonstrated. In defiance his former band performed as Starship Jefferson, but shortly after became Starship. Both Thomas and Freiberg left during these antagonistic times, leaving Slick the remaining original member after the incredible changes of the past few years. The new line-up added Denny Baldwin on drums and recorded *Knee Deep In The Hoopla* in 1985, which became their most successful album since *Red Octopus*. Two singles from the album 'We Built This City' (written by Bernie Taupin) and 'Jane' both reached number 1 in the USA. The following year they reached the top spot on both sides of the Atlantic with the theme from the film *Mannequin*, 'Nothing's Gonna Stop Us Now'. Their image is now of slick perpetrators of AOR, performing immaculate music for the MTV generation (on which China Kantner was a presenter). Now having gone full circle, Grace Slick departed in 1989 to join Kaukonen, Casady, Balin and Kantner in . . . the Jefferson Airplane.
Albums: *Dragonfly* (1974), *Red Octopus* (1975), *Spitfire* (1976), *Earth* (1978), *Freedom At Point Zero* (1979), *Modern Times* (1981), *Winds Of Change* (1982), *Nuclear Furniture* (1984); as Starship *Knee Deep In The Hoopla* (1985), *No Protection* (1987), *Love Among The Cannibals* (1989). Compilations: featuring Jefferson Airplane and Starship *Flight Log (1966-1976)* (1977), *Gold* (1979).

Jeffreys, Garland

b. 1944, Brooklyn, New York, USA. Singer/songwriter Jeffreys first gained attention in 1973 with a critically-acclaimed self-titled album that contained the anthemic 'Wild In The Streets'. Jeffreys, of mixed racial background, studied art in Italy before deciding to concentrate on music. He first performed solo around New York and in 1966 formed a band called Grinder's Switch (not the US southern rock band of a similar name that recorded in the 70s). Jeffreys spent the early 70s going back to performing solo and honed a sound that crossed elements of rock, folk, reggae, salsa and soul. His 1973 Atlantic Records debut album contained frank songs of New York street life and the struggle for acceptance and survival Jeffreys witnessed and experienced in his youth. It was not commercially successful, yet 'Wild In The Streets' became a staple on FM radio. Jeffreys re-recorded the song for his next album. *Ghost Writer*, his debut

for A&M Records in 1977, another critical favourite, made a minor dent in the charts. That pattern continued throughout the late 70s and 80s; Jeffreys recorded two more albums for A&M before switching to Epic in 1981 and recording three more albums. Ironically, considering the critical praise he had gathered for his writing, his only chart single in the USA was a remake of ? and the Mysterians' '96 Tears' in 1981. He has enjoyed success outside the USA, however, and the 1981 single 'Matador' reached the Top 10 in some European countries. That same year, Jeffreys employed the services of Graham Parker's backing band, the Rumour on his *Rock And Roll Adult* album. This respected artist has, in the past, enjoyed the support of various illustrious musicians including David Sanborn, Phoebe Snow, Herb Alpert, James Taylor, Luther Vandross, David Bromberg and Dr. John.
Albums: *Grinder's Switch Featuring Garland Jeffreys* (1970), *Garland Jeffreys* (1973), *Ghost Writer* (1977), *One-Eyed Jack* (1978), *American Boy And Girl* (1979), *Escape Artist* (1981), *Rock And Roll Adult* (1981), *Guts For Love* (1983).

Jethro Tull

Jethro Tull was formed in Luton, England in 1967 when Ian Anderson (b. 10 August 1947, Edinburgh, Scotland; vocals/flute) and Glenn Cornick (b. 24 April 1947, Barrow-in-Furness, Cumbria, England; bass), members of a visiting Blackpool blues group, John Evan's Smash, became acquainted with Mick Abrahams (b. 7 April 1973, Luton, Bedfordshire, England; guitar/vocals) and Clive Bunker (b. 12 December 1946, Blackpool, Lancashire, England; drums), Abrahams' colleague in local attraction, McGregor's Engine, completed the original line-up which made its debut in March the following year with 'Sunshine Day'. This commercially-minded single, erroneously credited to Jethro Toe, merely hinted at developments about to unfold. A residency at London's famed Marquee club and a sensational appearance at that summer's Sunbury Blues Festival confirmed a growing reputation, while 'Song For Jeffrey', the quartet's first release for the Island label, introduced a more representative sound. Abrahams' rolling blues licks and Anderson's distinctive, stylized voice combined expertly on *This Was* - for many Tull's finest collection. Although the material itself was derivative, the group's approach was highly exciting, with Anderson's propulsive flute playing, modelled on jazzman Raahsan Roland Kirk, particularly effective. The album reached the UK

Ian Anderson of Jethro Tull

Top 10, largely on the strength of Tull's live reputation in which the singer played an ever-increasing role. His exaggerated gestures, long, wiry hair, ragged coat and distinctive, one-legged stance cultivated a compulsive stage personality to the extent that, for many spectators, Jethro Tull was the name of this extrovert frontman and the other musicians merely his underlings. This impression gained credence through the group's internal ructions. Mick Abrahams left in November 1968 and formed Blodwyn Pig. When future Black Sabbath guitarist Tony Iommi proved incompatible, Martin Barre (b. 17 November 1946) joined Tull for *Stand Up*, their excellent, chart-topping, second album. The group was then augmented by John Evan (b. 28 March 1948; keyboards), the first of Anderson's Blackpool associates to be invited into the line-up. *Benefit*, the last outwardly blues-based album, duly followed and this period was also marked by the group's three UK Top 10 singles, 'Living In The Past', 'Sweet Dream' (both 1969) and 'The Witch's Promise' (1970). Cornick then quit to form Wild Turkey and Jeffrey Hammond-Hammond (b. 30 July 1946), already a legend in Tull's lexicon through their debut single, 'Jeffrey Goes To Leicester Square' and 'For Michael Collins, Jeffrey And Me', was brought in for *Aqualung*. Possibly the group's best-known work, this ambitious concept album featured Anderson's musings on organized religion and contained several tracks

which remained long-standing favourites, including 'My God' and 'Locomotive Breath'.

Clive Bunker, the last original member, bar Anderson, left in May 1971. A further John Evan-era acolyte, Barriemore Barlow (b. 10 September 1949), replaced him as Jethro Tull entered its most controversial period. Although *Thick As A Brick* topped the US chart and reached number 5 in the UK, critics began questioning Anderson's reliance on obtuse concepts. However, if muted for this release, the press reviled *A Passion Play*, damning it as pretentious, impenetrable and the product of an egotist and his neophytes. Such rancour obviously hurt. Anderson retorted by announcing an indefinite retirement, but continued success in America, where the album became Tull's second chart-topper, doubtlessly appeased his anger. *War Child*, a US number 2, failed to chart in the UK, although *Minstrel In The Gallery* proved more popular. *Too Old To Rock 'N' Roll, Too Young To Die* marked the departure of Hammond-Hammond in favour of John Glascock (b. 1953, London, England, d. 17 November 1979), formerly of the Gods, Toe Fat and Chicken Shack. Subsequent releases, *Songs From The Wood* and *Heavy Horses*, reflected a more pastoral sound as Anderson abandoned the gauche approach marking many of their predecessors. David Palmer, who orchestrated each Tull album, bar their debut, was added as a second keyboards player as the group embarked on another highly-successful phase

culminating in November 1978 when a concert at New York's Madison Square Garden was simultaneously broadcast around the world by satellite. However, Glascock's premature death in 1979 during heart surgery ushered in a period of uncertainty, culminating in an internal re-alignment. In 1980 Anderson began a projected solo album, retaining Barre and new bassist Dave Pegg (ex-Fairport Convention), but adding Eddie Jobson (ex-Curved Air and Roxy Music; keyboards) and Marc Craney (drums). Longtime cohorts Barlow, Evan and Palmer were left to pursue their individual paths. The finished product, *A*, was ultimately issued under the Jethro Tull banner and introduced a productive period which saw two more group selections, plus Anderson's solo effort, *Walk Into Light*, issued within a two-year period. Since then Jethro Tull has continued to record and perform live, albeit on a lesser scale, using a nucleus of Anderson, Barre and Pegg. *Catfish Rising* in 1991, although a disappointing album was a return to their blues roots. The singer has also become a renowned entrepreneur, owning tracts of land on the west coast of Scotland and the highly-successful Strathaird Salmon processing plant.
Albums: *This Was* (1968), *Stand Up* (1969), *Benefit* (1970), *Aqualung* (1971), *Thick As A Brick* (1972), *A Passion Play* (1973), *War Child* (1974), *Minstrel In The Gallery* (1975), *Too Old To Rock 'N' Roll Too Young To Die* (1976), *Songs From The Wood* (1977), *Heavy Horses* (1978), *Live - Bursting Out* (1978), *Storm Watch* (1979), *A* (1980), *The Broadsword And The Beast* (1982), *Under Wraps* (1984), *Crest Of A Knave* (1987), *Rock Island* (1989), *Live At Hammersmith* (1991), *Catfish Rising* (1991). Compilations: *Living In The Past* (1972), *M.U.: Best Of Jethro Tull* (1976), *Repeat, The Best Of Jethro Tull - Volume II* (1977), *Original Masters* (1985), *20 Years Of Jethro Tull* (1988, box set). Ian Anderson solo: *Walk Into The Light* (1983).

Jigsaw

Barrie Bernard (b. 27 November 1944, Coventry, Midlands, England; bass), Tony Campbell (b. 24 June 1944, Rugby, Midlands, England; guitar), Des Dyer (b. 22 May 1948, Rugby, Midlands, England; vocals/drums) and Clive Scott (b. 24 February 1945, Coventry, Midlands, England; keyboards/vocals) became Jigsaw in 1966. Bernard came from Pinkerton's Assorted Colours, while Campbell had previously played in the Mighty Avengers. Scott and Dyer were a successful songwriting team - Engelbert Humperdinck

covered their material - but it took the band nine years and 13 singles before their big hit, 'Sky High'. It was the theme to *The Man From Hong Kong*, and was the first release on the band's own label Splash. 'Sky High' was a worldwide hit. It was number 1 twice in Japan, thanks to a popular wrestler adopting it as his theme tune. Jigsaw enjoyed continuing success there, but elsewhere their star shone less brightly and in 1977 'If I Have To Go Away' only reached number 36 in the UK.
Albums: *Leathersdale Farm* (1970), *Sky High* (1975), *Jigsaw* (1977).

Jilted John

Rabid Records, a new wave label based in Manchester, England, received a recording of 'Jilted John', composed and performed by a thespian named Graham Fellowes. Rabid released this semi-monologue concerning the woes of a young lover, and were soon so overwhelmed by demand that EMI had to take over its marketing in 1978. Fellowes slipped into his Jilted John character in media interviews - a few similarly gormless appearances on BBC television's *Top Of The Pops* pushed the record to number 4 in the UK chart - and necessitated the issue of an album and an 'answer' single by John's rival, Gordon The Moron. After this episode, however, Fellowes returned to his acting career which has since included roles in the UK soap opera *Coronation Street* and a northern stage production of a play concerning John Lennon.
Album: *True Love Stories* (1978).

Joel, Billy

b. 9 May 1949, Hicksville, Long Island, New York, USA. Joel, a classically-trained pianist, joined his first group, the Echoes, in 1964. Four years later he left them in favour of the Hassels, a popular Long Island act signed to United Artists. Billy appeared on both of their albums, *The Hassels* and *Hour Of The Wolf*, before breaking away with drummer Jon Small to form Attila. The duo completed an self-titled album before moving in separate directions. A demo of Joel's original compositions led to the release of his debut album, *Cold Spring Harbor*, but its progress was marred by insufficient promotion. However, when 'Captain Jack', a new song recorded for a radio broadcast, became an 'underground' hit, Columbia Records traced Billy to California and signed him to a long-term contract. The title track to *Piano Man*, became a US Top 30 single in 1973 and sowed the seeds of a highly successful recording career.

Billy Joel

However, Joel refused to bow to corporate demands for commercially-minded material and despite enjoying hits with two subsequent albums, *Street Life Serenade* and *Turnstiles*, it was not until 1977 that Billy's fortunes flourished with the release of *The Stranger* which eventually surpassed *Bridge Over Troubled Water* as Columbia's best-selling album. Its best-known track, 'Just The Way You Are' later won two Grammy awards for Song Of The Year and Record Of The Year. This romantic ballad has since become a standard, and was a major UK hit for Barry White in 1978. Joel's 1979 album, *52nd Street*, spawned another smash single, 'My Life' while the singer's first US number 1, 'It's Still Rock 'N' Roll To Me' came from a subsequent release, *Glass Houses*. His image as a popular, uncontroversial figure was shaken with *The Nylon Curtain*, which featured two notable 'protest' compositions, 'Allentown' and 'Goodnight Saigon'. However he returned to simpler matters in 1984 with *An Innocent Man* which included the effervescent best-seller 'Uptown Girl'. This memorable single topped the UK charts and confirmed the artist's status as an international performer. Joel and his wife, model Chrissie Brinkley spend a great deal of their time avoiding the media's fascination with them. Although his recent output has been less prolific, Joel continues to score the occasional hit single, maintaining his standing in the pop world. A perfectionist by nature, he has also indicated a desire to pursue a wider musical style. In 1991 Joel was awarded an honourary doctorate at Fairfield University, Connecticut.

Albums: *Cold Spring Harbor* (1972), *Piano Man* (1973), *Street Life Serenade* (1975), *Turnstiles* (1976), *The Stranger* (1977), *52nd Street* (1978), *Glass Houses* (1980), *Songs In The Attic* (1981), *The Nylon Curtain* (1982), *An Innocent Man* (1983), *The Bridge* (1986), *Kohyept - Live In Leningrad* (1987), *Storm Front* (1989). Compilations: *Greatest Hits Vol 1 & 2* (1985).

John, Elton

b. Reginald Kenneth Dwight, 25 March 1947, Pinner, Middlesex, England. At the age of four, the young Reg started taking piano lessons. This launched a talent, which via the Royal Academy Of Music led him to become the most successful rock pianist in the world, one of the richest men in Britain and one of the world's greatest rock stars. John formed his first band Bluesology in the early 60s and turned professional in 1965 when they secured enough work backing touring American soul artists. Long John Baldry joined the band in 1966, which included Elton Dean on saxophone and Caleb Quaye on lead guitar. As the forceful Baldry became the leader, Elton became disillusioned with being a pub pianist and began to explore the possibilities of a music publishing contract. Following a meeting set up by Ray Williams of Liberty Records at Dick James Music, the shy Elton first met Bernie Taupin, then an unknown writer from Lincolnshire. Realising they had uncannily similar musical tastes they began to communicate by post only, and their first composition 'Scarecrow' was completed. This undistinguished song was the first to bear the John/Taupin monicker; Elton had only recently adopted this name, having dispensed with Reg Dwight in favour of the more saleable title borrowed from the first names of his former colleagues Dean and Baldry.

In 1968 John and Taupin were signed by Dick James, formerly of Northern Songs, to be staff writers for his new company DJM at a salary of £10 per week. The songs were slow to take off, although Roger Cook released their 'Skyline Pigeon' and Lulu sang 'I've Been Loving You Too Long' as a possible entry for the Eurovision Song Contest. One hopes that Elton was not too depressed when he found that 'Boom-Bang-A-Bang' was the song chosen in its place. While the critics liked his own single releases, none were selling. Only 'Lady Samantha' came near to breaking the chart, which is all the more perplexing as it was an excellent commercial-sounding record. In June 1969 *Empty Sky* was released, and Elton was still ignored, although the reviews were reasonably favourable. During the next few months he played on sessions with the Hollies (notably the piano on 'He Ain't Heavy He's My Brother') and made budget recordings for cover versions released in supermarkets.

Finally, his agonisingly long wait for recognition came the following year when Gus Dudgeon produced the outstanding *Elton John*. Among the tracks were 'Border Song' and the classic 'Your Song'. The latter provided Elton's first UK hit, reaching number 2, and announced the emergence of a major talent. The momentum was maintained with *Tumbleweed Connection* but the following soundtrack *Friends* and the live *17-11-70* were major disappointments to his fans. These were minor setbacks, as over the next few years Elton John became a superstar. His concerts in America were legendary as he donned ridiculous outfits and outrageous spectacles. At one stage between 1972

Elton John

and 1975 he had seven consecutive number 1 albums, variously spawning memorable hits including 'Rocket Man', 'Daniel', 'Saturday Night's Alright For Fighting', 'Goodbye Yellow Brick Road', 'Candle In The Wind' and the powerful would-be suicide note, 'Someone Saved My Life Tonight'.

He was partly responsible for bringing John Lennon and Yoko Ono back together again following his Madison Square Garden concert in 1975 and became Sean Lennon's godfather. In 1976 he topped the UK charts with a joyous duet with Kiki Dee, 'Don't Go Breaking My Heart', and released a further two million selling albums *Here And There* and *Blue Moves*. The phenomenal pattern continued as Elton courted most of the rock *cognoscenti*. Magazine articles peeking into his luxury home revealed an astonishing wardrobe, and a record collection so huge that he would never be able to listen to all of it. By 1979 the John/Taupin partnership went into abeyance as Bernie moved to Los Angeles. Elton started writing with pianist and bandleader Tony Osborne's son, Gary. The partnership produced few outstanding songs however. The most memorable during that time was the solo 'Song For Guy', a beautiful instrumental written in tribute to the Rocket Records motorcycle messenger who was tragically killed.

Elton entered an uncomfortable phase in his life; he remained one of pop's most newsworthy figures, openly admitting his bisexuality and personal insecurities about his weight and baldness. It was this vulnerability that made him such a popular personality. His consumerism even extended to rescuing his favourite football club, Watford. He purchased the club and invested money in it, and under his patronage their fortunes changed positively. His albums during the early 80s were patchy, and only when he started working exclusively with Taupin again did his record sales pick up. The first renaissance album was *Too Low For Zero* in 1983 which scaled the charts as did the triumphant 'I'm Still Standing'. Elton ended the year in much better shape and married Renate Blauel the following February. During 1985 he appeared at Wham's farewell concert, and the following month he performed at the historic Live Aid giving a particularly strong performance; now as one of rock's elder statesmen. He completed the year with another massive album, *Ice On Fire*.

In January 1986 he and Taupin contested a lengthy court case for back royalties against DJM. However, the costs of the litigation were prohibitive and the victory at best pyrrhic. Towards the end of that year Elton collapsed onstage in Australia and entered an Australian hospital for throat surgery in January. During this time the UK gutter press were having a field day, speculating on Elton's possible throat cancer and his rocky marriage. The press had their pound of flesh when it was announced that Renate and Elton had separated. In 1988 he released the excellent *Reg Strikes Back* and the fast-tempo boogie 'I Don't Want To Go On With You Like That'. Meanwhile the *Sun* newspaper made serious allegations against the singer, which prompted a libel suit. Considering the upheavals in his personal life and regular sniping by the press Elton sounded in amazingly good form and was performing with the energy of his early 70s' extravaganzas. In September, almost as if he were closing a chapter of his life, Elton auctioned at Sotheby's 2,000 items of his personal memorabilia including his boa feathers, 'Pinball Wizard' boots and hundreds of pairs of spectacles. In December 1989, John accepted a settlement (reputedly £1 million, although never confirmed) from the *Sun*, thus forestalling one of the most bitter legal disputes in pop history. He appeared a sober figure, now divorced, he concentrated on music and recorded another outstanding record *Sleeping With The Past*. In April 1991 the *Sunday Times* announced that Elton had entered the top 200 wealthiest people in Britain. With or without money Elton John is a star, an outstanding songwriter and with the Beatles and Rolling Stones is Britain's most successful artists of all time He has ridden out all intrusions into his private life from the media with considerable dignity and enormous popularity.

Albums: *Empty Sky* (1969), *Elton John* (1970), *Tumbleweed Connection* (1971), *Friends* (1971, film soundtrack), *17-11-70* (1971), *Madman Across The Water* (1972), *Honky Chateau* (1972), *Don't Shoot Me I'm Only The Piano Player* (1973), *Goodbye Yellow Brick Road* (1973), *Caribou* (1974), *Captain Fantastic And The Brown Dirt Cowboy* (1975), *Rock Of The Westies* (1975), *Here And There* (1976), *Blue Moves* (1976), *A Single Man* (1978), *Victim Of Love* (1979), *Lady Samantha* (1980), *21 At 33* (1980), *The Fox* (1981), *Jump Up* (1982), *Too Low For Zero* (1983), *Breaking Hearts* (1984), *Ice On Fire* (1985), *Leather Jackets* (1986), *Live In Australia* (1987), *Reg Strikes Back* (1988), *Sleeping With The Past* (1989), *The One* (1992). Compilations: *Greatest Hits* (1974), *Greatest Hits Volume 2* (1980), *Love Songs* (1982), *The Very Best Of Elton John* (1990).

Further reading: *Elton*, Philip Norman.

John, Robert

b. Robert John Pedrick Jnr., 1946, Brooklyn, New York, USA. In 1958, when he was aged 12, Bobby Pedrick (as he was named on record then) charted with his debut 'White Bucks And Saddle Shoes'. He recorded without success on Shell in 1960 and Duel in 1962 and fronted Bobby And The Consoles on Diamond a year later. As a soloist again, this high tenor recorded on MGM in 1965 and on their Verve subsidiary in 1966. After a name change to Robert John he hit the Hot 100 in 1968 on Columbia and 1970 on A&M. His first big success was a falsetto revival of 'The Lion Sleeps Tonight' (produced by a member of the Tokens whose original of the song also reached the charts), which made number 3 in the US charts in 1972 on Atlantic. Yet again he had a period of little activity until 1979 when he scored his biggest success with his own composition 'Sad Eyes' on EMI. The record spent six months in the US chart reaching number 1 and was also his only UK Top 40 entry. After a couple of lower chart records, he moved to Motown and was last in the Top 100 with a revival of 'Bread And Butter' in 1983, stretching his span of hits to 25 years.
Album: *Robert John* (1979).

Johns, Glyn

b. c.1940. Having embarked on a short-lived singing career releasing singles on Pye and Immediate in the 60s, Johns began a concurrent path as an engineer. He assisted Shel Talmy on several sessions before establishing his name as a producer through an association with the Steve Miller Band. Their fruitful partnership resulted in four exceptional albums (including *Sailor*)which showcased a crafted, timeless sound, which complemented Miller's innovative ideas. Johns was also involved in the recording of the Beatles' *Sgt. Pepper's Lonely Hearts Club Band* and *Let It Be*, while Led Zeppelin, Joe Cocker and Traffic also called on his talents. Post-production work on the Rolling Stones' *Get Yer Ya Yas Out* collection resulted in further collaborations with the group on *Sticky Fingers*, *Exile On Main Street* and *Black And Blue*. During the 70s Johns achieved due respect with his productions for the Who, the Faces, Eric Clapton and Joan Armatrading. His connection with the Eagles, which spanned the group's first three albums, was fundamental in establishing this highly-successful country-rock group's sound and style. Johns' frantic schedule lessened during the succeeding decade as he embarked on a lower-key approach with newer acts, including Nine Below

Zero, Live Wire and, more recently, Helen Watson. Johns' work is now largely determined by artists he respects. In 1992 he was working with David Crosby at his studio in Sussex, England.

Journey

This US rock group was formed in 1973 by ex-Santana members Neil Schon (guitar) and Greg Rolie (keyboards) plus Ross Valory (ex-Steve Miller band; bass) and Aynsley Dunbar (drums). George Tickner was added later as rhythm guitarist and lead vocalist. On New Year's Eve the same year, they made their live debut in front of 10,000 people at San Fransisco's Winterland. The following day they played to 10 times as many at an open-air festival in Hawaii. Initially they specialized in jazz-rock, complete with extended and improvised solo spots. This style can clearly be heard on their first three albums. The switch to highly sophisticated pomp-rock occurred with the recording of *Infinity*. At this juncture, Tickner left and was replaced by ex-Alien Project vocalist Steve Perry. In addition, Roy Thomas Baker was brought in as producer to give the band's sound a punchy and dynamic edge. The album was a huge success reaching number 21 on the *Billboard* album charts. Dunbar was unhappy with this new style and quit, to be replaced by Steve Smith. *Evolution* followed and brought the band their first Top 20 hit, 'Lovin', Touchin', Squeezin''. *Captured* was a double live album that surprised many of the critics, being far removed from their technically excellent and clinically produced studio releases; instead, it featured cranked-up guitars and raucous hard rock, eventually peaking at number 9 in the US album chart. Founder member Rolie departed after its release, to be replaced by Jonathan Cain, who had previously played with the Babys. Cain's arrival was an important landmark in Journey's career, as his input on the writing side added a new dimension to the bands sound. *Escape* was the pinnacle of the band's success, reaching number 1 and staying in the chart for over a year. It also spawned three US Top 10 hit singles in the form of 'Who's Crying Now', 'Don't Stop Believin'', and 'Open Arms'. The follow-up *Frontiers* was also successful, staying for nine weeks at the number 2 position on the *Billboard* album chart; 'Separate Ways', culled as a single from it climbed to number 8 in the US singles chart.
After a series of internal disputes the band reduced to a three-man nucleus of Schon, Cain and Perry to record *Raised On Radio*. This was to become Journey's last album, before Schon and Cain joined

forces with John Waite's Bad English in 1988. A *Greatest Hits* compilation was posthumously released to commemorate the band's demise.

Albums: *Journey* (1975), *Look Into The Future* (1976), *Next* (1977), *Infinity* (1978), *Evolution* (1979), *In The Beginning* (1979), *Departure* (1980), *Dream After Dream* (1980), *Captured* (1981), *Escape* (1981), *Frontiers* (1983), *Raised On Radio* (1986). Compilation: *Greatest Hits* (1988).

Joy Division

Originally known as Warsaw, this Manchester post-punk outfit comprised of Ian Curtis (b. July 1956, Macclesfield, Cheshire, England, d. 18 May 1980; vocals), Bernard Dicken/Albrecht (b. 4 January 1956, Salford, Manchester, England; guitar/vocals), Peter Hook (b. 13 February 1956, Manchester, England; bass) and Steven Morris (b. 28 October 1957, Macclesfield, Cheshire, England; drums). Borrowing their name from the prostitution wing of a concentration camp, Joy Division emerged in 1978 as one of the most important groups of their era. After recording a regionally available EP, *An Ideal For Living*, they were signed to Manchester's recently formed Factory Records and placed in the hands of producer Martin Hannett. Their debut *Unknown Pleasures*, was a raw, intense affair, with Curtis at his most manically arresting in the insistent 'She's Lost Control'. With its stark, black cover, the album captured the group still coming to terms with the recording process, but displaying a vision that was piercing in its clinical evocation of an unsettling disorder. With Morris's drums employed as a lead instrument, backed by the leaden but compulsive bass lines of Hook, the sound of Joy Division was distinctive and disturbing. By the time of their single 'Transmission' the quartet had already established a strong cult following, which increased after each gig. Much of the attention centred on the charismatic Curtis, who was renowned for his neurotic choreography, like a demented marionette on wires. By the autumn of 1979, however, Curtis's performances were drawing attention for a more serious reason. On more than one occasion he suffered an epileptic seizure and blackouts onstage, the illness seemed to worsen with the group's increasingly demanding live schedule. On 18 May 1980, the eve of Joy Division's proposed visit to America, Ian Curtis was found hanged. The verdict was suicide. A note was allegedly found bearing the words: 'At this moment I wish I were dead. I just can't cope anymore'.

The full impact of the tragedy was underlined shortly afterwards, for it quickly became evident that Curtis had taken his life at the peak of his creativity. While it seemed inevitable that the group's posthumously released work would receive a sympathetic reaction, few could have anticipated the quality of the material that emerged in 1980. The single, 'Love Will Tear Us Apart' was probably the finest of the year, a haunting account of a fragmented relationship, sung by Curtis in a voice that few realized he possessed. The attendant album, *Closer*, was faultless, displaying the group at their creative peak. With spine-tingling cameos such as 'Isolation' and the extraordinary 'Twenty-Four Hours' the album eloquently articulated a sense of despair, yet simultaneously offered a therapeutic release. Instrumentally, the work showed maturity in every area and is deservedly regarded by many critics as the most brilliant rock album of the 80s. The following year, a double album, *Still* collected the remainder of the group's material, most of it in primitive form. Within months of the Curtis tragedy, the remaining members sought a fresh start as New Order.

Albums: *Unknown Pleasures* (1979), *Closer* (1980), *Still* (1981), *The Peel Sessions* (1986).

Judas Priest

This group was formed in Birmingham, England, in 1970 by guitarist K.K. Downing and close friend, bassist Ian Hill. As another hopeful, struggling young rock band, they played their first gig in Essington in 1971 with a line-up completed by Alan Atkins (vocals) and John Ellis (drums). The name Judas Priest came from Atkins's previous band before he joined up with Hill and Downing, but it was retained as the best choice. Consistent gigging continued with Alan Moore taking over on drums only to be replaced at the end of 1971 by Chris Campbell. 1972 was spent mostly on the road in the UK, and in 1973 both Atkins and Campbell departed leaving the nucleus of Hill and Downing once more. At this point, their fortunes took a turn for the better. Vocalist Rob Halford and drummer John Hinch from the band Hiroshima joined the unit. More UK shows followed as the bands following grew steadily. In 1974 the they toured abroad for the first time in Germany and the Netherlands, and returned home to a record deal with the small UK label, Gull. The band recruited second guitarist Glenn Tipton and then in September 1974, *Rocka Rolla* was released. They were very disappointed with the recording, and the album failed to make any impact.

In 1975, the bands appearance at the Reading Festival went down well. Hinch left at this point to be replaced by the returning Alan Moore. *Sad Wings Of Destiny*, was an improvement on the debut, having been produced by the band. The album received good reviews, but their financial situation was desperate.

A worldwide contract with CBS saved the day, and *Sin After Sin* was a strong and positive album, with Simon Philips sitting in for the departed Moore. The band then visited America for the first time with drummer Les Binks, who appears on *Stained Class*, an album which showed Priest going from strength to strength. *Killing Machine* yielded the first UK hit single 'Take On The World', and featured shorter, punchier, but still extremely heavy songs. *Unleashed In The East* was recorded on the 1979 Japanese tour, and in that year, Les Binks was replaced on drums by Dave Holland of Trapeze. After major tours with both Kiss and AC/DC, Priest's popularity was beginning to gather momentum. *British Steel* smashed into the UK album charts at number 3, and contained the hit singles 'Breaking The Law' and 'Living After Midnight'. After appearing at the 1980 Castle Donington Monsters of Rock festival, they began recording *Point Of Entry*. It provided the hit single 'Hot Rockin', and was followed by sell-out UK and US tours. The period surrounding *Screaming For Vengeance* was phenomenally successful for the band. The hit single 'You've Got Another Thing Comin' was followed by a lucrative six month US tour with the album going platinum in the USA. *Screaming For Vengeance* was Priest's heaviest album, and *Defenders Of The Faith* did well to match it. *Turbo* was slightly more commercial and not particularly well received. *Ram It Down* was pure heavy metal by comparison, but by this time their popularity had begun to wane. Dave Holland was replaced by Scott Travis for *Painkiller* which was a *bone fide* return to form. Although not as universally popular as before, Priest were still a big live attraction and a top class metal band. Judas Priest are in many ways the epitome of heavy metal; screaming guitars and screaming vocalist, all clad in studs and leather. They laid the groundwork for much of the metal genre, and it is their enduring talent and popularity that has made them known worldwide as one of the ultimate metal bands.

Albums: *Rocka Rolla* (1974), *Sad Wings Of Destiny* (1976), *Sin After Sin* (1977), *Stained Class* (1978), *Killing Machine* (1978), *Unleashed In The East* (1979), *British Steel* (1980), *Point Of Entry* (1981), *Screaming For Vengeance* (1982), *Defenders Of The Faith* (1984), *Turbo* (1986), *Priest Live* (1987), *Ram It Down* (1988), *Painkiller* (1990).

Juicy Lucy

Juicy Lucy was formed in 1969 when three ex-members of the Misunderstood - Ray Owen (vocals), Glen 'Ross' Campbell (steel guitar) and Chris Mercer (tenor saxophone) - were augmented by Neil Hubbard (guitar), Keith Ellis (bass) and Pete Dobson (bass). The sextet enjoyed a surprise hit single with their fiery reading of Bo Diddley's 'Who Do You Love', a track featured on the group's first, and best-known, album. The cover became a sexist classmate of Jimi Hendrix's *Electric Ladyland*, and featured a naked busty woman languishing on a banquet table, amid a glut of various sliced and squashed fruits. Owen was later replaced by former Zoot Money singer Paul Williams, one of several changes afflicting the group. Their brand of blues-rock became more predictable as one by one the original cast dropped out. A fourth album, *Pieces*, was completed by a re-shaped unit of Williams, Mick Moody (guitar), Jean Roussel (keyboards) and ex-Blodwyn Pig members Andy Pyle (bass) and Ron Berg (drums), but this was to be the final line-up of Juicy Lucy, which broke up soon afterwards.

Albums: *Juicy Lucy* (1969), *Lie Back And Enjoy It* (1970), *Get A Whiff A This* (1971), *Pieces* (1972). Compilation: *Who Do You Love: The Best Of* (1990).

K

K-Tel Records

This Minneapolis-based company was the pioneer of television-advertised mail-order compilation albums in the early 70s. Among its best sellers were a *Hooked On* (*Country*, *Rock*, etc.) series and a sequence of nostalgic albums entitled *Back To The 40s*, *50s*, and *60s*. K-Tel soon set up foreign branches in Canada, Germany, Holland, Japan, Australia and New Zealand. It moved into the UK in May 1972, revolutionizing music marketing by licensing original versions of hit singles for a *20 Dynamic Hits* album which was heavily promoted on television at a cost of £250,000. Earlier current hits compilations had used soundalike cover versions of chart records. Soon K-Tel was followed by companies such as Arcade, Telstar and Ronco. By the mid-70s, however, K-Tel had extended into single artist compilations and concept albums (*Great Italian Love Songs*, *Country Comforts*). Within a couple of years, the major record companies were marketing numerous greatest hits albums although K-Tel's *Chart Hits* series continued to sell in hundreds of thousands. In 1983, EMI and Virgin launched their *Now That's What I Call Music* series, albums crammed full of recent hits and a direct copy of the original K-Tel concept. The high cost of television advertising and the highly competitive marketplace led to the failure of several companies including Ronco (1984) and Stylus (1990). In 1990, K-Tel also closed down its UK record company (but not the video distributor) and sold its Australian label. In the USA, K-Tel narrowly escaped bankruptcy in 1984 but returned with successful rap and breakdance compilations. In the late 80s, it set up new labels, signing jazz organist Jimmy McGriff, rapper MC Smooth and purchased the Marshall Tucker Band's catalogue.

Kandidate

This expansive UK disco and soul group came together in 1976 comprising members from two previous soul bands: Hot Wax (who went on to become Hi Tension) and 70% Proof. They were signed to Mickie Most's RAK label and he also produced their recordings. Their debut 'Don't Wanna Say Goodnight' was a minor hit in 1978 and this was followed by three more charting singles, including the number 11 hit, 'I Don't Wanna Lose You' (1979). The line-up of the band was Teeroy (vocals/keyboards), Ferdi (bass), Alex Bruce (percussion), St Lloyd Phillips (drums/vocals), Tamby (guitar/vocals), Phil Fearon (guitar) and Bob Collins (percussion/vocals). Of these, only Fearon (b. 30 July 1956, Jamaica) had any further chart success after Kandidate split. He built his own recording studio and had a string of hits in the mid-80s under his own name and the group name, Galaxy.

Kansas

This US group was formed in 1972 after David Hope (b. c.1951, Kansas, USA; bass) and Phil Ehart (b. 1951, Kansas, USA; drums/percussion) changed the name of their band, White Clover to Kansas, recruiting Kerry Livgren (b. 18 September 1949, Kansas, USA; guitar/vocals), Robert Steinhardt (b. c.1951, Michigan, USA; violin/strings/vocals), Steve Walsh (b. c.1951, St. Joseph, Missouri, USA; keyboards/vocals) and Richard Williams (b. c.1951, Kansas, USA; guitars). Although an American band, Kansas were heavily influenced from the outset, by British rock of the time, such as Yes and Genesis, and this was evident in the lyrics of their primary songwriter, Walsh. Kansas released their debut in 1974, and the following two albums attained gold record status, guaranteeing the band a high profile in the USA although no Kansas albums made the charts in the UK. By 1977, the band had grown somewhat tired of the progressive rock pigeon-hole into which the music press was forcing them, and decided to try a more commercial approach. Their popularity was confirmed on 27 June 1978 when they attended a ceremony at the Madison Square Gardens in New York at which the organization UNICEF named the band Deputy Ambassadors of Goodwill. In the early 80s, Walsh decided to leave the band since he was not happy with the increasingly commercial sound they were producing. He released the solo *Schemer Dreamer*, which featured other members of Kansas. He was replaced by John Elefante (b. c.1958, Levittown, New York, USA; keyboards/vocals) who wrote four of the songs on *Vinyl Confessions*. The band split in 1983, following two unsuccessful albums. Livgren and Hope had become born-again Christians, the former releasing *Seeds Of Change*, a commercially disastrous solo album based on his religious experiences. In October 1986, Walsh, Ehart and Williams re-formed Kansas with Steve Morse, lately of Dixie Dregs, (guitar) and Billy Greer (bass). This reunion was celebrated with the release of *Power*, an album

Kansas

that rejected the jazz–rock feel of earlier releases in favour of a heavier sound.

Albums: *Kansas* (1974), *Songs For America* (1975), *Masque* (1975), *Leftoverture* (1976), *Point Of Know Return* (1977), *Two For The Show* (1978), *Monolith* (1979), *Audio-Visions* (1980), *Vinyl Confessions* (1982), *Drastic Measures* (1983), *Power* (1986), *In The Spirit Of Things* (1988). Compilation: *The Best Of Kansas* (1984).

KC And The Sunshine Band

This racially-integrated band was formed in Florida, USA in 1973 by Harry Wayne (KC) Casey (b. 31 January 1951, Hialeah, Florida, USA; vocals, keyboards) and Richard Finch (b. 25 January 1954, Indianapolis, Indiana, USA; bass). Arguably the cornerstone of the Miami-based TK label, the duo wrote, arranged and produced their own group's successes, as well as those of singer George McCrae. The Sunshine Band enjoyed several hits, including 'Queen Of Clubs' (1974, UK Top 10), three consecutive US number 1s with 'Get Down Tonight', 'That's The Way (I Like It)' (both 1975) and '(Shake, Shake, Shake,) Shake Your Body' (1976), each of which displayed an enthusiastic grasp of dance-based funk. The style was exaggerated to almost parodic proportions on 'I'm Your Boogie Man' (1977, a US number 1) and 'Boogie Shoes' (1978), but a crafted ballad, 'Please Don't Go', in 1979, not only reversed this bubblegum trend, but was a transatlantic smash in the process (a UK number 1 in 1992 for K.W.S.). That same year KC duetted with Teri DeSario on the US number 2 hit, 'Yes, I'm Ready' on the Casablanca label. Although the group numbered as many as 12 on its live appearances, its core revolved around Jerome Smith (b. 18 June 1953, Hialeah, Florida, USA; guitar), Robert Johnson (b. 21 March 1953, Miami, Florida, USA; drums) and its two songwriters. The team moved to CBS/Epic after the collapse of the TK organization in 1980. Any benefit this accrued was hampered by a head-on car crash in January 1982 which left Casey paralysed for several months. Their fortune changed the following year when the group found themselves at the top of the UK charts with 'Give It Up'. It did not reach the US charts until the following year, and was by then credited to 'KC'. Casey and Finch subsequently seem to have lost the art of penning radio-friendly soul/pop.

Albums: *Do It Good* (1974), *KC And The Sunshine Band* (1975), as the Sunshine Band *The Sound Of Sunshine* (1975), *Part Three* (1976), *I Like To Do It* (1977), *Who Do Ya Love* (1978), *Do You Wanna Go Party* (1979), *Painter* (1981), *All In A Night's Work* (1983). Compilations: *Greatest Hits* (1980), *The Best Of* (1990). Solo albums: Wayne Casey/KC *Space Cadet* (1981), *KC Ten* (1984).

Kenny

Former employees at a banana warehouse in Enfield, Middlesex, England, Richard Driscoll (vocals), Yan Style (guitar), Christopher Lacklison (keyboards), Chris Redburn (bass) and Andy Walton (drums) were collectively known as Chufff (sic), a group of glam-rock latecomers who, after a 1974 showcase at London's exclusive Speakeasy, signed with manager Peter Walsh. In doing so, they acquired a new name - and a producer in Mickie Most who, with the highest calibre of session musicians, arrangers and songwriters at his disposal, guided them with mathematical precision to transient success. This was despite the confusion of an Irish singer called Kenny who was also signed to Most's Rak Records at this time. Chris Spedding and Clem Cattini were among those heard anonymously on the group Kenny's four UK smashes. All inconsequentially catchy and topped with a trademark falsetto in unison with Driscoll, these were 'The Bump' (a dance craze ditty that fought off competition from a b-side version by the Bay City Rollers) 'Fancy Pants', 'Baby I Love You OK' and autumn 1975's Top 20 swansong, Bill Martin and Phil Coulter's 'Julie Ann'. This chart run was rounded off neatly when the hits and some makeweight tracks were lumped together on a collection which bubbled under the album Top 50 in January 1976. They later provided the backing to the theme tune to Thames Television's popular *Minder* series, sung by Dennis Waterman. Album: *The Sound Of Super K* (1975).

Kilburn And The High Roads

An important link between 'pub rock' and punk, Kilburn And The High Roads were formed in November 1970 by art lecturer Ian Dury (b. 12 May 1942, Upminster, Essex, England; vocals) and Russell Hardy (b. 9 September 1941, Huntingdon, Cambridgeshire, England; piano). As a frontman, Dury cut an almost Dickensian figure with his growling, half-spoken vocals, squat figure, polio stricken leg and a withered hand, encased in a black leather glove. In fact, throughout the band's entire history their visual image was the antithesis of the prevalent glitter and glam-pop fashion. The initial line-up included Ted Speight (guitar), Terry Day (drums) and two former members of the Battered Ornaments, George Khan (saxophone) and Charlie Hart (bass). By 1973, despite a series of fluctuating line-ups, Dury and Russell had eventually settled down with a collection of musicians comprising: Keith Lucas (b. 6 May 1950, Gosport, Hampshire, England; guitar - a former art-school pupil of Dury's), Davey Payne (b. 11 August 1944, Willesden, London, England; saxophone), David Newton-Rohoman (b. 21 April, 1948, Guyana, South America; drums) and Humphrey Ocean (bass). The last would subsequently leave the Kilburns to concentrate on a successful career as an artist and be replaced by Charlie Sinclair in January 1974. The group's early repertoire consisted of rock 'n' roll favourites mixed with early 50s Tin Pan Alley pop, but this was later supplemented and supplanted by original material utilizing Dury's poetry, mostly depicting the loves and lives of every day east London folk. The Kilburns were, by this point, enshrined on London's 'pub rock' circuit. Managed by Charlie Gillett, they completed an album for the Raft label. This good fortune suffered a setback when the album's release was cancelled after the label went bankrupt. Warner Brothers, the parent company, chose to drop the group from its roster (but later released the sessions as *Wotabunch* in the wake of Dury's solo success). By late spring 1974, Gillett had left the scene, as had Hardy, who was replaced by Rod Melvin. Later that year they signed to the Dawn label, and released two superb singles, 'Rough Kids'/'Billy Bentley (Promenades Himself In London)' and 'Crippled With Nerves'/'Huffety Puff'. The subsequent album, *Handsome*, released the following year, was a huge disappointment, largely due to the bland production which captured little of the excitement and irreverence of a Kilburn's gig. The album marked the end of this particular era as the group then disintegrated. Keith Lucas embraced punk with the formation of 999, performing under the name of Nick Cash, while Dury, Melvin and Payne became founder members of a revitalized unit, Ian Dury And The Kilburns. Ted Speight was also involved in this transitional band, during which time the singer introduced 'What A Waste' and 'England's Glory', two songs better associated with Ian Dury And The Blockheads, the group with which he later found greater, long-deserved success.

Albums: *Handsome* (1975), *Wotabunch* (1978). Compilation: *The Best Of Kilburn And The High Roads* (1977).

King Crimson

Arguably progressive rock's definitive exponents,

King Crimson was formed in January 1969 out of the ashes of the eccentric Giles, Giles And Fripp. Robert Fripp (b. 1946, Wimbourne, Dorset, England; guitar) and Mike Giles (b. 1 March 1942; Bournemouth, Dorset, England; drums) were joined by Ian McDonald (b. 25 June 1946, London, England; keyboards), before former Gods member Greg Lake (b. 10 November 1948, Bournemouth, Dorset, England; vocals/bass), completed the first official line-up. A fifth addition to the circle, Pete Sinfield, supplied lyrics to the guitarist's compositions. The group's debut album, *In The Court Of The Crimson King*, drew ecstatic praise from critics and a glowing, well-publicized testimonial from the Who's Pete Townshend. An expansive use of mellotron suggested a kinship with the Moody Blues, but Fripp's complex chord progressions, and the collection's fierce introduction '21st Century Schizoid Man', revealed a rare imagination.

This brief courtship with critical popularity ended with *In The Wake Of Poseidon*. Damned as a repeat of its predecessor, the album masked internal strife which saw McDonald And Giles depart to work as a duo and Greg Lake leave to found Emerson, Lake And Palmer. Having resisted invitations to join Yes, Fripp completed the album with various available musicians including Gordon Haskell (vocals) and Mel Collins (saxophone), both of whom remained in the group for *Lizard*. Drummer Andy McCullough completed this particular line-up, but both he and Haskell left the group when the sessions terminated. Boz Burrell (bass/vocals - Fripp taught Burrell how to play the instrument) and Ian Wallace (drums) replaced them before the reshaped quartet embarked on a punishing touring schedule. One studio album, *Islands*, and a live selection, *Earthbound*, emanated from this particular version of King Crimson which collapsed in April 1972. Collins, Wallace and Burrell then pursued studio-based careers although the bassist later found fame with Bad Company. With Sinfield also ousted from the ranks, Fripp began fashioning a new, more radical line-up. John Wetton (b. 12 June 1950, Derby, England), formerly of Family, assumed the role of bassist/vocalist while Bill Bruford left the more lucrative ranks of Yes to become King Crimson's fourth drummer. Percussionist Jamie Muir and violinist David Cross (b. 23 April 1949, Plymouth, Devon, England) completed the innovative unit unveiled on *Larks Tongues In Aspic*, but were discarded over the next two years until only Fripp, Wetton and Bruford remained for the exemplary *Red*.

King Crimson

'King Crimson is completely over for ever and ever' Fripp declared in October 1974 as he embarked on an idiosyncratic solo career. However, in 1981 the guitarist took a surprisingly retrograde step, resurrecting the name for a unit comprising himself, Bruford, Tony Levin (bass) and Adrian Belew (guitar). The albums which followed, *Discipline*, *Beat* and *Three Of A Perfect Pair*, showed both adventure and purpose, belying the suspicion that the group would rest on previous laurels. It was, however, a temporary interlude and Fripp subsequently resumed his individual pursuits and established a new unit, the League Of Gentlemen. King Crimson, a group which married invention and ambition while avoiding the trappings prevailing in rock's experimental arena, may nonetheless prove his crowning achievement.
Albums: *In The Court Of The Crimson King* (1969), *In The Wake Of Poseidon* (1970), *Lizard* (1970), *Islands* (1971), *Earthbound* (1972), *Larks Tongues In Aspic* (1973), *Starless And Bible Black* (1974), *Red* (1974), *USA* (1975), *Discipline* (1981), *Beat* (1982), *Three Of A Perfect Pair* (1984). Compilations: *A Young Person's Guide To King Crimson* (1976), *The Compact King Crimson* (1986), *The Essential King Crimson - Frame By Frame* (1991).

Kirkpatrick, John

b. 8 August 1947, Chiswick, London, England. Kirkpatrick is often held to be the master player of the accordion, melodeon and the concertina. Having spent some time in the early Steeleye Span line-up, he went on to be involved with folk-rock recordings of the 70s. He has toured and recorded with a veritable who's who of the folk-rock establishment, in particular Ashley Hutchings, Richard Thompson and Martin Carthy. Kirkpatrick also performed with Brass Monkey. *A Really High Class Band* included 'The Cherry Tree Carol' and Sir John Betjeman's 'A Shropshire Lad'. Kirkpatrick regularly records and performs with Sue Harris (b. 17 May 1949, Coventry, Warwickshire, England), who is known for her hammer dulcimer and oboe playing. They first started working together in 1971. Harris was, for a time, a member of the English Country Blues Band, and has contributed incidental music for television, theatre and radio, including *The Canterbury Tales* on BBC Radio 4. Kirkpatrick, Harris and Carthy were in one of the early line-ups of the Albion Band. Kirkpatrick also played on *Night Owl* by Gerry Rafferty in 1979, and, in 1988, on Pere Ubu's *The Tenement Year*. By complete contrast, and highlighting Kirkpatrick's wide

diversity, he also formed the Shropshire Bedlams Morris Dance team. In recent years, Kirkpatrick has toured as a trio with the two fine melodeon players Riccardo Tesi from Italy and Marc Perrone from France. Harris and Kirkpatrick also performed and recorded with Umps And Dumps, which included Derek Pearce (percussion), Tufty Swift (melodeon) and Alan Harris (banjo). Other commitments, such as performing with the Richard Thompson Band and his involvement with the National Theatre production of *Lark Rise To Candleford* have reduced Kirkpatrick's solo touring. In 1991, he presented a six-week radio series for the BBC, *Squeezing Around The World*, which featured many of the world's leading squeezebox players. Harris and Kirkpatrick have now started working, as a trio with Dave Whetstone (melodeon/guitar).
Albums: *Jump At The Sun* (1972), with Sue Harris *The Rose Of Britain's Isle* (1974), with Ashley Hutchings *The Compleat Dancing Master* (1974), with Harris *Among The Many Attractions At The Show Will Be A Really High Class Band* (1976), *Plain Capers* (1976), with Harris *Shreds And Patches* (1977), *Going Spare* (1978), with Harris *Facing The Music* (1980), with Umps And Dumps *The Moon's In A Fit* (1980), *Three In A Row - The English Melodeon* (1984), *Blue Balloon* (1987), *Sheepskins* (1988), with Harris *Stolen Ground* (1989). Solo album: Sue Harris *Hammers And Tongues* (1978).

Kiss

Following the demise of Wicked Lester, Kiss was formed in 1972 by Paul Stanley (b. Stanley Eisen, 20 January 1950, New York, USA; rhythm guitar/vocals) and Gene Simmons, (b. Gene Klein, 25 August 1949, New York, USA; bass/vocals) who went on to recruit Peter Criss (b. Peter Crisscoula, 20 December 1945, New York, USA; drums/vocals) and Ace Frehley (b. Paul Frehley, 27 April 1950, New York, USA; lead guitar/vocals) At their second show at the Hotel Diplomat, Manhattan, 1973, Flipside producer, Bill Aucoin offered the band a management deal, and within two weeks they were signed to Neil Bogart's recently established Casablanca Records. In just over a year, Kiss had released their first three albums with a modicum of success. In the summer of 1975 their fortunes changed with the release of *Alive* which spawned their first US hit single 'Rock 'N' Roll All Nite'. The appeal of Kiss has always been based on their live shows: the garish greasepaint make-up, outrageous costumes, and over-the-top pyrotechnic stage effects, along with

Kiss

their hard-rocking anthems, combined to create what was billed as 'The Greatest Rock 'n' Roll Show On Earth'. The live success caused a dramatic upswing in record sales, and *Alive* became their first certified platinum album in the USA. *Destroyer* proved just as successful, and also gave them their first US Top 10 single, earning Peter Criss a major songwriting award for the uncharacteristic ballad 'Beth'. Subsequent releases *Rock And Roll Over*, *Love Gun* (their first album to attain platinum status in the USA), and *Alive II* confirmed Kiss as major recording artists.

By 1977 Kiss had topped the prestigious Gallup poll as the most popular act in the USA. They had become a marketer's dream. Kiss merchandise included: make-up kits, masks, board games, and pinball machines. *Marvel Comics* produced two super-hero cartoon books, and even a full length science-fiction film, *Kiss Meet The Phantom Of The Park* was produced. The ranks of their fan club, the Kiss Army, had swollen to a six figure number. In 1978, all four group members each produced a solo album which were released on the same day, a feat never before achieved and never since matched. This represented the biggest shipment of albums from one 'unit' to record stores in the history of music. The albums received a varying degree of success; Ace Frehley's record came out on top and included the US hit single 'New York Groove'.

Gene Simmons, whose album featured an impressive line-up of guests, including Cher, Donna Summer, Bob Seger and Janis Ian, had a hit single in the UK with 'Radioactive', which reached Number 41 in 1978. After the release of *Dynasty* in 1979, which featured the worldwide hit single 'I Was Made For Lovin' You', cracks appeared in the ranks. Peter Criss left to be replaced by session player Anton Fig, who had previously appeared on Ace Frehley's solo album. Fig played drums on the 1980 release *Unmasked* until a permanent replacement was found in the form of New York born, Eric Carr, who made his first appearance during the world tour of 1980. Carr's debut appearance came on *Music From The Elder*, an album that represented a radical departure from traditional Kiss music and included several ballads, an orchestra and a choir. It was a brave attempt to break new ground but failed to capture the imagination of the record-buying public. Frehley, increasingly disenchanted with the musical direction of the band finally left in 1983. The two albums prior to his departure had featured outside musicians. Bob Kulick, who had contributed to the studio side of *Alive II* and played on Stanley's solo album, supported the lead work to the four previously unreleased tracks on the *Killers* compilation of 1982 and Vincent Cusano (later to become Vinnie Vincent) was responsible for the lead guitar on the 1982 release, *Creatures Of The Night*. By 1983, the popularity of the band was waning and drastic measures were called for. The legendary make-up which had concealed their true identities for almost 10 years was removed on MTV in the USA. Vinnie Vincent made his first official appearance on *Lick It Up*, an album which saw Kiss with their first Top 10 hit in the UK. The resurgence of the band continued with *Animalize*. Vincent had been replaced by Mark St. John (b. Mark Norton) who was a seasoned session player and guitar tutor. His association with the band was short lived for he was tragically struck down by Reiters Syndrome. Bruce Kulick, the brother of long-time Kiss cohort Bob, was drafted in as a temporary replacement on the 1984 European Tour and subsequently became a permanent member when it became apparent that St. John would not be able to continue as a band member. Further commercial success was achieved with *Asylum* and *Crazy Nights*, the latter featuring their biggest UK hit single 'Crazy, Crazy Nights' which peaked at number 4 in 1987 and this was followed by a further two Top 40 hit singles 'Reason To Live' and 'Turn On The Night'. *Hot In The Shade* succeeded their third compilation album, *Smashes, Thrashes And Hits,* and included their highest charting hit single in the US, 'Forever', which reached number 4 in 1990. Work on a new Kiss album with producer Bob Ezrin was delayed following Eric Carr's illness due to complications from cancer. He died in 1991, in New York at the age of 41. Despite this setback, Kiss contributed a cover of Argent's classic 'God Gave Rock 'N' Roll To You' to the soundtrack of the film, *Bill And Ted's Bogus Journey*. With a history spanning three decades, Kiss have been one of the most influential groups in hard-rock history.

Albums: *Kiss* (1974), *Hotter Than Hell* (1974), *Dressed to Kill* (1975), *Alive* (1975), *Destroyer* (1976), *Rock And Roll Over* (1976), *Love Gun* (1977), *Alive II* (1977), *Dynasty* (1979), *Unmasked* (1980), *Music From The Elder* (1981), *Creatures Of The Night* (1982), *Lick It Up* (1983), *Animalize* (1984), *Asylum* (1985), *Crazy Nights* (1987), *Hot In The Shade* (1989), *Revenge* (1992). Compilations: *Double Platinum* (1978), *Killers* (1982), *Smashes, Thrashes And Hits* (1988), *Revenge* (1992).

Kool And The Gang

Originally formed as a quartet, the Jazziacs, by Robert 'Kool' Bell (b. 8 October 1950, Youngstown, Ohio, USA; bass), Robert 'Spike' Mickens (b. Jersey City, New Jersey, USA; trumpet), Ronald 'The Captain' Bell (b. 1 November 1951, Youngstown, Ohio, USA; saxophone) and Dennis 'D.T.' Thomas (b. 9 February 1951, Jersey City, New Jersey, USA; saxophone). Based in Jersey City, this aspiring jazz group opened for acts such as Pharaoh Sanders and Leone Thomas. They were later joined by Charles 'Claydes' Smith (b. 6 September 1948, Jersey City, New Jersey, USA; guitar) and 'Funky' George Brown (b. 5 January 1949, Jersey City, New Jersey, USA; drums), and as the Soul Town Band, moderated their early direction by blending soul and funk, a transition completed by 1969 when they settled on the name Kool And The Gang. The group crossed over into the US pop chart in 1973 and initiated a run of 19 stateside Top 40 hits on their own De-Lite label starting with 'Funky Stuff', a feat consolidated the following year with a couple of Top 10 hits 'Jungle Boogie' and 'Hollywood Swinging'. They continued to enjoy success although their popularity momentarily wavered in the latter half of the 70s as the prominence of disco strengthened. In 1979 the Gang added vocalists, James 'J.T.' Taylor (b. 16 August 1953, Laurens, South Carolina, USA) and Earl Toon Jnr., with Taylor emerging as the key member in a new era of success for the group, which coincided with their employment of an outside producer. Eumire Deodato refined the qualities already inherent in the group's eclectic style and together they embarked on a series of highly successful international hits including 'Ladies Night' (1979), 'Too Hot' (1980), and the bubbling 'Celebration', a 1980 platinum disc and US pop number 1 - later used by the media as the homecoming theme for the returning American hostages from Iran. Outside the USA they achieved parallel success and proved similarly popular in the UK where 'Get Down On It' (1981), 'Joanna' (1984) and 'Cherish' (1985) each reached the Top 5. The arrival of Taylor also saw the group's albums achieving Top 30 status in their homeland for the first time, with *Celebrate!* (1980) reaching the Top 10. Their longevity was due, in part, to a settled line-up. The original six members remained with the group into the 80s and although newcomer Toon left, Taylor blossomed into an ideal frontman. This core was later supplemented by several auxiliaries, including Amir Bayyan (keyboards), Clifford Adams (trombone) and Michael Ray (trumpet). This idyllic situation was finally undermined by Taylor's departure in 1988 and he was replaced by three singers, former Dazz Band member Skip Martin plus Odeen Mays and

Kool And The Gang

Gary Brown. Taylor released a solo album in 1989, *Sister Rosa*, while the same year the group continued recording with the album *Sweat*. The compilation set, *The Singles Collection* shows that Taylor left behind him one of the most engaging, and successful of soul/funk catalogues.

Albums: *Kool And The Gang* (1969), *Live At The Sex Machine* (1971), *Live At P.J.s* (1971), *Music Is The Message* (1972), *Good Times* (1973), *Wild And Peaceful* (1973), *Light Of Worlds* (1974), *Spirit Of The Boogie* (1975), *Love And Understanding* (1976), *Open Sesame* (1976), *The Force* (1977), *Everbody's Dancin'* (1978), *Ladies' Night* (1979), *Celebrate!* (1980), *Something Special* (1981), *As One* (1982), *In The Heart* (1983), *Emergency* (1984), *Victory* (1986), *Forever* (1986), *In The Heart* (1988), *Sweat* (1989). Compilations: *The Best Of Kool And The Gang* (1971), *Kool Jazz* (1974), *Kool And The Gang Greatest Hits!* (1975), *Kool Kuts* (1982), *Twice As Kool* (1983), *The Singles Collection* (1988).

Kraftwerk

The word 'unique' is over-used in rock music, but Kraftwerk have a stronger claim than most to the tag. Ralf Hutter (b. 1946, Krefeld, Germany; organ) and woodwind student Florian Schneider-Esleben (b. 1947, Düsseldorf, Germany; woodwind) met while they were studying improvised music in Düsseldorf, Germany. They drew on the influence of experimental electronic forces such as composer Karlheinz Stockhausen and Tangerine Dream to create minimalist music on synthesizers, drum machines and tape recorders. Having previously recorded an album with Organisation (*Tone Float*), Hutter and Schneider formed Kraftwerk with Klaus Dinger and Thomas Homann and issued *Highrail*, after which Dinger and Homann left to form Neu. Their first two

Kraftwerk

albums, released in Germany, were later released in the UK as an edited compilaton in 1972. Produced by Conny Plank (later to work with Ultravox and the Eurythmics), the bleak, spartan music provoked little response. After releasing a duo set, *Ralf And Florian*, Wolfgang Flur (electronic drums) and Klaus Roeder (guitar/violin/keyboards) join the group. *Autobahn* marked Kraftwerk's breakthrough and established them as purveyors of hi-tech, computerized music. The title track, running at more than 22 minutes, was an attempt to relate the monotony and tedium of a long road journey. An edited version reached the Top 10 in the US and UK charts. In 1975, Roeder was replaced by Karl Bartos. *Radioactivity* was a concept album based on the sounds to be found on the airwaves. *Trans-Europe Express* and *The Man-Machine* were strong influences on new-wave groups like the Human League, Tubeway Army (Gary Numan), Depeche Mode and Orchestral Manoeuvres In The Dark, while David Bowie claimed to be have long been an admirer. The *New Musical Express* said of *Man Machine*: 'It is the only completely successful visual/aural fusion rock has produced so far'. Kraftwerk spent three years building their own Kling Klang studios in the late 70s, complete with, inevitably, scores of computers. The single 'The Model', from *Computer World*, gave the band a surprise hit when it topped the UK charts in 1981 and it led to a trio of hits, including 'Showroom Dummies' and 'Tour De France', a song that was featured in the film *Breakdance* and became the theme for the cycling event of the same name in 1983. *Electric Cafe* was seen as a pioneering dance record and the group was cited as a major influence on a host of dance artists from Afrika Bambaataa to the respected producer Arthur Baker. In 1990, Flur departed to be replaced by Fritz Hijbert. They achieved further UK chart success with 'The Robots' which was accompanied by the eerie display of Kraftwerk look-alike robots. Kraftwerk's best known songs were collected together in 1991 on the double, *The Mix*, aimed chiefly at the dance market by EMI. 'I think our music has to do with emotions. Technology and emotion can join hands . . .' said Hutter in 1991.
Albums: *Highrail* (1971), *Var* (1972), *Autobahn* (1974), *Radioactivity* (1975), *Trans-Europe Express* (1977), *The Man-Machine* (1978), *Computer World* (1981), *Electric Cafe* (1986), *The Mix* (1991). Compilations: *Kraftwerk* (1973, a UK compilation of the first two releases).

Kristofferson, Kris

b. 22 June 1936, Brownsville, Texas USA. Kristofferson, a key figure in the 'New Nashville' of the 70s, began his singing career in Europe. While studying at Oxford University in 1958 he briefly performed for impresario Larry Parnes as Kris Carson while for five years he sang and played at US Army bases in Germany. As Captain Kristofferson, he left the army in 1965 to concentrate on songwriting. He worked as a cleaner at the CBS studios in Nashville, until Jerry Lee Lewis became the first to record one of his songs, 'Once More With Feeling'. Johnny Cash soon became a champion of Kristofferson's work and it was he who persuaded Roger Miller to record 'Me And Bobby McGee' (co-written with Fred Foster) in 1969. With its atmospheric opening, 'Busted flat in Baton Rouge, waiting for a train/feeling nearly faded as my jeans', the bluesy song was a country hit and became a rock standard in the melodramatic style by Janis Joplin and the Grateful Dead. Another classic among Kristofferson's early songs was 'Sunday Morning Coming Down', which Cash recorded. In 1970, Kristofferson appeared at the Isle of Wight pop festival while Sammi Smith was charting with the second of his major compositions, the passionate 'Help Me Make It Through The Night', which later crossed over to the pop and R&B audiences in Gladys Knight's version. Knight was also among the numerous artists who covered the tender 'For The Good Times', a huge country hit for Ray Price, while 'One Day At A Time' was a UK number 1 for Lena Martell in 1979. Kristofferson's own hits began with 'Loving Her Was Easier (Than Anything I'll Ever Do Again)' and 'Why Me', a ballad which was frequently performed in concert by Elvis Presley. In 1973, Kristofferson married singer Rita Coolidge and recorded three albums with her before their divorce six years later. Kristofferson had made his film debut in *Cisco Pike* (1971) and also appeared with Bob Dylan in *Pat Garrett And Billy The Kid*, but he achieved movie stardom when he acted opposite Barbra Streisand in a 1976 re-make of the 1937 picture *A Star Is Born*. For the next few years he concentrated on his film career but returned to country music with *The Winning Hand*, which featured duets with Brenda Lee, Dolly Parton and Willie Nelson. A further collaboration, *Highwaymen*, (with Nelson, Cash and Waylon Jennings) headed the country chart in 1985. The four musicians subsequently toured as the Highwaymen and issued a second collaborative album in 1991. A campaigner for radical causes, Kristofferson starred in the post-nuclear television drama *Amerika* (1987) and came up with hard-hitting political commentaries on *Third World Warrior*. Kristofferson compared and performed at the Bob Dylan Tribute Concert in 1992, during which he gave Sinead O'Conner a sympathetic shoulder to cry on after she was booed off stage.

Albums: *Kristofferson* (1970), *The Silver-Tongued Devil And I* (1971), *Me And Bobby McGee* (1971), *Border Lord* (1972), *Jesus Was A Capricorn* (1972), with Rita Coolidge *Full Moon* (1973), *Spooky Lady's Sideshow* (1974), with Coolidge *Breakaway* (1974), *Who's To Bless...And Who's To Blame* (1975), *Surreal Thing* (1976), five tracks on *A Star Is Born* (1976, film soundtrack), *Easter Island* (1977), with Coolidge *Natural Act* (1979), *The Winning Hand* (1983), with Willie Nelson *Music From Songwriter* (1984, film soundtrack), with Nelson, Johnny Cash, Waylon Jennings *Highwaymen* (1985), *Repossessed* (1986), *Third World Warrior* (1990), with Nelson, Cash, Jennings *Highwaymen II* (1991). Compilations: *Songs Of Kristofferson* (1977), *Country Store* (1988).

L

La Dusseldorf

This cult German group was founded by guitarist/vocalist Klaus Dinger, formerly of Neu. Comprising Thomas Dinger (percussion/vocals), Hans Lampe (percussion/synthesizer/keyboards), Nikolaus Van Rhein (keyboards), Harald Konietzo (bass) and Andreas Schell (piano), they completed *La Dusseldorf*, originally issued in 1976, but it was denied a UK release until 1978, when it was licensed to the WEA/Radar label. The group maintained the insistent pulsebeat of Neu, but offered a much fuller sound, shown to great effect on *Viva*. With Schell now musically superfluous, the set acknowledged the concurrent punk movement without deflecting from La Dusseldorf's individuality, but it failed to reap due commercial rewards. *Individuellos* maintained the Dingers brothers' capacity for surprise and inventiveness, but their unique version of German rock was increasingly obscured by the electro-dance styles of Kraftwerk and D.A.F. and the unit was subsequently dissolved.
Albums: *La Dusseldorf* (1976), *Viva* (1978), *Individuellos* (1981).

Lake, Greg

b. 10 November 1948, Poole, Dorset, England. Greg Lake is a vocalist and bass guitarist of great ability. He started to play the guitar at the age of 12, earning small amounts of money by entertaining customers at his local bingo hall. At 15, he left school to pursue a career as a draughtsman, but by the age of 17 had played as a full-time musician with both Shame and the Gods. In 1968, he was contacted by Robert Fripp and Michael Giles (b. 1942, Bournemouth, England), who had heard of his musical abilities and of the peculiar choir-like tone of his voice, and was invited to form King Crimson with them. With King Crimson, Lake played at the Rolling Stones' Hyde Park, free concert on 5 July 1969, and the high profile of this occasion guaranteed the band almost overnight fame. However, during the recording of *In The Wake Of Poseidon*, he left to join Emerson, Lake And Palmer. This trio quickly gained a reputation for being one of the most technically skilled bands of the 70s. Keith Emerson (b. 1 November 1944, Todmorden, England;

keyboards) and Carl Palmer (b. 20 March 1951, Birmingham, England; drums/percussion) made up the outfit which first played at the Isle of Wight festival in 1970. The band set up their own record label, Manticore, but despite considerable commercial success, they temporarily disbanded in 1974. Lake resurfaced around Christmas time 1975 when he released what was to become one of the most perennially-popular Christmas singles with 'I Believe In Father Christmas' (co-written with King Crimson/ELP lyricist Pete Sinfield) - the song carried on the ELP tradition of including a passage of popular classical music with Prokofiev's 'Sleigh Bell Ride'. This single, which reached number 2 in the UK, was so successful that it was re-released in both 1982 and 1983. 1977 saw Lake collaborating with Sinfield again to write blues-oriented songs such as 'Closer To Believing' on *Works, Volumes 1 And 2* by the reformed Emerson, Lake And Palmer. A huge tour followed this project, during the course of which the trio were accompanied by a full symphony orchestra. They disbanded for a second time in 1980, and Lake released the solo *Greg Lake* the following year. The album peaked at number 62 in both UK and US charts. The Greg Lake Band, which lasted from June 1981 to April 1982 included Gary Moore (guitar), Tommy Eyre (keyboards), Tristram Margetts (bass) and Ted McKenna (drums, former Rory Gallagher group and later MSG). Another solo album was released in 1983 for Chrysalis, but this time failed completely. In September 1983, Lake replaced John Wetton in Asia, but he left shortly afterwards. In 1984, he renewed his relationship with Emerson, and in 1985 *Emerson, Lake And Powell* was released, the latter name belonging to Cozy Powell who had played drums for the likes of Rainbow and Whitesnake. This combination lasted until 1987 when Powell departed. A new drummer, Richard Berry, was recruited for the release of the unsuccessful 1988 *To The Power Of Three*. By 1992, the original trio were back together, recording and performing again.
Albums: *Greg Lake* (1981), *Manoeuvres* (1983).

Lane, Ronnie

b. 1 April 1946, London, England. A founder member of the Small Faces and Faces, Lane left for a highly-stylized solo career in 1973. He formed a backing group, Slim Chance, which included (Benny) Gallagher And (Graham) Lyle, and scored a UK Top 20 hit with the effervescent 'How Come?', in 1974. In the same year 'The Poacher' was a UK Top 40 hit, but the group were unable to maintain their chart success. Ronnie's debut, *Anymore For Anymore*, was a finely-honed mixture of good-time original songs and folksy cover versions, the most impressive of which was Lane's reading of Derroll Adams' 'Roll On Babe'. Lane's progress, however, faltered on an ambitious tour, the Passing Show, with its attendant fire-eaters and jugglers. Financial burdens caused its abandonment and the original Slim Chance broke up in disarray. A new line-up was later convened around Brian Belshaw (bass - formerly of Blossom Toes), Steve Simpson (guitar/mandolin), Ruan O'Lochlainn (keyboards/saxophone), Charlie Hart (keyboards/accordion) and Colin Davey (drums). Two excellent albums, *Ronnie Lane's Slim Chance* and *One For The Road*, confirmed the promise of that first collection. The singer disbanded his group in 1977, although several ex-members, including Gallagher, Lyle and Hart, appeared on *Rough Mix*, Ronnie's excellent collaboration with Who guitarist Pete Townshend. This critically acclaimed release was preceded by *Mahoney's Last Stand*, a less satisfying venture with former Faces member Ron Wood. Although Lane completed another stylish collection, *See Me* in 1979, his progress was blighted by the debilitating disease, multiple sclerosis. Over the years Lane's condition has deteriorated considerably. Recent reports have indicated that he is now living in comparative poverty and efforts have been made to raise money for him through various rock benefits. The singer currently lives in Austin, Texas with his wife and children. Despite his illness, he still manages to tour in the USA and embarked on a tour in Japan during 1990.

Albums: *Anymore For Anymore* (1973), *Ronnie Lane's Slim Chance* (1974), *One For The Road* (1975), with Ron Wood *Mahoney's Last Stand* (1976), with Pete Townshend *Rough Mix* (1977), *See Me* (1979).

Leandros, Vicky

b. 1950, Greece. Leandros was raised in Hamburg, Germany, and groomed for showbusiness with a disciplined regime of vocal, classical guitar and ballet lessons. Managed by her songwriting father Leo, she recorded her first single (as 'Vicky') in 1965 and had become quite well known in northern Europe by 1967 when she was chosen to perform Luxembourg's entry in the Eurovision Song Contest. 'L'Amour Est Bleu' (Love Is Blue) finished 4th and was a massive hit in 19 countries, but the Leandros original fell behind instrumental versions by Jeff Beck and Paul Mauriat in the UK

and the USA. Vicky emerged as a huge attraction in such diverse territories as Canada and Japan - where she received 1968's *Prix Du Disque* - and any disappointment over 'L'Amour Est Bleu' was mitigated when her 'Apres Toi' was the winning Eurovision song for Luxembourg in 1972. Translated as 'Come What May', it almost topped the UK chart. In its afterglow, 'The Love In Your Eyes' and 1973's 'When Bouzoukis Played' were minor UK hits. The most far-reaching benefit of this episode, however, was the broadening of Vicky's concert itinerary and fame.

Selected albums: *Apres Toi* (1974), *My Favourite Songs In Greek* (1975), with Nana Mouskouri and Demis Roussos *Greek Songs* (1979), *Love Is Alive* (1981).

Lear, Amanda

b. Amanda Tapp, 1941. This tall, blonde jet-setter of Russian descent performed in burlesque as 'Peki d'Oslo' in her teens prior to a short marriage to Alain-Philippe Malignac, a French record producer. In the 70s, she was linked romantically to Bryan Ferry, Oliver Tobias, John Bentley - and, especially, surrealist Salvadore Dali for whom she modelled. She secured a recording contract after an introduction by Marianne Faithfull to David Bowie resulted in Bowie insisting that his Mainman management sign her. After singing lessons from his former teacher, Florence Wiese-Norberg, she was launched as a 'White Disco Queen' (in competition with Grace Jones), amid publicity that cast unfounded doubts about her gender and provocative photographs portraying her in cutaway black leotards and high leather boots. Another trademark was her husky vocals likened to 'gargling with rusty nails' on singles such as 'Follow Me', which earned her one of four gold discs awarded her for chart success in continental Europe. Propositions that she star in a film based on the anti-Soviet *Oktobriana* cartoon were not pursued, and despite occasional recording sessions she re-launched herself in the 80s as a painter.

Albums: *I Am A Photograph* (1978), *Sweet Revenge* (1978), *Never Trust A Pretty Face* (1979), *Diamonds For Breakfast* (1980), *Tam Tam* (1984), *Secret Passion* (1987).

LeBlanc And Carr

A duo consisting of Lenny LeBlanc (b. 17 June 1951, Leominster, Massachusetts, USA) and Pete Carr (b. 22 April 1950, Daytona Beach, Florida, USA), this act enjoyed one chart album and a handful of singles in the late 70s, including the US

Amanda Lear

Top 20 single 'Falling'. Carr had formerly been a member of Hourglass the pre-Allman Brothers Band, featuring Duane and Gregg Allman. He later became a session musician and met LeBlanc in Muscle Shoals, Alabama, USA while recording sessions. Both musicians released solo albums with no success, and in 1978 they teamed up for *Midnight Light*, on the Big Tree label. From that album, three singles were released, each making the charts. 'Falling' was the second one, ascending to number 18. When the album's title track failed to follow its predecessor up the charts, the duo split up, each returning to session work. LeBlanc later turned to Christian music.

Album: *Midnight Light* (1978).

Led Zeppelin

This pivotal quartet was formed in October 1968 by British guitarist Jimmy Page (b. 9 January 1944, Heston, Middlesex, England) on the demise of his former band, the Yardbirds. John Paul Jones (b. John Baldwin, 31 January 1946, London, England; bass/keyboards), a respected arranger and session musician, replaced original member Chris Dreja, but hopes to incorporate vocalist Terry Reid floundered on a contractual impasse. The singer unselfishly recommended Robert Plant (b. 26 August 1947, Birmingham, England), then frontman of struggling Midlands act Hobbstweedle, who in turn introduced drummer, John Bonham (b. 31 May 1947, Birmingham, England, d. 25 September 1980) when first choice B.J. Wilson opted to remain with Procol Harum. The quartet gelled immediately and having completed outstanding commitments under the name 'New Yardbirds', became Led Zeppelin following an off-the-cuff quip by the Who's Keith Moon, who remarked when rating their prospects that they would probably go down like a lead Zeppelin.

Armed with a prestigious contract with Atlantic Records, the group toured the USA supporting Vanilla Fudge prior to the release of their explosive debut *Led Zeppelin*, which included several exceptional original songs, including; 'Good Times, Bad Times', 'Communication Breakdown', 'Dazed And Confused' - a hold-over from the Yardbirds' era, and skilled interpretations of R&B standards 'How Many More Times?' and 'You Shook Me'. The set vied with Jeff Beck's *Truth* as the definitive statement of English heavy blues/rock, but Page's meticulous production showed a greater grasp of basic pop dynamics, resulting in a clarity redolent of 50s rock 'n' roll. His staggering dexterity was matched by Plant's expressive, beseeching voice, a combination that flourished on *Led Zeppelin II*. The group was already a headline act, drawing sell-out crowds across the USA, when this propulsive collection confirmed an almost peerless position. The introductory track, 'Whole Lotta Love', a thinly-veiled rewrite of Willie Dixon's 'You Need Love', has since become a classic, while 'Livin' Lovin' Maid' and 'Moby Dick', Bonham's exhibition piece, were a staple part of the quartet's early repertoire. Elsewhere, 'Thank You' and 'What Is And What Should Never Be' revealed a greater subtlety, a factor emphasized more fully on *Led Zeppelin III*. Preparation for this set had been undertaken at Bron-Y-Aur cottage in Snowdonia (immortalized in 'Bron-Y-Aur Stomp') and a resultant pastoral atmosphere permeated the acoustic-based selections, 'That's The Way' and 'Tangerine'. 'The Immigrant Song' and 'Gallow's Pole' reasserted the group's traditional fire and the album's release confirmed Led Zeppelin's position as one of the world's leading attractions. In concert, Plant's sexuality and Adonis-like persona provided the perfect foil to Page's more mercurial character, yet both individuals took full command of the stage, the guitarist's versatility matched only by the singer's unfettered roar.

Confirmation of the group's ever-burgeoning strengths appeared on *Led Zeppelin IV*, also known as 'Four Symbols', the 'Runes Album' or 'Zoso', in deference to the fact the set bore no official title. It included the anthemic 'Stairway To Heaven', a *tour de force*, viewed as the unit's finest performance and which became their in-concert finale in 1975. The latter song is arguably the definitive heavy-rock song, it continues to win polls and the memorable introduction remains every guitar novice's first hurdle. The approbation granted this ambitious piece initially obscured other contents, but the propulsive 'When The Levee Breaks' is now lauded as a masterpiece, particularly for Bonham's drumming, which later became the subject of widespread sampling. 'Black Dog' and 'Rock 'N' Roll' were Zeppelin at their immediate energetic best, while 'The Battle Of Evermore' was marked by a contribution by singer Sandy Denny. However, the effusive praise this album generated was notably more muted for *Houses Of The Holy*. Critics queried its musically diverse selection - the set embraced folksy ballads, reggae and soul - yet when the accustomed power was unleashed, notably on 'No Quarter', the effect was inspiring.

A concurrent US tour broke all previous attendance records, the proceeds from which

Led Zeppelin

helped finance an in-concert film, issued in 1976 as *The Song Remains The Same*, and the formation of the group's own record label, Swan Song, allowed Led Zeppelin total artistic freedom. Bad Company, the Pretty Things and Maggie Bell were also signed to the company. *Physical Graffiti*, a double set, gave full rein to the quartet's diverse interests with material ranging from compulsive hard-rock ('Custard Pie' and 'Sick Again') to pseudo-mystical experimentation ('Kashmir'). The irrepressible 'Trampled Underfoot' joined an ever-growing lexicon of peerless performances while 'In My Time Of Dying' showed an undiminished grasp of progressive blues. Sell-out appearances in the UK followed the release, but rehearsals for a projected world tour were abandoned in August 1975 when Plant sustained multiple injuries in a car crash. A new album was prepared during his period of convalescence, although problems over artwork delayed its release. Advance orders alone assured *Presence* platinum status, yet the set was regarded as a disappointment and UK sales were noticeably weaker. The 10-minute maelstrom, 'Achilles Last Stand', was indeed a remarkable performance, but the remaining tracks were competent rather than fiery and lacked the accustomed sense of grandeur. In 1977, Led Zeppelin began its rescheduled US tour, but on 26 July news reached Robert Plant that his six-year-old son, Karac, had died of a viral infection. The remaining dates were cancelled amid speculation that the group would break up.

They remained largely inactive for over a year, but late in 1978 flew to Abba's Polar recording complex in Stockholm. Although lacking the definition of earlier work, *In Through The Out Door* was a strong collection on which John Paul Jones emerged as the unifying factor. Two concerts at Britain's Knebworth Festival were the prelude to a short European tour on which the group unveiled a stripped-down act, inspired, in part, by the punk explosion. Rehearsals were then undertaken for another US tour, but in September 1980, Bonham was found dead following a lengthy drinking bout. On 4 December, Swansong announced that the group had officially retired, although a collection of archive material, *Coda*, was subsequently issued. Jones later became a successful producer, notably with the Mission, while Plant embarked on a highly-successful solo career, launched with *Pictures At Eleven*. Page scored the film *Death Wish 2* and, after a brief reunion with Plant and the Honeydrippers project in 1984, he inaugurated the short-lived Firm with Paul Rogers. He then formed the Jimmy Page Band with John Bonham's

son, Jason, who in turn drummed with Led Zeppelin on their appearance at Atlantic's 25th Anniversary Concert in 1988. Despite renewed interest in the group's career, particularly in the wake of the retrospective *Remasters*, entreaties to make this a permanent reunion have been resisted. Although their commercial success is unquestionable, Led Zeppelin is now rightly recognized as one of the most influential bands of the rock era and their catalogue continues to provide inspiration to successive generations of musicians.

Albums: *Led Zeppelin* (1969), *Led Zeppelin II* (1969), *Led Zeppelin III* (1970), *Led Zeppelin IV* (1971), *Houses Of The Holy* (1973), *Physical Graffiti* (1975), *Presence* (1976), *The Song Remains The Same* (1976, film soundtrack), *In Through The Out Door* (1979), *Coda* (1982). Compilation: *Remasters* (1990).

Further reading: *Hammer Of The Gods*, Stephen Davis. *Led Zeppelin: A Celebration*, Dave Lewis.

Lee, Alvin

b. 19 December 1944, Nottingham, England. Guitarist Lee began his professional career in the Jaybirds, a beat-trio popular both locally and in Hamburg, Germany. In 1966, an expanded line-up took a new name, Ten Years After, and in turn became one of Britain's leading blues/rock attractions with Lee's virtuoso solos its main attraction. His outside aspirations surfaced in 1973 with *On The Road To Freedom*, a collaboration with American Mylon Lefevre, which included support from George Harrison, Steve Winwood and Mick Fleetwood. When Ten Years After disbanded the following year, the guitarist formed Alvin Lee & Co. with Neil Hubbard (guitar), Tim Hinkley (keyboards), Mel Collins (saxophone), Alan Spenner (bass) and Ian Wallace (drums). Having recorded the live *In Flight*, Lee made the first of several changes in personnel, but although he and Hinkley were joined by Andy Pyle (bass, ex-Blodwyn Pig) and Bryson Graham (drums) for *Pump Iron!*, the group struggled to find its niche with the advent of punk. Lee toured Europe fronting Ten Years Later (1978-80) and the Alvin Lee Band (1980-81), before founding a new quartet, known simply as Alvin Lee, with Mick Taylor (guitar, ex-John Mayall/Rolling Stones), Fuzzy Samuels (bass, ex-Crosby, Stills, Nash And Young) and Tom Compton (drums). This promising combination promoted *RX-5*, but later split. In 1989, Lee reconvened the original line-up of Ten Years After to record *About Time*. Lee

Alvin Lee

released *Zoom* in 1992 with Sequel Records, after finding the majaor companies were not interested. Although the record offered nothing new, it was a fresh and well-produced record, and featured George Harrison on backing vocals.

Albums: with Mylon Lefevre *On The Road To Freedom* (1973), *In Flight* (1974), *Pump Iron!* (1975), *Rocket Fuel* (1978), *Ride On* (1979), *Free Fall* (1980), *RX-5* (1981), *Detroit Diesel* (1986), *Zoom* (1992).

Leonard, Deke

b. Roger Leonard, Wales. A veteran of a small, but thriving, Welsh beat group scene, Leonard was a member of Lucifer And The Corncrakers, the Jets, the Blackjacks, the Jets (again), the Smokeless Zone and the Dream prior to replacing Vic Oakley in the Bystanders in 1968. Concurrently, this close-harmony group had decided to pursue a more progressive direction and became Man on the newcomer's arrival. Influenced by Mickey Green of the Pirates and Bo Diddley, Leonard's guitar work and compositional skill was crucial in their evolution from concept album acolytes to free-flowing improvisers. He left the group in 1972, following the release of *Live At The Padgett Rooms, Penarth* and immediately recorded an impressive solo album, *Iceberg*. This inspired the formation of a permanent group which coincidentally supported Man on tour, but a disappointing second album, *Kamikaze*, doomed the project. Leonard subsequently rejoined his former colleagues, where he remained until their break-up in 1976. The guitarist completed a third album in 1981 and has continued to pursue a career in less fashionable enclaves, both as a solo attraction, and as a member of the reformed Man. In the early 90s, Deke additionally turned his hand to journalism, writing album reviews for *Vox*.

Albums: *Iceberg* (1973), *Kamikaze* (1974), *Before Your Very Eyes* (1981).

Levi Smiths Clefs

Formed Adelaide, Australia in 1966. The Levi Smiths Clefs were Barrie McAskill. McAskill formed the band and has presided over its history and destiny during its subsequent phases. McAskill, possessing one of the country's most distinct and raspy voices, led the troupe through two decades of change, with many talented members, his main love being soul and R&B-based material. The band held residencies at popular discos and clubs in both Melbourne and Sydney, and provided the music at a consistently high level. Perhaps the band's failing

was that they did not record more often, nor did they write much original material. Their one album did contain several originals, but the strongest song was a Beatles cover. The list of musicians that passed through the ranks is considerable. Of these, one of the most notable was the 1968 line-up which became Fraternity with the addition of Bon Scott in his pre-AC/DC days, and which recorded two albums. The 1969 band became Tully and the 1971 big band provided members for SCRA - an 11-piece Chicago/Blood Sweat And Tears-styled band that released two albums. The 1972 line-up became Mighty Mouse briefly before assuming the name Chain. McAskill still performs in Sydney, bringing the band together as required by various promoters.

Album: *Empty Monkey* (1970).

Lewie, Jona

b. c.1943, England. A former member of Brett Marvin And The Thunderbolts and Terry Dactyl And The Dinosaurs, Lewie was one of several unconventional artists signed to the Stiff label. *On The Other Hand There's A Fist* maintained the quirky approach of earlier acts, but despite an appearance on the highly-publicized *Be Stiff* tour, the artist remained largely unknown until 1980 when 'You'll Always Find Me In The Kitchen At Parties' broached the UK Top 20. A follow-up release, 'Stop The Cavalry', reached number 3 later that year when its nostalgic brass arrangement proved popular in the Christmas market. However, a subsequent album, *Heart Skips Beat*, failed to consolidate this success. 'Stop The Cavalry' continues to be an annual favourite during the Christmas season, thanks to its inclusion on compilation albums.

Albums: *On The Other Hand There's A Fist* (1978), *Heart Skips Beat* (1982). Compilations: *Gatecrasher* (1979).

Lewis, Linda

b. London, England. Linda's first steps in the entertainment business were made as a pre-teen actress. She had bit-parts in fashionable 60s films, *Help* and *A Taste Of Honey*. She quit acting and school to play in bands, and soon formed her own, White Rabbit. In 1967, she first achieved recognition in Europe with Ferris Wheel, before becoming a leading session singer in the early 70s. She had an exceptionally good range (5 octaves), and she had already recorded for David Bowie, Al Kooper and Cat Stevens when she had her first UK Top 20 hit. 'Rock-A-Doodle-Doo' was a self-

Linda Lewis

penned pop song, with the gimmick of a deep Helen Shapiro-style verse and a leap to a petulant little girl voice in the chorus. *Lark* offered a good example of her brand of soft soul. Any momentum gained was stalled when the Raft label went out of business. Her highest UK chart position came in 1975 with a cover of the Betty Everett hit, 'It's In His Kiss (Shoop Shoop Song)' reaching number 6. The accompanying album, *Not A Little Girl Anymore*, reached the Top 40. The remainder of the 70s saw her achieve two minor hits with 'Baby I'm Yours' (1976) and 'I'd Be Surprisingly Good For You' (1979), but she continued her session work, and put in appearances for Steve Harley, Chris Spedding, Mike Batt, Rod Stewart and Rick Wakeman in the late 70s. She had been married to Jim Cregan (ex-Family), for some time, but sadly her career floundered with personal problems.
Albums: *Hacienda View* (1970), *Say No More* (1971), *Lark* (1972), *Fathoms Deep* (1973), *Heart Strings* (1974), *Not A Little Girl Anymore* (1975), *Woman Overboard* (1977), *A Tear And A Smile* (1983).

Lieutenant Pigeon

Hailing from Coventry, England, this novelty group evolved from the minor league outfit, Stavely Makepiece. Lieutenant Pigeon's line-up comprised Robert Woodward (piano), Stephen Johnson (bass) and Nigel Fletcher (drums). Their single 'Mouldy Old Dough', an instrumental occasionally punctuated by the deadpan refrain of the title, was issued in January 1972. Almost forgotten, it was revived the following autumn and topped the UK charts for four weeks. The single had actually been recorded in Woodward's front room and featured his mother Hilda on piano. Although strong candidates for the one-hit-wonder tag, the group managed one more UK Top 20 hit, 'Desperate Dan', before returning to obscurity.

Lightfoot, Gordon

b. 17 November 1938, Orillia, Ontario, Canada. Lightfoot moved to Los Angeles during the 50s where he studied at Hollywood's Westlake College of Music. Having pursued a short-lived career composing jingles for television, the singer began recording demos of his own compositions which, by 1960, owed a considerable debt to folksingers Pete Seeger and Bob Gibson. Lightfoot then returned to Canada and began performing in Toronto's Yorktown coffee houses. His work was championed by several acts, notably Ian And Sylvia and Peter, Paul And Mary. Both recorded the enduring 'Early Morning Rain', which has since become a standard, while the latter group also enjoyed a hit with his 'For Lovin' Me'. Other successful compositions included 'Ribbon Of Darkness', which Marty Robbins took to the top of the US country chart, while such renowned artists as Bob Dylan, Johnny Cash, Elvis Presley and Jerry Lee Lewis have all covered Lightfoot's songs. Having joined the Albert Grossman management stable, the singer made his debut in 1966 with the promising *Lightfoot. The Way I Feel* and *Did She Mention My Name* consolidated the artist's undoubted promise, but it was not until 1970 that he made a significant commercial breakthrough with *Sit Down Young Stranger*. Producer Lenny Waronker added an edge to Lightfoot's approach which reaped an immediate benefit with a US Top 5 hit, 'If You Could Read My Mind'. The album also included the first recording of Kris Kristofferson's 'Me And Bobbie McGee'. A series of crafted albums enhanced his new-found position and in 1974 the singer secured a US number 1 with the excellent 'Sundown'. Two years later 'The Wreck Of The Edmund Fitzgerald' peaked at number 2, but although Lightfoot continued to record mature singer-songwriter-styled material, his increasing reliance on safer, easy-listening perspectives proved unattractive to a changing rock audience. Gordon Lightfoot nonetheless retains the respect of his contemporaries, although his profile lessened quite considerably during the 80s.
Albums: *Lightfoot* (1966), *The Way I Feel* (1967), *Did She Mention My Name* (1968), *Back Here On Earth* (1969), *Sunday Concert* (1969), *Sit Down Young Stranger* aka *If You Could Read My Mind* (1970), *Summer Side Of Life* (1971), *Don Quixote* (1972), *Old Dan's Records* (1972), *Sundown* (1974), *Cold On The Shoulder* (1975), *Summertime Dream* (1976), *Endless Wire* (1978), *Dream Street Rose* (1980), *Shadows* (1982), *Salute* (1983), *East Of Midnight* (1986). Compilations: *The Very Best Of Gordon Lightfoot* (1974), *Gord's Gold* (1975), *The Best Of Gordon Lightfoot* (1981).

Lighthouse

Lighthouse was formed in the USA by Skip Prokop, one-time drummer in the Paupers, a respected Canadian rock band. His subsequent association with the Al Kooper/Mike Bloomfield *Super Session* project secured Prokop's reputation and inspired the inception of this new group. Lighthouse also featured guitarist Ralph Cole, a veteran of several Michigan-based units, and an

Lindisfarne

ambitious string and horn section. Initially compared favourably with Chicago, a series of personnel changes undermined what potential Lighthouse offered and consequently later albums lacked direction. Al Wilmot, the one-time bassist with SRC, joined the act towards the close of its career, but the group had folded by the end of 70s. Albums: *Lighthouse* (1969), *Peacing It All Together* (1970), *Suite Feeling* (1970), *One Fine Morning* (1971), *Thoughts Of Moving On* (1972), *Live* (1972), *Sunny Days* (1972), *Can Feel It* (1974), *Good Day* (1974). Solo album: Skip Prokop *All Growed Up* (1977).

Limmie And The Family Cooking

Led by Limmie Snell (b. Dalton, Alabama, USA), this vocal trio was hugely popular on the UK disco scene in the mid-70s. Limmie's first musical influence was gospel but at the age of 11 he made a series of novelty records as Lemmie B. Good. He next formed a singing group with his sisters Jimmy and Martha. After an initial recording for Phil Spector's Scepter label, they were signed to Avco, where Steve Metz and Sandy Linzer produced the catchy 'You Can Do Magic', a UK Top 10 hit in 1973. This was followed by the less successful 'Dreamboat', but the next year the trio had another

UK best seller with a revival of the Essex's 1963 hit 'A Walking Miracle'. More pop than soul, Limmie And the Family Cooking next recorded a version of the 50s hit 'Lollipop'. Despite its failure, the group remained a favourite with British disco audiences and appeared on soul revival bills in the UK over the next decade.

Lindisfarne

This Newcastle, UK-based quintet - Alan Hull (b. 20 February 1945, Newcastle-Upon-Tyne, Tyne And Wear, England; vocals/guitar/piano), Simon Cowe (b. 1 April 1948, Jesmond Dene, Tyne And Wear, England; guitar), Ray Jackson (b. 12 December 1948, Wallsend, Tyne And Wear, England; harmonica/mandolin), Rod Clements (b. 17 November 1947, North Shields, Tyne And Wear, England; bass/violin) and Ray Laidlaw (b. 28 May 1948, North Shields, Tyne And Wear, England; drums) - was originally known as the Downtown Faction, but took the name Lindisfarne in 1968. Their debut *Nicely Out Of Tune*, was issued the following year and this brash mixture of folk-rock and optimistic harmonies is arguably the group's most satisfying set. The album contained the wistful and lyrically complex 'Lady Eleanor'. Their popularity flourished with the release of *Fog*

On The Tyne the humorous title track celebrating life in Newcastle and containing such verses as; 'Sitting in a sleazy snack-bar sucking sickly sausage rolls'. The number 1 album's attendant single, 'Meet Me On The Corner' reached the UK Top 5 in 1972 where it was followed by a re-released 'Lady Eleanor'. *Fog On The Tyne* was produced by Bob Johnston, and although they pursued this relationship on a third selection, *Dingly Dell*, the group was unhappy with his work and remixed the set prior to release. The final results were still disappointing, creatively and commercially, and tensions within the line-up were exposed during an ill-fated tour of the USA. In 1973, Laidlaw, Cowe and Clements left for a new venture, Jack The Lad. Kenny Craddock (keyboards), Charlie Harcourt (guitar), Tommy Duffy (bass) and Paul Nichols (drums) were brought in as replacements but this reconstituted line-up lacked the charm of its predecessor and was overshadowed by Alan Hull's concurrent solo career. A 1974 release, *Happy Daze*, offered some promise, but Lindisfarne was disbanded the following year. The break, however, was temporary and the original quintet later resumed working together. They secured a recording deal with Mercury Records and in 1978 enjoyed a UK Top 10 single with 'Run For Home'. Despite further releases, Lindisfarne was unable to repeat this success and subsequently reached an artistic nadir with *C'mon Everybody*, a medley of rock 'n' roll party favourites with six of the group's own best-known songs saved for the finale. In November 1990, Lindisfarne were back in the UK charts, joined together with the England international footballer, and fellow Geordie, Paul Gascoigne. Their re-worked, and inferior, version of 'Fog On The Tyne' reached number 2. Although they are now restricted to only the occasional chart success, the group's following remains strong, particularly in the north-east of England, and is manifested in their annual Christmas concerts.

Albums: *Nicely Out Of Tune* (1970), *Fog On The Tyne* (1971), *Dingly Dell* (1972), *Lindisfarne Live* (1973), *Roll On Ruby* (1973), *Happy Daze* (1974), *Back And Fourth* (1978), *Magic In The Air* (1978), *The News* (1979), *Sleepless Nights* (1982), *Lindisfarne Tastic Live* (1984), *Lindisfarne Tastic Volume 2* (1984), *Dance Your Life Away* (1984), *C'mon Everybody* (1987), *Amigos* (1989). Compilations: *Take Off Your Head* (1974), *Finest Hour* (1975), *Singles Album* (1981).

Little Feat

The compact rock 'n' roll funk displayed by Little Feat put them out of step with atypical, early 70s, Californian rock bands. By combining elements of country, folk, blues, soul and boogie they unwittingly created a sound that became their own, and has to date never been replicated or bettered. The band comprised Lowell George (b. 13 April 1945, Hollywood, California, USA, d. 29 June 1979) who had already found experience with the earthy garage band the Standells and with the Mothers Of Invention, plus, Roy Estrada (b. Santa Ana, California, USA; bass), Bill Payne (b. 12 March 1949, Waco, Texas, USA; keyboards) and Richie Haywood (drums). Although they signed to the mighty Warner Brothers label in 1970, no promotional push was given to the band until their second album in 1972. The public later latched on to the debut, *Little Feat*. It remains a mystery why the band were given such a low profile. George had already been noticed as potentially a major songwriter; two of his songs were taken by the Byrds, 'Truck Stop Girl' and 'Willin''.

The debut sold poorly, and quite inexplicably, so did their second and third albums. The band were understandably depressed and began to fragment. Lowell began writing songs with John Sebastian amid rumours of a planned supergroup adding Phil Everly. Fortunately, their record company made a further advance to finance *Feats Don't Fail Me Now*; the revised band was now Paul Barrere (b. 3 July 1948, Burbank, California, USA; guitar), Kenny Gradney (b. New Orleans, Louisiana, USA; bass) and Sam Clayton (b. New Orleans, Louisiana, USA; percussion). Deservedly, they made the album charts in the USA, although the excellent material was no better than their three previous albums. *Feats Don't Fail Me Now* marked the growth of other members as credible songwriters and George's role began to diminish. The European critics were unanimous in praising the band in 1975 on the 'Warner Brothers Music Show'. This impressive package tour contained Graham Central Station, Bonaroo, Tower Of Power, Montrose, Little Feat and the headliners, the Doobie Brothers, who were then enjoying unprecedented acclaim and success. Without exaggeration, Little Feat blew everyone off the stage with a series of outstanding concerts, and from that moment on they could do no wrong. *The Last Record Album* in 1975 contained Lowell's finest (albeit short), winsome love song, 'Long Distance Love'; the sparseness of the guitar playing and the superb change of tempo with drum and

Little Feat

bass, created a song that courted melancholy and tenderness. The opening question and answer line 'Ah Hello, give me missing persons, tell me what is it that you need, I said oh, I need her so, you've got to stop your teasing', is full of emotional pleading.

George meanwhile was over indulging with drugs and his contribution to *Time Loves A Hero* was minimal. Once again they delivered a great album, featuring the by now familiar and distinctive cover artwork by Neon Park. Following the double live *Waiting For Columbus*, the band disintegrated and George started work on his solo album, *Thanks, I'll Eat It Here*, (which sounded like a Little Feat album); two notable tracks were 'Missing You', and '20 Million Things To Do'. During a solo concert tour George had a heart attack and died; years of abuse had taken their toll. The remaining band reformed for a benefit concert for his widow and at the end of a turbulent year the barrel was scraped to release *Down On The Farm*. The record became a considerable success, as did the compilation *Hoy-Hoy*.

In 1988, almost a decade after they broke up, the band re-formed and *Let It Roll* became their biggest album by far. The band had ex-Pure Prairie League Craig Fuller taking Lowell's place, and the musical direction was guided by the faultless keyboard of Bill Payne. A second set from the re-formed band came in 1990, and although it disappointed many, it added fuel to the theory that this time they intended to stay together. *Shake Me Up* finally buried the ghost of George, as the critics accepted that the band are a credible force once again.

Albums: *Little Feat (1971), Sailin' Shoes* (1972), *Dixie Chicken* (1973), *Feats Don't Fail Me Now* (1974), *The Last Record Album* (1975), *Time Loves A Hero* (1977), *Waiting For Columbus* (1978), *Down On The Farm* (1979), *Let It Roll* (1988), *Representing The Mambo* (1990), *Shake Me Up* (1991). Compilation: *Hoy Hoy* (1981), *As Time Goes By - The Best Of Little Feat* (1986). Solo album: Lowell George *Thanks I'll Eat It Here* (1979).

Little River Band

Prior to the success of AC/DC, Air Supply, Men At Work and INXS, the Little River Band were probably Australia's most successful international rock band. Evolving out of the group Mississippi, who had previously spent much time working in London, former members Graham Goble (b. 15 May 1947, Adelaide, South Australia, Australia; guitar), Beeb Birtles (b. Gerard Birtlekamp, 28 November 1948, Amsterdam, Netherlands; guitar) and Derek Pellicci (drums) met up with Glen Shorrock (b. 30 June 1944, Rochester, Kent, England; vocals) in Melbourne in 1975. With a name change to the Little River Band and the addition of Rick Formosa (guitar) and Roger McLachlan (bass) the band boasted years of experience and chose the US west coast harmony and guitar sound as their major influence. They had immediate success in Australia with their first single and album. Under the guidance of Glen Wheatley (ex-Masters Apprentices), the band was soon aiming for the overseas market, the USA in particular, and by the end of 1976 they had enjoyed their first appearance in the US charts. With Formosa and McLachlan being replaced respectively by David Briggs (b. 26 January 1951, Melbourne, Victoria, Australia) and George McArdle (b. 30 November 1954, Melbourne,

Little River Band

Victoria, Australia), the second album *Diamantina Cocktail* went gold in the USA in 1977, the first time an Australian act had managed this. The band followed this with another hugely successful album in 1978, *Sleeper Catcher*, and they found themselves also selling well in Latin-America and Europe, especially France. The band's popularity waned a little in Australia but continued unabated in the USA. In 1983, lead vocalist Glen Shorrock left to pursue a solo career and was replaced by John Farnham, one of Australia's most popular singers. By 1986 Farnham had left to pursue his solo career and the band continued with a low profile, playing live occasionally at up-market venues but still releasing records. In 1988, with the return of Shorrock, the group signed to MCA Records, releasing *Get Lucky* two years later.

Albums: *Little River Band* (1975), *After Hours* (1976), *Diamantina Cocktail* (1977), *Sleeper Catcher* (1978), *First Under The Wire* (1979), *Backstage Pass* (1980), *Time Exposure* (1981), *The Net* (1983), *Playing To Win* (1984), *No Reins* (1986), *Monsoon* (1988), *Too Late To Load* (1989), *Get Lucky* (1990). Compilation: *Greatest Hits* (1982).

Liverpool Express

Liverpool Express centred on singer/guitarist Billy Kinsley (b. 28 November 1946, Liverpool, England), veteran of 60s groups the Merseybeats, the Merseys and the Swinging Blue Jeans. He later formed Rockin' Horse with songwriter Jimmy Campbell, before embarking on a solo career in 1973 with 'Annabella'. Liverpool Express evolved out of the club group Kinsley had been working with and this new venture made its debut in 1975 with 'Smile (My Smiler's Smile)'. The quartet scored four chart hits between 1976-77, two of which, 'You Are My Love' and 'Every Man Must Have A Dream', reached the UK Top 20. The resulting touring schedule brought success in South America and on the European continent. A brief hiatus was followed by a modest UK chart position for 'So What?' in 1983. Liverpool Express have continued to perform and record into the 90s.

Albums: *Tracks* (1977), *Dreamin'* (1977, issued only in South America), *ELX* (1978, issued only in Europe).

Lobo

b. Roland Kent Lavoie, 31 July 1943, Tallahassee, Florida, USA. Lobo was the pseudonym of Roland Lavoie a singer-songwriter who was successful in the early 70s. He was raised in the town of Winter Haven, Florida, where he began his musical career as a member of the Rumors. He apprenticed in several other groups during the 60s as well, notably, the Legends from Tampa, Florida, which included Gram Parsons and Jim Stafford; who would also enjoy success in the early 70s with two US Top 10 hits, produced by Lavoie. (Other members of the Legends included Gerald Chambers and Jon Corneal, the latter remaining an

Nils Lofgren

associate of Parsons for many years.) Lavoie also performed with bands called the Sugar Beats and Me And The Other Guys, neither of which had any success outside of their region. In 1971, former Sugar Beats member Phil Gernhard signed Lavoie, calling himself Lobo (Spanish for wolf) to Big Tree Records, where he was an executive, and released their first single, 'Me And You And A Dog Named Boo'. It reached number 5 in the US and launched a successful series of singles. The song became his only hit in the UK, where it reached number 4. Back to back Top 10 hits in 1972, 'I'd Love You To Want Me' and 'Don't Expect Me To Be Your Friend', were the last major hits for Lobo. However, he continued to chart with Big Tree until 1975 (six albums also charted, but only the second, *Of A Simple Man,* in 1972, made the Top 40). In 1979, Lobo resurfaced on MCA Records, 'Where Were You When I Was Falling In Love', reached number 23. After the end of that decade his recording career ended.
Albums: *Introducing Lobo* (1971), *Of A Simple Man* (1972), *Calumet* (1973), *Just A Singer* (1974), *A Cowboy Afraid Of Horses* (1975), *Lobo* (1979). Compilation: *The Best Of Lobo* (1975).

Lofgren, Nils

b. 21 June 1951, Chicago, Illinois, USA. In the late 60s, Lofgren first recorded as Paul Dowell And The Dolphin before forming Grin. The latter made

several excellent albums during the early 70s and although a critics' favourite they never quite managed to receive the recognition they deserved. Lofgren, meanwhile, was already branching out into other ventures after making a guest appearance on Neil Young's *After The Goldrush*. He briefly teamed-up with Young's backing group Crazy Horse for their critically-acclaimed debut album. Lofgren's association with Young continued in 1973 when he was invited to join the *Tonight's The Night* tour. By now, Lofgren was a highly-respected guitarist and it was widely speculated that he might be joining the Rolling Stones as Mick Taylor's replacement. Instead, he signed to A&M Records as a solo artist and recorded a self-titled album, which included the tribute 'Keith Don't Go (Ode To The Glimmer Twin)'. The album was applauded on its release, as were Lofgren's solo tours during which he would astound audiences with his acrobatic skills, often propelling himself in the air from a trampoline. An 'official bootleg' from the tour *Back It Up* captured some of the excitement. Lofgren's *Cry Tough*, displayed his power as a writer, arranger and musician. It was a best seller on both sides of the Atlantic and momentarily placed Lofgren on a level with the other acclaimed new guitar-playing artists such as Bruce Springsteen. With *I Came To Dance* and *Nils*, the singer/guitarist consolidated his position without breaking any new ground. The latter included some lyrics from Lou Reed which added some bite to the proceedings. By the end of the 70s, Lofgren left A&M and found himself recording for the MCA subsidiary, Backstreet. By the early 80s, his reputation as a solo artist had declined and it was generally accepted that his real genius lay as a 'right-hand man' to other artists. In early 1983 he embarked on Neil Young's *Trans* tour and the following year joined Bruce Springsteen's E Street Band. By this point, his solo standing was such that he was recording for an independent label, Towerbell. During the late 80s, he continued tò work with Springsteen, but also undertook occasional low-key solo tours. In 1991, he ended a six-year hiatus from recording with *Silver Lining*, which included guest appearances from Springsteen and various members of Ringo Starr's All Starr Band.

Albums: *Nils Lofgren* (1975), *Back It Up (Official Bootleg)* (1976), *Cry Tough* (1976), *I Came To Dance* (1977), *Night After Night* (1977), *Nils* (1979), *Night Fades Away* (1981), *Wonderland* (1983), *Flip* (1985), *Code Of The Road* (1986), *Silver Lining* (1991).

Lomax, Jackie

b. 10 May 1944, Wallasey, Merseyside, England. A former vocalist with the 60s beat group the Undertakers, Lomax began a new career in America when this respected Liverpool unit disbanded. Spells with two short-lived bands, the Mersey Lads and the Lost Souls, preceded a return to England where the singer worked with his own group, the Lomax Alliance, and as a solo act. Two strong, but unsuccessful, singles followed before he was signed to the fledgling Apple label but his opening release, 'Sour Milk Sea', written for him by George Harrison, was unfortunately overshadowed by hits for stablemates the Beatles and Mary Hopkin. Jackie's debut *Is This What You Want*, featured contributions from a host of star names including Harrison, Paul McCartney, Ringo Starr and Eric Clapton. The artist's stylish compositions and superb voice were equal to such esteemed company. Sadly, Apple's internal problems doomed his undoubted potential and following an interlude as part of the elusive Heavy Jelly, Lomax returned to America where he completed two more excellent albums, *Home Is In My Head* and *Three*. In 1973, the singer joined the British-based Badger, a group formed by ex-Yes organist, Tony Kaye. Lomax helped transform them from a progressive rock band into a more soulful aggregation, exemplified on *White Lady*, which was produced by Allen Toussaint and consisted solely of Jackie's songs. Badger then split into two factions, with Lomax and bassist Kim Gardner instigating an offshoot unit named after the album. Jackie subsequently resumed his solo career, but the releases which followed were disappointing and the ill-luck which had often dogged this worthwhile performer further undermined his career. Lomax did resurface in 1990 as one of several acts contributing to the 'tribute' album *True Voices* wherein he sang a version of Tim Buckley's 'Devil Eyes'.

Albums: *Is This What You Want* (1969), *Home Is In My Head* (1971), *Three* (1972), with Badger *White Lady* (1974), *Livin' For Lovin'* (1976), *Did You Ever* (1977).

Love Unlimited

Formed in 1969 in San Pedro, California, USA, under the aegis of singer/producer Barry White, the group consisted of Diane Taylor, Linda James and her sister Glodean James who married White on 4 July 1974. The trio scored an early hit with 'Walkin' In The Rain With The One I Love' (1972), an imaginatively arranged performance which married contemporary soul to the aura of the now-passed girl-group genre, reminiscent of the Shangri-Las. Love Unlimited's later releases included 'It May Be Winter Outside, (But In My Heart It's Spring)' (1973) and 'Under The Influence Of Love' (1974), both of which White had previously recorded with Felice Taylor. The care the producer lavished on such releases equalled that of his own, but despite further R&B hits, 'I Belong To You' (1974) was the trio's final US pop chart entry.

Albums: *Love Unlimited* (1972), *Rhapsody In Blue* (1973), *Under The Influence Of...* (1973), *In Heat* (1974), *He's All I Got* (1977), *Love Is Back* (1980).

M

McCartney, Paul

b. 18 June 1942, Liverpool, England. Although commitments to the Beatles not unnaturally took precedence, bassist/vocalist McCartney nonetheless pursued several outside projects during this tenure. Many reflected friendships or personal preferences, ranging from production work for Cliff Bennett, Paddy, Klaus And Gibson and the Bonzo Dog Doo-Dah Band to appearances on sessions by Donovan, Paul Jones and Steve Miller. He also wrote 'Woman' for Peter And Gordon under the pseudonym Bernard Webb, but such contributions flourished more freely with the founding of Apple Records, where Paul guided the early careers of Mary Hopkin and Badfinger and enjoyed cameos on releases by Jackie Lomax and James Taylor. However, despite this well-documented independence, the artist ensured a critical backlash by timing the release of *McCartney* to coincide with that of the Beatles' *Let It Be* and his announced departure from the group. His low-key debut was labelled self-indulgent, yet its intimacy was a welcome respite from prevailing heavy rock, and in 'Maybe I'm Amazed', offered one of Paul's finest songs. *Ram*, credited to McCartney and his wife Linda (b. Linda Eastman, 24 September 1942, Scarsdale, New York, USA), was also maligned as commentators opined that the singer lacked an acidic riposte to his often sentimental approach. The album nonetheless spawned a US number 1 in 'Uncle Albert/Admiral Halsey', while an attendant single, 'Another Day', reached number 2 in the UK. Drummer Denny Seiwell, who had assisted on these sessions, was invited to join a projected group, later enhanced by former Moody Blues' member Denny Laine. The quartet, dubbed Wings, then completed *Wildlife*, another informal set marked by an indifference to dexterity and the absorption of reggae and classic rock 'n' roll rhythms. Having expanded the line-up to include Henry McCullough (ex-Grease Band; guitar), McCartney took the group on an impromptu tour of UK colleges, before releasing three wildly contrasting singles, 'Give Ireland Back To The Irish' (banned by the BBC), 'Mary Had A Little Lamb' and 'Hi Hi Hi'/'C Moon' (all 1972). The following year, Wings completed 'My Love', a sculpted ballad in the accepted McCartney

tradition, and *Red Rose Speedway*, to that date his most formal set. Plans for the unit's fourth album were undermined by the defection of McCullough and Seiwell, but the remaining trio emerged triumphant from a series of productive sessions undertaken in a Lagos studio.

Band On The Run was undeniably a major achievement, and did much to restore McCartney's faltering reputation. Buoyed by adversity, the artist offered a passion and commitment missing from earlier albums and, in turn, reaped due commercial plaudits when the title song and 'Jet' reached both US and UK Top 10 positions. The lightweight, 'Junior's Farm' provided another hit single before a reconstituted Wings, which now included guitarist Jimmy McCulloch (ex-Thunderclap Newman and Stone The Crows) and Joe English (drums), completed *Venus And Mars*, *Wings At The Speed Of Sound* and the expansive on-tour collection, *Wings Over America*. Although failing to scale the artistic heights of *Band On The Run*, such sets re-established McCartney as a major figure and included best-selling singles such as 'Listen To What The Man Said' (1975), 'Silly Love Songs' and 'Let 'Em In' (both 1976). Although progress was momentarily undermined by the departures of McCulloch and English, Wings enjoyed its most spectacular success with 'Mull Of Kintyre' (1977), a saccharine paean to Paul and Linda's Scottish retreat which topped the UK charts for nine consecutive weeks and sold over 2.5 million copies in Britain alone. Although regarded as disappointing, *London Town* nevertheless included 'With A Little Luck', a US number 1, but although Wings' newcomers Laurence Juber (guitar) and Steve Holly (drums) added weight to *Back To The Egg*, it, too, was regarded as inferior. Whereas the group was not officially disbanded until April 1981, McCartney's solo recordings, 'Wonderful Christmastime' (1979), 'Coming Up' (1980) and *McCartney II*, already heralded a new phase in the artist's career. However, if international success was maintained through duets with Stevie Wonder ('Ebony And Ivory'), Michael Jackson ('The Girl Is Mine') as well as 'Say Say Say' and 'Pipes Of Peace', attendant albums were marred by inconsistency. McCartney's feature film, *Give My Regards To Broadstreet*, was maligned by critics, a fate befalling its soundtrack album, although the optimistic ballad, 'No More Lonely Nights', reached number 2 in the UK. The artist's once-prolific output then noticeably waned, but although his partnership with 10cc guitarist Eric Stewart gave *Press To Play* a sense of direction, it failed to halt a significant commercial decline. *Choba B CCCP*, a collection of favoured 'oldies' solely intended for release in the USSR, provided an artistic respite and publicity, before a much-heralded collaboration with Elvis Costello produced material for the latter's *Spike* and McCartney's own *Flowers In The Dirt*, arguably his strongest set since *Venus And Mars*. Paradoxically, singles culled from the album failed to chart significantly, but a world tour, on which Paul and Linda were joined by Robbie McIntosh (ex-Pretenders; guitar), Wix (keyboards), Hamish Stuart (ex-Average White Band; bass/vocals) and Chris Whitten (drums), showed that McCartney's power to entertain was stil intact. By drawing on material from the Beatles, Wings and solo recordings, this enduring artist demonstrated a prowess which spans over a quarter of a century. The extent of his diversity was emphasized by his collaboration with Carl Davis on the classical 'Liverpool Oratorio', which featured opera singer Dame Kiri Tekanewa. In 1993 amid rumours of a reunion with Harrison and Starr he released *Off The Ground*.

Albums: *McCartney* (1970), *McCartney II* (1980), *Tug Of War* (1982), *Pipes Of Peace* (1983), *Give My Regards To Broad Street* (1984), *Press To Play* (1986), *Choba B CCCP* (1989), *Flowers In The Dirt* (1989), *Tripping The Live Fantastic* (1990), *Unplugged - The Official Bootleg* (1991), *Off The Ground* (1993). As Wings *Ram* (1971), *Wildlife* (1971), *Red Rose Speedway* (1973), *Band On The Run* (1973), *Venus And Mars* (1975), *Wings At The Speed Of Sound* (1976), *Wings Over America* (1976), *London Town* (1978), *Back To The Egg* (1979). Compilations: *Wings Greatest* (1978), *All The Best* (1987).
Further reading: *McCartney: The Biography*, Chet Flippo.

McClinton, Delbert

b. 4 November 1940, Lubbock, Texas, USA. This white R&B artist honed his craft working in a bar band, the Straitjackets, backing visiting blues giants such as Sonny Boy Williamson, Howlin' Wolf, Lightnin' Hopkins and Jimmy Reed. McClinton made his first recordings as a member of the Ron-Dels, and was noted for his distinctive harmonica work on Bruce Channel's 'Hey Baby', a Top 3 single in the UK and number 1 in the US in 1962. Legend has it that on a tour of the UK with Channel, McClinton met a young John Lennon and advised him on his harmonica technique, resulting in the sound heard on 'Love Me Do'. Relocating to Los Angeles in the early 70s,

McClinton emerged in a partnership with fellow Texan Glen Clark, performing country/soul. They achieved a degree of artistic success, releasing two albums before splitting, with Delbert embarking on a solo career. His subsequent output reflects several roadhouse influences. Three gritty releases, *Victim Of Life's Circumstances*, *Genuine Cowhide* and *Love Rustler,* offered country, R&B and southern-style funk, while a 1980 release, *Keeper Of The Flame*, contained material written by Chuck Berry and Don Covay, as well as several original songs, including loving re-makes of two compositions from the Delbert and Glen period. Emmylou Harris scored a C&W number 1 with McClinton's 'Two More Bottles Of Wine' in 1978 and 'B Movie Boxcar Blues' was used in the John Belushi-Dan Aykroyd film, *The Blues Brothers*. His 1980 album, *The Jealous Kind*, contained his solitary hit single, a Jerry Williams song, 'Givin' It Up For Your Love' which reached the US Top 10. After a lay-off for much of the 80s, this rootsy and largely underrated figure made a welcome return in 1989 with the fiery, *Live From Austin*.

Albums: as Delbert And Glen *Delbert And Glen* (1972), *Subject To Change* (1973). Solo *Victim Of Life's Circumstances* (1975), *Genuine Cowhide* (1976), *Love Rustler* (1977), *Second Wind* (1978), *Keeper Of The Flame* (1979), *The Jealous Kind* (1980), *Plain' From The Heart* (1981), *Live From Austin* (1989), *I'm With You* (1990). Archive collection: *Very Early Delbert McClinton With The Ron-Dels* (1978).

McCrae, George

b. 19 October 1944, West Palm Beach, Florida, USA. A member of a vocal group, the Stepbrothers, while at elementary school, McCrae later joined the Jivin' Jets. This unit broke up on his induction into the US Navy, but was reformed by the singer on completing his service in 1967. McCrae's wife, Gwen McCrae, joined the line-up, but after six months the couple began work as a duo. Together they recorded two singles, the second of which, 'Lead Me On', won Gwen a contract as a solo artist with Columbia Records. She received sole credit on the song's ensuing re-release which reached the R&B Top 40. McCrae then began managing his wife's career, but following an R&B Top 20 hit with 'For Your Love' (1973), the pair resumed their singing partnership. McCrae was responsible for one of soul's memorable releases when Gwen failed to meet a particular studio session. He was obliged to sing lead on 'Rock Your Baby', a melodic composition written and produced by Harry

Wayne (KC) Casey and Rick Finch, the two protagonists of KC And The Sunshine Band. This soaring, buoyant song topped both the US and UK charts, while two further releases, 'I Can't Leave You Alone' (1974) and 'It's Been So Long' (1975) also reached the UK Top 10. McCrae's work was less well-received at home but he continued to manage and record with his wife, appearing on her US number 1 R&B hit 'Rockin' Chair' (1975). In 1984, George McCrae enjoyed a final minor UK chart entry with 'One Step Closer (To Love)', but was still recording and touring in the early 90's.
Albums: *Rock Your Baby* (1974), *George McCrae i* (1975), *Diamond Touch* (1977), *George McCrae ii* (1978), *We Did It* (1979). With Gwen McCrae *Together* (1975), *One Step Closer To Love* (1984). Compilation: *The Best Of George McCrae* (1984).

McDonald, Country Joe

b. 1 January 1942, El Monte, California, USA. Named Joe in honour of Joseph Stalin by his politically active parents, McDonald became immersed in Berkeley's folk and protest movement during the early 60s. In 1964, he made a low-key album with fellow performer Blair Hardman, and later founded the radical pamphlet, *Rag Baby*. An early copy included a four-track record which featured the original version of the singer's celebrated anti-Vietnam War song, 'I Feel Like I'm Fixin' To Die Rag'. In 1965, he formed the Instant Action Jug band, which later evolved into Country Joe And The Fish. This influential acid-rock band was one of the era's finest, but by 1969, McDonald had resumed his solo career. Two tribute albums, *Thinking Of Woody Guthrie* and *Tonight I'm Singing Just For You* (a selection of C&W favourites) presaged his first original set, *Hold On, It's Coming*, which was recorded in London with several British musicians. This was followed by *Quiet Days In Clichy*, the soundtrack to a film of Henry Miller's novel, and *War, War, War*, an evocative adaptation of the work of poet Robert Service. The acclaimed *Paris Sessions* was a critical success, but subsequent releases lacked the artist's early purpose. He has remained a popular live attraction and his commitment to political and environmental causes is undiminished, as exemplified on a 1989 release, *Vietnam Experience*.
Albums: *Country Joe And Blair Hardman* (1964), *Thinking Of Woody Guthrie* (1969), *Tonight I'm Singing Just For You* (1969), *Hold On It's Coming* (1971), *Quiet Days In Clichy* (1971), *War, War, War* (1971), *Incredible Live* (1972), *The Paris Sessions* (1973), *Country Joe* (1975), *Paradise With An Ocean*

View (1976), *Love Is A Fire* (1976), *Goodbye Blues* (1977), *Rock 'N' Roll From Planet Earth* (1978), *Leisure Suite* (1979), *On My Own* (1980), *Into The Fray* (1982), *Child's Play* (1983), *Animal Tracks* (1983), *Peace On Earth* (1989), *Vietnam Experience* (1989). Compilations: *The Best Of Country Joe McDonald* (1973), *The Essential Country Joe McDonald* (1976), *Collectors' Items* (1981).

McGuinness Flint

Formed in 1969 by Tom McGuinness (b. 2 December 1941, London, England; bass, ex-Manfred Mann) and Hughie Flint (b. 15 March 1942; drums, ex-John Mayall). Dennis Coulson (keyboards), Benny Gallagher (b. Largs, Scotland; guitar/vocals), Graham Lyle (b. Largs, Scotland; guitar/vocals) and Paul Rutherford (saxophone) completed the original line-up, although the latter dropped out the following year. The group enjoyed immediate success with 'When I'm Dead And Gone' and 'Malt And Barley Blues', both of which reached the UK Top 5 and established their brand of light, folksy pop. Two excellent albums confirmed their undoubted promise, although a succession of disastrous live performances undermined progress. Further problems occurred in 1971, when principle songwriters Gallagher And Lyle left to pursue a career as a duo, but although Dixie Dean (bass/harmonica), John Bailey (guitar) and Neil Innes (piano, ex-Bonzo Dog Doo-Dah Band) replaced them, the group broke up at the end of the year. A resurrection of sorts occurred in 1972, when Coulson, Dean, McGuinness and Flint recorded *Lo And Behold*, a selection of Bob Dylan songs unavailable commercially. Coulson was then replaced by Lou Stonebridge, and with the addition of guitarist Jim Evans, a revamped McGuinness Flint re-emerged the following year. Two more albums were completed, but the unit was unable to recapture that first flush of success and broke up in 1975. Flint, Stonebridge and McGuinness later enjoyed fruitful periods with the Blues Band, albeit at different times.
Albums: *McGuinness Flint* (1971), *Happy Birthday Ruthie Baby* (1971), *Lo And Behold* (1972), *Rainbow* (1973), *C'est La Vie* (1974).

Mackay, Andy

b. 23 July 1946, London, England. Originally a classical musician, Mackay switched to rock, and while at Reading University, played saxophone in R&B group, the Nova Express. After answering an advertisement placed by Bryan Ferry, Mackay was offered a place in Roxy Music. Within a year and a half, the group were acclaimed as one of the most exciting new prospects on the UK rock scene. Much of their power came from the breathtaking saxophone work of Mackay. Such was his credibility that, in 1974, he was given leave to release a solo album, *In Search Of Eddie Riff*. With a wealth of backing musicians, including Brian Eno, Phil Manzanera, Eddie Jobson, Paul Thompson and John Porter, Mackay recorded an instrumental album on which he demonstrated his musical talent. It was an idiosyncratic work containing a selection of rock numbers and updated classics such as Jimmy Ruffin's 'What Becomes Of The Broken Hearted?' and the Beatles' 'The Long And Winding Road'. The classical pieces featured an arrangement of Schubert's 'An Die Musik' and a startling adaptation of Wagner's 'Ride Of The Valkyries'. The musical concoction was completed by some self-penned compositions, most notably, 'Pyramid Of The Night (Past, Present And Future)'. When Roxy Music temporarily retired during 1976-78, Mackay composed the music for the television series *Rock Follies*. He also worked with Mott The Hoople, John Cale and Pavlov's Dog and produced and played on Eddie And The Hot Rods' reworking of 'Wooly Bully'. In 1978, a second album of saxophone instrumentals emerged with *Resolving Contradictions*. In the wake of Roxy's final split, Mackay formed the Explorers with Phil Manzanera and released an album of the same title, which sold moderately.

Albums: *In Search Of Eddie Riff* (1974), *Resolving Contradictions* (1982), *The Explorers* (1985).

Further reading; *Electronic Music*, Andy Mackay.

McLean, Don

b. 2 October, 1945, New Rochelle, New York, USA. McLean began his recording career performing in New York clubs during the early 60s. A peripatetic singer for much of his career, he was singing at elementary schools in Massachusettts when he wrote a musical tribute to Van Gogh in 1970. After receiving rejection slips from countless labels, his debut *Tapestry* was issued by Mediarts that same year, but failed to sell. United Artists next picked up his contract and issued an eight-minutes plus version of 'American Pie'. A paean to Buddy Holly, full of symbolic references to other performers such as Elvis Presley and Bob Dylan, the song topped the US chart and reached number 2 in the UK. The album of the same name was also an enormous success. In the UK, 'Vincent' fared even better than in his home country, reaching number 1. By 1971, McLean was acclaimed as one

of the most talented and commercial of the burgeoning singer-songwriter school emerging from the USA. According to music business legend, the song 'Killing Me Softly With His Song' was written as a tribute to McLean, and was subsequently recorded by Lori Lieberman and Roberta Flack. McLean's affection for Buddy Holly was reiterated in 1973, with a successful cover of 'Everyday'. Meanwhile, his song catalogue was attracting attention, and Perry Como registered a surprise international hit with a cover of McLean's 'And I Love You So'. Despite his promising start, McLean's career foundered during the mid-70s, but his penchant as a strong cover artist held him in good stead. In 1980, he returned to the charts with a revival of Roy Orbison's 'Crying' (UK number 1/US number 2). Thereafter, his old hits were repackaged and he toured extensively. As the 80s progressed, he moved into the country market, but remained popular in the pop mainstream. In 1991, his 20-year-old version of 'American Pie' unexpectedly returned to the UK Top 20, once again reviving interest in his back catalogue.

Albums: *Tapestry* (1970), *American Pie* (1971), *Don McLean* (1973), *Playin' Favorites* (1974), *Homeless Brother* (1974), *Solo* (1976), *Prime Time* (1977), *Chain Lightning* (1980), *Believers* (1982), *Love Tracks* (1987). Compilations: *The Very Best Of Don McLean* (1980), *Don McLean's Greatest Hits - Then And Now* (1987), *The Best Of Don McLean* (1991).

McWilliams, David

b. 4 July 1945, Cregagh, Belfast, Northern Ireland. The subject of an overpowering publicity campaign engineered by his manager Phil Solomon, McWilliams was featured on the front, inside and back covers of several consecutive issues of the *New Musical Express,* which extolled the virtues of a new talent. He was incessantly plugged on the pirate Radio Caroline. Much was made of his rebellious youth and affinity with Irish music, yet the singer's debut release, 'Days Of Pearly Spencer'/'Harlem Lady', revealed a grasp of pop's dynamics rather than those of folk. The former song was both impressive and memorable, as was the pulsating follow-up, '3 O'Clock Flamingo Street', but McWilliams was unable to shake the 'hype' tag which accompanied his launch. His manager believed that Williams was a more promising protege than his other star artist, Van Morrison of Them, but his faith was unrewarded. Williams disliked live performance and failed to show his true talent in front of an audience.

Neither single charted and a period of reassessment followed before the artist re-emerged the following decade with a series of charming, folk-influenced collections. In April 1992 Marc Almond took 'Days Of Pearly Spencer' back into the UK charts.
Albums: *David McWilliams Sings* (1967), *David McWilliams Volume 2* (1967), *Days Of Pearly Spencer* (1971), *Lord Offaly* (1972), *The Beggar And The Priest* (1973), *Living Is Just A State Of Mind* (1974), *David McWilliams* (1977), *Don't Do It For Love* (1978), *Wounded* (1982). Compilation: *Days Of Pearly Spencer* (1971).

Magma

This challenging Parisian combo was assembled in the late 60s by classically-trained drummer Christian Vander to perform a lengthy oratorio expressing laudable anxiety about the future of our abused planet. Much of its libretto was in the language of Kobaia, Earth's imaginary rival world. The first fifth of the work filled Magma's first two albums, but by 1973's overblown *Mekanik Destrucktiw Kommandoh* (for which a choir was hired) the idea was wearing thin. The group's line-up included Vander's singing wife Stella and Klaus Blasquiz, whose *bel canto* baritone became Magma's most identifiable idiosyncrasy. Apart from Vander, the most representative instrumental line-up during the band's 10-year history was Gabriel Federow (guitar), Didier Lockwood (violin), Jean-Paul Asseline (keyboards), Benoit Widemann (keyboards) and Bernard Paganotti (bass). After transferring from A&M Records to Utopia in the summer of 1975, Giorgio Gomelsky, the new label's supremo, was often heard smiting percussion on subsequent discs, such as an in-concert offering from the French capital's Taverne de l'Olympia.
Rather than individual pieces, it was the sound of Magma's records that mattered. Among the most apparent of stylistic reference points were the John Coltrane/Ornette Coleman end of jazz and the stubbornly chromatic tonalities of Stravinsky, Bartok and Stockhausen - hardly the stuff of hit singles. Musical and lyrical themes and leitmotivs connected each album à la Mothers Of Invention - even if Magma's humour was radically different from that of the US act. Continued repackaging of the band's output has enhanced their reputation.
Albums: *Magma* (1970), *1001 Centigrade* (1971), *Mekanik Destructiw Kommandoh* (1973), *Kohntarkosz* (1974), *Live* (1975), *Udu Wudu* (1976), *Edits* (1977). Compilations include *Retrospective* (1979).

Mahavishnu Orchestra

Led by guitarist John McLaughlin, (b. 4 January 1942, Yorkshire, England), between 1972 and 1976 the Mahavishnu Orchestra played a leading part in the creation of jazz/rock fusion music. Mahavishnu was the name given to McLaughlin by his Hindu guru Snr i Chimnoy, and the group's early work showed the influence of Indian ragas. The first line-up included several musicians who had played on McLaughlin's previous solo album, *Inner Mounting Flame*. The high-energy electric music created by keyboardist Jan Hammer, ex-Flock violinist Jerry Goodman, bassist Rick Laird and drummer Billy Cobham made *Birds Of Fire* a Top 20 hit in the USA. After releasing the live *Between Nothingness And Eternity*, whose lengthy 'Dreams' sequence featured spectacular duetting between the guitarist and Cobham, McLaughlin split the group. A year later he re-formed Mahavishnu with an entirely new personnel. Jean-Luc Ponty replaced Goodman, Narada Michael Walden took over on drums, with Gayle Moran on keyboards/vocals, and there was also a four-piece string section. This group made *Apocalypse* with producer George Martin. In 1975, Ponty left and keyboardist Stu Goldberg played on the final albums. McLaughlin next decided to pursue classical Indian music more rigorously in the acoustic quartet Shakti, but Cobham and Hammer in particular carried on the Mahavishnu approach to jazz/rock in their later work. Moran played with Chick Corea's Return To Forever while Walden became a noted soul music producer in the 80s.
Albums: *The Inner Mounting Flame* (1972), *Birds Of Fire* (1973), *Between Nothingness And Eternity* (1973), *Apocalypse* (1974), *Visions Of The Emerald Beyond* (1975), *Inner Worlds* (1976).

Mahogany Rush

Recovering in hospital from a bad drugs experience, Frank Marino claimed he was visited by an apparition of Jimi Hendrix. After leaving hospital he picked up a guitar for the first time and was able to play Hendrix riffs. The group was formed in Montreal during 1970 when Marino recruited bassist Paul Harwood and drummer Jim Ayoub to fulfil his desire to work in a power trio format. Their first three albums were derivative in the extreme; every component of Hendrix's unique style had been dismantled, adapted, then re-built under their own song titles. Nevertheless, they were not condemned as copyists, but instead, were revered for paying tribute to the great man in such an honest and sincere fashion. By 1976,

Marino had started to develop his own style, based on the extension of the Hendrix tricks he had already acquired. This is clearly evident on *Mahogany Rush IV* and *World Anthem*, released in 1976 and 1977, respectively. Eventually he outgrew the Hendrix comparisons as his own style began to dominate the band's material. The name was amended to Frank Marino and Mahogany Rush, then to Frank Marino, following the release of *What's Next* and the departure of Ayoub.

Albums: *Maxoom* (1971), *Child Of The Novelty* (1974), *Strange Universe* (1975), *Mahogany Rush IV* (1976), *World Anthem* (1977), *Live* (1978), *Tales Of The Unexpected* (1979), *What's Next* (1980).

Main Ingredient

This New York-based trio, Donald McPherson (b. 9 July 1941, d. 4 July 1971), Luther Simmons Jnr. (b. 9 September 1942) and Tony Sylvester (b. 7 October 1941, Panama) made their recording debut in 1965. One of several groups using the name 'the Poets', they decided to become the Main Ingredient and signed with producer Bert DeCoteaux, whose lush arrangements provided the requisite foil for their excellent harmonies. This skill was particularly apparent on such early releases as 'I'm So Proud' (1970), 'Spinning Around (I Must Be Falling In Love)' and 'Black Seeds Keep On Growing' (both 1971). McPherson died from leukaemia in 1971 and, ironically, it was his replacement, Cuba Gooding, who sang on the group's million-seller 'Everybody Plays The Fool'. Although the Ingredient went on to enjoy further commercial success, their work grew increasingly bland and lacked the purpose of those early releases. Gooding embarked on a solo career with Motown in 1977, but reunited with Sylvester and Simmons in 1979, continuing to record under the Main Ingredient name into the 80s.

Albums: *The Main Ingredient LTD* (1970), *Black Seeds* (1971), *Tasteful Soul* (1971), *Bitter Sweet* (1972), *Afrodisiac* (1973), *Euphrates River* (1974), *Rolling Down A Mountainside* (1975), *Shame On The World* (1975), *Music Maxiums* (1977), *Ready For Love* (1980), *I Only Have Eyes For You* (1981), *I Just Wanna Love You* (1989).

Major Surgery

A four-piece outfit based in Croydon, Surrey, England, during the latter part of the 70s, Major Surgery comprised Don Weller, Tony Marsh (drums), Bruce Collcutt (bass guitar) and Jimmy Roche (guitar). Roche had a blues background, having been a brief member of an early Colosseum line-up; he subsequently joined East Of Eden, where he played with Weller. This pair also played together in Boris prior to forming Major Surgery. Thus Major Surgery drew on the blues, rock, and *avant garde* music, reconstituting them as a muscular blend of intellectual electric jazz.

Album: *First Cut* (1977).

Mallard

This short-lived group was the result of an acrimonious split between Captain Beefheart and the most renowned of his backing groups, the Magic Band. Their split had occurred in 1974, following the release of *Unconditionally Guaranteed*. Bill Harkleroad (aka Zoot Horn Rollo; guitar), Mark Boston (aka Rockette Morton; bass) and Ed Marimba (aka Art Tripp III; drums) formed Mallard with vocalist Sam Galpin, but although their debut album offered a glimpse of the inspired interplay shown on their previous incarnation, its overall lack of passion justified Beefheart's assertion that he taught the two guitarists by rote. Tripp was replaced by George Draggota for a second Mallard album, *In A Different Climate*. This set was an even greater disappointment and the group broke up soon after its release.

Albums: *Mallard* (1975), *In A Different Climate* (1977).

Man

Man evolved from the Bystanders, a Swansea-based group specializing in close harmony pop. They latterly grew tired of this direction and, by 1969, were performing a live set at odds with their clean-cut recordings. Producer John Schroeder was inclined to drop the unit from his roster, but on hearing this contrary material, renewed their contract on the understanding they pursue a more progressive line. Micky Jones (b. 7 June 1946, Merthyr Tydfil, Mid-Glamorgan, Wales; lead guitar/vocals), Deke Leonard (b. Roger Leonard, Wales; guitar), Clive John (guitar/keyboards), Ray Williams (bass) and Jeff Jones (drums) completed Man's debut, *Revelation*, a concept album based on evolution. One of the tracks, 'Erotica', became a substantial European hit, but the single, which featured a simulated orgasm, was denied a British release. Man abandoned much of *Revelation*'s gimmicky frills for *2ozs Of Plastic With A Hole In The Middle*, which captured something of the group's live fire. Having suppressed the British feel prevalent on that first outing, the quintet was establishing its improvisatory preferences, akin to those associated with America's 'west coast' bands,

exemplified by the Quicksilver Messenger Service. The first in a flurry of line-up changes began when Martin Ace (bass) and Terry Williams (drums) joined the group. *Man* and *Do You Like It Here, Are Your Settling In?* contained several established stage favourites, including 'Daughter Of The Fireplace' and 'Many Are Called But Few Get Up', but the band only prospered as a commercial force with the release of *Live At the Padgett Rooms, Penarth*. This limited-issue set created considerable interest but coincided with considerable internal unrest. With the departure of Deke Leonard in pursuit of a solo career, the 1972 line-up of Micky Jones, Clive John, Will Youatt (b. Michael Youatt, 16 February, 1950, Swansea, West Glamorgan, Wales; bass/vocals), Phil Ryan (b. 21 October 1946, Port Talbot, West Galmorgan, Wales; keyboards) and Terry Williams (b. 11 January 1948, Swansea, West Glamorgan, Wales) released what is generally considered to be Man's most popular album, the live set, *Be Good To Yourself...At Least Once A Day*, which contained lengthy guitar/keyboard work-outs typified by the classic track 'Bananas'. The next album, *Back To The Future* gave Man their highest UK album chart position, which was almost emulated the following year with *Rhinos, Winos And Lunatics*. The latter saw the return of Leonard and found Man at the height of their success. During this period the nomadic habits of various members were unabated due to the comings and goings between variously related groups such as Help Yourself, the Neutrons, Alkatraz and the Flying Aces. Throughout the band's history, Mickey Jones was Man's unifying factor as they lurched from one change to the next. Following the group's success in the USA promoting their well-received album, *Slow Motion*, an ill-fated project with Quicksilver's John Cippolina resulted in the unsatisfactory *Maximum Darkness*. The group's demise came in 1976 when, after the release of the *Welsh Connection*, having lost their momentum, the group ground to a halt. During the late 80s, Jones, Leonard, Ace and drummer John 'Pugwash' Weathers (ex-Gentle Giant), resuscitated the Man name, regularly appearing on the UK pub/club circuit and on the Continent. Terry Williams had in the meantime found security in Rockpile and Dire Straits. Much-loved, the band's activities are still chronicled in Michael Heatley's fanzine, *The Welsh Connection*.
Albums: *Revelation* (1969), *2ozs Of Plastic With A Hole In The Middle* (1969), *Man* aka *Man 1970* (1970), *Do You Like It Here Are You Settling In?* (1971), *Live At The Padgett Rooms, Penarth* (1972),

Be Good To Yourself...At Least Once A Day (1972), *Back To The Future* (1974), *Rhinos, Winos And Lunatics* (1975), *Slow Motion* (1975), *Maximum Darkness* (1976), *The Welsh Connection* (1976), *All's Well That Ends Well* (1977). Compilations: *Golden Hour* (1973), *Green Fly* (1986), *Perfect Timing (The UA Years: 1970-75)* (1991).

Manassas

The multi-talented Stephen Stills founded this highly-regarded unit in October 1971, during sessions for a projected album. Chris Hillman (guitar/vocals), Al Perkins (pedal steel guitar), both formerly of the Flying Burrito Brothers, and percussionist Jo Lala joined the singer's regular touring band of Paul Harris (b. New York City, New York, USA; keyboards), Calvin Samuels (bass) and Dallas Taylor (drums), although Samuels was latterly replaced by Kenny Passarelli. The group's disparate talents were best displayed in their remarkably accomplished live shows and on *Manassas*, a diverse double-album selection brilliantly encompassing country, rock, R&B and latin styles. The septet displayed a remarkable unity of purpose despite the contrasting material, a cohesion which endowed the set with its lasting quality. *Down The Road* could not match the standards set by the debut and Manassas was brought to an end in September 1973, with the sudden departure of Hillman, Perkins and Harris for the ill-fated Souther Hillman Furay Band.
Albums: *Manassas* (1972), *Down The Road* (1973).

Manchester, Melissa

b. 15 February 1951, the Bronx, New York, USA. A former staff writer at Chappel Music and back-up singer for Bette Midler, Manchester launched her own career in 1973 with *Home To Myself*. Her intimate style showed a debt to contemporary New York singer/songwriters, but later releases, including her self-titled third album, were more direct. This collection, produced by Richard Perry and Vini Poncia, yielded the artist's first major hit, 'Midnight Blue' (US Top 10), and set the pattern for her subsequent direction which, if carefully performed, lacked the warmth of those early recordings. Success as a performer and songwriter continued into the 70s and 80s. 'Whenever I Call You Friend', co-written with Kenny Loggins, was a best-selling single for him in 1978, while in 1979 Melissa's second US Top 10 was achieved with 'Don't Cry Out Loud' (composed by Carole Bayer Sager and Peter Allen). Three years later she scored another hit with 'You Should Hear How She

Talks About You'. Although she has since diversified into scriptwriting and acting, Manchester remains a popular recording artist.

Albums: *Home To Myself* (1973), *Bright Eyes* (1974), *Melissa* (1975), *Better Days And Happy Endings* (1976), *Help Is On The Way* (1976), *Singin'* (1977), *Don't Cry Out Loud* (1978), *Melissa Manchester* (1979), *For The Working Girl* (1980), *Hey Ricky* (1982), *Emergency* (1983), *Mathematics* (1985). Compilation: *Greatest Hits* (1983).

Mandel, Harvey

b. 11 March 1945, Detroit, Michigan, USA. This fluent, mellifluous guitarist was one of several young aspirants learning their skills in Chicago clubs. A contemporary of Paul Butterfield and Michael Bloomfield, Mandel was a member of both the Charlie Musselwhite and Barry Goldberg blues bands, before moving to the west coast in 1967. His debut album, *Christo Redentor*, was released the following year. This wholly instrumental set, which included contributions from Musslewhite, Graham Bond, and the Nashville musicians later known as Area Code 615, is arguably the guitarist's definitive release, but *Righteous* and *Baby Batter* are equally inventive. Between 1969 and 1971, Mandel was a member of Canned Heat wherein he struck an empathy with bassist Larry Taylor. Both subsequently joined John Mayall for *USA Union* and *Back To The Roots* before the guitarist formed the short-lived Pure Food And Drug Act. He also remained a popular session musician, contributing to albums by Love, the Ventures and Don 'Sugarcane' Harris during this highly prolific period. Mandel continued to record his stylish solo albums throughout the early 70s, and was one of several candidates mooted to replace Mick Taylor in the Rolling Stones. The results of his audition are compiled on the group's 1976 album, *Black And Blue*. This dalliance with corporate rock was Harvey's last high-profile appearance. In 1985 he signed a recording deal with the newly-founded Nuance label, but no new release has been forthcoming.

Albums: *Christo Redentor* (1968), *Righteous* (1969), *Games Guitars Play* (1970), *Baby Batter* aka *Electric Progress* (1971), with other artists *Get Off In Chicago* (1972), *The Snake* (1972), with Dewey Terry *Chief* (1973), *Shangrenade* (1973), *Feel The Sound Of* (1974). Compilations: *Feel The Sound Of Harvey Mandel* (1974), *Best Of* (1975).

M&O Band

This studio act was assembled by studio owner and producer Muff Murfin and his engineer and assistant Colin Owen. Murfin, who ran a recording studio at the back of a department store in Worcester, England, recorded many acts under various names before becoming involved with the burgeoning northern soul scene in the mid-70s. A specialist at duplicating sounds, he recorded tracks for Disco Demand under names like the Jezebelles and the Sounds Of Lancashire and also worked with Wigan's Ovations. He then built the Old Smithy studio in his large garden and produced television personality John Asher's 1975 Top 20 revival of 'Let's Twist Again'. In 1976 he covered Eddie Drennon's 'Let's Do The Latin Hustle' as the M&O Band and made it a bigger hit. He was accused of sampling part of Drennon's track on his record which he took as a compliment on his close duplication of Drennon's rhythm track. The publicity, however, harmed the act and future records failed to chart. Today Murfin continues to run a successful studio and publishing operation.

Manfred Mann's Earth Band

The fourth incarnation of Manfred Mann (the second being only a change of singer) has been the longest, surviving for almost 20 years. The original Earth Band was formed after Mann's bold attempt at jazz/rock with Manfred Mann Chapter Three had proved financially disastrous. The new band was comprised of Manfred (b. Michael Lubowitz, 21 October 1940, Johannesburg, South Africa; keyboards), Mick Rogers (vocals/guitar), Colin Pattenden (bass) and Chris Slade (drums). Their debut was with the Bob Dylan song 'Please Mrs Henry' and following its poor showing they quickly released a version of Randy Newman's 'Living Without You', again to apathy. Whilst the band gradually won back some of the fans who had deserted the Chapter Three project, it was not until their third offering, *Messin'*, that both success and acclaim arrived. The title track was a long, rambling but exciting piece, reminiscent of Chapter Three, but the band hit the mark with a superb interpretation of Holst's Jupiter, entitled 'Joybringer'. It became a substantial UK hit in 1973. From then on the band forged ahead with gradual rather than spectacular progress and built a loyal following in Europe and America. Their blend of rock still contained strong jazz influences, but the sound was wholeheartedly accessible and rock based. *Solar Fire* featured yet another Dylan song, 'Father Of Day', complete with heavenly choir. Rogers departed in 1976. Just as Bruce Springsteen fever started, the band had a

Manhattans

transatlantic hit with a highly original reading of his 'Blinded By The Light' with vocals from Chris Thompson. The record, with its lengthy, spacey instrumental introduction, reached the top spot in the US chart and worldwide sales exceeded two million.

The Roaring Silence became the band's biggest album, and featured the most assured line-up to date. Other hits followed, including the Robbie Robertson/John Simon composition 'Davey's On The Road Again' in 1978 and Dylan's 'You Angel You' and 'Don't Kill It Carol' in 1979. Further personnel changes came with Pat King (bass), ex-Wings and East Of Eden drummer Geoff Britton and Steve Waller, a seemingly unlikely candidate, formerly with Gonzalez. After a lengthy absence, they made the US chart in 1984 with 'Runner', featuring the vocals of the returning Mick Rogers. Mann's homage to his former homeland *Somewhere In Afrika* was well received that year, although *Criminal Tango*, a collection of non-originals, *Budapest* and *Masque* were commercial failures. The band remain highly popular in Germany and retain the respect of the critics, having never produced a poor album during their long career. Albums: *Manfred Mann's Earth Band* (1972), *Glorified Magnified* (1972), *Messin'* (1973), *Get Your Rocks Off* (1973), *Solar Fire* (1973), *The Good Earth* (1974), *Nightingales And Bombers* (1975), *The Roaring Silence* (1976), *Watch* (1978), *Angel Station* (1979), *Chance* (1980), *Somewhere In Afrika* (1983), *Budapest* (1984), *Criminal Tango* (1986), *Masque* (1987). Compilations: *The New Bronze Age* (1977), *Manfred Mann's Earth Band 1971-1991* (c.90s).

Manhattans

Formed in 1962 in Jersey City, New Jersey, USA, about 10 miles south of New York City's borough of Manhattan, the Manhattans were a soul group whose greatest success came during the 70s. The original members were lead vocalist George Smith, bass singer Winfred 'Blue' Lovett (b. 16 November 1943), tenor Edward Bivins (b. 15 January 1942), tenor Kenneth Kelley (b. 9 January 1943) and baritone Richard Taylor. Specializing in smooth ballads, the group recorded first for the Newark, New Jersey-based Carnival label, on which they placed eight singles on the US R&B charts, beginning with 1965's 'I Wanna Be (Your Everything)'. In 1969, they changed to Deluxe Records, on which they recorded their first Top 10 R&B hit, 'One Life To Live', in 1972. In 1971, Smith died, and was replaced by Gerald Alston (b. 8 November 1942). The group left Deluxe for Columbia in 1973, where their now-sweetened soul style resulted in a string of Top 10 R&B hits, including the 1976 number 1 'Kiss And Say Goodbye', which also made number 1 on the pop charts, and 1980's 'Shining Star' (number 4 R&B/number 5 pop). After 1983's number 4 'Crazy', the group's chart popularity waned, although they continued to release recordings for Columbia. Taylor left the group in 1977 and was not replaced; he died in 1988.

Albums: *Dedicated To You* (c.60s), *For You And Yours* (c.60s), *With These Hands* (1970), *A Million To One* (1972), *There's No Me Without You* (1973), *Summertime In The City* (1974), *That's How Much I Love You* (1975), *The Manhattans* (1976), *It Feels So Good* (1977), *There's No Good In Goodbye* (1978), *Love Talk* (1979), *Greatest Hits* (1980), *After Midnight* (1980), *Black Tie* (1981), *Best Of* (1981), *Follow Your Heart* (1981), *Forever By Your Side* (1983), *Back To Basics* (1986), *Sweet Talk* (1989).

Manhattan Transfer

The original band was formed in 1969, performing good-time, jugband music. By 1972, the only surviving member was Tim Hauser (b. 1940, Troy, New York, USA; vocals), accompanied by Laurel Masse (b. 1954, USA; vocals) Alan Paul (b. 1949, Newark, New Jersey, USA; vocals) and Janis Siegel (b. 1953, Brooklyn, New York, USA; vocals). Although they covered a variety of styles, their trademark was their use of exquisite vocal harmony. Like their Atlantic stablemate, Bette Midler, they were selling nostalgia, and they were popular on the New York cabaret circuit. An unlikely pop act, they nonetheless charted on both sides of the Atlantic. It was symptomatic of their lack of crossover appeal that the hits were different in the UK and the USA. Their versatility splintered their audience. Fans of the emotive ballad, 'Chanson D'Amour', were unlikely to go for the brash gospel song 'Operator', or a jazz tune like 'Tuxedo Junction'. In 1979, Cheryl Bentyne replaced Masse without noticeably affecting the vocal sound. Their stunning version of Weather Report's 'Birdland' remains a modern classic. The power of Manhattan Transfer is in their sometimes breathtaking vocal abilities, strong musicianship and slick live shows.

Albums: *Jukin'* (1971/75), *Manhattan Transfer* (1975), *Coming Out* (1976), *Pastiche* (1978), *Live* (1978), *Extensions* (1979), *Mecca for Moderns* (1981), *Bodies And Souls* (1983), *Bop Doo-wop* (1985), *Vocalese* (1985), *Live In Tokyo* (1987), *Brazil* (1988). Compilation: *Best Of Manhattan Transfer* (1983).

Manhattan Transfer

Solo album: Janis Siegel *Experiment In White* (1982).

Manilow, Barry

b. Barry Alan Pinkus, 17 June 1946, Brooklyn, New York, USA. Manilow studied music at the Juilliard School and worked as an arranger for CBS-TV. During the 60s, he also became a skilled composer of advertising jingles. In 1972 he became accompanist to Bette Midler, then a cult performer in New York's gay bath-houses. Manilow subsequently arranged Midler's first two albums and gained his own recording contract with Bell. After an unsuccessful debut album, he took the booming ballad 'Mandy' to number 1 in America. The song had previously been a UK hit for its co-writer Scott English, as 'Brandy'. This was the prelude to 10 years of remarkable hit parade success. With his strong, pleasant tenor, well-constructed love songs and ingratiating manner in live shows, Manilow was sneered at by critics but adored by his fans, who were predominantly female. Among the biggest hits were 'I Write The Songs' (composed by the Beach Boys' Bruce Johnston, 1976), 'Looks Like We Made It' (1977) by Richard Kerr, the upbeat 'Copacabana' (1978) and 'I Made It Through The Rain' (1981). *2am*

Paradise Cafe and *Swing Street* marked a change of direction as Manilow underlined his jazz credentials in collaborations with Gerry Mulligan and Sarah Vaughan. He also appeared on Broadway in two one-man shows, the second of which, 1991's *Showstoppers* was a schmaltzy tribute to great songwriters of the past. During the 80s, Manilow was invited by the widow of one of those writers, Johnny Mercer, to set to music lyrics unpublished during Mercer's lifetime. A selection of these were recorded by Nancy Wilson on her 1991 album, *With My Lover Beside Me*.

Albums: *Barry Manilow* (1973), *Barry Manilow II* (1974), *Tryin' To Get The Feeling* (1975), *This One's For You* (1976), *Live* (1977), *Even Now* (1978), *One Voice* (1979), *Barry* (1980), *If I Should Love Again* (1981), *Barry Live In Britain* (1982), *2am Paradise Cafe* (1984), *Swing Street* (1988), *Songs To Make The Whole World Sing* (1989), *Live On Broadway* (1990). *Showstoppers* (1991).

Manuel And His Music Of The Mountains

Orchestra leader Geoff Love (b. 1916, d. July 1991) initially used the above name pseudonymously. The British-born son of a black American dancer, he took to music at an early age and by the late 50s/early 60s joined Joe Loss and

Barry Manilow

Ted Heath as one of the country's leading bandleaders. Love's Manuel appellation allowed him an artistic freedom to draw influence from South American music and, although early releases did not reveal its creator's identity (Love was 'unmasked' during a cameo appearance on BBC television's *Juke Box Jury*), such recordings later became the natural outlet for his talents. A prodigious output, notably for EMI's prestigious *Studio Two* stereo series, ensured that the attraction remained one of Britain's most popular light orchestral attractions throughout the 60s and 70s.

Albums: *Manuel And His Music Of The Mountains* (c.60s), *Mountain Carnival* (c.60s), *Ecstasy* (c.60s), *Mountain Fiesta* (c.60s), *Blue Waters* (1966), *Reflections* (1969), *This Is Manuel* (1971), *Carnival* (1971), *Mardi Gras* (1972), *Shangri-La* (1973), *Sun, Sea And Sky* (1973), *Y Viva Espana* (1974), *You, The Night And Music* (1975), *El Bimbo* (1975), *Manuel And The Voices Of Mountains* (1975), *Masquerade* (1976), *Mountain Fire* (1977), *Blue Tangos* (1977), *Bossa Nova* (1978), *Cha Cha* (1978), *Music Of Manuel* (1978), *Supernatural* (1979), *Viva Manuel* (1979), *Manuel Movie Hits* (1979), *Fiesta* (1980), *Digital Spectacular* (1981), *Bolero* (1984), *Latin Hits* (1988). Compilation: *The Very Best Of Manuel* (1976).

Marley, Bob, And The Wailers

This legendary Jamaican vocal group originally comprised six members: Robert Nesta Marley (b. 6 February 1945, St. Anns, Jamaica, d. 11 May 1981, Miami, Florida, USA), Bunny Wailer (b. Neville O'Riley Livingston, 10 April 1947, Kingston, Jamaica), Peter Tosh (b. Winston Hubert McIntosh, 19 October 1944, Westmoreland, Jamaica, d. 11 May 1987, Kingston, Jamaica), Junior Braithwaite, Beverley Kelso, and Cherry Smith. Bob Marley And The Wailers are the sole Jamaican group to have achieved global superstar status together with genuine penetration of world markets. The original vocal group was formed during 1963. After extensive tuition with the great vocalist Joe Higgs, they began their recording career later that year for Coxsone Dodd, although Marley had made two singles for producer Leslie Kong in 1962 - 'Judge Not' and 'One Cup Of Coffee'. Their first record, released just before Christmas 1963 under the group name Wailing Wailers, went to number 1 on the JBC Radio chart in January 1964, holding that position for the ensuing two months and reputedly selling over 80,000 copies. This big local hit was followed by 'It Hurts To Be Alone', featuring Junior

Braithwaite on lead vocal, and 'Lonesome Feeling', with lead vocal by Bunny Wailer. During the period 1963-66, the Wailers made over 70 tracks for Dodd, over 20 of which were local hits, covering a wide stylistic base; from covers of US soul and doo-wop with ska backing to the newer, less frantic rude-boy sounds which presaged the development of rock steady, and including songs which Marley would re-record in the 70s. In late 1965, Braithwaite left to go to America, and Kelso and Smith also departed that year. On 10 February 1966, Marley married Rita Anderson, at the time a member of the Soulettes, later to become one of the I-Threes and a solo vocalist in her own right. The next day he left to join his mother in Wilmington, Delaware, returning to Jamaica in October 1966. The Wailers were now a vocal trio; they continued with Dodd through 1967, recording the local hit 'Bend Down Low' at Studio One late in the year. In 1968 they began releasing self-produced music on their own label, Wail 'N' Soul, later Tuff Gong. This output, amongst the rarest, least re-issued Wailers music, catches the group on the brink of a new maturity; for the first time there were overtly Rasta songs. By the end of that year, following Bunny Wailer's release from prison, they were making demos for Danny Sims, the manager of soft-soul singer Johnny Nash, who would hit the UK charts in April of 1972 with the 1968 Marley composition 'Stir It Up'. This association proved incapable of supporting them, and they began recording for producer Leslie Kong, who had already enjoyed international success with Desmond Dekker, the Pioneers, and Jimmy Cliff. Kong released several singles and an album called *The Best Of The Wailers* in 1970. By the end of 1969, wider commercial success still eluded them. Marley, who had spent the summer of 1969 working at the Chrysler car factory in Wilmington, Delaware, returned to Jamaica, and the trio began a collaboration with Lee Perry that was to prove crucially important to their future development. Not only would Perry help focus the trio's rebel stance more effectively, but they would work with the bass and drum team of the Barrett brothers, Aston 'Family Man' (b. 22 November 1946, Kingston, Jamaica) and Carlton (b. 17 December 1950, Kingston, Jamaica, d. 1987, Kingston, Jamaica), who would become an integral part of the Wailers' sound.

The music Bob Marley And The Wailers made with Perry during 1969-71 represents possibly the height of their respective collective powers. Combining brilliant new songs like 'Duppy

Bob Marley

Conqueror', 'Small Axe' and 'Sun Is Shining' with definitive reworkings of old material, backed by the innovative rhythms of the Upsetters and the equally innovative influence of Perry, the body of work made stands as a high point in Jamaican music. It was also the blueprint for Bob Marley's international success. The group continued to record for their own Tuff Gong label after the Perry sessions and came to the attention of Chris Blackwell, then owner of Island Records. Island had released much of the Wailers' early music from the Studio One period, although the label had concentrated on the rock market since the late 60s. Their first album for the company, *Catch A Fire* (1973), was packaged like a rock album, utilized and targetted at the album market in which Island had been very successful. The band arrived in the UK in April 1973 to tour and appear on television. In July 1973, they supported Bruce Springsteen at Max's Kansas City club in New York. Backed by an astute promotional campaign, *Catch A Fire* sold well enough to warrant issue of *Burnin'*, adding Earl 'Wire' Lindo to the group, which signalled a return to a militant, rootsy approach unencumbered by any rock production values whatsoever.

The rock/blues guitarist Eric Clapton covered 'I Shot The Sheriff' from this album, taking the tune to the number 9 position in the UK chart during the autumn of 1974, and reinforcing the impact of the Wailers in the process. Just as the band was poised on the brink of wider success internal differences caused Tosh and Livingston to depart, both embarking on substantial solo careers, and Lindo left to join Taj Mahal. The new Wailers band, formed mid-1974, included Marley, the Barrett brothers and Bernard 'Touter' Harvey on keyboard, with vocal harmonies by the I-Threes, comprising Marcia Griffiths, Rita Marley and Judy Mowatt. This line-up, with later additions, would come to define the so-called 'international' reggae sound that Bob Marley and the Wailers played until Marley's death in 1981. In establishing that form, not only on the series of albums recorded for Island but also by extensive touring, the band moved from the mainstream of Jamaican music into the global market. As the influence of Bob Marley spread, not only as a musician but also as a symbol of success from the so-called 'Third World', the music made locally pursued its own distinct course. 1975 was the year in which the group consolidated their position, with the release of the massively successful *Natty Dread* and the rapturously-received concerts at London Lyceum.

These concerts attracted both black and white patrons; the crossover had begun. At the end of the year, Marley scored his first UK chart hit, the autobiographical 'No Woman No Cry'. His first official live album, comprising material from the Lyceum concerts, was also released this year. He continued to release an album a year until his death, at which time a spokesman for Island Records estimated worldwide sales of $190 million. Marley survived an assassination attempt on 3rd December 1976, leaving Jamaica for 18 months early in 1977. In July he had an operation in Miami to remove cancer cells from his right toe.

His albums *Exodus* and *Kaya* enjoyed massive international sales. In April 1978, he played the Peace Concert in Kingston, bringing the two leaders of the violently-warring Jamaican political parties together in a largely symbolic peacemaking gesture. The band then undertook a huge worldwide tour that took in the USA, Canada, Japan, Australia and New Zealand. His own label, Tuff Gong, was expanding its interests, developing new talent. The album *Survival* was released to the usual acclaim, being particularly successful in Africa. The song 'Zimbabwe' was covered many times by African artists. In 1980, Marley and the Wailers played the momentous concert in the newly-liberated Zimbabwe to an audience of 40,000. In the summer of 1980, his cancer began to spread; he collapsed at Madison Square Garden during a concert. Late in 1980 he began treatment with the controversial cancer specialist, Dr Josef Issels. By May 3, the doctor had given up. Marley flew to Miami, Florida, where he died in May 1981. His global success had been an inspiration to all Jamaican atists; his name became synonymous with Jamaican music, of which he had been the first authentic superstar. His contribution is thus immense: his career did much to focus attention on Jamaican music and establish credibility for it. In addition, he was a charismatic performer, a great singer and superb songwriter; inevitably that has been a hard act to follow for other Jamaican artists. Marley was rightly celebrated in 1992 with the release of an outstanding CD box set chronicling his entire career.

Albums: *The Wailing Wailers* (c.1970), *The Best Of The Wailers* (1970), *Soul Rebels* (1970), *African Herbsman* (1973), *Catch A Fire* (1973), *Burnin'* (1973), *Soul Revolution* (c.1973), *Soul Revolution II* (c.1973), *Rasta Revolution* (1974), *The Best Of Bob Marley And The Wailers* (1974), *Natty Dread* (1975), *Live At The Lyceum* (1975), *Rastaman Vibration* (1976), *Exodus* (1977), *The Birth Of A Legend*

(1977), *Early Music* (1977), *Kaya* (1978), *Babylon By Bus* (1978), *Survival* (1979), *Uprising* (1980), *Chances Are* (1981), *Marley, Tosh, Livingston & Associates* (1981), *Bob Marley Interviews* (1982), *Confrontation* (1983), *In The Beginning* (1984), *Legend* (1984), *Talking Blues* (1991), *Songs Of Freedom* (4CD box set 1992).

Further reading: *Bob Marley*, Stephen Davis. *Catch A Fire*, Timothy White.

Marriott, Steve

b. 30 January 1947, London, England, d. 20 April 1991, Essex, England. As a child actor, Marriott appeared in *The Famous Five* television series in the late 50s and made a West End theatre debut as the Artful Dodger in Lionel Bart's *Oliver!* in 1962. That same year, Decca engaged him as an Adam Faith soundalike for two unsuccessful singles. Next, as singing guitarist in the Moments, he had another miss with a sly cover of the Kinks' 'You Really Got Me' for the USA market. Then followed Steve Marriott and the Frantic Ones (amended to just the Frantics). This venture was, however, less lucrative than his daytime job in an East Ham music equipment shop where, in 1964, he met fellow mod Ronnie Lane (bass) with whom he formed the Small Faces after recruiting Kenney Jones (drums) and ex-Moment Jimmy Winston (keyboards). Knock-kneed and diminutive, Steve emerged as the outfit's public face, attacking the early smashes with a strangled passion revealing an absorption of R&B, and an exciting (if sometimes slipshod) fretboard style that belied the saccharine quality of such songs as 'Sha-La-La-La-Lee' and 'My Mind's Eye'. With Lane, he composed the unit's later output as well as minor hits for Chris Farlowe and P.P. Arnold.

On leaving the Small Faces in 1969, Marriott, as mainstay of Humble Pie, acquired both a solitary UK Top 20 entry and a reputation for boorish behaviour on BBC's *Top Of The Pops* before building on his previous group's small beginnings. In North America, by 1975, he earned a hard-rock stardom accrued over 22 USA tours when Humble Pie disbanded. He put himself forward as a possible replacement when Mick Taylor left the Rolling Stones, played concerts with his All-Stars (which included Alexis Korner) and recorded a patchy solo album before regrouping the Small Faces, but poor sales of two 'comeback' albums blighted their progress. A link-up with Leslie West was mooted and a new Humble Pie released two albums but, from the early 80s, Marriott was heard mostly on the European club circuit, fronting

various short-lived bands, including Packet Of Three, with a repertoire that hinged on past glories. Shortly before he perished in a fire in his Essex home in April 1991, Marriot had been attempting to reconstitute Humble Pie with Peter Frampton. Frampton was among the many famous friends attending the funeral where the Small Faces' 'All Or Nothing' was spun as Steve Marriott's requiem.

Album: *Marriott* (1975).

Marshall Tucker Band

Formed in 1971 in South Carolina, USA, the Marshall Tucker Band was a 'southern-rock' style outfit which maintained modest popularity from the early to late 70s. The band consisted of Toy Caldwell (b. 1948, Spartanburg, South Carolina, USA; lead guitarist), his brother, Tommy Caldwell, (b. 1950, Spartanburg, South Carolina, USA; bass), vocalist/keyboardist Doug Gray, rhythm guitarist George McCorkle, saxophonist/flautist Jerry Eubanks and drummer Paul Riddle. There was no member named Marshall Tucker; the group was named after the owner of the room in which they practiced their music. Like the Allman Brothers Band, Wet Willie and several others, the band signed with Capricorn Records and established the southern-rock style that emphasized lengthy improvisations built around soul-influenced rock and boogie songs. Prior to the formation of the Marshall Tucker Band, from 1962-65, Toy Caldwell had played with a local group called the Rants. He was in the Marines from 1965-69, and then the Toy Factory, which also included Gray and Eubanks. McCorkle (another ex-Rant), Riddle and Tommy Caldwell were then added in 1972, and the new name was adopted. The group's first Capricorn album was self-titled and reached number 29 in the US in 1973. The following year *A New Life* and *Where We All Belong* were released, a two-album set featuring one studio and one live disc. Their highest-charting album, *Searchin' For A Rainbow*, came in 1975. Their first single to chart was 'This Ol' Cowboy', also in 1975.

Most of the group's albums were gold or platinum sellers through 1978, and the 1977 single 'Heard It In A Love Song' was their best-selling, reaching number 14 (although they were primarily considered an 'album' band). Following their 1978 *Greatest Hits* album, the band switched to Warner Brothers Records and released three final chart albums through 1981. The group continued to perform after the death of Tommy Caldwell in an auto crash on 28 April 1980, but never recaptured

Steve Marriott

their 70s success. (Caldwell was replaced by Franklin Wilkie, ex-Toy Factory) By the early 80s they had largely disappeared from the national music scene. They released new albums, first on Mercury Records in 1988, and then on Sisapa Records in 1990, with no notable success. All of the group's Capricorn albums were reissued on the AJK Music label in the USA in the late 80s.

Albums: *The Marshall Tucker Band* (1973), *A New Life* (1974), *Where We All Belong* (1974), *Searchin' For A Rainbow* (1974), *Long Hard Ride* (1976), *Carolina Dreams* (1977), *Together Forever* (1978), *Greatest Hits* (1978), *Running Like The Wind* (1979), *Tenth* (1980), *Dedicated* (1981), *Tuckerized* (1981), *Just Us* (1983), *Still Holdin' On* (1988), *Southern Spirit* (1990).

Martell, Lena

A much-loved British cabaret singer, her polished interpretations of contemporary, easy-listening items popularized by others - with a bias towards country-tinged material - filled 13 Pye albums that rose successively higher in the national list throughout the 70s to culminate with 1979's prosaically-titled *Lena's Music Album*. The latter included Kris Kristofferson's 'One Day At A Time'. Produced, like all her output, by her bandleader, George Elrick, it was issued as a single and, blessed by many spins on BBC Radio 2, spent three weeks at number 1 - her sole entry in the UK singles chart. An ill-advised attempt at 'Don't Cry For Me Argentina' and the title track of 1980's *Beautiful Sunday* - a revival of a Daniel Boone hit - were among subsequent misses, but her albums still reached the Top 50 until her retirement in the late 80s.

Selected albums: *That Wonderful Sound Of Lena Martell* (1974), *The Best Of Lena Martell* (1977), *The Lena Martell Collection* (1978), *Lena's Music Album* (1979), *By Request* (1980), *Beautiful Sunday* (1980).

Martyn, John

b. Iain McGeachy, 11 September 1948, New Malden, Surrey, England, to musically-minded parents. At the age of 17, he started his professional career under the guidance of folk artist Hamish Imlach. The long, often bumpy journey through Martyn's career began when he arrived in London, where he was signed instantly by the astute Chris Blackwell, whose fledgling Island Records was just finding major success. Martyn became the first white solo artist on the label. His first album, the jazz/blues tinged *London Conversation* (1968), was released amidst a growing folk scene which was

beginning to shake off its traditionalist image. The jazz influence was confirmed when, only nine months later, *The Tumbler* was released. A bold yet understated album, it broke many conventions of folk music, featuring the flute and saxophone of jazz artist Harold MacNair. The critics began the predictable Bob Dylan comparisons, especially as the young Martyn was not yet 20. Soon afterwards, Martyn married singer Beverly Kutner, and as John and Beverly Martyn they produced two well-received albums, *Stormbringer* and *Road To Ruin*. The former was recorded in Woodstock, USA, with a talented group of American musicians, including Levon Helm of the Band and keyboard player Paul Harris. Both albums were relaxed in approach and echoed the simple peace and love attitudes of the day, with their gently naive sentiments. Martyn the romantic also became Martyn the drunkard, and so began his conflict. The meeting with jazz bassist Danny Thompson, who became a regular drinking companion, led to some serious boozing and Martyn becoming a 'Jack the Lad'. Hard work in the clubs, however, was building his reputation, but it was the release of *Bless The Weather* and *Solid Air* that established him as a concert hall attraction. Martyn delivered a unique combination of beautifully slurred vocals and a breathtaking technique using his battered acoustic guitar played through an echoplex unit, together with sensitive and mature jazz arrangements. The track 'Solid Air' was written as a eulogy to his friend singer/songwriter Nick Drake who had committed suicide in 1974. Martyn was able to pour out his feelings in the opening two lines of the song: 'You've been taking your time and you've been living on solid air. You've been walking the line, you've been living on solid air'. Martyn continued to mature with subsequent albums, each time taking a step further away from folk music. *Inside Out* and the mellow *Sunday's Child* both confirmed his important musical standing, although commercial success still eluded him. Frustrated by the music business in general, he made and produced *Live At Leeds* himself. The album could be purchased only by writing to John and Beverly at their home in Hastings; they personally signed every copy of the plain record sleeve upon despatch. Martyn's dark side was beginning to get the better of him, and his alcohol and drug intake put a strain on his marriage. *One World*, in 1977, has subtle references to these problems in the lyrics, and, with Steve Winwood guesting on most tracks, the album was warmly received. Martyn, however, was going through serious problems and would not produce a new work until three years later when, following the break up of his marriage, he delivered the stunning *Grace And Danger* produced by Phil Collins. This was the album in which Martyn bared all to his listeners, a painfully emotional work, which put the artist in a class of his own. Following this collection Martyn ended his association with Chris Blackwell. Martyn changed labels to WEA and delivered *Glorious Fool* and *Well Kept Secret*, also touring regularly with a full-time band including the experienced Max Middleton on keyboards and the talented fretless bassist, Alan Thompson. These two albums had now moved him firmly into the rock category and, in live performance, his much- revered acoustic guitar playing was relegated to only a few numbers, such as his now-classic song 'May You Never', subsequently recorded by Eric Clapton. Martyn's gift as a lyricist, however, had never been sharper, and he injected a fierce yet honest seam into his songs.

On the title track to *Glorious Fool* he wrote a powerful criticism of the former American president, Ronald Reagan (in just one carefully repeated line Martyn states, 'Half the lies he tells you are not true'). Following another home-made live album *Philentropy,* Martyn returned to Island Records and went on to deliver more quality albums. *Sapphire*, with his evocative version of 'Somewhere Over The Rainbow', reflected a happier man, now re-married. The world's first commercially released CD single was Martyn's 'Angeline', a superbly crafted love song to his wife, which preceded the album *Piece By Piece* in 1986. With commercial success still eluding him, Martyn slid into another alcoholic trough until 1988, when he was given a doctor's ultimatum. He chose to dry out and live, returning in 1990 with *The Apprentice*. Martyn has retained his cult following for over 20 years, and remains a critics' favourite. It is difficult to react indifferently to his important work as a major artist; although he has yet to receive major commercial success.

Albums: *London Conversation* (1968), *The Tumbler* (1968), *Stormbringer* (1970), *The Road To Ruin* (1970), *Bless The Weather* (1971), *Solid Air* (1973), *Inside Out* (1973), *Sunday's Child* (1975), *Live At Leeds* (1975), *One World* (1977), *Grace And Danger* (1980), *Glorious Fool* (1981), *Well Kept Secret* (1982), *Philentrophy* (1983), *Sapphire* (1984), *Piece By Piece* (1986), *Foundations* (1987), *The Apprentice* (1990), *Cooltide* (1991), *BBC Radio 1 Live In Concert* (1992), *Couldn't Love You More* (1992).

Compilations: *So Far So Good* (1977), *The Electric John Martyn* (1982).

Marvin, Brett And The Thunderbolts

This UK skiffle-cum-jugband act was comprised of Graham Hine (guitar/vocals), Jim Pitts (guitar/vocals/harmonica), John Lewis aka Jona Lewie (keyboards/vocals), Pete Gibson (trombone/vocals/percussion), Dave Arnott (drums) and percussionists Keith Trussell and Big John Randall. Their debut album aroused novelty-based interest, but the unit only enjoyed commercial success after adopting the pseudonym Terry Dactyl And The Dinosaurs. An ensuing single, 'Seaside Shuffle', reached number 2 in 1972, but the Thunderbolts reverted to their original name when subsequent releases failed to emulate its success. Lewie embarked on a solo career following the group's break-up.

Albums: *Brett Marvin And The Thunderbolts* (1970), *Twelve Inches Of Brett Marvin* (1971), *Best Of Friends* (1971), *Alias Terry Dactyl* (1972), *Ten Legged Friend* (1973).

Mason, Dave

b. 10 May 1946, Worcester, England. Mason, the former guitarist of local band the Hellions, met Steve Winwood when he was employed as a road manager for the Spencer Davis Group. This legendary 60s R&B band was weakened in 1967 when Winwood, together with Mason, formed Traffic. They found instant success as one of the leaders of progressive pop in the late 60s, and went on to develop into a highly regarded unit in the 70s. Mason joined and left the band on numerous occasions. He subsequently settled in America and enjoyed considerable success as a solo artist. His excellent debut album, *Alone Together*, proved to be his most critically acclaimed work, and featured strong musical support from Leon Russell, Rita Coolidge and former Traffic colleague Jim Capaldi. Mason's melodic flair and fine guitar playing came to the fore on all eight tracks. The original record package was a triple fold, cut-out, hole-punched cover which attempted to encourage the listener to hang it on the wall. His second venture without Traffic was a collaboration with 'Mama' Cass Elliot. The record suffered from poor marketing and indifferent reviews. By 1973, Mason had permanently settled in America, and he signed a long-term contract with CBS. The first record, *It's Like You Never Left*, put him back in favour. The recruitment of a number of name LA musicians gave the album a full and varied sound. Graham

Nash, Greg Reeves, Jim Keltner, Carl Radle, Lonnie Turner and Stevie Wonder were just some of the artists who participated. Mason found greater success in his adopted country, and produced a series of successful records throughout the 70s. The albums formed a steady pattern that contained mostly Mason originals, regularly sprinkled with competent versions of oldies. 'All Along The Watchtower', 'Bring It On Home To Me', 'Crying, Waiting, Hoping' were just three of the songs he sympathetically interpreted. Mason kept a relatively low-profile during the 80s, making one album in 1987 on the small Voyager label. He was last heard on American television singing on a beer commercial.

Albums: *Alone Together* (1970), *Dave Mason And Cass Elliot* (1971), *Headkeeper* (1972), *Dave Mason Is Alive!* (1973), *It's Like You Never Left* (1973), *Dave Mason* (1974), *Split Coconut* (1975), *Certified Live* (1976), *Let It Flow* (1977), *Mariposa De Oro* (1978), *Old Crest On A New Wave* (1980). Compilations: *The Best Of Dave Mason* (1974), *Dave Mason At His Best* (1975), *The Very Best Of Dave Mason* (1978).

Further reading: *Keep On Running: The Steve Winwood Story*, Chris Welch. *Back In The High Life: A Biography Of Steve Winwood*, Alan Clayson.

Matchbox

Named after a Carl Perkins' classic, Matchbox were one of several 70s rock 'n' roll revivalist bands from the UK to make the jump from club favourites to chart stars. The band was formed in 1971 by two former members of Contraband - bassist Fred Poke and his brother-in-law Jimmy Redhead. They were joined by an old school friend of Poke's called Steve Bloomfield. Capable of playing almost any stringed instrument, Bloomfield had made a living as a session player for Pye and was on several Mungo Jerry hits. Matchbox's debut single came out on Dawn in 1973, after which Redhead's departure left a line-up of Wiffle Smith (vocals), Rusty Lipton (piano), Bob Burgos (drums), Bloomfield (guitars), and Poke (bass). They subsequently recorded *Riders In The Sky* for Charly. (They had previously recorded a Dutch only album on Rockhouse.) Smith and Lipton then departed, and former Cruisers vocalist Gordon Waters joined. The band were signed to a minor label and completed *Setting The Woods On Fire* in just over two days in October 1977, but as the record company were virtually bankrupt Chiswick took over its distribution. By this time however, Matchbox had signed up with Raw Records - which issued a single - and this led to

complications. Chiswick did not promote the band because Matchbox were not signed to the label, and Raw declined to promote them because they did not own the album. In desperation the group bought themselves out of their contract and signed a new deal with Magnet. At this point they had been joined by vocalist Graham Fenton, previously with the Wild Bunch, the Houseshakers and the Hellraisers, and now Redhead returned, along with another guitarist Gordon Scott. The first Magnet single, 'Black Slacks', missed out, but the second - a Steve Bloomfield original called 'Rockabilly Rebel' - made the charts. A string of hit singles followed. One further line-up change came about when Bloomfield decided he did not want to tour anymore, and Dick Callan was brought in as a replacement for live appearances. Apart from Matchbox recordings, the group also put out a version of Freddie Cannon's 'Palisades Park' under the pseudonym Cyclone. Steve Bloomfield released a solo album entitled *Rockabilly Originals*. The group is known as Major Matchbox outside the UK.

Albums: *Riders In The Sky* (1978), *Setting The Woods On Fire* (1979), *Matchbox* (1980), *Midnite Dynamos* (1980), *Flying Colours* (1981), *Crossed Line* (1983), *Going Down Town* (1985).

Matthews Southern Comfort

Formed in 1969 by former Fairport Convention singer/guitarist Iain Matthews, the group comprised Mark Griffiths (guitar), Carl Barnwell (guitar), Gordon Huntley (pedal steel guitar), Andy Leigh (bass) and Ray Duffy (drums). After signing to EMI Records, they recorded their self-titled debut album in late 1969. Country-tinged rather than folk, it nevertheless displayed Matthews' songwriting talents. In the summer of 1970, their next album, *Second Spring* reached the UK Top 40 and was followed by a winter chart-topper, 'Woodstock'. The single had been written by Joni Mitchell as a tribute to the famous festival that she had been unable to attend. Already issued as a single in a harde -rocking vein by Crosby, Stills, Nash & Young, it was a surprise UK number 1 for Matthews Southern Comfort. Unfortunately, success was followed by friction within the group and, two months later, Matthews announced his intention to pursue a solo career. One more album by the group followed, after which they truncated their name to Southern Comfort. After two further albums, they disbanded in the summer of 1972.

Albums: *Matthews Southern Comfort* (1969), *Second Spring* (1970), *Later That Same Year* (1970). As

Southern Comfort: *Southern Comfort* (1971), *Frog City* (1971), *Stir Don't Shake* (1972).

Medicine Head

John Fiddler (b. 25 September 1947, Darlaston, Staffordshire, England; guitar/vocals) and Peter Hope-Evans (b. 28 September 1947, Brecon, Powys, Wales; harmonica/jew's harp) were constrained to the small clubs of England's midlands, until a demo tape brought the duo to pioneering BBC disc jockey John Peel's Dandelion label. Their debut album, *New Bottles Old Medicine,* offered delicate, sparse, atmospheric songs, and crude, rumbustious R&B, a contrast maintained on a second set, *Heavy On The Drum*. The duo enjoyed a surprise hit single when '(And The) Pictures In The Sky' reached number 22 in 1971, but their progress faltered when Hope-Evans left the group. Ex-Yardbird Keith Relf, at this point Medicine Head's producer, joined Fiddler and drummer John Davies for the group's third album, *Dark Side Of The Moon*. Hope-Evans and Fiddler resumed their partnership in 1972, although session musicians were employed on their subsequent album, *One And One Is One*. The title track became a number 3 UK hit in 1973, while a second single, 'Rising Sun', reached number 11; as

a result, the line-up was expanded to include Roger Saunders (b. 9 March 1947, Barking, Essex, England; guitar), Ian Sainty (bass) and ex-Family member Rob Townsend (b. 7 July 1947, Leicester, Leicestershire, England; drums). Further ructions followed the release of *Thru' A Five* and by 1976, Medicine Head was again reduced to the original duo. *Two Man Band* (1976) marked the end of their collaboration. Fiddler then joined British Lions, which otherwise comprised former members of Mott The Hoople, and recorded several solo singles before fronting 'reformed' Yardbirds, Box Of Frogs, in 1983. He currently works as a solo act. Hope-Evans assisted Pete Townshend on his *White City* soundtrack (1985), and later played in several part-time groups.
Albums: *Old Bottles New Medicine* (1970), *Heavy On The Drum* (1971), *Dark Side Of The Moon* (1972), *One And One Is One* (1973), *Thru' A Five* (1974), *Two Man Band* (1976). Compilations: *Pop History Volume XXV* (1973), *Medicine Head* (1976).

Melanie

b. Melanie Safka, 3 February 1947, New York, USA. One of the surprise discoveries of the 1969 Woodstock Festival with her moving rendition of 'Beautiful People', Melanie briefly emerged as a

Medicine Head

force during the singer/songwriter boom of the early 70s. Although often stereotyped as a winsome 'earth-mother', much of her work had a sharp edge with a raging vocal style very different from her peers. Her first US hit, the powerful 'Lay Down' (1970), benefitted from the glorious backing of the Edwin Hawkins Singers. In Britain, she broke through that same year with a passionate and strikingly original version of the Rolling Stones' 'Ruby Tuesday'. *Candles In The Rain*, was a best seller on both sides of the Atlantic, with an effective mixture of originals and inspired cover versions. 'What Have They Done To My Song, Ma?' gave her another minor hit, narrowly outselling a rival version from the singalong New Seekers. Her last major success came in 1971 with 'Brand New Key', which reached number 1 in the USA and also proved her biggest hit in Britain. In 1972, Melanie founded Neighbourhood Records, and its parochial title seemed to define her career thereafter. Marginalized as a stylized singer/songwriter, she found it difficult to retrieve past glories. Sporadic releases continued, however, and she has often been seen playing charity shows and benefit concerts all over the world.

Selected albums: *Born To Me* (1969), *Affectionately Melanie* (1969), *Candles In The Rain* (1970), *Leftover Wine* (1970), *The Good Book* (1971), *Gather Me* (1971), *Garden In The City* (1972), *Stoneground Words* (1972), *Melanie At Carnegie Hall* (1973), *Madrugada* (1974), *As I See It Now* (1975), *From The Beginning* (1975), *Sunset And Other Beginnings* (1975), *Photogenic - Not Just Another Pretty Face* (1978), *Ballroom Streets* (1979), *Arabesque* (1982), *Seventh Wave* (1983), *Cowabonga - Never Turn Your Back On A Wave* (1989).

Melvin, Harold, And The Blue Notes

Formed in Philadelphia in 1954, the Blue Notes - Harold Melvin (b. 25 June 1939, Philadelphia, Pennsylvania, USA), Bernard Wilson, Jesse Gillis Jnr., Franklin Peaker and Roosevelt Brodie - began life as a doo-wop group. In 1960, they scored a minor hit with a ballad, 'My Hero', but failed to make a significant breakthrough despite several excellent singles. By the end of the decade only Melvin and Wilson remained from that early group, with John Atkins and Lawrence Brown completing the line-up. Two crucial events then changed their fortunes. Theodore 'Teddy' Pendergrass, drummer in the Blue Notes backing band, was brought into the frontline as the featured vocalist in place of the departing Atkins. A fifth singer, Lloyd Parkes, also joined the group which

was then signed by producers Gamble And Huff, whose sculpted arrangements and insistent rhythm tracks provided the perfect foil for the Pendergrass voice. His imploring delivery was best heard on 'If You Don't Know Me By Now' (1972), an aching ballad which encapsulated the intimacy of a relationship. Further singles, including 'The Love I Lost (1973) and 'Where Are All My Friends' (1974), enhanced Teddy's reputation and led to his demand for equal billing in the group. Melvin's refusal resulted in the singer's departure. However, while Pendergrass remained contracted to Philadelphia International and enjoyed considerable solo success, Melvin And The Blue Notes, with new singer David Ebo, moved to ABC Records. Despite securing a UK Top 5 hit with 'Don't Leave Me This Way' and a US R&B Top 10 hit with 'Reaching For The World' in 1977, the group was unable to recapture its erstwhile success. By the early 80s, they were without a recording contract, but continued to enjoy an in-concert popularity.

Albums: *Harold Melvin And The Blue Notes* (1972), *Black And Blue* (1973), *To Be True* (1975), *Wake Up Everybody* (1975), *Reaching For The World* (1977), *Now Is The Time* (1977), *Blue Album* (1980), *All Things Happen In Time* (1981). Compilations: *All Their Greatest Hits!* (1976), *Greatest Hits - Collector's Item* (1985), *Golden Highlights Of Harold Melvin* (1986).

Memphis Horns

The Memphis Horns, an off-shoot of the Mar-Keys, boasted a fluid line-up throughout its history. The mainstays, trumpeter Wayne Jackson and tenor saxophonist Andrew Love, guided the group through its period at the Stax and Hi studios. Augmented by James Mitchell (baritone saxophone), Jack Hale (trombone) and either Ed Logan or Lewis Collins (tenor saxophone), the Horns appeared on releases by Al Green, Ann Peebles, Syl Johnson and many others. The group's eponymous debut album featured several members of the Dixie Flyers and, during the mid-70s, the Horns secured four R&B hits including 'Get Up And Dance' and 'Just For Your Love'. The 1978 album *Memphis Horns II*, featured as guest vocalists, Michael McDonald, Anita Pointer and James Gilstrap. The Memphis Horns are, however, better recalled for their contributions to many of southern soul's finest moments. Andrew Love and Wayne Jackson maintained the Memphis Horns' name throughout the 80s and made appearances on U2's *Rattle And Hum* and Keith Richards' *Talk Is Cheap* (both in 1988). In 1990, the duo joined the Robert Cray band.

Albums: *Memphis Horns* (1971), *High On Music* (1976), *Get Up And Dance* (1977), *Memphis Horns Band II* (1978), *Welcome To The Memphis Horns* (1979).

MFSB

'Mother, Father, Sister, Brother' or MFSB (and there was a less flattering alternative), was the houseband employed by producers Gamble And Huff. Jesse James, Bobby Martin, Norman Harris, Ronnie Baker, Earl Young, Roland Chambers and Karl Chambers came to prominence as the uncredited performers on 'The Horse', a hit for Cliff Nobles And Co. in 1968. As the James Boys, the septet replicated with a cash-in release, 'The Mule', and the unit also recorded under other names, including the Music Makers and Family. It was as the instrumental muscle behind the Philadelphia International stable and artists such as the O'Jays and Harold Melvin And The Blue Notes that the group garnered its reputation. 'TSOP (The Sound Of Philadelphia)', the theme from television's *Soul Train* show, was a million-selling single in 1974, but later releases failed to match its exuberance and purpose. Undeniably rhythmic and undoubtedly competent, MFSB nonetheless lacked the focal point that the Three Degrees' voices provided on those early successes.

Albums: *MFSB* (1973), *Love Is The Message* (1974), *Universal Love* (1975), *Philadelphia Freedom!* (1975), *Summertime* (1976), *The End Of Phase 1* (1977), *The Gamble-Huff Orchestra* (1979), *Mysteries Of The World* (1981).

Middle Of The Road

Originally known as Los Caracas when they performed throughout Europe, this Scottish quartet featured singer Sally Carr, backed by Ian Lewis, Eric Lewis and Ken Andrew. An astute cover of a novelty Continental song 'Chirpy Chirpy Cheep Cheep' saw them outsell a rival version by Mac And Katie Kissoon and hog the UK number 1 spot for five weeks during the summer of 1971. The follow-up, 'Tweedle Dee, Tweedle Dum' (a song about two feuding Scottish clans) had already reached the top in Sweden, Denmark and Norway prior to its UK release, where it climbed to number 2. Further lightweight hits in the early 70s included 'Soley Soley', 'Sacramento' and 'Samson And Delilah', paving the way for many successful seasons in cabaret.

Albums: *Chirpy Chirpy Cheep Cheep* (c.70s), *Drive On* (c.70s).

Midler, Bette

b. 1 December 1945, Paterson, New Jersey, USA. As a singer, comedienne and actress, Midler rose to fame with an outrageous, raunchy stage act, and became known as 'The Divine Miss M', 'Trash With Flash' and 'Sleaze With Ease'. Her mother, a fan of the movies, named her after Bette Davis. Raised in Hawaii, at school, as one of the few white students, and the only Jew, she 'toughened up fast, and won an award in the first grade for singing 'Silent Night'. Encouraged by her mother, she studied theatre at the University of Hawaii, and worked in a pineapple factory and as a secretary in a radio station before gaining her first professional acting job in 1965, in the movie, *Hawaii*, playing the bit part of a missionary wife who is constantly sick. Moving to New York, she held jobs as a glove saleswoman in Stern's Department Store, a hat-check girl and a go-go dancer before joining the chorus of the hit Broadway Musical, *Fiddler On The Roof*, in 1966. In February 1967, Midler took over one of the leading roles, as Tzeitel, the eldest daughter, and played the part for the next three years. While singing late-night after the show at the Improvisation Club, a showcase for young performers, she was noticed by an executive from the David Frost television show, and subsequently appeared several times with Frost, and on the *Merv Griffin Show*. After leaving *Fiddler On The Roof*, she appeared briefly in the Off-Broadway Musical, *Salvation*, and worked again as a go-go dancer in a Broadway bar, before taking a $50-a-night job at the Continental Baths, New York, singing to male homosexuals dressed in bath towels. Clad in toreador pants, or sequin gowns, strapless tops and platform shoes, uniforms of a bygone age, she strutted her extravagant stuff, singing songs from the 40s, 50s, and 60s - rock, blues, novelties - even reaching back to 1929 for the Harry Akst/Grant Clarke ballad, 'Am I Blue?', a hit then for Ethel Waters. News of these somewhat bizarre happenings soon got round, and outside audiences of both sexes, including show people, were allowed to view the show. Offers of other work flooded in, including the opportunity to appear regularly on Johnny Carson's *Tonight* show. In May 1971, she played the dual roles of the Acid Queen and Mrs Walker in the Seattle Opera Company's production of the rock opera, *Tommy* and, later in the year, made her official New York nightclub debut at the Downstairs At The Upstairs, the original two-week engagement being extended

Bette Midler

to 10, to accommodate the crowds. During the following year, she appeared with Carson at the Sahara in Las Vegas, and in June played to standing room only at Carnegie Hall in New York. In November, her first album, *The Divine Miss M,* was released by Atlantic Records, and is said to have sold 100,000 copies in the first month. It contained several of the cover versions which she featured in her stage act such as the Andrew Sisters' 'Boogie Woogie Bugle Boy', the Dixie Cups' 'The Chapel Of Love', the Shangri-Las' 'The Leader Of The Pack' and Bobby Freeman's 'Do You Want To Dance?'. The pianist on most of the tracks was Barry Manilow, who was Midler's accompanist and musical director for three years in the early 70s. The album bears the dedication: 'This is for Judith'. Judith was Midler's sister who was killed in a road accident on her way to meet Bette when she was appearing in *Fiddler On The Roof*. Midler's second album, *Bette Midler*, also made the US Top 10. In 1973, Midler received the After Dark Award for Performer Of The Year and, during the 70s, attained superstar status, able to fill concert halls throughout the USA. In 1979, she had her first starring role in the movie *The Rose*, roughly based on the life of rock singer Janis Joplin. Midler was nominated for an Academy Award as 'Best Actress', and won two Golden Globe Awards for her performance. Two songs from the film, the title track (a million-seller), and 'When A Man Loves A Woman', and the soundtrack album, entered the US charts, as did the album from Midler's next film, *Divine Madness*, a celluloid version of her concert performance in Pasadena, California. After all the success of the past decade, things started to go wrong in the early 80s. In 1982, the aptly-named black comedy, *Jinxed!*, was a disaster at the box office, amid rumours of violent disagreements between Midler and her co-star Ken Wahl and director Don Siegel. Midler became persona non-grata in Hollywood, and suffered a nervous breakdown. She married Martin Von Haselberg, a former commodities broker, in 1984, and signed to a long-term contract to the Walt Disney Studios, making her come-back in the comedy, *Down And Out In Beverly Hills* (1985), with Nick Nolte and Richard Dreyfuss. During the rest of the decade she eschewed touring, and concentrated on her acting career in a series of raucous comedy movies such as *Ruthless People* (1986) co-starring Danny De Vito; *Outrageous Fortune* (1987) and *Big Business* (1988). In 1988, *Beaches*, the first film to be made by her own company, All Girls Productions (their motto

is, 'We hold a grudge'), gave her one of her best roles, and the opportunity to sing songs within the context of the story. These included standards such as 'Ballin' The Jack', Cole Porter's 'I've Still Got My Health', 'The Glory Of Love', 'Under The Boardwalk', and a deliberately tasteless tale about the invention of the brassiere, 'Otto Titsling'. Also included was 'Wind Beneath My Wings', by Larry Henley and Jeff Silbar, which reached number 1 in the US charts. Midler's recording won Grammys in 1990 for 'Record Of The Year' and 'Song Of The Year'. In 1990, Midler appeared in *Stella*, a remake of the classic weepie, *Stella Dallas*, in which she performed an hilarious mock striptease among the bottles and glasses on top of a bar; and *Scenes From A Mall*, a comedy co-staring Woody Allen. Her appearance alongside actor James Caan in *For The Boys* (1991), which she co-produced, earned her a Golden Globe award for Best Actress. In the same year, she released *Some People's Lives*, her first non-soundtrack album since the 1983 flop, *No Frills*. It entered the US Top 10, and one of the tracks, 'From A Distance', had an extended chart life in the USA and UK. By 1991, she was planning to revive her musical career and start touring again, although, on the evidence of 'From A Distance', with its references to the Almighty, the days of the brassy, loud-mouthed cabaret star would seem to be a thing of the past.
Albums: *The Divine Miss M* (1972), *Bette Midler* (1973), *Songs For The New Depression* (1976), *Live At Last* (1977), *Broken Blossom* (1977), *Thighs And Whispers* (1979), *The Rose* (1979, film soundtrack), *Divine Madness* (1980, film soundtrack), *No Frills* (1983), *Beaches* (1989, film soundtrack), *Some People's Lives* (1990).
Further reading: *Bette Midler*, R. Baker. *A View From A Broad*, Bette Midler. *The Saga Of Baby Divine*, Bette Midler.

Miles, Buddy
b. 5 September 1945, Omaha, Nebraska, USA. A teenage prodigy, this powerful, if inflexible drummer was a veteran of several touring revues prior to his spell with soul singer Wilson Pickett. In 1967, Miles joined the Electric Flag at the behest of guitarist Mike Bloomfield, whose subsequent departure left the drummer in control. Although the group collapsed in the wake of a disappointing second album, Miles retained its horn section for his next venture, the Buddy Miles Express. This exciting unit also included former Mitch Ryder guitarist Jim McCarthy. Their first album, *Expressway To Your Skull*, was full of

Buddy Miles

driving, electric soul rhythms which had the blessing of Jimi Hendrix, who produced the album and wrote the sleeve notes. In 1969, Miles joined Jimi Hendrix in the ill-fated Band Of Gypsies. The drummer then continued his own career with the Buddy Miles Band and the rumbustious *Them Changes* album, the title track of which was a minor US hit. As an integral part of the artist's career, the song was not only featured on the *Band Of Gypsies* album, but provided one of the highlights of Miles' 1972 collaboration with Carlos Santana, which was recorded live in an extinct Hawaiian volcano. Having participated in an ill-fated Electric Flag reunion, the drummer continued his prolific rock/soul output with a variety of releases. Despite enjoying a seemingly lower profile during the 80s, Miles has been the guiding musical force behind the phenomenally successful California Raisins, a cartoon group inspired by television advertising.

Albums: as the Buddy Miles Express *Expressway To Your Skull* (1968), *Electric Church* (1969); as the Buddy Miles Band *Them Changes* (1970), *We Got To Live Together* (1970), *Message To The People* (1971), *Live* (1971); with Carlos Santana *Carlos Santana and Buddy Miles! Live!* (1972); solo *Chapter VII* (1973), *Booger Bear* (1973), *All The Faces Of*

Buddy Miles (1974), *More Miles Per Gallon* (1975), *Bicentennial Gathering* (1976), *Sneak Attack* (1981).

Miles, John

b. 23 April 1949, Jarrow, Tyne And Wear, England. Miles achieved international fame in 1976 with the classic rock ballad 'Music' ('music was my first love and it will be my last/the music of tomorrow, the music of the past'). His beginnings in the music business found him manufacturing toilet signs by day, but by night performing in a semi-pro band called the Influences which also included Paul Thompson (later in Roxy Music) and Vic Malcolm (later in Geordie). After this band split, Miles formed his own John Miles Band, who were successful in their native north east and also recorded for the groups own Orange label. In 1975, Miles and bassist Bob Marshall moved to London and were signed to Decca. Recruiting Barry Black (and later adding pianist Gary Moberly) they reached the UK Top 20 with the Alan Parson produced 'Highfly'. The 1976 epic length follow-up 'Music' reached number 3 and earned the band an American tour with Elton John. The accompanying album portrayed Miles as a moody, James Dean figure and the artist came across as such when defending his composition

John Miles

from quarters of the music press who unfairly ridiculed the artist as pretentious. He had two further UK hits in 'Remember Yesterday' (Top 40, 1976) and 'Slow Down' (Top 10, 1977), but Miles was forever linked with his self-confessional epic. This ultimately proved to be a burden on Miles' development and although he continued to record into the 80s, he was never able to brush off the memory of that song. 1983's *Play On*, Miles was using a 40-piece orchestra and Elton John's old producer Gus Dudgeon. By 1986 he was recording for the Valentino label.

Albums: *Rebel* (1976), *Stranger In The City* (1977), *Zaragon* (1978), *More Miles Per Hour* (1979), *Miles High* (1981), *Play On* (1983), *Transition* (1985).

Miller, Frankie

b. 1950, Glasgow, Scotland. Miller commenced his singing career in the late 60s group, the Stoics. Along with Robin Trower, Jim Dewar and Clive Bunker, he formed the short-lived Jude, whose potential was never captured on vinyl. With Brinsley Schwarz as his backing unit, Miller recorded his first solo album, *Once In A Blue Moon*, in 1972. The following year he moved to New Orleans to work with Allen Toussaint on the highly regarded *High Life*, which displayed Miller's throaty, blues-styled vocals to considerable effect. Although the album did not sell well, it provided hit singles for both Three Dog Night and Bette Wright. By 1975, Miller had formed a full-time band featuring Henry McCullough, Mick Weaver, Chrissie Stewart and Stu Perry. Their album, *The Rock*, was a solid effort, but met with middling sales. With a completely new band comprising Ray Minhinnit (guitar), Charlie Harrison (bass), James Hall (keyboards) and Graham Deacon (drums), Miller next recorded *Full House*. The band of the same name lasted a year before Miller reverted to a solo excursion for *Perfect Fit*. The latter provided a surprise Top 10 UK hit with 'Darlin'', but Miller could not build on that success. His frequent change of musicians and producers has resulted in an erratic career which has always remained tantalisingly short of a major leap into the top league of white blues performers. Nevertheless, his live performances are as popular as ever, while his back catalogue has grown substantially over the years.

Albums: *Once In A Blue Moon* (1972), *High Life* (1973), *The Rock* (1975), *Full House* (1977), *Double Trouble* (1978), *Falling In Love* (1979), *Perfect Fit* (1979), *Easy Money* (1980), *Standing On The Edge* (1982), *Rockin' Rollin' Frankie Miller* (1983), *Hey,* *Where Ya Goin'* (1984), *Dancing In The Rain* (1986).

Millican And Nesbitt

Alan Millican and Tom Nesbitt worked as coal miners for 20 years in Northumberland, the northern-most county in England and, in their spare time, sang as a duo in the local workingmen's clubs. In 1973, they appeared on the UK's top television talent show, *Opportunity Knocks*, and captured the hearts of millions with their sentimental rendition of 'Vaya Con Dios', which was light years away from Les Paul And Mary Ford's 1953 UK Top 10 version. They won their heat, and returned to the programme nine times in all. With 'Vaya Con Dios', they rubbed shoulders with Gary Glitter and Diana Ross in the UK chart for a few weeks, and had a minor hit with the follow-up, 'For Old Times Sake'. Voted 1973's top new talent by the Variety Club of Great Britain, they had hit albums with *Millican And Nesbitt* (which featured golden oldies such as 'Paper Roses', 'Keep A Light At The Window' and 'The Old Lamplighter') and *Everybody Knows Millican And Nesbitt*. During the late 70s, they also released *Golden Hour Of Millican And Nesbitt*, *Canadian Sunset* and *Country Roads*, before returning to the clubs.

Minnelli, Liza

b. Liza May Minnelli, 12 March 1946, Hollywood, California, USA. An extremely vivacious and animated actress, singer and dancer, in films, concerts, musical shows and television. She was named Liza after the Gershwin song, and May after the mother of her film-director father, Vincente Minnelli. Liza's mother was show-business legend Judy Garland. On the subject of her first name, Miss Minnelli is musically quite precise: 'It's Liza with an 'z', not Lisa with a 's'/'Cos Liza with a 'z' goes zzz, not sss'. She spent a good deal of her childhood in Hollywood, where her playmates included Mia Farrow. At the age of two-and-a-half, she made her screen premiere in the closing sequence of *In The Good Old Summer Time*, as the daughter of the musical film's stars, Garland and Van Johnson. When she was seven, she danced on the stage of the Palace Theatre, New York, while her mother sang 'Swanee'. In 1962, after initially showing no interest in a show-business career, Minnelli served as an apprentice in revivals of the musicals, *Take Me Along* and *The Flower Drum Song*, and later played Anne Frank in a stock production. By the following year she was accomplished

Frankie Miller

enough to win a Promising Personality Award for her third lead performance in an Off-Broadway revival of the 1941 Blane/Martin Musical, *Best Foot Forward*, and later toured in road productions of *Carnival*, *The Pajama Game*, and *The Fantasticks*. She also made her first album, *Liza! Liza!* which sold over 500,000 copies after it was released in 1964. In November of that year, Minnelli appeared with Judy Garland at the London Palladium. Comparatively unknown in the UK, she startled the audience with dynamic performances of songs such as 'The Travellin' Life' and 'Gypsy In My Soul'; - almost 'stealing' the show from the more experienced artist. Her first Broadway show, and an early association with songwriters John Kander and Fred Ebb, came with *Flora And The Red Menace* (1965), for which she was given a Tony Award, though the show closed after only 87 performances. In 1966, she made her New York cabaret debut at the Plaza Hotel to enthusiastic reviews and, in 1967, married Australian singer/songwriter, Peter Allen. Her film career started in 1968, with a supporting role in Albert Finney's first directorial effort, *Charlie Bubbles*, and in 1969, she was nominated for an Academy Award for her performance as Pookie Adams in the film of John Nichols' novel, *The Sterile Cuckoo*. She took time off from making her third film, *Tell Me That You Love Me, Junie Moon*, to attend the funeral of her mother, who died in 1969. In the following year she and Peter Allen announced their separation.

In 1972, Liza Minnelli became a superstar. The film of Kander and Ebb's Broadway hit, *Cabaret*, won nine Oscars, including Best Film and, for her role as Sally Bowles, Minnelli was named Best Actress and appeared on the front covers of *Newsweek* and *Time* magazines in the same week. She also won an Emmy for her television Special, *Liza With A Z*, directed by Bob Fosse. Her concerts were sell-outs; when she played the Olympia, Paris, they dubbed her 'la petite Piaf Americano'. In 1973, she met producer/director Jack Haley Jnr. while contributing to his film project, *That's Entertainment*. Haley's father had played the Tin Man in Judy Garland's most famous picture, *The Wizard Of Oz*. Haley Jnr and Minnelli married in 1974, and in the same year she broke Broadway records and won a special Tony Award for a three-week series of one-woman shows at the Winter Garden. Her next two movies, *Lucky Lady* and *A Matter Of Time* received lukewarm reviews, but she made up for these in 1977, with her next film project, *New York, New York*. Co-starring with

Robert DeNiro, and directed by Martin Scorsese, Minnelli's dramatic performance as a young band singer in the period after World War II was a personal triumph. This was the last film she made until *Arthur* (1981), in which she played a supporting role to Dudley Moore. The musical theme for *Arthur*, 'Best You Can Do', was co-written by her ex-husband, Peter Allen. A renewed association with Kander and Ebb for the Broadway musical, *The Act* (1977), was dismissed by some critics as being little more than a series of production numbers displaying the talents of Liza Minnelli. She won another Tony Award, but collapsed from exhaustion during the show's run. In 1979, she was divorced from Jack Haley Jnr., and married Italian sculptor, Mark Gero. Rumours were appearing in the press which speculated about her drug and alcohol problems, and for a couple of years she was virtually retired. In 1984, she was nominated for yet another Tony for her performance on Broadway in *The Rink*, with Chita Rivera, but dropped out of the show to seek treatment for drug and alcohol abuse at the Betty Ford Clinic in California. She started her comeback in 1985, and the following year, on her 40th birthday, opened to a sold-out London Palladium, the first time she had played the theatre since that memorable occasion in 1964; she received the same kind of reception that her mother did then. In the same year, back in the USA, Minnelli won the Golden Globe Award as Best Actress in *A Time To Live*, a television adaptation of the true story, *Intensive Care*, by Mary-Lou Weisman. During the late 80s, she joined Frank Sinatra and Sammy Davis Jnr. for a world tour, dubbed *The Ultimate Event!*, and in 1989 collaborated with the UK pop group, the Pet Shop Boys, on the album, *Results*. A single from the album, Stephen Sondheim's composition, 'Losing My Mind', gave Liza Minnelli her first chart entry, reaching the UK Top 10. She also appeared with Dudley Moore in *Arthur 2: On The Rocks*. In 1990, she started work on the film version of the successful British comedy musical, *Stepping Out*, co-starring Julie Walters. Minnelli's career in film and music has enabled her to transcend the title, 'Judy Garland's daughter'.

Albums: *Best Foot Forward* (1963, stageshow soundtrack), *Liza! Liza!* (1964), *It Amazes Me* (1965), *The Dangerous Christmas Of Red Riding Hood* (1965, film soundtrack), with Judy Garland *'Live' At The London Palladium* (1965), *Flora The Red Menace* (1965, film soundtrack), *There Is A Time* (1966), *New Feelin'* (1970), *Cabaret* (1972,

film soundtrack), *Liza With A 'Z'* (1972, television soundtrack), *Liza Minnelli The Singer* (1973), *Live At The Winter Garden* (1974), *Lucky Lady* (1976), *Tropical Nights* (1977), *Live! - At Carnegie Hall* (1988), *Results* (1989).
Further reading: *Liza*, James Robert Parish.

Mitchell, Joni

b. Roberta Joan Anderson, 7 November 1943, Fort McLeod, Alberta, Canada. After studying art in Calgary, this singer-songwriter moved to Toronto in 1964, where she married Chuck Mitchell in 1965. The two performed together at coffee houses and folk clubs, playing several Mitchell originals including 'The Circle Game'. The latter inspired fellow Canadian Neil Young to write the reply 'Sugar Mountain', a paean to lost innocence that Mitchell herself included in her sets during this period. While in Detroit, the Mitchells met folk singer Tom Rush, who unsuccessfully attempted to persuade Judy Collins to cover Joni's 'Urge For Going'. He later recorded the song himself, along with the title track of his next album, *The Circle Game*. The previously reluctant Collins also brought Mitchell's name to prominence by covering 'Michael From Mountains' and 'Both Sides Now' on her 1967 album *Wildflowers*.
Following her divorce in 1967, Mitchell moved to New York and for a time planned a career in design and clothing, selling Art Nouveau work. Her success on the New York folk circuit paid her bills, however, and she became known as a strong songwriter and engaging live performer, backed only by her acoustic guitar and dulcimer. After appearing at the Gaslight South folk club in Coconut Grove, Florida, the astute producer Joe Boyd took her to England, where she played some low-key venues. Her trip produced several songs, including the comical tribute to 'London Bridge', based on the traditional nursery rhyme. The song included such lines as 'London Bridge is falling up/Save the tea leaves in my cup . . .' Other early material included the plaintive 'Eastern Rain', 'Just Like Me' and 'Brandy Eyes', which displayed Mitchell's love of sharp description and internal rhyme. Mitchell was initially discovered by budding manager Elliot Roberts at New York's Cafe Au Go-Go, and shortly afterwards in Coconut Grove by former Byrds member, David Crosby. She and Crosby became lovers, and he went on to produce her startling debut album *Songs To A Seagull*. Divided into two sections, 'I Came To The City' and 'Out Of The City And Down

To The Seaside', the work showed her early folk influence which was equally strong on the 1969 follow-up *Clouds*, which featured several songs joyously proclaiming the possibilities offered by life, as well as its melancholic side. 'Chelsea Morning' presented a feeling of wonder in its almost childlike appreciation of everyday observations. The title of the album was borrowed from a line in 'Both Sides Now', which had since become a massive worldwide hit for Judy Collins. The chorus ('It's love's illusions I recall/I really don't know love at all') became something of a statement of policy from Mitchell, whose analyses of love - real or illusory - dominated her work. With *Clouds,* Mitchell paused for reflection, drawing material from her past ('Tin Angel', 'Both Sides Now', 'Chelsea Morning') and blending them with songs devoted to new-found perplexities. If 'I Don't Know Where I Stand' recreates the tentative expectancy of an embryonic relationship, 'The Gallery' chronicles its decline, with the artist as the injured party. The singer, however, was unsatisfied with the final collection, and later termed it her artistic nadir.
Apart from her skills as a writer, Mitchell was a fine singer and imaginative guitarist with a love of open tuning. Although some critics still chose to see her primarily as a songwriter rather than a vocalist, there were already signs of important development on her third album, *Ladies Of The Canyon*. Its title track, with visions of antique chintz and wampum beads, mirrored the era's innocent naivety, a feature also prevailing on 'Willy', the gauche portrait of her relationship with singer Graham Nash. Mitchell is nonetheless aware of the period's fragility, and her rendition of 'Woodstock' (which she never visited), a celebration of the hippie dream in the hands of Crosby, Stills, Nash And Young, becomes a eulogy herein. With piano now in evidence, the music sounded less sparse and the lyrics more ambitious. portraying the hippie audience as searchers for some lost Edenic bliss ('We are stardust, we are golden . . . and we've got to get ourselves back to the garden'). With 'For Free' (later covered by the Byrds), Mitchell presented another one of her hobbyhorses - the clash between commercial acceptance and artistic integrity. Within the song, Mitchell contrasts her professional success with the uncomplicated pleasure that a street performer enjoys. The extent of Mitchell's commercial acceptance was demonstrated on the humorous 'Big Yellow Taxi', a sardonic comment on the urban disregard for ecology. The single was a surprise Top 20 hit and

Joni Mitchell

was even more surprisingly covered by Bob Dylan. Following a sabbatical, Mitchell returned with her most introspective work to date, *Blue*. Less melodic than her previous albums, the arrangements were also more challenging and the material self-analytical to an almost alarming degree. Void of sentimentality, the work also saw her commenting on the American Dream in 'California' ('That was a dream some of us had'). Austere and at times anti-romantic, *Blue* was an essential product of the singer/songwriter era. On *Blue,* the artist moved from a purely folk-based perspective to that of rock, as the piano, rather than guitar, became the natural outlet for her compositions. Stephen Stills (guitar/bass), James Taylor (guitar), 'Sneaky' Pete Kleinow (pedal steel) and Russ Kunkel (drums) embellished material inspired by an extended sojourn travelling in Europe, and if its sense of loss and longing echoed previous works, a new maturity instilled a lasting resonance to the stellar inclusions, 'Carey', 'River' and the desolate title track. Any lingering sense of musical restraint was thrown off with *For The Roses*, in which elaborate horn and woodwind sections buoyed material on which personal themes mixed with third-person narratives. The dilemmas attached to fame and

performing, first aired on 'For Free', reappeared on the title song and 'Blonde In The Bleachers' while 'Woman Of Heart And Mind' charted the reasons for dispute within a relationship in hitherto unexplored depths. 'You Turn Me On, I'm A Radio' gave Mitchell a US Top 30 entry, but a lengthy two-year gap ensued before *Court And Spark* appeared. Supported by the subtle, jazz-based LA Express, Mitchell offered a rich, luxuriant collection, marked by an increased sophistication and dazzling use of melody. The sweeping 'Help Me' climbed to number 7 in the US in 1974, bringing its creator a hitherto unparalleled commercial success. The emergence of Mitchell as a well-rounded rock artist was clearly underlined on *Court And Spark* with its familiar commentary on the trials and tribulations of stardom ('Free Man In Paris'). The strength of the album lay in the powerful arrangements courtesy of Tom Scott, and guitarist Robben Ford, plus Mitchell's own love of jazz rhythms, most notably on her amusing version of Annie Ross' 'Twisted'.

The quality of Mitchell's live performances, which included stadia gigs during 1974, was captured on the live album *Miles Of Aisles*.

In 1975, Mitchell produced the startling *The*

Hissing Of Summer Lawns, which not only displayed her increasing interest in jazz, but also world music. Her most sophisticated work to date, the album was less concerned with introspection than a more generalized commentary on American mores. In 'Harry's House', the obsessive envy of personal possessions is described against a swirling musical backdrop that captures an almost anomic feeling of derangement. The Burundi drummers feature on 'The Jungle Line' in which African primitivism is juxtaposed alongside the swimming pools of the Hollywood aristocracy. 'Edith And The Kingpin' offers a startling evocation of mutual dependency and the complex nature of such a relationship ('His right hand holds Edith, his left hand holds his right/what does that hand desire that he grips it so tight?'). Finally, there was the exuberance of the opening 'In France They Kiss On Main Street' and a return to the theme of 'For Free' on 'The Boho Dance'. The album deserved the highest acclaim, but was greeted with a mixed reception on its release, which emphasized how difficult it was for Mitchell to break free from her 'acoustic folk singer' persona. *The Hissing Of Summer Lawns* confirmed this newfound means of expression. Bereft of an accustomed introspective tenor, its comments on suburban values were surprising, yet were the natural accompaniment to an ever-growing desire to expand stylistic perimeters. However, although *Hejira* was equally adventurous, it was noticeably less ornate, echoing the stark simplicity of early releases. The fretless bass of Jaco Pastorius wrought an ever-present poignancy to a series of confessional compositions reflecting the aching restlessness encapsulated in 'Song For Sharon', an open letter to a childhood friend. The same sense of ambition marked with *Hejira*, Mitchell produced another in-depth work which, though less melodic and texturous than its predecessory, was still a major work. The dark humour of 'Coyote', the sharp observation of 'Amelia' and the lovingly cynical portrait of Furry Lewis, 'Furry Sings The Blues', were all memorable. The move into jazz territory continued throughout 1978-79, first with the double album, *Don Juan's Reckless Daughter,* and culminating in her collaboration with Charlie Mingus. The latter was probably Mitchell's bravest work to date, although its invention was not rewarded with sales and was greeted with suspicion by the jazz community. On *Mingus,* she adapted several of the master musician's best-known compositions. It was an admirable, but flawed, ambition, as her often-reverential lyrics failed to convey the music's erstwhile sense of spontaneity. 'God Must Be A Boogie Man' and 'The Wolf That Lives In Lindsay', for which Joni wrote words and music, succeeded simply because they were better matched.

A live double album, *Shadows And Light* featured Pat Metheny and Jaco Pastorius among the guest musicians. Following her marriage to bassist Larry Klein, Mitchell appeared to wind down her activities. Finally, she signed a long-term contract with Geffen Records and the first fruits of this deal were revealed on *Wild Things Run Fast* in 1972. A more accessible work than her recent efforts, it also lacked the depth and exploratory commitment of its predecessors. The opening song, 'Chinese Cafe', remains one of her finest compositions, blending nostalgia to shattered hopes, but the remainder of the set was musically ill-focussed, relying on unadventurous, largely leaden arrangements. Its lighter moments were well-chosen, however, particularly on the humorous reading of Leiber And Stoller's 'Baby, I Don't Care'. The Thomas Dolby produced *Dog Eat Dog* was critically underrated and represented the best of her 80s work. Despite such hi-tech trappings, the shape of the material remained constant with 'Impossible Dreamer' echoing the atmosphere of *Court And Spark*. Elsewhere, 'Good Friends', an uptempo duet with Michael McDonald, and 'Lucky Girl', confirmed Mitchell's newfound satisfaction and contentment. In interviews, Mitchell indicated her intention to pursue a career in painting, a comment which some took as evidence of the loss of her musical muse. *Chalk Mark In A Rain Storm* continued in a similar vein, while including two notable reworkings of popular tunes, 'Cool Water', which also featured Willie Nelson, and 'Corrina Corrina', herein retitled 'A Bird That Whistles'. Their appearance inferred the change of perspective contained on *Night Flight Home*, issued in 1991 following a three-year gap. Largely stripped of contemporaneous clutter, this acoustic-based collection invoked the intimacy of *Hejira*, thus allowing full rein to Mitchell's vocal and lyrical flair. Its release coincided with the artist's avowed wish to pursue her painting talents - exhibitions of her 80s canvases were held in London and Edinburgh - and future musical directions remain, as always, open to question. Her remarkable body of work encompasses the changing emotions and concerns of a generation: from idealism to adulthood responsibilities, while baring her soul on the traumas of already public relationships. That she does so with insight and melodic flair accounts for a deserved longevity. With *Chalk Mark In A Rainstorm* and *Night Ride Home*, Mitchell reiterated the old themes in a more relaxed style without ever threatening a new direction. Still regarded as one of the finest singer/songwriters of her generation, Mitchell has displayed more artistic depth and consistency than most of her illustrious contemporaries from the 70s. The creatively quiet decade that followed has done little to detract from her importance and she remains one of popular music's most articulate and keen voices.

Albums: *Songs To A Seagull* (1968), *Clouds* (1969), *Ladies Of The Canyon* (1970), *Blue* (1970), *For The Roses* (1972), *Court And Spark* (1974), *Miles Of Aisles* (1975), *The Hissing Of Summer Lawns* (1975), *Hejira* (1976), *Don Juan's Reckless Daughter* (1978), *Mingus* (1979), *Shadows And Light* (1980), *Wild Things Run Fast* (1982), *Dog Eat Dog* (1985), *Chalk Mark In A Rainstorm* (1988), *Night Ride Home* (1991).

Modern Lovers

Formed in Boston, Massachusetts, USA, the Modern Lovers revolved around the talents of uncompromising singer/songwriter Jonathan Richman (b. May 1951, Boston, Massachusetts, USA). The group, which included Jerry Harrison (b. 21 February 1949, Milwaukee, Wisconsin, USA; guitar - later of Talking Heads), Ernie Brooks (bass) and future Cars drummer David Robinson, offered an inspired amalgamation of 50s pop, garage bands, girl groups and the Velvet Underground, a style which both engendered a cult following and attracted the interest of ex-Velvet member John Cale, then a staff producer at Warner Brothers. However, having completed a series of demos, a disillusioned Richman disbanded the line-up and retreated to Boston, although Cale marked their association by recording his protege's composition, 'Pablo Picasso', on *Helen Of Troy* (1975). In 1976, the unfinished tracks were purchased by the newly-founded Beserkley label, which remixed the masters, added two new performances and released the package as *The Modern Lovers*. The company also signed Richman, whose new album, *Jonathan Richman And The Modern Lovers*, was confusingly issued within months of the first selection. The second set revealed a less intensive talent, and his regression into almost child-like simplicity was confirmed on *Rock 'N' Roll With The Modern Lovers*. Richman's new group - Leroy Radcliffe (guitar), Greg 'Curly' Kerenen (bass) and D. Smart (drums) - was purely

acoustic and featured a repertoire which, by including 'The Ice-Cream Man', 'Hey There Little Insect', 'The Wheels On The Bus' and 'I'm A Little Aeroplane', was deemed enchanting or irritating, according to taste. The Modern Lovers nonetheless enjoyed two surprise UK hits with 'Roadrunner' and 'Egyptian Reggae', which reached numbers 11 and 5, respectively, in 1977. However, as the unit was undeniably a vehicle for Richman's quirky vision, the Modern Lovers' name was dropped the following year when the singer embarked on a solo tour. He has nonetheless revived the title on occasions, notably on *It's Time For Jonathan Richman And The Modern Lovers* and *Modern Lovers 88*.

Albums: *The Modern Lovers* (1976), *Jonathan Richman And The Modern Lovers* (1976), *Rock 'N' Roll With The Modern Lovers* (1977), *The Modern Lovers Live* (1977), *It's Time For Jonathan Richman And The Modern Lovers* (1986), *Modern Lovers 88* (1988). Compilations: *The Original Modern Lovers* (1981, early recordings), *Jonathan Richman And The Modern Lovers - 23 Great Recordings* (1990).

Moments

Formed in Hackensack, New Jersey, USA in the late 60s, this distinctive sweet soul trio comprised Al Goodman (b. 31 March 1947, Jackson, Mississippi, USA; ex-Vipers and Corvettes), Harry Ray (b. 15 December 1946, Longbranch, New Jersey, USA; ex-Sounds Of Soul and Establishment) and William Brown (b. 30 June 1946, Atlanta, Georgia, USA; ex-Broadways and Uniques). The falsetto-led, 50s-style harmony vocal group recorded for Sylvia Robinson's Stang label. According to Goodman, the original group led by Mark Greene was replaced by Ray, Goodman and Brown in 1969, after their first hit 'Not On The Outside'. It was this trio's fourth R&B Top 20 hit, 'Love On A Two-Way Street' in 1970, that gave them their biggest pop hit, reaching number 3 in the US charts. They had a further 21 R&B chart records, which included their self-penned Top 20 hit 'Sexy Mama' in 1973, and the R&B number 1 'Look At Me (I'm In Love)' in 1975. Their first UK success came in 1975 with 'Girls', made with fellow Stang group the Whatnauts. They had two further UK Top 10s: 'Dolly My Love' in 1975 and 'Jack In The Box' in 1977, neither of which charted in the USA. In 1979, they joined Polydor as Ray, Goodman And Brown.

Albums: *Not On The Outside* (1969), *A Moment With The Moments* (1970), *Moments Live At The*

New York State Women's Prison (1971), *Love At The Miss Black America Pageant* (1971), *Those Sexy Moments* (1974), *Look At Me* (1975), *Moments With You* (1976), *Sharp* (1978). Compilations: *Moments Greatest Hits* (1970), *Best Of The Moments* (1974), *Greatest Hits* (1987), *Moments* (1988).

Motors

The Motors were based around the partnership of Nick Garvey (b. 26 April 1951, Stoke-on-Trent, Staffordshire, England) and Andy McMaster (b. 27 July 1947, Glasgow, Scotland) who first met in the pub rock band Ducks Deluxe. McMaster had a long career in pop music, having played in several bands in the 60s including the Sabres, which also featured Frankie Miller. McMaster released a solo single, 'Can't Get Drunk Without You', on President, and joined Ducks Deluxe in November 1974. Garvey was educated at Kings College in Cambridge and was an accomplished pianist, oboeist and trumpeter. Before he joined Ducks Deluxe in December 1972 he had acted as a road manager for the Flamin' Groovies. The pair left the Ducks early in 1975, just a few months before the unit disbanded. Garvey joined a group called the Snakes (along with future Wire vocalist Rob Gotobed) and they released one single. McMaster, meanwhile, went to work for a music publisher. Garvey's friend and manager Richard Ogden suggested that Garvey form his own band in order to record the songs he had written. This led to him contacting McMaster and in January 1977 they recorded demos together. The following month they recruited Ricky Wernham (aka Ricky Slaughter) from the Snakes on drums, - he is the cousin of Knox from the Vibrators. Guitarist Rob Hendry was quickly replaced by Bram Tchaikovsky and the Motors were up and running. They made their live debut at the Marquee Club, London in March 1977 and signed to Virgin in May.

A tour with the Kursaal Flyers and the Heavy Metal Kids led to the release of their debut single, 'Dancing The Night Away', and first album, produced by Mutt Lange. However, it was their second single, 'Airport', which became a huge hit in the UK. It is widely used to this day as a stock soundtrack when television programmes show film clips of aeroplanes taking off or landing. Despite this success, the group were already burning out. After performing at Reading in August the Motors decided to concentrate on writing new material. Wernham took the opportunity to leave, while Tchaikovsky formed his own band with the intention of returning to the Motors, though he never did. Garvey and McMaster eventually re-emerged with some new material for *Tenement Steps*. It was recorded with the assistance of former Man bassist Martin Ace, and drummer Terry Williams (ex-Man and Rockpile, future Dire Straits). After *Tenement Steps* the Motors seized up, but both Garvey and McMaster have since released solo singles.

Albums: *The Motors I* (1977), *Approved By The Motors* (1978), *Tenement Steps* (1980). Compilation: *Greatest Hits* (1981).

Mott The Hoople

Having played in a number of different rock groups in Hereford, England during the late 60s, the founding members of this promising ensemble comprised: Overend Watts (b. Peter Watts, 13 May 1947, Birmingham, England; vocals/bass), Mick Ralphs (b. 31 March 1944, Hereford, England; vocals/guitar), Verden Allen (b. 26 May 1944, Hereford, England; organ) and Dale Griffin (b. 24 October 1948, Ross-on-Wye, England; vocals/drums). After dispensing with their lead singer Stan Tippens, they were on the point of dissolving when Ralphs sent a demo tape to Island Records producer Guy Stevens. He responded enthusiastically, and after placing an advertisement in *Melody Maker* auditioned a promising singer named Ian Hunter (b. 3 June 1946, Shrewsbury, England; vocals/keyboards/guitar). In June 1969 Stevens christened the group Mott The Hoople, after the novel by Willard Manus. Their self-titled debut album had a very strong Bob Dylan influence, most notably in Hunter's nasal vocal inflexions and visual image. With his corkscrew hair and permanent shades Hunter bore a strong resemblance to vintage 1966 Dylan and retained that style for his entire career. The first album, with its M.C. Escher cover illustration, included interesting reworkings of the Kinks' 'You Really Got Me' and Sonny Bono's 'Laugh At Me' and convinced many that Mott would become a major band. Their next three albums trod water, however, and it was only their popularity and power as a live act which kept them together. Despite teaming up with backing vocalist Steve Marriott on the George 'Shadow' Morton-produced 'Midnight Lady', a breakthrough hit remained elusive. On 26 March 1972, following the departure of Allen, they quit in disillusionment. Fairy godfather David Bowie convinced them to carry on, offered his assistance as producer, placed them under the wing of his manager, Tony De

Mott The Hoople

Fries, and even presented them with a stylish UK hit: 'All The Young Dudes'. The catchy 'Honaloochie Boogie' maintained the momentum but there was still one minor setback when Ralphs quit to form Bad Company. With new members Morgan Fisher and Ariel Bender (Luther Grosvenor) Mott enjoyed a number of further UK hits including 'All The Way From Memphis' and 'Roll Away The Stone'. During their final phase, Bowie's sideman Mick Ronson joined the group in place of Grosvenor (who had departed to join Widowmaker). Preparations for a European tour in late 1974 were disrupted when Hunter was hospitalized suffering from physical exhaustion, culminating in the cancellation of the entire tour. When rumours circulated that Hunter had signed a deal instigating a solo career, with Ronson working alongside him, the upheaval led to an irrevocable rift within the group resulting in the stormy demise of Mott The Hoople. With the official departure of Hunter and Ronson, the remaining members, Watts, Griffin and Fisher, were determined to carry on, working simply as Mott.

Albums: *Mott The Hoople* (1969), *Mad Shadows* (1970), *Wild Life* (1971), *Brain Capers* (1971), *All The Young Dudes* (1972), *Mott* (1973), *The Hoople* (1974), *Live* (1974). Selected compilations: *Rock And Roll Queen* (1972), *Greatest Hits* (1975), *Shades Of Ian Hunter - The Ballad Of Ian Hunter And Mott The Hoople* (1979), *Two Miles From Heaven* (1980). Further reading: *The Diary Of A Rock 'N' Roll Star*, Ian Hunter.

Mountain

Mountain were one of the first generation heavy metal bands, formed by ex-Vagrants guitarist Leslie West (b. Leslie Weinstein, 22 October 1945, Queens, New York, USA) and bassist Felix Pappalardi (b. 1939, Bronx, New York, USA, d. 17 April 1983) in New York 1968. Augmented by drummer Corky Laing and Steve Knight on keyboards they played the Woodstock festival in 1970, releasing *Mountain Climbing* shortly afterwards. Featuring dense guitar lines from West and the delicate melodies of Pappalardi, they quickly established their own sound, although Cream influences were noticeable in places. The album was an unqualified success, peaking at number 17 in the *Billboard* album chart in November 1970. Their next two albums built on this foundation, and the band refined their style into an amalgam of heavy riffs, blues-based rock and extended guitar and keyboard solos. *Nantucket Sleighride* and *Flowers Of Evil* made the *Billboard* charts at numbers 16 and 35, respectively. A live album followed, which included interminably long solos and was poorly received. The group temporarily disbanded to follow separate projects. Pappalardi returned to producing, while West and Laing teamed up with Cream's Jack Bruce to record as the trio (West, Bruce And Laing). In the autumn of 1974, Mountain rose again with Alan Schwartzberg and Bob Mann replacing Laing and Knight to record *Twin Peaks*, live in Japan. This line-up was short-lived as Laing rejoined for the recording of the disappointing studio album *Avalanche*. The band collapsed once more and West concentrated on his solo career again. Pappalardi was shot and killed by his wife in 1983. Two years later, West and Laing resurrected the band with Mark Clarke (former Rainbow and Uriah Heep bassist) and released *Go For Your Life*. They toured with Deep Purple throughout Europe in 1985, but split up again soon afterwards.

Albums: *Mountain Climbing* (1970), *Nantucket Sleighride* (1971), *Flowers Of Evil* (1971), *The Road Goes On Forever-Mountain Live* (1972), *Best Of* (1973), *Twin Peaks* (1974), *Avalanche* (1974), *Go For Your Life* (1985).

Mr. Big

With their name taken from an album track by the disbanded Free, Jeff Dicken (vocals), Pete Crowther (guitar), Robert Hirschman (bass) and John Burnip (drums) attempted to fill this market void by ploughing a hard rock furrow with a similar blues-derived stalk. On stage, hirsute Dicken's tight-trousered gyrations ensured a healthy cluster of fans round the central microphone as the group garnered a grassroots following on the British and European club circuit, and an EMI contract, in 1975. More touring ensured that their two albums sold well without actually making the charts, though the second spawned the singles 'Romeo' and 'Feel Like Calling Home' which reached the UK Top 40. By 1977, Burnip had been replaced by Vincent Chaulk and then John Marter, and Crowther was replaced by Edward Carter. Despite enriching their sound on record with keyboards, the group were categorized as another outmoded 'heavy' act as they drowned in the rip-tide of punk.

Albums: *Sweet Silence* (1975), *Mr. Big* (1977).

Mr. Bloe

'Groovin' With Mr. Bloe', an instrumental dominated by harmonica, was put together by pianist Zack Laurence and issued on DJM Records, a division of Dick James Music. It was prevented from topping the UK chart in the summer of 1970 by Mungo Jerry's 'In The Summertime'. The Mr.

Bloe project was abandoned after efforts including 'Anyway You Want It', 'One More Time' fell on deaf ears, despite contributions of compositions by Elton John and other James associates. The influence of the hit single was felt, nevertheless, in 1977 on the overall sound of 'A New Career In A New Town' on David Bowie's *Low*.

Album: *Groovin' With Mr Bloe* (1973).

Mu

A Californian band of legendary obscurity, Mu named themselves after the lost continent of Mu (of which the Hawaiian islands are the remnants). Their only album, recorded in 1971, is a magical mix of oriental blues guitar, underground rock rhythms and Beach Boys harmonies. They comprised Merrell Fankhauser (guitar/vocal), who claimed he had composed the Surfaris' 1963 hit 'Wipe Out', Jeff Cotton (guitar/vocal), who had played on Captain Beefheart's *Strictly Personal* (1968) and *Trout Mask Replica* (under the name Antennae Jimmy Semens), Larry Willey (bass/vocals) and Randy Wimer (drums). United Artists gave the record an official release in 1974. The group set up their own MU label, which was financed by their own banana and papaya plantation on the island of Maui, where the group lived a communal hippie-life searching for the lost continent.

Album: *Mu* (1971).

Mud

Originally formed in 1966, this lightweight UK pop outfit comprised Les Gray (b. 9 April 1946, Carshalton, Surrey, England; vocals), Dave Mount (b. 3 March 1947, Carshalton, Surrey, England; drums/vocals), Ray Stiles (b. 20 November 1946, Carshalton, Surrey, England; bass guitar/vocals) and Rob Davis (b. 1 October 1947, Carshalton, Surrey; lead guitar/vocals). Their debut single for CBS, 'Flower Power', was unsuccessful but they continued touring for several years. The group's easy-going pop style made them natural contenders for appearances on *The Basil Brush Show*, but still the hits were not forthcoming. Eventually, in early 1973, they broke through in the UK with 'Crazy' and 'Hypnosis'. Their uncomplicated blend of pop and rockabilly brought them an impressive run of 12 more Top 20 hits during the next three years, including three UK number 1 hits: 'Tiger Feet', 'Lonely This Christmas' and 'Oh Boy'. The group continued in cabaret, but their membership atropied after the hits had ceased. Gray attempted a solo career with little success, while Stiles turned

Mud

up unexpectedly in 1988 as a latter-day member of the Hollies at the time of their belatedly chart-topping 'He Ain't Heavy He's My Brother'.
Albums: *Mud Rock* (1974), *Mud Rock Vol. 2* (1975), *Use Your Imagination* (1975), *It's Better Than Working* (1976), *Mudpack* (1978), *Rock On* (1978), *As You Like It* (1979), *Mud* (1983). Compilation: *Mud's Greatest Hits* (1975), *Let's Have A Party* (1990).

Muldaur, Maria

b. Maria Grazia Rosa Domenica d'Amato, 12 September 1943, Greenwich Village, New York, USA. Her name was changed to Muldaur when she married Geoff Muldaur, with whom she performed in the Jim Kweskin Jug Band. Although her mother was fond of classical music, Muldaur grew up liking blues and big band sounds. The 60s scene in Greenwich Village thrived musically, and she first joined the Even Dozen Jug Band, playing alongside John Sebastian, Stefan Grossman, Joshua Rifkin and Steve Katz. After leaving them she teamed up with the Jim Kweskin Jug Band. After two albums together, they split up, and Geoff and Maria were divorced in 1972. *Maria Muldaur*, her first solo effort, went platinum in the USA. It contained the classic single 'Midnight At The

Oasis', which featured an excellent guitar solo by Amos Garrett. The album reached number 3 in the US charts in 1974, with the single making the US Top 10. A follow-up, 'I'm A Woman', made the Top 20 in the US charts in 1975. Muldaur toured the USA in 1975, and shortly after played in Europe for the first time. The US Top 30 album, *Waitress In A Donut Shop*, featured the songs of contemporary writers such as Kate And Anna McGarrigle, and with the assistance of musicians including Amos Garrett and J.J.Cale, she created a stronger jazz influence on the album. With sales of her records in decline, she was dropped by WEA, and since then has concentrated on recording with smaller labels such as Takoma, Spindrift, Making Waves and the Christian label Myrhh with whom she released *There Is A Love*. Shortly after *Live In London* was released, the label, Making Waves, folded. *On The Sunny Side* appeared on the largely unknown Music For Little People label. She has never been able to completely match the success of 'Midnight At The Oasis', but her soulful style of blues, tinged with jazz is still in demand.
Albums: *Maria Muldaur* (1973), *Waitress In A Donut Shop* (1974), *Sweet Harmony* (1976), *Southern Winds* (1978), *Open Your Eyes* (1979), *Gospel Nights* (1980), *There Is A Love* (1982), *Sweet And Slow*

(1984), *Transblucency* (1985), *Live In London* (1987), *On The Sunny Side* (1991).

Mungo Jerry

Mungo Jerry - Ray Dorset (vocals/guitar), Colin Earl (piano/vocals), Paul King (banjo/jug/guitar/vocals) and Mike Cole (bass) - was a little-known skiffle-cum-jug band which achieved instant fame following a sensational appearance at 1970's Hollywood Pop Festival, in Staffordshire, England, wherein they proved more popular than headliners the Grateful Dead, Traffic and Free. The group's performance coincided with the release of their debut single, 'In The Summertime', and the attendant publicity, combined with the song's nagging commerciality, resulted in a runaway smash. It topped the UK chart and, by the end of that year alone, global sales had totalled six million. Despite an eight-month gap between releases, Mungo Jerry's second single, 'Baby Jump', also reached number 1. By this time Mike Cole had been replaced by John Godfrey and the group's jug band sound had grown appreciably heavier. A third hit, in 1971, 'Lady Rose', showed a continued grasp of melody (the maxi-single also included the controversial 'Have A Whiff On Me' which was banned by the BBC). This successful year concluded with another Top 20 release, 'You Don't Have To Be In The Army To Fight In The War'. Paul King and Colin Earl left the group in 1972 and together with bassist Joe Rush, an early member of Mungo Jerry, formed the King Earl Boogie Band. Dorset released a solo album, *Cold Blue Excursions* prior to convening a new line-up with John Godfrey, Jon Pope (piano) and Tim Reeves (drums). The new line-up scored another Top 3 hit in 1973 with 'Alright Alright Alright', but the following year the overtly sexist 'Longlegged Woman Dressed In Black' became the group's final chart entry. Dorset continued to work with various versions of his creation into the 80s, but was never able to regain the group's early profile. A short-lived collaboration with Peter Green and Vincent Crane under the name Katmundu resulted in a rather disappointing album, *A Case For The Blues* (1986), but Ray did achieve further success when he produced 'Feels Like I'm In Love' for singer Kelly Marie. This former Mungo b-side became a UK number 1 in August 1980.

Albums: *Mungo Jerry* (1970), *Electronically Tested* (1971), *You Don't Have To Be In The Army To Fight In The War* (1971), *Boot Power* (1972), *Long Legged Woman* (1974), *Impala Saga* (1976), *Lovin' In The Alleys, Fightin' In The Streets* (1977), *Ray Dorset And Mungo Jerry* (1978), *Six Aside* (1979), *Together Again* (1981). Compilations: *Greatest Hits* (1973), *Golden Hour* (1974), *File* (1977), *The Early Years* (1992). Solo albums: Ray Dorset *Cold Blue Excursion* (1972); Paul King *Been In The Pen Too Long* (1972); the King Earl Boogie Band *Trouble At Mill* (1972).

Murray, Anne

b. 20 June 1946, Springhill, Nova Scotia, Canada. This doctor's daughter enjoyed local celebrity for her trained singing, which was accompanied by her own piano accompaniment. Nevertheless, she regarded music as a pastime when she graduated to New Brunswick University prior to a post as a physical training instructor at a Prince Edward Island school. In 1964 she was persuaded to audition for *Sing Along Jubilee*, a regional television show, but was selected instead for the same network's *Let's Go*, hosted by Bill Langstroth (her future husband). Income from a residency on the programme and solo concerts was sufficient for Murray to begin entertaining professionally in a vaguely folk/country rock style, though she could also acquit herself admirably with both R&B and mainstream pop material. Like Linda Ronstadt - seen by some as her US opposite number - she was mainly an interpreter of songs written by others. Issued by Arc Records, 1968's *What About Me*, created sufficient impact to interest Capitol Records, who signed her to a long term contract. From *This Was My Way*, an arrangement of Gene MacLellan's remarkable 'Snowbird', soared into *Billboard*'s Top 10 (and was also her biggest UK hit). Despite regular appearances on Glen Campbell's *Goodtime Hour* television series, subsequent releases - including the title track to *Talk It Over In The Morning* - sold only moderately until 1973 when she scored another smash hit with 'Danny's Song', composed by Kenny Loggins (with whom she duetted 11 years later on 'Nobody Loves Me Like You Do', a country chart-topper). Although finishing 1976 as *Billboard*'s second most successful female artist, family commitments necessitated a brief period of domesticity before 1978's 'You Needed Me' won her a Grammy award. While revivals of Bobby Darin's 'Things' and the Monkees' 'Daydream Believer' were aimed directly at the pop market, it was with the country audience that she proved most popular. 'He Thinks I Still Care' (originally a b-side) became her first country number 1. However, between 'Just Another Woman In Love', 'Could I Have This

Dance' (from the film *Urban Cowboy*), 1983's bold
'A Little Good News' and other country hits, she
had also recorded a collection of children's ditties
(*Hippo In My Tub*), commensurate with her
executive involvement with Canada's Save The
Children Fund. In 1989 Springhill's Anne Murray
Center was opened in recognition for her tireless
work for this charity.

Albums: *What About Me* (1968), *This Was My Way*
(1970), *Snowbird* (1970), *Anne Murray* (1971), *Talk
It Over In The Morning* (1971), *Annie* (1972), *Anne
Murray And Glen Campbell* (1972), *Danny's Song*
(1973), *Love Song* (1974), *Country* (1974), *Highly
Prized Possession* (1974), *Together* (1975), *Love Song*
(1975), *Keeping In Touch* (1976), *Let's Keep It That
Way* (1977), *Hippo In My Tub* (1979), *New Kind Of
Feeling* (1979), *I'll Always Love You* (1980),
Somebody's Waiting (1980), *Where Do You Go To
When You Dream* (1981), *Christmas Wishes* (1981),
The Hottest Night Of The Year (1982), *A Little Good
News* (1983), *Heart Over Mind* (1985), *Something To
Talk About* (1986), *Talk It Over In The Morning*
(1986), *Christmas Wishes* (1986), *Songs Of The Heart*
(1987), *Harmony* (1989). Compilations: *A Country
Collection* (1980), *Greatest Hits* (1980), *The Very Best
Of Anne Murray* (1981), *Special Collection* (1990).

N

Nash, Graham

b. 2 February 1942, Blackpool, Lancashire, England. Guitarist/vocalist Nash embraced music during the skiffle boom. He formed the Two Teens with classmate Allan Clarke in 1955, but by the following decade the duo, now known as Ricky And Dane, had joined local revue Kirk Stephens And The Deltas. In 1961 they broke away to found the Hollies, which evolved from provincial status into one of Britain's most popular 60s attractions with Nash's shrill voice cutting through their glorious harmony vocals. Although their early hits were drawn from outside sources, Nash, Clarke and guitarist Tony Hicks subsequently forged a prolific songwriting team. However, Graham's growing introspection, as demonstrated by 'King Midas In Reverse' (1967), was at odds with his partners' pop-based preferences and the following year he left to join 'supergroup' Crosby, Stills And Nash. Nash's distinctive nasal tenor instilled a sense of identity to the trio's harmonies, and although his compositional talent was viewed as lightweight by many commentators, 'Marrakesh Express' (originally written for the Hollies), 'Teach Your Children' and 'Just A Song Before I Go', were all highly successful when issued as singles. *Songs For Beginners* confirmed the artist's unpretentious, if naive style with material weaving political statements, notably 'Chicago', to personal confessions. Stellar support from his girlfriend Rita Coolidge, plus Jerry Garcia and Dave Mason brought precision to a set which silenced many of Nash's critics. However, the stark and dour *Wild Tales*, recorded following the murder of Nash's girlfriend Amy Gosage, proved less successful and not unnaturally lacked the buoyancy of its predecessor; nevertheless it contained some strong material, including 'Prison Song' and 'Another Sleep Song'. Graham then spent the remainder of the decade as half of Crosby And Nash, or participating in the parent group's innumerable reunions. He devoted considerable time and effort to charitable and political projects, including *No Nukes* and *M.U.S.E.*, but a regenerated solo career was undermined by the poor reception afforded *Earth And Sky*. Having completed a brief spell in a rejuvenated Hollies (1983), Nash resumed his on-off commitments to Crosby, Stills, Nash And Young and to date has only released one further solo effort. The perplexing *Innocent Eyes* matched Nash with modern technology: a surfeit of programmed drum machines. The record sounded synthesized and over-produced and was rejected by the critics and public. Nash's first love has always been CS&N, and history has shown that his best post-Hollies work has been unselfishly saved for group rather than solo activities. Nash's own stability has enabled him to help his colleagues through numerous problems; he takes much of the credit for David Crosby's recovery from drug addiction.

Albums: *Songs For Beginners* (1971), *Wild Tales* (1973), *Earth And Sky* (1980), *Innocent Eyes* (1986).

Further reading: *Crosby, Stills And Nash*, Dave Zimmer.

National Health

This group was formed in August 1975 by Phil Miller (guitar) and Dave Stewart (organ), former members of Hatfield And The North. Amanda Parsons (vocals), Alan Gowen (synthesizer), Mont Campbell (ex-Egg; bass) and Bill Bruford (ex-Yes and King Crimson; drums) completed the group's original line-up, but the following year Neil Murray joined in place of Campbell who had opted for session work. National Health continued the quintessential English progressive rock style forged by Soft Machine, Caravan and Matching Mole, but despite judicious live appearances, failed to reap the same commercial rewards. Pip Pyle replaced Bruford prior to the recording of *National Health*, but further changes in the unit's line-up preceded *Of Queues And Cures*. Such instability doomed the group's commercial progress, although they remained a popular live attraction until the end of the decade. Stewart subsequently enjoyed a successful solo career recreating classic 60s singles with singers Colin Blunstone and Barbara Gaskin, in turn confirming the demise of National Health as a serious proposition. Despite continued interest from the Continent, the group was then disbanded.

Albums: *National Health* (1978), *Of Queues And Cures* (1978), *D.S. Al Coda* (1982).

Nazareth

Formed in 1968 in Dunfermline, Fife, Scotland, Nazareth evolved out of local attraction, the Shadettes. Dan McCafferty (vocals), Manny Charlton (guitar), Pete Agnew (bass) and Darrell Sweet (drums) took their new name from the opening line in 'The Weight', a contemporary hit

Graham Nash

for the Band. After completing a gruelling Scottish tour, Nazareth opted to move to London. *Nazareth* and *Exercises* showed undoubted promise, while a third set, *Razamanaz*, spawned two UK Top 10 singles in 'Broken Down Angel' and 'Bad Bad Boy' (both 1973). New producer Roger Glover helped focus the quartet's brand of melodic hard-rock, and such skills were equally prevalent on *Loud 'N' Proud*. An unlikely rendition of Joni Mitchell's 'This Flight Tonight' gave the group another major chart entry, while the Charlton-produced *Hair Of The Dog* confirmed Nazareth as an international attraction. Another cover version, this time of Tomorrow's 'My White Bicycle', was a Top 20 entry and although *Rampant* did not yield a single, the custom-recorded 'Love Hurts', originally a hit for the Everly Brothers, proved highly successful in the US and Canada. Nazareth's popularity remained undiminished throughout the 70s but, having tired of a four-piece line-up, they added guitarist Zal Cleminson, formerly of the Sensational Alex Harvey Band, for *No Mean City*. Still desirous for change, the group invited Jeff 'Skunk' Baxter, late of Steely Dan and the Doobie Brothers, to produce *Malice In Wonderland*. While stylistically different from previous albums, the result was artistically satisfying. Contrasting ambitions then led to Cleminson's amicable departure, but the line-up was subsequently augmented by former Spirit keyboard player, John Locke. Baxter also produced the experimental *The Fool Circle*, while the group's desire to capture their in-concert fire resulted in *'Snaz*. Glasgow guitarist Billy Rankin had now joined the group, but dissatisfaction with touring led to Locke's departure following *2XS*. Rankin then switched to keyboards, but although Nazareth continued to enjoy popularity in the US and Europe, their stature in the UK was receding. Bereft of a major recording deal, Nazareth suspended their career during the late 80s, leaving McCafferty free to pursue solo ambitions. A comeback album in 1992 with the addition of Billy Rankin produced the outstanding *No Jive*, yet Nazareth's past low profile in the UK will demand a lot of live work to capitalize on this success.

Albums: *Nazareth* (1971), *Exercises* (1972), *Razamanaz* (1973), *Loud 'N' Proud* (1974), *Rampant* (1974), *Hair Of The Dog* (1975), *Close Enough For Rock 'N' Roll* (1976), *Play 'N' The Game* (1976), *Expect No Mercy* (1977), *No Mean City* (1978), *Malice In Wonderland* (1980), *The Fool Circle* (1981), *'Snaz* (1981), *2XS* (1982), *Sound Elixir* (1983), *The Catch* (1984), *Play The Game* (1985), *No Jive* (1992). Compilations: *Greatest Hits* (1975), *Hot Tracks* (1976), *20 Greatest Hits: Nazareth* (1985), *Anthology: Nazareth* (1988).

Nesmith, Michael

b. Robert Michael Nesmith, 30 December 1942, Houston, Texas, USA. Although best-known as a member of the Monkees, Nesmith enjoyed a prolific career in music prior to this group's inception. During the mid-60s folk boom he performed with bassist John London as Mike and John, but later pursed work as a solo act. Two singles, credited to Michael Blessing, were completed under the aegis of New Christy Minstrels' mastermind Randy Sparks, while Nesmith's compositions, 'Different Drum' and 'Mary Mary' were recorded, respectively, by the Stone Poneys and Paul Butterfield. Such experience gave the artist confidence to demand the right to determine the Monkees' musical policy and his sterling country-rock performances were the highlight of the group's varied catalogue. In 1968 he recorded *The Witchita Train Whistle Sings*, an instrumental set, but his independent aspirations did not fully flourish until 1970 when he formed the First National Band. Former colleague London joined Orville 'Red' Rhodes (pedal steel) and John Ware (drums) in a group completing three exceptional albums which initially combined Nashville-styled country to the leader's acerbic pop, (*Magnetic South*), but later grew to encompass a grander, even eccentric interpretation of the genre (*Nevada Fighter*). The band disintegrated during the latter's recording and a Second National Band, on which Nesmith and Rhodes were accompanied by Johnny Meeks (bass; ex-Gene Vincent and Merle Haggard) and Jack Panelli (drums), completed the less impressive *Tantamount To Treason*. The group was disbanded entirely for the sarcastically-entitled *And The Hits Just Keep On Comin'*, a haunting, largely acoustic, set regarded by many as the artist's finest work. In 1972 he founded the Countryside label under the aegis of Elektra Records, but despite critically-acclaimed sets by Iain Matthews, Garland Frady and the ever-present Rhodes, the project was axed in the wake of boardroom politics. The excellent *Pretty Much Your Standard Ranch Stash* ended the artist's tenure with RCA, following which he founded a second label, Pacific Arts. *The Prison*, an allegorical narrative which came replete with a book, was highly criticized upon release, although recent opinion has lauded its ambition. Nesmith reasserted his commercial status in 1977 when 'Rio', culled from *From A Radio Engine To The Photon Wing*, reached the UK Top 30. The attendant video signalled a growing interest in the visual arts which flourished following *Infinite Rider On The Big Dogma*, his biggest selling US release. In 1982 *Elephant Parts* won the first ever Grammy for a video, while considerable acclaim was engendered by a subsequent series, *Michael Nesmith In Television Parts*, and the film *Repo Man*, which the artist financed. Having refused entreaties to join the Monkees' 20th Anniversary Tour, this articulate entrepreneur continues to pursue his various diverse interests including a highly successful video production company (Pacific Arts), while rumours of new recordings continue to proliferate.

Albums: *The Wichita Train Whistle Sings* (1968), *Magnetic South* (1970), *Loose Salute* (1971), *Nevada Fighter* (1971), *Tantamount To Treason* (1972), *And The Hits Just Keep On Comin'* (1972), *Pretty Much Your Standard Ranch Stash* (1973), *The Prison* (1975), *From A Radio Engine To The Photon Wing* (1977), *Live At The Palais* (1978), *Infinite Rider On The Big Dogma* (1979). Compilations: *The Best Of Mike Nesmith* (1977), *The Newer Stuff* (1989).

New Riders Of The Purple Sage

Formed in 1969 the New Riders was initially envisaged as a part-time spin-off from the Grateful Dead. Group members Jerry Garcia (pedal steel guitar), Phil Lesh (bass) and Mickey Hart (drums) joined John Dawson (b. 1945, San Francisco, California, USA; guitar/vocals) and David Nelson (b. San Francisco, California, USA; guitar), mutual associates from San Francisco's once-thriving traditional music circuit. Although early live appearances were viewed as an informal warm-up to the main attraction, the New Riders quickly established an independent identity through the strength of Dawson's original songs. They secured a recording deal in 1971, by which time Dave Torbert had replaced Lesh, and Spencer Dryden (b. 7 April 1943, New York City, New York, USA), formerly of Jefferson Airplane, was installed as the group's permanent drummer. *New Riders Of The Purple Sage* blended country-rock with hippie idealism, yet emerged as a worthy companion to the parent act's lauded *American Beauty*. Sporting one of the era's finest cover's (from the renowned Kelley/Mouse studio), the stand-out track was 'Dirty Business'. This lengthy 'acid country' opus that featured some memorable guitar feedback. The final link with the Dead was severed when an over-committed Garcia made way for newcomer Buddy Cage (b. Canada). *Powerglide* introduced the

punchier, more assertive sound the group now pursued which brought commercial rewards with the highly popular *The Adventures Of Panama Red*. Torbert left the line-up following *Home, Home On The Road* and was replaced by Skip Battin, formerly of the Byrds. In 1978 Dryden relinquished his drumstool in order to manage the band; while sundry musicians then joined and left, Dawson and Nelson remained at the helm until 1981. The New Riders were dissolved following the disastrous *Feelin' Alright*, although the latter musician subsequently resurrected the name with Gary Vogenson (guitar) and Rusty Gautier (bass). Nelson meanwhile resumed his association with the Dead in the Jerry Garcia Acoustic Band, and supervised several archive New Riders sets for the specialist Relix label.

Albums: *New Riders Of The Purple Sage* (1971), *Powerglide* (1972), *Gypsy Cowboy* (1972), *The Adventures Of Panama Red* (1973), *Home, Home On The Road* (1974), *Brujo* (1974), *Oh, What A Mighty Time* (1975), *New Riders* (1976), *Who Are These Guys* (1977), *Marin County Line* (1978), *Feelin' Alright* (1981), *Friend Of The Devil* (1991). Compilations: *The Best Of The New Riders Of The Purple Sage* (1976), *Before Time Began* (1976), *Vintage NRPS* (1988).

New Seekers

Ex-Seeker Keith Potger's television appearances with the trendier New Edition, in 1970, left a peculiar aftertaste for the old quartet's fans. Wisely, he retreated to the less public role of manager, leaving the stage to Eve Graham (b. 19 April 1943, Perth, Scotland), Lyn Paul (b. 16 February 1949, Manchester, England) - both former Nocturnes - Peter Doyle (b. 28 July 1949, Melbourne, Australia), Paul Layton (b. 4 August 1947, Beaconsfield, England) and Marty Kristian (b. 27 May 1947, Leipzig, Germany), a Latvian who had been raised in Australia. The male contingent played guitars in concert but the act's main strengths were its interweaving vocal harmonies and a clean, winsome image. Their entertainments also embraced dance and comedy routines. Initially they appealed to US consumers who thrust a cover of Melanie's 'Look What They've Done To My Song Ma' and 'Beautiful People' - all unsuccessful in Britain - high up the *Billboard* Hot 100. A UK breakthrough came with 'Never Ending Song Of Love' which reached number 2, and, even better, a re-write of a Coca-Cola commercial, 'I'd Like To Teach The World To Sing', topping foreign charts too, and overtaking the Hillside Singers' original

New Riders Of The Purple Sage

New Seekers

version in the States. Their Eurovision Song Contest entry, 'Beg Steal Or Borrow' and the title track of 1972's *Circles* were also hits, but revivals of the Fleetwoods' 'Come Softly To Me' and Eclection's 'Nevertheless' were among 1973 singles whose modest Top 40 placings were hard-won, though the year ended well with another UK number 1 in 'You Won't Find Another Fool Like Me'. With its follow-up, 'I Get A Little Sentimental Over You' likewise hurtling upwards in spring 1974, the five disbanded with a farewell tour of Britain. Two years later, however, the lure of a CBS contract brought about a reformation - minus Lyn Paul who had had a minor solo hit in 1975 - but no subsequent single could reconjure a more glorious past and, not-so-New anymore, the group broke up for the last time in 1978.

Albums: *Beautiful People* (1971), *We'd Like To Teach The World To Sing* (1971, US issue), *New Colours* (1972), *We'd Like To Teach The World To Sing* (1972, UK issue), *Never Ending Song Of Love* (1972), *Circles* (1972), *Now* (1973), *Pinball Wizards* (1973), *Together* (1974). Compilations: *15 Great Hits* (1983), *The Best Of The New Seekers* (1985), *Greatest Hits* (1987).

New York Dolls

One of the most influential rock bands of the last 20 years, the New York Dolls pre-dated the punk and sleaze-metal movements which followed long after their own demise. Formed in 1972, the line-up stabilized with David Johansen (vocals), Johnny Thunders (guitar), Arthur Harold Kane (bass), Sylvain Sylvain (guitar/piano) and Jerry Nolan (drums), the last two having replaced Rick Rivets and Billy Murcia (who died in November 1972). The band sported an outrageous, glam-rock image: lipstick, high-heels and tacky leather outfits being the norm. Underneath, they were a first rate rock 'n' roll band, dragged up on the music of Stooges, Rolling Stones and MC5. Their self-titled debut, released in 1973, is a minor landmark in rock history, oozing attitude, vitality and controversy from every note. It was met with widespread critical acclaim, but this never transferred to commercial success. The follow-up, *Too Much Too Soon*, was an appropriate title and indicated that alcohol and drugs were beginning to take their toll. The album is a charismatic collection of punk/glam-rock anthems, delivered with a chaotic coolness, that has yet to be equalled. It received a unanimous thumbs down from the music press and the band began to implode shortly afterwards. Johansen embarked on a solo career and Thunders formed Heartbreakers. The Dolls continued for a short time with Blackie Lawless (now W.A.S.P.'s

New York Dolls

vocalist) on guitar, before eventually grinding to a halt in 1975. Jerry Nolan died as a result of a stroke on 14 January 1992 whilst undergoing treatment for pneumonia and meningitis. *Red Patent Leather* is a poor quality and posthumously-released live recording from May 1975.

Albums: *New York Dolls* (1973), *Too Much Too Soon* (1974), *Red Patent Leather* (1984). Compilation: *Lipstick Killers* (1983).

Newton-John, Olivia

b. 26 September 1948, Cambridge, England. Her showbusiness career began when she won a local contest to find 'the girl who looked most like Hayley Mills' in 1960 after the Newton-Johns had emigrated to Australia. Later she formed the Sol Four with schoolfriends. Though this vocal group disbanded, the encouragement of customers who heard her sing solo in a cafe led her to enter - and win - a television talent show. The prize was a 1966 holiday in London during which she recorded her debut single, Jackie De Shannon's 'Till You Say You'll Be Mine' after a stint in a duo with Pat Carroll. Staying on in England, Olivia became part of Toomorrow, a group created by bubblegum-pop potentate Don Kirshner, to fill the gap in the market left by the disbanded Monkees (not to be confused with Tomorrow). As well as a science-fiction movie and its soundtrack, Toomorrow was also responsible for 'I Could Never Live Without Your Love,' a 1970 single, produced by the Shadows' Bruce Welch - with whom Olivia was romantically linked. Although Toomorrow petered out, Newton-John's link with Cliff Richard and the Shadows was a source of enduring professional benefit. A role in a Richard movie, tours as special guest in *The Cliff Richard Show*, and a residency - as an comedienne as well as a singer - on BBC television's *It's Cliff!* guaranteed steady sales of her first album, and the start of a patchy British chart career with a Top 10 arrangement of Bob Dylan's 'If Not For You' in 1971. More typical of her output were singles such as 'Take Me Home Country Roads',penned by John Denver, 'Banks Of The Ohio' and, from the late John Rostill of the Shadows, 1973's 'Let Me Be There'. This last release sparked off by an appearance on the USA's *The Dean Martin Show* and crossed from the US country charts to the Hot 100, winning her a controversial Grammy for Best Female Country Vocal. After an uneasy performance in 1974's Eurovision Song Contest, Newton-John became omnipresent in North America, first as its most popular country artist, though her standing in pop improved considerably after a chart-topper with 'I Honestly Love You,'

Olivia Newton-John

produced by John Farrar, another latter-day Shadow (and husband of the earlier mentioned Pat Carroll), who had assumed the task after the estrangement of Olivia and Bruce.

Newton-John also became renowned for her duets with other artists, notably in the movie of the musical 'Grease' in which she and co-star John Travolta featured 'You're The One That I Want'. This irresistibly effervescent song became one of the most successful UK hit singles in pop history, topping the charts for a stupendous nine weeks. The follow-up, 'Summer Nights' was also a UK number 1 in 1978. Her 'Xanadu', the film's title opus with the Electric Light Orchestra, was another global number 1. However, not such a money-spinner was a further cinema venture with Travolta (1983's 'Two Of A Kind'). Neither was 'After Dark,' a single with the late Andy Gibb in 1980 nor *Now Voyager* a 1984 album with his brother Barry. With singles like 'Physical' (1981) and the 1986 album *Soul Kiss* on Mercury Records she adopted a more raunchy image in place of her original perky wholesomeness.

During the late 80s/early 90s much of her time was spent,along with Pat (Carroll) Farrar, running her Australian-styled clothing business, Blue Koala. Following *The Rumour*, Olivia signed to Geffen for the release of a collection of children's songs and rhymes, *Warm And Tender*. The award of an OBE preceded her marriage to actor and dancer Matt Lattanzi; she remains a showbusiness evergreen although this was clouded in July 1992, when it was announced that she is undergoing treatment for cancer.

Albums: *If Not For You* (1971), *Let Me Be There* (1973), *Olivia Newton-John* (1973), *If You Love Me Let Me Know* (1974), *Music Makes My Day* (1974), *Long Live Love* (1974), *Have You Never Been Mellow?* (1975), *Clearly Love* (1975), *Come On Over* (1976), *Don't Stop Believin'* (1976), *Making A Good Thing Better* (1977), with various artists *Grease* (1978, film soundtrack), *Totally Hot* (1978), with the Electric Light Orchestra *Xanadu* (1980, film soundtrack), *Physical* (1981), with various artists *Two Of A Kind* (1983, film soundtrack), *Soul Kiss* (1986), *The Rumour* (1988), *Warm And Tender* (1990). Compilations: *Olivia Newton-John's Greatest Hits* (1977, US MCA issue), *Greatest Hits* i (1978, UK EMI issue), *Olivia's Greatest Hits, Volume 2* (1982, US MCA issue), *Greatest Hits* ii (1982, UK EMI issue).

Nicholas, Paul

Actor/singer Nicholas served a musical apprenticeship as pianist with Screaming Lord Sutch and the Savages. Then known as Paul Dean, he embarked on a singing career in 1964, but later changed his name to Oscar when this venture proved unsuccessful. Despite access to exclusive songs by Pete Townshend ('Join My Gang') and David Bowie ('Over The Wall We Go' - a comment on a contemporary rash of prison outbreaks), this second appellation brought no commercial comfort. However, it was during this period that the artist began his long association with manager Robert Stigwood, and he developed a career in pop musicals, appearing in some of the best onstage productions of the era. His debut in the love/rock musical *Hair* was followed by *Jesus Christ Superstar*. He appeared in Ken Russell's *Lisztomania* and had a major role in the film *Stardust,* starring David Essex. His recent stage appearances have been in *Cats* and the less-than - triumphant *Pirates*. Prior to that Nicholas finally achieved pop single success with several disco-style numbers for his mentor's RSO label. 'Dancing With The Captain' and 'Grandma's Party' reached the UK Top 10 in 1976, but his musical career increasingly took a subordinate role to thespian ambitions. Nicholas has since become a highly popular actor on television, performing light comedy and dramatic roles with confidence.

Albums: *Paul Nicholas* (1977), *Just Good Friends* (1986).

Nightingale, Maxine

b. 2 November 1952, Wembley, London, England. Although Maxine made her recording debut in 1968, early acclaim was garnered from a series of roles in the stage productions of *Hair, Jesus Christ Superstar* and *Godspell*. She resumed a solo career during the 70s, scoring an international hit with the compulsive 'Right Back Where We Started From'. This infectious performance, featured heavily in Paul Newman's cult movie *Slapshot*, reached number 8 in the UK and number 2 in the US, but although 'Love Hit Me' also reached the UK Top 20, the singer was unable to sustain consistent success. 'Lead Me On', a flop at home, climbed to number 5 in the USA in 1979, but proved to be her last substantial release.

Albums: *Right Back Where We Started From* (1976), *Love Hit Me* (1977), *Night Life* (1977), *Love Lines* (1978), *Lead Me On* (1979), *Bittersweet* (1981), *It's A Beautiful Thing* (1982).

Nilsson

b. Harry Edward Nelson, 15 June 1941, Brooklyn,

Paul Nicholas

New York, USA. Nelson moved to Los Angeles as an adolescent and later undertook a range of different jobs before accepting a supervisor's position at the Security First National Bank. He nonetheless pursued a concurrent interest in music, recording demos of his early compositions which were then touted around the city's publishing houses. Producer Phil Spector drew on this cache of material, recording 'Paradise' and 'Here I Sit' with the Ronettes and 'This Could Be The Night' with the Modern Folk Quartet. None of these songs was released contemporaneously, but such interest inspired the artist's own releases for the Tower label. These singles - credited to 'Nilsson' - included 'You Can't Take Your Love Away From Me' and 'Good Times' (both 1966). The following year the Yardbirds recorded his 'Ten Little Indians', and Nilsson finally gave up his bank job upon hearing the Monkees' version of another composition, 'Cuddly Toy', on the radio. He secured a contract with RCA Records and made his album debut with the impressive *Pandemonium Shadow Show*. The selection was not only notable for Nilsson's remarkable three-octave voice, it also featured 'You Can't Do That', an enthralling montage of Beatles' songs which drew considerable praise from John Lennon and inspired their subsequent friendship. The artist's own compositions continued to find favour with other acts; the Turtles recorded 'The Story Of Rock 'N' Roll', Herb Alpert and Blood, Sweat And Tears covered 'Without Her', while Three Dog Night enjoyed a US chart-topper and gold disc with 'One'. Nilsson's own version of the last-named song appeared on *Ariel Ballet* - a title derived from his grandparents' circus act - which also included the singer's rendition of Fred Neil's 'Everybody's Talking'. This haunting recording was later adopted as the theme to the film *Midnight Cowboy* and gave Nilsson his first US Top 10 hit. *Harry* included 'The Puppy Song', later a smash for David Cassidy, while *Nilsson Sings Newman* comprised solely Randy Newman material and featured the songwriter on piano. This project was followed by *The Point*, the soundtrack to a full-length animated television feature, but Nilsson's greatest success came with *Nilsson Schmilsson* and its attendant single, 'Without You'. His emotional rendition of this Badfinger-composed song sold in excess of 1 million copies, topping both the US and UK charts and garnering a 1972 Grammy for Best Male Pop and Rock Vocal Performance. Having completed the similarly-styled *Son Of Schmilsson*, this idiosyncratic performer confounded

expectations with *A Little Touch Of Schmilsson In The Night,* which comprised beautifully orchestrated standards including 'Makin' Whoopee' and 'As Time Goes By'. Nilsson's subsequent career was blighted by well-publicized drinking with acquaintances John Lennon, Keith Moon and Ringo Starr. Lennon produced Nilsson's *Pussy Cats* (1974), an anarchic set fuelled by self-indulgence, which comprised largely pop classics, including 'Subterranean Homesick Blues', 'Save The Last Dance For Me' and 'Rock Around The Clock'. Starr meanwhile assisted the artist on his film soundtrack, *Son Of Dracula*. Ensuing releases proved inconsistent, although a 1976 adaptation of *The Point*, staged at London's Mermaid Theatre, was highly successful, and marked the reunion of former Monkees Davy Jones and Mickey Dolenz. By the 80s Nilsson had largely retired from music altogether, preferring to pursue business interests, the most notable of which was a film distribution company based in California's Studio City. However, in 1988 RCA released *A Touch More Schmilsson In The Night* which, in common with its 1973 predecessor, offered the singer's affectionate renditions of popular favourites, including two of E.Y. Harburg's classics, 'It's Only a Paper Moon' and 'Over The Rainbow'. The unyielding paradox of Nilsson's career is that despite achieving recognition as a superior songwriter, his best-known and most successful records were penned by other acts.
Albums: *Pandemonium Shadow Show* (1967), *Ariel Ballet* (1968), *Harry* (1969), *Skidoo* (1969, film soundtrack), *Nilsson Sings Newman* (1970), *The Point* (1971), *Nilsson Schmilsson* (1971), *Son Of Schmilsson* (1972), *A Little Touch Of Schmilsson In The Night* (1973), *Son Of Dracula* (1974), *Duit On Mon Dei* (1975), *The Sandman* (1975), *That's The Way It Is* (1976), *Knillssonn* (1977), *Night After Night* (1979), *Flash Harry* (1980), *A Touch More Schmilsson In The Night* (1988). Compilations: *Early Years* (c.1970), *Ariel Pandemonium Ballet* (1973), *Early Tymes* (1977), *Nilsson's Greatest Music* (1978), *Harry And...* (1979), *Diamond Series: Nilsson* (1988).

Nolans

This highly-popular Irish family group featured Tommy, Anne, Denise, Maureen (b. 14 June 1954), Brian, Linda (b. 23 February 1959), Bernadette (b. 17 October 1960) and Coleen Nolan. The Nolans lived in Dublin until 1962 when they emigrated to Blackpool. Parents Tommy and Maureen Nolan were singers and gradually brought their offspring into the act. In

Nolans

1963 the entire family debuted as 'the Singing Nolans'. The girls later decided to turn professional and, after recording a Christmas EP, issued their debut album in 1980. After moving to London, the group was streamlined to Anne, Denise, Linda, Bernadette and young Maureen. Their act proved very popular on UK television and variety shows. After recording a second album in 1977 and touring America with Engelbert Humperdinck, Denise decided to pursue a solo career. Continuing as a quartet, the sisters signed to CBS and were widely tipped to represent the UK in the Eurovision Song Contest but lost out to Black Lace. After a minor hit single with 'Spirit Body And Soul', Anne married and left the group. She was replaced by the younger sister, Denise, and the quartet changed their name from the Nolan Sisters to the Nolans. A massive hit with the catchy 'I'm In The Mood For Dancing' brought them worldwide renown and even topped the charts in Japan. Further UK Top 10 hits followed with 'Gotta Pull Myself Together' and 'Attention To Me'. Meanwhile, Linda married former Harmony Grass drummer Brian Hudson and retired from the group. She was replaced by Anne, who had left two years earlier. Phenomenal success in Japan and Eire coincided with further minor chart appearances in the UK, as well as best-selling albums. Coleen, Bernadette and Denise have each recorded solo singles, while Linda and Coleen enjoyed a minor hit as the Young And Moody Band with 'Don't Do That'.

Albums: *The Singing Nolans* (1972), *The Nolan Sisters* (1977), *20 Giant Hits* (1978), *Best Of The Nolan Sisters Vol. 1* (1979), *Best Of The Nolan Sisters Vol 2* (1979), *Nolan Sisters* (1979), *The Nolan Sisters Collection* (1980), *Making Waves* (1980), *Portrait* (1982), *Altogether* (1982), *Harmony* (1983), *I'm In The Mood For Dancing* (1983), *Girls Just Wanna Have Fun* (1984), *Love Songs* (1985), *Tenderly* (1986).

Nucleus

The doyen of British jazz-rock groups, Nucleus was formed in 1969 by trumpeter Ian Carr. He was joined by Chris Spedding (guitar, ex-Battered Ornaments), John Stanley Marshall (drums) and Karl Jenkins (keyboards). The quartet was signed to the distinctive progressive outlet, Vertigo, and their debut, *Elastic Rock*, is arguably their exemplary work. The same line-up completed *We'll Talk About It Later*, but Spedding's subsequent departure heralded a bewildering succession of changes which undermined the group's potential. Carr nonetheless remained its driving force, a factor reinforced when *Solar Plexus*, a collection the trumpeter had intended as a solo release, became the unit's third album. In 1972 both Jenkins and Marshall left the group to join fellow fusion act, Soft Machine, and Nucleus became an inadvertent nursery for this 'rival' ensemble. Later members Roy Babbington and Alan Holdsworth also defected, although Carr was able to maintain an individuality despite such damaging interruptions. Subsequent albums, however, lacked the innovatory purpose of those first releases and Nucleus was dissolved during the early 80s. Nucleus took the jazz/rock genre further into jazz territory with skill, melody and a tremendous standard of musicianship. Their first three albums are vital in any comprehensive collection.

Albums: *Elastic Rock* (1970), *We'll Talk About It later* (1970), *Solar Plexus* (1971), *Belladonna* (1972), *Labyrinth* (1973), *Roots* (1973), *Under The Sun* (1974), *Snake Hips Etcetera* (1975), *Direct Hits* (1976), *In Flagrante Delicto* (1978), *Out Of The Long Dark* (1979), *Awakening* (1980), *Live At The Theaterhaus* (1985).

Nugent, Ted

b. 13 December 1949, Detroit, Michigan, USA. Excited by 50s rock 'n' roll, Nugent taught himself the rudiments of guitar playing at the age of 8. As a teenager he played in the Royal Highboys and Lourds, but this formative period ended in 1964 upon his family's move to Chicago. Here, Nugent assembled the Amboy Dukes, which evolved from garage-band status into a popular, hard-rock attraction. He led the group throughout its various permutations, assuming increasing control as original members dropped out of the line-up. In 1974 a revitalized unit - dubbed Ted Nugent And The Amboy Dukes - completed the first of two albums for Frank Zappa's Discreet label, but in 1976 the guitarist abandoned the now-anachronistic suffix and embarked on a fully-fledged solo career. Derek St. Holmes (guitar), Rob Grange (bass) and Cliff Davies (drums) joined him for *Ted Nugent* and *Free For All*, both of which maintained the high-energy rock of previous incarnations. However, it was as a live attraction that Nugent made his mark - he often claimed to have played more gigs per annum than any other artist or group. Ear-piecing guitar work and vocals - 'If it's too loud you're too old' ran one tour motto - were accompanied by a cultivated 'wild man' image, where the artist would appear in loin-cloth and headband, brandishing the bow and arrow with which he claimed to hunt food for his family. The aggression of a Nugent concert was captured on the platinum selling *Double Live Gonzo*, which featured many of his best-loved stage numbers, including 'Cat Scratch Fever', 'Motor City Madness' and the enduring 'Baby Please Don't Go'. Charlie Huhn (guitar) and John Sauter (bass) replaced St. Holmes and Grange for *Weekend Warriors*, and the same line-up remained intact for *State Of Shock* and *Scream Dream*. In 1981 Nugent undertook a worldwide tour fronting a new backing group, previously known as the D.C. Hawks, comprising of Mike Gardner (bass), Mark Gerhardt (drums) and three guitarists; Kurt, Rick and Verne Wagoner. The following year the artist left Epic for Atlantic Records, and in the process established a new unit which included erstwhile sidemen Derek St. Holmes (vocals) and Carmine Appice (drums; ex-Vanilla Fudge). Despite such changes, Nugent was either unwilling, or unable, to alter the formula which had served him so well in the 70s. Successive solo releases offered little new and the artist drew greater publicity for appearances on talk shows and celebrity events. In 1989 Nugent teamed up with Tommy Shaw (vocals/guitar, ex-Styx), Jack Blades (bass, ex-Night Ranger) and Michael Cartellone (drums) to form the successful 'supergroup', Damn Yankees.

Albums: with the Amboy Dukes *Call Of The Wild* (1973), *Tooth, Fang And Claw* (1974), solo *Ted Nugent* (1975), *Free For All* (1976), *Cat Scratch Fever* (1977), *Double Live Gonzo* (1978), *Weekend Warriors* (1978), *State Of Shock* (1979), *Scream Dream* (1980), *Intensities In Ten Cities* (1981), *Nugent* (1982), *Penetrator* (1984), *Little Miss Dangerous* (1986), *If You Can't Lick 'Em...Lick 'Em* (1988). Compilations: *Great Gonzos: The Best Of Ted Nugent* (1981), *Anthology: Ted Nugent* (1986).

O

Ohio Players

Formed in Dayton, Ohio, USA in 1959, this multi-talented unit originated from three members of the Ohio Untouchables, Leroy 'Sugarfoot' Bonner, Clarence 'Satch' Satchell and Marshall Jones. They forged a reputation as a powerful instrumental group by providing the backing vocals to the Falcons, whose R&B classic, 'I Found A Love' (1962), featured singer Wilson Pickett. The Players began recording in their own right that same year, but did not achieve a notable success until the following decade when they embarked on a series of striking releases for the Westbound label after brief sessions for both Compass and Capitol Records. The group's experimental funk mirrored the work George Clinton had forged with Funkadelic for the same outlet and in 1973 the septet - Bonner, Satchell, Jones, Jimmy 'Diamond' Williams, Marvin 'Merv' Pierce, Billy Beck, Ralph 'Pee Wee' Middlebrook - scored a massive R&B hit with the irrepressible 'Funky Worm'. The Players later switched to Mercury where their US hits included 'Fire' (1974), 'Sweet Sticky Thing' and 'Love Rollercoaster' (1975), all of which topped the soul and pop charts. 'Who'd She Coo?' became the group's last substantial hit the following year and although success did continue throughout the rest of the 70s, their releases grew increasingly predictable. The group had become renowned for their sexually explicit album covers, however, their musical credibility was such that the unit's version of 'Over The Rainbow' was played at Judy Garland's funeral. Williams and Beck left the line-up in 1979 to form a new group Shadow. A re-shaped Ohio Players recorded throughout the 80s, and scored a minor soul hit in 1988 with 'Sweat'.
Albums: *First Impressions* (1968), *Observations In Time* (1968), *Pain* (1972), *Pleasure* (1973), *Ecstasy* (1973), *Skin Tight* (1974), *Climax* (1974, a collection of out-takes), *Fire* (1974), *Honey* (1975), *Contradiction* (1976), *Angel* (1977), *Mr. Mean* (1977), *Jass-Ay-Lay-Dee* (1978), *Everybody Up* (1979), *Tenderness* (1981), *Ouch!* (1982), *Graduation* (1985). Compilations: *Greatest Hits* (1975), *Rattlesnake* (1975), *Ohio Players Gold* (1976), *Ohio Players* (1977).

O'Jays

The core of this long-standing soul group, Eddie Levert (b. 16 June 1942) and Walter Williams (b. 25 August 1942), sang together as a gospel duo prior to forming the Triumphs in 1958. This doo-wop influenced quintet was completed by William Powell, Bill Isles and Bobby Massey and quickly grew popular around its hometown of Canton, Ohio. The same line-up then recorded as the Mascots before taking the name the O'Jays after Cleveland disc jockey Eddie O'Jay, who had given them considerable help and advice. Having signed to Imperial in 1963, the O'Jays secured their first hit with 'Lonely Drifter', which was followed by an imaginative reworking of Benny Spellman's 'Lipstick Traces' (1965) and 'Stand In For Love' (1966). Despite gaining their first R&B Top 10 entry with 'I'll Be Sweeter Tomorrow (Than I Was Today)' (1967), the group found it difficult to maintain a constant profile, and were cut to a four-piece following Isles' departure. In 1968 the group met producers (Kenny) Gamble And (Leon) Huff with whom they recorded, unsuccessfully, on the duo's short-lived Neptune label. The line-up was reduced further in 1972 when Bobby Massey left. Paradoxically the O'Jays then began their most fertile period when Gamble and Huff signed them to Philadelphia International. The vibrant 'Back Stabbers', a US Top 3 hit, established the group's style, but the preachy 'Love Train', with its plea for world harmony, established the 'protest' lyrics of later releases 'Put Your Hands Together' (1973) and 'For The Love Of Money' (1974). *Back Stabbers* is a classic album and arguably the finest cohesive example of Gamble And Huff's outstanding work.
In 1975 Sammy Strain joined the line-up from Little Anthony And The Imperials when ill health forced William Powell to retire from live performances. This founder member continued to record with the group until his death on 25 April 1976. 'Message In Our Music' (1976) and 'Use Ta Be My Girl' (1977) confirmed the O'Jays continued popularity as they survived many of Philly soul's changing fortunes. But as the genre felt the ravages of fashion so the group also suffered. The early 80s were commercially fallow, until *Love Fever* (1985) restated their direction with its blend of funk and rap. Two years later the O'Jays were unexpectedly back at the top of the soul chart with 'Lovin' You', confirming their position as one of soul music's most durable groups.
Albums: *Comin' Through* (1965), *Soul Sounds*

O'Jays

(1967), *O'Jays* (1967), *Full Of Soul* (1968), *Back On Top* (1968), *The O'Jays In Philadelphia* (1969), *Back Stabbers* (1972), *Ship Ahoy* (1973), *Live In London* (1974), *Survival* (1975), *Family Reunion* (1975), with the Moments *The O'Jays Meet The Moments* (1975), *Message In The Music* (1976), *Travelin' At The Speed Of Thought* (1977), *So Full Of Love* (1978), *Identify Yourself* (1979), *Year 2000* (1980), *My Favourite Person* (1982), *When When I See You Again* (1983), *Love And More* (1984), *Love Fever* (1985), *Close Company* (1985), *Let Me Touch You* (1987), *Serious* (1990), *Emotionally Yours* (1991). Compilations: *Collectors' Items* (1977), *Greatest Hits* (1984). *Working On Your Case* (1985), *From The Beginning* (1984), *Reflections In Gold 1973-1982* (1988).

Oldfield, Mike

b. 15 May 1953, Reading, Berkshire, England. Multi-instrumentalist Oldfield will forever be remembered for a piece of symphonic length music he wrote before his 20th birthday. *Tubular Bells* sold 12 million copies world-wide and topped the charts in the USA and UK, staying in both for more than five years. He began his career providing acoustic guitar accompaniment to folk songs sung by his older sister, Sally Oldfield, who would often appear in Reading's pubs and clubs with Marianne Faithfull. Mike and Sally recorded *Sallyangie* together before he left to join Kevin Ayers And The Whole World, with whom he played bass and guitar for a short period. He continued working on his own material and produced a demo of instrumental music which later became *Tubular Bells*. Several record companies rejected the piece but entrepreneur Richard Branson, the head of Virgin stores, recognized its marketing potential. He asked Oldfield to re-record the demo in the recently-acquired Manor Studios and it became one of Virgin's first releases. The 49-minute long piece was a series of basic melodies from folk, rock and classical sources which featured an array of different instruments, all played by Oldfield, and was introduced by guest master of ceremonies, Viv Stanshall. Excerpts from it were used in the horror film, *The Exorcist*, and a shortened version was released as a single in 1974.

On *Hergest Ridge* he attempted to capture Berkshire's pastoral beauty and largely succeeded, although matching the impact of *Tubular Bells* was clearly impossible and many critics dubbed the album 'Son of Tubular Bells' because of the similarity. It reached the top of the UK charts but,

like all his subsequent album releases, it did not chart in the USA. Along with arranger, Dave Bedford, a former collaborator of Kevin Ayers, he scored *Tubular Bells* and a version recorded by the Royal Philharmonic Orchestra was released in 1975. *Ommadawn* featured the uillean pipes playing of the Chieftains' Paddy Moloney and a team of African drummers. It sold well but the critical response was that his introspective music had become over-formularized over the three albums. Virgin also saw the records as complementary works and packaged them together in 1976 as *Boxed*. Oldfield had two consecutive Christmas hits in 1975 and 1976 with the traditional 'In Dulci Jubilo' and 'Portsmouth', played on the hornpipe and familiar to the UK public because of its use as theme tune to the children's' television programme, *Blue Peter*.

Around 1977-78, the shy, withdrawn Oldfield underwent a programme of self-assertiveness with the Exegesis method. The result was a complete reversal of personality and Oldfield took the opportunity in music press interviews to retaliate, almost to the point of parody, to accusations of limp, neo-hippy blandness and strongly defended himself against pillorying by the nascent punk movement. *Incantations* drew strongly on disco influences and *Exposed* was recorded at various concerts where Oldfield played with up to 50 other musicians. *Platinum*, *QE2* and *Five Miles Out* caught Oldfield slightly out of step with his contemporaries as he tried to hone his songwriting and avoid repeating himself. Hall And Oates recorded a version of 'Family Man', which had missed out as a single for Oldfield, and it became a Top 20 hit in the UK in 1983. Oldfield began working with soprano Maggie Reilly and she sang on the hit 'Moonlight Shadow' from *Crises*. After *Discovery* he wrote the music for the award-winning film *The Killing Fields*. On *Islands* he was joined by guest vocalists Bonnie Tyler, Kevin Ayers and Roger Chapman (Family/Chapman Whitney). Even though he was now writing to a more standard pop structure, Oldfield found himself no longer in vogue and his music was largely portrayed in the music press as anachronistic. *Earth Moving*, with contributions from Maggie Reilly, Anita Hegerland and Chris Thompson (ex-Manfred Mann) failed to challenge the prevailing modern view. It appears that *Tubular Bells* will always ring rather too loudly and diminish most of Oldfield's other work, certainly in terms of commercial acceptance, but he continues releasing records welcomed by a large cult following which apparently cares little about his low profile and the scarcity of live appearances. 1992 has found him working with Trevor Horn on *Tubular Bells II* to mark the 20th anniversary of the original album.

Albums: with Sally Oldfield *Sallyangie* (1968), *Tubular Bells* (1973), *Hergest Ridge* (1974), with the Royal Philharmonic Orchestra *The Orchestral Tubular Bells* (1975), *Ommadawn* (1975), *Incantations* (1978), *Exposed* (1979), *Platinum* (1979), *QE2* (1980), *Five Miles Out* (1982), *Crises* (1983), *Discovery* (1984), *The Killing Fields* (1984, film soundtrack), *Islands* (1987), *Earth Moving* (1989), *Amarok* (1990), *Heaven's Open* (1991). Compilations: *Boxed* (1976), *The Complete Mike Oldfield* (1985).

Osibisa

Formed in London in 1969 by three Ghanaian and three Caribbean musicians, Osibisa played a central role in developing an awareness of African music - in their case, specifically, West African highlife tinged with rock - among European and North American audiences in the 70s. Since then, Osibisa have suffered the fate of many once-celebrated 70s African-oriented performers. Their pioneering blend of rock and African rhythms has either been overlooked or downgraded for its lack of roots appeal. There is, in truth, some justification for this: Osibisa's style was too closely hitched to western rock to survive the passing of that lumbering wagon, and too much of a fusion to survive the scrutiny of western audiences who, from the early 80s onwards, were looking for 'authentic' African music. But the group's towering achievements in the 70s should not be denigrated. The Ghanaian founder members of Osibisa - Teddy Osei (saxophone), Sol Amarfio (drums) and Mac Tontoh (trumpet, Osei's brother) - were seasoned members of the Accra highlife scene before they moved to London to launch their attack on the world stage. Osei and Amaflio had played in the Star Gazers, a top Ghanaian highlife band, before setting up the Comets, who scored a large West African hit with their 1958 single 'Pete Pete'. Tontoh was also a member of the Comets, before joining the Uhuru Dance Band, one of the first outfits to bring elements of jazz into Ghanaian highlife.

The other founder members of Osibisa were Spartacus R, a Grenadian bass player, Robert Bailey (b. Trinidad; keyboards) and Wendel Richardson (b. Antigua; lead guitar). They were joined soon after their formation by the Ghanaian

percussionist Potato. In 1962, Osei moved to London, where he was eventually given a scholarship by the Ghanaian government to study music. In 1964, he formed Cat's Paw, an early blueprint for Osibisa which blended highlife, rock and soul. In 1969, feeling the need for more accomplished African musicians within the line-up, he persuaded Tontoh and Amarfio to join him in London, where towards the end of the year Osibisa was born. The venture proved to be an immediate success, with the single 'Music For Gong Gong' a substantial hit in 1970 (three other singles would later make the British Top 10: 'Sunshine Day', 'Dance The Body Music' and 'Coffee Song'). Osibisa's self-titled debut album in 1971 also scored heavily. The timing of its release was fortuitous: rock music, after having been revitalized in the 60s, was in a creative slump, demanding passive, sometimes catatonic audiences for whom dancing was not only uncool but in many cases physically impossible, such was the extent of the fashionable ingestion of narcotic substances. Disco had yet to make its mark. Osibisa stepped into the breach with a music whose rock references, in the guitar solos and chord structures, combined with vibrant African cross rhythms to attract an immediate public response. Osibisa became almost an household name, with their albums to be found in student bed-sits across the country. But the band's true power only fully came across on stage, when African village scenarios and a mastery of rhythm and melody summoned up an energy and spirit lacking in other branches of Western pop. Their best work, *Woyaya*, like their debut stalled outside the UK Top 10 (at number 11). The title track was covered by Art Garfunkel, who produced a sensitive arrangement. The group followed up their onslaught on the UK by making inroads into many other countries' charts and touring circuits, and during the mid and late 70s they spent much of their time on extended world tours, capturing particularly large audiences in Japan, India, Australia and, of course, throughout Africa. In 1977 they were headliners at the Lagos-based Festac 77, the pan-African Olympics of music and culture, and in 1980 performed a special concert at the Zimbabwean independence celebrations. By this time, however, Osibisa's star was firmly in decline in Europe and the USA, as disco overwhelmed African music as the accepted invitation to dance. The band continued touring and releasing records, but to steadily diminishing audiences. Business problems followed. After an initial signing to MCA, Osibisa had changed labels

Donny Osmond

several times, ending with Bronze. The moves reflected their growing frustration with British business, as each label in turn tried to persuade them to adapt their music to the disco style and thus maximize their appeal. Osibisa were prepared to make some concessions but, to their credit (and sadly, their financial debit) only up to a point. Beyond that they were not prepared to abandon their roots, culture or pride. In the mid-80s, the group directed their attention to the state of the music business in Ghana, planning a studio and theatre complex which came to nothing following the withdrawal of state funding, and helping in the promotion of younger highlife artists. In 1984, Tontoh formed a London band to back three visiting Ghanaian musicians - A.B. Crentsil, Eric Agyeman and Thomas Frempong. An album, *Highlife Stars*, followed on Osibisa's own Flying Elephant label.

Now effectively disbanded, Osibisa occasionally stage reunion concerts.

Albums: *Osibisa* (1971), *Heads and Woyaya* (both 1972), *Happy Children* (1973), *Superfly TNT* (1974), *Welcome Home* (1976), *Ojah Awake* (1976), *Black Magic Night* (1977), *Mystic Energy* (1980), *Celebration* (1983), *Live At The Marquee* (1984). Compilation: *The Best Of Osibisa* (1974).

Osmond, Donny

b. Donald Clark Osmond, 9 December 1957, Ogden, Utah, USA. The most successful solo artist to emerge from family group, the Osmonds, Donny was particularly successful at covering old hits. His first solo success came in the summer of 1971 with a version of Billy Sherrill's 'Sweet And Innocent', which reached the US Top 10. The follow-up, a revival of Goffin/King's 'Go Away Little Girl' (previously a hit for both Steve Lawrence and Mark Wynter) took Osmond to the top of the US charts. 'Hey Girl', once a success for Freddie Scott, continued his US chart domination, which was now even more successful than that of the family group. By the summer of 1972, Osmondmania reached Britain, and a revival of Paul Anka's 'Puppy Love' gave Donny his first UK number 1. The singer's clean-cut good looks and perpetual smile brought him massive coverage in the pop press, while a back catalogue of hit songs from previous generations sustained his chart career. 'Too Young' and 'Why' both hit the UK Top 10, while 'The Twelfth Of Never' and 'Young Love' both reached number 1. His material appeared to concentrate on the pangs of adolescent love, which made him the perfect teenage idol for the period. In 1974, Donny began a series of duets with his sister Marie Osmond, which included

Little Jimmy Osmond

Osmonds

more UK Top 10 hits with 'I'm Leaving It All Up To You' and 'Morning Side Of The Mountain'. It was clear that Donny's teen appeal was severely circumscribed by his youth and in 1977 he tried unsuccessfully to reach a more mature audience with *Donald Clark Osmond*. Although minor hits followed, the singer's appeal was waning alarmingly by the late 70s. After the break-up of the group in 1980, Donny went on to star in the Broadway musical *Little Johnny Jones* and ceased recording after the mid-70s. A decade later a more rugged Osmond returned with 'I'm In It For Love' and the more successful 'Soldier Of Love', which reached the US Top 30. Most agreed that his attempts at mainstream rock were much more impressive than anyone might have imagined.

Albums: solo *The Donny Osmond Album* (1971), *To You With Love* (1971), *Portrait Of Donny* (1972), *Too Young* (1972), *My Best Of You* (1972), *Alone Together* (1973), *A Time For Us* (1973), *Donny* (1974), *Discotrain* (1976), *Donald Clark Osmond* (1977), *Soldier Of Love* (1988), *Eyes Don't Lie* (1991); with Marie Osmond: *I'm Leaving It All Up To You* (1974), *Make The World Go Away* (1975), *Donny And Marie - Featuring Songs From Their Television Show* (1976), *Deep Purple* (1976), *Donny And Marie - A New Season* (1977), *Winning Combination* (1978), *Goin' Coconuts* (1978).

Osmond, Little Jimmy

b. 16 April 1963, Canoga Park, California, USA. The youngest member of the Osmonds family, Jimmy unexpectedly emerged as a pre-teen idol in 1972. Overweight and cute, he was launched at the peak of Osmondmania and topped the Christmas charts in the UK with his singalong 'Long-Haired Lover From Liverpool'. In doing so, he became, at nine years of age, the youngest individual ever to reach number 1 in the UK up until that time. He returned to the charts during the next two years with Lavern Baker's old hit 'Tweedle Dee' and Eddie Hodges' 'I'm Gonna Knock On Your Door'. His brief popularity in Britain was eclipsed by fan mania in Japan where he was known as 'Jimmy Boy'. When the hits ceased and he grew up, he became successful as an entrepreneur and rock impresario.

Album: *Killer Joe* (1972).

Osmond, Marie

b. 13 October 1959, Ogden, Utah, USA. Following the success of her elder siblings in the Osmonds, Marie launched her own singing career in late 1973. Her revival of Anita Bryant's 'Paper Roses' reached the US Top 5 and did even better in the UK, peaking at number 2. Following two solo albums, she successfully collaborated with her brother Donny Osmond on a series of duets. They enjoyed a transatlantic Top 10 hit with a version of Dale And Griffin's 'I'm Leaving It All Up To You' and repeated that achievement with a cover of Tommy Edwards' 'Morning Side Of The Mountain'. Marie simultaneously continued her solo career with a reworking of Connie Francis's 'Who's Sorry Now?' The brother and sister duo next moved into the country market with a version of Eddy Arnold's 'Make The World Go Away'. By early 1976, their popularity was still strong and they featured in a one-hour variety television show titled *Donny And Marie*. The programme spawned a hit album and another UK/US hit with a revival of Nino Tempo And April Stevens' 'Deep Purple'. By 1977, the Mormon duo were covering Tamla/Motown material, duetting on Marvin Gaye And Tammi Terrell's 'Ain't Nothing Like The Real Thing'. The duets continued until 1978 and their last significant success was a cover of the Righteous Brothers' '(You're My) Soul And Inspiration'. That same year, Donny and Marie starred together in the movie *Goin' Coconuts*. Following the break-up of the Osmonds the sister continued with her own television series *Marie*. Thereafter, she moved successfully into country music and recorded several albums for the Curb label.

Albums: solo *Paper Roses* (1974), *In My Little Corner Of The World* (1974), *Who's Sorry Now?* (1975), *This Is The Way That I Feel* (1977), *There's No Stopping Your Heart* (1986), *I Only Wanted You* (1987), *All In Love* (1988); with Donny Osmond *I'm Leaving It All Up To You* (1974), *Make The World Go Away* (1975), *Donny And Marie - Featuring Songs From Their Television Show* (1976), *Deep Purple* (1976), *Donny And Marie - A New Season* (1977), *Winning Combination* (1978), *Goin' Coconuts* (1978).

Osmonds

This famous family all-vocal group from Ogden, Utah, USA comprised Alan Osmond (b. 22 June 1949), Wayne Osmond (b. 28 August 1951), Merrill Osmond (b. 30 April 1953), Jay Osmond (b. 2 March 1955) and Donny Osmond (b. 9 December 1957). The group first came to public notice following regular television appearances on the top-rated *Andy Williams Show*. From 1967-69, they also appeared on television's *Jerry Lewis Show*. Initially known as the Osmond Brothers they

recorded for Andy Williams' record label Barnaby. By 1971, their potential was recognized by Mike Curb, who saw them as likely rivals to the star-studded Jackson 5. Signed to MGM Records, they recorded the catchy 'One Bad Apple', which topped the US charts for five weeks. Before long, they became a national institution, and various members of the family including Donny Osmond, Marie Osmond and Little Jimmy Osmond enjoyed hits in their own right. As a group, the primary members enjoyed a string of hits, including 'Double Lovin'', 'Yo Yo' and 'Down By The Lazy River'. By the time Osmondmania hit the UK in 1972, the group peaked with their ecologically-conscious 'Crazy Horses', complete with intriguing electric organ effects. Their clean-cut image and well-scrubbed good looks brought them immense popularity among teenagers and they even starred in their own cartoon series. Probably their most ambitious moment came with the evangelical concept album, *The Plan,* in which they attempted to express their Mormon beliefs. Released at the height of their success, the album reached number 6 in the UK. During the early to mid-70s, they continued to release successive hits, including 'Going Home', 'Let Me In' and 'I Can't Stop'. Their sole UK number 1 as a group was 'Love Me For A Reason', composed by Johnny Bristol. Their last major hit in the UK was 'The Proud One' in 1975, after which their popularity waned. The individual members continued to prosper in varying degrees, but the family group disbanded in 1980. Two years later, the older members of the group re-formed without Donny, and moved into the country market. During the mid-80s, they appeared regularly at the Country Music Festival in London, but their recorded output lessened.
Selected albums: *Osmonds* (1971), *Homemade* (1971), *Phase-III* (1972), *The Osmonds 'Live'* (1972), *Crazy Horses* (1972), *The Plan* (1973), *Our Best To You* (1974), *I'm Still Gonna Need You* (1975), *The Proud One* (1975), *Around The World - Live In Concert* (1975), *Brainstorm* (1976), *The Osmonds Christmas Album* (1976), *Today* (1985). Compilation: *The Osmonds Greatest Hits* (1977).

O'Sullivan, Gilbert

b. Raymond O'Sullivan, 1 December 1946, Waterford, Eire. O'Sullivan's family moved to Swindon, England, during his childhood and after attending art college there, the singer was signed to CBS Records. Under the name Gilbert he issued the unsuccessful 'What Can I Do?' and soon moved on to Phil Solomon's Major Minor label,

where 'Mr Moody's Garden' also failed. Seeking a new manager, Gilbert wrote to the starmaking Gordon Mills, who had already launched Tom Jones and Engelbert Humperdinck to international success. Mills was impressed by the demo tape enclosed and relaunched the artist on his new MAM label under the name Gilbert O'Sullivan. The debut 'Nothing Rhymed' had some clever lyrics and a strong melody. It reached the UK Top 10 in late 1970 and television audiences were amused or puzzled by the sight of O'Sullivan with his pudding basin haircut, short trousers and flat cap. The 'Bisto Kid' image was retained for the first few releases and the singer initially acted the part of an anti-star. At one point, he was living in the grounds of Mills' Weybridge house on a meagre £10-a-week allowance. His hit-making potential was undeniable and his ability to pen a memorable melody recalled the urbane charm of Paul McCartney. Early UK successes included 'We Will', 'No Matter How I Try' and 'Alone Again (Naturally)'. Any suspicions that O'Sullivan's charm was largely parochial were dashed when the latter single broke through in America, peaking at number 1 and selling over a million copies. The debut album, *Himself*, was also highly accomplished and included the radio favourite 'Matrimony', which would have provided a sizeable hit if released as a single. O'Sullivan went on to become one of the biggest selling artists of 1972. That year he enjoyed two consecutive UK number 1s with 'Clair' (written in honour of Mills's daughter) and 'Get Down'. These singles also reached the US Top 10. By this time, O'Sullivan's image had radically changed and he began to appreciate the superstar trappings enjoyed by Mills' other acts.
O'Sullivan's second album, *Back To Front*, reached number 1 in the UK and his appeal stretched across the board, embracing teen and adult audiences. For a time, he seemed likely to rival and even excel Elton John as Britain's most successful singer/songwriter export. Although further hits were forthcoming with 'Ooh Baby', 'Happiness Is Me And You' and 'Christmas Song', it was evident that his appeal had declined by the mid-70s. Following the UK Top 20 hit 'I Don't Love You But I Think I Like You' in the summer of 1975, his chart career ceased. After a spectacular falling out with Mills, he left MAM and returned to CBS, the label that had launched his career. Five years on, only one hit, 'What's In A Kiss?', emerged from the association. Minus Mills, it seemed that the superstar of the mid-70s was incapable of rekindling his once illustrious career. His

Gilbert O'Sullivan

disillusionment culminated in a High Court battle against his former manager and record company which came before Justice Mars Jones in the spring of 1982. The judge not only awarded O'Sullivan substantial damages and had all agreements with MAM set aside, but decreed that all the singer's master tapes and copyrights should be returned. The case made legal history and had enormous repercussions for the British music publishing world. Despite his court victory over the starmaking Mills, however, O'Sullivan failed to re-establish his career subsequently.

Albums: *Himself* (1971), *Back To Front* (1972), *I'm A Writer Not A Fighter* (1973), *Stranger In My Own Backyard* (1974), *Southpaw* (1977), *Off Centre* (1980), *Life And Rhymes* (1982), *Frobisher Drive* (1988). Compilations: *Greatest Hits* (1976), *20 Golden Greats* (1981), *20 Of The Very Best* (1981), *20 Golden Pieces Of Gilbert O' Sullivan* (1985), *16 Golden Classics* (1986).

Otway, John

b. 2 October, 1952, Aylesbury, Buckinghamshire, England. The enigmatic madcap John Otway first came to prominence in the early 70s with his guitar/fiddle-playing partner Wild Willie Barrett. Otway's animated performances and unusual vocal style caught the attention of Pete Townshend, who produced the duo's first two Track label singles, 'Murder Man' and 'Louisa On A Horse'. Extensive gigging, highlighted by crazed and highly entertaining stage antics, won Otway and Barrett a loyal collegiate following and finally a minor hit with 'Really Free' in 1977. Its b-side, 'Beware Of The Flowers ('Cause I'm Sure They're Going To Get You Yeh)' was equally appealing and eccentric and augured well for further hits. Although Otway (with and without Barrett) soldiered on with syllable-stretching versions of Tom Jones's 'Green Green Grass Of Home' and quirky novelty workouts such as 'Headbutts', he remains a 70s curio, still locked into the UK college/club circuit.

Albums: *John Otway And Wild Willie Barrett* (1977), *Deep And Meaningless* (1978), *Where Did I Go Right* (1979), *Way And Bar* (1980), *All Balls And No Willy* (1982), *The Wimp And The Wild* (1989). Compilations: *Gone With The Bin Or The Best Of Otway And Barre* (1981), *Greatest Hits* (1986).

Further reading: *Cor Baby That's Really Me*, John Otway.

Our Kid

This school-aged Liverpool based quartet were Kevin Rown (b. 1964), Brian Farrell (b. 1963), Terry McCreight (b. 1961) and Terry Beccino (b. 1961). The well choreographed and groomed young vocal group were winners on UK television's top talent show *New Faces* and were quickly signed up by Polydor Records. Their first single 'You Just Might See Me Cry' in 1976,

which was penned by the hit team of Roger Greenaway and Barry Mason, shot to the runner-up position on the UK chart. The future looked very bright for the polished and youthful foursome. However, the local educational authorities intervened and, because of their age, banned them from various television and live appearances. They had two more singles on Polydor but when neither charted they returned to their studies.
Album: *Our Kid* (1975).

Outlaws

Formed in Tampa, Florida, USA in 1974, the Outlaws comprised Billy Jones (guitar), Henry Paul (guitar), Hugh Thomasson (guitar), Monty Yoho (drums) and Frank O'Keefe (bass) - who was superceded by Harvey Arnold in 1977. With Thomasson as main composer, they were respected by fans (if not critics) for a strong stage presentation and artistic consistency which hinged on an unreconstructed mixture of salient points from the Eagles, Allman Brothers and similarly guitar-dominated, denim-clad acts of the 70s. The first signing to Arista, their 1975 debut album - produced by Paul A. Rothchild - reached number 13 in *Billboard*'s chart. The set included the riveting lengthy guitar battle 'Green Grass And High Tides', which was the highlight of the group's live act. Singles success with 'There Goes Another Love Song' and 'Lady In Waiting' (the title track of their second album) was followed by regular touring. A coast-to-coast tour in 1976 and further less publicized work on the road necessitated the hire of a second drummer, David Dix, who was heard on 1978's in-concert *Bring It Back Alive* - the first without Paul (replaced by Freddy Salem) whose resignation was followed in 1979 by those of Yoho and Arnold. In 1981 the band was on the edge of the US Top 20 with the title track of *Ghost Riders* - a revival of Vaughn Monroe's much-covered ballad - but, when this proved their chart swansong, the outfit - with Thomasson the only remaining original member - disbanded shortly after *Les Hombres Malo*. Following modest success with two albums by the Henry Paul Band, its leader rejoined Thomasson in a reformed Outlaws who issued *Soldiers Of Fortune* in 1986.
Albums: *The Outlaws* (1975), *Lady In Waiting* (1976), *Hurry Sundown* (1977), *Bring It Back Alive* (1978), *Playin' To Win* (1978), *In The Eye Of The Storm* (1979), *Ghost Riders* (1980), *Les Hombres Malo* (1982), *Soldiers Of Fortune* (1986). Compilations: *Greatest Hits Of The Outlaws/High Tides Forever* (1982), *On The Run Again* (1986).

P

Pablo Cruise

Formed in 1973, this San Francisco-based group was founded when two ex-members of Stoneground, Cory Lerois (b. California, USA; keyboards) and Steve Price (b. California, USA; drums), were joined by Dave Jenkins (b. Florida, USA; guitar) and Bud Cockrell (b. Missouri, USA; bass) from It's A Beautiful Day. *Pablo Cruise* enjoyed critical acclaim for its astute blend of rich, jazz-influenced textures and accomplished instrumental work and while *Lifeline* enhanced this reputation, the quartet reaped commercial rewards when 'Whatcha Gonna Do?' from *A Place In The Sun* reached number 6 in the US singles chart. 'Love Will Find A Way' achieved the same position the following year, while promoting *Worlds Away* into the US Top 10, while 'Don't Want To Live Without It' also entered the Top 30 as the group adroitly added elements of disco to an already cosmopolitan approach. Former Santana bassist Bruce Day joined the group for *Part Of The Game*, replacing Cockrell, but he in turn was supplanted by John Pierce and second guitarist Angelo Rossi. Although *Reflector*, a collaboration with veteran R&B producer Tom Dowd, generated another hit in 'Cool Love', Pablo Cruise was increasingly viewed as moribund in the wake of the 'new wave'. Internal problems led to further wholesale changes and a period of inactivity followed the release of *Out Of Our Hands*, after which the line-up reverted to that of the original quartet.
Albums: *Pablo Cruise* (1975), *Lifeline* (1976), *A Place In The Sun* (1977), *Worlds Away* (1978), *Part Of The Game* (1979), *Reflector* (1981), *Out Of Our Hands* (1983).

Paper Lace

This UK pop group was formed in 1969, and comprised Michael Vaughan (b. 27 July 1950, Sheffield, England; guitar), Chris Morris (b. 1 November 1954, Nottingham, England), Carlo Santanna (b. 29 July 1947, nr. Rome, Italy; guitar), Philip Wright (b. 19 April 1948, Nottingham, England; drums/lead vocals) and Cliff Fish (b. 13 August 1949, Ripley, England; bass). All were residents of Nottingham, England, the lace manufacturing city that lent their mainstream pop

group its name. A season at Tiffany's, a Rochdale club, led to television appearances, but a passport to the charts did not arrive until a 1974 victory in *Opportunity Knocks*, the ITV talent contest series, put their winning song, Mitch Murray and Peter Callender's 'Billy Don't Be A Hero', on the road to a UK number 1. Hopes of emulating this success in the USA were dashed by Bo Donaldson And The Heywoods' cover. The follow-up, 'The Night Chicago Died', set in the Prohibition era, was untroubled by any such competition and topped the US charts, narrowly missing out in the UK by peaking at number 3. 'The Black-Eyed Boys', a UK number 11 hit from Murray and Callender was the group's last taste of chart success - apart from a joint effort with local football heroes, Nottingham Forest FC, for the 1978 singalong, 'We've Got The Whole World In Our Hands'.
Albums: *Paper Lace And Other Bits Of Material* (1974), *First Edition* (1975). Compilation: *The Paper Lace Collection* (1976).

Paris

This US power-trio was put together in 1975 by former Fleetwood Mac guitarist Bob Welch and ex-Jethro Tull bassist Glenn Cornick. Adding Thom Mooney on drums, they signed to Capitol Records in 1976 and released their self-titled debut album. Weaving mystical lyrical tapestries, within psychedelic, blues-based progressive rock, their strange and tormented style was ignored at the time of release, and remains an odd curio even today. Hunt Sales replaced Mooney on *Big Towne 2061* and the band adopted a more mainstream approach, with the lyrics taking on a religious emphasis. This also failed to find an audience and the band went their separate ways soon after its release. Welch embarked on what was to become a highly successful solo career.
Albums: *Paris* (1975), *Big Towne 2061* (1976).

Park, Simon

b. March 1946, Market Harborough, Leicestershire, England. A graduate of music at Winchester College, Oxford, Park began playing piano at the age of five. In 1972 he was commissioned to write the theme music to the new television detective thriller series *Van Der Valk*. The theme, called 'Eye Level', and credited to the Simon Park Orchestra, was initially released during the first series, but it only reached number 41 in the UK charts. Viewing figures for the second series increased and the theme was re-released by public demand. This time it climbed all the way to the top and became the final number 1 for EMI/Columbia label. Simon Park went on to produce a number of albums containing a mixture of originals and orchestrated classics.

Albums: *Eye Level* (1973), with the Ingman Orchestra *Something In Air* (1974), *Venus Fly Trap* (1975), *Danger UXB* (1979).

Parker, Graham

b. 18 November 1950, London, England. Having begun his career in aspiring soul groups the Black Rockers and Deep Cut Three, R&B vocalist Parker undertook menial employment while completing several demo tapes of his original songs. One such collection came to the attention of David Robinson, owner of a small recording studio within a building housing the north London, Hope & Anchor pub. Impressed, he pieced together a backing group - Brinsley Schwarz (guitar/vocals), Bob Andrew (keyboards/vocals), both ex-Brinsley Schwarz, Martin Belmont (guitar/vocals, ex-Ducks Deluxe), Andrew Bodnar (bass) and Steve Goulding (drums) - known collectively as the Rumour, and the new aggregation joined the dying embers of the 'pub rock' scene. The patronage of Radio London disc jockey Charlie Gillett helped engender a recording deal and both *Howlin' Wind* and *Heat Treatment* received almost universal acclaim. Parker's gritty delivery was both tough and passionate, placing the singer on a level with US contemporaries Bruce Springsteen and Southside Johnny And The Asbury Jukes. Although the artist also enjoyed two chart entries with *The Pink Parker* EP (1977) and 'Hold Back The Night' (1978). His momentum was effectively stalled by the divided critical opinion to the commercial *Stick To Me*, and a live-double set, *The Parkerilla*. While the public gave the them a UK Top 40 hit with 'Hey Lord, Don't Ask Me Questions' and despite both albums attaining UK Top 20 status, many felt Parker and the Rumour were losing their original fire and bitter wrangles with his record company further undermined progress. *Squeezing Out Sparks*, his debut for Arista Records (in the USA), reclaimed former glories and was lauded in both *Rolling Stone* and *Village Voice*. Persistent contradictions between the critics and chart positions added fuel to the confusion in the group line-up. Their most successful UK chart album, 1980's *The Up Escalator* (released on Stiff Records in the UK), would mark the end of Parker's partnership with the Rumour. With the break-up, any magic that had remained from the early days had truly gone. The remainder of the 80s was spent rebuilding his career and personal life in the USA. In 1988 *Mona Lisa's Sister* proved a dramatic return-to-form rightly praised for its drive and sense of purpose. Ex-Rumour bassist Andrew Bodner joined former Attractions Steve Nieve (keyboards) and Pete Thomas (drums) for *Human Soul*, an ambitious concept albums split between sides labelled 'real' and 'surreal'. This surprising departure indicates Parker's increasing desire to expand the perimeters of his exhilarating style. Into the 90s, Parker proved fully capable, and confident, of performing to large audiences solo, with acoustic guitar or with full backing. In early 1992 he changed record labels once more by signing to Capitol Records in the USA.

Albums: *Howlin' Wind* (1976), *Heat Treatment* (1976), *Stick To Me* (1977), *The Parkerilla* (1978), *Squeezing Out Sparks* (1979), *The Up Escalator* (1980), *Another Grey Area* (1982), *The Real McCaw* (1983), *Steady Nerves* (1985), *Mona Lisa's Sister* (1988), *Human Soul* (1989), *Live! Alone In America* (1989), *Struck By Lightning* (1991). Compilation: *The Best Of Graham Parker And The Rumour* (1980).

Parliament(s)

This exceptional US vocal quintet was formed in 1955 by George Clinton (b. 22 July 1941, Kannapolis, North Carolina, USA), Raymond Davis (b. 29 March 1940, Sumter, South Carolina, USA), Calvin Simon (b. 22 May 1942, Beckley, West Virginia, USA), Clarence 'Fuzzy' Haskins (b. 8 June 1941, Elkhorn, West Virginia, USA) and Grady Thomas (b. 5 January 1941, Newark, New Jersey, USA). George Clinton's interest in music did not fully emerge until his family moved to the urban setting of Plainfield, New Jersey. Here, he fashioned the Parliaments after the influential doo-wop group, Frankie Lymon And The Teenagers. Two singles, 'Poor Willie' and 'Lonely Island' mark this formative era, but it was not until 1967 that Clinton was able to secure a more defined direction with the release of '(I Wanna) Testify'. Recorded in Detroit, the single reached the US Top 20, but this promise was all but lost when Revilot, the label to which the band was signed, went out of business. All existing contracts were then sold to Atlantic, but George preferred to abandon the Parliaments' name altogether in order to be free to sign elsewhere. Clinton took the existing line-up and its backing group to Westbound Records, where the entire collective recorded as Funkadelic. However, the outstanding problem over their erstwhile title was resolved in 1970, and the same musicians were signed to the

Invictus label as Parliament. This group unleashed the experimental and eclectic *Osmium* (1970) before securing an R&B hit with the irrepressible 'Breakdown'. For the next three years the 'Parliafunkadelicament Thang' would concentrate on Funkadelic releases, but disagreements with the Westbound hierarchy inspired Parliament's second revival. Signed to the Casablanca label in 1974, the group's first singles, 'Up For The Down Stroke', 'Chocolate City' and 'P. Funk (Wants To Get Funked Up)' were marginally more mainstream than the more radical material Clinton had already issued, but the distinctions became increasingly blurred. Some 40 musicians were now gathered together under the P. Funk banner, including several refugees from the James Brown camp including Bootsy Collins, Fred Wesley and Maceo Parker, while live shows offered elements of both camps. Parliament's success within the R&B chart continued with 'Give Up The Funk (Tear The Roof Off The Sucker)' (1976), and two 1978 best-sellers, 'Flashlight' and 'Aqua Boogie (A Psychoalphadiscobetabioaquadoloop)', where the group's hard-kicking funk was matched by the superlative horn charts and their leader's unorthodox vision. Their last chart entry was in 1980 with 'Agony Of Defeet', after which Clinton decided to shelve the Parliament name again when problems arose following Polygram's acquisition of the Casablanca catalogue.

Albums: as Parliament *Osmium* (1970), *Up For The Down Stroke* (1974), *Chocolate City* (1975), *Mothership Connection* (1976), *The Clones Of Doctor Funkenstein* (1976), *Parliament Live - P. Funk Earth Tour* (1977), *Funkentelechy Vs The Placebo Syndrome* (1977), *Motor-Booty Affair* (1978), *Gloryhallastoopid (Or Pin The Tale On The Funky)* (1979), *Trombipulation* (1980). Compilation: *Parliament's Greatest Hits* (1984), *The Best Of Parliament* (1986).

Parton, David

This singer/songwriter and producer was based in Stoke, England. Parton was the mainstay of the group Strange Fox, who were taken under the wing of Tony Hatch in the early 70s. Parton discovered the group Sweet Sensation and together with Hatch wrote and produced their hits, including the 1974 UK number 1 'Sad Sweet Dreamer'. Since he had a voice similar to Stevie Wonder, he was the ideal choice to cover Wonder's 'Isn't She Lovely', when Stevie decided he did not want to release his version on a single. Parton's version on Pye Records shot into the UK Top 10 in 1977 but it was to be his sole hit as an singer. He continues to work in production and songwriting in Stoke.

Partridge Family

David Cassidy (b. 12 April 1950, New York City, New York, USA), and his real life step-mother actress Shirley Jones (b. 31 March 1934, Smithton, Pennsylvania, USA), were the only members of the fictitious television family group to be heard on their records. Jones, who had starred in hit film musicals like *Oklahoma!*, *Carousel* and *The Music Man* married David's father actor Jack Cassidy in 1956. *The Partridge Family*, a humorous series about a family pop group (based loosely on the Cowsills) started on US television on 25 September 1970. It was an instant hit and sent their debut single 'I Think I Love You' to the top of the chart. In less than two years the fake family, whose records were produced by Wes Farrell, had put another six singles and albums into the US Top 40, including the Top 10 successes, 'Doesn't Somebody Want To Be Wanted' and 'I'll Meet You Halfway'. When their US popularity began to wane the series took off in the UK, giving them five UK Top 20 hits, most of which were less successful Stateside. The show made Cassidy a transatlantic teen idol and he also had a run of solo hits. By the time the television series ended in 1974 the hits for both acts had dried up.

Albums: *The Partridge Family Album* (1970), *Up To Date* (1971), *A Partridge Family Christmas Card* (1971), *The Partridge Family Sound Magazine* (1972), *The Partridge Family Shopping Bag* (1972), *The Partridge Family Notebook* (1972), *Crossword Puzzle* (1973). Compilations: *The Partridge Family At Home With Their Hits* (1972), *Only A Moment Ago* (1975).

Pasadena Roof Orchestra

Britain's most commercially successful traditional jazz-based act of the 70s was formed in the mid-60s by baker John Arthey (bass) as a larger, slicker recreation of a 20s ragtime band than that of the Temperance Seven. Among its mainstays were John Parry (vocals), arranger Keith Nichols (piano), Mac White (clarinet) and trumpeters Clive Baker, Enrico Tomasino and Mike Henry. Transient members included Viv Stanshall (euphonium). Despite much interest from London's music press - especially the *Melody Maker* - the Orchestra had no major record hits but their albums did brisk business in foyers on the European college circuit and at the more prestigious jazz festivals where they commanded high fees as a popular attraction of considerable longevity.

Albums: *The Show Must Go On* (1977), *A Talking Picture* (1978), *Night Out* (1979), *Puttin' On The Ritz* (1983), *Fifteen Years On* (1985), *Good News* (1987), *On Tour* (1987), *Happy Feet* (1988). Compilatons: *Anthology* (1978), *Everythin' Stops For Tea* (1984), *C'mon Along And Listen To* (1986), *Isn't It Romantic* (1987), *Collection* (1987), *Top Hat, White Tie And Tails* (1988).

Paton, Tam

b. Prestonpans, Scotland. Paton's involvement in the music business began during the early 60s when he played piano in Scottish showband, the Crusaders. After they split he was persuaded to form a new 10-piece showband known as the Tam Paton Orchestra, which had a residency at Edinburgh's Palais de Dance. In 1967, he was approached by two young kids, Alan and Derek Longmuir, who had recently formed a group called the Saxons. By the time he auditioned them, however, they had changed their name to the Bay City Rollers. Paton managed the group who had an ever-shifting line-up over the next few years. It was not until 1971 that they received their big break when Paton persuaded a posse of record company talent spotters to witness their act in Edinburgh. Initially signed to Tony Calder's production company, they released their work through Dick Leahy's Bell Records. In the meantime, Paton retained another group, Kip, who served as a pool of replacements. Briefly, he had a managerial tie-up with Peter Walsh after which the Rollers swiftly became the biggest pop sensation of their day. The press predictably caricatured Paton as an aggressive hirer/firer and puppetmaster. Several people attempted to buy out Paton's interests in the Rollers but he always refused to surrender power. For Paton, the Rollers were not merely a business asset but the embodiment of all his frustrated dreams and ambitions. Sadly, the dream ended in the late 70s when the Rollers good boy image was exposed as a myth. Worse was to follow for Paton who was sentenced to three years' imprisonment at Edinburgh High Court for committing indecent acts with a number of youngsters aged between 15 and 20 years, supplying them with stupefying liquor and allowing blue movies to be shown at his home. His fall was undoubtedly the most spectacular of any manager in pop music history.

Paul, Billy

b. Paul Williams 1 December 1934, Philadelphia, Pennsylvania, USA. Although Paul had been an active singer in the Philadelphia area since the 50s, singing in jazz clubs and briefly with Harold Melvin And The Blue Notes, it was not until he met producer Kenny Gamble that his career prospered. After signing to the Neptune label, he enjoyed a successful spell on the Philadelphia International label. His instinctive jazz-based delivery provided an unlikely foil for the label's highly structured, sweet-soul sound but Paul's impressive debut hit, 'Me And Mrs Jones', nonetheless encapsulated the genre. A classic confessional tale of infidelity, Billy's unorthodox style enhanced the ballad's sense of guilt. His later releases included 'Thanks For Saving My Life' (1974), 'Let's Make A Baby' (1976) and 'Let 'Em In' (1977), the last of which adapted the Paul McCartney hit to emphasize lyrical references to Dr. Martin Luther King. Billy continued to make excellent records but his last chart entry, to date, came in 1980 with 'You're My Sweetness'.
Albums: *Ebony Woman* (1970), *Going East* (1971), *360 Degrees Of Billy Paul* (1972), *Feelin' Good At The Cadillac Club* (1973), *War Of The Gods* (1973), *Live In Europe* (1974), *Got My Head On Straight* (1975), *When Love Is New* (1975), *Let 'Em In* (1976), *Only The Strong Survive* (1977), *First Class* (1979) *Lately* (1985), *Wide Open* (1988). Compilation: *Billy Paul's Greatest Hits* (1983).

Pavlov's Dog

Formed in St. Louis, Missouri, USA in 1973, the group initially comprised David Surkamp (vocals/guitar), Siegfried Carver (violin), Steve Scorfina (guitar, ex-REO Speedwagon), David Hamilton (keyboards), Doug Rayburn (mellotron/bass) and Mike Safron (drums). They were initially signed to the ABC label, for whom they recorded *Pampered Menial* under the aegis of Blue Öyster Cult producer Sandy Pearlman. The sextet was then traded to Columbia in exchange for Poco and their impressive debut album reappeared on this new outlet. The set focused on Surkamp's remarkable high voice, pitched somewhere between those of Jon Anderson and Tiny Tim, which soared through the group's exceptional compositions in tandem with Carver's mesmerizing violin. Although not a commercial success, *Pampered Menial* enjoyed a considerable cult following, in particular for 'Julia', its memorable opening track. The following album, *At The Sound Of The Bell* introduced several changes within the group, the most crucial of which was the loss of Carver. Guitarist Tom Nickeson had been added to the line-up while

Safron was replaced by Bill Bruford, formerly of Yes and King Crimson. Although of a high quality, this second set lacked the distinctive panache of its predecessor and failed to reverse waning fortunes. The group split up soon afterwards, but despite considerable interest, Surkamp's subsequent work has been confined to a collaboration with singer/songwriter Iain Matthews.
Albums: *Pampered Menial* (1974), *At The Sound Of The Bell* (1975).

Payne, Freda

b. Freda Charcilia Payne, 19 September 1945, Detroit, Michigan, USA. Schooled in jazz and classical music, this urbane singer attended the Institute Of Musical Arts and worked with Pearl Bailey prior to recording her debut album in 1963 for MGM Records. Payne signed to Holland/Dozier/Holland's label Invictus and her first recording, 'The Unhooked Generation' introduced a new-found soul style, but it was the magnificent follow-up, 'Band Of Gold' (1970), which established Payne's reputation. This ambiguous wedding-night drama was a US number 3 and UK number 1 and prepared the way for several more excellent singles in 'Deeper And Deeper', 'You Brought The Joy' and 'Bring The Boys Home', an uncompromising anti-Vietnam anthem. Ensuing releases lacked that early purpose and were marred by Payne's increasingly unemotional delivery. The singer moved to ABC/Dunhill (1974), Capitol (1976) and Sutra (1982), but Payne was also drawn to television work and would later host a syndicated talk show, 'For You Black Woman'.
Albums: *After The Lights Go Down And Much More* (1963), *Band Of Gold* (1970), *Contact* (1971), *Reaching Out* (1973), *Payne And Pleasure* (1974), *Out Of Payne Comes Love* (1975), *Stares And Whispers* (1978) *Supernatural High* (1978). Compilations: *The Best Of Freda Payne* (1972), *Reaching Out* (1973), *Deeper And Deeper* (1989).

Pearl Harbor And The Explosions

Formed in San Francisco, California in 1979, this much-touted attraction was centred on vocalist Pearl Harbor (b. 1958, Germany, of a Filipino mother), who, as Pearl E. Gates, had previously been a dancer in the Tubes live show. She subsequently joined Jane Dornacker in Leila And The Snakes, before taking the group's rhythm section - Hilary Stench (bass) and John Stench (drums) - in this new act. Their act continued the theatricality of the Tubes, but Gates was more interested in conventional rock 'n' roll. To this end she recruited Peter Bilt (guitar) and formed Pearl Harbor And The Explosions in October 1978. They specialized in old fashioned rock 'n' roll/rockabilly spiced with 'new wave' energy. Their debut single 'Drivin'' (which was later covered by Jane Aire And The Belvederes) came out on the independent 415 Records label and became an cult hit. Its success encouraged Warner Brothers to sign the group. Their self-titled debut was a strong, promising work, but the group failed to complete a follow-up. They split in June 1980 leaving Pearl to continue with a solo album *Don't Follow Me I'm Lost* under her new name Pearl Harbor. The album was produced by Nicky Gallagher (former member of Ian Dury's Blockheads). The Stench brothers joined ex-Jefferson Airplane guitarist Jorma Kaukonen in Vital Parts, before embarking on an association with cult *avant garde* act Chrome.
Albums: *Pearl Harbor And The Explosions* (1979), as Pearl Harbor *Don't Follow Me, I'm Lost* (1981).

Peebles, Ann

b. 27 April 1947, East St. Louis, Missouri, USA. An impromptu appearance at the Rosewood Club in Memphis led to Peebles' recording deal. Bandleader Gene Miller took the singer to producer Willie Mitchell whose skills fashioned an impressive debut single, 'Walk Away' (1969). Anne's style was more fully shaped with 'Part Time Love' (1970), an irresistibly punchy reworking of the Clay Hammond-penned standard, while powerful original songs, including 'Slipped Tripped And Fell In Love' (1972) and 'I'm Gonna Tear Your Playhouse Down' (1973), later recorded by Paul Young and Graham Parker, confirmed her promise. Her work matured with the magnificent 'I Can't Stand The Rain', which defined the Hi Records sound and deservedly ensured the singer's immortality. Donald Bryant, Peebles' husband and a songwriter of ability, wrote that classic as well as '99 lbs' (1971). Later releases, '(You Keep Me) Hangin' On' and 'Do I Need You', were also strong, but Peebles was latterly hampered by a now-established formula and sales subsided. 'If You Got The Time (I've Got The Love)' (1979) was the singer's last R&B hit, but her work nonetheless remains among the finest in the 70s soul canon.
Albums: *This Is Ann Peebles* (1969), *Part Time Tove* (1971), *Straight From The Heart* (1972), *I Can't Stand The Rain* (1974), *Tellin' It* (1976), *If This Is Heaven* (1978), *Handwriting On The Wall* (1979), *Call Me* (1989). Compilations: *I'm Gonna Tear Your*

Playhouse Down (1985), *99 lbs* (1987), *Greatest Hits* (1988).

Pendergrass, Teddy

b. Theodore Pendergrass, 26 March 1950, Philadelphia, Pennsylvania, USA. Pendergrass joined Harold Melvin And The Blue Notes in 1969, when they invited his group, the Cadillacs, to work as backing musicians. Initially their drummer, Teddy had become the featured vocalist within a year. His ragged, passionate interpretations brought distinction to such releases as 'I Miss You' and 'If You Don't Know Me By Now'. Clashes with Melvin led to an inevitable split and in 1976 Pendergrass embarked on a successful solo career, remaining with the Philadelphia International label. His skills were most apparent on slower material which proved ideal for the singer's uncompromisingly sensual approach, which earned him a huge following amongst women. 'The Whole Town's Laughing At Me' (1977), 'Close The Door' (1978) and 'Turn Off The Lights' (1979) stand among the best of his early work and if later releases were increasingly drawn towards a smoother, more polished direction, Pendergrass was still capable of creating excellent records, including a moving rendition of 'Love TKO', a haunting Womack And Womack composition. However, his life was inexorably changed in 1982, following a near-fatal car accident which left the singer confined to a wheelchair, although his voice was intact. Nonetheless, after months of physical and emotional therapy, he was able to begin recording again. 'Hold Me' (1984), Teddy's debut hit on his new outlet, Asylum, also featured Whitney Houston, while further success followed with 'Love 4/2' (1986) and 'Joy' (1988).

Albums: *Teddy Pendergrass* (1977), *Life Is A Song Worth Singing* (1978), *Teddy* (1979), *Teddy Live! (Coast To Coast)* (1979), *T.P.* (1980), *It's Time For Love* (1981), *This One's For You* (1982), *Heaven Only Knows* (1983), *Love Language* (1984), *Workin' It Back* (1985), *Joy* (1988). Compilations: *Greatest Hits* (1987), *Teddy Pendergrass* (1989), *Truly Blessed* (1991).

Pere Ubu

Formed in Cleveland, Ohio, USA in 1975, and taking their name from Alfred Jarry's surrealist play, Pere Ubu evolved from several of the region's experimental groups, including Rocket From The Tombs and Foggy And The Shrimps. Their initial line-up, comprising David Thomas (vocals), Peter Laughner (guitar), Tom Herman (guitar/bass/organ), Tim Wright (guitar/bass), Allen Ravenstine (synthesizer/saxophone) and Scott Krauss (drums) completed the compulsive '30 Seconds Over Tokyo', while a second single, 'Final Solution', was recorded following Ravenstine's departure. Wright and Laughner then left the fold, but new bassist Tony Maimone augmented the nucleus of Thomas, Herman and Krauss before the prodigal Ravenstine returned to complete the most innovative version of the group. Two more singles, 'Street Waves' and 'The Modern Dance', were released before the quintet secured an international recording deal. Their debut, *The Modern Dance*, was an exceptional collection, blending new-wave art-rock with early Roxy Music. Rhythmically, the group evoked Captain Beefheart's Magic Band while Thomas's vocal gymnastics were both distinctive and compelling. Two further releases, *Dub Housing* and *New Picnic Time*, maintained this sense of adventure although the demonstrable power of that debut set was gradually becoming diffuse. Nonetheless, the three albums displayed a purpose and invention which deservedly received considerable critical approval.

In 1979 Tom Herman was replaced by former Red Crayola guitarist Mayo Thompson, who introduced a sculpted, measured approach to what had once seemed a propulsive, intuitive sound. *The Art Of Walking*, was deemed obtuse, and the group became pigeon-holed as both difficult and inconsequential. A dissatisfied Kraus left the line-up, and Anton Fier (ex-Feelies) joined Pere Ubu for the disappointing *Song Of The Bailing Man*. This lightweight selection appeared following the release of *The Sound Of The Sand*, David Thomas's first solo album, and reflected a general disinterest in the parent group's progress. Maimone then joined Krauss in Home And Garden, Herman surfaced with a new group, Tripod Jimmie, while Ravenstine and Thompson collaborated within a restructured Red Crayola. Thomas meanwhile enjoyed the highest profile with a further five albums.

By 1985 both Maimone and Ravenstine were working with the singer's new group, the Wooden Birds. Scott Kraus set the seeds of a Pere Ubu reunion by appearing for an encore during a Cleveland concert. 'It walked like a duck, looked like a duck, quacked like a duck, so it was a duck,' Thomas later remarked and by the end of 1987, the Ubu name had been officially re-instated. Jim Jones (guitar) and Chris Cutler (drums) completed the new line-up for the exceptional *Tenement Year*, which coupled the charm of earlier work with a newfound accessibility. *Cloudland* emphasized this enchanting direction although the group's age-old instability still threatened their long-term ambitions. Both Cutler and Ravenstine left the line-up. The latter was replaced by Eric Drew Feldman, formerly of Captain Beefheart. Pere Ubu's ultimate fate depends on their ability to contain their disparate personalities and individual ambitions.

Albums: *The Modern Dance* (1977), *Dub Housing* (1978), *Datapanik In The Year Zero* (1979), *New Picnic Time* (1979), *The Art Of Walking* (1980), *390 Degrees Of Simulated Stereo - Ubu Live: Volume 1* (1981), *Song Of The Bailing Man* (1982), *The Tenement Year* (1988), *One Man Drives While The Other Man Screams - Live Volume 2: Pere Ubu On Tour* (1989), *Cloudland* (1989), *Worlds In Collision* (1991). Compilation: *Terminal Tower* (1985).

Perry, Richard

b 18 June 1942, Brooklyn, New York City, New York, USA. His work with artists ranging from Barbra Streisand and Carly Simon to Tiny Tim and Captain Beefheart made Perry the 'name' producer of the 70s. As a teenager he sang with New York group the Legends whose members included Goldie Zelkowicz (aka Genya Ravan). He began songwriting with Kenny Vance and produced singles for the Kama Sutra and Red Bird labels. In 1967 Perry moved to Los Angeles, producing the debut album of Captain Beefheart And The Magic Band before joining Warner Brothers as a staff producer. In two years with the label, Perry displayed his versatility by supervising recordings by Tiny Tim, Ella Fitzgerald, actor Theodore Bikel and all-female rock group, Fanny. Next, he undertook the project which catapulted him into the forefront of US producers. Columbia Records wished to bring Broadway musical star Barbra Streisand to a mass audience and Perry chose a selection of contemporary material for the *Stoney End* album. The title track became a USTop 10 hit. Harry Nilsson, Carly Simon ('You're So Vain'), Ringo Starr, Leo Sayer and Diana Ross were among the other artists he worked with before setting up his own label, Planet, in 1978. Its most successful signing was the Pointer Sisters, who recorded six albums for the label before moving to RCA in 1986. Perry's later work included *Rock, Rhythm And Blues* (1989), a various artists album including contributions from Chaka Khan, the Pointer Sisters and Rick James.

Persuasions

Formed in the Bedford-Stuyvesant area in New York City, this talented group has continued the a cappella tradition despite prevalent trends elsewhere. Jerry Lawson (b. 23 January 1944, Fort Lauderdale, Florida, USA; lead), Joseph 'Jesse' Russell (b. 25 September 1939, Henderson, North Carolina, USA; tenor), Little Jayotis Washington (b. 12 May 1941, Detroit, Michigan, USA; tenor), Herbert 'Tubo' Rhoad (b. 1 October 1944, Bamberg, South Carolina, USA; baritone) and Jimmy 'Bro' Hayes (b. 12 November 1943, Hopewell, Virginia, USA; bass) began working together in 1966. Having recorded for Minit, the Persuasions gained prominence four years later with *Accapella*, a part live/part studio album released on Frank Zappa's Straight label. Their unadorned voices were later heard on several superb collections including, *Street Corner Symphony* and *Chirpin'*, while the group also supplied harmonies on Joni Mitchell's *Shadows And Light* (1980). During 1973-74, Willie C. Daniel replaced Jayotis Washington in the group. On 8 December 1988 Rhoad died, leaving a four-man group. The Persuasions continue to pursue this peerless path, winding sinewy harmonies around such varied songs as 'Slip Sliding Away' and 'Under The Boardwalk'.

Albums: *Accapella* (1970), *We Came To Play* (1971), *Street Corner Symphony* (1972), *Spread The Word* (1972), *We Still Ain't Got No Band* (1973), *More Than Before* (1974), *I Just Wanna Sing With My Friends* (1974), *Chirpin'* (1977), *Comin' At Ya* (1979), *No Frills* (1984), *Stardust* (1987), *Good News* (1988).

Peters And Lee

After Lennie Peters (b. 1939, London, England, d. 1992) was blinded at the age of 16, an accident which put paid to his ambitions to become a boxer, he began singing and playing piano in pubs around the Islington area of London. Dianne Lee (b. c.1950, Sheffield, Yorkshire, England) was a dancer with her cousin as the Hailey Twins and after Lennie and Dianne met on a tour of clubs they decided to form a duo. This popular club and Holiday Camp act subsequently entered and won UK Independent Television's *Opportunity Knocks*. Their blend of Tony Bennett and Ray Charles numbers made them one of the most popular winners of the talent show which led to the number 1 single, the country-flavoured 'Welcome Home' (1973). The accompanying *We Can Make It* also reached number 1 - it was the first time since

the Beatles that a single and album from a single act had simultaneously held the UK number 1 spots. Whilst becoming regulars on the television variety show circuit, the duo earned three Top 20 singles followed in the ensuing years, including the number 3 hit 'Don't Stay Away Too Long' (1974). After a brief split in 1981, the duo re-formed in the late 80s and maintained their position as one of the UK's major cabaret artists until 1992 when it was announced that Peters was suffering from cancer.
Selected albums: *By Your Side* (1973), *We Can Make It* (1973), *Rainbow* (1974), *Favourites* (1975), *Invitation* (1976), *Serenade* (1976), *Smile* (1977), *Remember When* (1980), *The Farewell Album* (1980), *Through All The Years* (1992). Compilations: *Spotlight On Peters And Lee* (1979). Solo album: Lennie Peters *Unforgettable* (1981).

Philadelphia International Records

Founded in Philadelphia, Pennsylvania, USA in 1971, this much-respected record company defined the sweet, melodic style of early 70s urban soul. Initiators Gamble And Huff were already renowned songwriters and producers through collaborations with Jerry Butler, the Soul Survivors and the Intruders, although several early ventures into label ownership, notably with Gamble and Neptune, had folded prematurely. They nonetheless established a distinctive sound which eschewed Tamla/Motown's cavernous bass lines in favour of a smooth, string-laden, silky approach, fashioned on Burt Bacharach's early work with Dionne Warwick, but embellished with lush orchestration and arrangements often obscuring the punch of a crack rhythm section. Armed with a marketing and distribution deal with Columbia Records, Gamble and Huff founded Philadelphia International knowing the parent company would exploit the white market, leaving the duo free to concentrate their energies on black radio stations. The result was a series of marvellous cross-over hits, including 'Love Train' and 'Backstabbers' (the O'Jays), 'Me And Mrs Jones' (Billy Paul) and 'If You Don't Know Me By Now' (Harold Melvin And The Blue Notes), while the label's cool, sculpted formula was echoed by Blue Magic, the (Detroit) Spinners and the Stylistics. The duo's houseband - Roland Chambers and Norman Harris (guitars), Vince Montana (vibes), Ronnie Baker (bass) and Earl Young (drums) - also appeared on releases by the Delfonics and First Choice, while David Bowie used their Sigma Sound studio to record *Young Americans*. The rise of disco undermined the freshness of 'Philly Soul', but a

recurrent controversy of payola allegations did more to undermine the company's collective confidence. Charges against Huff - that he offered inducements in exchange for airplay - were dropped in 1976, but Gamble was fined $2,500, although commentators have viewed the indictment as racially motivated. Philadelphia International continued to function in the 80s, but its pre-eminent position was usurped by a new generation of black acts. It nonetheless set benchmarks for quality and style in the same way as Motown had done during the previous decade.
Compilations: *Philadelphia Classics* (1978), *The Philadelphia Story* (1986, 14 album box-set), *TSOP: The Sound Of Philadelphia* (1988), *The Philadelphia Years, Volume One* (1989), *The Philadelphia Years Volume 2* (1989).

Phoenix

This UK group rose up from the ashes of Argent in 1975. The band comprised John Verity (vocals/guitar), Robert Henrit (drums) and Jim Rodford (keyboards/bass). The trio continued in much the same vein as before; hard-rock infused with melody and a keen sense of dynamics. They debuted with a self-titled album in 1976 and landed the support slot to Ted Nugent's UK tour. The band went down a storm live, but this was never translated into album sales. They split up after just 12 months together. In 1979 Verity and Henrit re-formed Phoenix with Russ Ballard (keyboards/vocals), Bruce Turgon (bass), Ray Minnhinnett (guitar) and Michael Des Barres (vocals). This short-lived collaboration produced *In Full View*, a non-descript melodic rock album that sold poorly. The band disintegrated shortly afterwards, with Verity and Henrit joining Charlie and then later forming Verity, under the vocalists own surname.
Albums: *Phoenix* (1976), *In Full View* (1979).

Piblokto!

Piblokto! was the second backing group formed by poet/songwriter/singer Pete Brown (b. 25 December 1940, London, England). Drummer Rob Tait was retained from Brown's previous unit, the Battered Ornaments, and the line-up was completed by Jim Mullen (guitar), Dave Thompson (keyboard/saxophone) and Roger Bunn (bass). The quintet recorded their debut album, *Things May Come And Things May Go, But The Art School Dance Goes On Forever*, with the help of augmented musicians, and the collection remains one of the finest of the progressive era. Brown's

Peters And Lee

lyricism coupled with excellent musicianship from all of the various line-ups resulted in several classic moments including 'High Flying Electric Bird' and 'Flying Hero Sandwich'.

Bunn was replaced by Steve Glover prior to a second release, *Thousands On A Raft*, but this excellent album marked the end of Brown's association with Mullen, Thompson and Tait. The singer's sadness over their departure was captured on 'My Last Band', his first single with a new Piblokto! - Glover, Brian Breeze (guitar), Phil Ryan (keyboards) and John 'Pugwash' Weathers (drums). Sadly this line-up also proved unstable; Taff Williams and Ed Spevock replaced Breeze and Glover, but Piblokto! folded in 1971 when Brown began a brief association with Graham Bond.

Albums: *Things May Come And Things May Go But The Art School Dance Goes On Forever* (1970), *Thousands On A Raft* (1971). Compilation: with the Battered Ornaments *My Last Band* (1977).

Pickettywitch

Naming their London-based outfit after a Cornish village, singers Polly Brown and Maggie Farran and their turnover of backing musicians came to public attention in 1969 via ITV's *Opportunity Knocks* television talent show with 'Solomon Grundy', composed and arranged by Tony Macauley and John McLeod. This filled the b-side of the outfit's debut single, 'You Got Me So I Don't Know' but it was their second Pye single, 'The Same Old Feeling' that took them into UK Top 5 during the spring of 1970. With choreographed head movements peculiar to themselves, Pickettywitch promoted '(It's Like A) Sad Old Kinda Movie' and 'Baby I Won't Let You Down' to lesser effect on *Top Of The Pops* and on the cabaret circuit. Polly Brown was also in the news for her publicized romance with disc jockey, Jimmy Saville. After further Macauley-McLeod creations like 'Bring A Little Light Into My World', 'Summertime Feeling' and 'Waldo P. Emerson Jones' plus an album, the group split up - though a new Pickettywitch containing neither Farran nor Brown tried again in the mid-70s. As a soloist, Brown re-entered the British charts in 1974 with 'Up In A Puff Of Smoke', and a later single, 'Honey Honey' was a US hit. Farran subsequently headed a successful London publicity agency.

Album: *Pickettywitch* (1970).

Piglets

Another of Jonathan King's (b. Kenneth King, 6 December 1944, England) pseudonyms, the Piglets followed in the wake of UK hits under his own name ('Everyone's Gone To The Moon', 'Let It All Hang Out', 'Lazy Bones', 'Hooked On A Feeling', and 'Flirt'), as Sakkarin ('Sugar Sugar'), and the Weathermen ('It's The Same Old Song'). Recorded in November 1971 by King and a variety of session men, the Piglets came up with 'Johnny Reggae', which encapsulated the current trend for reggae within a poppy novelty framework perfectly suited to the early 70s. 'Johnny Reggae' quickly became King's fastest selling record to date and reached number 3 on the Bell label in November 1971. The follow-up, 'This Is Reggae' appeared in 1972 on King's UK label which he started in July. It was not a hit and the only other related release was on Bell later in the year - 'Johnny Reggae's Don't Get Your Knickers In A Twist', at which juncture the Piglets were sent to market whilst King created: Shag, Bubblerock, 53rd and 3rd, One Hundred Ton And A Feather, Sound 9418, Father Apraphart and the Smurfs.

Pigsty Hill Light Orchestra

This group formed to play at Fred Wedlock's New Years Party in 1968. All the members came from various well-known UK folk groups: Dave Creech (b. 4 March 1938, Bristol, England; trumpet/vocals/jug/trumpet mouthpiece) from the Elastic Band, Barry Back (b. 10 April 1944, Bristol, England, d. 2 April 1992; guitar/vocals/kazoo) and Andy Leggett (31 March 1942, Much Wenlock, Shropshire, England; vocals/guitar/brass) from the Alligator Jug Thumpers, and John Turner (b. 2 January 1947, Bristol, Avon, England; vocals/bass) from the Downsiders folk group. The party, held at the Troubadour club in Clifton, Bristol, England, became the birthplace of the Pigsty Hill Light Orchestra. The style of music was loosely based on jazz and blues from the 20s and 30s, and a variety of unorthodox instruments were employed to produce what became a highly original sound. Whether it be a paraffin funnel, ballcock sections from toilets, jugs and so on, they played it. In 1970, they released *Phlop!*, and *Melody Maker* voted them one of the bands most likely to succeed. The following year, they made their first Cambridge Folk Festival appearance. Fred Wedlock's *The Folker* and *Frollicks*, released in 1971 and 1973 respectively, featured members from the PHLO. Sadly, after a busy time playing the club and college circuit both at home and abroad, the group disbanded in May 1979. During that time, there had been various personnel changes, Turner had left in 1970, and Back departed in 1972. That same

year the group were augmented by Dave Paskett (b. Dave Paskett Smith, 3 June 1944, Potters Bar, Hertfordshire, England; vocals/guitar), who remained for only two years, and John Hays (percussion/vocals), who stayed until 1979. In 1974, with the departure of both Leggett and Paskett, Chris Newman (b. 30 October 1952, Stevenage, Hertfordshire, England; guitar/bass) joined, as did Henry Davies (bass/brass). More changes occurred in 1975 with the departure of Davies, when Ricky Gold (bass) joined them. A year later, in 1976, Robert Greenfield (b. 14 May 1949, Norfolk, England; guitar) joined as Newman had now left the group. Finally, after Greenfield left in 1978, they were joined by Patrick Small (guitar/kazoo/vocals). Bill Cole (bass), joined the group for a short while, and appeared on *Piggery Joker*. He had also played with the Ken Colyer band. Despite the fairly frequent changes in their line-up, the group were still able to secure a strong and loyal following, and continued recording. A chance telephone call came in 1988, asking Back to resurrect the line-up for a 'one-off' booking at the Village Pump Festival, Trowbridge, Wiltshire. The group, this time, included Hannah Wedlock, Fred's daughter, on vocals. In 1990, the band played the Sidmouth Folk Festival, and at the Tonder Festival, in Denmark, when they were on the bill with Peggy Seeger and Arlo Guthrie. The group are again playing clubs and festivals, and have reached a new audience, to add to those who knew them first time round. True to form, more changes occurred with the departure of both Small and Wedlock in December 1991. They were replaced by Jim Reynolds (b. 15 August 1950, Bristol, Avon, England; vocals/guitar) and Dave Griffiths (b. 23 August 1948, Leeds, West Yorkshire, England; mandolin/fiddle, bass/washboard), reverting the five-piece group to its early jug band sound.
Albums: *Phlop!* (1970), *Piggery Joker* (1972), *The Pigsty Hill Light Orchestra* (1976), *Back On The Road Again* (1991).

Pilot

Formed in Edinburgh, Scotland, in 1973, Pilot initially consisted of David Paton (b. 29 October 1951, Edinburgh; bass/vocals) and Billy Lyall (b. 26 March 1953, Edinburgh; synthesizer/piano/flute andvocals), two former members of the Bay City Rollers and Stuart Tosh (b. 26 September 1951, Aberdeen, Scotland; drums). The trio won a contract with EMI Records after recording a series of demos in London. Session guitarist Ian Bairnson

(b. 3 August 1953, Shetland Isles, Scotland) was recruited in the autumn of 1974. Having secured a Top 20 hit with 'Magic', the group reached the number 1 spot in 1975 with 'January', a simple, but perfectly crafted pop song. The group enjoyed two minor chart entries with 'Call Me Round' and 'Just A Smile', but their increasingly lightweight style quickly palled. Tosh left to join 10cc, while Bairnson and Paton pursued studio careers, which included sessions for Kate Bush's debut *The Kick Inside* (1978) and several recordings for Alan Parsons and Chris DeBurgh. Billy Lyall recorded a solo album, which featured several former colleagues, and later joined Dollar. In December 1989, he died weighing less than five stone, a victim of an AIDS-related illness.
Albums: *From The Album Of The Same Name* (1974), *Second Flight* (1975), *Morin Heights* (1976), *Two's A Crowd* (1977). Compilation: *The Best Of Pilot* (1980).

Pink Fairies

The name 'Pink Fairies' was initially applied to a fluid group of musicians later known as Shagrat. The original Tolkein-inspired appellation was resurrected in 1970 when one of their number, Twink (b. John Alder), erstwhile drummer in Tomorrow and the Pretty Things, joined former Deviants Paul Rudolph (guitar/vocals), Duncan Sanderson (bass/vocals) and Russell Hunter (drums). The Fairies' debut album, *Never Neverland*, was a curious amalgamation of primeval rabble-rousing ('Say You Love Me') and English psychedelia ('Heavenly Man'). It also featured 'Do It' and 'Uncle Harry's Last Freak Out', two songs which became fixtures of the group's live set as they became stalwarts of the free festival and biker circuits. Twink left the band in 1971 and the remaining trio completed the disappointing *What A Bunch Of Sweeties* with the help of Trevor Burton from the Move. Rudolph, later to join Hawkwind, was briefly replaced by Mick Wayne before Larry Wallis joined for *Kings Of Oblivion*, the group's most exciting and unified release. The trio split up in 1974, but the following year joined Rudolph and Twink for a one-off appearance at London's Chalk Farm Roundhouse. A farewell tour, with Sanderson, Wallis and Hunter, extended into 1977, by which time Martin Stone (ex-Chilli Willi And The Red Hot Peppers) had been added to the line-up. The Pink Fairies were then officially dissolved, but the original line-up, without Rudolph, but including Wallis, were reunited in 1987 for *Kill 'Em 'N' Eat 'Em* before

Pilot

going their separate ways again.

Albums: *Never Neverland* (1971), *What A Bunch Of Sweeties* (1972), *Kings Of Oblivion* (1973), *Live At The Roundhouse* (1982), *Previously Unreleased* (1984), *Kill 'Em 'N' Eat 'Em* (1987). Compilations: *Flashback* (1975), *Pink Fairies* (1991).

Planxty

This early 70s Irish group originally featured Christy Moore (b. 7 May 1945, Dublin, Eire; guitar/vocals), Donal Lunny (guitar/bouzouki/synthesizer), Liam O'Flynn (uilleann pipes) and Andy Irvine (guitar/mandolin/bouzouki/vocals). After two albums, Lunny left, to be replaced by Johnny Moynihan (bouzouki). In 1974, Moore left and was replaced by Paul Brady (b. 19 May 1947, Co. Tyrone, Northern Ireland; vocals/guitar). The name Planxty is an Irish word for an air that is written to thank or honour a person. The group remained highly popular throughout its existence and their records sold well. Moynihan then left to join De Danann. After splitting up, the original group re-formed, this time with Matt Molloy (flute), who later joined the Chieftains in September 1979. Moore and Lunny departed once more in 1981 to form Moving Hearts. *Words And Music* featured the Bob Dylan song 'I Pity The Poor Immigrant'. The group were only ever formed as an extension of the various group members' solo commitments, and though they were always in demand at festivals, personal career moves saw an end to the line-up. By the time *The Best Of Planxty Live* emerged, they were pursuing solo projects.

Albums: *Planxty* (1972), *The Well Below The Valley* (1973), *Cold Blow And The Rainy Night* (1974), *After The Break* (1979), *The Woman I Loved So Well* (1980), *Timedance* (1981), *Words And Music* (1983), *The Best Of Planxty Live* (1987). Compilations: *The Planxty Collection* (1976), *The High Kings Of Tara* (1980), *Ansi!* (1984).

Plastic Ono Band

Formed in 1969, the Plastic Ono band initially served as an alternative outlet for John Lennon and his wife Yoko Ono during the fractious final days of the Beatles. The group's debut single, 'Give Peace A Chance', was recorded live in a Montreal hotel room during the much-publicized 'Bed-In' and featured an assortment of underground luminaries attending this unconventional anti-war protest. A more structured group - Lennon, Ono, Eric Clapton (guitar), Klaus Voorman (bass) and

Alan White (drums) - was assembled for a Canadian concert captured on *Live Peace In Toronto 1969*. This audio-verité release contrasted Yoko's free-form and lengthy 'Don't Worry Kyoto' with several rock 'n' roll standards and a preview airing of 'Cold Turkey', the nerve-twitching composition which became the second Plastic Ono single when the Beatles spurned John's initial offer. Bereft of the cosy sentiments of 'Give Peace A Chance', this tough rocker failed to emulate its predecessor's number 2 position, a fact noted by Lennon when he returned his MBE in protest at British passivity over conflicts in Biafra and Vietnam. An expanded version of the group performed at the Lyceum in London during a UNICEF benefit and the Plastic Ono name was also used in a supporting role on several ensuing John and Yoko releases, notably *John Lennon: The Plastic Ono Band*, the artist's first, and arguably finest, solo album. Inspired by Arthur Janov's Primal Scream Therapy, the album was a veritable exorcism of all Lennon's past demons, and a harrowing yet therapeutic glimpse into the abyss of his soul from the bleak atheism of 'God' to the Oedipal 'Mother', the self-mocking 'Working Class Hero', the elegiac child-like wonderment of 'Remember', the confrontation with the self in 'Isolation' and the spine-chilling, macabre nursery rhyme ending, 'My Mummy's Dead'. Voorman was the sole survivor from the earlier version of the Plastic Ono Band, which had included George Harrison and Ringo Starr. Although the epithet also appeared on *Imagine*, *Sometime In New York City* and *Walls And Bridges* (where it was dubbed the Plastic Ono Nuclear Band), it simply applied to whichever musicians had made contributions and had ceased to have any real meaning.

Albums: *Live Peace In Toronto 1969* (1969), *John Lennon: The Plastic Ono Band* (1970), *Sometime In New York City* (1972, also contains the group's live Lyceum concert recording).

Poco

This US group formed as Pogo in the summer of 1968 from the ashes of the seminal Buffalo Springfield, which along with the Byrds was pivotal in the creation of country-rock. The band comprised Richie Furay (b. 9 May 1944, Yellow Springs, Ohio, USA; vocals/guitar), Randy Meisner (b. 8 March, 1946, Scottsbluff, Nebraska, USA; vocal/bass), George Grantham (b. 20 November 1947, Cordell, Oklahoma, USA; drums/vocals), Jim Messina (b. 30 October 1947, Harlingen, Texas, USA; vocals/guitar) and Rusty Young (b. 23 February 1946, Long Beach, California, USA; vocals/pedal steel guitar). Following an objection from Walt Kelly, the copyright owner of the Pogo cartoon character, they adopted the infinitely superior name, Poco. Poco defined as a musical term means 'a little' or 'little by little'. Their debut *Pickin' Up The Pieces* was arguably more country than rock, but its critical success made Poco the leaders of the genre. Meisner departed (later to co-found the Eagles) following a disagreement and *Poco* was released by the remaining quartet, again to critical applause, and like its predecessor made a respectable showing mid-way in the US Top 100. The album's landmark was an entire side consisting of a latin-styled, mainly instrumental suite, 'El Tonto De Nadie Regresa'. On this Rusty Young pushed the capabilities of pedal steel to its limit with an outstanding performance, and justifiably became one of America's top players. The energetically live *Deliverin'* made the US Top 30, the band having added the vocal talent of Timothy B. Schmit (b. 30 October 1947, Sacramento, California, USA; bass/vocals) and from the Illinois Speed Press, Paul Cotton (b. 26 February 1943, Los Angeles, California, USA; vocal/guitar). The departing Jim Messina then formed a successful partnership, Loggins And Messina, with Kenny Loggins. The new line-up consolidated their position with *From The Inside*, but it was the superb *A Good Feelin' To Know* that became their most critically acclaimed work. Contained on this uplifting set are some of Furay's finest songs; there were no weak moments, although worthy of special mention are the title track and the sublime 'I Can See Everything'. Another strong collection, *Crazy Eyes*, included another Furay classic in the 10-minute title track. Richie was tempted away by a lucrative offer to join a planned supergroup with Chris Hillman and J.D. Souther. Poco meanwhile persevered, still producing fine albums, but with moderate sales. Looking over their shoulder, they could see their former support band the Eagles carrying away their mantle.

During the mid-70s the stable line-up of Cotton, Schmit, Grantham and Young released three excellent albums, *Head Over Heels*, *Rose Of Cimarron* and *Indian Summer*. Each well-produced record contained a palatable mix of styles with each member except Grantham, an accomplished writer, and as always their production standards were immaculate. Inexplicably the band were unable to broach the US Top 40, and like Furay, Schmit was tempted away to join the monstrously successful Eagles. Grantham left shortly after and the future

looked decidedly bleak. The recruitment from England of two new members, Charlie Harrison (bass/vocals)and Steve Chapman (drums/vocals), seemed like artistic suicide, but following the further addition of American Kim Bullard on keyboards, they released *Legend* in 1978. Justice was seen to be done; the album made the US Top 20, became a million-seller and dealt them two major hit singles, 'Crazy Love' and 'Heart Of The Night'. This new stable line-up made a further four albums with gradually declining success. Poco sounded particularly jaded on *Ghost Town* in 1982; the magic had evaporated. A contract-fulfilling *Inamorata* was made in 1984. Fans rejoiced to see Richie Furay, Grantham and Schmit together again, and although it was a fine album it sold poorly. Poco then disappeared. Five years later rumours circulated of a new Poco, and lo, Furay, Messina, Meisner, Grantham and Young returned with the exhilarating *Legacy*. Ironically, after all the years of frustration, this was one of their biggest albums, spawning further hit singles. Poco remain, along with the Eagles, the undefeated champions of country-rock.
Albums: *Pickin' Up The Pieces* (1969), *Poco* (1970), *Deliverin'* (1970), *From The Inside* (1971), *A Good Feelin' To Know* (1972), *Crazy Eyes* (1973), *Seven* (1974), *Cantamos* (1974), *Head Over Heels* (1975), *Live* (1976), *Rose Of Cimarron* (1976), *Indian Summer* (1977), *Legend* (1978), *Under The Gun* (1980), *Blue And Gray* (1981), *Cowboys And Englishmen* (1982), *Ghost Town* (1982), *Inamorata* (1984), *Legacy* (1989). Compilations: *The Very Best Of Poco* (1975), *Crazy Loving: The Best Of Poco 1975-1982* (1989), *The Forgotten Trail* (1991).

Poppy Family

This Canadian folk-rock quartet was fronted by Terry Jacks (b. Winnipeg, Manitoba, Canada) and Susan Jacks (b. Susan Peklevits, Vancouver, British Columbia, Canada). Vancouver-based Terry led local group the Chessmen before teaming with, and later marrying, singer Peklevits. They later added guitarist/organist Craig MacCaw and percussionist Satwan Singh (who had played tabla with Ravi Shankar). The group had a transatlantic Top 10 hit with Terry's song 'Which Way You Goin' Billy' in 1970, which they had recorded and originally released in the UK the previous year. They had four more US chart entries before Terry and Susan divorced and went separate ways professionally in 1973. Although Susan's voice was the main feature of the Poppy Family her later recordings on Mercury and Epic had little success.

Terry however had further success with a plaintive version of a Jacques Brel and Rod McKuen song 'Seasons In The Sun'.
Albums: *Which Way You Goin' Billy* (1970), *Poppyseeds* (1971).

Preston, Billy

b. 9 September 1946, Houston, Texas, USA. Preston's topsy-turvy musical career began in 1956 when he played organ with gospel singer, Mahalia Jackson and appeared in the film *St Louis Blues* as a young W.C. Handy. As a teenager he worked with Sam Cooke and Little Richard and it was during the latter's 1962 European tour that Billy first met the Beatles with whom he would later collaborate. Preston established himself as an adept instrumentalist recording in his own right, especially on the driving 'Billy's Bag'. He also appeared frequently as a backing musician on the US television show, *Shindig*. After relocating to Britain as part of the Ray Charles' revue he was signed to Apple in 1969. George Harrison produced his UK hit, 'That's The Way God Planned It', and Preston also contributed keyboards to the Beatles' 'Get Back' and *Let It Be*. The following year he made a guest appearance at the Concert For Bangla Desh. He subsequently moved to A&M Records where he had a successful run of hit singles, with 'Outa-Space' (1972), a US number 1 in 1973 with 'Will It Go Round In Circles', 'Space Race' (1973), and another US number 1 in 1974 with 'Nothing From Nothing'. His compositional talents were also in evidence on 'You Are So Beautiful', a US Top 10 hit for Joe Cocker. Preston meanwhile continued as a sideman, most notably with Sly And The Family Stone and on the 1975 Rolling Stones' US tour. A sentimental duet with Syreeta, 'With You I'm Born Again', was an international hit in 1980. In 1989 preston toured with Ringo Starr's All Star Band and recorded for Ian Levine's Motor City label in 1990-91, including further collaborations with Syreeta. He was arrested on a morals charge in the USA during 1991.
Albums: *Gospel In My Soul* (1962), *The Most Exciting Organ Ever* (1965), *Early Hits Of 1965* (1965), *The Apple Of Their Eye* (1965), *The Wildest Organ In Town!* (1966), *That's The Way God Planned It* (1969), *Greazee Soul* (1969), *Encouraging Words* (1970), *I Wrote A Simple Song* (1971), *Music Is My Life* (1972), *Everybody Likes Some Kind Of Music* (1973), *The Kids & Me* (1974), *Live European Tour* (1974), *It's My Pleasure* (1975), *Do What You Want* (1976), *Billy Preston* (1976), *A Whole New*

Billy Preston with Joe Cocker

Thing (1977), *Soul'd Out* (1977), *Gospel In My Soul* (1977), with Syreeta *Fast Break* (1979), *Late At Night* (1979), *Behold* (1980), *Universal Love* (1980), *The Way I Am* (1981), *Billy Preston & Syreeta* (1981), *Pressin' On* (1982). Compilations: *The Best Of Billy Preston* (1988), *Collection* (1989).

Previn, Dory

b Dory Langdon, 27 October 1937, Woodbridge, New Jersey, USA, she was the daughter of a musician who became a child singer and dancer in New Jersey, graduating to musical theatre as a chorus line member. Her abilities as a songwriter next brought Langdon work composing music for television programmes. After moving to Hollywood, she met and married André Previn in 1959, the year in which he composed the tune 'No Words For Dory'. Now a lyricist for movie soundtracks, Dory Previn worked with Andre, Elmer Bernstein and others on songs for such films as *Pepe*, *Two For The Seesaw*, and *Valley Of The Dolls*, whose theme tune was a big hit for Dionne Warwick in 1967. By now the Previns had separated and in the late 60s Dory turned to more personal lyrics, publishing a book of poems before launching a recording career with United Artists. Produced by Nik Venet, her early albums were noted for angry, intimate and often despairing material like 'The Lady With The Braid' and 'Who Will Follow Norma Jean ?'. The title track of *Mary*

C. Brown & The Hollywood Sign was based on a true story of a suicide attempt and was turned by Previn into a stage musical. In 1974, she left U.A. for Warner Brothers where Joel Dorn produced the 1976 album,. In that year she also published her memoirs, *Midnight Baby*.
Albums: *On My Way To Where* (1970), *Mythical Kings & Iguanas* (1971), *Reflections In A Mud Puddle* (1971), *Mary C. Brown & The Hollywood Sign* (1972), *Live At Carnegie Hall* (1973), *Dory Previn* (1975), *We Are Children Of Coincidence And Harpo Marx* (1976), *1 AM Phone Calls* (1977).
Further reading: *Midnight Baby*, Dory Previn.

Protheroe, Brian

b. Salisbury, Wiltshire, England. This showbusiness jack-of-all-trades was a trainee laboratory technician, moonlighting in a provincial folk group, before becoming a professional thespian. Earnings as a recording artist were an adjunct to those in repertory acting, but his mid-70s albums were more pleasant and less coyly self-centred than those of others more famous who had cornered the student bedsit market. The title track of *Pinball* - wracked flashes of London's Soho low-life - was his only UK hit. Backed on record by Barry Morgan (drums) and Brian Odgers (bass), Protheroe was a proficient guitarist and pianist, and a tuneful vocalist both in the studio - and onstage as shown by his success in 1976's West End rock

Brian Protheroe

musical, *Leave Him To Heaven*. He has also appeared as 'Macheath' in a London production of John Gay's *The Beggar's Opera* in 1980, and, later, in Dublin, Eire as 'Captain Von Trapp' in *The Sound Of Music*. He has also composed music for many pantomimes at his local Stratford East theatre. By the 90s, he was better known as an excellent actor appearing in British television drama appearances which included leading roles in *Not A Penny More Not A Penny Less*, *Shrinks* and *Natural Lies*. He has also been seen in films, notably *Superman* and *A Nightingale Sang In Berkeley Square*. Albums: *Pinball* (1974), *Pick Up* (1975), *I/You* (1976).

Pure Prairie League

Formed in 1971, this US country rock group comprised Craig Lee Fuller (vocals/guitar), George Powell (vocals/guitar), John Call (pedal steel guitar), Jim Lanham (bass) and Jim Caughlin (drums). Their self-titled debut album was a strong effort, which included the excellent 'Tears', 'You're Between Me' (a tribute to McKendree Spring) and 'It's All On Me'. The work also featured some novel sleeve artwork, using Norman Rockwell's portrait of an ageing cowboy as a symbol of the Old West. On *Pure Prairie League*, the figure was seen wistfully clutching a record titled 'Dreams Of Long Ago'. For successive albums, the cowboy would be portrayed being ejected from a saloon, stranded in a desert and struggling with a pair of boots. The image effectively gave Pure Prairie League a brand name, but by the time of their *Bustin' Out*, Fuller and Powell were left to run the group using session musicians. This album proved their masterwork, one of the best and most underrated records produced in country rock. Its originality lay in the use of string arrangements, for which they recruited the services of former David Bowie acolyte Mick Ronson. His work was particularly effective on the expansive 'Boulder Skies' and 'Call Me Tell Me'. A single from the album, 'Amie', was a US hit and prompted the return of John Call, but when Fuller left in 1975 to form American Flyer, the group lost its major writing talent and inspiration. Powell continued with bassist Mike Reilly, lead guitarist Larry Goshorn and pianist Michael Connor. Several minor albums followed and the group achieved a surprise US Top 10 hit in 1980 with 'Let Me Love You Tonight'. Fuller is now with Little Feat.
Albums: *Pure Prairie League* (1972), *Bustin' Out* (1972), *Two Lane Highway* (1975), *If The Shoe Fits* (1976), *Dance* (1976), *Live!! Takin' The Stage* (1977), *Just Fly* (1978), *Can't Hold Back* (1979), *Firin' Up* (1980), *Something In The Night* (1981). Compilation: *Pure Prairie Collection* (1981).

Q

Quatro, Suzi

b. 3 June 1950, Detroit, Michigan, USA. From patting bongos at the age of seven in her father's jazz band, she graduated to go-go dancing in a pop series on local television. With an older sister, Patti (later of Fanny) she formed the all-female Suzi Soul And The Pleasure Seekers in 1964 for engagements that included a tour of army bases in Vietnam. In 1971, her comeliness and skills as bass guitarist, singer and chief show-off in Cradle were noted by Mickie Most who persuaded her to record Nicky Chinn-Mike Chapman songs for his RAK label in England. Backed initially by Britons Alastair McKenzie (keyboards), Dave Neal (drums) and her future husband, ex-Nashville Teens member Len Tuckey (guitar), a second RAK single, 1973's 'Can The Can', topped hit parades throughout the world at the zenith of the glam-rock craze - of which rowdy Suzi, androgynous in her glistening biker leathers, became an icon. Her sound hinged mostly on a hard rock chug beneath lyrics in which scansion overruled meaning ('the 48 crash/is a silken sash bash'). The team's winning streak with such as '48 Crash', 'Daytona Demon' and 'Devil Gate Drive' - a second UK number 1 - faltered when 'Your Mama Won't Like Me' stuck outside the Top 30, signalling two virtually hitless years before a mellower policy brought a return to the Top 10 with 'If You Can't Give Me Love'. Quatro's chart fortunes in Britain have since lurched from 'She's In Love With You' at number 11 to 1982's 'Heart Of Stone' at a lowly 68. 'Stumblin' In' - a 1978 duet with Smokie's Chris Norman - was her biggest US Hot 100 strike (number 8) but barely touched the UK Top 40. By the late 80s, her output had reduced to pot-shots like teaming up with Reg Presley of the Troggs for a disco revival of 'Wild Thing'. More satisfying than tilting for hit records, however, was her development as a singing actress - albeit in character as 'Leather Tuscadero' in *Happy Days*, a cameo in ITV's *Minder* and as the quick-drawing heroine of a 1986 London production of Irving Berlin's *Annie Get Your Gun*.

Selected albums: *Suzi Quatro* (1973), *Suzi Quatro's Greatest Hits* (1980), *Main Attraction* (1983), *Saturday Night Special* (1987), *Rock 'Til Ya Drop* (1988).

Queen

Arguably Britain's most consistently successful group of the past two decades, Queen began life as a glam rock unit in 1972. Brian May (b. 19 July 1947, Twickenham, Middlesex, England; guitar) and Roger Taylor (b. Roger Meddows-Taylor, 26 July 1949, Kings Lynn, Norfolk, England; drums) had been playing in a college group called Smile with bassist Tim Staffell. When the latter left to join Humpty Bong (featuring former Bee Gees drummer Colin Petersen), May and Taylor elected to form a new band with vocalist Freddie Mercury (b. Frederick Bulsara, 5 September 1946, Zanzibar, Africa, d. 24 November 1991). Early in 1971 bassist John Deacon (b. 19 August 1951, Leicester, England) completed the line-up. Queen were signed to EMI late in 1972 and launched the following spring with a gig at London's Marquee club. Soon after the failed single, 'Keep Yourself Alive', they issued a self-titled album, which was an interesting fusion of 70s glam and late 60s heavy rock. Queen toured extensively and recorded a second album which fulfilled their early promise by reaching the UK Top 5. Soon after, 'Seven Seas Of Rhye' gave them their first hit single, while *Sheer Heart Attack* consolidated their commercial standing. The title track from the album was also the band's first US hit. The pomp and circumstance of Queen's recordings and live act were embodied in the outrageously camp theatrics of the satin-clad Mercury, who was swiftly emerging as one of rock's most notable showmen during the mid-70s.

1975 was to prove a watershed in the group's career. After touring the Far East, they entered the studio with producer Roy Thomas Baker and completed the kitsch epic 'Bohemian Rhapsody', in which Mercury succeeded in transforming a seven-minute single into a mini-opera. The track was both startling and unique in pop and dominated the Christmas charts in the UK, remaining at number 1 for an astonishing nine weeks. The power of the single was reinforced by an elaborate video production, highly innovative for its period and later much copied by other acts. An attendant album, *A Night At The Opera*, was one of the most expensive and expansive albums of its period and lodged at number 1 in the UK, as well as hitting the US Top 5. Queen were now aspiring to the superstar bracket. Their career thereafter was a carefully marketed succession of hit singles, annual albums and extravagantly produced stage shows. *A Day At The Races* continued the bombast, while the catchy 'Somebody To Love'

Suzi Quatro

Queen

and anthemic 'We Are The Champions' both reached number 2 in the UK. Although Queen seemed in danger of being stereotyped as over-produced glam rock refugees, they successfully brought some eclecticism to their singles output with the rockabilly 'Crazy Little Thing Called Love' and disco-influenced 'Another One Bites The Dust' (both US number 1s). The group's soundtrack for the movie *Flash Gordon* was another success, typical of their pretentious approach. By the close of 1981, Queen were back at number 1 in the UK for the first time since 'Bohemian Rhapsody' with 'Under Pressure' (a collaboration with David Bowie). After a flurry of solo ventures, the group returned in fine form in 1984 with the satiric 'Radio Gaga', followed by the histrionic 'I Want To Break Free'. A performance at 1985's Live Aid displayed the group at their most professional and many acclaimed them the stars of the day. Coincidentally, their next single was 'One Vision', an idealistic song in keeping with the spirit of Live Aid. Queen's recorded output lessened during the late 80s as they concentrated on extra-curricular ventures. The space between releases did not effect the group's popularity, however, as was proven in 1991 when 'Intuition' entered the UK chart at number 1. Laden with powerful harmonies, and faultless musicianship, held together with May's biting guitar virtuosity and the

spectacular Mercury; Queen were one of the greatest rock acts. The career of the group effectively ended with the death of lead singer Freddie Mercury on 24 November 1991. 'Bohemian Rhapsody' was immediately reissued to raise money for AIDS research projects, and soared to the top of the British charts. A memorial concert for Freddie Mercury took place at London's Wembley Stadium in the spring of 1992, featuring an array of stars including Liza Minnelli, Elton John, Guns N' Roses, George Michael, David Bowie and Annie Lennox.
Albums: *Queen* (1973), *Queen II* (1974), *Sheer Heart Attack* (1974), *A Night At The Opera* (1975), *A Day At The Races* (1976), *News Of The World* (1977), *Jazz* (1978), *Live Killers* (1979), *The Game* (1980), *Flash Gordon* (1980), *Hot Space* (1982), *A Kind Of Magic* (1986), *Live Magic* (1986), *The Miracle* (1989), *Queen At The Beeb* (1989), *Innuendo* (1991). Compilations: *Greatest Hits* (1981), *The Works* (1984), *The Complete Works* (1985), *Greatest Hits Vol. 2* (1991).

Quintessence

Although formed by virtue of advertisements in *Melody Maker*, this briefly-popular act encapsulated the spiritual ambitions prevalent among sections of the UK 60s 'underground' movement. The original line-up - Raja Ram (b. Ron Rothfield;

vocals/flute), Shiva Shankar (aka Shiva Jones; vocals/keyboards), Alan Mostert (lead guitar), Maha Dev (rhythm guitar), Sambhu Babaji (bass) and Jake Milton (drums) - was forged following rehearsals at London's Notting Hill's All Saints Hall and their ensuing debut, *In Blissful Company*, captured the sextet's rudimentary blend of jazz/rock and Eastern philosophies. Mostert's powerful guitar style endeared the group to the progressive audience, but a commitment to religious themes was maintained on *Dive Deep* and *Self*. The departures of Shankar and Maha Dev - the former resurfaced in the similarly-styled Kala - robbed Quintessence of a sense of purpose and the group split up following the release of *Indweller*.

Albums: *In Blissful Company* (1969), *Quintessence* (1970), *Dive Deep* (1970, *Self* (1971), *Indweller* (1972).

Quiver

This under-rated group evolved from the ruins of Junior's Eyes, one of UK's more inventive progressive rock bands. Tim Renwick (guitar) and Honk (bass) founded the new unit, but when the latter dropped out, the line-up was completed by Pete Thomas (bass), formerly of Village, ex-Cochise drummer John 'Willie' Wilson' and guitarist/songwriter Cal Batchelor. Quiver hold the distinction of being the first group to play at London's famous Rainbow Theatre. Their two albums showcase a grasp of melodic rock, similar to American acts such as the Doobie Brothers, while sharing an affinity with the early Brinsley Schwarz. Neither release made a commercial impact and in 1973 all of the group, except Batchelor, agreed to amalgamate with the Sutherland Brothers. Renwick, meanwhile, joined 747, a short-lived pub-rock band, before forming Kicks, an equally brief ensemble.

Albums: *Quiver* (1971), *Gone In The Morning* (1972).

R

Racing Cars

From his Manchester, England audio shop, ex-Mindbenders Bob Land (bass) was persuaded to re-enter showbusiness in 1975 with Graham Headley Williams (guitar), Gareth Mortimer (guitar), Roy Edwards (keyboards) and Robert Wilding (drums). Released by Chrysalis, their records included bit-parts for session pianist Geraint Watkins, American saxophonist Jerry Jumonville, the Bowles Brothers Band (on vocal harmonies) and Swinging Blue Jeans guitarist Ray Ennis. Reaching number 39 in the UK album list, the band's debut *Downtown Tonight* also produced an unexpected Top 20 entry with the ballad 'They Shoot Horses Don't They'. No more hits were forthcoming but the group were sufficiently established in the colleges to issue two further albums.
Albums: *Downtown Tonight* (1976), *Weekend Rendezvous* (1977), *Bring On The Night* (1978).

Rafferty, Gerry

b. 16 April 1947, Paisley, Scotland. The lengthy career of the reclusive Rafferty started as a member of the Humblebums with Billy Connolly and Tam Harvey in 1968. After its demise through commercial indifference, Transatlantic Records offered him a solo contract. The result was *Can I Have My Money Back?*, a superb blend of folk and gentle pop music, featuring one of the earliest cover paintings from the well-known Scottish artist 'Patrick' (playwright John Byrne). Rafferty showed great promise as a songwriter with the rolling 'Steamboat Row' and the plaintive and observant, 'Her Father Didn't Like Me Anyway', but the album was a commercial failure. Rafferty's next solo project came after an interruption of seven years, four as a member of the brilliant but turbulent Stealers Wheel, and three through litigation over managerial problems. Much of this is documented in his lyrics both with Stealers Wheel and as a soloist. *City To City* in 1978 raised his profile and gave him a hit single that created a classic song with probably the most famous saxophone introduction in pop music, performed by Raphael Ravenscroft. 'Baker Street' became a multi-million seller and narrowly missed the top of the charts. The album sold similar numbers and Rafferty became a reluctant star. He declined to perform in the USA even though his album was number 1. The follow-up *Night Owl* was almost as successful, containing a similar batch of strong songs with intriguing lyrics and haunting melodies. Rafferty's output has been sparse during the 80s and none of his recent work has matched his earlier songs. He made a single contribution to the film *Local Hero* and produced the Top 3 hit for the Proclaimers with 'Letter From America' in 1987. Joe Egan added harmony vocals to his 1993 album which was accompanied by a rare tour.
Albums: *Can I Have My Money Back* (1971), *City To City* (1978), *Night Owl* (1979), *Snakes And Ladders* (1980), *Sleepwalking* (1982), *North And South* (1988), *On A Wing And A Prayer* (1993). Selected compilations: *Early Collection* (1986), *Blood And Glory* (1988).

Rainbow

In 1974, guitarist Ritchie Blackmore (b. 14 April 1945, Weston-Super-Mare, England; guitar) left Deep Purple, forming Rainbow the following year. His earlier involvement with American band Elf, led to his recruitment of Elf's Ronnie James Dio (vocals), Mickey Lee Soule, (keyboards), Craig Gruber on bass and Gary Driscoll as drummer. Their debut, *Ritchie Blackmore's Rainbow*, was released in 1975, and was undeservedly seen by some as a poor imitation of Deep Purple. Rainbow was intended to go in a different musical direction to Deep Purple. The constant turnover of personnel was representative of Blackmore's quest for the ultimate line-up and sound. Dissatisfaction with the debut album led to a new line-up being assembled. Jimmy Bain took over from Gruber, and Cozy Powell replaced Driscoll. With Tony Carey on keyboards, *Rainbow Rising* was released, an album far more confident than its predecessor. Shortly after this, Bain and Carey left, being replaced by Bob Daisley and David Stone respectively. It was when Rainbow moved to America that difficulties between Dio and Blackmore came to a head, resulting in Dio's departure from the band in 1978. His replacement was Graham Bonnet, whose only album with Rainbow, *Down To Earth*, saw the return as bassist of Roger Glover, the man Blackmore had forced out of Deep Purple in 1973. The album was a marked departure from the Dio days, and while it is often considered one of the weaker Rainbow albums, it did provide an enduring single, 'Since You've Been Gone', written and originally recorded by Russ Ballard. Bonnet and Powell soon became victims of another reorganization of

Rainbow's line-up. New vocalist Joe Lynn Turner brought a much more American feel to the band, introducing a commercial sound to *Difficult To Cure*, the album which produced the big hit, 'I Surrender'. Thereafter the band went into decline as their increasingly middle-of-the-road albums were ignored by the fans. In 1984 the Rainbow project was ended following the highly popular Deep Purple reunion. The compilation *Finyl Vinyl* appeared in 1986, and featured several different incarnations of Rainbow and some unreleased recordings.

Albums: *Ritchie Blackmore's Rainbow* (1975), *Rainbow Rising* (1976), *Live On Stage* (1977), *Long Live Rock And Roll* (1978), *Live In Germany* (1976, 1990), *Down To Earth* (1979), *Difficult To Cure* (1981), *Straight Between The Eyes* (1982), *Bent Out Of Shape* (1983). Compilation: *Finyl Vinyl* (1986).

Rak Records

Mickie Most (b. Michael Peter Hayes, June 1938, Aldershot, Surrey, England) started out in the music business as a performer who had a string of successes in South Africa in the 60s (with Mickie Most And The Playboys). He came home from constant touring of that country and became a producer, working with everyone from the Animals to Donovan. In the late 60s he decided to introduce the American selling style of rack-jobbing to the UK. This is where the salesman sets up a rack of albums for sale in places outside of record shops such as garages and supermarkets. To achieve this he formed Rak Records - the 'c' dropped from Rack as he thought it looked less harsh. Unfortunately supermarkets were not keen on the idea - although within a decade it was a commonplace outlet - but Most chose to keep the company name. In 1970 he decided to form a production company but initially he had no artists signed as all the people he was working with were already on the books of other companies. However, this changed in 1970 when he released Rak's first single - Julie Felix singing the Paul Simon-penned 'If I Could (El Condor Pasa)'. This was followed by a release from Peter Noone whom Most knew from producing Herman's Hermits. Rak quickly became big business, picking up Hot Chocolate from Apple, Alexis Korner's CCS - Collective Consciousness Society (whose version of 'Whole Lotta Love' was the theme music to *Top Of The Pops* for the best part of a decade), the Australian folk group New World (soon to be implicated in the Janie Jones 'sex for airplay' scandal), and dozens of teenybop groups like

Rainbow

Kenny, Suzi Quatro, Mud, the Arrows and Smokie. Songwriters and producers like Nicky Chinn and Mike Chapman had many hits through Rak, and at one point the company was situated in Charles Street, Mayfair, next door to the equally successful Bell Records (Gary Glitter, Bay City Rollers, etc.) causing some people to dub it 'teen-pan alley'. At the same time as running Rak, Most also became famous as a panelist on the talent show *New Faces*. As the teeny bop era passed into punk, Rak became less prolific with the hits though they bounced back briefly in the 80s with Kim Wilde.

Ram Jam

Formed in the mid-70s, Ram Jam was an east coast group best known for its one Top 20 single, 'Black Betty', in 1977. That song was the focus of a boycott by some black groups, which considered it offensive to black women, even though it had been written by Huddie 'Leadbelly' Ledbetter, the legendary black folk and blues singer. The group consisted of guitarist Bill Bartlett (b. 1949), bassist Howie Blauvelt (formerly a member of Billy Joel's early group the Hassles), singer Myke Scavone and drummer Pete Charles. Bartlett had earlier been lead guitarist with the Lemon Pipers. After leaving that group, Bartlett retired from music for some time, before recording a demo of the Leadbelly song. Released on Epic Records, it reached number 18, but the group never had another hit. In the UK they succeeded twice, in 1977 (number 7) and in 1990 a re-mix version made number 13 making them a quite extraordinary one-hit-wonder.

Albums: *Ram Jam* (1977), *Portrait Of An Artist As A Young Ram* (1978).

Ramones

The Ramones, comprising Johnny Ramone (b. John Cummings, 8 October 1951, Long Island, New York, USA; guitar), Dee Dee Ramone (b. Douglas Colvin, 18 September 1952, Vancouver, British Columbia, Canada; bass) and Joey Ramone (b. Jeffrey Hyman, 1952; drums) made their debut at New York's Performance Studio on 30 March 1974. Two months later manager Tommy Ramone (b. Tommy Erdelyi, 29 January 1952, Budapest, Hungary) replaced Joey on drums, who then switched to vocals. The quartet later secured a residency at the renowned CBGB's club where they became one of the city's leading proponents of punk rock. The fever-paced *Ramones* was a startling first album. Its high-octane assault drew from 50s kitsch and 60s garage-bands, while leather jackets, ripped jeans and an affected dumbness enhanced their music's cartoon-like quality. The group's debut appearance in London in July 1976 influenced a generation of British punk musicians, while *The Ramones Leave Home*, which included 'Suzie Is A Headbanger' and 'Gimme Gimme Shock Treatment', confirmed the sonic attack of its predecessor. *Rocket To Russia* was marginally less frenetic as the group's novelty appeal waned, although 'Sheena Is A Punk Rocker' gave the group their first UK Top 30 hit, in 1977. In May 1978 Tommy Ramone left to pursue a career in production and former Richard Hell drummer Marc Bell, now Marky Ramone, replaced him for *Road To Ruin* as the band sought to expand their appealing, but limited, style. They took a starring role in the trivial *Rock 'N' Roll High School* film, a participation which led to their collaboration with producer Phil Spector. The resultant release, *End Of The Century*, was a curious hybrid, and while Johnny baulked at Spector's laborious recording technique, Joey, whose penchant for girl-group material gave the Ramones their sense of melody, was less noticeably critical. The album contained a sympathetic version of the Ronettes' 'Baby I Love You' which became the group's biggest UK hit single when it reached the Top 10.

The Ramones entered the 80s looking increasingly anachronistic, unable or unwilling to change. *Pleasant Dreams*, produced by Graham Gouldman, revealed a group now outshone by the emergent hard-core acts they had inspired. However, *Subterranean Jungle* showed a renewed purpose which was maintained sporadically on *Animal Boy* and *Halfway To Sanity*, the former containing 'Bonzo Goes To Bitburg', a hilarious riposte to Ronald Reagan's ill-advised visit to a cemetery containing graves of Nazi SS personnel. Although increasingly confined to pop's fringes, a revitalized line-up - Joey, Johnny, Marky and newcomer C.J. - undertook a successful 1990 US tour alongside fellow CBGB's graduate Deborah Harry and Talking Heads' offshoot Tom Tom Club.

Albums: *Ramones* (1976), *The Ramones Leave Home* (1977), *Rocket To Russia* (1977), *Road To Ruin* (1978), *It's Alive* (1979), *End Of The Century* (1980), *Pleasant Dreams* (1981), *Subterranean Jungle* (1983), *Too Tough To Die* (1984), *Animal Boy* (1986), *Halfway To Sanity* (1987), *Brain Drain* (1989), *Loco Live* (1991). Compilation: *Ramones Mania* (1988), *All The Stuff And More (Volume One)* (1990).

Ramones

Rare Bird

Steve Gould (vocals/saxophone/bass) and Dave Kaffinette (keyboards) fronted this British group throughout its recording career. Graham Field (organ) and Mark Ashton (drums) completed the line-up featured on *Rare Bird*, which included their memorable 1970 hit single, 'Sympathy'. Although this atmospheric protest ballad only reached the lower reaches of the UK Top 30, it proved highly popular on the Continent and has since become a cult favourite. The group came under the wing of Tony Stratton-Smith, but failed to translate their European charm into further success at home. Gould and Kaffinette were joined by Andy Curtis (guitar) and Fred Kelly (percussion) for *Epic Forest*, but despite initial promise, this restructured line-up failed to revitalize Rare Bird's increasingly ailing fortunes.

Albums: *Rare Bird* (1969), *As Your Mind Flies By* (1970), *Epic Forest* (1972), *Somebody's Watching* (1973), *Born Again* (1974), *Rare Bird* (1975). Compilations: *Sympathy* (1976), *Rare Bird - Polydor Special* (1977).

Rare Earth

Saxophonist Gil Bridges and drummer Pete Rivera formed their first R&B band, the Sunliners, in Detroit in 1961. Bassist John Parrish joined in 1962; guitarist Rod Richards and keyboards player Kenny James followed in 1966. After years of playing in local clubs, they were signed to Motown in 1969, where they were renamed Rare Earth after the label's newly-formed progressive rock subsidiary. They scored immediate success with a rock-flavoured version of the Temptations' hit 'Get Ready', which reached the US Top 10. The single was edited down from a 20-minute recording which occupied one side of their debut album: it showcased the band's instrumental prowess, but also typified their tendency towards artistic excess. A cover of another Temptations' classic, '(I Know) I'm Losing You', brought them more success in 1970, as did original material like 'Born To Wander' and 'I Just Want To Celebrate'. But Rare Earth had already suffered the first in a bewildering series of personnel changes which dogged their progress over the next decade, as Rod Richards and Kenny James were replaced by Ray Manette and Mark Olson respectively, and Ed Guzman was added on percussion. This line-up scored several minor US hits in the early 70s, until internal upheavals in 1973 led to a complete revamp of the band's style. The Temptations' mentor, Norman Whitfield, produced the highly-regarded *Ma* that year, with new band leader Peter Hoorelbeke on vocals. By the release of *Back To Earth* in 1975, he in turn had been supplanted by Jerry La Croix. Subsequent releases proved commercially unsuccessful, though the band continued to record and tour into the 80s. Former members Peter Hoorelbeke, Gil Bridges and Michael Urso later combined as Hub for an album on Capitol Records. At the turn of the decade the line-up comprised, Gil Bridges, Ray Monette, Edward Guzman, Wayne Baraks, Rick Warner, Dean Boucher, Randy Burghdoff. They joined Ian Levine's Motor City label in 1990 and issued 'Love Is Here And Now You've Gone'. The band continue to be hugely successful in Germany.

Albums: *Get Ready* (1969), *Ecology* (1970), *One World* (1971), *In Concert* (1971), *Willie Remembers* (1972), *Ma* (1973), *Back To Earth* (1975), *Midnight Lady* (1976), *Rare Earth* (1977), *Band Together* (1978), *Grand Slam* (1978).

Raspberries

Formed in 1970, this popular 70s US group evolved from several aspiring Ohio-based bands. The original line-up included two former members of Cyrus Erie, Eric Carmen (b. 11 August 1949, Cleveland, Ohio, USA; vocals, guitar, keyboards) and Marty Murphy (guitar), as well as ex-Choir drummer Jim Bonfanti (b. 17 December 1948, Windber, Pennsylvania, USA). Murphy was quickly replaced by Wally Bryson (b. 18 July 1949, Gastonia, North Carolina, USA), a veteran of both groups, who in turn introduced John Alleksic. However the latter was removed in favour of Dave Smalley (b. 10 July 1949, Oil City, Pennsylvania, USA; guitar, bass), another ex-Choir acolyte. The Raspberries' love of the Beatles was apparent on their debut 'Don't Wanna Say Goodbye'. Its melodic flair set the tone of 'Go All The Way', a gorgeous slice of Anglophilia which rose to number 5 in the US chart. *Raspberries* confirmed the quartet's undoubted promise, but it was on *Fresh*, released a mere four months later, that their talent fully blossomed. Here the group's crafted harmonies recalled those of the Beach Boys and Hollies, while a buoyant *joie de vivre* was apparent on such memorable songs as 'Let's Pretend' and 'I Wanna Be With You'. This cohesion, sadly, was not to last and while *Side 3* included wider influences drawn from the Who and Small Faces, it also reflected a growing split between Carmen and the Bonfanti/Smalley team who were summarily fired in 1973. Scott McCarl (guitar) and Michael McBride (drums, ex-Cyrus Erie) completed the new Raspberries' line-up which debuted the following year with the gloriously ambitious 'Overnight Sensation'. The attendant album, cheekily entitled *Starting Over*, contained several equally memorable songs, but it was clear that Carmen now required a broader canvas for his work. He disbanded the group in 1975 and embarked on an intermittently successful solo career, while Bryson resurfaced in two disappointing pop/rock bands, Tattoo and Fotomaker.

Albums: *Raspberries* (1972), *Fresh* (1972), *Side 3* (1973), *Starting Over* (1974). Compilations: *Raspberries' Best Featuring Eric Carmen* (1976), *Overnight Sensation - The Very Best Of The Raspberries* (1987).

Real Thing

This Liverpool-based group has its origins in the Mersey boom. Lead singer Eddie Amoo was a former member of the Chants, whose excellent beat singles garnered considerable praise. Although they failed to chart, the Chants continued to record for various labels until the name was ultimately dropped. The Real Thing emerged in 1976 with 'You To Me Are Everything' which reached number 1 in the UK. Their next release, 'Can't Get By Without You' continued their brand of commercial sweet soul, but later singles were less successful until a more forthright performance in 1979 with the *Star Wars*-influenced, 'Can You Feel The Force', took the group back into the Top 5 establishing their popularity with the British disco audience. Since then the Real Thing's new material has fared less well, although remixes of those first two hits charted 10 years after their initial release, both reaching the UK Top 10.

Albums: *The Real Thing* (1976), *Four From Eight* (1977), *Step Into Our World* (1978), *Can You Feel The Force* (1979).

Redbone

A North American Indian band formed in 1968, Redbone included brothers Pat and Lolly Vegas (both b. Fresno, California, USA), who had already pursued minor performing careers. Lolly had recorded as early as 1961, while together the brothers completed *At The Haunted House*, as well as several singles. The duo were also successful songwriters, and a compulsive dance-based composition, 'Niki Hoeky', was interpreted by such diverse acts as P.J. Proby and Bobbie Gentry. Redbone, an Anglicized cajun epithet for half-breed, was completed by Tony Bellamy (b. Los

Angeles, California, USA; rhythm guitar/vocals) and Peter DePoe (b. Neah Bay Reservation, Washington, USA; drums). DePoe, whose native name was 'Last Walking Bear', had been for some time a ceremonial drummer on his reservation. With Pat on bass and Lolly on guitar and vocals, the group initially backed several different artists, including Odetta and John Lee Hooker, before embarking on an independent direction. The quartet scored an international hit with 'Witch Queen Of New Orleans', which owed much to the then-popular southern, or Cajun 'swamp-rock' style. In 1974 they enjoyed their sole million-seller, 'Come And Get Your Love', but the group was unable to transform their taught, but rhythmic, style into a consistent success.

Albums: *Redbone* (1970), *Potlatch* (1970), *Witch Queen Of New Orleans* (1971), *Message From A Drum* (1972), *Already Here* (1972), *Wovoka* (1974), *Beaded Dreams Through Turquoise Eyes* (1974), *Cycles* (1978). Compilations: *Come And Get Your Redbone* (1975), *Best Of Redbone* (1976), *Rock Giants* (1982).

Reddy, Helen

b. 25 October 1942, Melbourne, Victoria Australia, Reddy was a big-voiced interpreter of rock ballads whose 'I Am Woman' became a feminist anthem. From a show business family, she was a child performer and had starred in her own television show before winning a trip to New York in an Australian talent show in 1966. There, an appearance on the influential *Tonight Show* led to a recording contract with Capitol and a 1971 hit single with 'I Don't Know How To Love Him' from Andrew Lloyd Webber and Tim Rice's *Jesus Christ Superstar*. The following year, the powerful 'I Am Woman' was a US million-seller and over the next five years, Reddy had a dozen further hit singles. Among them were the contrasting number 1s, Alex Harvey's modern country ballad 'Delta Dawn' (1973), and the chilling, dramatic 'Angie Baby' in 1974. Her 1976 song 'I Can't Hear You No More' was composed by Carole King and Gerry Goffin while Reddy's final Top 20 record was a revival of Cilla Black's 1964 hit 'You're My World', co-produced by Kim Fowley. Reddy also became a well-known television personality, hosting the *Midnight Special* show for most of the 70s, taking a cameo role in *Airport 75* and starring in the 1978 film *Pete's Dragon*. She also sang 'Little Boys', the theme song for the film *The Man Who Loved Women* (1983).

Albums: *I Don't Know How To Love Him* (1971),

Real Thing

Helen Reddy (1971), *I Am Woman* (1972), *Long Hard Climb* (1973), *Love Song For Jeffrey* (1974), *Free And Easy* (1974), *No Way To Treat A Lady* (1975), *Music Music* (1976), *Ear Candy* (1977), *We'll Sing In The Sunshine* 1978, *Live In London* (1979), *Reddy* (1979), *Take What You Find* (1980), *Play Me Out* (1981), *Imagination* (1983), *Take It Home* (1984). Compilation: *Helen Reddy's Greatest Hits* (1975).

Redwing

Redwing originated in a Colorado trio, Tim Tom And Ron, which featured Timothy B. Schmit (b. 30 October 1947, Sacramento, California, USA; guitar/bass/vocals), Tom Phillips (guitar/pedal steel/vocals) and Ron Flogel (guitar/vocals). They developed into the Contenders with the addition of George Hullin (drums), but this surf-based unit took the name the New Breed when the group embraced a garage-cum-folk/rock direction. The same quartet moved to Sacramento, California where they were later known as both Never Mind and Glad. Schmit joined Poco as bassist in 1970 and was replaced by Andrew Samuels. Securing a permanent bass player would plague the band for years, and while Samuels, normally a lead guitarist, often performed the bass duties in the studio, this role was tackled by various personnel and on occasion calling upon the erstwhile member Schmit to stand in. This reshaped line-up evolved to become Redwing, and the masters of a self-financed album secured a deal with Fantasy Records. The band's sound embraced a taut, melodic style, based on country-rock which was to become identifiable with California in the ensuing years. However their five albums were marred by inconsistency. The group was unable to garner a significant following, and split up following the release of *Beyond The Sun And Stars*.
Albums: *Redwing* (1971), *What This Country Needs* (1972), *Take Me Home* (1973), *Dead Or Alive* (1974), *Beyond The Sun And Stars* (1975).

Reed, Lou

b. Louis Firbank, 2 March 1942, Freeport, Long Island, New York, USA. A member of several high-school bands, Reed made his recording debut with the Shades in 1957. Their 'So Blue' enjoyed brief notoriety when played by influential disc jockey Murray The K, but was lost in the plethora of independent singles released in this period. Having graduated from Syracuse University, Reed took a job as a contract songwriter with Pickwick Records which specialized in cash-in, exploitative recordings. His many compositions from this era included 'The Ostrich' (1965), a tongue-in-cheek dance song which so impressed the label hierarchy that Reed formed the Primitives to promote it as a single. The group also included a recent acquaintance, John Cale, thus sewing the early seeds of the Velvet Underground. Reed led this outstanding unit between 1966 and 1970, contributing almost all of the material and shaping its ultimate direction. His songs, for the most part, drew on the incisive discipline of R&B, while pointed lyrics displayed an acerbic view of contemporary urban life. Reed's departure left a creative vacuum within the group, yet he too seemed drained of inspiration following the break. He sought employment outside of music and two years passed before *Lou Reed* was released. Recorded in London with British musicians, including Steve Howe and Rick Wakeman, the set boasted some excellent songs - several of which were intended for the Velvet Underground - but was marred by an indistinct production. Nonetheless, an attendant UK tour with the Tots, a group of New York teenagers, was an artistic success.
David Bowie, a longtime Velvets' aficionado, oversaw *Transformer*, which captured a prevailing mood of decadence. Although uneven, it included the classic 'Walk On The Wild Side', a homage to transexuals and social misfits drawn to artist/film-maker Andy Warhol. This explicit song became a surprise hit, reaching the UK Top 10 and US Top 20 in 1973, but Reed refused to become trapped by the temporary nature of the genre and returned to the dark side of his talents with *Berlin*. By steering a course through sado-masochism, attempted suicide and nihilism, the artist expunged his newfound commerciality and challenged his audience in a way few contemporaries dared. Yet this period was blighted by self-parody and while a crack back-up band built around guitarists Dick Wagner and Steve Hunter provided undoubted muscle on the live *Rock 'N' Roll Animal*, *Sally Can't Dance* showed an artist bereft of direction and purpose. Having sanctioned a second in-concert set, Reed released the stark *Metal Music Machine*, an electronic, atonal work spaced over a double album. Savaged by critics upon release, its ill-synchronized oscillations have since been lauded by elitist sections of the *avant garde* fraternity, while others view its release as a work of mischief in which Reed displayed the ultimate riposte to careerist convention. It was followed by the sedate *Coney Island Baby*, Reed's softest, simplest collection to date, the inherent charm of which

Lou Reed

was diluted on *Rock 'N' Roll Heart*, a careless, inconsequential collection which marked an artistic nadir. However its successor, *Street Hassle*, displayed a rejuvenated power, resuming the singer's empathy with New York's subcultures. The title track, later revived by Simple Minds, was undeniably impressive, while 'Dirt' and 'I Wanna Be Black' revealed a wryness missing from much of the artist's solo work. Although subsequent releases, *The Bells* and *Growing Up in Public*, failed to scale similar heights, they offered a newfound sense of maturity. Reed entered the 80s a stronger, more incisive performer, buoyed by a fruitful association with guitarist Robert Quine, formerly of Richard Hell's Void-Oids. *The Blue Mask* was another purposeful collection and set a pattern for the punchy, concise material found on *Legendary Hearts* and *Mistrial*.

However, despite the promise these selections offered, few commentators were prepared for the artistic rebirth found on *New York*. Here the sound was stripped to the bone, accentuating the rhythmic pulse of compositions which focused on the seedy low-life that Reed excels in chronicling. His lyrics, alternately pessimistic or cynical, reasserted the fire of his best work as the artist regains the power to paint moribund pictures which neither ask, nor receive, pity. *New York* was a splendid return to form and created considerable interest in his back catalogue. *Songs For 'Drella*, was a haunting epitaph for Andy Warhol on which Reed collaborated with John Cale. Its showed another facet of the dramatic regeneration that places this immensely talented artist back at rock's cutting edge.

Albums: *Lou Reed* (1972), *Transformer* (1972), *Berlin* (1973), *Rock 'N' Roll Animal* (1974), *Sally Can't Dance* (1974), *Metal Machine Music* (1975), *Lou Reed Live* (1975), *Coney Island Baby* (1976), *Rock 'N' Roll Heart* (1976), *Street Hassle* (1978), *Live - Take No Prisoners* (1978), *The Bells* (1979), *Growing Up In Public* (1980), *The Blue Mask* (1982), *Legendary Hearts* (1983), *New Sensations* (1984), *Live In Italy* (1984), *Mistrial* (1986), *New York* (1989), *Magic And Loss* (1992), with John Cale *Songs For 'Drella* (1990). Selected compilations: *Walk On The Wild Side - The Best Of Lou Reed* (1977), *Rock 'N' Roll Diary 1967-1980* (1980), *I Can't Stand It* (1983), *New York Superstar* (1986).

Further reading: *Lou Reed: Growing Up In Public*, Peter Doggett.

Refugee

After growing restless with the direction in which

his group Jackson Heights was heading, Lee Jackson saw in Patrick Moraz (b. 24 June 1948, Morges, Switzerland) the chance to rekindle the style of music that he and drummer, Brian 'Blinky' Davidson, had pursued successfully in the Nice. Signed by Charisma Records, Refugee was launched with a blaze of publicity in the summer of 1973, but their sole album drew inevitable, and often unfavourable, comparisons with the band it attempted to emulate. Ironically, this promising combination was dealt a blow very similar to the one Jackson and Davidson had experienced when Keith Emerson had left the Nice. With Yes scouting around for a new member to replace Rick Wakeman, their eyes fell upon Moraz and by August 1974 he had accepted their offer, leaving Refugee in tatters, after which Jackson and Davidson parted company.
Album: *Refugee* (1974).

Reid, Neil

b. 1960, Motherwell, Scotland. By the age of eight Reid was already singing in public, at a Christmas party for Old Age Pensioners. His uncle played keyboards in Scottish Working Men's clubs and from the age of 10 Reid joined him as a singer. A teacher encouraged him to enter the television talent contest *Opportunity Knocks*, a contest he would go on to win three times. He recorded the weepy 'Mother Of Mine' (written by Bill Parkinson of the band P.A.T.C.H.) which became a massive hit in 1972 while Reid was not yet a teenager. Follow-ups included 'That's What I Want To Be' and 'With Every Passing Day'. For the remaining years of his youth he was a big attraction to both young teens and their parents and toured the UK, Europe and South Africa. The death of his grandfather coincided with his increasing interest in Christianity, and he became disillusioned with the fickle world of showbusiness where producers consistently expected him to sing like a 12-year-old. He took a break and worked in a fast food restaurant before a brief return during the 80s. He turned his back on performance once again, and is now an insurance salesman living in Blackpool, Lancashire, with his family.
Albums: *Neil Reid* (1972), *Smile* (1972), *I'll Walk With God* (1973).

Renaissance

In 1968, former Yardbirds Jim McCarty (b. 25 July 1943, Liverpool, England; drums) and Keith Relf (b. 22 March 1943, Richmond, Surrey, England; vocals/acoustic guitar) reunited as Together for two self-composed singles that in their pastoral lyricism and acoustic emphasis anticipated the more lucrative Renaissance in which they were joined by ex-Nashville Teens John Hawken (keyboards), Louis Cennamo (bass/vocals) and Relf's sister Jane (vocals). Produced by Paul Samwell-Smith (another Yardbirds veteran), their promising debut album embraced folk, classical and *musique concrète* reference points. However, though McCarty played and co-wrote tracks on *Prologue*, he and the others had abandoned Renaissance who continued with Annie Haslam (vocals), Robert Hendry (guitar/vocals), John Tout (keyboards), Jonathan Camp (bass/vocals) and Terry Slade (drums). As the last was replaced by Terence Sullivan in 1975, so Hendry was two years earlier by Mike Dunford, who provided melodies to poet Betty Thatcher's lyrics for *Ashes Are Burning* and later records which met with greater commercial acclaim in North America than Europe - so much so that the group found it more convenient to take up US residency. Indeed, *Turn Of The Cards* was not available in Britain until a year after its release in the USA, and the group's only concert recording was from Carnegie Hall with the New York Philharmonic. An orchestra had also augmented a Renaissance interpretation of Rimsky-Korsakov's *Scheherazade* featuring the stunning vocal harmonies that were to enliven *A Song For All Seasons* which became their biggest UK seller in the wake of a Top 10 entry for its 'Northern Lights' (1978). Haslam recorded the solo *Annie In Wonderland* but 1979's *Azur D'Or* was the only other album by Renaissance or its associates to make even a minor impression in the UK. In 1980, the band weathered the departures of Sullivan and Tout as pragmatically as they had worse upheavals in the past - and, indeed, Renaissance's considerable cult following has since taken many years to dwindle.
Albums: *Renaissance* (1969), *Prologue* (1972), *Ashes Are Burning* (1973), *Turn Of The Cards* (1974), *Scheherazade And Other Stories* (1975), *Live At Carnegie Hall* (1976), *Novella* (1977), *A Song For All Seasons* (1978), *Azur D'Or* (1979), *Camera Camera* (1981), *Time Line* (1983).

REO Speedwagon

Formed in Champaign, Illinois, USA in 1970 when pianist Neil Doughty (b. 29 July 1946, Evanston, Illinois, USA) and drummer Alan Gratzer (b. 9 November 1948, Syracuse, New York, USA) were joined by guitarist and songwriter Gary Richrath (b. 10 October 1949, Peoria, Illinois, USA). Although still in its

REO Speedwagon

embryonic stage, the group already had its unusual name which was derived from an early American fire-engine, designed by one Ransom E. Olds. Barry Luttnell (vocals) and Greg Philbin (bass) completed the line-up featured on *REO Speedwagon*, but the former was quickly replaced by Kevin Cronin (b. 6 October 1951, Evanston, Illinois, USA). The quintet then began the perilous climb from local to national prominence, but despite their growing popularity, particularly in America's mid-west, REO was initially unable to complete a consistent album. Although *REO Two* and *Ridin' The Storm Out* eventually achieved gold status, disputes regarding direction culminated in the departure of their second vocalist. Michael Murphy took his place in 1974, but when ensuing albums failed to generate new interest, Cronin rejoined his former colleagues. Bassist Bruce Hall (b. 3 May 1953, Champaign, Illinois, USA) was also brought into a line-up acutely aware that previous releases failed to reflect their in-concert prowess. The live *You Get What You Play For* overcame this problem to become the group's first platinum disc, a distinction shared by its successor, *You Can Tune A Piano, But You Can't Tuna Fish.* However, sales for *Nine Lives* proved disappointing, inspiring the misjudged view that REO had peaked. Such impressions were banished in 1980 with the release of *Hi Infidelity*, a crafted, self-confident collection which topped the US album charts and spawned a series of highly-successful singles. An emotive ballad, 'Keep On Lovin' You', reached number 1 in the US and number 7 in the UK, while its follow-up, 'Take It On The Run' also hit the US Top 5. However, a lengthy tour in support of the album proved creatively draining and *Good Trouble* is generally accepted as one of REO's least worthy efforts. Aware of its faults, the quintet withdrew from the stadium circuit and having rented a Los Angeles warehouse, enjoyed six months of informal rehearsals during which time they regained a creative empathy. *Wheels Are Turning* recaptured the zest apparent on *Hi Infidelity* and engendered a second US number 1 in 'Can't Fight This Feeling'. *Life As We Know It* emphasized the group's now accustomed professionalism, and while too often dubbed 'faceless', or conveniently bracketed with other in-concert 70s favourites Styx and Kansas, REO Speedwagon have proved the importance of a massive, secure, grass roots following.

Albums: *REO Speedwagon* (1971), *REO Two* (1972), *Ridin' The Storm Out* (1973), *Lost In A Dream* (1974), *This Time We Mean It* (1975), *REO* (1976), *REO Speedwagon Live/You Get What You Play For* (1977), *You Can Tune A Piano But You*

Can't Tuna Fish (1978), *Nine Lives* (1979), *Hi Infidelity* (1980), *Good Trouble* (1982), *Wheels Are Turning* (1984), *Life As We Know It* (1987). Compilations: *A Decade Of Rock 'N' Roll 1970-1980* (1980), *A Second Decade Of Rock 'N' Roll 1981-1991* (1991).

Return To Forever

This jazz group featured Chick Corea (b. 12 June 1941, Chelsea, Massachusetts, USA; keyboards), Joe Farrell (b. 16 December 1937, Chicago Heights, Illinois, USA, d. 10 January 1986; soprano saxophone/flute), Flora Purim (b. 6 March 1942, Rio de Janeiro, Brazil; vocals), Stanley Clarke (b. 30 June 1951, Philadelphia, USA; bass/electric bass), and Airto Moreira (b. 5 August 1941, Itaiopolis, Brazil; percussion). Formed by Chick Corea in 1971, Return To Forever began as a Latin-influenced fusion band, mixing the wild vocals of Purim with the tight, funk-edged slapping bass of Clarke to create a new sound. The group toured and made two commercially successful albums before disbanding in 1973. Keeping Clarke, Corea immediately put together the second of what was to be three successive Return To Forever bands. Hiring Bill Connors to play electric guitar (soon replaced by Earl Klugh and then Al DiMeola), and drummer Lenny White, the second band was much more of a rock-orientated outfit. Producing a harder overall sound, and aided by Corea's adoption of various electronic keyboard gadgetry, the new band achieved massive popularity, particularly with rock audiences, and its 1976 *Romantic Warrior* quickly became its best-selling album. The third and final Return To Forever was a huge but not altogether successful departure from what had come before. Corea put together a 13-piece band that included small string and brass sections, as well as Clarke and Farrell from the original band. A soft, unchallenging music resulted, and Return To Forever refined itself out of existence in 1980. Corea, Clarke, DiMeola, and White joined up for a single tour in 1983.
Albums: *Light As A Feather* (1972), *Return To Forever* (1973), *Where Have I Known You Before?* (1974), *Romantic Warrior* (1976), *Live: The Complete Concert* (1977).

Rich Kids

Formed in the UK during September 1977, the Rich Kids were the subject of exceptional initial interest. Centred on bassist Glen Matlock (b. 27 August 1956), a former member of the seminal Sex Pistols, his eminent role was emphasized by the inclusion of two 'unknown' musicians, Steve New (guitar/vocals) and Rusty Egan (drums). The group was later completed by Midge Ure, disillusioned frontman of struggling pop group, Slik, and this unusual mixture engendered criticism from unsympathetic quarters. The Rich Kids distanced themselves from punk, and their meagre releases were generally mainstream in execution. Indeed the group's ebullience recalled a 60s bonhomie, but this merely compounded criticism of their 'power pop' approach. The quartet was unable to transform their energy to record, while tension between Matlock and Ure increased to the extent that they were constantly squabbling. The group split up in November 1978, but denied the fact until free of contractual obligations. Egan and Ure later formed Visage, while their former colleagues pursued several low-key projects.
Album: *Ghosts Of Princes In Towers* (1978).

Richman, Jonathan

b. May 16 1951, Boston, Massachussetts, USA. Richman rose to prominence during the early 70s as leader of the Modern Lovers. Drawing inspiration from 50s pop and the Velvet Underground, the group initially offered a garage-band sound, as evinced on their UK hit 'Roadrunner' and the infectious instrumental 'Egyptian Reggae' in 1977. However, Richman increasingly distanced himself from electric music and latterly embraced an acoustic-based direction. He disbanded the group in 1978 to pursue an idiosyncratic solo career in which his naive style was deemed charming or irritating according to taste. His songs, including 'Ice Cream Man', 'My Love Is A Flower (Just Beginning To Bloom)', showed a child-like simplicity which seemed oblivious to changes in trends around him. Richman exhumed the Modern Lovers' name during the 80s without any alteration to his style and the artist continues to enjoy considerable cult popularity.
Albums: *Jonathan Richman And The Modern Lovers* (1977), *Back In Your Life* (1979), *The Jonathan Richman Songbook* (1980), *Jonathan Sings* (1984), *Its Time For Jonathan Richman And The Modern Lovers* (1986), *Jonathan Richman & Barence Whitfield* (1988), *Modern Lovers 88* (1988), *Jonathan Richman* (1989), *Jonathan Sings Country* (1990). Compilation: *23 Great Recordings* (1990).

Riperton, Minnie

b. 8 November 1947, Chicago, Illinois, USA, d. 12 July 1979. A former singer with the Gems,

Riperton recorded under the name 'Andrea Davis' prior to joining the Rotary Connection. She remained with this adventurous, black pop/psychedelic group between 1967 and 1970, before embarking on a solo career. In 1973 the singer began working with Wonderlove, Stevie Wonder's backing group. Two years later he returned this compliment, producing Minnie's *Perfect Angel*, and contributing two original compositions to the selection. However, it was 'Loving You', a song written by Riperton and her husband,Richard Rudolph, which brought international success, (US number 1/UK number 2) in 1975. This delicate performance featured the artist's soaring multi-octave voice, but set a standard later releases found hard to emulate. Riperton died from cancer in July 1979.

Albums: *Come To My Garden* (1969), *Perfect Angel* (1974), *Adventures In Paradise* (1975), *Stay In Love* (1977), *Minnie* (1979), *Love Lives Forever* (1980). Compilation: *The Best Of Minnie Riperton* (1981).

Robinson, Tom

b 1 July 1950, Cambridge, England. Robinson's wayward youth included the study of oboe, clarinet and bass guitar, and a spell in Finchden Manor, a readjustment centre in Kent, where he met guitarist Danny Kurstow with whom he formed his first group, Davanq, in 1971. However, two years later, as Cafe Society, he, Hereward Kaye and Ray Doyle were signed to the Kinks' Konk label. In 1974, *Cafe Society* was recorded with help from Ray Davies and Mick Avory. During the taping of an intended second album, administrative discord was manifested in what was now the Tom Robinson Band's on-stage mocking of Davies, and, later, the Kinks' reciprocal dig at Robinson in a 1977 b-side, 'Prince Of The Punks' - with whom Robinson's Band had been categorized (not entirely accurately) when contracted by EMI the previous year. Konk, nevertheless, retained publishing interests in 13 Robinson numbers. Some of these were selected for TRB's *Power In The Darkness* debut and attendant UK Top 40 singles - notably the catchy '2468 Motorway'. Backed by keyboardist Mark Ambler, drummer 'Dolphin' Taylor plus the faithful Kurstow, lead singer Robinson nurtured a homosexual image. His active support of many radical causes riddled his lyrical output but the gravity of 'Summer Of 79' and 'Up Against The Wall' was mitigated by grace-saving humour. The quartet's *Rising Free* EP, for example, contained the singalong 'Glad To Be Gay' anthem - which was also a highlight of both TRB's 1978 benefit concert for the Northern Ireland Gay Rights and One Parent Families Association, and Robinson's solo set during a Lesbian and Gay Rights March in Washington in 1979, shortly after parting with his Band. This had followed a disappointed critical and market reaction to *TRB2* (supervised by Todd Rundgren) - on which the sloganeering was overdone and the musical performance tepid. While Kurstow joined ex-Sex Pistol Glen Matlock in the Spectres, Robinson led the short-lived Section 27 and began songwriting collaborations with Elton John and Peter Gabriel. By 1981, he had relocated to Berlin to record the solo *North By Northwest* and work in alternative cabaret and fringe theatre. Professionally, this period proved fruitful - with 1982's strident 'War Baby' and evocative 'Atmospherics' in the UK Top 40, and a revival of Steely Dan's 'Ricki Don't Lose That Number', from *Hope And Glory*, which fared as well as the original in the same chart. However, when *Still Loving You* produced no equivalent of even this modest triumph Robinson, now a contented father, regrouped his original band. Subsequent engagements were viewed by many as akin to a nostalgia revue - and certainly several old favourites were evident the Berlin concert set, *Last Tango*. However, Robinson's articulate and lyrical eloquence suggest that further solid work may lie ahead.

Albums: *Power In The Darkness* (1978), *TRB2* (1979), *Sector 27* (1980), *North By Northwest* (1982), *Hope And Glory* (1984), *Still Loving You* (1986), *Last Tango* (1989).

Roches

Sisters Maggie (b. 26 October 1951, Detroit, Michigan, USA) and Terre Roche (b. 10 April 1953, New York City, New York, USA) began singing a mixture of traditional, doo-wop and barbershop quartet songs in New York clubs in the late 60s. Their first recording was as backing singers on Paul Simon's 1972 album, *There Goes Rhymin' Simon*. Through Simon, the duo recorded an album for CBS in 1975 which attracted little attention. The following year, the Roches became a trio with the addition of the distinctive voice of younger sister Suzzy (b. New York City, New York, USA) to Terre's soprano and Maggie's deep alto. With Maggie's compositions, by turns whimsical and waspish, featuring strongly they became firm favourites on New York's folk club scene. A Warner Brothers recording deal followed and Robert Fripp produced the self-titled album,

Tom Robinson

which included compositions by each of the sisters and remains their strongest recording. Among the many lyrical extravaganzas were Maggie's best-known song of infidelity 'The Married Men' (later covered by Phoebe Snow), Terre's poignant and autobiographical 'Runs In The Family' and 'We', the trio's a cappella opening number at live performances. The highly commercial 'Hammond Song' was arguably the star track (featuring a fine Fripp solo). *Nurds* another Fripp production featured the extraordinary 'One Season' wherein the trio manage to sing harmony almost a cappella but totally (and deliberately) out of tune. (Harmony vocalists will appreciate that this is extremely difficult). *Keep On Doing*, maintained a high standard including a refreshing burst of Handel's 'Hallelujah Chorus' and Maggie's tragic love song 'Losing You'. If the Roches ever had strong desires on the charts *Another World* was potentially the album to do it. Featuring a full rock-based sound this remains an undiscovered gem including the glorious title track and a cover of the Fleetwoods' 'Come Softly To Me'. Throughout the 80s, the Roches continued to perform in New York and appeared occasionally at European folk festivals. They also wrote and performed music for theatre productions and the 1988 film *Crossing Delancy*. *Speak* went largely unnoticed in 1989. Their next album was a memorable Christmas gift, *Three Kings*. Containing traditional yuletide songs and carols it displayed clearly the Roches exceptional harmony. *A Dove* in 1992 featured the 'Ing' Song' a brilliant lyrical exercise with every word ending with ing. They remain a highly original unit with a loyal cult following.

Albums: *Seductive Reasoning* (1975), *The Roches* (1979), *Nurds* (1980), *Keep On Doing* (1982), *Another World* (1985), *Speak* (1989), *Three Kings* (1990), *A Dove* (1992).

Roden, Jess

This former member of the respected 60s band the Alan Bown Set formed Bronco in 1970. Their brand of US-influenced rock was too derivative and they folded after two albums for Island Records. He then joined former Doors' members, John Densmore and Robby Krieger in the Butts Band. His solo debut *Jess Roden* in 1974 prompted him to form the Jess Roden Band, and he made the well-received *You Can Keep Your Hat On* in 1976. Roden returned in 1980 as part of the Rivets, who released an undistinguished album. Roden now lives in New York working as a graphic artist.

Albums: *Jess Roden* (1974), *You Can Keep Your Hat On* (1976).

Romeo, Max

b. Max Smith, c.1947, Jamaica. It was Romeo who first introduced Britain to the concept of rude reggae when his 'Wet Dream', which, despite a total radio ban, reached number 10 in the UK charts. He toured the UK several times in the space of a year and issued two albums: *A Dream* being the best selling. However, despite other similarly-styled singles like 'Mini Skirt Vision', he did not enjoy chart success again. Romeo was, essentially, something of a gospel singer with the ability to convey a revivalist fervour on his records such as 'Let The Power Fall' (a Jamaican political anthem in 1972) and 'Pray For Me'. Furthermore, he had an ability to get the trials, tribulations and amusements of Jamaican life into a song, as evinced by 'Eating Competition', 'Sixpence' and 'Aily And Ailaloo'. In 1972 Romeo began a liason with producers Lee Perry and Winston 'Niney' Holness, and from this point on his records had a musical fire to match his apocalyptical vision and contrasting humour: 'Babylose Burning', 'Three Blind Mice', 'The Coming Of Jah' all maintained his star status in Jamaica between 1972 and 1975. *Revelation Time* was one of the best albums of 1975, and 1976's *War Ina Babylon* was hailed by the rock press as one of the all-time classic reggae albums. However, Perry had much to do with those records' artistic success, and following a much-publicized split between the pair - with Perry recording 'White Belly Rat' about Max, and scrawling 'Judas' over the singer's picture in Perry's studio - Romeo was cast adrift without musical roots. *I Love My Music*, recorded with the help of Keith Richards was a flop, and the stronger *Reconstruction* fared no better. A move to New York's Bullwackies' label in the early 80s did little to reverse his fortunes, and by the late 80s Max Romeo's name was forgotten in the mainstream reggae market. However, in the spring of 1992, London producer Jah Shaka recorded *Fari, Captain Of My Ship* on Maxie Records, an unabashed, Jamaican-recorded roots album generally reckoned to be Romeo's best for over 15 years.

Albums: *A Dream By Max Romeo* (1970), *Let The Power Fall* (1972), *Revelation Time* (1975), *War Ina Babylon* (1976), *Reconstruction* (1978), *I Love My Music* (1979), *Rondos* (1980), *Fari, Captain Of My Ship* (1992).

Ronco Records

For over a decade, Ronco was one of the leading television marketing companies for pop albums. Originally a Canadian firm selling carpet cleaners and other household products it branched out into music in the 70s, arriving in the UK in 1972, shortly after its main rival K-Tel. The first Ronco success was *20 Star Tracks*, followed by *That'll Be The Day*, a compilation of 50s hits timed to coincide with the hit film starring David Essex and Ringo Starr. Released in 1973, it became the label's only number 1. Ronco later released soundtrack albums, having the greatest success with *Stardust,* the movie sequel to *That'll Be The Day* and *The Stud*, a Joan Collins vehicle. However, most of its 70s releases were collections of tracks from various musical styles - rock, black music, disco and military bands. Some of Ronco's biggest sellers came from single artist albums, by MOR stars. In 1976, its Max Bygraves release, *100 Gold Greats* reached the UK Top 10, while two Lena Martell albums were almost as successful. The increased competition from mainstream record companies in the television advertising sphere eventually caused the collapse of Ronco in 1984. Its former general manager Tony Naughton went on to found Stylus Music, another television merchandising label which in turn crashed after five years.

Ronson, Mick

b. Hull, Yorkshire, England.This UK guitarist, was originally a member of David Bowie's backing group Hype, in February 1970. Bowie later renamed the group, the Spiders From Mars and achieved international success, with Ronson playing lead on the pivotal albums, *The Man Who Sold The World*, *Hunky Dory*, *The Rise And Fall Of Ziggy Stardust And The Spiders From Mars* and *Aladdin Sane*. Ronson embarked on a short-lived and unsuccessful solo career towards the end of 1973, initiated by Bowie's decision to quit touring at the time. Recording two competent rock albums, he found it difficult to accept the lack of success as a solo artist and joined Mott The Hoople in 1974. They only recorded the single 'Saturday Gigs' with Ronson, before a major personnel change ensued. Lead vocalist, Ian Hunter, departed to start a solo career and Ronson followed. He subsequently appeared with Bob Dylan in the famous Rolling Thunder Revue. The remaining members shortened the name to Mott and recruited new members. The Hunter-Ronson partnership has lasted over 15 years, but it is only on the latest *YUIORTA* album, that Ronson has received equal billing on the sleeve with Hunter. In 1991, Ronson underwent treatment for cancer, and in 1992 he appeared with Bowie at the Freddy Mercury Aids Benefit concert.
Albums: *Slaughter On Tenth Avenue* (1974), *Play Don't Worry* (1975).

Roogalator

One of the first of the 70s R&B revivalist bands (along with Dr Feelgood), Roogalator were led by American Danny Adler. He left the USA in the early 70s having played guitar for Bootsy Collins and various jazz and blues musicians. He arrived in London and in 1972 put together the first line-up of Roogalator. Over the years numerous personnel were involved including key names like Paul Riley (of Chilli Willi And The Red Hot Peppers), and Bobby Irwin (of the Strutters, the Sinceros, and various Nick Lowe bands). They came under the management of Robin Scott (later the brains behind M) and in 1973 recorded their best-known track - 'Cincinatti Fat Back' - for a BBC radio session. This was eventually released as an EP by Stiff in 1976. Scott then formed the Do It label in order to release an album by the band whose new line-up was Adler (guitar/vocals), Nick Plytas (keyboards), Julian Scott (bass), and Justin Hilkdreth (drums). Adler also ran a simultaneous career with the De Luxe Blues Band.
Album: *Play It By Ear* (1978).

Rose Royce

Formed in the USA as a multi-purpose backing group, the original nine-piece worked under a variety of names. In 1973 Kenji Brown (guitar), Victor Nix (keyboards), Kenny Copeland, Freddie Dunn (trumpets), Michael Moore (saxophone), Lequient 'Duke' Jobe (bass), Henry Garner and Terrai Santiel (drums) backed Edwin Starr as Total Concept Limited, before supporting Yvonne Fair as Magic Wand. This line-up later became the regular studio band behind the Undisputed Truth and Temptations, before embarking on their own recording career following the addition of singer Gwen Dickey. The group took the name Rose Royce in 1976 when they recorded the successful soundtrack to the motion picture *Car Wash*, the title song of which was a platinum-selling single. Two further songs from the film reached the R&B Top 10 before the band joined producer Norman Whitfield's label. Two atmospheric releases, 'Wishing On A Star' and 'Love Don't Live Here Anymore' (both 1978) reached the Top 3 in the

UK despite disappointing sales at home. This feature continued the following year with 'Is It Love You're After', another UK Top 20 record. Their popularity in Britain was verified in 1980 when the *Greatest Hits* collection reached number 1 in the album charts. Since then the group has continued to record, but their releases have only reached the lower reaches of the charts.

Albums: *Car Wash* (1976), *In Full Bloom* (1977), *Rose Royce Strikes Again!* (1978), *Rainbow Connection IV* (1979), *Golden Touch* (1981), *Jump Street* (1981), *Stronger Than Ever* (1982), *Music Magic* (1984), *The Show Must Go On* (1985), *Fresh Cut* (1987). Compilations: *Greatest Hits* (1980), *Is It Love You're After* (1988).

Ross, Diana

b. Diane Ernestine Ross, 26 March 1944, Detroit, USA. While still in high school Ross became the fourth and final member of the Primettes, who recorded for Lu-Pine in 1960, signed to Motown Records in 1961 and then changed their name to the Supremes. She was a backing vocalist on the group's early releases, until Motown supremo Berry Gordy insisted that she become their lead singer, a role she retained for the next six years. In recognition of her prominent position in the Supremes, she received individual billing on all their releases from 1967 onwards. Throughout her final years with the group, Ross was being groomed for a solo career under the close personal supervision of Gordy, with whom she was rumoured to have romantic links. In late 1969, he announced that Ross would be leaving the Supremes, and she played her final concert with the group in January 1970. Later that year Ross began a long series of successful solo releases, with the chart-topping 'Ain't No Mountain High Enough'. In April 1971, she married businessman Robert Silberstein, but they were divorced in 1976 after renewed speculation about her relationship with Gordy.

As she continued to enjoy success with lightweight love songs in the early 70s, Motown's plan to widen Ross's appeal led her to host a television special, *Diana!*, in 1971. In 1972, she starred in Motown's film biography of Billie Holiday, *Lady Sings The Blues*, winning an Oscar nomination for her stirring portrayal of the jazz singer's physical decline into drug addiction. But subsequent starring roles in *Mahogany* (1975) and *The Wiz* (1978) drew a mixed critical response. In 1973, Ross released an album of duets with Marvin Gaye, though allegedly the pair did not meet during the recording of the project. She scored another USA number 1 with 'Touch Me In The Morning', and repeated that success with the theme song from *Mahogany* in 1975. 'Love Hangover' in 1976 saw her moving into the contemporary disco field, a shift of direction that was consolidated on the 1980 album *Diana*, produced by Nile Rodgers and Bernard Edwards of Chic. By now, Ross was as much a media personality as a soul singer, winning column inches for her liaison with Gene Simmons of Kiss. There was also intense speculation about the nature of her relationship with Michael Jackson, whose career she had helped to guide since 1969.

After months of rumour about her future, Ross left Motown in 1981, and signed contracts with RCA for North America, and Capitol for the rest of the world. She formed her own production company and had further hits. A reworking of Frankie Lymon's 'Why Do Fools Fall In Love' and Michael Jackson's 'Muscles' confirmed her pre-eminence in the field of disco-pop. During the remainder of the 80s only 'Missing You', a tribute to the late Marvin Gaye, brought her the success to which she had become accustomed. In Britain, however, she achieved a number 1 hit in 1986 with 'Chain Reaction', an affectionate re-creation of her days with the Supremes written and produced by the Bee Gees. In 1986, Ross married a Norwegian shipping magnate, effectively quashing renewed rumours that she might wed Berry Gordy and return to Motown. Since then, she has won more publicity for her epic live performances, notably an open-air concert in New York's Central Park in a torrential storm, than for her sporadic releases of new material, which continue to occupy the lighter end of the black music market. Her most recent offering *Force Behind The Power* was a dull and unambitious album, far more attention was paid to her greatest hits package.

Albums: *Reach Out* (1970), *Everything Is Everything* (1970), *Diana!* (1971), *Surrender* (1971), *Lady Sings The Blues* (1972), *Touch Me In The Morning* (1973), with Marvin Gaye *Diana And Marvin* (1973), *Last Time I Saw Him* (1973), *Live At Caesar's Palace* (1974), *Mahogany* (1975), *Diana Ross* (1976), *An Evening With Diana Ross* (1977), *Baby It's Me* (1977), *Ross* (1978), *The Boss* (1979), *Diana* (1980), *To Love Again* (1981), *Why Do Fools Fall In Love* (1981), *Silk Electric* (1982), *Ross* (1983), *Swept Away* (1984), *Eaten Alive* (1985), *Red Hot Rhythm 'N' Blues* (1987), *Working Overtime* (1989), *Greatest Hits Live* (1989), *Force Behind The Power* (1991).

Diana Ross

Rough Trade Records

Initially based near west London's Portobello Road, the Rough Trade retail shop opened in February 1976, just months prior to the rise of the punk rock phenomenon. Owned by Geoff Travis (b. 2 February 1952, Stoke Newington, London, England), it was an important outlet for punk and independent releases from the UK and USA. Travis's empathy for this musical revolution helped build the shop's reputation as a leading source for import material, British independent releases, complimentary reggae releases and as a selling point for the proliferation of music fanzines. The demand for outlets generated by bands inspired the formation of a distribution network and label, and the Rough Trade record label was launched two years later with the release of 'Paris Maquis' by Metal Urbain, which anticipated the 'Industrial' style flourishing later in the decade. Subsequent releases by reggae artist Augustus Pablo and *avant garde* act Cabaret Voltaire confirmed Rough Trade's reputation as an outlet for diverse talent. Stiff Little Fingers, Young Marble Giants, Aztec Camera, the Raincoats, the Go-Betweens, the Fall, Scritti Politti and the Pop Group maintained the company's reputation as purveyors of challenging music, while a succession of excellent recordings by the Smiths combined perception with popular acclaim, making the group the company's biggest asset for much of its history. The label also became the natural outlet for several US acts, ranging from the guitar-orientated Feelies, Dream Syndicate, the idiosyncratic Jonathan Richman and Camper Van Beethoven, to the experimental styles of Pere Ubu and the offbeat country/folk of Souled American. Many defections to major labels most notably Aztec Camera and Scritti Politti undermined the pitfalls bedevilling independent outlets and in 1984, under the aegis of the giant Warner Brothers corporation, Travis established Blanco Y Negro on which acts who preferred the security of a major company could nonetheless enjoy the intimacy of an independent. Jesus And Mary Chain, Everything But The Girl and Dinosaur Jnr have been among the label's signings, confirming Travis as one of Britain's most astute executives. Rough Trade Records continued to serve as the natural outlet for independently-minded acts throughout the 80s, but defection to EMI by the aforementioned Smiths was a significant loss. Hopes were then pinned on the Sundays, but the collapse of the Rough Trade distribution network in 1991 put the label's fate in jeopardy. However, a trimming down of staff and operations found the company steadying its position and subsequent recordings by artists such as Robert Wyatt suggest that its long-term future as a haven for adventurism is still assured.

Album: *Wanna Buy A Bridge?* (1980).

Roussos, Demis

b. 15 June 1947, Alexandria, Egypt. This multi-lingual Greek's father was a semi-professional classical guitarist, and his mother a singer. At music college in Athens, Roussos mastered trumpet, double bass, organ and bouzouki. These talents were put to commercial use with his founder membership of Aphrodite's Child in 1963. Following 1968's million-selling 'Rain And Tears', he began a career as a solo vocalist which, after a slow start, hit its stride with *Forever And Ever*, a chart success in Europe. 'Happy To Be On An Island In The Sun', climbed into the UK Top 5 but it seemed as if the new sensation had dwindled as both 'Can't Say How Much I Love You' the follow-up and the second album struggled in their respective listings. However, Roussos was to return with a vengeance in 1976 with self-produced *The Roussos Phenomenon*, the first EP to top the UK singles chart. That same year, 'When Forever Has Gone' peaked at number 2. Within months, he bade farewell to the Top 40 with the EP *Kyrila*. Although general consumer reaction to subsequent releases has been modest, the impact of their perpetrator on theatre box office takings has been immense. Roussos has lent a high euphonious tenor to essentially middle-of-the-road material. Style transcends content when, with dramatic *son et lumiere* effects and garbed in billowing robes, his Grand Entrance - like Zeus descending from Olympus - still leaves an indelible impression on every packed audience before he sings even a note. Selected albums: *Forever And Ever* (1974), *Souvenirs* (1975), *Happy To Be* (1976), *My Only Fascination* (1976), *The Magic Of Demis Roussos* (1977), *Man Of The World* (1980), *Love And Life* (1978), *Magic* (1981), *Demis* (1982), *Greatest Hits* (1984), *The Golden Voice Of Demis Roussos* (1988), *My Friend The Wind* (1989).

Roxy Music

This highly regarded and heavily influential UK group came together in January 1971 with a line-up comprising Bryan Ferry (b. 26 September 1945, Washington, Co. Durham, England; vocals/keyboards); Brian Eno (b. Brian Peter George St. Baptiste de la Salle Eno, 15 May 1948, Woodbridge, Suffolk, England;

Phil Manzanera of Roxy Music

electronics/keyboards); Graham Simpson (bass) and Andy Mackay (b. 23 July 1946, England). Over the next year, several new members came and went including drummer Dexter Lloyd, guitarist Roger Bunn and former Nice guitarist David O'List. By early 1972, a relatively settled line-up emerged with the recruitment of Paul Thompson (b. 13 May 1951, Jarrow, Northumberland, England; drums) and Phil Manzanera (b. Philip Targett Adams (b. 31 January 1951, London, England; guitar). Roxy's self-titled 1972 debut album for Island Records was a musical pot pourri, with Ferry's 50s-tinged vocals juxtaposed alongside distinctive 60s rhythms and 70s electronics. The novel sleeve concept underlined Roxy's art school background, while the group image (from 50s quiffs to futurist lurex jackets) emphasized their stylistic diversity. Reviews verged on the ecstatic, acclaiming the album as one of the finest debuts in living memory. Ferry's quirky love songs were often bleak in theme but strangely effervescent, fusing romanticism with bitter irony. On 'If There Was Something', for example, a quaint melody gradually descends into marvellous cliche ('I would do anything for you . . . I would climb the ocean blue') and bathos ('I would put roses round your door . . . growing potatoes by the score'). 'The Bob (Medley)' was another clever touch; a montage of war-time Britain presented in the form of a love song. As a follow-up to their first album, the group issued 'Virginia Plain', a classic single combining Ferry's cinematic interests and love of surrealistic art. During the same period, Simpson departed and thereafter Roxy went through a succession of bassists, including John Porter, John Gustafson, John Wetton, Rik Kenton, Sal Maida, Rick Wills and Gary Tibbs.

After failing to break into America, the group scored a second UK Top 10 hit with 'Pyjamarama' and released For Your Pleasure, produced by Chris Thomas. Another arresting work, the album featured the stunning 'Do The Strand', arguably the group's most effective rock workout, with breathtaking saxophone work from Mackay. 'Beauty Queen' and 'Editions Of You' were contrastingly strong tracks and the album's centrepiece was 'In Every Dream Home Λ Heartache', Ferry's paean to an inflatable rubber doll and a chilling evocation of consumerist alienation. On 21 June 1973, Eno left, following a series of disagreements with Ferry over his role in the group. The replacement was former Curved Air violinist Eddie Jobson, who willingly accepted the role of hired musician rather than taking on full membership. After taking time off to record a solo album of cover versions, Ferry took Roxy on a nation-wide tour to promote the excellent Stranded. 'Street Life', the first album track to be issued as a single, proved another Top 10 hit. The song neatly summed up his contradictory attitude to city life: 'You may be stranded if you stick around — and that's really something'. The epic 'A Song For Europe', with a melody borrowed from George Harrison's 'When My Guitar Gently Weeps', was another tour of alienation. The most complex and rewarding piece on the album, however, was 'Mother Of Pearl', a macrocosm of Ferry's lounge-lizard image, complete with plastic goddesses and lifeless parties.

Following his second solo album, Ferry completed work on Roxy's fourth album, Country Life, another strong set ranging from the uptempo single 'All I Want Is You' to the aggressive 'The Thrill Of It All' and the musically exotic 'Triptych'. In the USA, the album sleeve was withdrawn due to its risqué portrayal of two semi-naked women, and Roxy took advantage of the controversy by undertaking two consecutive US tours. Their hopes of capturing stadium-sized audiences ultimately remained unfulfilled. In spite of a challenging pilot single, 'Love Is The Drug', Roxy's next album, Siren, proved a major disappointment, lacking the charm and innovation of its predecessors. Only 'Both Ends Burning', which hinted at a disco direction, gave evidence of real vocal passion. The album was followed by a three-year gap during which the individual members pursued various solo projects. The 1979 comeback, Manifesto, received mixed reviews but included two excellent hit singles, 'Angel Eyes' and the fatalistic 'Dance Away'. The succeeding Flesh And Blood was a more accomplished work with some strong arrangements, including a reworking of Wilson Pickett's 'In The Midnight Hour' and an unusual interpretation of the Byrds' 'Eight Miles High'. Two UK hit singles were also in attendance: 'Over You' and 'Oh Yeah (On The Radio)'. In 1981 Roxy finally achieved their first number 1 single with 'Jealous Guy', an elegiac tribute to its recently assassinated composer John Lennon. The following year, Roxy released their final album Avalon, which topped the album charts and was praised by most critics. Roxy Music left behind a substantial body of work whose sheer diversity contributed significantly to the multifarious musical styles that followed in their wake.

Albums: Roxy Music (1972), For Your Pleasure

(1973), *Stranded* (1973), *Country Life* (1974), *Siren* (1975), *Viva! Roxy Music* (1976), *Manifesto* (1979), *Flesh And Blood* (1980), *Avalon* (1981). Compilations: *Greatest Hits* (1977), *The First Seven Albums* (1981), *The Atlantic Years 1973-1980* (1983), *Street Life - 20 Great Hits* (1986), *The Ultimate Collection* (1988).

Further reading: *Roxy Music: Style With Substance - Roxy's First Ten Years*, Johnny Rogan.

Royal Scots Dragoon Guards

One of the more unlikely records to top the UK charts during the 70s was an instrumental version of the traditional 'Amazing Grace', already a hit courtesy of Judy Collins' evocative reading. The Pipes, Drums And Military Band of the Royal Scots Dragoon Guards had first recorded their haunting version on the album *Farewell To The Greys* their tribute to the Royal Scots Greys. The stirring bagpipes caught the attention of BBC Radio 2, however, and they began playing 'Amazing Grace' which received a favourable response from radio listeners. By April 1972, the song was number 1, where it stayed for a lengthy five weeks. Two further hits followed that same year, 'Heykens Serenade/The Day Is Over' and 'Little Drummer Boy', before the Dragoon Guards ended their chart run.

Album: *Farewell To The Greys* (1972), *Amazing Grace* (1972), *The Amazing Sound Of The Royal Scots Dragoon Guards* (1984), *Golden Sounds Of The Royal Scots Dragoon Guards* (1984), *Royal Scots Dragoon Guards* (1986). Compilation: *Spotlight On The Royal Scots Dragoon Guards* (1984).

Rubettes

Former songwriters of the Pete Best Four, Wayne Bickerton and Tony Waddington created the Rubettes from session musicians after their composition, 'Sugar Baby Love', was rejected by existing acts. A fusion of 50s revivalism and glam-rock, it gave the new group's career a flying start by topping the UK charts and climbing into the US Top 40 in 1974. The song was mimed on television and promoted in concert by Alan Williams (b. 22 December 1950, Welwyn Garden City, Hertfordshire, England; vocals/guitar), Tony Thorpe (b. 20 July 1947, London, England; guitar), Bill Hurd (b. 11 August 1946, London, England; keyboards), Mick Clarke (b. 10 August 1948, Grimsby, Humberside, England; bass) and John Richardson (b. 3 May 1947, Dagenham, Essex, England). Despite adverse publicity when it was revealed that a Paul Da Vinci had warbled the punishing falsetto lead vocal on 'Sugar Baby Love', the five stayed together and were able to continue as hit parade contenders and touring attractions – particularly in Britain and northern Europe - for another three years. 'Tonight', 'Juke Box Jive', 'I Can Do It' and lesser hits mixed mainly Waddington-Bickerton and band originals. Five years after their grand exit with 1977's countrified 'Baby I Know' in the domestic Top 10, Williams returned from obscurity to sing lead on the Firm's 'Arthur Daley (E's Alright)', a chartbusting paean to the main character in the television series *Minder*.

Albums: *We Can Do It*, (1975), *Impact* (1982), *Best Of The Rubettes*, (1983).

Rubinoos

The Rubinoos carried on the great pop tradition of UK bands like the Hollies and the Beatles and that espoused by other American acts like the Raspberries. They were formed in the Bay Area of San Francisco, California, in 1973 by Tommy 'TV' Dunbar and Jon Rubin, who were thrown out of high school together and enrolled in a so-called Progressive School where they learnt to smoke illegal substances. They called themselves the Rubinoos after Jon's surname, Rubin acting as vocalist while Dunbar played guitar. They were joined by Royse Ader on bass and Donn Spindit on drums. Their early set consisted of covers including the Archies' 'Sugar Sugar'. The Rubinoos were often pelted with vegetables until the American new wave scene helped make 60s pop respectable again. Dunbar's brother Rob was in a band called Earthquake and their manager, Matthew Kaufman, helped get the Rubinoos gigs. He also added them to his impressive roster on Beserkley Records. Their debut single in 1977 (produced by Kaufman) was a version of Tommy James And The Shondells 'I Think We're Alone Now'. Both this, and their self-penned but similarly styled 'I Wanna Be Your Boyfriend', were much vaunted but not hits. They became a popular live attraction particularly for their showstopping 'Rock And Roll Is Dead (And We Don't Care)'. Regardless of their lack of major success they ploughed on though Ader left in 1980 and by the time of their 1983 mini-album, *Party Of Two*, they were just a duo of Rubin and Dunbar. However, the four original members re-formed in 1988.

Albums: *The Rubinoos* (1977), *Rubinoos In Wax* (1979), *Back To The Drawing Board* (1979), *Party Of Two* (1983).

Rufus

This Chicago-based group evolved from the American Breed when three original members, Al Ciner (guitar), Charles Colbert (bass) and Lee Graziano (drums), were joined by Kevin Murphy (keyboards), Paulette McWilliams (vocals), Ron Stockard and Dennis Belfield. Initially known as Smoke, then Ask Rufus, it was several months before a stable unit evolved. Graziano made way for Andre Fisher, but the crucial change came when Chaka Khan (b. Yvette Marie Stevens, 23 March 1953, Great Lakes Naval Training Station, Illinois, USA) joined in place of McWilliams. The group, now known simply as Rufus, signed with the ABC label in 1973, but made little headway until a chance encounter with Stevie Wonder during sessions for a second album. Impressed by Khan's singing, he donated an original song, 'Tell Me Something Good' which, when issued as a single, became a gold disc. It began a run of exceptional releases, including 'You Got The Love' (1974), 'Sweet Thing' (1975) and 'At Midnight (My Love Will Lift You Up)' (1977), all of which topped the R&B chart. By this time Rufus had stabilized around Khan, Murphy, Tony Maiden (guitar), Dave Wolinski (keyboards), Bobby Watson (bass) and John Robinson (drums), but it was clear that the singer was the star attraction. She began recording as a solo act in 1978, but returned to the fold in 1980 for *Masterjam*, which contained 'Do You Love What You Feel', a further number 1 soul single. Khan continued to pursue her own career and perform with Rufus, who secured an international hit in 1983 with 'Ain't Nobody'. The song was written by Wolinski, by now an established figure in soul circles through his work on Michael Jackson's *Off The Wall*. The distinction between Chaka Khan's successful solo recordings and her work with Rufus has become blurred over the years, but it remains arguable whether or not she achieved the same empathy elsewhere.
Albums: *Rufus* (1973), *Rags To Rufus* (1974), *Rufusized* (1974), *Rufus Featuring Chaka Khan* (1975), *Ask Rufus* (1977), *Street Player* (1978), *Numbers* (1979), *Masterjam* (1979), *Party 'Til You're Broke* (1981), *Camouflage* (1981), *Live - Stompin' At The Savoy* (1983).

Rumour

Formed in 1975, the Rumour served as the backing group to Graham Parker. Brinsley Schwarz (guitar/vocals) and Bob Andrews (keyboards/vocals), both ex-Brinsley Schwarz, were joined by Martin Belmont (guitar, ex-Ducks Deluxe), Andrew Bonar (bass) and Steve Goulding (drums) in a unit supplying the necessary punch to the singer's R&B ambitions. Their own aspirations were realized in 1977 with the release of *Max*, but a sense of individuality only fully emerged on *Frogs, Sprouts, Clogs And Krauts* which included the single 'Emotional Traffic'. However, as the parent attraction fell from commercial favour, so too did the career of the Rumour whose independent recordings ended with *Purity Of Essence*.
Albums: *Max* (1977), *Frogs, Sprouts, Clogs And Krauts* (1979), *Purity Of Essence* (1980).

Runaways

Formed in 1975, the Runaways were initially the product of producer/svengali Kim Fowley and teenage lyricist Kari Krome. Together they pieced together an adolescent girl-group following several auditions in the Los Angeles area. The original line-up consisted of Joan Jett (b. 22 September 1958, Philadelphia, Pennsylvania, USA; guitar/vocals), Micki Steele (bass - later of the Bangles) and Sandy West (drums), but was quickly bolstered by the addition of Lita Ford (b. 23 September 1959, London, England; guitar/vocals) and Cherie Currie (vocals). The departure of Steele prompted several replacements, the last of which was Jackie Fox who had failed her original audition. Although originally viewed as a vehicle for compositions by Fowley and associate Mars Bonfire (b. Dennis Edmonton), material by Jett and Krome helped assert the quintet's independence. *The Runaways* showed a group indebted to the 'glam-rock' of the Sweet and punchy pop of Suzie Quatro, and included the salutary 'Cherry Bomb'. *Queens Of Noise* repeated the pattern, but the strain of touring - the quintet were highly popular in Japan - took its toll of Jackie Fox, who left the line-up and abandoned music altogether. As Jackie Fuchs she later became a qualified attorney, and remains her career today. Personality clashes resulted in the departure of Cherie Currie, whose solo career stalled following the failure of her debut, *Beauty's Only Skin Deep*. Guitarist/vocalist Vicki Blue and bassist Laurie McAllister completed a revitalized Runaways, but the latter was quickly dropped. Subsequent releases lacked the appeal of the group's early work which, although tarred by both novelty and sexual implications, nonetheless showed a sense of purpose. The Runaways split in 1980 but both Jett and Ford later enjoyed solo careers, the former of which engendered considerable commercial success during the 80s. In

1985 the mischievous Fowley resurrected the old group's name with an all-new personnel. This opportunistic concoction split up on completing *Young And Fast*.

Albums: *The Runaways* (1976), *Queens Of Noise* (1977), *Live In Japan* (1977), *Waitin' For The Night* (1977), *And Now...The Runaways* (1979), *Flamin' Schoolgirls* (1982), *Young And Fast* (1987).

Rundgren, Todd

b. 22 June 1948, Philadelphia, Pennsylvania, USA. One of rock's eccentric talents, Rundgren began his career in local bar-band Woody's Truck Stop, before forming the Nazz in 1967. This acclaimed quartet completed three albums of anglophile pop/rock before disintegrating in 1970. Rundgren sought solace as an engineer - his credits included *Stage Fright* by the Band - before recording *Runt*, a name derived from his nickname. Brothers Hunt and Tony Sales (drums and bass respectively), later of Tin Machine, joined the artist on a set deftly combining technical expertise with his love of melody. This exceptionally accomplished album spawned a US Top 20 hit in 'We Got To Get You A Woman' and paved the way for the equally charming *The Ballad Of Todd Rundgren*. However, it was with *Something/Anything?* that this performer truly flourished. The first three sides were entirely his own creation - as writer, singer, musician and producer - and contained some of Rundgren's most popular songs, including 'I Saw The Light' and 'It Wouldn't Have Made Any Difference'. Although the final side was devoted to an indulgent 'pop opera', the set is rightly regarded as one of the landmark releases of the early 70s. *A Wizard, A True Star* offered a similarly dazzling array of styles, ranging from a suite of short song-snippets to a medley of soul ballads, including 'I'm So Proud' and 'Ooh Baby Baby'. *Todd*, a second double-set, proved equally ambitious, although its erratic content suggested that Rundgren was temporarily bereft of direction. His riposte was Utopia, a progressive rock ensemble which initially featured three musicians on keyboards/synthesizers - Moogy Klingman, M. Frog Labat and Ralph Shuckett - John Segler, then Kasim Sulton, (bass) and John Wilcox (drums). Although Roger Powell latterly assumed all keyboard duties, the group's penchant for lengthy instrumental interludes and semi-mystical overtones remained intact.

A popular live attraction, Utopia taxed the loyalties of Rundgren aficionados, particularly when their unrepentant self-indulgence encroached into the artist's 'solo' work, notably on *Initiation*. *Faithful*

did reflect a return to pop with 'Love Of The Common Man' and 'The Verb To Love', while acknowledging Todd's inspirational roots with note-for-note remakes of several 60s classics, including 'If Six Was Nine' (Jimi Hendrix), 'Good Vibrations' (the Beach Boys) and 'Strawberry Fields Forever' (the Beatles). In 1977 Utopia released *Ra* and *Oops! Wrong Planet*, the latter of which had Rundgren taking a less prominent role. He nonetheless maintained a frenetic workload and having already established his credentials as a producer with the New York Dolls, Grand Funk Railroad and Hall And Oates, commenced work on Meatloaf's *Bat Out Of Hell*, which has since become one of the best-selling albums of all time. The artist also began recording *Hermit Of Mink Hollow*, a superb set recalling the grasp of pop offered on *Something/Anything?* and deservedly lauded by critics. Rundgren entered the 80s determined to continue his eclectic path. Utopia's *Deface The Music* was a dazzling pastiche of Beatles' music from 'I Wanna Hold Your Hand' to 'Tomorrow Never Knows' while another 'solo' set, *Healing*, flirted with ambient styles. His earlier profligacy lessened as the decade progressed but retained the capacity to surprise, most notably on the inventive *Aceppella*. Production work for XTC joined later recordings in proving his many talents have remained as true as ever.

Albums: *Runt* (1970), *The Ballad Of Todd Rundgren* (1971), *Something/Anything?* (1972), *A Wizard, A True Star* (1973), *Todd* (1974), *Initiation* (1975), *Faithful* (1976), *Hermit Of Mink Hollow* (1978), *Back To The Bars* (1978), *Healing* (1981), *The Ever Popular Tortured Artist Effect* (1983), *A cappella* (1985), *POV* (1985), *Nearly Human* (1989), *Second Wind* (1991). Compilations: *Anthology: Todd Rundgren* (1988). With Utopia *Todd Rundgren's Utopia* (1974), *Another Live* (1975), *Ra* (1977), *Oops! Wrong Planet* (1977), *Adventures In Utopia* (1980), *Deface The Music* (1980), *Swing To The Right* (1982), *Utopia* (1982), *Oblivion* (1984).

Rush

This Canadian heavy rock band comprised of Geddy Lee (b. 29 July 1953, Willowdale, Toronto, Canada; keyboards/bass/vocals), Alex Lifeson (b. 27 August 1953, British Columbia, Canada; guitar) and John Rutsey (drums). From 1969-72 they performed in Toronto playing a brand of Cream inspired material. but they gained more recognition when they supported the New York Dolls in 1973. In 1974 they took the name Rush and released *Rush* on Mercury Records following its success on

the independent Moon Records. The same year, Neil Peart (b. 12 September 1952, Hamilton, Ontario, Canada; drums), who was to be the main songwriter of the band, replaced Rutsey, and Rush undertook their first full tour of the USA. Rush's music is typified by Lee's oddly high-pitched voice, a tremendously powerful guitar sound, especially in the early years, and a great interest in science fiction and fantasy. This is most notable in the now classic 1976 concept album, *2112*, based on the work of novelist/philosopher Ayn Rand, which has as its central theme the idea of freewill and individualism. By 1979 Rush were immensely successful worldwide, and the Canadian Government gave them the title of official Ambassadors of Music. As the 80s progressed Rush altered their image from the science fiction dominated tracks to become more sophisticated, clean-cut and undoubtedly intellectual music-makers. Some early fans criticised the band's seeming determination to progress musically with each new album, while others lauded their very iconoclasm. Now major artists worldwide, they still sell large numbers of records despite rarely playing outside their native Canada. Often criticized for being lyrically pretentious, Rush have weathered the storm and remain Canada's leading rock band.
Albums: *Rush* (1974), *Fly By Night* (1975), *Caress Of Steel* (1975), *2112* (1976), *All The World's A Stage* (1976), *A Farewell To Kings* (1977), *Archives* (1978), *Hemispheres* (1978), *Permanent Waves* (1980), *Rush Through Time* (1980), *Moving Pictures* (1981), *Exit: Stage Left* (1981), *Signals* (1982), *Grace Under Pressure* (1984), *Power Windows* (1985), *Hold Your Fire* (1987), *Presto* (1989), *Roll The Bones* (1991).

Rushen, Patrice

b. 30 September 1954, Los Angeles, California, USA. Rushen grew up in Los Angeles and attended the University of Southern California. She started learning classical piano when she was three, and turned to jazz in her teens. A group with which she was playing, won an award for young musicians at Monterey in 1972. She played with a host of artists, including Abbey Lincoln, Donald Byrd and Sonny Rollins, before joining Lee Ritenour's group in 1977.
Her career a solo singing artist which commenced in the late 70s as a pop/soul artist, bore fruit on the Elektra label. The US R&B Top 20 hit 'Hang It Up' (1978) was followed by 'Haven't You Heard' (US R&B number 7/US pop Top 30, 1979). The latter, plus 'Never Gonna Give You Up (Won't

Let You Be)' were minor UK hits in the early 80s, but were eclipsed by the Top 10 'Forget Me Nots'. Despite a tailing off in UK/US pop chart action from then on, Rushen continued to score regularly on the US R&B/soul charts. She gained notable chart success with 'Feel So Real (Won't Let Go)' (number 3, 1984) and 'Watch Out (number 9, 1987). After a period of label change, to Arista Records, she has given increased attention to her singing, and her predominantly bop-based playing, has given way to a fusion style. In 1988 she played with the Wayne Shorter/Carlos Santana group.
Albums: *Prelusion* (1974), *Before The Dawn* (1975), *Shout It Out* (1977), with Sonny Rollins *The Way I Feel* (1976), with Lee Ritenour *Sugarloaf Express* (1977), with John McLaughlin *Johnny McLaughlin, Electric Guitarist* (1978), *Patrice* (1979), *Pizzazz* (1979), *Let There Be Funk* (1980), *Posh* (1980), *Straight From The Heart* (1982), *Now* (1984), *Breaking All The Rules* (1986). *Watch Out!* (1987).

Russell, Leon

b. 2 April 1941, Lawton, Oklahoma, USA. The many talents of Russell include that of singer, songwriter, producer, arranger, entrepreneur, record company executive and multi-instrumentalist. While he tasted great honours as a solo star in the early 70s, it is his all-round contribution, much of it in the background, that has made him a vitally important figure in rock music for more than 30 years. His impressive career began, after having already mastered piano and trumpet as a child, when he played with Ronnie Hawkins and Jerry Lee Lewis in the late 50s. He became a regular session pianist for the pivotal US television show *Shindig* as well as being present on most of the classic Phil Spector singles, including the Ronettes, Crystals and the Righteous Brothers. James Burton is reputed to have taught him the guitar around this time. He has appeared on hundreds of major singles right across the music spectrum, playing with a plethora of artists, including Frank Sinatra, Bobby Darin, the Byrds, Herb Alpert and Paul Revere. He formed his own unit Asylum Choir in 1968 together with Marc Benno and formed a cultist duo that was a commercial disaster. He befriended Delaney And Bonnie and created the famous Mad Dogs And Englishmen tour, which included Joe Cocker. Cocker recorded Russell's 'Delta Lady' during this time, to great success. Russell founded his own label Shelter Records with UK producer Denny Cordell and released the self-titled debut which received unanimous critical approbation. His own

Leon Russell

session players included Steve Winwood, George Harrison, Eric Clapton, Charlie Watts, Bill Wyman and Ringo Starr. Following further session work including playing with Bob Dylan and Dave Mason, he appeared at the historic Concert for Bangla Desh in 1971 and was forced to rest the following year when he suffered a nervous and physical breakdown.

He returned in 1972 with the poignantly stunning *Carney*. This US number 2, million seller, was semi-autobiographical using the circus clown theme as an analogy to his own punishing career. The following year Russell delivered a superb country album, *Hank Wilson's Back*, acknowledging his debt to classic country singers. That year he released an album by his future wife, Mary McCreary, and in 1974 an excellent version of Tim Hardin's 'If I Were A Carpenter'. Leon concentrated on his own career more and more and in 1977 was awarded a Grammy for his song 'This Masquerade', which made the US Top 10 the previous year for George Benson. A partnership with Willie Nelson produced a superb country album in 1979; it became one of his biggest albums. The single 'Heartbreak Hotel' topped the US country chart, endorsing Russell's acceptance as a country singer. An excursion into bluegrass resulted in the 1981 live set with the New Grass Revival. Following *Hank Wilson's Volume II* in 1984 Leon became involved with his own video production company. Now white-haired, he resembles Tolkein's Gandalf. He returned in 1992 with the disappointing *Anything Will Happen*. Russell has already earned his retirement twice over and his place in the history books. If there were such a trophy he would be a contender for the 'most outstanding all-round contribution to rock' music award.'

Albums: *Look Inside The Asylum Choir* (1968), *Leon Russell* (1970), *Leon Russell And The Shelter People* (1971), *Asylum Choir II* (1971), *Carney* (1972), *Leon Live* (1973), *Hank Wilson's Back, Vol.1* (1973), *Stop All That Jazz* (1974), *Looking Back* (1974), *Will O' The Wisp* (1975), *Wedding Album* (1976), *Make Love To The Music* (1977), *Americana* (1978), with Willie Nelson *One For The Road* (1979), *Live And Love* (1979), with the New Grass Revival *The Live Album* (1981), *Hank Wilson Vol.II* (1984), *Anything Will Happen* (1992). Compilation: *Best Of Leon* (1976).

Rutles

The product of satirists Neil Innes (ex-Bonzo Dog Doo-Dah Band) and Eric Idle, formerly of the comedy team *Monty Python's Flying Circus*, the Rutles, was an affectionate and perceptive parody of the Beatles' career, which emerged from the duo's *Rutland Weekend Television* BBC comedy series. Innes played Ron Nasty (Lennon), Idle played Dirk McQuickly (McCartney), while Rikki Fataar (ex-Beach Boys) and John Halsey (ex-Patto) completed the line-up as Stig O'Hara (Harrison) and Barry Wom (Starr) respectively. The Rutles' film, *All You Need Is Cash*, and attendant album deftly combined elements drawn from both founder members' past work. Innes' songs re-created the different, and indeed, contrasting, styles of music the Beatles offered, ranging from the Mersey pop of 'I Must Be In Love' and 'Ouch!' to the psychedelia of 'Piggy In The Middle'. Mick Jagger and Paul Simon made excellent cameo appearances while George Harrison enjoyed a small acting role. The project is now rightly regarded, alongside Spinal Tap, as one of rock's most lasting parodies and the Rutles were themselves lampooned in 1991 when maverick New York label Shimmy Disc produced *Rutles Highway Revisited* wherein its roster performed a unique interpretation of the original album.

Album: *The Rutles* (1978).

S

Sad Cafe

Formed in 1976, Sad Cafe originally consisted of Paul Young (vocals), Ian Wilson (guitar), Mike Hehir (guitar), Lenni (saxophone), Vic Emerson (keyboards), John Stimpson (bass) and David Irving (drums). They evolved out of two Manchester groups, Gyro and Mandala, although Young had previously sung in an earlier beat group, the Toggery Five. Their debut *Fanx Ta Ra*, introduced the group's blend of hard-rock riffs and adult pop, but it was a second collection, *Misplaced Ideals*, which brought them international success when one of its tracks, 'Run Home Girl', became a US hit. *Facades*, produced by 10cc guitarist Eric Stewart, contained 'Every Day Hurts', a UK Top 3 single in 1979, and two further Top 40 entries the following year, 'Strange Little Girl' and 'My Oh My'. John Stimpson had became the group's manager in August 1980 and his place in the line-up was taken by Des Tong. However, despite enjoying a handful of minor hits, Sad Cafe were unable to sustain their early success although they continued to record, intermittently, throughout the 80s.
Albums: *Fanx Ta Ra* (1977), *Misplaced Ideals* (1978), *Facades* (1979), *Sad Cafe* (1980), *Live* (1981), *Ole* (1981), *The Politics Of Existing* (1986), *Whatever It Takes* (1989).

Sager, Carole Bayer

b. 1946, New York City, New York, USA. Sager's career as a hit songwriter stretches over three decades, from the catchy pop of 'Groovy Kind Of Love' to the charity ballad 'That's What Friends Are For', which has raised over $1m. for AIDS research. She began songwriting in the early 60s while as a student at New York's High School of Music and Art. Sager was talent-spotted by Don Kirshner and signed to his Screen Gems publishing company, with her first big hit coming in 1966 with 'Groovy Kind Of Love'. Co-written by Toni Wine, the song was first recorded by Patti Labelle and the Bluebelles, but it became an international best-seller in the version by the Mindbenders. It was equally successful when revived by Phil Collins for the soundtrack of *Buster* in 1989. In 1970, Sager wrote lyrics for the Broadway musical *Georgy* before co-writing 'Midnight Blue', Melissa

Manchester's 1975 US Top 10 hit. Her own recording career had begun on Metromeadia in 1972, and in 1976 Richard Perry produced 'You're Moving Out Today'. Co-written with Bette Midler, it was a UK Top 10 hit on Elektra Records. Even more successful was the dramatic 'When I Need You', a chart-topper for Leo Sayer on both sides of the Atlantic. 1979 brought a Broadway hit when Sager collaborated with Marvin Hamlisch on 'They're Playing Our Song', a semi-autobiographical piece about the romantic entanglement of a songwriting team. In 1981, she recorded for CBS, having her biggest US hit with 'Stronger Than Before'. Her most important partnership has turned out to be with Burt Bacharach, with whom Sager wrote the Oscar-winning 'Arthur's Theme' a big hit for Christopher Cross. She subsequently married Bacharach and collaborated with him on 'That's What Friends Are For', which became a US number 1 hit in 1986 when recorded by Dionne Warwick And Friends. Other notable Sager compositions from the 80s include 'Nobody Does It Better' (the James Bond film theme recorded by Carly Simon) and the Patti Labelle/Michael McDonald duet 'On My Own'.
Albums: *Carole Bayer Sager* (1977), *Too* (1978), *Sometimes Late At Night* (1981).

Sailor

Sailor were formed in 1974 by songwriter and acoustic guitarist George Kajanus (b. Georg Hultgren, Norway) who, apart from claiming to be a Norwegian prince, was a member of the folk rock group Eclection. The remainder of Sailor comprised Phil Pickett (b. Germany; nickleodeon) and Grant Serpell (b. Maidenhead, England; drums). They were signed to CBS/Epic Records who released their debut 'Traffic Jam'. A projected 1975 tour with Mott was expected to bring the group success; however, it was cancelled when Mott split. Subsequent tours with Kiki Dee and Cockney Rebel did have the desired effect. They reached number 2 in the UK charts with the sparkling 'A Glass Of Champagne'. They had two more hits with 'Girls Girls Girls' and 'One Drink Too Many' before the onset of punk overwhelmed them, but they continued gigging. The line-up underwent some changes but Marsh and Pickett were still on board by 1982. Kajanus formed the offshoot group Data in 1980 and they made three albums under that name. In 1983, Pickett acted as keyboard player and songwriter for Culture Club and his 'Karma Chameleon' was an international hit for them; though he was later sued by the

Carol Bayer Sager with Burt Bacharach

writers of Jimmy Jones' 'Handy Man' for alleged plagiarism. Pickett went on to write and perform ITV's 'Olympic Games Theme' in 1984 and produce Thereze Bazaar's solo album that same year. The group reformed in 1991, releasing their first album in 13 years.

Albums: *Sailor* (1974), *Trouble* (1975), *The Third Step* (1976), *Checkpoint* (1977), *Hideaway* (1978), *Dressed For Drowning* (1980), *Sailor* (1991). Compilation: *Greatest Hits* (1978).

Santana

This US group were the pioneers of Afro-Latin rock, head and shoulders above all pretenders to the throne. Santana emerged as part of the late 60s San Francisco new wave scene, which they rapidly transcended. Over the past 25 years the leader Carlos Santana (b. 20 July 1947, Autlan de Navarro, Mexico) has introduced jazz and funk into his unique blend of polyrhythmic music. Carlos owns the name, and has maintained his role as leader through a constant change of personnel, yet fully maintaining the Santana sound of 1967. The original line-up consisted of Gregg Rolie, Michael Shrieve, David Brown, Marcus Malone and Mike Carabello. Later important members were José Chepito Areas, Neal Schon, Tom Coster, Armando Peraza, Raul Rekow, Graham Lear, Orestes Vilato and Coke Escovedo. Santana was a regional favourite by 1969 and Carlos appeared on Al Kooper and Mike Bloomfield's *The Live Adventures Of. . .* The Woodstock Festival of 1969 was the band's major breakthrough; their performance gave rock fans a first taste of 'Cubano rock' and was one of the highlights.

The first three albums are outstanding examples of the genre. *Santana, Abraxas* and *Santana III* spent months high in the US charts, the latter two staying at number 1 for many weeks. These albums included numerous, memorable and fiery tracks including 'Jingo', Tito Puente's 'Oye Como Va', a definitive version of Peter Green's 'Black Magic Woman' and possibly the most sensual rock instrumental of all time; 'Samba Pa Ti'. On this Carlos plays a solo that oozes sexuality over an irresistible slow Latin beat. *Caravanserai* marked a change of style as Rolie and Schon departed to form Journey. This important album is almost a single suite showing a move towards jazz in the mode of Miles Davis' *In A Silent Way*. At that time Carlos became a disciple of Sri Chimnoy and, after befriending fellow guitarist John McLaughlin, he released the glorious *Love Devotion And Surrender*. During that year he released a messy live album

with soul/funk drummer Buddy Miles. All these albums were considerable hits. *Welcome* (featuring vocalist Leon Thomas and guest John McLaughlin) and *Borboletta* (with guests Flora Purim and Stanley Clarke) were lesser albums. He returned to hard Latin rock with the excellent *Amigos* in 1977. A version of the Zombies 'She's Not There' became a hit single from *Moonflower* in 1977. In his parallel world Carlos was maintaining a jazz-fusion path with a series of fine albums, the most notable was *The Swing Of Delight* with Herbie Hancock and Wayne Shorter. *Zebop!* in 1981 was a *tour de force*, and Santana's guitar playing was particularly impressive, with a clarity not heard since the earliest albums. The hit single from this collection was the admirable Russ Ballard song 'Winning'. The solo *Havana Moon* featured guests, Willie Nelson and Booker T. Jones, although the difference between what is solo Santana and band Santana has become almost irrelevant as Carlos is such an iconoclastic leader. *Beyond Appearances* in 1985 maintained his considerable recorded output. The same year he toured with Bob Dylan to ecstatic audiences. Carlos scored the music for *La Bamba* in 1986 and reunited with Buddy Miles in 1987 to record *Freedom*. Any association with the name Santana is a positive one; whether as the band or solo, Carlos Santana is an outstanding figure in rock music.

Albums: *Santana* (1969), *Abraxas* (1970), *Santana III* (1971), *Caravanserai* (1972), *Carlos Santana And Buddy Miles! Live!* (1972), *Love Devotion Surrender* (1973), *Welcome* (1973), *Borboletta* (1974), *Illuminations* (1974), *Lotus* (1975), *Amigos* (1976), *Festival* (1977), *Moonflower* (1977), *Inner Secrets* (1978), *Marathon* (1979), *Oneness: Silver Dreams, Golden Reality* (1979), *The Swing Of Delight* (1980), *Zebop!* (1981), *Shango* (1982), *Havana Moon* (1983), *Beyond Appearances* (1985), *La Bamba* (1986), *Freedom* (1987), *Blues For Salvador* (1987), *Persuasion* (1989), *Spirits Dancing In The Flesh* (1990). Compilations: *Greatest Hits* (1974), *Viva Santana - The Very Best* (1986), *Viva Santana* (1988, triple album), *The Very Best Of Santana, Volumes 1 And 2* (1988).

Sassafras

A band that never achieved major league success, they nevertheless built up a loyal following by extensively touring the UK during the 70s. Hailing from Wales, their line-up featured Terry Bennett (vocals), Dai Shell (guitar), Ralph Evans (guitar), Ricky John (bass) and Robert Jones (drums). They recorded three albums of straightforward boogie

rock, similar in style to Status Quo.
Albums: *Expecting Company* (1973), *Whealin' And Dealin'* (1976), *Riding High* (1976).

Sayer, Leo

b. 21 May 1948, Shoreham-on-Sea, England. Sayer fronted the Terraplane Blues Band while as a Sussex art student before moving to London, where he supplemented his wages as an illustrator by street busking and via floor spots in folk clubs. In 1971, he formed Patches with drummer Dave Courtney to whose melodies he provided lyrics. Speculating in artist management, Courtney's former employer, Adam Faith found the group ultimately unimpressive and chose only to promote its animated X-factor - Sayer. During initial sessions at Roger Daltrey's studio, the Who's vocalist was sufficiently impressed by the raw material to record some Courtney-Sayer numbers himself. These included 'Giving It All Away', Daltrey's biggest solo hit. After a miss with 'Why Is Everybody Going Home', Sayer reached the UK number 1 spot with 1973's exuberant 'The Show Must Go On' but immediate US success was thwarted by a chart-topping cover by Three Dog Night. Seeing him mime the song in a clown costume and pan-caked face on BBC television's *Top Of The Pops*, some dismissed Sayer as a one-shot novelty, but he had the last laugh on such detractors when his popularity continued into the next decade. After 'One Man Band' and 'Long Tall Glasses' - the US Hot 100 breakthrough - came the severing of Sayer's partnership with Courtney in 1975 during the making of *Another Year*. With a new co-writer in Frank Furrell (ex-Supertramp) from his backing group, Sayer rallied with the clever 'Moonlighting'. Though the year ended on a sour note with an ill-advised version of the Beatles' 'Let It Be', 1976 brought a US million-seller in 'You Make Me Feel Like Dancing' just as disco sashayed near its *Saturday Night Fever* apogee. From 1977's *Endless Flight* (produced by fashionable Richard Perry), the non-original ballad, 'When I Need You', marked Sayer's commercial peak at home - where the BBC engaged him for two television series. However, with the title track of *Thunder In My Heart* halting just outside the UK Top 20, hits suddenly became harder to come by with 1978's 'I Can't Stop Lovin' You' and telling revivals of Buddy Holly's 'Raining In My Heart' and Bobby Vee's 'More Than I Can Say' the only unequivocal smashes as his 1983 chart swansong (with 'Till You Come Back To Me') loomed nearer. Nevertheless, even 1979's fallow period for

singles was mitigated by huge returns for a compilation. By the late 80s Sayer was bereft of a recording contract, having severed his longstanding relationship with Chrysalis Records and was reduced to self-financing his UK tours. A legal wrangle with his former manager, Adam Faith, resulted in Sayer reportedly receiving £650,000 in lost royalties. His recording career recommenced in 1990 after signing to EMI and was reunited with producer Alan Tarney. Indications of a revival in his chart fortunes remain to be seen; however, this artist has been written off twice before, in 1973 and 1979, and critics should not be so quick to do so again.
Albums: *Silver Bird* (1974), *Just A Boy* (1974), *Another Year* (1975), *Endless Flight* (1976), *Thunder In My Heart* (1977), *Leo Sayer* (1978), *Here* (1979), *Living In A Fantasy* (1980), *World Radio* (1982), *Have You Ever Been In Love* (1983), *Cool Touch* (1990). Compilation: *The Very Best Of Leo Sayer* (1979).

Scaggs, Boz

b. William Royce Scaggs, 8 June 1944, Ohio, USA. Scaggs was raised in Dallas, Texas, where he joined fellow guitarist Steve Miller in a high-school group, the Marksmen. The musicians maintained this partnership in the Ardells, a group they formed at the University of Wisconsin, but this early association ended when Scaggs returned to Texas. Boz then formed an R&B unit, the Wigs, whom he took to London in anticipation of a more receptive audience. The group broke up when this failed to materialize and the guitarist headed for mainland Europe where he forged a career as an itinerant folk-singer. Scaggs was particularly successful in Sweden, where he recorded a rudimentary solo album, *Boz*. This interlude in exile ended in 1967 when he received an invitation from his erstwhile colleague to join the fledgling Steve Miller Band. Scaggs recorded two albums with this pioneering unit but left for a solo career in 1968. *Boz Scaggs*, recorded at the renowned Fame studios in Muscle Shoals, was a magnificent offering and featured sterling contributions from Duane Allman, particularly on the extended reading of Fenton Robinson's 'Loan Me A Dime'. Over the next five years, Boz forged an exemplary soul/rock direction with several excellent albums, including *My Time* and *Slow Dancer*. Skilled production work from Glyn Johns and Johnny Bristol reinforced a high quality, but it was not until 1976, and the smooth *Silk Degrees*, that this was translated into commercial success. A slick

Leo Sayer

session band, which later became Toto, enhanced some of Scaggs' finest compositions, including 'Lowdown' (a US chart number 3 hit), 'What Can I Say?' and 'Lido Shuffle', each of which reached the UK Top 30. The album also featured 'We're All Alone', which has since become a standard. Paradoxically the singer's career faltered in the wake of this exceptional album and despite enjoying several hit singles during 1980, Scaggs maintained a low profile during the subsequent decade. It was eight years before a new selection, *Other Roads* appeared.

Albums: *Boz* (1966), *Boz Scaggs* (1969), *Moments* (1971), *Boz Scaggs And Band* (1971), *My Time* (1972), *Slow Dancer* (1974), *Silk Degrees* (1976), *Two Down Then Left* (1977), *Middle Man* (1980), *Other Roads* (1988). Compilation: *Hits!* (1980).

Schulze, Klaus

Born in Germany, Schulze is one of the fathers of modern electronic music. Originally a drummer, he was a founder member of Tangerine Dream in 1967 and played on the group's debut. His debut solo album was on the Ohr subsidiary of Hansa Records but much of his later work appeared on his own Brain label. During the late 70s he recorded on synthesizer with Stomu Yamash'ta (*Go Two*) and was the first musician to perform live at the London Planetarium. He also toured with Arthur Brown, who sang on *Dune*, an album inspired by Frank Herbert's cult science fiction novel. In the 80s Schulze concentrated on recording albums whose titles and mesmeric synthesized compositions were the essence of 'new age' music. In 1987, he recorded the soundtrack for the film *Babel* with Andreas Grosser.

Albums: *Irrlicht* (1972), *Cyborg* (1973), *Blackdance* (1974), *Picture Music* (1974), *Timewind* (1975), *Moondawn* (1976), *Body Love* (1977), *Mirage* (1977), *Body Love II* (1977), *X* (1978), *Blanche* (1979), *Dune* (1979), *Live* (1980), *Dig It* (1980), *Trancefer* (1981), *Rock On* (1981), *Audentity* (1983), *Drive Inn* (1984), *Aphrica* (1984), *Angst* (1985), *Dreams* (1987), *Babel* (1987, film soundtrack), *En=Trance* (1988), *The Dresden Performance* (1991).

Scott, Tom

b. 19 May 1948, Los Angeles, California, USA. Scott's mother - Margery Wright - was a pianist, his father - Nathan Scott - a film and television composer. Scott played clarinet in high school and won a teenage competition with his Neoteric Trio at the Hollywood Bowl in 1965. He learned all the saxophones and played in the studios for TV shows

such as *Ironside*. He performed on Roger Kellaway's *Spirit Feel* in 1967, playing fluent alto and soprano over a proto-fusion encounter of hard bop and rock music. As a member of Spontaneous Combustion in 1969, he played on *Come And Stick Your Head In*, an experimental record in the jazz-rock idiom. His own records - *Honeysuckle Breeze* (1967) and *Rural Still Life* (1968) - presented a tight, forceful jazz funk. From his early 20s he wrote prolifically for television and films (including *Conquest Of The Planet Of The Apes*), his sound becoming the blueprint for LA copshow soundtracks: urgent, funky, streamlined. His band, the LA Express, became one of the most successful fusion bands of the 70s. Joni Mitchell used them as her backing band on *Miles Of Aisles* (and guested on 1975's *Tom Cat*) and George Harrison played slide guitar on *New York Connection*. 1987's *Streamlines* showed that Scott had not lost his sound, but an interest in samples of ethnic instruments had given his music a more world-music feel.

Albums: *Honeysucle Breeze* (1967), *Rural Still Life* (1968), with Spontaneous Combustion *Come And Stick Your Head In* (1969), *Tom Scott & the LA Express* (1974), *Tom Cat* (1975), *New York Connection* (1975), *Blow It Out* (1977), *Apple Juice* (1981), *Desire* (1982), *Streamlines* (1987).

Scott-Heron, Gil

b. 1 April 1949, Chicago, Illinois, USA. Raised in Jackson, Tennessee, by his grandmother, Scott-Heron moved to New York at the age of 13 and had published two novels (*The Vulture*, *The Nigger Factory*) plus a book of poems by the time he was 12. He met musician Brian Jackson when both were students at Lincoln University, Pennsylvania, and in 1972 they formed the Midnight Band to play their original blend of jazz, soul and prototype rap music. *Small Talk At 125th And Lenox* was mostly an album of poems (from his book of the same name), but later albums showed Scott-Heron developing into a skilled songwriter whose work was soon covered by other artists: for example, Labelle recorded his 'The Revolution Will Not Be Televised' and Esther Phillips made a gripping version of 'Home Is Where The Hatred Is'. In 1973 he had a minor hit with 'The Bottle'. *Winter In America*, on the Strata East label, and *The First Minute Of A New Day*, for Arista, were heavily jazz-influenced, but later Arista albums had Scott-Heron exploring more pop-oriented formats, and in 1976 he scored a hit with the disco-based protest single 'Johannesburg'. One of his best records of the 80s, *Reflections*, featured a fine version of Marvin Gaye's 'Inner City Blues'; but his strongest songs were generally his own barbed political diatribes, in which he confronted issues such as nuclear power, apartheid and poverty and made a series of scathing attacks on American politicians. Richard Nixon, Gerald Ford, Barry Goldwater and Jimmy Carter were all targets of his trenchant satire and his anti-Reagan rap 'B-Movie' gave him another small hit in 1982. An important precursor of today's rap artists, Scott-Heron once described Jackson (who left the band in 1980) and himself as 'interpreters of the black experience'.

Albums: *Small Talk At 125th And Lenox* (1972), *Free Will* (1973), *Pieces Of A Man* (1974), *Winter In America* (1975), *The First Minute Of A New Day* (1975), *From South Africa To South Caroline* (1975), *It's Your World* (1976), *Bridges* (1977), *Secrets* (1978), *1980* (1980), *Real Eyes* (1980), *Reflections* (1981), *Moving Target* (1982). Compilations: *The Revolution Will Not Be Televised* (1975), *The Mind Of Gil Scott-Heron* (1978), *The Best Of Gil Scott-Heron* (1984).

Seals And Crofts

A duo consisting of Jim Seals (b. 17 October 1941, in Sidney, Texas, USA) and Dash Crofts (b. 14 August 1940 in Cisco, Texas, USA), Seals and Crofts were one of the most popular soft rock-pop acts of the 70s. The pair first worked together in 1958 as guitarist (Seals) and drummer (Crofts) for Texan singer Dean Beard, with whom they recorded a number of singles that did not chart. When Beard was asked to join the Champs, of 'Tequila' fame, Seals and Crofts came along, relocating to Los Angeles. They stayed with the Champs until 1965, when Crofts returned to Texas. The following year, Seals joined a group called the Dawnbreakers, and Crofts returned to Los Angeles to join as well. Both Seals and Crofts converted to the Baha'i religion in 1969 (10 years later they would leave the music business to devote themselves to it full-time). Following the split of the Dawnbreakers, Seals and Crofts continued as an acoustic music duo (Seals played guitar, saxophone and violin, Crofts guitar and mandolin), recording their first album, which did not chart, for the Talent Associates label. Meanwhile, the pair performed live and built a following. In 1970 *Down Home*, made the charts and led to a label change to Warner Brothers Records. Their second album for that company, 1972's *Summer Breeze*, made number 7 on the US charts and the title single reached number 6. ('Summer Breeze' also provided the

Isley Brothers with a UK Top 20 hit in 1974.) It was followed in 1973 by their best-selling *Diamond Girl*, which also yielded a number 6 title single. They maintained their popularity throughout the mid-70s, coming up with yet another number 6 single, 'Get Closer', in 1976. Following the release of the 1978 album *Takin' It Easy* and the same-titled single, which became their final chart entries, Seals and Crofts retired from music to devote themselves to their faith.

Albums: *Seals And Crofts* (1970), *Down Home* (1970), *Year Of Sunday* (1972), *Summer Breeze* (1972), *Diamond Girl* (1973), *Unborn Child* (1974), *I'll Play For You* (1975), *Get Closer* (1976), *Sudan Village* (1976), *One On One* (1977, film soundtrack), *Takin' It Easy* (1978). Compilations: *Greatest Hits* (1975).

Sea Train

The original Sea Train line-up - John Gregory (guitar/vocals), Richard Greene (violin), Donald Kretmar (saxophone/bass), Andy Kulberg (bass/flute) and Roy Blumenfeld (drums) - evolved from the New York-based Blues Project and this particular quintet completed the previous group's contractual obligations with the *Planned Obsolescence* album. The unit's first official self-titled album was released in 1969. By this point the group had been augmented by lyricist James T. Roberts and this imaginative collection fused such seemingly disparate elements as rock, bluegrass and Elizabethan-styled folksiness. Internal problems sadly doomed this quirky line-up, and after approximately 25 members had passed through the band, a stable Sea Train line-up emerged with only Kulberg and Greene remaining from the initial band. The three newcomers were Lloyd Baskin (keyboards/vocals), Larry Atamanuk (drums) and former Earth Opera member Peter Rowan (guitar/vocals). A second album, also entitled *Sea Train*, was recorded in London under the aegis of George Martin, as was their third collection, *Marblehead Messenger*. Both albums displayed an engaging, eclectic style, but were doomed to commercial indifference. The departure of Rowan and Greene to the critically acclaimed Muleskinner was a severe blow and although Kulberg and Baskin persevered by bringing Peter Walsh (guitar), Bill Elliott (keyboards) and Julio Coronado (drums) into the group, a fourth release, *Watch*, was a major disappointment. When Sea Train latterly disbanded, Kulberg pursued a career composing for numerous television shows.

Albums: *Sea Train* (1969), *Sea Train* (1970),

Marblehead Messenger (1971), *Watch* (1973).

Sensational Alex Harvey Band

Formed in 1972 when veteran vocalist Alex Harvey (b. 5 February 1935, Glasgow, Scotland, d. 4 February 1981) teamed with struggling Glasgow group, Tear Gas. Zal Cleminson (b. 4 May 1949; guitar), Hugh McKenna (b. 28 November 1949; keyboards), Chris Glen (b. 6 November 1950, Paisley, Renfrewshire, Scotland; bass) and Ted McKenna (b. 10 March 1950; drums) gave the singer the uncultured power his uncompromising rasp required and were the perfect foil to the sense of drama he created. Armed with a musical and cultural heritage, Harvey embarked on a unique direction combining elements of rock, R&B and the British music hall. He created the slum-kid Vambo, celebrated pulp fiction with 'Sergeant Fury' and extolled a passion for 'b-movie' lore in 'Don't Worry About The Lights Mother, They're Burning Big Louie Tonight'. *Framed*, SAHB's debut, was accompanied by a period of frenetic live activity. *Next*, reflected a consequent confidence which was especially apparent on the title track, a harrowing, atmospheric rendition of a Jacques Brel composition. The quintet continued their commercial ascendancy with *The Impossible Dream* and *Tomorrow Belongs To Me*, while enhancing their in-concert reputation with a series of excellent and increasingly ambitious stage shows. Harvey's presence was a determining factor in their visual appeal, but Cleminson's intelligent use of clown make-up and mime brought yet another factor to the unit's creative think-tank. *Live* encapsulated this era, while SAHB's irreverence was made clear in their exaggerated reading of Tom Jones' hit 'Delilah', which gave the group a UK Top 10 single. Its success inspired *The Penthouse Tapes*, which featured such disparate favourites as 'Crazy Horses' (the Osmonds) 'School's Out' (Alice Cooper) and 'Goodnight Irene' (Leadbelly). The group enjoyed another hit single with 'Boston Tea Party' (1976), but the rigorous schedule extracted a toll on their vocalist. He entered hospital to attend to a recurring liver problem, during which time the remaining members recorded *Fourplay* as SAHB (Without Alex). Hugh McKenna was then replaced by Tommy Eyre and in August 1977 Harvey rejoined the group to complete *Rock Drill*. However, three months later he walked out on his colleagues during a rehearsal for BBC's *Sight And Sound* programme and despite the ill-feeling this caused, it was later accepted that his return had been premature given the extent of his illness.

Despite pursuing a solo career at a more measured pace, Harvey died as a result of a heart attack on 4 February 1981. Ted McKenna, Cleminson and Glen had meanwhile formed the short-lived Zal, with Billy Rankin (guitar) and Leroi Jones (vocals), but this ill-starred ensemble struggled in the face of punk and split up in April 1978. McKenna later joined Rory Gallagher and MSG, while Cleminson was briefly a member of Nazareth.
Albums: *Framed* (1972), *Next* (1973), *The Impossible Dream* (1974), *Tomorrow Belongs To Me* (1975), *Live* (1975), *The Penthouse Tapes* (1976), *SAHB Stories* (1976), *Rock Drill* (1978). Compilations: *Big Hits And Close Shaves* (1977), *Collectors Items* (1980), *The Best Of The Sensational Alex Harvey Band* (1984), *The Legend* (1985), *Anthology - Alex Harvey* (1986), *Collection - Alex Harvey* (1986). SAHB (Without Alex): *Fourplay* (1977).

Sex Pistols

This incandescent UK punk group came together under the aegis of entrepreneur Malcolm McLaren during the summer of 1975. Periodically known as the Swankers, with lead vocalist Wally Nightingale, they soon metamorphosed into the Sex Pistols with a line up comprising: Steve Jones (b. 3 September 1955, London, England; guitar), Paul Cook (b. 20 July 1956, London, England; drums), Glen Matlock (b. London, England; bass) and Johnny Rotten (b. John Lydon, 30 January 1956, London, England; vocals). By 1976, the group was playing irregularly around London and boasted a small following of teenagers, whose spiked hair, torn clothes and safety pins echoed the new fashion that McLaren was transforming into commodity. The group's gigs became synonymous with violence, which reached a peak during the 100 Club's Punk Rock Festival when a girl was blinded in a glass-smashing incident involving the group's most fearful follower, Sid Vicious. The adverse publicity did not prevent the group from signing to EMI Records later that year when they also released their first single, 'Anarchy In The UK'. From Rotten's sneering laugh at the opening of the song to the final seconds of feedback, the single was a riveting debut. The Pistols promoted the work on London Weekend Television's *Today* programme, which ended in a stream of four-letter abuse that brought the group banner headlines in the following morning's tabloid press. More controversy ensued when the group's 'Anarchy' tour was decimated and the single suffered distribution problems and bans from shops. Eventually, it peaked at number 38 in the UK charts. Soon after, the group was dropped from EMI in a blaze of publicity. By February 1977, Matlock was replaced by that punk caricature Sid Vicious (b. John Simon Ritchie, 10 May 1957, London, England, d. 2 February 1979). The following month, the group was signed to A&M Records outside the gates of Buckingham Palace. One week later, A&M cancelled the contract, with McLaren picking up another parting cheque of £40,000. After reluctantly signing to the small label Virgin, the group issued 'God Save The Queen'. The single tore into the heart of British Nationalism at a time when the populace was celebrating the Queen' Jubilee. Despite a daytime radio ban the single rose to number 1 in the NME chart. The Pistols suffered for their art as outraged royalists attacked them whenever they appeared on the streets. A third single, the melodic 'Pretty Vacant' (largely the work of the departed Matlock) proved their most accessible single to date and restored them to the Top 10.

By the winter the group hit again with 'Holidays In The Sun' and issued their controversially-titled album, Never Mind The Bollocks - Here's The Sex Pistols. The work rocketed to number 1 in the UK album charts amid partisan claims that it was a milestone in rock. In truth, it was a more patchy affair, containing a preponderance of previously released material which merely underlined that the group was running short of ideas. An ill-fated attempt to capture the group's story on film wasted much time and revenue, while a poorly received tour of America fractured the Pistols' already strained relationship. In early 1978, Rotten announced that he was leaving the group after a gig in San Francisco. According to the manager Malcolm McLaren he was fired. McLaren, meanwhile, was intent on taking the group to Brazil in order that they could be filmed playing with the train robber Ronnie Biggs. Vicious, incapacitated by heroin addiction, could not make the trip, but Jones and Cook were happy to indulge in the publicity stunt. McLaren mischievously promoted Biggs as the group's new lead singer and another controversial single emerged: 'God Save The Pistols'. It was later retitled 'No One Is Innocent (A Punk Prayer)' and issued as a double a-side with Vicious's tuneless rendition of the Frank Sinatra standard 'My Way'. McLaren's movie was finally completed by director Julien Temple under the title The Great Rock 'n' Roll Swindle. A self-conscious rewriting of history, it callously wrote Matlock out of the script and saw the unavailable Rotten relegated to old footage.

While the film was being completed, the Pistols' disintegration was completed. Vicious, now the centre of the group, recorded a lame version of Eddie Cochran's 'C'mon Everybody' before returning to New York. On 12 October 1978, his girlfriend Nancy Spungen was found stabbed in his hotel room and Vicious was charged with murder. While released on bail, he suffered a fatal overdose of heroin and died peacefully in his sleep on the morning of 2 February 1979. Virgin Records continued to issue the desultory fragments of Pistols work that they had on catalogue, including the appropriately titled compilation, Flogging A Dead Horse. The group's impact as the grand symbol of UK punk rock has ensured their longevity. The unholy saga appropriately ended in the High Court a decade on in 1986 when Rotten and his fellow ex-Pistols won substantial damages against their former manager.

Albums: Never Mind The Bollocks - Here's The Sex Pistols (1977). Compilations: The Great Rock 'N' Roll Swindle (1979), Some Product - Carri On Sex Pistols (1979), Flogging A Dead Horse (1980).

Sha Na Na

Spearheading the US rock 'n' roll revivalism that began in the late 60s, the group emerged from Columbia University in 1968 with a repertoire derived exclusively from the 50s, and a choreographed stage act that embraced a jiving contest for audience participants. Looking the anachronistic part - gold lame, brilliantine cockades, drainpiped hosiery et al - the initial line-up consisted of vocalists Scott Powell, Johnny Contardo, Frederick Greene, Don York and Richard Joffe; guitarists Chris Donald, Elliot Cahn and Henry Gross; pianists Scott Symon and John Bauman, plus Bruce Clarke (bass), Jocko Marcellino (drums) and - the only musician with a revered past - saxophonist Leonard Baker (ex-Danny And The Juniors). Surprisingly, there were few personnel changes until a streamlining to a less cumbersome 10-piece in 1973. The band were launched internationally by a show-stealing appearance at 1969's Woodstock Festival (that was included in the subsequent film and album spin-offs) but their onstage recreations of old sounds did not easily translate on disc - especially if the original versions had emotional significance for the listener. From 1972's The Night Is Still Young, 'Bounce In Your Buggy' - one of few self-composed numbers - was the closest the outfit ever came to a hit (though Gross would enjoy a solo US smash in 1976 with 'Shannon'). Nevertheless, the approbation of the famous was manifest in Keith Moon's compering of a Sha Na Na bash in 1971 and John Lennon's choice of the band to open his One-For-One charity concert in New York a year later. By 1974, however, their act had degenerated to a dreary repetition that took its toll in discord, nervous breakdowns and more unresolvable internal problems culminating in a fatal heroin overdose by Vincent Taylor, a latter-day member. Yet Sha Na Na's early example enabled archivist-performers such as Darts, Shakin' Stevens and the Stray Cats to further the cause of a seemingly outmoded musical form.

Selected albums: *The Night Is Still Young* (1972), *Rock And Roll Revival* (1977), *Sha Na Na Is Here To Stay* (1985), *Rockin' And A Rollin'* (1987). Compilation: *20 Greatest Hits* (1989).

Sham 69

Originally formed in London, England in 1976, this five-piece skinhead/punk-influenced group comprised Jimmy Pursey (vocals), Albie Slider (bass), Neil Harris (lead guitar), Johnny Goodfornothing (rhythm guitar) and Billy Bostik (drums). Pursey was a fierce, working-class idealist, an avenging angel of the unemployed, who sacked most of the above line-up within a year due to their lack of commitment. A streamlined aggregation featuring Dave Parsons (guitar), Dave Treganna (bass) and Mark Cain (drums) helped Pursey reach the UK charts with a series of anthemic hits including 'Angels With Dirty Faces', 'If The Kids Are United', 'Hurry Up Harry' and 'Hersham Boys'. Although Pursey championed proletarian solidarity, his rabble-rousing all too often brought violence and disruption from a small right-wing faction causing wary promoters to shun the group. After a troubled couple of years attempting to reconcile his ideals and their results, Pursey elected to go solo, but his time had passed. The group reformed in the early 90s and performed at punk nostalgia/revival concerts.

Albums: *Tell Us The Truth* (1978), *That's Life* (1978), *Adventures Of The Hersham Boys* (1979).

Showaddywaddy

When two promising Leicestershire groups fused their talents in 1983, the result was an octet comprising Dave Bartram (vocals), Billy Gask (vocals), Russ Fields (guitar), Trevor Oakes (guitar), Al James (bass), Rod Teas (bass), Malcolm Allured (drums) and Romeo Challenger (drums). Showaddywaddy personified the easy-listening dilution of rock 'n' roll and rockabilly and their visual appeal and showmanship won them talent contests and, more importantly, a contract with Bell Records. Initially penning their own hits, they charted steadily, but after reaching number 2 with Eddie Cochran's 'Three Steps To Heaven', the cover version game was begun in earnest. Fifteen of their singles reached the UK Top 20 during the late 70s but the seemingly foolproof hit formula ran dry in the following decade when the rock 'n' roll revival had passed.

Albums: *Step Two* (1975), *Trocadero* (1976), *Showaddywaddy* (1977), *Red Star* (1977), *Crepes And Drapes* (1979), *Bright Lights* (1980), *Good Times* (1981), *Living Legends* (1983).

Shusha

b. Shusha Guppy, 7 January 1940, Teheran, Iran. This songwriter, singer and author emigrated to France at the age of 16, and was educated at the Sorbonne in Paris, studying Oriental Languages and Philosophy. Having married an English author during the 60s, she relocated to London. Although she had trained and studied as an opera singer, her interest lay in a range of musical styles from medieval folk through 16th century ballads, to the works of writers such as Jacques Brel and Joan Baez. Shusha garnered a good deal of critical praise for a number of her recordings during the 70s, and made a number of television and radio appearances. In 1973, she travelled with the nomadic Bakhtiari tribe in Iran, making two films. The first, *People Of The Wind*, a documentary about the migration of the tribe across the mountains, won an Oscar nomination for best documentary in 1977. A soundtrack album from the film was later released in the USA. The second film was a short of Shusha singing during the journey. Never predictable, her albums varied in content. *From East To West* saw a collaboration with arranger Paul Buckmaster, setting traditional Persian songs to a jazz/rock setting. *Here I Love You*, by comparison, was an album of her own songs, while. *Durable Fire* featured songs by English poets, including William Shakespeare and Ted Hughes.

Albums: *Song Of Long-Time Lovers* (1972), *Persian Love Songs And Mystic Chants* (1973), *Shusha* (1974), *This Is The Day* (1974), *Before The Deluge* (1975), *From East To West* (1978), *Here I Love You* (1980), with various artists *Lovely In The Dances-Songs Of Sydney Carter* (1981), *Durable Fire* (1983), *Strange Affair* (1987).

Further reading: *The Blindfold Horse-Memories Of A Persian Childhood*, Shusha Guppy, *A Girl In Paris*, Shusha Guppy, *Looking Back*, Shusha Guppy.

Labi Siffre

Siffre, Labi

Siffre was born and brought up in Bayswater, London, England to an English mother and Nigerian father. He first took employment as a mini-cab driver and delivery man but practised guitar whenever he could, going on to study music harmonics. He played his first gigs as one of a trio of like-minded youngsters, before taking up a nine-month residency at Annie's Rooms. His tenure completed, he travelled to Cannes, France, and played with a variety of soul musicians and bands. He returned to the UK in the late 60s to score solo hits in 1971 with 'It Must Be Love' (later covered by Madness) and 'Crying Laughing, Loving, Lying'. Although 'Watch Me' in 1972 was his last hit of the 70s, he made a spectacular comeback in 1987 with the anthemic '(Something Inside) So Strong'.

Album: *Labi Siffre* (1970), *Singer And The Song* (1971), *Crying, Laughing, Loving, Lying* (1972), *So Strong* (1988), *Make My Day* (1989). Compilation: *The Labi Siffre Collection* (1986).

Sill, Judee

This Los Angeles-based artist first attracted attention for her work with the city's folk-rock fraternity. An early composition, 'Dead Time Bummer Blues', was recorded by the Leaves, whose bassist, Jim Pons, later joined the Turtles. He introduced Sill to Blimp, the group's publishing company, the fruit of which was 'Lady O', their finest late-period performance. The song also appeared on *Judee Sill*, the artist's poignant debut, which was largely produced by Pons in partnership with another ex-Leave, John Beck. Graham Nash supervised the sole exception, 'Jesus Was A Crossmaker', which drew considerable comment over its lyrical content and was one of the songs Sill featured on a rare UK television appearance. *Heart Food* continued this uncompromising individual's quest for excellence and deftly balanced upbeat, country-tinged compositions with dramatic emotional ballads. A gift for melody suggested a long, successful career, but Judee Sill subsequently abandoned full-time music.

Albums: *Judee Sill* (1971), *Heart Food* (1973).

Silver Convention

This studio group was created by Munich-based producers Silvester Levay and Michael Kunze. After scoring a UK hit in 1975 with 'Save Me', they went on to reach number 1 in the USA with 'Fly, Robin, Fly'. The international fame persuaded the duo to audition some girl singers to adopt the Silver Convention name and the lucky trio were Linda Thompson (ex-Les Humphries Singers), Ramona Wulf (formerly a solo artist) and Penny McLean. This 'second generation' Silver Convention proved more than a match for their anonymous studio counterparts and achieved transatlantic Top 10 success with the infectious 'Get Up And Boogie (That's Right)', one of the most distinctive disco numbers of the period. A significant line-up change followed with the departure of Thompson, replaced by Rhonda Heath. Further minor hits followed until the group quietly disbanded in the late 70s.

Albums: *Save Me* (1975), *Silver Convention* (1976), *Madhouse* (1976), *Golden Girls* (1977). Compilation: *Silver Convention: Greatest Hits* (1977).

Simon, Carly

b. 25 June 1945, New York City, New York, USA. Simon became one of the most popular singer-songwriters of the 70s and achieved equal success with film music in the 80s. In the early 60s she played Greenwich Village clubs with her sister Lucy. As the Simon Sisters they had one minor hit with 'Winkin' Blinkin And Nod' (Kapp Records 1964) and recorded two albums of soft folk and children's' material. After the duo split up, Carly Simon made an unsuccessful attempt to launch a solo career through Albert Grossman (then Bob Dylan's manager) before concentrating on songwriting with film critic Jacob Brackman. In 1971, two of their songs, the wistful 'That's The Way I've Always Heard It Should Be' and the Paul Samwell-Smith produced 'Anticipation' were US hits for Simon. Her voice was given a rock accompaniment by Richard Perry on her third album which included her most famous song, 'You're So Vain', whose target was variously supposed to be Warren Beatty and/or Mick Jagger, who provided backing vocals. The song was a million-seller in 1972 and nearly two decades later was reissued in Britain after it had been used in a television commercial. *No Secrets* remains her most applauded work, and featured among numerous gems, 'The Right Thing To Do'.

Simon's next Top 10 hit was an insipid revival of the Charlie And Inez Foxx song 'Mockingbird' on which she duetted with James Taylor to whom she was married from 1972-83. Their marriage was given enormous coverage in the US media, rivalling that of Richard Burton and Elizabeth Taylor. Their divorce received similar treatment as Carly found solace with Taylor's drummer Russell Kunkel. *Hotcakes* became US Top 3 album in

Carly Simon

1972. During the latter part of the 70s, Simon was less prolific as a writer and recording artist although she played benefit concerts for anti-nuclear causes. Her most successful records were the James Bond film theme. 'Nobody Does It Better', written by Carole Bayer Sager and Marvin Hamlisch and 'You Belong To Me', a collaboration with Michael McDonald, both in 1977. During the 80s, Simon's worked moved away from the singer-songwriter field and towards the pop mainstream. She released two albums of pre-war Broadway standards (*Torch* and *My Romance*) and increased her involvement with films. Her UK hit 'Why' (1982) was written by Chic and used in the movie *Soup For One* while she appeared in *Perfect* with John Travolta. But her biggest achievement of the decade was to compose and perform two of its memorable film themes. Both 'Coming Around Again' (from *Heartburn*, 1986) and the Oscar-winning 'Let The River Run' (from *Working Girl*, 1989) demonstrated the continuing depth of Simon's songwriting talent while the quality of her previous work was showcased on a 1988 live album and video recorded in the open air at Martha's Vineyard, Massachusetts. In 1990, her career came full circle when Lucy Simon was a guest artist on *Have You Seen Me Lately ?*

Albums: as the Simon Sisters *The Simon Sisters* (1964), *Cuddlebug* (1965); solo *Carly Simon* (1971), *Anticipation* (1972), *No Secrets* (1972), *Hotcakes* (1974), *Playing Possum* (1975), *Another Passenger* (1976), *Boys In The Trees* (1978), *Spy* (1979), *Come Upstairs* (1980), *Torch* (1981), *Hello Big Man* (1983), *Spoiled Girl* (1985), *Coming Around Again* (1987), *Greatest Hits Live* (1988), *My Romance* (1990), *Have You Seen Me Lately ?* (1990). Compilation: *The Best Of Carly Simon* (1975).

Simon, Paul

b. Paul Frederic Simon, 13 October 1941, Newark, New Jersey, USA. Simon first entered the music business with partner Art Garfunkel in the duo Tom and Jerry. In 1957, they scored a US hit with the rock 'n' roll influenced 'Hey Schoolgirl'. After one album, they split up in order to return to college. Although Simon briefly worked with Carole King recording demonstration discs for minor acts, he did not record again until the early 60s. Employing various pseudonyms, Simon enjoyed a couple of minor US hits during 1962-63 as Tico And The Triumphs ('Motorcycle') and Jerry Landis ('The Lone Teen-Ranger'). After moving to Europe in 1964, Simon busked in Paris and appeared at various folk clubs in London.

Upon returning to New York, he was signed to CBS Records by producer Tom Wilson and reunited with his erstwhile partner Garfunkel. Their 1964 recording *Wednesday Morning 3 AM*, which included 'The Sound Of Silence' initially failed to sell, prompting Simon to return to London. While there, he made *The Paul Simon Songbook*, a solo work, recorded on one microphone with the astonishingly low budget of £60. Among its contents were several of Simon's most well-known compositions, including 'I Am A Rock', 'A Most Peculiar Man' and 'Kathy's Song'. The album was virtually ignored until Tom Wilson altered Simon's artistic stature overnight. Back in the USA, the producer grafted electric instrumentation on to Simon And Garfunkel's acoustic recording of 'Sound Of Silence' and created a folk-rock classic that soared to the top of the US charts. Between 1965 and 70, Simon And Garfunkel became one of the most successful recording duos in the history of popular music. The partnership ended amid musical disagreements and a realization that they had grown apart.

After the break-up, Simon took songwriting classes in New York and prepared a stylistically diverse solo album, *Paul Simon* (1972). The work incorporated elements of latin, reggae and jazz and spawned the hit singles 'Mother And Child Reunion' and 'Me And Julio Down By The Schoolyard'. One year later, Simon returned with the much more commercial *There Goes Rhymin' Simon* which enjoyed massive chart success and included two major hits, 'Kodachrome' and 'Take Me To The Mardi Gras'. A highly successful tour resulted in *Live Rhymin'*, which featured several Simon And Garfunkel standards. This flurry of creativity in 1975 culminated in the chart-topping *Still Crazy After All These Years* which won several Grammy awards. The wry '50 Ways To Leave Your Lover', taken from the album, provided Simon with his first number 1 single as a soloist, while the hit 'My Little Town' featured a tantalizing duet with Garfunkel. A five-year hiatus followed during which Simon took stock of his career. He appeared briefly in Woody Allen's movie *Annie Hall*, recorded a hit single with Garfunkel and James Taylor ('Wonderful World'), released a *Greatest Hits* package featuring the catchy 'Slip Slidin' Away' and switched labels from CBS to Warner Brothers. In 1980, he released the ambitious *One Trick Pony*, from his film of the same name. The movie included cameo appearances by the Lovin' Spoonful and Tiny Tim but was not particularly well-received even though it was far more literate than most 'rock-related' films. In the wake of that project, Simon suffered a long period of writer's block, which was to delay the recording of his next album.

Meanwhile, a double-album live reunion of Simon And Garfunkel recorded in Central Park was issued and sold extremely well. It was intended to preview a studio reunion, but the sessions were subsequently scrapped. Instead, Simon concentrated on his next album, which finally emerged in 1983 as *Hearts And Bones*. An intense and underrated effort, it sold poorly despite its evocative hit single 'The Late Great Johnny Ace' (dedicated to both the doomed 50s star and the assassinated John Lennon). Simon was dismayed by the album's lack of commercial success and critics felt that he was in a creative rut. That situation altered during 1984 when Simon was introduced to the enlivening music of the South African black townships. After an appearance at the celebrated USA For Africa recording of 'We Are The World', Simon immersed himself in the music of the Dark Continent. *Graceland* (1986) was one of the most intriguing and commercially successful albums of the decade with Simon utilizing musical contributions from Ladysmith Black Mambazo, Los Lobos, Linda Ronstadt and Rockie Dopsie And The Twisters. The project and subsequent tour was bathed in controversy due to accusations (misconceived according to the United Nations Anti-Apartheid Committee) that Simon had broken the cultural boycott against South Africa. The success of the album in combining contrasting cross-cultural musical heritages was typical of a performer who had already incorporated folk, R&B, calypso and blues into his earlier repertoire. The album spawned several notable hits, 'The Boy In The Bubble', 'You Can Call Me Al' and 'Graceland'. Although *Graceland* seemed a near impossible work to follow up, Simon continued his pan-cultural investigations with *The Rhythm Of The Saints*, which incorporated African and Brazilian musical elements.
Albums: *The Paul Simon Songbook* (1965), *Paul Simon* (1972), *There Goes Rhymin' Simon* (1973), *Live Rhymin'* (1974), *Still Crazy After All These Years* (1975), *One Trick Pony* (1980, film soundtrack), *Hearts And Bones* (1983), *Graceland* (1986), *The Rhythm Of The Saints* (1990). Compilation: *Greatest Hits, Etc.* (1977).
Further reading: *The Boy In The Bubble*, Patrick Humphries.

Sister Sledge
Debra (b. 1955), Joan (1957), Kim (1958) and Kathie Sledge (1959) were all born and raised in Philadelphia, Pennsylvania, USA. They started their recording career in 1971 and spent a short time working as backing singers before enjoying a series of minor R&B hits between 1974-77. Two years later they entered a fruitful relationship with Chic masterminds Nile Rodgers and Bernard Edwards which resulted in several sparkling singles including 'He's The Greatest Dancer', 'We Are Family' and 'Lost In Music', each of which reached the the UK Top 20 in 1979. The Sisters then left the Chic organization and began to produce their own material in 1981. Although success in the United States waned, the quartet retained their UK popularity and two remixes of former hits served as a prelude to 'Frankie', a simple but irrepressible song which reached number 1 in 1985. Since then however, Sister Sledge have been unable to maintain this status.
Albums: *Circle Of Love* (1975), *Together* (1977), *We Are Family* (1979), *Love Somebody Today* (1980), *All American Girls* (1981), *The Sisters* (1982), *Bet Cha Say That To All The Girls* (1983), *When The Boys Meet The Girls* (1985). Compilation: *Greatest Hits* (1986).

Skellern, Peter
b. 14 March 1947, Bury, Lancashire, England. Skellern played trombone in a school band and served as organist and choirmaster in a local church before attending the Guildhall School of Music, from which he graduated with honours in 1968. Because 'I didn't want to spend the next 50 years playing Chopin', he joined March Hare which, as Harlan County, recorded a country-pop album before disbanding in 1971. Married with two children, Skellern worked as a hotel porter in Shaftesbury, Dorset, before striking lucky with a self-composed UK number 3 hit, 'You're A Lady'. *Peter Skellern, Not Without A Friend* - was all original bar Hoagy Carmichael's 'Rockin' Chair' - and another hit single with the title track to 1975's *Hold On To Love* established Skellern as a purveyor of wittily-observed if homely love songs of similar stamp to Gilbert O'Sullivan. He earned the approbation of the ex-Beatle coterie which, already manifested in Derek Taylor's production of *Not Without A Friend*, was further demonstrated when George Harrison assisted on *Hard Times*; the title number was later recorded by Starr. A minor hit in 1978 with 'Love Is The Sweetest Thing' (featuring Grimethorpe Colliery Band) was part of a tribute

Sister Sledge

to Fred Astaire that won a Music Trades Association award for Best MOR Album of 1979. Skellern subsequently wrote and performed six autobiographical programmes for BBC television, followed by a series of musical plays (*Happy Endings*) and also hosted the chat show *Private Lives*, in 1983. In 1984, he formed Oasis with Julian Lloyd Webber, Mary Hopkin and guitarist Bill Lovelady in an attempt to fuse mutual classical and pop interests but the group's recordings have yet to make major impact.

Albums: *Peter Skellern With Harlan County* (1971), *Peter Skellern* (1972), *Not Without A Friend* (1973), *Holding My Own* (1974), *Hold On To Love* (1975), *Hard Times* (1976), *Skellern* (1978), *Astaire* (1979), *Still Magic* (1980), *Happy Endings* (1981), *A String Of Pearls* (1982), *Lovelight* (1987). Compilations: *Introducing. . .Right From The Start* (1981), *Best Of Peter Skellern* (1985).

Slade

Originally recording as the 'N Betweens, this UK quartet comprised Noddy Holder (b. Neville Holder, 15 June 1946, Walsall, West Midlands, England; vocals/guitar), Dave Hill (b. 4 April 1952, Fleet Castle, Devon, England; guitar), Jimmy Lea (b. 14 June 1952, Wolverhampton, West Midlands, England; bass) and Don Powell (b. 10 September 1950, Bilston, West Midlands, England; drums). During the spring of 1966, they performed regularly in the Midlands, playing an unusual mixture of soul standards, juxtaposed with a sprinkling of hard-rock items. A chance meeting with producer Kim Fowley led to a one-off single, 'You Better Run', released in August 1966. Two further years of obscurity followed until their agent secured them an audition with Fontana Records' A&R head Jack Baverstock. He insisted that they change their name to Ambrose Slade and it was under that monicker that they recorded *Beginnings*. Chaff on the winds of opportunity, they next fell into the hands of former Animals' bassist turned manager, Chas Chandler. He abbreviated their name to Slade and oversaw their new incarnation as a skinhead group for the stomping 'Wild Winds Are Blowing'. Their image as 'bovver boys', complete with cropped hair and Dr Marten boots, provoked some scathing press from a media sensitive to youth culture violence. Slade persevered with their skinhead phase until 1970 when it was clear that their notoriety was passe. While growing their hair and cultivating a more colourful image, they retained their aggressive musicianship and screaming vocals for the bluesy

'Get Down Get With It', which reached number 20 in the UK.

Under Chandler's guidance, Holder and Lea commenced composing their own material, relying on distinctive riffs, a boot-stomping beat and sloganeering lyrics, usually topped off by a deliberately misspelt title. 'Coz I Luv You' took them to number 1 in the UK in late 1971, precipitating an incredible run of chart success which was to continue uninterrupted for the next three years. After the average 'Look Wot You Dun' (which still hit number 4) they served up a veritable beer barrel of frothy chart-toppers including 'Take Me Bak 'Ome', 'Mama Weer Al Crazee Now', 'Cum On Feel The Noize' and 'Skweeze Me Pleeze Me'. Their finest moment was 1977's 'Merry Xmas Everybody', one of the great festive rock songs.

Unpretentious and proudly working class, the group appealed to teenage audiences who cheered their larynx-wrenching singles and glorified in their garish yet peculiarly masculine forays into glam rock. Holder, clearly no sex symbol, offered a solid, cheery image, with Dickensian side whiskers and a hat covered in mirrors, while Hill took tasteless dressing to marvellous new extremes. Largely dependent upon a young, fickle audience, and seemingly incapable of spreading their parochial charm to the USA, Slade's supremacy was to prove ephemeral. They participated in a movie *Slade In Flame*, which was surprisingly impressive, and undertook extensive tours, yet by the mid-70s they were yesterday's teen heroes. The ensuing punk explosion made them virtually redundant and prompted in 1977 the appropriately titled, *Whatever Happened To Slade*. Undeterred they carried on just as they had done in the late 60s, awaiting a new break. An appearance at the 1980 Reading Festival brought them credibility anew. This performance was captured on the *Slade Alive At Reading '80* EP which pushed the group into the UK singles chart for the first time in three years. Their festive 'Merry Xmas Everybody' was re-recorded and charted that same year, (the first in a run of seven consecutive years, subsequently in it's original form). Slade returned to the Top 10 in January 1981 with 'We'll Bring The House Down' and they have continued to gig extensively, being rewarded in 1983 with the number 2 hit, 'My Oh My', followed up the next year with 'Run Run Away', a UK number 7 and their first US Top 20 hit, and the anthemic 'All Join Hands' (number 15). Slade are one of the few groups to have survived the heady days of glitter and glam with

Slade

Smokie

their reputation intact and are regarded with endearing affection by a wide spectrum of age groups.

Albums: as Ambrose Slade *Ambrose Slade - Beginnings* (1969), *Ballzy* (1969); as Slade *Play It Loud* (1970), *Slade Alive* (1972), *Slayed* (1972), *Old, New, Borrowed And Blue* (1974), *Stomp Your Hands, Clap Your Feet* (1974, US title), *Slade In Flame* (1974, film soundtrack), *Nobody's Fool* (1976), *Whatever Happened To Slade?* (1977), *Slade Alive Vol. 2* (1978), *Return To Base* (1979), *We'll Bring The House Down* (1981), *Till Deaf Us Do Part* (1981), *Slade On Stage* (1982), *Slade Alive* (1983), *The Amazing Kamikaze Syndrome* (1983), *Rogues Gallery* (1985), *Crackers - The Slade Christmas Party Album* (1985), *You Boyz Make Big Noize* (1987). Compilations: *Sladest* (1973), *Slade Smashes* (1980), *Slade's Greats* (1984), *Keep Your Hands Off My Power Supply* (1984, US title), *Wall Of Hits* (1991).

Smokie

This UK pop band from Bradford, Yorkshire, featured Chris Norman (vocals), Terry Utley (guitar), and Alan Silson (bass). The three were previously together in 1966 with a band titled the Elizabethans. Pete Spencer replaced their original drummer shortly afterwards. Turning professional in 1968, they changed their name to Kindness, performing at holiday camps and ballrooms. A variety of record company contracts failed to ignite any hit singles, however. Along the way they changed their name to Smokey, but it was not until they joined Rak Records, where Mickie Most introduced them to songwriters Chinn And Chapman, that they saw any success. They then scored frequently with 'If You Think You Know How To Love Me' and 'Don't Play Your Rock 'n' Roll To Me' in 1975, after which they changed the spelling of their name to Smokie. Their 1976 version of the Chinn/Chapman composition 'Living Next Door To Alice', originally recorded by New World, became a hit in the face of opposition from the burgeoning punk scene. Norman, meanwhile, joined fellow Rak artist Suzi Quatro on the 1978 hit duet 'Stumblin' In'. By 1978 and *The Montreux Album*, the band, through Norman and Spencer, were taking a greater share of writing credits, but this coincided with a drop in their fortunes. They bounced back briefly in 1980 with a cover of Bobby Vee's 'Take Good Care Of My Baby', but this proved to be their last hit. Norman and Spencer moved on to writing for other artists including fellow Rak teenybop groups, and both Kevin Keegan's 'Head Over Heels' and the England World Cup Squad's 'This Time We'll Get It Right'.

Albums: *Smokie/Changing All The Time* (1975), *Bright Lights And Back Alleys* (1977), *The Montreux Album* (1978). Compilations: *Greatest Hits* (1977), *Smokie's Hits* (1980).

Snafu

Snafu

Formed in 1973 by former Freedom vocalist and percussionist Bobby Harrison (b. 28 June 1943, East Ham, London, England) using the nucleus of the musicians who appeared on his solo album *Funkest* (1970). The name of the band came from an old Royal Air Force expression; Situation Normal - All Fucked Up. The original members were Colin Gibson (b. 21 September 1949, Newcastle-Upon-Tyne, Tyne & Wear, England; bass), Peter Solly (b. 19 October 1948, Hampstead, London, England; keyboards/synthesizers), Terry Popple (b. 21 July 1946, Stockton On Tees, Co Durham, England; drums) and Mick Moody (b. 30 August 1950, Middlesbrough, Cleveland, England; guitar). Snafu played solidly constructed heavy rock, and fitted well into the receptive music scene of the early 70s. All the members had previously made names as reputable session musicians, particularly the north-east trio of Gibson, Popple and Moody who would later show up on albums by such artists as Alan Hull and Graham Bonnett.
Albums: *Snafu* (1974), *Situation Normal* (1974), *All Funked Up* (1975).

Sondheim, Stephen

b. Stephen Joshua Sondheim, 22 March 1930, New York, USA. Sondheim is generally regarded as one of the most influential popular music composers of the 70s and 80s. Born into an affluent family, his father was a prominent New York dress manufacturer, Sondheim studied piano and organ sporadically from the age of seven. When he was 10, his parents divorced, and he spent some time at military school. His mother's friendship with the Oscar Hammerstein family in Philadelphia enabled Sondheim to meet the lyricist, who took him under his wing and educated him in the art of writing for the musical theatre. After majoring in music at Williams College, Sondheim graduated in 1950 with the Hutchinson Prize For Musical Composition, a two-year fellowship, which enabled him to study with the innovative composer Milton Babbit. During the early 50s, he contributed material to television shows such as *Topper*, and wrote the songs for a proposed Broadway musical, *Saturday Night* (1955), which was never staged due to the death of producer Lemuel Ayres. Sondheim also wrote the incidental music for the play, *Girls Of Summer* (1956). His first major success was as a lyric writer, with Leonard Bernstein's music, for the 1957 Broadway hit musical, *West Side Story*. Initially, Bernstein was billed as co-lyricist, but had his name removed before the New York opening, giving Sondheim full credit. The show ran for nearly 1,000 performances on Broadway, and eclipsed in London. The songs included 'Jet Song', 'Maria', 'Something's Coming', 'Tonight', 'America', 'One Hand, One Heart', 'I Feel Pretty', 'Somewhere' and 'A Boy Like That'. A film version was released in 1961 and there were New York revivals in 1968 and 1980. Productions in London during in 1974 and 1984 were also significant in that it marked the first of many collaborations between Sondheim and producer Harold Prince.

It was another powerful theatrical figure, David Merrick, who mounted *Gypsy* (1959), once again a Laurents-Robbins project, based on stripper Gypsy Rose Lee's book, *Gypsy: A Memoir*, and considered by some to be the pinnacle achievement of the Broadway musical stage. Sondheim was set to write both music and lyrics, before the show's star Ethel Merman demanded a more experienced composer. Jule Styne proved to be acceptable, and Sondheim concentrated on the lyrics, which have been called his best work in the musical theatre, despite the critical acclaim accorded his later shows. *Gypsy's* memorable score included 'Let Me Entertain You', 'Some People', 'Small World', 'You'll Never Get Away From Me', 'If Momma Was Married', 'All I Need Is The Girl', 'Everything's Coming Up Roses', 'Together, Wherever We Go', 'You Gotta Have A Gimmick' and 'Rose's Turn'. Merman apparently refused to embark on a long London run, so the show was not mounted there until 1973. Angela Lansbury scored a personal triumph then as the domineering mother, Rose, and repeated her success in the Broadway revival in 1974. In 1989, both the show and its star, Tyne Daly (well known for television's *Cagney and Lacey*), won Tony Awards in the 30th anniversary revival, which ran through until 1991. Rosalind Russell played Rose in the 1962 movie version, which received lukewarm reviews. For *Gypsy*, Sondheim had interrupted work on *A Funny Thing Happened On The Way To The Forum* (1962), to which he contributed both music and lyrics. Based on the plays of Plautus, it has been variously called, 'a fast moving farce', 'a vaudeville-based Roman spoof' and 'a musical madhouse'. Sondheim's songs, which included the prologue, 'Comedy Tonight' ('Something appealing, something appalling/Something for everyone, a comedy tonight!') and 'Everybody Ought To Have A Maid', celebrated moments of joy or desire but punctuated the thematic action. The show won several Tony awards, including 'Best Musical' and

'Best Producer' but nothing for Sondheim's score. The show was revived on Broadway in 1972 with Phil Silvers in the leading role, and had two London productions (1963 and 1986), both starring British comedian Frankie Howerd. A film version, starring Zero Mostel and Silvers, dropped several of the original songs. *Anyone Can Whistle* (1964), 'a daft moral fable about corrupt city officials', with an original book by Laurents, and songs by Sondheim, lasted just a week. The critics were unanimous in their condemnation of the musical with a theme that 'madness is the only hope for world sanity'. The original cast recording, which included 'Simple', 'I've Got You To Lean On', 'A Parade In Town', 'Me And My Town' and the appealing title song, was made after the show closed, and became a cult item.

Sondheim was back to 'lyrics only' for *Do I Hear A Waltz?* (1965). The durable Broadway composer, Richard Rodgers, supplied the music for the show that he described as 'not a satisfying experience'. In retrospect, it was perhaps underrated. Adapted by Arthur Laurents from his play, *The Time Of The Cuckoo*, the show revolved around an American tourist in Venice, and included 'Moon In My Window', 'This Week's Americans', 'Perfectly Lovely Couple' and 'Here We Are Again'. Broadway had to wait until 1970 for the next Sondheim musical, the first to be directed by Harold Prince. *Company* had no plot, but concerned 'the lives of five Manhattan couples held together by their rather excessively protective feelings about a 'bachelor friend'. Its ironic, acerbic score included 'The Little Things You Do Together' ('The concerts you enjoy together/Neighbours you annoy together/Children you destroy together...'), 'Sorry-Grateful', 'You Could Drive A Person Crazy', 'Have I Got A Girl For You?', 'Someone Is Waiting', 'Another Hundred People', 'Getting Married Today', 'Side By Side By Side', 'What Would We Do Without You?', 'Poor Baby', 'Tick Tock', 'Barcelona', 'The Ladies Who Lunch' ('Another chance to disapprove, another brilliant singer/Another reason not to move, another vodka stinger/I'll drink to that!') and 'Being Alive'. With a book by George Furth, produced and directed by Prince, the musical numbers staged by Michael Bennett, and starring Elaine Stritch and Larry Kert (for most of the run), *Company* ran for 690 performances. It gained the New York Drama Critics' Circle Award for Best Musical, and six Tony Awards, including Best Musical, and Best Music and Lyrics for Sondheim, the first awards of his Broadway career. The marathon recording session for the original cast album, produced by Thomas Z. Shepard, was the subject of a highly-acclaimed television documentary.

The next Prince-Bennett-Sondheim project, with a book by James Goldman, was the mammoth *Follies* (1971), 'the story of four people in their early 50s: two ex-show girls from the *Weismann Follies*, and two stage-door-Johnnies whom they married 30 years ago, who attend a reunion, and start looking backwards...'. It was a lavish, spectacular production, with a cast of 50, and a Sondheim score which contained 22 'book' songs, including 'Who's That Woman?' (sometimes referred to as the 'the mirror number'), 'Ah Paris!', 'Could I Leave You?', 'I'm Still Here' ('Then you career from career, to career/I'm almost through my memoirs/And I'm here!'); and several 'pastiche' numbers in the style of the 'great' songwriters such as George Gershwin and Dorothy Fields ('Losing My Mind'); Cole Porter ('The Story Of Lucy and Jessie'); Romberg and Friml ('One More Kiss'); Jerome Kern ('Loveland'); Irving Berlin (the prologue, 'Beautiful Girls') and De Sylva, Brown, and Henderson ('Broadway Baby'). Although the show received a great deal of publicity and gained the Drama Critics Circle Award for Best Musical, plus seven Tony awards, it closed after 522 performances with the loss of its entire $800,000 investment. A spokesperson commented: 'We sold more posters than tickets'. *Follies In Concert*, with the New York Philharmonic, played two performances in September 1985 at the Lincoln Centre, and featured several legendary Broadway names such as Carol Burnett, Betty Comden, Adolph Green, Lee Remick, Barbara Cook. The show was taped for television, and generated a much-acclaimed RCA album, which compensated for the disappointingly truncated recording of the original show. The latter did not reach London until 1987, when the young, Cameron Mackintosh, produced a 'new conception' with Goldman's revised book, and several new songs replacing some of the originals. It closed after 600 performances, because of high running costs. *A Little Night Music* (1973), was the first Sondheim-Prince project to be based on an earlier source, in this instance, Ingmar Bergman's film, *Smiles Of A Summer Night*. It was set at the turn of the century, in Sweden; an operetta, with all the music in three quarter time, or multiples thereof. The critics saw in it echoes of Mahler, Ravel, Rachmaninoff, Brahms, and even Johann Strauss. The score contained Sondheims's first song hit for which he wrote both words and music, 'Send In The Clowns'. Other songs included 'Liaisons', 'A Weekend In The Country', 'The Glamorous Life', 'In Praise Of Women', 'Remember' and 'Night Waltz'. The show ran for 601 performances, and was a healthy financial success. It gained the New York Drama Critics Award for Best Musical, and five Tony awards, including Sondheim's music and lyrics for a record third time in a row. The London run starred Jean Simmons, while Elizabeth Taylor played Desiree in the 1978 movie version.

On the back of the show's 1973 Broadway success, and the composer's increasing popularity, a benefit concert, *Sondheim: A Musical Tribute*, was mounted at the Shubert Theatre, featuring every available performer who had been associated with his shows, singing familiar, and not so familiar, material. *Pacific Overtures* (1976), was, perhaps, Sondheim's most daring and ambitious musical to date. John Weidman's book purported to relate the entire 120 years history of Japan, from Commodore Perry's arrival in 1856, to its emergence as the powerful industrial force of the 20th century. The production was heavily influenced by the Japanese Kabuki Theatre. The entire cast were Asian, and Sondheim used many Oriental instruments to obtain his effects. Musical numbers included 'Chrysanthemum Tea', 'Please Hello', 'Welcome To Kanagawa', 'Next', 'Someone In A Tree' and 'The Advantages Of Floating In The Middle Of The Sea'. The show closed after 193 performances, losing its entire budget of over half-a-million dollars, but it still won the Drama Critics Circle Award for Best Musical. It was revived, off-Broadway, in 1984.

The next Broadway project bearing Sondheim's name was much more successful, and far more conventional. *Side By Side By Sondheim* (1977), an anthology of some of his songs, started out at London's Mermaid Theatre the year before. Starring the original London cast of Millicent Martin, Julia McKenzie, David Kernan and Ned Sherrin, the New York production received almost unanimously favourable notices, and proved that many of Sondheim's songs, when presented in this revue form, removed from the sometimes bewildering librettos, could be popular items in their own right. In complete contrast, was *Sweeney Todd, The Demon Barber Of Fleet Street* (1979), Hugh Wheeler's version of the grisly tale of a 19th century barber who slits the throats of his clients, and turns the bodies over to Mrs Lovett (Angela Lansbury), who bakes them into pies. Sondheim's 'endlessly inventive, highly expressive score',

considered to be near-opera, included the gruesome, 'Not While I'm Around', 'Epiphany', 'A Little Priest', the more gentle 'Pretty Women' and 'My Friends'. Generally accepted as one of the most ambitious Broadway musicals ever staged ('a staggering theatrical spectacle'; 'one giant step forward for vegetarianism'), *Sweeney Todd* ran for over 500 performances, and gained eight Tony awards, including Best Musical, Score and Book.

In 1980, it played in London for four months, and starred Denis Quilley and Sheila Hancock. *Merrily We Roll Along* (1981), with a book by George Furth, based on the 1934 play by George S. Kaufman and Moss Hart, was probably the nearest that Sondheim reached to writing a 'good, old fashioned musical comedy'. Despite a run of only 16 performances, the pastiche score contained some 'insinuatingly catchy numbers'. It also marked the end, for the time being, of Sondheim's association with Harold Prince, who had produced and directed nearly all of his shows. Depressed and dejected, Sondheim threatened to give up writing for the theatre. However, in 1982, he began working with James Lapine, who had attracted some attention for his direction of the off-Broadway musical, *The March Of The Falsettos* (1981).

The first fruits of the Sondheim-Lapine association, *Sunday In The Park With George* also started off-Broadway, as a Playwrights Horizon workshop production, before opening on Broadway in 1984. Inspired by George Seurat's 19th century painting, *Sunday Afternoon On The Island Of La Grande Jatte*, with book and direction by Lapine, the two-act show starred Mandy Patinkin and Bernadette Peters, and an 'intriguingly intricate' Sondheim score that included 'Finishing The Hat', 'Lesson No.8', and 'Move On'. The run of a year-and-a-half was due in no small part to energetic promotion by the *New York Times*, which caused the theatrical competition to dub the show, *Sunday In The Times With George*. In 1985, it was awarded the coveted Pulitzer Prize for Drama, and in 1990 became one of the rare musicals to be staged at London's Royal National Theatre. In 1987, Sondheim again received a Tony award for *Into the Woods*, a musical fairy tale of a baker and his wife, who live under the curse of a wicked witch, played by Bernadette Peters. The critics called it Sondheim's most accessible show for many years, with a score that included 'Cinderella At The Grave', 'Hello, Little Girl' and 'Children Will Listen'. It won the New York Drama Critics Circle, and Drama Desk Awards, for Best Musical, and a Grammy for Best Original Cast album. 'Angry', rather than accessible, was the critics' verdict of *Assassins*, with a book by John Weidman, which opened for a limited run off-Broadway early in 1991. Dubbed by *Newsweek*: 'Sondheim's most audacious, far out and grotesque work of his career', it 'attempted to examine the common thread of killers and would-be killers from John Wilkes Booth, the murderer of Lincoln, through Lee Harvey Oswald to John Hinckley Jnr, who shot Ronald Reagan'. The pastiche score included 'Everybody's Got The Right', 'The Ballad Of Booth' and 'The Ballad Of Czolgosz'.

Besides his main Broadway works over the years, Sondheim provided material for many other stage projects, such as the music and lyrics for *The Frogs* (1974), songs for the revue *Marry Me A Little* and a song for the play *A Mighty Man Is He*. He also contributed the incidental music to *The Girls Of Summer*, 'Come Over Here' and 'Home Is the Place' for Tony Bennett. In addition, Sondheim wrote the incidental music for the play *Invitation To A March*, the score for the mini-musical *Passionella*, the lyrics (with Mary Rodgers' music) for *The Mad Show* and new lyrics for composer Leonard Bernstein's 1974 revival of *Candide*. Sondheim's film work included the music for *Stravinsky*, *Reds* and *Dick Tracy*. Sondheim also wrote the screenplay, with Anthony Perkins, for *The Last Of Sheila*, a film 'full of impossible situations, demented logic and indecipherable clues', inspired by his penchant for board games and puzzles of every description. For television, Sondheim wrote the music and lyrics for *Evening Primrose*, which starred Perkins, and made his own acting debut in 1974, with Jack Cassidy, in a revival of the George S. Kaufman-Ring Lardner play, *June Moon*. While never pretending to write 'hit songs' (apparently the term 'hummable' makes him bristle), Sondheim has nevertheless had his moments in the charts with songs such as 'Small World' (Johnny Mathis); 'Tonight' (Ferrante And Teicher); 'Maria' and 'Somewhere' (P.J.Proby); 'Send In The Clowns' (Judy Collins), and 'Losing My Mind' (Liza Minnelli). Probably Sondheim's greatest impact on records, apart from the Original Cast albums which won seven Grammys, was Barbra Streisand's, *The Broadway Album*, in 1985. Seven tracks, involving eight songs, were Sondheim's (two in collaboration with Bernstein), and he re-wrote three of them for Streisand, including 'Send In The Clowns'. *The Broadway Album* stayed at number 1 in the US charts for three weeks, and sold over three million copies. Other gratifying moments for Sondheim occurred in 1983 when he was voted a member of the American Academy and Institute of Arts and Letters, and again in 1990, when he became Oxford University's first Professor of Drama. As for his contribution to the musical theatre, opinions were sharply divided. John Podhoretz in the *Washington Times* said that 'with *West Side Story*, the musical took a crucial, and in retrospect, suicidal step into the realm of social commentary, and created a self-destructive form in which characters were taken to task and made fun of, for doing things like bursting into song'. Others, like Hal Prince said that, in his day, Stephen Sondheim was the best in the world.

Further reading: *Sondheim & Co.*, Craig Zadan. *Sondheim And The American Musical*, Paul Sheran and Tom Sutcliffe. *Song By Song By Sondheim (The Stephen Sondheim Songbook)*, edited by Sheridan Morley. *Sunday In the Park With George*, Stephen Sondheim and James Lapine.

Soul, David

b. David Solberg, 28 August 1943, Chicago, Illinois, USA. Under his *nom de theatre*, this handsome blond was a folk singer before trying his hand at acting. In 1966, he combined both talents with 30 appearances on US television's Merv Griffin Show as a masked vocalist ('The Covered Man') before less anonymous roles in *Here Comes The Bride*, *Streets Of San Francisco* and *Encyclopaedia Britannica Presents*. He is, however, best remembered as 'Ken Hutchinson' in *Starsky And Hutch*. A spin-off from this 70s television detective series was the projection of Solberg as a pop star via a recording career which began with 1976's 'Don't Give Up On Us' - composed and produced by Tony Macauley - at number 1 both at home and in the UK. Though a one-hit-wonder in the USA, Britain was good for another year or so of smashes which included another chart-topper in 'Silver Lady' (co-written by Geoff Stephens). Most of Soul's offerings were in a feathery, moderato style with limpid orchestral sweetening and sentimental lyrics. His name remains synonymous with the mid-late 70s.

Albums: *David Soul* (1976), *Playing To An Audience Of One* (1977).

Soul Children

This group was formed as a vehicle for the song writing talents of Isaac Hayes and David Porter in Memphis, Tennessee, USA. Comprising of Anita Louis (b. 24 November 1949, Memphis, Tennessee, USA), Shelbra Bennett (b. Memphis,

Tennessee, USA), John 'Blackfoot' Colbert (b. 20 November 1946, Greenville, Mississippi, USA) and Norman West (b. 30 October 1939, Monroe, Louisiana, USA), they first surfaced in 1968 with 'Give 'Em Love'. This excellent Hayes/Porter composition established their startling vocal interplay which, at times, suggested a male/female Sam And Dave. Although artistically consistent, only three of the group's singles, 'The Sweeter He Is' (1969), 'Hearsay' (1970) and 'I'll Be The Other Woman' (1973), reached the US R&B Top 10. The Soul Children were later reduced to a trio and moved to Epic when their former outlet, Stax, went into liquidation. Colbert later found fame under the name J. Blackfoot when one of his releases, 'Taxi', was a 1983 hit in both the US and UK.

Albums: *Soul Children* (1969), *Best Of Two Worlds* (1971), *Genesis* (1972), *Friction* (1974), *The Soul Years* (1974), *Finders Keepers* (1976), *Where Is Your Woman Tonight* (1977), *Open Door Policy* (1978).

Southside Johnny And The Asbury Jukes

R&B fanatic Southside Johnny (b. John Lyons, 4 December 1948, New Jersey, USA) sang with the Blackberry Booze Band in the late 60s before teaming up with the Asbury Jukes with school friends Billy Rush (guitar), Kevin Kavanaugh (keyboards), Kenneth Pentifallo (bass) and Alan 'Doc' Berger (drums), plus transient members of a horn section. Popular in Upstage, Stone Poney and other parochial clubs, they sought a wider audience via a 1976 promotional album, *Live At The Bottom Line*, which helped facilitate a contract with Epic. Like another local lad, Bruce Springsteen, the outfit bolstered their reputation with practical demonstrations of credible influences by enlisting Ronnie Spector, Lee Dorsey, and black vocal groups of the 50s on *I Wanna Go Home* and its follow-up, *This Time It's For Real*. Both were weighted further with Springsteen sleeve notes and songs as well as production supervision by his guitarist (and ex-Juke) Steve Van Zandt. After *Hearts Of Stone* failed to reach a mass public, Epic let the band go with the valedictory *Having A Party* - essentially a 'best of' compilation.

Mitigating this setback were increasing touring fees that permitted sensational augmentation with saxophonists Carlo Novi and Stan Harrison, trumpeters Ricki Gazda and Tony Palligrosi, and ex-Diana Ross trombonist Richard Rosenberg, as well as an additional guitarist in Joel Gramolini and replacement drummer Steve Becker. A debut on Mercury, 1979's *The Jukes* sold well as did *Love Is*

A Sacrifice in 1980 but, for all the polished production by Barry Beckett many felt that much nascent passion had been dissipated. Possibly, this was traceable to the borrowing of the horns by Van Zandt for his Disciples Of Soul, and the exits of Pentifallo - and Berger, writer (with Lyons and Rush) of the band's original material. The in-concert *Reach Out And Touch The Sky* (with its fiery Sam Cooke medley) halted a commercial decline that resumed with later studio efforts - though radio interest in a revival of Left Banke's 'Walk Away Renee' (from *At Least We Got Shoes*) and a Jersey Artists For Mankind charity single (organized by Lyons) suggests that all might not yet be lost. They halted the decline in 1991 with *Better Days*. This lyrically nostalgic album contained a Springsteen song 'Walk You All The Way Home' in addition to Steve Van Zandt's numerous contributions.

Albums: *I Don't Wanna Go Home* (1976), *This Time It's For Real* (1977), *Hearts Of Stone* (1978), *The Jukes* (1979), *Love Is A Sacrifice* (1980), *Reach Out And Touch The Sky* (1981), *Trash It Up! Live* (1983), *In The Heat* (1984), *At Least We Got Shoes* (1986), *Better Days* (1991). Compilation: *Having A Party* (1979).

Sparks

Ex-child actors and veterans of Los Angeles' Urban Renewal Project, vocalist Russell Mael and his elder brother Ron (keyboards) led Halfnelson in 1968 (with renowned rock critic John Mendelssohn on drums). By 1971, this had evolved into Sparks in which the Maels were joined by Earle Mankay (guitar), Jim Mankay (bass) and Harley Fernstein (drums). At the urging of Todd Rundgren - their eventual producer - Albert Grossman signed them to Bearsville. While it emitted a regional US hit in 'Wonder Girl,' Sparks' debut album sold poorly - as did the subsequent *A Woofer In Tweeter's Clothing*. A stressful club tour of Europe - during which they were often heckled - amassed, nonetheless, a cult following in glam-rock England where the Maels emigrated in 1973 to gain an Island recording contract and enlist a new Sparks from native players. Drummer 'Dinky' Diamond from Aldershot's Sound Of Time was a mainstay during this period but among many others passing through the ranks were guitarist Adrian Fisher from Toby and Jook's bass player Ian Hampton. Overseen by Muff Winwood, this Anglo-American edition of Sparks notched up eight UK chart entries, starting with 1974's unprecedented and startling 'This Town Ain't Big

Enough For Both Of Us' from *Kimono My House*. With eccentric arrangements in the Roxy Music vein, 'Amateur House' and later singles were also notable for Ron's lyrical idiosyncracies as well as wide stereo separation between the bass guitar section and Russell's twittering falsetto. Their appeal hinged visually on the disparity between creepy Ron's conservative garb and 'Hitler' moustache, and Russell's bubbly androgyny. *Propaganda* was a stylistic departure but the basic formula was unaltered. Sparks' over-dependence on this combined with an unsteady stage act to provoke fading interest in further merchandise - despite strategies like hiring Tony Visconti to supervise 1975's *Indiscreet*, and the Maels' return to California to make *Big Beat* with expensive LA session musicians.

Sparks engineered a transient comeback to the British Top 20 in 1977 with two singles from *Number One In Heaven*, produced by Giorgio Moroder - and 1981's 'When I'm With You' (from *Terminal Jive*) sold well in France. Later, the brothers succeeded in the US Hot 100 - particularly with 1983's 'Cool Places,' a tie-up with the Go-Go's' guitarist Jane Wiedlin - which intimates that their future may hold more surprises.

Albums: *Sparks* (1971), *A Woofer In Tweeter's Clothing* (1972), *Kimono My House* (1974), *Propaganda* (1974), *Indiscreet* (1975), *Big Beat* (1978), *Number One In Heaven* (1979), *Terminal Jive* (1980), *Whoop That Sucker* (1981), *Angst In My Pants* (1982), *Sparks In Outer Space* (1983). Compilation: *Best Of Sparks* (1979).

Spear, Roger Ruskin

b. England. A founder member of the Bonzo Dog Doo-Dah Band, Ruskin Spear's use of robots and electric props provided enduring visual images to accompany the musical, lyrical and humorous antics of his colleagues. His creations were similar to another great eccentric, Professor Bruce Lacey, a former member of the Alberts, a group whose approach anticipated that of the Bonzos. In 1970, Spear briefly joined Viv Stanshall's new unit, biG GRunt, before embarking on a solo career. He toured as a one man show with his *Giant Kinetic Wardrobe* and recorded two solo albums which were as entertaining as they were bizarre. *Electric Shocks* contained a cast which included *Melody Maker* journalists Chris Welch and Roy Hollingsworth, rock group the Flamin' Groovies and former Bonzos, Sam Spoons and Dave Clague, while *Unusual* featured assistance from Help Yourself, a quartet signed to the same label as

Spear. However, although this extraordinary artist continued to make sporadic appearances, his profile diminished as the 70s progressed.

Albums: *Electric Shocks* (1972), *Unusual* (1973).

Spedding, Chris

b. 17 June 1944, Sheffield, Yorkshire, England. An underestimated talent, this inventive guitarist began his career in a beat group, the Vulcans, prior to following a haphazard path touring in country bands and supporting cabaret attractions on the cruise ship Himalaya. Spells backing Alan Price and Paul Jones preceded Spedding's involvement in the Battered Ornaments where he established a reputation for technique and imagination. The guitarist was subsequently heard on Jack Bruce's *Songs For A Tailor*, and on early releases by Nucleus, a leading jazz-rock ensemble. Session work for Lulu, John Cale, Dusty Springfield and others was interspersed by two low-key solo albums, *Backward Progression* and *The Only Lick I Know*. Spedding also formed the much-touted Sharks with former Free bassist Andy Fraser, but internal ructions undermined the group's potential. The guitarist resumed studio work in 1975, but also joined Roy Harper in Trigger, the singer's short-lived backing band. Spedding's clinical approach resulted in several career-based anomalies. He donned the requisite costume to perform with the Wombles and contrived an ill-fitting leather-boy image for a series of pop punk singles under the guidance of producer Mickie Most. 'Motor-Biking', in 1975, provided the UK Top 20 single the guitarist doubtlessly deserved, but these unusual interludes have discoloured perception of his other work.

Albums: *Backward Progression* (1971), *The Only Lick I Know* (1972), *Chris Spedding* (1976), *Hurt* (1977), *Guitar Graffiti* (1978), *I'm Not Like Everybody Else* (1980), *Friday The 13th* (1981), *Enemy Within* (1986). Compilations: *Motorbikin': The Best Of Chris Spedding* (1991), *Just Plug Him In!* (1991).

Springfield, Rick

b. Richard Springthorpe, 23 August 1949, Sydney, Australia. The son of an army officer, Springfield's musical interests developed while living in England in the early 60s and on his return to Australia he played guitar and piano in the house band of a Melbourne club. At the end of the 60s, Springfield played with the Jordy Boys, Rock House and the MPD Band before joining Zoot. The group had several hits with Springfield compositions before he turned solo with the number 1 single 'Speak To

The Sky'. He moved to the USA in 1972 where he was groomed to become a new teenybop idol and a new version of 'Speak To The Sky' was a Top 20 US hit. After contractual disputed kept him inactive for two years, he joined Wes Farrell's Chelsea label where Elton John's rhythm section Dee Murray (bass) and Nigel Olsson (drums) backed him on *Wait For The Night*. Soon afterwards the label collapsed and Springfield began a new career as a television actor. After guest appearances in *The Rockford Files*, *Wonder Woman* and *The Six Million Dollar Man*, he landed a leading role in the soap opera *General Hospital*. This exposure helped to give him a series of big hits on RCA Records in 1981-82 including 'Jessie's Girl' which reached number 1 and the Top 10 records 'I've Done Everything For You', and 'Don't Talk To Strangers'. The later hit 'Love Somebody' came from the 1984 film *Hard To Hold* in which Springfield played a rock singer. The next year a reissue of one 1978 track, ('Bruce'; a tale about being mistaken for Bruce Springsteen) was a Top 30 hit and later Springfield albums were equally popular in America.

Albums: *Beginnings* (1972), *Comic Book* (1974), *Heroes* (1974), *Wait For The Night* (1976), *Working Class Dog* (1981), *Success Hasn't Spoiled Me Yet* (1982), *Living In Oz* (1983), *Tao* (1985), *Rock Of Life* (1988).

Squeeze

Formed in the south east London area of Deptford in 1974, Squeeze came to prominence in the late 70s riding on the new wave created by the punk movement. Original members Chris Difford (b. 4 November 1954, London, England; guitar/lead vocals), Glenn Tilbrook (b. 31 August 1957, London, England; guitar/vocals) and Julian 'Jools' Holland (b. 24 January 1958; keyboards) named the group after a disreputable Velvet Underground album. With the addition of Harry Kakoulli (bass), and original drummer Paul Gunn replaced by sessions drummer Gilson Lavis (b. 27 June 1951, Bedford, England), Squeeze released an EP *Packet Of Three* in 1977 on the Deptford Fun City label and produced by former Velvets member John Cale. The EP's title in itself reflected the group's main songwriters, Chris Difford and Glenn Tilbrook's pre-occupation for the underside side of life. The EP led to a major contract with A&M Records and a UK Top 20 hit in 1978 with 'Take Me I'm Yours'. Minor success with 'Bang Bang' and 'Goodbye Girl' that same year was followed in 1979 by two number 2 hits with 'Cool For Cats'

and 'Up The Junction'. Difford's lyrics were by now beginning to show an acute talent in capturing the flavour of contemporary south London life with a sense of the tragi-comic. This began to fully flower with the release of 1980's *Argy Bargy* which spawned the singles 'Another Nail In My Heart' (UK Top 20) and 'Pulling Mussels (From A Shell)'. The set was Squeeze's most cohesive album to date, having finally thrown off any remaining traces of a punk influence they now displayed one of the finest 'kitchen sink' lyrics since Ray Davies' finest work. The album also featured the group's new bass player, John Bentley (b. 16 April 1951).

In 1980, Holland left for a solo career that included performing and recording with his own band Jools Holland And The Millionaires (which displayed his talent for the 'boogie-woogie' piano style) and, to a larger extent, hosting the UK television show *The Tube*. His replacement was singer/pianist Paul Carrack, formerly with pub-rock band Ace. He appeared on *East Side Story* which was co-produced by Elvis Costello. Carrack stamped his mark on the album with his performance on 'Tempted' and with the success of 'Labelled With Love' a UK Top 5 hit, the album became the band's most successful to date. Carrack departed soon after to join Carlene Carter's group and was replaced by Don Snow (b. 13 January 1957, Kenya, ex-Sinceros). The follow-up *Sweets From A Stranger* was an uneven affair, although it did spawn the superb 'Black Coffee In Bed'.

At the height of the group's success, amid intense world tours, including selling out New York's Madison Square Garden, Difford And Tilbrook dissolved the group. However, the duo continued to compose together releasing an album in 1984. The following year they re-formed the band with Lavis, the returning Holland and a new bass player, Keith Wilkinson. *Cosi Fan Tutti Frutti* was hailed as a return to form, and although not supplying any hit singles, the tracks 'King George Street', 'I Learnt How To Pray' and Difford/Holland's 'Heartbreaking World' stood out well. In 1987, Squeeze achieved their highest position in the UK singles chart for almost six years when 'Hourglass' reached number 16 and subsequently gave the group their first US Top 40 hit, reaching number 15. '853-5937' also earned them a US Top 40 hit. The accompanying album *Babylon And On* featured contributions from former Soft Boy and one of Robyn Hitchcock's Egyptians, Andy Metcalfe (horns/keyboards/moog). After the release of 1989's *Frank*, which contained one of the most

Squeeze

sensitive lyrics ever written by a man about menstruation ('She Doesn't Have To Shave'), Holland departed once again to concentrate on television work. With Matt Irving joining as a second keyboards player, Squeeze released a live album, *A Round And A Bout*, on their old Deptford Fun City label in 1990 before signing a new record deal with Warner Brothers. The release of Play confirmed, and continued, Chris Difford and Glenn Tilbrook's reputation as one of the UK's finest songwriting teams.

Albums: *Squeeze* (1978), *Cool For Cats* (1979), *Argy Bargy* (1980), *East Side Story* (1981), *Sweets From A Stranger* (1982), *Cosi Fan Tutti Frutti* (1985), *Babylon And On* (1987), *Frank* (1989), *A Round And About* (1990), *Play* (1991). Compilations: *Singles 45 And Under* (1982), *Squeeze Greatest Hits* (1992).

Squire, Chris

b. 4 March 1948, London, England. An accomplished bass player who has made his name with supergroup Yes, having played with them for over 20 years. Yes was formed after Squire, then a member of the Syn, met Jon Anderson in a London music club. The original line-up consisted of Anderson (b. 25 October 1944, Accrington, Lancashire, England; vocals), an extremely gifted vocalist and composer; Peter Banks (b. England; guitar), also a former member of the Syn; Bill Bruford (b. 17 May 1948, London, England; drums); Tony Kaye (b. England; organ), and Squire. Anderson, Banks and Squire had been in a band called Mabel Greer's Toyshop in the last years of the 60s. Yes endured various personnel changes throughout the 70s, with Squire acting as a solid foundation for the band. By the mid-80s the line-up had been completely revamped by Squire with Anderson's help. In 1977, Squire and another band member, Alan White (b. 14 June 1949, Pelton, Co. Durham, England; drums), appeared on Rick Wakeman's solo, *Criminal Record*. There music matured as the decade progressed, Squire quickly becoming one of the best bassists to emerge from England. Some of the material the band put out could be described as pretentious, such as the highly esoteric *Tales From Topographic Oceans* which was based on Shastric Scriptures. In the mid-70s, each member of Yes undertook a solo project, Squire releasing the successful *Fish Out Of Water*. In 1981 the break-up of the band was confirmed. Although Squire and White rehearsed with Robert Plant and Jimmy Page, formerly of Led Zeppelin, nothing came of this project apart from Squire and White releasing 'Run With The Fox' which failed to chart. The following year Squire and White

formed Cinema with South-African guitarist Trevor Rabin and Tony Kaye. Rabin was an unsatisfactory vocalist, being replaced by Jon Anderson. Since the band was virtually identical to one of the early Yes line-ups, it was decided that they should call themselves by that name once more. However, by 1988 Yes had split into two warring factions with Squire owning the name, thereby forcing the other members to tour under the rather longer-winded title of Anderson, Bruford, Wakeman And Howe. It was Squire's version of Yes which released *Big Generator* in 1988.
Album: *Fish Out Of Water* (1975).

Stackridge

Using a bizarre mixture of dustbin lids and rhubarb stalks as stage props, Stackridge were once acclaimed as the 'West Country Beatles' and enjoyed a brief vogue in the early 70s. The group was formed in Bristol in 1969 as Stackridge Lemon by Jim 'Crun' Walter (bass) and Andy Davis (b. Andrew Cresswell-Davis; keyboards) who recruited James Warren (guitar) and Billy Sparkle (drums) through a newspaper advertisement. Lead singer and flautist Mike 'Mutter' Slater had been in a local folk duo. Adding violinist Mike Evans, they developed an idiosyncratic folk-rock style with whimsical lyrics on songs like 'Dora The Female Explorer', their debut single for MCA Records in 1971. Over the next three years, Stackridge toured throughout Europe and appeared at the 1972 Reading Festival with a troupe of St. Trinians-style dancers. Slater invented a dance craze, 'Do The Stanley' but left the group shortly before the release of the George Martin-produced *The Man In The Bowler Hat*.
Stackridge now added session player Keith Bowkett (keyboards) and former Audience and Sammy member Keith Gemmell on saxophone and flute. They changed labels to Elton John's Rocket in 1974 but despite Slater's return for Mr Mick, lack of commercial success caused the band to split in 1976. While Slater left the music business, Evans toured with visiting country stars and later played in the trio at Bath Pump Room. Davis played guitar on two albums by ex-String Driven Thing vocalist Kimberley Beacon and in 1979 formed the Korgis with Warren. The group made three albums for Rialto and had UK hits with 'If I Had You' (1979) and 'Everybody's Got To Learn Sometime' (1980). Warren later made *Burning Questions* (Sonet 1987) while Davis toured with Tears For Fears before recording the 'new age'-

style *Clevedon Pier* for MMC, the label owned by Peter Van Hooke, who had played drums with Stackridge in the mid-70s.
Albums: *Stackridge* (1971), *Friendliness* (1972), *The Man In The Bowler Hat* (1974), *Extravaganza* (1974), *Mr Mick* (1976).

Stackwaddy

This group was formed in Manchester, England in 1969 by Mick Stott (lead guitar) and Stuart Banham (bass), previously of the New Religion. John Knail (vocals/harmonica) and Steve Revell (drums) completed the new act's line-up which first drew attention for an impressive appearance at Buxton's 1969 Progressive Blues Festival. Stackwaddy were later signed to UK disc jockey John Peel's Dandelion label. Both *Stackwaddy* and *Bugger Off*, revealed aspirations similar to British 60s' R&B groups, played in an uncluttered, irreverent, but exciting style. Included were versions of the Pretty Things' 'Rosalyn', Frank Zappa's 'Willie The Pimp' and the wryly-titled 'Meat Pies Have Come But The Band's Not Here Yet', but Stackwaddy's guttural music proved unfashionable and the original group split up. However, between 1973-76 Barnham led a revamped line-up comprising of Mike Sweeny (vocals), Wayne Jackson (bass) and Kevin Wilkinson (drums).
Albums: *Stackwaddy* (1971), *Bugger Off* (1972).

Stafford, Jim

b. 16 January c.1946, Florida, USA. Stafford had a series of novelty hits in the mid-70s, but his career began as a member of the Legends which also included Gram Parsons and Lobo (Kent Lavoie). Working with Miami producer Phil Gernhard, Stafford signed to MGM as a solo singer, releasing 'Swamp Witch' in 1973. A minor hit, it was followed by the million-selling 'Spiders And Snakes', which used a swamp-rock sound reminiscent of Tony Joe White to tell a humorous tale. The song was composed by David Bellamy of the Bellamy Brothers. In 1974, Stafford tried a soft ballad which a twist, 'my Girl Bill' (his biggest UK hit) and another zany number, 'Wildwood Weed' which reached the US Top 10. Both were co-produced by Lobo. The same strand of humour ran through Stafford's 1975 singles 'Your Bulldog Drinks Champagne' and 'I Got Drunk And Missed It'. By now a minor celebrity, Stafford hosted a networked summer variety show from Los Angeles, where he met and married Bobbie Gentry. Such later records as 'Jasper' (Polydor

1976), co-written with Dave Loggins, and 'Turns Loose Of My Leg' (Warner Brothers/Curb 1977) were only minor hits but Stafford continued to record into the 80s for labels such as Elektra, Town House and CBS.

Albums: *Jim Stafford* (1974), *Spiders and Snakes* (1974), *Not Just Another Pretty Fool* (1975).

Stafford, Jim

b. 16 January c.1946, Florida, USA. Stafford had a series of novelty hits in the mid-70s, but his career began as a member of the Legends which also included Gram Parsons and Lobo (Kent Lavoie). Working with Miami producer Phil Gernhard, Stafford signed to MGM as a solo singer, releasing 'Swamp Witch' in 1973. A minor hit, it was followed by the million-selling 'Spiders And Snakes', which used a swamp-rock sound reminiscent of Tony Joe White to tell a humorous tale. The song was composed by David Bellamy of the Bellamy Brothers. In 1974, Stafford tried a soft ballad which a twist, 'my Girl Bill' (his biggest UK hit) and another zany number, 'Wildwood Weed' which reached the US Top 10. Both were co-produced by Lobo. The same strand of humour ran through Stafford's 1975 singles 'Your Bulldog Drinks Champagne' and 'I Got Drunk And Missed It'. By now a minor celebrity, Stafford hosted a networked summer variety show from Los Angeles, where he met and married Bobbie Gentry. Such later records as 'Jasper' (Polydor 1976), co-written with Dave Loggins, and 'Turns Loose Of My Leg' (Warner Brothers/Curb 1977) were only minor hits but Stafford continued to record into the 80s for labels such as Elektra, Town House and CBS.

Albums: *Jim Stafford* (1974), *Spiders And Snakes* (1974), *Not Just Another Pretty Fool* (1975).

Stanshall, Vivian

b. 21 March 1943, Shillingford, Oxfordshire, England. Stanshall's love of pre-war ephemera, trad jazz and an art school prankishness was instrumental in shaping the original tenor of the Bonzo Dog Doo-Dah Band. This satirical unit was one of the most inventive groups to emerge from the 60s, but fell foul of the eclectic pursuits of its divergent members. Stanshall's first offering following the Bonzo's collapse was 'Labio Dental Fricative', a single credited to the Sean Head Showband, an impromptu unit which included guitarist Eric Clapton. A second release, a brazenly tongue-in-cheek rendition of Terry Stafford's 'Suspicion', featured Vivian Stanshall And His

Gargantuan Chums, and was coupled to 'Blind Date', the singer's only recording with biG GRunt, the group he had formed with Roger Ruskin Spear, Dennis Cowan and 'Borneo' Fred Munt, three refugees from the immediate Bonzo Dog circle. Each band member, bar Munt, appeared on *Let's Make Up And Be Friendly*, the album the Bonzos belatedly completed to fulfil contractual obligations. Despite a handful of excellent live appearances, biG GRunt's undoubted potential withered to a premature end when Stanshall entered hospital following a nervous breakdown.

Men Opening Umbrellas, Vivian's debut album, was released in 1974. Steve Winwood was one of the many musicians featured on the record, inaugurating a working relationship which continued with the excellent 'Vacant Chair' on Winwood's solo debut *Steve Winwood* and contributions on *Arc Of A Diver*, his 1980 release for which Stanshall contributed several lyrics. Indeed, despite recording a punk-inspired version of Cliff Richard's 'The Young Ones', Viv achieved notoriety for his contributions to other outside projects, narrating Mike Oldfield's *Tubular Bells* and as a contributor to the BBC Radio 4 programme, *Start The Week*. It was while deputizing for the Radio 1 disc jockey John Peel that Stanshall developed his infamous monologue, *Rawlinson End*. This later formed the basis for the artist's 1978 release, *Sir Henry At Rawlinson End*, which later inspired a film of the same title and starred Trevor Howard. Stanshall has continued to tread his idiosyncratic path throughout the 80s. An album of songs, *Teddy Bears Don't Knit* was followed by another spoken-word release, *Henry At Ndidis Kraal*. In 1991, he continued the Rawlinson saga by staging at London's Bloomsbury Theatre, *Rawlinson Dogends*, which included in the show's backing band former Bonzo colleagues, Roger Ruskin-Spear and Rodney Slater. In recent years, Stanshall has carved out a separate career using his voice in advertising, making full use of his luxurious, stately tones. Vivian has remained one of England's most cherished eccentrics.

Albums: *Men Opening Umbrellas* (1974), *Sir Henry At Rawlinson End* (1978), *Teddy Bears Don't Knit* (1981), *Henry At Ndidis Kraal* (1984).

Stardust, Alvin

b. Bernard William Jewry, 27 September 1942, London, England. Jewry first enjoyed pop fame during the early 60s under the name Shane Fenton. When the arrival of the Beatles and the subsequent

Mersey beat explosion occurred, Fenton effectively retired from singing. In one of the more unlikely comebacks in British pop history, he re-emerged in 1973 as hit singer Alvin Stardust. Bedecked in menacingly black leather, with an image that fused Gene Vincent with Dave Berry, Stardust returned to the charts with the UK number 2 hit 'My Coo-Ca-Choo'. It was followed by the chart-topping 'Jealous Mind' which, like its predecessor, was composed by songwriter Peter Shelley. Two further UK Top 10 hits followed with 'Red Dress' and 'You You You' before until his chart career petered out with 'Tell Me Why' and 'Good Love Can Never Die'. The indomitable Stardust revitalized his career once more during the early 80s with the Top 10 successes 'Pretend' and the commemorative ballad 'I Feel Like Buddy Holly', which also mentioned Paul McCartney. Stardust ended 1984 with two further hits 'I Won't Run Away' and 'So Near Christmas' before once again falling from chart favour. He remains a popular star on the British showbusiness scene and in recent years, as a born-again Christian, presented and performed with on BBC television with Christian pop and rock acts.
Albums: *It's All Happening* (1963), *Good Rockin' Tonight* (1974), *I'm A Moody Guy* (1982), *I Feel Like... Alvin Stardust* (1984). Compilation: *Greatest Hits: Alvin Stardust* (1977), *20 Of The Best* (1987).

Starland Vocal Band

A quartet based in the Washington, DC, USA. Starland Vocal Band took one single, the novelty disco hit 'Afternoon Delight', to the top of the US charts in 1976. The band comprised of the husband-wife team Bill Danoff (b. 7 May 1946, Springfield, Massachusetts; USA) and Taffy Danoff (b. Kathleen Nivert, 24 October 1944, Washington, DC, USA), Jon Carroll (b. 1 March 1957, Washington, DC, USA) and Margot Chapman (b. 7 September 1957, Honolulu, Hawaii, USA). The group had its roots in a band called Fat City which included the Danoffs. The Starland Vocal Band were formed in late 1974 and opened for John Denver on his 1975 tour (Bill had earlier co-written the John Denver hit 'Take Me Home, Country Roads'); Denver subsequently signed them to his Windsong Records label. The dance song 'Afternoon Delight', about the pleasures of mid-day sex ('Sky rocket's in flight - afternoon delight'), was the band's breakthrough in May 1976 and spent 14 weeks in the US charts, peaking at number 1. They placed a self-titled album at number 20 and three other singles charted

but nothing came close to repeating the debut's success. Despite winning the Best New Artist and Best Vocal Arrangement Grammy awards, and being given a six-week television show of their own, the band's popularity declined and they broke up in 1980. Carroll later wrote the Linda Ronstadt hit, 'Get Closer', and eventually married Chapman; while the Danoffs divorced, but still worked together under the Fat City banner.
Albums: *Starland Vocal Band* (1976), *Rear View Mirror* (1977), *Late Nite Radio* (1978).

Starry Eyed And Laughing

This promising UK group formed in May 1973 as a duo: Tony Poole (b. 28 July 1952, Northampton, England; vocals/12 string guitar) and Ross McGeeney (b. 22 December 1950, Northamptonshire, England; vocals/lead guitar). Taking their name from a line in Bob Dylan's song 'Chimes Of Freedom', the group were initially hugely influenced by the Byrds, with Roger McGuinn-style jingle-jangle Rickenbacker guitar-work and vocals. After briefly performing with bassist Steve Hall and drummer Nick Brown, the group found more suitable replacements in the form of Iain Whitmore (b. 5 October 1953, Shoreham, Sussex, England) and Mike Wackford (b. 6 February 1953, Worthing, Sussex, England). After securing a contract with CBS Records in April 1974, the quartet issued a self-titled debut album the following September. The work was dominated by Poole/McGeeney compositions and critics duly noted the striking Byrds' flavouring. After a year on the road, the group completed *Thought Talk*, which was issued in October 1975. Although the title was taken from the Byrds' song 'I See You', the album was a less derivative, more mature work, with Poole showing his melodic excellence on 'One Foot In The Boat' and Whitmore emerging as a highly-talented writer on the orchestrated 'Fools Gold'. Following a promotional tour of the USA that autumn, the group suddenly fragmented. McGeeney was replaced by Roger Kelly, and Whitmore quit in the spring of 1976. A valedictory gig for the German television show *Rockpalast* saw McGeeney return, playing alongside Kelly. Later that year, Poole briefly shortened the group title to Starry Eyed and recorded a couple of commercial singles produced by Flo And Eddie, but the anticipated radio hits were not forthcoming and so the story ended.
Albums: *Starry Eyed And Laughing* (1974), *Thought Talk* (1975).

Staton, Candi

b. Hanceville, Alabama, USA. A former member of the Jewel Gospel Trio, Staton left the group, and her first husband, for a secular career. She was then discovered performing at a club by Clarence Carter, who took the singer to the Fame label. Carter wrote her debut hit, the uncompromising 'I'd Rather Be An Old Man's Sweetheart (Than A Young Man's Fool)', and helped guide the singer's early releases. Candi later began pursuing a country-influenced path, especially in the wake of her successful version of Tammy Wynette's 'Stand By Your Man'. Staton and Carter were, by now, married, although this relationship subsequently ended in divorce. Candi left Fame for Warner Brothers in 1974 but it was two years before 'Young Hearts Run Free', an excellent pop-styled hit, consolidated this new phase. 'Nights On Broadway', written by Bee Gees Barry, Maurice and Robin Gibb, then became a UK Top 10 single, although it unaccountably flopped in America. The singer has continued to enjoy intermittent UK success but US hits have been restricted to the R&B chart. 'You Lost The Love' a collaboration with the Force was a popular dancefloor track and a UK Top 40 hit in 1991. More recently Candi Staton has been recording in the gospel field.

Albums: *I'm Just A Prisoner* (1969), *Stand By Your Man* (1971), *Candi Staton* (1972), *Candi* (1974), *Young Hearts Run Free* (1976), *Music Speaks Louder Than Words* (1977), *House Of Love* (1978), *Chance* (1979), *Candi Staton* (1980), *Suspicious Minds* (1982), *Make Me An Instrument* (1985), *Love Lifted Me* (1988), *Stand Up And Be A Witness* (1990). Compilation: *Tell It Like It Is* (1986 - shared with Bettye Swann).

Status Quo

The origins of this durable and now-legendary attraction lie in the Spectres, a London-based beat group. Founder members Mike (later Francis) Rossi (b. 29 May 1949, Peckham, London, England; guitar/vocals) and Alan Lancaster (b. 7 February 1949. Peckham, London, England; bass) led the act from its inception in 1962 until 1967, by which time Roy Lynes (organ) and John Coughlan (b. 19 September 1946, Dulwich, London, England; drums) completed its line-up. The Spectres' three singles encompassed several styles of music, ranging from pop to brash R&B, but the quartet took a new name, Traffic Jam, when such releases proved commercially unsuccessful. A similar failure beset 'Almost But

Not Quite There', but the group was nonetheless buoyed by the arrival of Rick Parfitt aka Rick Harrison (b. 12 October 1948, Woking, Surrey, England; guitar/vocals), lately of cabaret attraction, the Highlights. The revamped unit assumed their 'Status Quo' appellation in August 1967 and initially sought work backing various solo artists, including Madeleine Bell and Tommy Quickly. Such employment came to an abrupt end the following year when the quintet's debut single, 'Pictures Of Matchstick Men', soared to number 7. One of the era's most distinctive performances, the song's ringing guitar pattern and *de rigueur* phasing courted pop and psychedelic affectations. A follow-up release, 'Black Veils Of Melancholy', exaggerated latter trappings at the expense of melody, but the group enjoyed another UK Top 10 hit with the jaunty 'Ice In The Sun', co-written by former 50s singer, Marty Wilde.

Subsequent recordings in a similar vein struggled to emulate such success, and despite reaching number 12 with 'Down The Dustpipe', Status Quo was increasingly viewed as a *passé* novelty. However, the song itself, which featured a simple riff and wailing harmonica, indicated the musical direction unveiled more fully on *Ma Kelly's Greasy Spoon*. The album included Quo's version of Steamhammer's 'Junior's Wailing', which had inspired this conversion to a simpler, 'boogie' style. Gone too were the satin shirts, frock coats and kipper ties, replaced by long hair, denim jeans and plimsolls. The departure of Lynes en route to Scotland - 'He just got off the train and that was the last we ever saw of him,' (Rossi) - brought the unit's guitar work to the fore, although indifference from their record company blighted progress. Assiduous live appearances built up a grass roots following and impressive slots at the Reading and Great Western Festivals (both 1972) signalled a commercial turning point. Now signed to the renowned Vertigo label, Status Quo scored a UK Top 10 hit that year with 'Paper Plane' but more importantly, reached number 5 in the album charts with *Piledriver*. A subsequent release, *Hello*, entered at number 1, confirming the group's emergence as a major attraction. Since that point their style has basically remained unchanged, fusing simple, 12-bar riffs to catchy melodies, while an unpretentious 'lads' image has proved equally enduring. Each of their 70s albums reached the Top 5, while a consistent presence in the singles' chart included such notable entries as 'Caroline' (1973), 'Down Down' (a chart topper in 1974), 'Whatever You Want' (1979) and 'Lies'/'Don't Drive My Car'

(1980). An uncharacteristic ballad, 'Living On An Island' (1979), showed a softer perspective while Quo also proved adept at adapting outside material, as evinced by their version of John Fogerty's 'Rockin' All Over The World' (1977). (The song was later re-recorded as 'Running All Over The World' to promote the charitable Race Against Time in 1988.)

The quartet undertook a lengthy break during 1980, but answered rumours of a permanent split with Just Supposin'. However, a dissatisfied Coughlan left the group in 1981 in order to form his own act, Diesel. Pete Kircher, (ex-Original Mirrors), took his place, but Quo was then undermined by the growing estrangement between Lancaster and Rossi and Parfitt. The bassist moved to Australia in 1983 - a cardboard cut-out substituted on several television slots - but he remained a member for the next two years. Lancaster's final appearance with the group was at Live Aid, following which he unsuccessfully took out a High Court injunction to prevent the group performing without him. Rossi and Parfitt secured the rights to the name 'Status Quo' and reformed the act around John Edwards (bass), Jeff Rich (drums) and keyboard player Andy Bown. The last-named musician, formerly of the Herd and Judas Jump, had begun his association with the group in 1973, but only now became an official member. Despite such traumas Quo continued to enjoy commercial approbation with Top 10 entries 'Dear John' (1982), 'Marguerita Time' (1983), 'In The Army Now' (1986) and 'Burning Bridges (On And Off And On Again)' (1988), while 1+9+8+2 was their fourth chart-topping album. Status Quo celebrated its silver anniversary in October 1991 by entering The Guinness Book Of Records having completed four charity concerts in four UK cities in the space of 12 hours. This ambitious undertaking, the subject of a television documentary, was succeeded by a national tour which confirmed the group's continued mass-market popularity. The much-loved Status Quo have carried a very large niche in music history by producing uncomplicated, unpretentious and infectious rock music.

Albums: Picturesque Matchstickable Messages (1968), Spare Parts (1969), Ma Kelly's Greasy Spoon (1970), Dog Of Two Head (1971), Piledriver (1973), Hello (1973), Quo (1974), On The Level (1975), Blue For You (1976), Status Quo Live! (1977), Rockin' All Over The World (1977), If You Can't Stand The Heat (1978), Whatever You Want (1979), Just Supposin' (1980), Never Too Late (1981), 1+9+8+2 (1982),

To Be Or Not To Be (1983), Back To Back (1983), In The Army Now (1986), Ain't Complaining (1988), Rock 'Til You Drop (1991). Compilations: Status Quo-tations (1969), The Best Of Status Quo (1973), The Golden Hour Of Status Quo (1973), Down The Dustpipe (1975), The Rest Of Status Quo (1976), The Status Quo File (1977), The Status Quo Collection (1978)), Twelve Gold Bars (1980), Spotlight On Status Quo Volume 1 (1980), Fresh Quota (1981), 100 Minutes Of Status Quo (1982), Spotlight On Status Quo Volume 2 (1982), From The Makers Of... (1983), Works (1983), To Be Or Not To Be (1983), Twelve Gold Bars Volume 1 & 2 (1984), Na Na Na (1985), Collection: Status Quo (1985), Quotations, Volume 1 (1987), Quotations, Volume 2 (1987), From The Beginning (1988), C.90 Collector (1989).

Further reading: Status Quo: The Authorised Biography; John Shearlaw.

Stealers Wheel

The turbulent, acrimonious and comparatively brief career of Stealers Wheel enabled the two main members Gerry Rafferty and Joe Egan to produce some memorable and inventive, relaxed pop music. During the early 70s. Rafferty (b. 16 April 1946, Paisley, Scotland) and long-time friend Joe Egan (b. c.1946 Scotland) assembled in London to form a British Crosby, Stills And Nash, together with Rab Noakes, Ian Campbell and Roger Brown. After rehearsing and negotiating a record contract with A&M Records. The band had already fragmented, before they entered the studio to meet with legendary producers Leiber And Stoller. Paul Pilnick (guitar), Tony Williams (bass) and ex-Juicy Lucy member Rod Coombes (drums) bailed out Rafferty and Egan; the result was a surprising success, achieved by the sheer quality of their songs and the blend of the two leaders' voices. 'Stuck In The Middle With You' is an enduring song reminiscent of mid-period Beatles, and it found favour by reaching the Top 10 on both sides of the Atlantic. While the song was high on the charts Rafferty departed and was replaced by former Spooky Tooth lead guitarist Luther Grosvenor (aka Ariel Bender). Rafferty had returned by the time the second album was due to be recorded, but the musical chairs continued as all the remaining members left the band, leaving Rafferty and Egan holding the baby. Various session players completed Ferguslie Park, astonishingly another superb, melodic and cohesive album. The album was a failure commercially and the two leaders set about completing their contractual obligations and recording their final work *Right Or Wrong*. Even with similarly strong material, notably the evocative 'Benidictus' and the arresting 'Found My Way To You', the album failed. Rafferty and Egan, disillusioned, buried the name forever. Management problems plagued their career and lyrics of these troubled times continued to appear on both Egan and Rafferty's subsequent solo work.

Albums: *Stealers Wheel* (1973), *Ferguslie Park* (1974), *Right Or Wrong* (1975). Compilation: *The Best Of Stealers Wheel* (1978).

Steamhammer

Kieran White (vocals/harmonica), Martin Pugh (lead guitar), Martin Quittenton (rhythm guitar), Steve Davy (bass) and Michael Rushton (drums) made their recording debut in 1969 with the excellent *Steamhammer*. The set featured an impressive group original, 'Junior's Wailing', which was later adopted by Status Quo during their transformation from pop group to boogie band. Pugh and Quittenton also contributed to Rod Stewart's first debut, *An Old Raincoat Won't Let You Down*, and the latter guitarist subsequently remained with the singer, co-writing the million-selling 'Maggie May', and adding the song's distinctive mandolin sound. Pugh, White and Davy were then joined by Steve Jollife (saxophones/flute) and Mick Bradley (drums) for *Steamhammer Mk. II* which, although offering the blues-base of its predecessor, showed an increased interest in improvisation, as evidenced in the extended 'Another Travelling Tune'. This propensity for a more progressive direction was maintained on ensuing releases, the last of which was only issued in Europe where the group had amassed a considerable following. Defections, sadly, undermined their potential and Steamhammer broke up during the mid-70s.

Albums: *Steamhammer* (1969), *Steamhammer Mk. II* (1970), *Mountains* (1970), *Speech* (1972). Compilation: *This Is Steamhammer* (1972).

Steeleye Span

The roots of this pivotal English folk-rock group lay in several ill-fated rehearsals between Ashley 'Tyger' Hutchings (b. January 1945, London, England; bass, ex-Fairport Convention), Irish trio Sweeny's Men - Terry Woods (vocals/guitar/mandolin), Johnny Moynihan (vocals/fiddle) and Andy Irvine (vocals/mandolin) - and Woods' wife Gay (vocals/concertina/autoharp). When Moynihan

and Irvine subsequently retracted, the remaining musicians were joined by Tim Hart (vocals/guitar/dulcimer/harmonium) and Maddy Prior (vocals), two well-known figures in folk circles. Taking their name from a Lincolnshire waggoner celebrated in song, Steeleye Span began extensive rehearsals before recording the excellent *Hark, The Village Wait*. The set comprised of traditional material, expertly arranged and performed to encompass the rock-based perspective Hutchings helped create on the Fairport's *Liege And Lief*, while retaining the purity of the songs. The Woods then left to pursue their own career and were replaced by Martin Carthy (vocals/guitar) and Peter Knight (vocals/fiddle) for *Please To See The King* and *Ten Man Mop*. This particular line-up toured extensively, but the departure of Hutchings for the purist Albion Country Band signalled a dramatic realignment in the Steeleye camp. Carthy resumed his solo career when conflict arose over the extent of change and two musicians of a rock-based persuasion - Bob Johnson (guitar) and Rick Kemp (bass) - were brought in. The quintet also left manager/producer Sandy Robertson for the higher-profile of Jo Lustig, who secured the group's new recording deal with Chrysalis Records. Both *Below The Salt* and *Parcel Of Rogues*, displayed an electric content and tight dynamics, while the punningly-entitled *Now We Are Six*, which was produced by Jethro Tull's Ian Anderson, emphasized the terse drumming of newcomer Nigel Pegrum. The group enjoyed two hit singles with 'Gaudete' (1973) and 'All Around My Hat' (1975), the latter of which reached the UK Top and was produced by Mike Batt. However, the charm of Steeleye's early work was gradually eroding and although their soaring harmonies remained as strong as ever, experiments with reggae and heavier rock rhythms alienated rather than attracted prospective audiences. The group was 'rested' following the disappointing *Rocket Cottage* (1976), but reconvened the following year for *Storm Force Ten*. However, Knight and Johnson were otherwise employed and this line-up was completed by John Kirkpatrick (accordion) and the prodigal Martin Carthy. Although their formal disbanding was announced in March 1978, Steeleye Span has been resurrected on subsequent occasions. Hart, Prior and Carthy have also pursued successful solo careers.

Albums: *Hark, The Village Wait* (1970), *Please To See The King* (1971), *Ten Man Mop (Or Mr. Reservoir Strikes Again)* (1971), *Below The Salt* (1972), *Parcel Of Rogues* (1973), *Now We Are Six*

Steeleye Span

(1974), *Commoners Crown* (1975), *All Around My Hat* (1975), *Rocket Cottage* (1976), *Storm Force Ten* (1977), *Live At Last* (1978), *Sails Of Silver* (1980), *Back In Line* (1986), *Ten Man Mop* (1986). Compilations: *Individually And Collectively* (1972), *Steeleye Span Almanac* (1973), *Original Masters* (1977). *Time Span* (1978), *Best Of Steeleye Span* (1984), *Time Span* (1984), *Steeleye Span* (1985), *Portfolio* (1988), *Tempted And Tried* (1989), *The Early Years* (1989).

Steely Dan

The seeds of this much respected rock group were sewn at New York's Bard College where founder members Donald Fagen (keyboards/vocals) and Walter Becker (bass/vocals) were students. They subsequently forged a songwriting team and their many demos were later collected on several exploitative compilations. Formative versions of 'Brooklyn', 'Berry Town' and 'Parker's Band' - each of which were re-recorded on official Steely Dan releases - were recorded during this period. The duo also enjoyed a contemporaneous association with pop/harmony act Jay And The Americans, for which they adopted the pseudonyms Gus Marker and Tristan Fabriani. Becker and Fagen appeared on the group's last US Top 20 hit, 'Walkin' In The Rain' (1969), the albums *Wax Museum* and *Capture The Moment*, and accompanied the unit on tour. Group vocalist Jerry Vance and drummer John Discepolo joined the pair for *You Gotta Walk It Like You Talk It (Or*

You'll Lose That Beat), the soundtrack to a low-key movie. Denny Dias (guitar) also contributed to these sessions and he joined Fagen and Becker on their next project which evolved following an alliance with producer Gary Katz. Taking the name 'Steely Dan' from the steam-powered dildo in William Burroughs' novel *The Naked Lunch*, the trio was quickly expanded by the arrival of David Palmer (vocals ex-Myddle Class), Jeff 'Skunk' Baxter (guitar ex-Ultimate Spinach) and Jim Hodder (drums). The accomplished *Can't Buy A Thrill* was completed within weeks, but drew considerable critical praise for its deft melodies and immaculate musicianship. The title track and 'Do It Again' reached the US Top 20 when issued as singles and this newfound fame inspired the sarcasm of 'Show Biz Kids' on *Countdown To Ecstacy*.

Their second album was another undoubted classic of the 70s, and featured such bittersweet celebrations as 'The Boston Rag' and 'My Old School'. By this point Palmer had left the line-up following an uncomfortable US tour, but although Baxter declared the set superior to its predecessor, the same commercial approbation did not follow. This was reversed with the release of *Pretzel Logic*, Steely Dan's first US Top 10 album. Here Fagen and Becker drew more fully on their love of jazz, acquiring the riff of 'Rikki Don't Lose That Number' from Horace Silver's 'Song Of My Father' and recreating Duke Ellington's 'East St. Louis Toodle-O'. The former reached number 4 in the US charts. The group's clarity of purpose and enthralling dexterity was never so apparent, but internal conflicts simmered over a reluctance to tour, shown by Becker and, especially, Fagen who was unhappy with the in-concert role of frontman. Steely Dan's final live appearance was on 4 July 1974 and ensuing strife resulted in the departures of both Baxter and Hodder. The guitarist resurfaced in the Doobie Brothers, with whom he was already guesting, while the drummer reverted to session work. The faithful Dias joined newcomers Michael McDonald (keyboards/vocals) and Jeff Porcaro (drums) for *Katy Lied* which also featured cameos by guitarist Rick Derringer and saxophonist Phil Woods. The set was, however, greeted with disquiet as the transformation from active unit to purely studio creation resulted in crafted anonymity.

The Royal Scam redressed the balance and in its title track offered one of the group's most impressive tracks to date. Becker and Fagen were, by now, the sole arbiters of Steely Dan, with McDonald having followed Baxter into the Doobie Brothers and Dias and Porcaro opting for studio employment. The new collection boasted another series of sumptuous tunes and included 'Haitian Divorce', the group's lone Top 20 hit in Britain. *Aja* continued in a similar vein where an array of quality musicians - including Wayne Shorter, Jim Horn and Tom Scott - brought meticulousness to a set notable for the seemingly effortless, jazz/disco sweep evinced on 'Peg'. A similar pattern was unveiled on *Gaucho*, the release of which was marred by conflict between the group and record label over escalating recording costs. The latter's nervousness was assuaged when the album achieved platinum sales and an attendant single, 'Hey Nineteen', reached the US Top 10. However, Becker and Fagen had now tired of their creation and in June 1981 they announced the break-up of their partnership. The following year Fagen released *The Nightfly*, a superb collection which continued where his erstwhile group had ended. Producer Katz supervised the accustomed cabal of Los Angeles session musicians to create a sound and texture emphasizing the latter's dominant role in later Steely Dan releases. Becker meanwhile produced albums for China Crisis and Rickie Lee Jones, but in May 1990 the pair were reunited in New York's Hit Factory studio to collaborate on material for a forthcoming Fagen project. 'We're not working as Steely Dan,' stated Becker, but aficionados were undoubtedly heartened by news of their rekindled partnership.

Albums: *Can't Buy A Thrill* (1972), *Countdown To Ecstacy* (1973), *Pretzel Logic* (1974), *Katy Lied* (1975), *The Royal Scam* (1976), *Aja* (1977), *Gaucho* (1980). Compilations: *You Gotta Walk It Like You Talk It (Or You'll Lose That Beat)* (1974, early recordings), *Greatest Hits* (1979), *Gold* (1982), *A Decade Of Steely Dan* (1985), *Reelin' In The Years* (1985), *Berry Town* (1986), *Sun Mountain* (1986, early Becker/Fagen material), *Old Regime* (1987, early Becker/Fagen material), *Stone Piano* (1988, early Becker/Fagen material), *Gold (Expanded Edition)* (1991).

Stevenson, B.W.

b. Louis C. Stevenson, 5 October 1949, Dallas, Texas, USA, d. 28 April 1988. B.W. Stevenson (the initials stood for Buckwheat) was best remembered for his 1973 US Top 10 single 'My Maria'. Stevenson performed with local Texas rock bands as a teenager, before attending college and then joining the Air Force. Upon his discharge, Stevenson returned to the club scene, particularly in the burgeoning Austin, Texas area. Although he considered himself a blues and rock singer, he was signed to RCA Records as a country artist and released 'Shambala', a song which charted but did not fare as well as the version by rockers Three Dog Night. Stevenson and Daniel Moore's 'My Maria' became a number 9 pop hit (oddly missing the country charts), and the album of the same title reached number 45, also in 1973. Stevenson continued to record, placing two further singles on the charts in the 70s (the latter, 'Down To The Station', for Warner Brothers Records). He also recorded for MCA Records. Stevenson died following heart surgery in April 1988.
Albums: *B.W. Stevenson* (1972), *Lead Free* (1972), *My Maria* (1973), *Calabasas* (1974), *Lost Feeling* (1977), *Lifeline* (1980).

Stewart, Rod

b. Roderick David Stewart, 10 January 1945, Highgate, London, England. The leading British rock star of the 70s started his career as an apprentice professional with Brentford Football Club; over the years Stewart has made it known that football is his second love. Following a spell roaming Europe with folk artist Wizz Jones in the early 60s he returned to join Jimmy Powell And The Five Dimensions in 1963. This frantic R&B band featured Rod playing furious harmonica, reminiscent of James Cotton and Little Walter. As word got out, he was attracted to London and was hired by Long John Baldry in his band the

Hoochie Coochie Men (formerly Cyril Davies All Stars). Without significant success outside the club scene, the band disintegrated and evolved into the Steampacket, with Baldry, Stewart, Brian Auger, Julie Driscoll, Mickey Waller and Rick Brown. Following a television documentary on the swinging mod scene, featuring Stewart, he collected his monicker 'Rod the Mod'. In 1965, he joined the blues-based Shotgun Express as joint lead vocalist with Beryl Marsden. The impressive line-up included Peter Green, Mick Fleetwood and Peter Bardens. By the following year, Stewart was well-known in R&B and blues circles, but it was joining the Jeff Beck Group that gave him national exposure. During his tenure with Beck he recorded two important albums, *Truth* and *Cosa Nostra-Beck Ola* and made a number of gruelling tours of America.

When the group broke up (partly through exhaustion) Stewart and Ron Wood joined the Faces, now having lost their smallest face Steve Marriot. Simultaneously, Rod had been signed as a solo artist to Phonogram, and he managed to juggle both careers expertly over the next six years. Though critically well-received, his first album sold only moderately; it was *Gasoline Alley* that made the breakthrough. In addition to the superb title track it contained the glorious 'Lady Day'. This album marked the beginning of the 'mandolin' sound supplied by the talented guitarist Martin Quittenton. Stewart became a superstar on the strength of his next two albums, *Every Picture Tells A Story* and *Never A Dull Moment*. Taken as one body of work, they represent Stewart at his best. His choice and exemplary execution of non-originals gave him numerous hits from these albums including; 'Reason To Believe' (Tim Hardin), 'I'm Losing You' (Temptations), 'Angel' (Jimi Hendrix). His own classics were the irresistible chart-topping magnum opus 'Maggie May' and the wonderful 'You Wear It Well', all sung in the now familiar frail, hoarse, croaky voice. In the mid-70s, following the release of the below average *Smiler*, Rod embarked on a relationship with the glamorous actress, Britt Ekland. Besotted with her, he allowed her to dictate his sense of dress, and for a while appeared in faintly ludicrous dungarees made out of silk and ridiculous 'Andy Pandy' jump suits. During this time Rod became the darling of the magazine and gutter press, a reputation he has unwillingly maintained through his succession of affairs with stunning blonde females. *Atlantic Crossing* was his last critical success for many years; it included the future football

crowd anthem and a number 1 'Sailing' (written by Gavin Sutherland) and a fine reading of Dobie Gray's 'Drift Away'. His albums throughout the second half of the 70s were patchy affairs although they became phenomenally successful, selling millions and in many cases they topped the charts world-wide. The high-spots during this disco glitzy phase were 'The Killing Of Georgie', Cat Stevens' 'First Cut Is The Deepest', 'Tonight's The Night' and 'You're In My Heart'. Other hits included 'Hot Legs' and the superbly immodest but irresistible number 1, 'D'Ya Think I'm Sexy'. 'Ole Ola', was adopted by the Scottish World Cup football team.

He entered the 80s newly married, to George Hamilton IV's ex-wife Alana, and maintained his momentum of regular hits and successful albums; his large body of fans ensured a chart placing irrespective of the quality. Throughout the 80s Rod spent his time jet-setting all over the world, attending parties and generally having a whale of a time. The press followed his marriage break-up, his long relationship with Kelly Emberg closely watching him for any lapses. In the background to his jack-the-lad persona was an artist who still had a good ear for a quality song, which surfaced throughout the decade with numbers like 'How Long' (Paul Carrick), 'Some Guys Have All The Luck' (Robert Palmer) and reunited with Jeff Beck, a superb performance of Curtis Mayfield's 'People Get Ready'. His biggest hits of the 80s were 'What Am I Gonna Do', 'Every Beat Of My Heart' and his best of the decade 'Baby Jane'. As the 90s got under way Stewart, now re-married indicated that he had settled down, and has found true love. His new guise has not affected his record sales; in April 1991 he was high on the UK chart with 'Rhythm Of My Heart' and had the best selling *Vagabond Heart*. Rod Stewart, one of the biggest 'superstars' of the century approaches 50 with confidence.

Albums: *An Old Raincoat Won't Let You Down* (1969), *Gasoline Alley* (1970), *Every Picture Tells A Story* (1971), *Never A Dull Moment* (1972), *Smiler* (1974), *Atlantic Crossing* (1975), *A Night On the Town* (1976), *Foot Loose And Fancy Free* (1977), *Blondes Have More Fun* (1978), *Foolish Behaviour* (1980), *Tonight I'm Yours* (1981), *Absolutely Live* (1982), *Body Wishes* (1983), *Camouflage* (1984), *Every Beat Of My Heart* (1986), *Out Of Order* (1988), *Vagabond* (1991). Compilations: *Sing It Again Rod* (1973), *The Best Of Rod Stewart* (1977, Mercury collection), *Greatest Hits* (1979), *The Best Of Rod Stewart* (1989, Warner Brothers collection),

Storyteller (1989).
Further reading; *Rod Stewart; A Biography*, Tim
Ewbank and Stafford Hildred.

Stiff Records

Britain's premier 'new wave' label of the 70s was
founded in 1976 by pub-rock producer and
promoter Dave Robinson and Andrew Jakeman,
tour manager of Dr Feelgood. The first release,
'Heart Of The City' by Nick Lowe, was financed
by a £400 loan from Dr Feelgood's singer Lee
Brilleaux. From 1976-77, the label released
material by a range of London-based pub and punk
rock bands such as Roogalator, Lew Lewis, the
Adverts and the Damned. Stiff also signed Elvis
Costello whose fourth single 'Watching The
Detectives' was the label's first hit. Costello had
achieved prominence as a member of Stiff's first
package tour of numerous British cities. Like its
1978 successor, the tour served to publicise and
popularise the label and its artists. During the early
days it was extremely hip to be seen wearing a Stiff
Tee-shirt bearing its uncompromising slogan, 'If it
isn't Stiff it ain't worth a fuck'. Towards the end of
1977, Stiff suffered a setback when Jakeman,
Costello and Nick Lowe left to join the Radar
label. However, Stiff's fortunes were transformed
by the success of Ian Dury whose anthem 'Sex And
Drugs And Rock 'n' Roll' had made little impact
when first issued in 1977. A year later, however,
'What A Waste' inaugurated a run of four hit
singles. Lene Lovich, Jona Lewie and Madness also
provided Top 20 records for the label in 1978-80,
when Robinson switched distribution from EMI to
CBS. In the early 80s, Stiff flirted with reggae
(Desmond Dekker) and soul (various productions
by Eddy Grant) but the bulk of its releases came
from artists on the eccentric fringe of the new
wave such as Tenpole Tudor and Wreckless Eric.
The company also issued one album from Graham
Parker before he moved to the larger RCA label.
There were also hits from the Belle Stars and Dave
Stewart with Barbara Gaskin. From the outset,
Robinson had been interested in new wave
developments in America and over the years Stiff
licensed material by such artists as Rachel Sweet,
Devo, the Plasmatics and Jane Aire. In 1984, Stiff
was merged with Island Records and Robinson
became managing director of both companies. This
coincided with the departure of Madness to start
their own label (Zarjazz), although Stiff's new
signing, the Pogues provided hits throughout the
mid-80s. The merger was not a success, however,
and in 1986 Robinson resumed control of an
independent Stiff, only to see it suffer an
immediate cash-crisis. The assets of the company,
which had a turnover of £4m at its peak, were sold
to ZTT Records for a reputed £300,000. Under
the new ownership there were initial releases from
the Pogues, hard bop drummer Tommy Chase and
female vocal group the Mint Juleps. But by the
90s, the pioneering Stiff had become simply a
reissue label.

Stills, Stephen

b. 3 January 1945, Dallas, Texas, USA. The often
dubbed 'musical genius' is better known for his
work with the pivotal Buffalo Springfield, and for
many years his association with David Crosby,
Graham Nash and Neil Young. After the
Springfield's break-up, Stills, at a loose end, joined
with Al Kooper and Mike Bloomfield for the
million-selling *Super Session*. His contributions
included Donovan's 'Season Of The Witch', on
which he played one of the decade's most famous
wah-wah guitar solos. His solo career began during
one of Crosby, Stills And Nash's many hiatuses.
Then living in England at Ringo Starr's former
home, Stills enlisted a team of musical
heavyweights to play on his self-titled debut which
reached the US Top 3 in 1970. This outstanding
album remains his best work, and is justifiably still
available. In addition to the irresistible hit single
'Love The One You're With' the album contains a
healthy mixture of styles, all demonstrating his
considerable dexterity as a songwriter, guitarist and
singer. The solo acoustic 'Black Queen' for
example, was reputedly recorded while Stills was
completely drunk, and yet his mastery of the (C.F.)
Martin acoustic guitar still prevails. All tracks reach
the listener, from the infectious 'Old Times Good
Times', featuring Jimi Hendrix to 'Go Back
Home', featuring Eric Clapton; it is unfair to single
out any track for they are all exemplary. On this
one album, Stills demonstrated the extent of his
powers. *Stephen Stills 2* was a similar success
containing the innocently profound 'Change
Partners', a brass re-working of the Springfield's
'Bluebird' and the brilliant yet oddly timed blues
number 'Nothing To Do But Today'. For a while
it appeared that Stills' solo career would eclipse that
of his CSNY involvement. His superbly eclectic
double album with Manassas and its consolidating
follow-up, made Stills an immensely important
figure during these years. Ultimately Stephen was
unable to match his opening pair of albums. While
Stills was an admirable effort, the subsequent live
album and *Illegal Stills* were patchy. His nadir came

Stephen Stills with Manassas

in 1978 when, following the break up of his marriage to French chanteuse Veronique Sanson he produced *Thoroughfare Gap*; a collection riddled with uninspired songs of self-pity. Only the title track was worthy of his name. No official solo release came until 1984, when Ahmet Ertegun reluctantly allowed Stills to put out *Right By You*. While the slick production did not appeal to all Stills aficionados, it proved to be his most cohesive work since *Stephen Stills 2*, although appealing more to the AOR market. The moderate hit 'Can't Let Go' featured both Stills and Michael Finnigan, exercising their fine voices to great effect. Since then the brilliant but erratic Stills has continued his stop-go career with Crosby, Nash, and occasionally Young. Stills released a solo acoustic self-financed work in 1991. *Stills Alone* was an excellent return to his roots and featured hoarse-voiced versions of the Beatles 'In My Life' and Bob Dylan's 'Ballad Of Hollis Brown'. As a guitarist, his work in 1992 with a rejuvenated Crosby, Stills And Nash was quite breathtaking, demonstrating those early accolades were not mis-judged.

Albums: with Al Kooper and Mike Bloomfield *Super Session* (1969), *Stephen Stills* (1970), *Stephen Stills 2* (1971), *Stills* (1975), *Illegal Stills* (1976), *Stephen Stills Live* (1900), *Thoroughfare Gap* (1978), *Right By You* (1984), *Stills Alone*. (1991).

Stone The Crows

Singer Maggie Bell and guitarist Leslie Harvey (younger brother of Alex Harvey), served their musical apprenticeships in Glasgow's Palais dancebands. In 1967 they toured American bases in Germany with a group which also included Bill and Bobby Patrick. The following year Bell and Harvey formed Power, houseband at the Burns Howff bar, which included Jimmy Dewar (bass) and John McGuinness (organ). Leslie subsequently toured America, augmenting another Glasgow-based group, Cartoone. This newly-formed quartet was managed by Peter Grant, whom the guitarist then brought to Scotland to view Power. Grant duly signed the group, who were renamed Stone The Crows on the addition of former John Mayall drummer, Colin Allen. The quintet's early blues-based albums were notable for both Bell and Dewar's expressive vocals and Harvey's textured, economic guitar work. However, an inability to match their live popularity with record sales led to disaffection and both McGuinness and Dewar left on completing *Ode To John Law*. Steve Thompson (bass) and Ronnie Leahy (keyboards) joined Stone The Crows for *Teenage Licks*, their most successful album to date. Bell was awarded the first of several top vocalist awards but this new-found momentum ended in tragedy. On 3 May 1972, Leslie Harvey died after being electrocuted onstage at Swansea's Top Rank Ballroom. Although the group completed a fourth album with Jimmy McCulloch from Thunderclap Newman, they lacked the heart to continue and broke up the following year.

Albums: *Stone The Crows* (1970), *Ode To John Law*

(1970), *Teenage Licks* (1971), '*Ontinuous Performance* (1972). Compilation: *Flashback - Stone The Crows* (1976).

Stories

This US pop group came together in the wake of the disbandment of the Left Banke. Multi-instrumentalist Michael Brown was searching for a strong, harmonic unit and brought together Ian Lloyd (b. Ian Buoncocglio, Seattle, USA; vocals), Steve Love (guitar) and Bryan Medley (drums). However, after completing their self-titled debut album in 1972, founding member Michael Brown dramatically quit. Determined to soldier on, the group recruited two new members, Ken Aaronson (bass) and Ken Bichel (piano) and in 1973 recorded *About Us*. An opportune cover of Hot Chocolate's UK hit 'Brother Louie' (itself inspired from the Richard Berry/Kingsmen classic 'Louie Louie') brought the Stories a surprise US number 1 hit. Two further US hits followed, 'Mammy Blue' and 'If It Feels Good, Do It', before the group abruptly split up. Lloyd alone registered some further success with the minor hit 'Slip Away' in 1979.
Albums: *Stories* (1972), *About Us* (1973).

Stranglers

One of the longest-surviving groups from the British new wave explosion of the late 70s, the Stranglers first rehearsed in Guildford as early as 1974. Two years later, the first full line-up emerged comprising: Hugh Cornwell (b. 28 August 1949, London, England; vocals/guitar), Jean Jacques Burnel (b. 21 February 1952, London, England; vocals/bass), Jet Black (b. Brian Duffy, 26 August 1943; drums) and Dave Greenfield. Following a tour supporting Patti Smith during 1976 and some favourable press reports (with comparisons with the Doors), the group were signed by United Artists Records. Courting controversy from the outset, the group caused a sensation and saw their date at London's Roundhouse cut short when Cornwell wore an allegedly obscene T-shirt. In February 1977, the Stranglers' debut single, '(Get A) Grip (On Yourself)' reached number 44 in the UK charts and inexplicably dropped out after only one week. According to the chart compilers, the sales were inadvertently assigned to another record, but it was too late to rectify the damage. 'Grip' saw the group at their early best. Bathed in swirling organ and backed by a throbbing beat, the single displayed Cornwell's gruff vocal to strong effect. The b-side, 'London Lady', was taken at a faster pace and

revealed the first signs of an overbearing misogynism that would later see them fall foul of the critics. Initially bracketed with punk, the Stranglers owed as much to their pub-rock background and it soon emerged that they were older and more knowing than their teenage contemporaries. Nevertheless their first album *IV Rattus Norvegicus* was greeted with enthusiasm by the rock press and sold extremely well. The near 'blasphemous' lyrics of 'Hanging Around' and the gruesome imagery of 'Down In The Sewer' seemingly proved less acceptable than the women-baiting subject matter of their next single, 'Peaches'. Banned by BBC radio, the song still charted thanks to airplay offered the b-side 'Go Buddy Go'. Rather than bowing to the feminist criticisms levelled against them, the group subsequently compounded the felony by introducing strippers at a Battersea Park, London concert. Journalists were treated even more cavalierly and the group were renowned for their violent antics. Having initially alienated the press, their work was almost universally derided thereafter. The public kept faith, however, and ensured that the Stranglers enjoyed a formidable run of hits over the next few years. The lugubrious protest 'Something Better Change' and faster paced 'No More Heroes' both reached the UK Top 10, while 'Five Minutes' and 'Nice 'N Sleazy' each entered the Top 20. In the background there were the usual slices of bad publicity. Burnel and Black were arrested for being drunk and disorderly before charges were dropped. Cornwell was not so fortunate and found himself sentenced to three months' imprisonment on drugs charges in January 1980. Within two months of his release, the group found themselves under arrest in Nice, France, after allegedly inciting a riot. Later that year they received a heavy fine in a French court.
The group's uncompromising outlaw image tended to distract from subtle changes that had been occurring in their musical repertoire. Their brave cover of the Burt Bacharach/Hal David standard 'Walk On By' (with an identical arrangement to the Doors' 'Light My Fire') reached number 21 in spite of the fact that 100,000 copies of the record had already been issued gratis with the album *Black And White*. Equally effective and contrasting was the melodic 'Duchess', which displayed the Stranglers' plaintive edge to surprising effect. Their albums also revealed a new diversity from *The Raven* (with its elaborate 3-D cover) to the genuinely strange *Themeninblack*. The latter was primarily Cornwell's concept, and introduced the

idea of extra-terrestrial hit-men who silence individuals that have witnessed UFO landings. For their next album, *La Folie*, the group were accompanied on tour by a ballet company. The album spawned the group's biggest hit, the evocative 'Golden Brown', with its startling, classical-influenced harpsichord arrangement. This paean to heroin reached the UK number 2 spot, resting just behind Buck Fizz's 'Land Of Make Believe'. Even at their most melodic the Stranglers ran into a minor furore when it was alleged that the song was concerned with heroin consumption. Fortunately, the theme was so lyrically obscure that the accusations failed to prove convincing enough to provoke a ban. Another single from *La Folie* was the sentimental 'Strange Little Girl', which also climbed into the UK Top 10. The melodic influence continued on 'European Female', but in spite of the hits, the group's subsequent albums failed to attract serious critical attention. As unremittingly ambitious as ever, the Stranglers' 1986 album *Dreamtime* was inspired by Aborigine culture and complemented their outsider image. Just as it seemed that their appeal was becoming merely cultish, they returned to their old style with a cover of the Kinks' 'All Day And All Of The Night'. It was enough to provide them with their first Top 10 hit for five years. Increasingly unpredictable, the group re-recorded their first single 'Grip' which ironically fared better than the original, reaching the Top 40 in January 1989.

Despite their small handful of solo ventures, it seemed unlikely that either Cornwell or Burnel would ever consider abandoning the group for solo careers. Perpetual derision by the press finally took its cumulative toll on the lead singer, however, and in the summer of 1990 Cornwall announced that he was quitting the group. Initial reports indicated that he was considering an acting career. Burnel, Black and Greenfield were left with the unenviable problem of finding an experienced replacement and deciding whether to retain the name Stranglers. Their task was made no easier by the realization that they had achieved one of the most stable and consistent group line-ups in rock history. Fifteen years on, it seems remarkable that this most anarchic of mid-70s groups should have turned into something of an institution.

Albums: *IV Rattus Norvegicus* (1977), *No More Heroes* (1977), *Black And White* (1978), *Live (X Cert)* (1979), *The Raven* (1979), *The Meninblack* (1981), *La Folie* (1981), *Feline* (1983), *Aural Sculpture* (1984), *Dreamtime* (1986), *All Live And All Of The Night* (1988). Compilation: *The Singles* (1989), *Greatest Hits: 1977-1990* (1990).

Strawbs

This versatile unit was formed in 1967 by guitarists Dave Cousins (b. 7 January 1945; guitar/banjo/piano/recorder) and Tony Hooper. They initially worked as a bluegrass group, the Strawberry Hill Boys, with mandolinist Arthur Phillips, but later pursued a folk-based direction. Truncating their name to the Strawbs, the founding duo added Ron Chesterman on bass prior to the arrival of singer Sandy Denny whose short spell in the line-up is documented in *All Our Own Work*. This endearing collection, released in the wake of Denny's success with Fairport Convention, features an early version of her exemplary composition, 'Who Knows Where The Time Goes'. Cousins, Hooper and Chesterman released their official debut, *Strawbs*, in 1968. This excellent selection featured several of the group's finest compositions, including 'Oh How She Changed' and 'The Battle', and was acclaimed by both folk and rock audiences. *Dragonfly*, was less well-received, prompting a realignment in the band. The original duo was joined by former Velvet Opera members John Ford (b. 1 July 1948, Fulham, London, England; bass/acoustic guitar) and Richard Hudson (b. Richard William Stafford Hudson, 9 May 1948, London, England; drums/guitar/sitar), plus Rick Wakeman (keyboards), a graduate of the Royal Academy of Music. The Strawbs embraced electric rock with *Just A Collection Of Antiques And Curios*, although critical analysis concentrated on Wakeman's contribution.

Such plaudits continued on *From The Witchwood* but the pianist grew frustrated within the group's framework and left to join Yes. He was replaced by Blue Weaver (b. 11 March 1947, Cardiff, South Glamorgan, Wales; guitar/autoharp/piano) from Amen Corner. Despite the commercial success generated by the outstanding *Grave New World*, tension within the Strawbs mounted, and in 1972, Hooper was replaced by Dave Lambert (b. 8 March 1949, Hounslow, Middlesex, England). Relations between Cousins and Hudson and Ford were also deteriorating and although 'Lay Down' gave the band its first UK Top 20 single, the jocular 'Part Of The Union', written by the bassist and drummer, became the Strawbs' most successful release. The group split following an acrimonious US tour. The departing rhythm section formed their own unit, Hudson-Ford while Cousins and Lambert brought in pianist John Hawken (ex-

Strawbs

Nashville Teens and Renaissance), Chas Cronk (bass) and former Stealers Wheel drummer Rod Coombes. However, a series of poorly-received albums suggested the Strawbs had lost both direction and inspiration. Cousins nonetheless presided over several fluctuating line-ups and continued to record into the 80s despite a shrinking popularity. In 1989, the group reunited, including the trio of Cousins, Hooper And Hudson, for the *Don't Say Goodbye*.

Albums: *Strawbs* (1969), *Dragonfly* (1970), *Just A Collection Of Antiques And Curios* (1970), *From The Witchwood* (1971), *Grave New World* (1972), *All Our Own Work* (1973 - as Sandy Denny And The Strawbs), *Bursting At The Seams* (1973), *Hero And Heroine* (1974), *Ghosts* (1975), *Nomadness* (1976), *Deep Cuts* (1976), *Burning For You* (1977), *Dead Lines* (1978), *Don't Say Goodbye* (1988). Compilations: *Strawbs By Choice* (1974), *Best Of The Strawbs* (1978).

Streetband

This British rock band of the late 70s, notable mainly for the membership of Paul Young (b. 17 January 1956, Luton, Bedfordshire, England). Having played in local group, Kat Kool And The Kool Kats, Young formed Streetband in 1977 with John Gifford (guitar/vocals), Mick Pearl (bass/vocals), Roger Kelly (guitar) and Vince Chaulk (drums, ex-Mr Big, whose biggest hit was 'Romeo' in 1977). The group's R&B-tinged music brought a recording deal with Logo Records. The debut album was produced by Chas Jankel, Ian Dury's songwriting partner. The first single, 'Hold On' had a novelty b-side, 'Toast' which gained airplay and became a Top 20 hit in 1978. Streetband returned to their hard-rocking approach for later singles and a second album which included Jools Holland playing keyboards. Lack of further commercial success precipitated the break-up of the group in 1979 when Young, Gifford and Pearl formed the soul group Q-Tips.

Albums: *London* (1979), *Dilemma* (1979).

Streetwalkers

After Family's farewell tour in autumn 1973, vocalist Roger Chapman and guitarist Charles Whitney, collaborated on *Streetwalkers* with help from guitarist Bob Tench (from the Jeff Beck Group) and members of King Crimson. These were among the *ad hoc* UK aggregation that backed Chapman and Whitney for a brief promotional tour - and Tench became the nucleus of a more fixed set-up when the pair recommenced operations as 'Streetwalkers'. With Jon Plotel (bass, ex-Casablanca) and Nicko McBain (drums), the group recorded *Downtown Flyers* which, like its predecessor, was far less self-consciously 'weird' than Family's output had been and, with Chapman's vibrato moderated, drew much inspiration from R&B and soul stylings. A popular attraction on the college circuit - especially in Germany - the quartet's *Red Card* reached the UK Top 20 but this triumph was dampened by internal difficulties. In July 1976, Plotel and Nicko were replaced by Michael Feat and David Dowie. Augmented by Brian Johnson on keyboards, Streetwalkers released the undistinguished *Vicious But Fair* before bowing out with a concert album in late 1977. However, the group survived in spirit via Chapman's subsequent stage performances with a new band, his three solo albums and his characteristically agonized singing in a television commercial for Brutus jeans.

Albums: *Streetwalkers* (1974), *Downtown Flyers* (1975), *Red Card* (1976), *Vicious But Fair* (1977), *Live* (1977).

Streisand, Barbra

b. 24 April 1942, New York City, New York, USA. From childhood Streisand was eager to make a career in show business, happily singing and 'playacting' for neighbours in Brooklyn, where she was born and raised. At the age of 15, she had a trial run with a theatrical company in upstate New York and by 1959, the year she graduated, was convinced that she could make a success of her chosen career. She still sang for fun, but was set on being a stage actress. The lack of opportunites in straight plays drove her to try singing instead and she entered and won a talent contest at The Lion, a gay bar in Greenwich Village. The prize was a booking at the club and this was followed by more club work, including an engagement at the Bon Soir which was later extended and established her as a fast-rising new singer. Appearances in off-Broadway revues followed, in which she acted and sang. Towards the end of 1961 she was cast in *I Can Get It For You Wholesale*, a musical play with songs by Harold Rome. The show was only moderately successful but Streisand's notices were excellent (as were those of another newcomer, Elliott Gould). She was invited to appear on an 'original cast' recording of the show, which was followed by another record date, to make an album of Rome's *Pins And Needles*, a show he had written 25 years earlier. The records and her Bon Soir appearances brought a television date and in 1962,

on the strength of these, Columbia Records offered her a recording date of her own. With arrangements by Peter Matz, who was also responsible for the charts used by Noël Coward at his 1955 Las Vegas appearance, Streisand made her first album, which included such songs as 'Cry Me A River', 'Happy Days Are Here Again' and 'Who's Afraid Of The Big, Bad Wolf?'. Within two weeks of the album's release, in February 1963, Streisand was the top-selling female vocalist in the USA. Two Grammy Awards followed, for Best Album and for Streisand as Best Female Vocalist (for 'Happy Days Are Here Again'). Streisand's career was now unstoppable.

She had more successful club appearances in 1963 and released another strong album, which she followed by opening for Liberace at Las Vegas and appearing at Los Angeles's Coconut Grove and the Hollywood Bowl. That same remarkable year she married Elliott Gould and she was engaged to appear in a forthcoming Broadway show, *Funny Girl*. Based upon the life of Fanny Brice, *Funny Girl* had a troubled pre-production history, but once it opened it proved to have all the qualities its principal producer, Ray Stark, (who had nurtured the show for 10 years), believed it to have. With songs by Jule Styne and Ray Merrill, amongst which were 'People' and 'Don't Rain On My Parade', the show was a massive success, running for 1,348 performances and giving Streisand cover stories in *Time* and *Life* magazines. Early in 1966 Streisand opened *Funny Face* in London but the show's run was curtailed when she became pregnant. During the mid-60s she starred in a succession of popular and award-winning television spectaculars. Albums of the music from these shows were big-sellers and one included her first composition, 'Ma Premiere Chanson'. In 1967, she went to Hollywood to make the film version of *Funny Girl*, the original Styne-Merrill score being extended by the addition of some of the songs Fanny Brice had performed during her own Broadway career. These included 'Second-Hand Rose' and 'My Man'. In addition to *Funny Girl*, Streisand's film career included roles in *Hello, Dolly!* and *On A Clear Day You Can See Forever*. The film of *Funny Girl* (1968) was a hit, with Streisand winning one of two Oscars awarded that year for Best Actress (the other winner was Katharine Hepburn).

By the time she came to the set to make her second Hollywood film, *Hello, Dolly!* (1969), Streisand had developed an unenviable reputation as a meddlesome perfectionist who wanted, and usually succeeded in obtaining, control over every aspect of the films in which she appeared. Although in her later films, especially those which she produced, her demands seemed increasingly like self-indulgence, her perfectionism worked for her on the many albums and stage appearances which followed throughout the 70s. This next decade saw changes in Streisand's public persona and also in the films she worked on. Developing her childhood ambitions to act, she turned more and more to straight acting roles, leaving the songs for her record albums and television shows. Among her films of the 70s were *The Owl And The Pussycat* (1970), *What's Up, Doc?* (1972), *The Way We Were* (1973), *Funny Lady* (1975), a sequel to *Funny Girl*, and *A Star Is Born* (1976). For the latter she co-wrote (with Paul Williams) a song, 'Evergreen', which won an Oscar as Best Song. Streisand continued to make well-conceived and perfectly executed albums, most of which sold in large numbers. She even recorded a set of the more popular songs written by classical composers such as Debussy and Schumann.

Although her albums continued to attract favourable reviews and sell well, her films became open season for critics and were markedly less popular with fans. The shift became most noticeable after *A Star Is Born* was released and its damaging self-indulgence was apparent to all. Nevertheless, the film won admirers and several Golden Globe Awards. She had an unexpected number 1 hit in 1978 with 'You Don't Bring Me Flowers', a duet with Neil Diamond, and she also shared the microphone with Donna Summer on 'Enough Is Enough', a disco number which reached Platinum, and with Barry Gibb on the album, *Guilty*. Her film career continued into the early 80s with *All Night Long* (1981) and *Yentl*, (1983) which she co-produced and directed. By the mid-80s Streisand's career appeared to be on cruise. However, she starred in and wrote the music for *Nuts* (1987), a film which received mixed reviews. Growing concern for ecological matters revealed themselves in public statements and on such occasions as the recording of her 1986 video/album, *One Voice*. In 1991 she was criticized for another directorial assignment on *Prince Of Tides*. As a performer, Streisand was one of the greatest showbiz phenomenons of the 60s. Her wide vocal range and a voice which unusually blends sweetness with strength, helps make Streisand one of the outstanding dramatic singers in popular music. Her insistence upon perfection has meant that her many records are exemplars for other singers. Her latest movie, *Prince Of Tides*, released in 1991, has been nominated for seven Oscars.

Albums: *The Barbra Streisand Album* (1962), *The Second Barbra Streisand Album* (1963), *Barbra Streisand: The Third Album* (1964), *Funny Girl* (1964), *People* (1964), *My Name Is Barbra* (1965), *Color Me Barbra* (1966), *Je M'Appelle Barbra* (1967), *What About Today?* (1969), *Stoney End* (1970), *Barbra Joan Streisand* (1971), *Classical Barbra* (1974), *Butterfly* (1975), *Lazy Afternoon* (1975), *Streisand Superman* (1977), *Songbird* (1978), *Wet* (1979), *Guilty* (1980), *One Voice* (1986).
Further reading: *Streisand: The Woman and the Legend*, James Spada. *Barbra Streisand, The Woman, The Myth, The Music*, Shawn Considine.

String-Driven Thing

With animated, shock-headed violinist Graham Smith their visual selling-point, Pauline Adams (vocals), her husband Chris (guitar/vocals) and Colin Wilson (guitar/bass) trod an idiosyncratically British rock path in the early 70s. Like acts of similar stamp, they were later augmented by a drummer - when Billy Fairley toughened up the sound on their second album which also featured new recruits Clare Sealey (cello) and Bill Hatje (who took over Wilson's bass duties). The band's performances on children's television proved surprisingly popular, and a wider fame was predicted. The departure of the Adamses and Hatje in 1974 was seen as unfortunate but by no means disastrous as the group were able to continue in recognizable form with, respectively, Kimberley Beacon, Graham White and James Exell for *Please Mind Your Head* - on which Henry McDonald (keyboards) and jazz saxophonist Alan Skidmore (then one of Georgie Fame's Blue Flames) were heard too. Even more iconoclastic was the appearance of *Oh Boy* regular Cuddley Dudley on mouth organ for their final album before Smith's defection to Van Der Graaf Generator in 1976 and String-Driven Thing's correlated sundering.
Albums: *String-Driven Thing* (1972), *Machine That Cried* (1973), *Please Mind Your Head* (1974), *Keep Yer 'And On It* (1975).

Stylistics

The Stylistics were formed in 1968 from the fragments of two Philadelphia groups, the Monarchs and the Percussions, by Russell Thompkins Jnr (b. 21 March 1951, Philadelphia, Pennsylvania, USA), Airrion Love (b. 8 August 1949, Philadelphia, Pennsylvania, USA), James

Stylistics

Smith (b. 16 June 1950, New York City, USA), Herbie Murrell (b. 27 April 1949, Lane, S. Carolina, USA) and James Dunn (b. 4 February 1950, Philadelphia, Pennsylvania, USA). The quintet's debut single, 'You're A Big Girl Now' was initially issued on a local independent, but became a national hit following its acquisition by the Avco label. The Stylistics were then signed to this outlet directly and teamed with producer/composer Thom Bell. This skillful musician had already worked successfully with the Delfonics and his sculpted, sweet soul arrangements proved ideal for his new charges. In partnership with lyricist Linda Creed, Bell fashioned a series of immaculate singles, including 'You Are Everything' (1971), 'Betcha By Golly Wow' and 'I'm Stone In Love With You' (both 1972), where Simpkins' aching voice soared against the group's sumptuous harmonies and a cool, yet inventive accompaniment. The style reached its apogee in 1974 with 'You Make Me Feel Brand New', a number 2 single in both the US and UK. This release marked the end of Bell's collaboration with the group who were now pushed towards the easy listening market. With arranger Van McCoy turning sweet into saccharine, the material grew increasingly bland, while Thompkins' falsetto, once heartfelt, now seemed contrived. Although their American fortune waned, the Stylistics continued to enjoy success in Britain with 'Sing Baby Sing', 'Can't Give You Anything (But My Love)' (both 1975) and '16 Bars' (1976), while a compilation album that same year, *The Best Of The Stylistics*,

became one of the UK's best-selling albums. Despite this remarkable popularity, purists labelled the group a parody of its former self. Ill-health forced Dunn to retire in 1978, whereupon the remaining quartet left Avco for a brief spell with Mercury. Two years later they were signed to the TSOP/Philadelphia International stable, which resulted in some crafted recordings reminiscent of their heyday, but problems within the company undermined the group's progress. Subsequent singles for Streetwise took the Stylistics into the lower reaches of the R&B chart, but their halcyon days now seem to be over.

Albums: *The Stylistics* (1971), *Round 2: The Stylistics* (1972), *Rockin' Roll Baby* (1973), *Let's Put It All Together* (1974), *Heavy* (UK title: *From The Mountain*) (1974), *Thank You Baby* (1975), *You Are Beautiful* (1975), *Fabulous* (1976), *Once Upon A Juke Box* (1976), *Sun And Soul* (1977), *Wonder Woman* (1978), *In Fashion* (1978), *Black Satin* (1979), *Love Spell* (1979), *Live In Japan* (1979), *The Lion Sleeps Tonight* (1979), *Hurry Up This Way Again* (1980), *Closer Than Close* (1981), *1982* (1982), *Some Things Never Change* (1985). Compilations *The Best Of The Stylistics* (1975), *Spotlight On The Stylistics* (1977).

Summer, Donna

b. Ladonna Gaines, 31 December 1948, Boston, Massachusetts, USA, Summer's 'Love To Love You Baby' made her the best-known of all 70s disco divas. Having sung with rock bands in Boston, Summer moved to Europe in 1968 and appeared in German versions of *Hair* and *Porgy And*

Bess and married Austrian actor Helmut Sommer, from whom she took her stage name. Summer's first records were 'Hostage' and 'Lady Of The Night' for Giorgio Moroder's Oasis label in Munich. They were local hits but it was 'Love To Love You Baby' (1975) which made her an international star. The track featured Summer's erotic sighs and moans above Moroder's hypnotic disco beats and it sold a million copies in the US on Neil Bogart's Casablanca label. In 1977, a similar formula took 'I Feel Love' to the top of the UK chart and 'Down Deep Inside', Summer's theme song for the film *The Deep* was a big international success. Her own film debut came the next year in *Thank God It's Friday* in which she sang another million-seller 'Last Dance'. This was the peak period of Summer's career as she scored three more US number 1s in 1978-79 with a revival of Jim Webb's 'MacArthur Park', 'Hot Stuff', 'Bad Girls' and 'No More tears (Enough Is Enough)' a duet with Barbra Streisand. The demise of disco coincided with a legal dispute between Summer and Bogart and in 1980 she signed to David Geffen's new company.

Her work now took on a more pronounced soul and gospel flavour - she had become a born-again Christian. Her only big hit during the early 80s was 'Love Is In Control (Finger On The Trigger)' in 1982, produced by Quincy Jones. After a three year absence from music, Summer returned in 1987 with a US and European tour. Her best-selling 1989 album for Warner Brothers was written and produced by Stock Aitken And Waterman while Clivilles & Cole worked on *Love Is Gonna Change.*

Albums: *Love To Love You Baby* (1975), *A Love Trilogy* (1976), *Four Seasons Of Love* (1976), *I Remember Yesterday* (1977), *Once Upon A Time* (1977), *Live And More* (1978), *Bad Girls* (1979), *The Wanderer* (1980), *Donna Summer* (1982), *She Works Hard For The Money* (1983), *Cats Without Claws* (1984), *All Systems Go* (1987), *Another Place And Time* (1989), *Love Is Gonna Change* (1990), *Mistaken Identity* (1991). Compilations: *On The Radio - Greatest Hits, Volumes 1 And 2* (1979), *Walk Away - Collector's Edition (The Best Of 1977-1980)* (1980), *The Best Of Donna Summer* (1990).

Supertramp

Many aspiring musicians would have envied the opportunity which was given to Supertramp in 1969. They were financed by the Dutch millionaire Stanley August Miesegaes, and this enabled Richard Davies (b. 22 July 1944, Swindon, Wiltshire, England; vocals/keyboards) to recruit, through the *Melody Maker,* the band of his choice.

Supertramp

He enlisted Roger Hodgson (b. 21 March 1950, Portsmouth, Hampshire, England; guitar), Dave Winthrop (b. 27 November 1948, New Jersey, USA; saxophone), Richard Palmer (guitar) and Bob Miller (drums). The debut *Supertramp* was an unspectacular affair of lengthy self-indulgent solos. The follow-up, *Indelibly Stamped* was similarly unsuccessful and meandering; the controversial cover created most interest, depicting a busty, naked tattooed female. The band were in dire straits when their fairy godfather departed, along with Winthrop and Palmer. They recruited ex-Alan Bown band members, John Helliwell (b. 15 February 1945, Todmorden, Yorkshire, England) and Dougie Thompson (b. 24 March 1951, Glasgow, Scotland) and from Bees Make Honey, Bob Benberg. They had a remarkable change in fortune as *Crime Of The Century* became one of the top-selling albums of 1974. The band had refined their keyboard dominated sound and produced an album that was well-reviewed. Their debut hit 'Dreamer' was taken from the album, while 'Bloody Well Right' was a Top 40 hit in the USA and went on to become one of their classic live numbers. The subsequent *Crisis? What Crisis?* and *Even In The Quietest Moments* were lesser works, being erratic in content. The choral 'Give A Little Bit', with its infectious acoustic guitar introduction was a minor transatlantic hit in 1977. Supertramp were elevated to the rock's first division with the faultless *Breakfast In America*. Four of the tracks became hits, 'The Logical Song', 'Take The Long Way Home', 'Goodbye Stranger' and the title track. The album stayed on top of the US charts for six weeks and became their biggest seller, with over 18 million copies to date. The obligatory live album came in 1980 and was followed by the R&B influenced *Famous Last Words*. Hodgson left shortly afterwards, unhappy with the bluesier direction the band were taking and he made two respectable solo albums; *In The Eye Of A Storm* and *Hai Hai*. Supertramp continued with occasional tours and infrequent albums. Their recent releases, however, have only found minor success.

Albums: *Supertramp* (1970), *Indelibly Stamped* (1971), *Crime Of The Century* (1974), *Crisis? What Crisis?* (1975), *Even In The Quietest Moments* (1977), *Breakfast In America* (1979), *Paris* (1980), *Famous Last Words* (1982), *Brother Where You Bound* (1985), *Free As A Bird* (1987), *Supertramp Live 88* (1988). Compilation: *The Autobiography Of Supertramp* (1986).

Sutherland Brothers (And Quiver)

Iain Sutherland (vocals/guitar/keyboards) and Gavin Sutherland (guitar/vocals) were signed to the Island label in 1972. Their first two albums *The Sutherland Brothers Band* and *Lifeboat*, continued the gift for melodic, folk-based pop, exemplified in 'The Pie', their excellent debut single. It was during this period that the duo composed and recorded the original version of 'Sailing', which later became a million-seller for Rod Stewart. Having completed their second album with the use of session musicians, the Sutherlands began seeking a permanent backing group. In 1973, they amalgamated with Quiver, Tim Renwick (guitar), Bruce Thomas (bass) and Willie Wilson (drums), and the ensemble, which also included pianist Pete Wood, was henceforth known as the Sutherland Brothers and Quiver. The meritorious *Dream Kid* celebrated their union and the expanded unit enjoyed a US Top 20 hit with 'You Got Me Anyway'. Thomas left the line-up prior to the release of *Beat Of The Street* (later joining Elvis Costello's Attractions) and was replaced, temporarily, by Tex Comer from Ace until Gavin Sutherland assumed the bassist role. Rod Stewart's success in 1975 with the Sutherland's 'Sailing' prompted CBS to sign the group. *Reach For The Sky*, released in 1975 and a UK Top 5 single, 'Arms Of Mary' augered well for the future. However, the Sutherlands seemed to lose direction during the punk upheaval and their songs lost an erstwhile sparkle and melodic twist. The Quiver connection was severed with the departure of Renwick and Wilson, and the name reverted to 'The Sutherland Brothers' with the release of *When The Night Comes*, in 1979. Four years later Iain Sutherland made his solo debut with *Mixed Emotions*.

Albums: The Sutherland Brothers; *The Sutherland Brothers Band* (1972), *Lifeboat* (1972), *When The Night Comes Down* (1979). The Sutherland Brothers Band And Quiver; *Dream Kid* (1973), *Beat Of The Street* (1974), *Reach For The Sky* (1975), *Slipstream* (1976), *Down To Earth* (1977). Compilation: *Sailing* (1976).

Sweet

The nucleus of the Sweet came together in 1966, when drummer Mick Tucker (b. 17 July 1949, Harlesden, London, England) and vocalist Brian Connolly (b. 5 October 1949, Hamilton, Scotland) played together in Wainwright's Gentlemen, a small-time club circuit band, whose repertoire comprised a mixture of Motown, R&B and

psychedelia. The pair broke away to form Sweetshop, later shortened to just Sweet, with Steve Priest (b. 23 February 1950, Hayes, Middlesex) on bass and Frank Torpey on guitar. After releasing four unsuccessful singles on Fontana and EMI, Torpey was replaced by Andy Scott (b. 30 June 1951, Wrexham, Wales) and the new line-up signed to RCA. The band were introduced to the writing partnership of Chinn And Chapman, who were to provide the band with a string of hit singles. Their initial success was down to bubblegum pop anthems such as 'Funny, Funny', 'Co-Co', 'Poppa Joe' and 'Little Willy'. However, the band were writing their own hard-rock numbers on the b-sides of these hits. This resulted in Chinn/Chapman coming up with heavier pop-rock numbers most notably the powerful 'Blockbuster', which reached number 1 in the UK at the beginning of 1973. The group's determinedly effete, glam-rock image was reinforced by a succession of Top 10 hits, including 'Hell Raiser', 'Ballroom Blitz', 'Teenage Rampage' and 'The Six Teens'.

Sweet decided to take greater control of their own destiny in 1974 and recorded the album *Sweet Fanny Adams*, without the assistance of Chinn and Chapman. The album charted at number 27, but disappeared again after just two weeks. The work marked a significant departure from their commercially-minded singles on which they had built their reputation. 'Set Me Free', 'Restless' and 'Sweet F.A.' epitomized their no-frills hard-rock style. *Desolation Boulevard* included the self-penned 'Fox On The Run' which was to hit number 2 in the UK singles chart. This gave the band confidence and renewed RCA's faith in the band as a commercial proposition. However, as Sweet became more of an albums band, the hit singles began to dry up, with 1978's 'Love Is Like Oxygen' being their last Top 10 hit. Following a move to Polydor, they cut four albums with each release making less impact than its predecessor. Their brand of melodic rock, infused with infectious hooks and brutal riffs, now failed to satisfy both the teenybopper and the more mature rock fan. Since 1982, various incarnations of the band have appeared from time to time, with any number from one to three of the original members in the line-up. The most recent of these was in 1989, when they recorded a live album at London's Marquee Club, with Paul Mario Day (ex-More) handling the vocals. Brian Connolly now suffers from a muscular disorder and his grim situation was warmed in 1992 with the incredible success of the film *Ballroom Blitz* and the subsequent renewed interest in the Sweet.

Albums: *Funny How Sweet Co Co Can Be* (1971), *Sweet* (1973), *Sweet Fanny Adams* (1974), *Desolation Boulevard* (1974), *Strung Up* (1975), *Give Us A Wink* (1976), *Off The Record* (1977), *Level Headed* (1978), *Cut Above The Rest* (1979), *Water's Edge* (1980), *Identity Crisis* (1982), *Live At The Marquee* (1989), *Blockbusters* (1989). Compilations: *Biggest Hits* (1972), *Sweet's Golden Greats* (1983), *Sweet 16 - It's, It's The Sweet's Hits* (1984), *Hard Centres - The Rock Years* (1987), *The Collection* (1989).

Sweet, Rachel

b. 1963, Akron, Ohio, USA. Rachel Sweet sang professionally at the age of five, working as a child model for television commercials in New York and as a support act to Mickey Rooney. At the age of 12 she recorded her first single, the country song 'Faded Rose', on the Derrick label which, along with her follow-up, 'We Live In Two Different Worlds' reached the lower regions of the *Billboard* Country charts. Under the tutelage of manager and songwriter Liam Sternberg, Rachel landed a contract with the pioneering independent UK label Stiff Records. The company had previously distributed a compilation album of Akron acts which included two tracks by the singer. For the Stiff 78 Tour with fellow labelmates Lene Lovich, Wreckless Eric, Jona Lewie and Mickey Jupp, Rachel's backing band were the Records. The single, a version of the Isaac Hayes/David Porter song 'B-A-B-Y', reached the UK Top 40. Sweet possessed a mature voice for someone still in her mid-teens. *Fool Around* saw her tackling Del Shannon's 'I Go To Pieces' and Elvis Costello's 'Stranger In The House' as well as several Sternberg originals. Rachel's obvious talents were dogged by persistent, but tenuous, accusations of her being marketed as 'jail-bait'. After parting with Sternberg in 1979, her second album presented Rachel with a harder image, complete with an advertising campaign bizarrely depicting her as a leather-jacketed, sullen, child abductor. Backed by Fingerprintz, the songs on the album contained cover versions of Lou Reed's 'New Age', Graham Parker's 'Fool's Gold' and the Damned's 'New Rose' as well as the usual quota of country rock. As with the first album, *Protect The Innocent* was a commercial failure, although this time it did not enjoy critical approbation. Her departure from Stiff to CBS saw the release of *...And Then He Kissed Me* which included the UK and US Top 40 hit duet with Rex Smith, 'Everlasting Love' in 1981.

Despite this encouraging start, the mismanaged talents of Rachel Sweet saw her fade from the scene.
Albums: *Fool Around* (1978), *Protect The Innocent* (1980), *...And Then He Kissed Me* (1981).

Sylvester

b. Sylvester James, 1946, Los Angeles, California, USA. Having moved to San Francisco in 1967, James joined the Cockettes, an androgynous theatrical group with whom he made his debut on New Year's Eve 1970. He subsequently pursed a career as 'Ruby Blue' before putting together the Hot Band with James Q. Smith (guitar), Bobby Blood (trumpet), Chris Mostert (saxophone), Kerry Hatch (bass) and Travis Fullerton (drums). The line-up later included vocalists Izora Rhodes and Martha Wash, now better known as the Weather Girls. Early recordings for the Blue Thumb label, coupled with an outrageous live show, secured James' local reputation, but his 'discovery' by former Motown producer Harvey Fuqua led to a much wider audience. In 1978 Sylvester scored two massive disco hits with 'You Make Me Feel (Mighty Real)' and 'Dance (Disco Heat)', performances marked by an unswerving urgency and the singer's soaring falsetto. The artist was adopted by the city's gay community, where later releases proved especially popular. Sylvester's excellent voice and skilled arrangements bestowed a lasting quality on his work, but he died of an AIDS-related illness in 1988. Jimmy Somerville subsequently recorded a version of *Mighty Real* as a tribute to this imaginative performer's talent.
Albums: With the Hot Band; *Sylvester And The Hot Band - Scratch My Flower* (1973), *Bazaar* (1973). Solo; *Sylvester* (1977), *Step II* (1978), *Stars* (1979), *Living Proof* (1979), *Sell My Soul* (1980), *Mighty Real* (1980), *Too Hot To Sleep* (1981), *Sylvester And Griffin* (1982), *All I Need* (1983), *Call Me* (1984), *M1015* (1984), *Mutual Attraction* (1987). Compilations: *Star - The Best Of Sylvester* (1989), *The Original Hits* (1989).

Syreeta

b. Rita Wright, Pittsburgh, Philadelphia, USA. Like Martha Reeves, Syreeta joined the staff of Motown Records as a secretary rather than a recording artist. In the mid-60s she sang occasional backing vocals on Motown sessions, and in 1967 Ashford and Simpson produced her debut single, 'I Can't Give Back The Love I Feel For You', which became a cult record among British soul fans. In 1968 she met Stevie Wonder, who encouraged her to begin songwriting. She co-wrote his 1970 hit 'Signed, Sealed, Delivered (I'm Yours)', and also commenced work on the song-cycle which became *Where I'm Coming From*. The couple were married on 14 September 1970, and although they were divorced just 18 months later, they continued to work together for several years. In 1972, Wonder produced *Syreeta*, a stunning collection of soft-soul and light-funk which showcased her fluent, joyous vocals. The collaboration allowed Stevie to experiment with studio techniques that he perfected on his own later projects, and also inspired one of his earliest pronouncements of black pride on the affecting ballad 'Black Maybe'. *Stevie Wonder Presents Syreeta* in 1974 continued the pair's close musical partnership, and produced a British hit in the reggae-flavoured 'Your Kiss Is Sweet'. The couple's last joint recording, 'Harm Our Love' in 1975, was also their most commercial, and its success in the UK and USA gave Syreeta a platform from which to build. She teamed up with G.C. Cameron for a disappointing album of duets before completing a more fulfilling partnership with Billy Preston, which produced the soundtrack for the film *Fast Break*, and a US and UK Top 10 hit, the sentimental love song, 'With You I'm Born Again'. Syreeta and Preston completed a further album project in 1981. Her solo recordings were less successful, and after the Jermaine Jackson-produced *The Spell* in 1983, she abandoned her career to concentrate on raising a family. In the late 80s, Syreeta recorded several tracks for Ian Levine's Motor City label, including a solo rendition of 'With You I'm Born Again' and new duets with Billy Preston.
Albums: *Syreeta* (1972), *Stevie Wonder Presents Syreeta* (1974), *One To One* (1977), with G.C. Cameron *Rich Love, Poor Love* (1977), with Billy Preston *Fast Break* (1979), *Syreeta* (1980), *Billy Preston And Syreeta* (1981), *Set My Love In Motion* (1981), *The Spell* (1983).

T

Talking Heads

One of the most critically acclaimed groups of the past two decades, Talking Heads pursued an idiosyncratic path of (often) uncompromising brilliance. After graduating from the Rhode Island School of Design, students David Byrne (b. 14 May 1952, Dumbarton, Scotland; vocals/guitar), Chris Frantz (b. Charlton Christopher Frantz, 8 May 1951, Fort Campbell, Kentucky, USA; drums) and Tina Weymouth (b. Martina Weymouth, 22 November 1950, Coronado, California, USA; bass) relocated to New York. In 1975, they lived and rehearsed in Manhattan and named themselves Talking Heads. After appearing at the club CBGBs, they were approached by Seymour Stein of Sire Records, who would eventually sign the group. Early in 1976, the line-up was expanded to include pianist Jerry Harrison (b. Jeremiah Harrison, 21 February 1949, Milwaukee, Wisconsin, USA), a former member of Jonathan Richman's Modern Lovers. The group's art school background, witty invention and musical unorthodoxy was evident on their intriguingly titled debut, 'Love Goes To Building On Fire'. After touring extensively, they issued *Talking Heads '77*, an exhilarating first album, which was widely praised for its verve and intelligence. The highlight of the set was the insistent 'Psycho Killer', a *tour de force*, in which singer Byrne displayed his deranged vocal dramatics to the full. His wide-eyed stare, jerky movements and onstage cool reminded many commentators of Anthony Perkins, star of Hitchcock's movie *Psycho*.

For their second album, the group turned to Brian Eno as producer. *More Songs About Buildings And Food* was a remarkable work, its title echoing Talking Heads' anti-romantic subject matter. Byrne's eccentric vocal phrasing was brilliantly complemented by some startling rhythm work and the songs were uniformly excellent. The climactic 'The Big Country' a satiric commentary on consumerist America, featured the scathing aside: 'I wouldn't live there if you paid me'. The album also featured one cover version, an interesting reading of Al Green's 'Take Me To The River', which was a minor hit. Eno's services were retained for the more opaque *Fear Of Music*, which included the popular 'Life During Wartime'. Byrne

next collaborated with Eno on *My Life In The Bush Of Ghosts*, before the group reunited for *Remain In Light*. The latter boasted the superb 'Once In A Lifetime', complete with 'found voices' and African polyrhythms. An edited version of the song provided one of the best hit singles of 1981. During the early 80s, the group's extra-curricular activites increased and while Byrne explored ballet on *The Catherine Wheel*, Franz and Weymouth found success with their spin-off project, Tom Tom Club. The live double *The Name Of This Band Is Talking Heads* served as a stop-gap until *Speaking In Tongues* appeared in the summer of 1983. As ambitious as ever, the album spawned the group's UK Top 10 single, 'Burning Down The House'. While touring with additional guitarist Alex Weir (formerly of the Brothers Four), the group were captured on film in *Stop Making Sense*, the soundtrack of which sold well. The excellent *Little Creatures*, a more accessible offering than their more experimental work, featured three strong singles in the title track, 'And She Was' and 'Road To Nowhere'. The latter brought the group their biggest chart hit and was accompanied by an imaginative and highly entertaining video. In 1986, Byrne moved more forcibly into movies with *True Stories*, for which Talking Heads provided the soundtrack; it was two more years before the group reconvened for *Naked*. Produced by Steve Lillywhite, the work included musical contributions from Level 42 producer Wally Badarou and guitarists Yves N'Djock and Johnny Marr (from the Smiths). Since then Talking Heads have branched out into various offshoot ventures; there was an official announcement of their break-up at the end of 1991.

Albums: *Talking Heads '77* (1977), *More Songs About Buildings And Food* (1978), *Fear Of Music* (1979), *Remain In Light* (1980), *The Name Of This Band Is Talking Heads* (1982), *Speaking In Tongues* (1983), *Stop Making Sense* (1984), *Little Creatures* (1985), *True Stories* (1986, film soundtrack), *Naked* (1988), *Sand In The Vaseline* (1992). Compilation: *Once In A Lifetime* (1992).

Tangerine Dream

Like Amon Duul and Can, Tangerine Dream were German-based purveyors of imaginative electronic music. There have been numerous line-ups since the band's formation in 1968, although Edgar Froese (b. 6 June 1944, Tilsit, East Prussia) has remained at the head of affairs throughout. After playing with college band the Ones, who released a single and performed for Salvador Dali at his villa,

Talking Heads

Froese put together Tangerine Dream with himself on guitar, Voker Hombach (flute/violin), Kirt Herkenber (bass) and Lanse Hapshash (drums). Heavily influenced by US bands like the Doors, Jefferson Airplane and the Grateful Dead, they performed live at various student counter culture events. By 1969 they had split and remained inactive until Froese recruited Steve Jollife (electric flute). He departed soon after, although he would return to the fold later. A debut album was recorded, for which Froese brought in Konrad Schnitzler and Klaus Schulze, who would later embark on a solo career for Virgin Records. Jazz drummer Christoph Franke (ex-Agitation Free) joined in 1971, as did organist Steve Schroyder. This line-up recorded *Alpha Centauri*, which combined space age rock in the style of Pink Floyd with classical structures. Peter Baumann (ex-Ants)

replaced Schroyder, and this became the band's first stable line-up, staying together until 1977.

Zeit saw the band's instrumentation incorporate new synthesizer technology, while *Atem* focused on atmospheric, restrained passages. Influential BBC disc jockey John Peel elected it the best album of 1983. *Phaedra* established their biggest foothold in the UK market when it reached number 15 in the album charts in 1974. Their attentions turned, however, to a series of soundtracks, while Froese released his first solo, *Aqua*. At the height of punk, and as one of the named targets of the insurrection, *Stratosfear* emerged. It was their most commercial album so far. Guitar, piano and harpsichord were all incorporated, taking the edge off the harsh electronics. After the hectic touring schedule of the following year, Baumann left to pursue his solo career. He would go on to form his own Private Music label, and, ironically, sign Tangerine Dream for releases in the USA. He was replaced by former member and multi-instrumentalist Jollife, as well as drummer Klaus Kreiger. The ensuing *Cyclone* featured vocals and lyrics for the first time, although they returned to instrumental work with *Force Majeure*. As the new decade dawned, the band became the first western combo to play in East Berlin. *Tangram* and *Exit* relied on melody more than their precursors, the latter featuring the emotive 'Kiev Mission', which included a message from the Russian Peace Movement. *Le Parc* used advanced sampling technology, which seemed to be a little at odds with the band's natural abilities. Schmoelling became the next to depart for a solo career in 1985, replaced by classically trained Paul Haslinger. Three years later Chris Franke, after 17 years service, followed Schmoelling's example. Computer programmer Ralf Wadephal took his place but when he left the band elected to continue as a duo. Although often criticized, the band are pivotal in refining a sound which effectively pioneered new-age ambient electronic music more than a decade later. Their importance in this field should not be underestimated.

Albums: (not including the multitude of soundtrack albums) *Electronic Meditation* (1970), *Alpha Centauri* (1971), *Zeit* (1972), *Atem* (1973), *Phaedra* (1974), *Rubycon* (1975), *Ricochet* (1975), *Stratosfear* (1976), *Encore* (1977), *Cyclone* (1978), *Force Majeure* (1979), *Tangram* (1980), *Quichotte* (1980), *Exit* (1981), *White Eagle* (1982), *Hyperborea* (1983), *Le Parc* (1985), *Underwater Sunlight* (1986), *Tyger* (1987), *Optical Race* (1988), *Lily On The Beach* (1989), *Melrose* (1990), *Rockoon* (1992). Compilation: *The Collection* (1987).

Taupin, Bernie

b. 22 May 1950, Sleaford, Lincolnshire, England. Taupin is recalled principally, as the title of his own memoirs affirms, as 'The One Who Writes The Words For Elton John', even though this lucrative partnership terminated in 1976, nearly a decade after the two independently answered a Liberty Records music press advertisement for new talent. Put together by A&R representative Ray Williams, John and Taupin (then fresh from school as a Lincolnshire farm labourer) were engaged as songwriters by Dick James Music. Initially, they collaborated by post; John putting melodies to Taupin's lines in which the sound of the words rather than their sense permeated early efforts such as 'When The First Tear Shows', an a-side by

Brian Keith (ex-Plastic Penny).

As John's career as a singing pianist took off, Taupin's output exuded a strong romanticism, most notably on the reflective 'Your Song,' John's chart debut. Taupin went on to produce David Ackles' *American Gothic*, which was a minor US chart entry in 1972. A couple of prosaically-named Taupin solo albums were thought expedient, but despite tuneful vocals and sterling accompaniment from guitarists Shawn Phillips and Caleb Quaye, his prominence as a performer was infinitely less than that of flamboyant Elton, the 'Captain Fantastic' of the autobiographical 1975 album - with Taupin as the 'Brown Dirt Cowboy'.

By then, Taupin was exploring the stance of 'the-outsider-versus-society', epitomized by North American outlaw themes reminiscent of the Band, and prevalent on 1970's *Tumbleweed Connection*. An advantage of his comparative facelessness was freedom to roam abroad. Taupin's perceptive observations and self-projections often converted into skilful librettos, as in 'Snookeroo,' an overview of a squandered youth in Liverpool, made-to-measure for Ringo Starr's *Goodnight Vienna*. Nevertheless, John's melodies saved the throwaway 'Your Sister Can't Twist,' and rendered unto trite couplets like 'Hollywood created a superstar/And pain was the price you paid' (from 'Candle In The Wind') an undeserved 'beautiful sadness'.

Free of John, Taupin's career became caught in the wealthy lethargy of Los Angeles. His own infrequent albums were overshadowed by additional collaborations with Alice Cooper (*From The Inside*) which featured 'How You Gonna See Me Now', an exorcism of the horrors of alcoholism. During this time he jointly composed the US number 1 'We Built This City' for Starship. During the 80s Taupin was reunited as Elton's principal lyricist and both the film *Two Rooms* and the accompanying album confirmed the John/Taupin musical partnership as one of the greatest of all time.

Albums: *Bernie Taupin* (1970), *Taupin* (1971), *He Who Rides The Tiger* (1980).
Further reading: *The One Who Writes The Words For Elton John*, Bernie Taupin. *Elton*, Philip Norman.

Tavares

This US group was formed in 1964 in New Bedford, Massachusetts, USA. The line-up consisted of five brothers, Ralph, Antone 'Chubby', Feliciano 'Butch', Arthur 'Pooch' and

Perry Lee 'Tiny' Tavares. Originally known as Chubby And The Turnpikes, the group assumed its family's surname in 1969. Although they lacked a distinctive lead voice or a characteristic sound, Tavares' undemanding blend of light soul and pop resulted in several commercial successes. The brothers' early run of R&B hits culminated in 1975 with 'It Only Takes A Minute', a soul chart-topper and a US pop Top 10 entry. The following year the group scored their sole million-seller in 'Heaven Must Be Missing An Angel' before enjoying further success with one of their strongest songs, 'Don't Take Away The Music'. Both of these singles reached number 4 in the UK where Tavares enjoyed an enduring popularity. 'Whodunit' (1977) was another major release, while 'More Than A Woman' (1978), a song from that year's box-office smash, *Saturday Night Fever*, gave the group their last significant hit. Tavares continued to reach the R&B lists until 1984, but their safe, almost old-fashioned style gradually fell from favour.
Albums: *Check It Out* (1974), *Hard Core Poetry* (1974), *In The City* (1975), *Sky High!* (1976), *Love Storm* (1977), *Future Bound* (1978), *Madam Butterfly* (1979), *Supercharged* (1980), *New Directions* (1982). Compilation: *The Best Of The Tavares* (1977).

Taylor, James

b. 12 March 1948, Boston, Massachusetts, USA. The embodiment of the American singer-songwriter from the late 60s and early 70s was the frail and troubled James Taylor. He was born into a wealthy family. His mother was a classically trained soprano and encouraged James and his siblings to become musical. As a child he wanted for nothing and divided his time between two substantial homes. He befriended Danny 'Kootch' Kortchmar at the age of 15 and won a local talent contest. As is often the case, boarding school education often suits the parents more than the child, and James rebelled from Milton Academy at the age of 16 to join his brother Alex in a rock band, the Fabulous Corsairs. At only 17 he committed himself to the McLean Mental Institution in Massachusetts. Following his nine-month stay he re-united with 'Kootch' and together they formed the commercially disastrous Flying Machine. At 18, now being supported by his parents in his own apartment, the seemingly affluent James drew the predictable crowd of hangers-on and emotional parasites. He experimented and soon was addicted to heroin. He had the drive to move out, and after several months of travelling he arrived in London

and found a flat in Notting Hill (which in 1968 was hardly the place for someone trying to kick a drug habit!). Once again 'Kootch' came to the rescue, and suggested Taylor take a demo tape to Peter Asher. 'Kootch' had supported Peter And Gordon on an American tour, and Asher was now looking for talent as head of the new Apple Records. Both Asher and Paul McCartney liked the work and the thin, weak and by now world-weary teenager was given the opportunity to record. *James Taylor* was not a success when released, even though classic songs like 'Carolina On My Mind' and 'Something In The Way She Moves' appeared on it.
Depressed and still hooked on heroin, Taylor returned to America, this time to the Austin Riggs Mental Institution. Meanwhile Asher, frustrated at the disorganized Apple, moved to America, and persevering with Taylor, he secured a deal with Warner Brothers and rounded up a team of supportive musician friends; 'Kootch', Leland Sklar, Russ Kunkel and Carole King. Many of the songs written in the institution appeared on the superlative *Sweet Baby James*. The album eventually spent two years in the US charts and contained a jewel of a song: 'Fire And Rain'. In this, he encapsulated his entire life, problems and fears; it stands as one of the finest songs of the era. Taylor received rave notices from critics and he was quickly elevated to superstardom. The follow-up *Mud Slide Slim And The Blue Horizon* consolidated the previous success and contained the definitive reading of Carole King's 'You've Got a Friend'. In 1972, now free of drugs, Taylor worked with the Beach Boys' Dennis Wilson on the cult drag-race film *Two Lane Blacktop* and released *One Man Dog* which contained another hit 'Don't Let Me Be Lonely Tonight'. Fortunately Taylor was not lonely for long; he married Carly Simon in the biggest show business wedding since Burton and Taylor. They duetted on a version of the Charlie And Inez Foxx hit, 'Mockingbird' which made the US Top 5 in 1974.
Taylor's albums began to form a pattern of mostly original compositions, mixed with an immaculately chosen blend of R&B, soul and rock 'n' roll classics. Ironically most of his subsequent hits were non-originals. Holland Dozier And Holland's 'How Sweet It Is', Otis Blackwell's 'Handy Man', Goffin And King's 'Up On The Roof'. Taylor was also displaying confidence and sparkling onstage wit, having a superb rapport with his audiences, where once his shyness was excruciating. Simon filed for divorce a decade after their marriage, but

James Taylor

Taylor accepted the breakdown and carried on with his profession. The assured Taylor is instrumentally captured by Pat Metheny's joyous composition 'James' recorded on Metheny's *Offramp* album in 1982. In 1985 Taylor released the immaculate *That's Why I'm Here* . The reason he is here as the lyric explains is; 'fortune and fame is such a curious game, perfect strangers can call you by name, pay good money to hear "Fire And Rain", again and again and again'. This one song says as much about James Taylor today as 'Fire And Rain' did many years ago. He has survived, he is happy, he is still creative and above all his concerts show that he is genuinely grateful to be able to perform.

Albums: *James Taylor* (1968), *Sweet Baby James* (1970), *James Taylor And The Original Flying Machine - 1967* (1970), *Mud Slide Slim And The Blue Horizon* (1971), *One Man Dog* (1972), *Walking Man* (1974), *Gorilla* (1975), *In The Pocket* (1976), *JT* (1977), *Flag* (1979), *Dad Loves His Work* (1981), *That's Why I'm Here* (1985), *Never Die Young* (1988), *New Moon Shine* (1991). Compilations: *Greatest Hits* (1976), *Classic Songs* (1987), *The Best Of James Taylor - The Classic Years* (1990).

Taylor, R. Dean

Toronto-born R. Dean Taylor remains the most successful white artist to emerge from the Motown Records stable. The protege of writer/producer Brian Holland, he worked on many of the mid-60s hits produced by the Holland/Dozier/Holland partnership, and later claimed to have helped compose several songs credited to them. He began his recording career in 1965, with 'Let's Go Somewhere', but found more success with two of his compositions for the Supremes, 'Love Child' and 'I'm Living In Shame', both of which brought a new realism into the group's work. In 1967, he recorded the classic soul number 'There's A Ghost In My House', which enjoyed cult status in Britain. A year later he released the evocative 'Gotta See Jane', which also charted in the UK that summer. His most memorable single was 'Indiana Wants Me', an effect-laden melodrama which climbed high in both the UK and US charts in 1970. Despite his popularity in Britain, where a revival of 'There's A Ghost In My House' reached the Top 3 in 1974, Taylor was unable to repeat this success with his subsequent recordings, either on his own Jane label in 1973, or with Polydor from 1974.

Albums: *I Think Therefore I Am* (1970), *Indiana Wants Me* (1971), *LA Sunset* (1975).

Television

Lead guitarist/vocalist Tom Verlaine (b. Thomas Miller, 13 December 1949, Mount Morris, New Jersey, USA) first worked with bassist Richard Hell (b. Richard Myers, 2 October 1949, Lexington, Kentucky, USA) and drummer Billy Ficca in the early 70s as the Neon Boys. By the end of 1973, with the addition of rhythm guitarist Richard Lloyd, they reunited as Television. Early the following year, they secured a residency at the Bowery club CBGB's and found themselves at the forefront of the New York new wave explosion. Conflicts between Verlaine and Hell led to the departure of the latter who would soon re-emerge with the Heartbreakers. Meanwhile, Television found a replacement bassist in Fred 'Sonic' Smith from Blondie. The new line-up recorded the raw but interesting 'Little Johnny Jewel' for their own label Ork Records. This led to their signing with Elektra Records for whom they recorded their debut album in 1977. *Marquee Moon* was largely ignored in their homeland, but elicited astonished, ecstatic reviews in the UK where it was applauded as one of rock's most accomplished debut albums. Verlaine's sneering, nasal vocal and searing, jagged twin guitar interplay with Lloyd were the hallmarks of Television's work, particularly on such stand-out tracks as 'Torn Curtain', 'Venus' and 'Prove It'. Although the group looked set for a long and distinguished career, the follow-up *Adventure* was a lesser work and the group split in 1978. Since then both Verlaine and Lloyd pursued solo careers with mixed results. In November 1991, Verlaine, Lloyd, Smith and Ficca revived Television and spent the ensuing time rehearsing for a come back album for Capitol Records. They made an appearance at the 1992 Glastonbury Festival.

Albums: *Marquee Moon* (1978), *Adventure* (1979), *The Blow Up* (1990, rec. live 1978).

10cc

The formation of 10cc in 1970 represented the birth of a Manchester supergroup. The line-up - Eric Stewart (b. 20 January 1945, Manchester, England; vocals/guitar), Lol Creme (b. Lawrence Creme, 9 September 1947, Manchester, England; vocals/guitar), Kevin Godley (b. 7 October 1945, Manchester, England; vocals/drums) and Graham Gouldman (b. 10 May 1945, Manchester, England; vocals/guitar) - boasted years of musical experience stretching back to the mid-60s. Stewart was a former member of both Wayne Fontana And The Mindbenders and the Mindbenders; Gouldman had

played in the Mockingbirds and written many hits for such artists as Herman's Hermits, the Yardbirds, the Hollies and Jeff Beck; Godley And Creme had worked in various session groups, including Hotlegs, which had spawned 10cc. After working with Neil Sedaka, the 10cc ensemble launched their own recording career on Jonathan King's UK label with the 50s doo-wop pastiche 'Donna'. The song reached number 2 in the UK chart, spearheading a run which continued almost uninterrupted until the end of the decade. 10cc specialized in reinterpreting pop's great tradition by affectionately adopting old styles and introducing them to new teenage audiences. At the same time, their wit, word play and subtle satire appealed to an older audience, who appreciated mild irony, strong musicianship and first rate production. The chart-topping 'Rubber Bullets', the high school romp 'The Dean And I', the sardonic 'Wall Street Shuffle', zestful 'Silly Love' and mock-philosophical 'Life Is A Minestrone' were all delightful slices of 70s pop and among the best singles of their time. In 1975, the group achieved their most memorable hit with the tragi-comic UK chart-topper 'I'm Not In Love', a song that also brought them success in the USA. The group continued its peak period with the mischievous 'Art For Art Sake' and bizarre travelogue 'I'm Mandy Fly Me' before internal strife undermined their progress. In 1976, the group split in half as Godley And Creme pursued work in video production and as a recording duo. Stewart and Gouldman retained the 10cc tag and toured with a line-up comprising Tony O'Malley (keyboards), Rick Fenn (guitar) and Stuart Tosh (drums). The streamlined 10cc continued to chart with the over-sweetened 'The Things We Do For Love' and the mock-reggae chart topper 'Dreadlock Holiday'. Nevertheless, it was generally agreed that their recordings lacked the depth, invention, humour and charm of the original line-up. The hits ceased after 1982 and Stewart and Gouldman went on to pursue other ventures. The former produced Sad Cafe and collaborated with Paul McCartney, while the more industrious Gouldman produced Gilbert O'Sullivan and the Ramones before forming the duo Wax, with Andrew Gold. 10cc issued a new album in 1992 after Gouldman and Stewart, writing songs with each other after a long break. Godley and Creme joined in during the recording, although they did not participate in any writing.
Albums: *10cc* (1973), *Sheet Music* (1974), *The Original Soundtrack* (1975), *How Dare You* (1976), *Deceptive Bends* (1977), *Live And Let Live* (1977), *Bloody Tourists* (1978), *Look Hear!* (1980), *Ten Out Of 10* (1981), *10cc In Concert* (1982), *Window In The Jungle* (1983), *Meanwhile* (1992). Compilations: *10cc - The Greatest Hits* (1975), *Greatest Hits 1972-1978* (1979).

Thin Lizzy

Formed in Dublin, Eire in 1969, this hard-rocking group comprised Phil Lynott (b. 20 August 1951, Dublin, Eire, d. 4 January 1986; vocals/bass), Eric Bell (b. 3 September 1947, Belfast, Northern Ireland; guitar) and Brian Downey (b. 27 January 1951, Dublin, Eire; drums). After signing to Decca, they issued two albums, neither of which charted. A change of fortune occurred after they recorded a novelty rock version of the traditional 'Whiskey In The Jar'. The single reached the UK Top 10 and popularized the group's blend of Irish folk elements and strident guitar work. The group underwent a series of line-up changes during early 1974. Bell was replaced by Gary Moore and two more temporary guitarists were recruited, Andy Gee and John Cann. The arrival of guitarists Brian Robertson (b. 12 September 1956, Glasgow, Scotland) and Scott Gorham (b. 17 March 1951, Santa Monica, California, USA) stabilized the group as they entered their most productive phase. A series of UK concerts throughout 1975 saw the group make considerable headway. 1976 was the breakthrough year with the acclaimed *Jailbreak* hitting the charts. The driving macho-celebrating 'The Boys Are Back In Town' reached the UK Top 10 and US Top 20 and was voted single of the year by the influential and discerning *New Musical Express*. In early 1977, Robertson was forced to leave the group due to a hand injury following a fight and was replaced by the returning Moore. Another UK Top 20 hit followed with the scathing 'Don't Believe A Word' from the album *Johnny The Fox*. Moore then returned to Colosseum and the recovered Robertson took his place. Both 'Dancin' In The Moonlight' and *Bad Reputation* were UK Top 10 hits and were soon followed by the excellent double album, *Live And Dangerous*. 1979 saw the group scaling new commercial heights with such Top 20 singles as 'Waiting For An Alibi' and 'Do Anything You Want To', plus the best-selling *Black Rose*. The tortuous line-up changes continued apace. Robertson again left and joined Wild Horses. Moore returned, but within a year was replaced by Midge Ure (formerly of Slik and the Rich Kids). By late 1979, the peripatetic Ure had moved on to Ultravox and was replaced by Snowy White. In

Thin Lizzy

early 1980, Lynott married Caroline Crowther, daughter of the television personality Leslie Crowther. After recording some solo work, Lynott reunited with Thin Lizzy for *Chinatown*, which included the controversial Top 10 single, 'Killer On The Loose'. The heavily-promoted *Adventures Of Thin Lizzy* maintained their standing, before White bowed out on *Renegade*. He was replaced by John Sykes, formerly of the Tygers Of Pan Tang. One more album, *Thunder And Lightning*, followed before Lynott split up the group in the summer of 1984. A posthumous live album, *Life-Live* was issued at the end of that year. Its title took on an ironically macabre significance two years later when Lynott died of heart failure and pneumonia after a drugs overdose. Four months later, in May 1986, Thin Lizzy reformed for the Self Aid concert organized in Eire by Bob Geldof, who replaced Lynott on vocals for the day.

Albums: *Thin Lizzy* (1971), *Shades Of Blue Orphanage* (1972), *Vagabonds Of The Western World* (1973), *Night Life* (1974), *Fighting* (1975), *Jailbreak* (1976), *Remembering - Part One* (1976), *Johnny The Fox* (1976), *Bad Reputation* (1977), *Live And Dangerous* (1978), *Black Rose* (1979), *The Continuing Saga Of The Ageing Orphans* (1979), *Renegade* (1981), *Rockers* (1981), *Thunder And Lightning* (1983), *Life-Live* (1983). Compilations: *Lizzy Killers* (1983), *The Collection* (1985), *The Best Of Phil Lynott And Thin Lizzy* (1987), *Dedication - The Best Of Thin Lizzy* (1991).
Further reading: *Phil Lynott: Dancing In The Moonlight*, Pamela McCleeve.

Thompson, Richard And Linda

This husband-and-wife folk/rock duo began performing together officially in 1972 although their association dated from the previous year.

Richard Thompson

When Richard Thompson (b. 3 April 1949, Totteridge & Whetsone, London, England; guitar/vocals) left Fairport Convention, he pursued a generally low-key path, performing in folk clubs and on various sessions, including *Rock On*, a collection of rock 'n' roll favourites which featured several Fairport acolytes. 'When Will I Be Loved?' was marked by a duet between Sandy Denny and Linda Peters, the latter of whom then provided vocals on Thompson's *Henry The Human Fly*. Richard and Linda then began a professional, and personal, relationship, introduced on *I Want To See The Bright Lights Tonight*. This excellent album contained several of Richard's best-known compositions, including the title track, 'Cavalry Cross' and the despondent 'End Of The Rainbow': 'Life seems so rosy in the cradle, but I'll be a friend, I'll tell you what's in store/There's nothing at the end of the rainbow/There's nothing to grow up for anymore'. The Thompsons toured with former-Fairport guitarist Simon Nicol as Hokey Pokey, which in turn evolved into a larger, more emphatic unit, Sour Grapes. The former group inspired the title of a second enthralling album which blended humour with social comment. Its release was the prelude to a frenetic period which culminated in *Pour Down Like Silver*, the Thompson's second album within 12 months. It reflected the couple's growing interest in the Sufi faith, but despite a sombre reputation, the set included several excellent compositions.

A three year hiatus in the Thompson's career ensued, broken only in 1977 by a series of live performances accompanied by fellow converts Ian Whiteman, Roger Powell and Mick Evans, all previously with Mighty Baby. Now signed to the Chrysalis label, *First Light* provided a welcome return and many commentators rate this album as the duo's finest. The follow-up release, *Sunnyvista*, was in comparison, a disappointment, despite the inclusion of the satiric title track and the angry and passionate 'You're Going To Need Somebody'. However, it led to the duo's departure from their record label. This second, if enforced, break ended with the superb *Shoot Out The Lights*, nominated by *Rolling Stone* as the best album of 1982. Indeed such a response suggested the Thompsons would now secure widespread success and they embarked on a US tour to consolidate this newly-won recognition. Despite this, the couple's marriage was breaking up and in June 1982 the duo made their final appearance together at Sheffield's South Yorkshire Folk Festival. Richard Thompson then resumed his critically-acclaimed solo career, while

Linda went on to record *One Clear Moment* (1985). Albums: *I Want To See The Bright Lights Tonight* (1974), *Hokey Pokey* (1975), *Pour Down Like Silver* (1975), *First Light* (1978), *Sunnyvista* (1979), *Shoot Out The Lights* (1982).

Three Degrees

Protegees of producer/songwriter Richard Barrett; Fayette Pickney, Linda Turner and Shirley Porter scored a US hit with their first single, 'Gee Baby (I'm Sorry)', in 1965. This Philadelphia-based trio secured further pop success the next year with 'Look In My Eyes', but struggled to sustain this momentum until 1970, when their emphatic reworking of the Chantels' standard, 'Maybe', returned them to the chart. By this point Sheila Ferguson and Valerie Holiday had joined the line-up in place of Turner and Porter. The Three Degrees' golden period came on signing with Philadelphia International. They shared vocals with MFSB on 'TSOP', the theme song to television's successful *Soul Train* show. This US pop and R&B number 1 preceded the trio's international hits, 'Year Of Decision' and 'When Will I See You Again?' (both 1974). These glossy performances were particularly popular in the UK, where the group continued to chart, notably with the Top 10 hits, 'Take Good Care Of Yourself' (1975), 'Woman In Love' and 'My Simple Heart' (both 1979). Helen Scott appeared on the 1976 album *Standing Up For Love*. Now signed to Ariola Records, the Three Degrees' releases grew increasingly bland as they emphasized the cabaret element suppressed in their early work. Fêted by royalty - Prince Charles stated they were his favourite group - the 80s saw the group resident in the UK where they were a fixture on the variety and supper-club circuit.

Albums: *Maybe* (1970), *Three Degrees* (1974), *International* (1975), *So Much In Love* (1975), *Take Good Care Of Yourself* (1975), *Three Degrees Live* (1975), *Three Degrees Live In Japan* (1975), *Standing Up For Love* (1977), *The Three Degrees* (1978), *New Dimensions* (1978), *3D* (1979), *Three Degrees And Holding* (1989). Compilations: *Gold* (1980), *Hits Hits Hits* (1981), *20 Golden Greats* (1984). Solo album: Fayette Pickney *One Degree* (1979).

Tonto's Expanding Headband

Americans Robert Margouleff and Malcolm Cecil pioneered the collaboration between Arp and Moog synthesizer and keyboard. 'Tonto' was an acronym for The Original New Tibrel Orchestra. Their first album was released by Embryo and licensed through Atlantic. In attaining the reputation of a cult classic, the album impressed Stevie Wonder sufficiently to request the duo to contribute substantially to *Innervisions* (1973) with Cecil also providing bass. Cecil also made an appearance that same year on Little Feat's *Dixie Chicken*. A follow-up to *Zero Time* in 1974 for Polydor, *It's About Time*, drew less plaudits. Both musicians carried on with session work throughout the 70s, recording alongside Billy Preston, Joan Baez and Steve Hillage.

Albums: *Zero Time* (1971), *It's About Time* (1974).

Tourists

A UK power-pop group of the late 70s, the Tourists were notable as the first setting in which the David A. Stewart-Annie Lennox partnership came into the spotlight. The band grew out of an earlier duo formed by ex-Longdancer guitarist Stewart (b. 9 September 1952, Sunderland, Tyne & Wear, England) with fellow Sunderland singer-songwriter Pete Coombes who had been a member of Peculiar Star. The pair played folk clubs and cabaret around Europe in 1974-76. Returning to London, they met Lennox (b 25 December 1954, Aberdeen, Scotland) a former Royal Academy of Music student who had toured with jazz-rock big band Red Brass. As Catch they made one single, 'Black Blood' (Logo 1977), before re-forming as the five-strong Tourists with Jim Toomey (drums) and Eddie Chin (bass). The first album appeared on Logo Records in 1979, recorded with German producer Conny Plank. All the songs, including two minor hit singles, were by Coombes, but the band's first real success came with a revival of the 1963 Dusty Springfield hit 'I Only Want To Be With You' and 'So Good To Be Back Home Again', which both reached the Top 10. After a contractual dispute with Logo, the Tourists made *Luminous Basement* for RCA, produced by Tom Allom at George Martin's studio in Montserrat. It sold poorly and after a final UK tour The band split in 1980. Coombes and Chin formed Acid Drops while Lennox and Stewart re-emerged the next year as the Eurythmics.

Albums: *The Tourists* (1979), *Reality Effect* (1979), *Luminous Basement* (1980).

Tower Of Power

Formed in 1967 in Oakland, California, USA, this durable group - Rufus Miller (vocals), Greg Adams (trumpet), Emilio 'Mimi' Castillo (b. Detroit, Michigan; saxophone), Steve Kupka (saxophone), Lenny Pickett (saxophone), Mic Gillette (horns), Willie Fulton (guitar), Francis Prestia (bass), Brent Byer (percussion) and David Garibaldi (drums) - was originally known as the Motowns/Motown Soul Band. One of several Bay Area outfits preferring soul to its prevalent acid-rock sound, Tower Of Power's debut album, *East Bay Grease* (1969) followed several popular appearances at San Francisco's Fillmore auditorium. Having now signed to the Warner Brothers label, the group's next two albums, *Bump City* and *Tower Of Power* produced a hit single each in 'You're Still A Young Man' and 'So Very Hard To Go', but their progress was hampered by a recurring vocalist problem. Miller was replaced, firstly by Rick Stevens and then Lenny Williams (b. 1945, San Francisco, California, USA), while the rhythm section also proved unstable. Curiously, the horn section stayed intact and was much in-demand for session work, a factor which doubtlessly kept the parent group intact despite dwindling commercial fortunes. 'Don't Change Horses (In The Middle Of A Stream)' (1974) was the group's last US Top 30 single, but although they switched to Columbia in 1976, the Power returned to Warners after three lacklustre albums. Still bedevilled by personnel changes, recordings under their own name are now infrequent, but the brass players remain part of the west coast backroom circle for their work with, amongst others, Huey Lewis and Phil Collins.

Albums: *East Bay Grease* (1970), *Bump City* (1971), *Tower Of Power* (1973), *Back In Oakland* (1974), *Urban Renewal* (1974), *In The Slot* (1975), *Live And Living In Colour* (1976), *Ain't Nothin' Stoppin' Us Now* (1976), *We Came To Play!* (1978), *Back On The Streets* (1979), *Tower Of Power* (1982), *Power* (1988), *Direct* (1988). Compilation: *What Is Hip?* (1986).

Trammps

This Philadelphia-based group was formed by Earl Young and Jimmy Ellis, two former members of the Volcanoes, who scored a local R&B hit with their 'Storm Warning' single. The duo was joined by Dennis Harris (guitar), Ron Kersey (keyboards), John Hart (organ), Stanley Wade (bass) and Michael Thompson (drums), taking their name from a jibe that 'all (they would) ever be is tramps.' Initially the group won its reputation updating 'standards' of which 'Zing Went The Strings Of My Heart' (1972) was a minor hit. They then followed a more individual direction on their own label, Golden Fleece, before scoring a major UK hit with the excellent 'Hold Back The Night' (1975). Two years later the Trammps completed

Tourists

their *tour de force*, 'Disco Inferno', which featured in the film *Saturday Night Fever*, and irrevocably linked their name to the dancefloor. By this point the line-up had undergone several changes. The group's instigators, Young and Ellis, remained at the helm, alongside Stan and Harold Wade and baritone Robert Upchurch. There changes could not, however, halt the Trammps' commercial slide when the disco bubble burst and their 80s' releases made little impression on either the soul or pop charts.

Albums: *The Legendary Zing Album* (1975), *Trammps* (1975), *Where The Happy People Go* (1976), *Disco Inferno* (1977), *Trammps III* (1977), *The Whole World's Dancing* (1979), *Mixin' It Up* (1980), *Slipping Out* (1981). Compilation: *The Best Of The Trammps* (1978).

Trapeze

Formed in Birmingham, England in 1968, Trapeze were one of several local acts signed to the Moody Blues' label, Threshold Records. John Jones (vocals), Mel Galley (guitar/vocals), Terry Rowley (guitar), Glen Hughes (bass) and Dave Holland (bass) recorded a self-titled debut album, before Jones and Rowley were dropped from the line-up. Trapeze completed *Medusa* and *You Are The Music* as a trio before Hughes replaced Roger Glover in Deep Purple in June 1973. However, the three musicians were latterly reunited, although the bassist dropped out in the midst of an ill-fated tour of the USA and embarked on a solo career. Galley and Holland then recruited Rob Kendrick (guitar) and Pete Wright (bass), issuing two albums for Warner Brothers before Pete Galby replaced Kendrick for a final Trapeze release entitled *Hold On/Running*.

Albums: *Trapeze* (1970), *Medusa* (1970), *You Are The Music...We're Just The Band* (1972), *Hot Wire* (1974), *Trapeze* (1975), *Hold On/Running* (1978). Compilation: *Final Swing* (1974).

Travers, Pat, Band

Canadian guitarist Pat Travers began his career playing in his brother's band and then in the Band. Having moved to London, Travers set up a band of his own consisting of Peter 'Mars' Cowling (bass) and drummer Roy Dyke (of Ashton, Gardner And Dyke). In 1976 they played at the Reading rock festival, and this led to greater recognition of their debut, *Pat Travers*. In 1977, Nicko McBrain, who subsequently joined Iron Maiden, replaced Roy Dyke. Travers himself turned his talents to songwriting, his music taking a more experimental turn, and being aided by other artists, including Scott Gorham. During their 1977 tour, Clive Edwards replaced McBrain, and Michael Dycke added another guitar. Guitarist Pat Thrall, who had been a member of Automatic Man, and Tommy Aldridge (drums), formerly of Black Oak Arkansas, were recruited to work on *Heat In The Street*, a very heavy, powerful sounding album. Their relationship with the band was short-lived, however; Thrall left and Aldridge departed in order to work with Ozzy Osbourne. Subsequent recordings featured Sandy Gennaro (drums) and Michael Shrieve, and were notable for their solid, blues-like sound. In 1984 the line-up of Pat Marchino (drums), Barry Dunaway (bass), Jerry Riggs (guitar) and Travers himself released *Hot Shot*, an album which was not a great commercial success. There was then a lengthy break in Travers' recording career until 1990 when he released *School Of Hard Knocks*. The following year Travers was working again with Thrall, Aldridge and Cowling, touring Japan along with Jerry Riggs and Scott Zymowski, and planning a reunion album.

Albums: *Pat Travers* (1976), *Makin' Magic* (1977), *Putting It Straight* (1977), *Heat In The Street* (1978), *Go For What You Know* (1979), *Crash And Burn* (1980), *Radio Active* (1981), *Black Pearl* (1982), *Hot Shot* (1984), *School Of Hard Knocks* (1990).

Travolta, John

b. 18 February 1954, Englewood, New Jersey, USA, of Italian-Irish ancestry. Travolta left school at the age of 16 to become an actor. After working in off-Broadway productions and Hollywood bit-parts, he landed a lead in *Welcome Back Cotter*, a nationally-transmitted television series. Hating to see this exposure go to waste, Midsong Records engaged the handsome young thespian as a recording artist. Three singles, notably 1976's 'Let Her In', cracked the US Top 40 which, with his film roles in such as *Devil's Rain* (1975), *The Boy In The Plastic Bubble* (1976) and *Carrie* (1976), readied the public for his *pièce de résistance* as the star of *Saturday Night Fever* which turned disco into a multi-national industry. Travolta's pop and cinema interests combined in 1978's *Grease* for which he was singularly well-prepared, having once toured in a stage version of this musical. From the soundtrack, his duets with co-star Olivia Newton-John, 'You're The One That I Want' and 'Summer Nights', were world-wide number 1hits with Travolta's solo highlights, 'Sandy' and 'Greased Lightning' also selling well. His chart career effectively ended after the fall of *Sandy* from album lists in 1979. *Staying Alive*, a 1983 sequel-of-sorts to *Saturday Night Fever*, was the most successful of Travolta's later movies, although he teamed up again with Newton-John in *Two Of A Kind* and they were heard on its tie-in album. He subsequently co-starred with Kirstie Allie in *Look Who's Talking*.

Albums: *Sandy* (1978), *Whenever I'm Away From You* (1978), *Two Of A Kind* (1983, film soundtrack). Compilation: *20 Golden Pieces* (1981).

T. Rex

Although initially a six-piece group, formed by Marc Bolan (b. Mark Feld, 30 July 1947, Hackney, London, England; vocals/guitar) in 1967 on leaving John's Children, the new venture was reduced to an acoustic duo when a finance company repossessed their instruments and amplifiers. Steve 'Peregrine' Took (b. 28 July, 1949, London, England; percussion) completed the original line-up which was originally known as Tyrannosaurus Rex. Nurtured by disc jockey John Peel, the group quickly became an established act on the UK 'underground' circuit through numerous live appearances. Bolan's quivering voice and rhythmic guitar-playing were ably supported by Took's frenetic bongos and the sound created was one of the most distinctive of the era. 'Debora', their debut single, broached the UK Top 40, while a follow-up, 'One Inch Rock', reached number 28, but Tyrannosaurus Rex found a wider audience with their albums. *My People Were Fair...* and *Prophets, Seers & Sages* encapsulated Bolan's quirky talent and while his lyrics, made obtuse by a sometimes impenetrable delivery, invoked pixies, fawns, the work of J.R.R. Tolkien and the trappings of 'flower-power', his affection for pop's tradition resulted in many memorable melodies. Bolan also published *The Warlock Of Love*, a collection of poems which entered the best-selling book lists.

Unicorn (1969) introduced a much fuller sound as Tyrannosaurus Rex began to court a wider popularity. Long-time producer Tony Visconti emphasized the supporting instruments - organ, harmonium, bass guitar and drumkit - while adding piano on 'Catblack', one of the more popular selections. However, tension between Bolan and Took led to the latter's departure and Mickey Finn (b. 3 June 1947), formerly with Hapshash And The Coloured Coat, took his place in 1970. The ensuing *A Beard Of Stars* completed the transformation into a fully-fledged electric group and while the lyrical content and shape of the songs remained the same, the overall sound was noticeably punchier and more direct. The most obvious example, 'Elemental Child', featured Bolan's long, almost frantic, guitar solo. The duo's name was truncated to T. Rex in October 1970. The attendant single, 'Ride A White Swan', rose to number 2, a success which confirmed an irrevocable change in Bolan's music. Steve Currie (bass) and Bill (Fifield) Legend (drums) formerly of Legend, the Epics and Bateson And Stott, were added to the line-up for 'Hot Love' and 'Get It On', both of which topped the UK charts, and *Electric Warrior*, a number 1 album. *T. Rextacy* became the watchword for pop's new phenomenon which continued unabated when 'Jeepster' reached number 2. However, the track was issued without Bolan's permission and in retort the singer left the Fly label to found his own T. Rex outlet. The pattern of hits continued throughout 1972 with two polished chart-toppers, 'Telegram Sam' and 'Metal Guru', and two number 2 hits, 'Children Of The Revolution' and 'Solid Gold Easy Action', while the now-anachronistic 'Debora' reached the Top 10 upon re-release. A documentary, *Born To Boogie*, filmed by Ringo Starr, captured this frenetic period, but although '20th Century Boy' and 'The Groover' (both 1973) were also substantial hits, they were the group's last UK Top 10 entries. Bolan's relationship with Visconti was severed following 'Truck On (Tyke)' and a tired predictability crept into the singer's work. Astringent touring of Britain, America, Japan and Australia undermined his creativity, reflected in the disappointing *Zinc Alloy... and Bolan's Zip Gun* albums.

American soul singer Gloria Jones, now Bolan's girlfriend, was added to the group, but a series of departures, including those of Currie, Legend and Finn, emphasized an internal dissent. Although 'New York City' bore a 'T. Rex' credit, the group had been officially declared defunct with session musicians completing future recordings. A series of minor hits - 'Dream Lady', 'London Boys' and 'Laser Love' - was punctuated by 'I Love To Boogie', which reached the UK Top 20, but its lustre was removed by charges of plagiarism. However unlike many contemporaries, Bolan welcomed the punk explosion, championing the Damned and booking Generation X on his short-lived television show, *Marc*. The series featured poignant reunions with David Bowie and John's Children singer Andy Ellison and helped halt Bolan's sliding fortunes. A working unit of Herbie Flowers (bass) and Tony Newman (drums) was formed in the wake of a new recording deal with RCA, but on 16 September 1977, Marc Bolan was killed when the car in which he was a passenger struck a tree. The first of several T. Rex related deaths, it was followed by those of Took (1980) and Currie (1981). A vociferous fan-club has kept Bolan's name alive through multiple reissues and repackages and the singer has retained a cult popularity. Although his spell as a top-selling act was brief, he was instrumental in restating pop values in the face of prevailing progressive trends.

Albums: as Tyrannosaurus Rex *My People Were Fair And Had Sky In Their Hair But Now They're Content To Wear Stars On Their Brows* (1968), *Prophets Seers & Sages, The Angels Of The Ages* (1968), *Unicorn* (1969), *A Beard Of Stars* (1970); as T. Rex *T. Rex* (1970), *Electric Warrior* (1971), *The Slider* (1972), *Tanx* (1973), *Zinc Alloy And The Hidden Riders Of Tomorrow Or A Creamed Cage In August* (1974), *Bolan's Zip Gun* (1975), *Futuristic Dragon* (1976), *Dandy In The Underworld* (1977), *T. Rex In Concert - The Electric Warrior Tour 1971* (1981). Compilations: *The Best Of T. Rex* (1971, contains Tyrannosaurus Rex material), *Bolan Boogie* (1972), *Great Hits* (1973), *Light Of Love* (1974), *Marc - The Words And Music 1947-1977* (1978), *Solid Gold T. Rex* (1979), *The Unobtainable T. Rex* (1980), *Children Of Ranr Suite* (1982), *Across The Airwaves* (1982), *Beyond The Rising Sun* (1984), *The Best Of The 20th Century Boy* (1985), *Dance In The Moonlight* (1985), *Billy Super Duper* (1985), *Till Dawn* (1985), *The T. Rex Collection* (1986), *Get It On* (1986), *A Crown Of Jewels* (1986), *The Singles Collection* (1987), *The Marc Shows* (1989).

Trower, Robin

b. 9 March 1947, London, England. Guitarist Trower spent his early career in the Paramounts, a popular Southend, Essex-based R&B/beat group which completed five singles between 1963 and 1965. Having briefly worked with a trio dubbed the Jam, he joined several colleagues from his earlier act in Procol Harum. Trower remained in this much-praised unit until 1971, when his desire to pursue a tougher musical style proved incompatible with their well-established grandiose inflections. He initially formed the short-lived Jude with Frankie Miller (vocals), Jim Dewar (bass/vocals) and Clive Bunker (drums, ex-Jethro Tull), but having retained Dewar (formerly with Lulu and Stone The Crows), founded the Robin Trower Band with drummer Reg Isidore. *Twice Removed From Yesterday* and *Bridge Of Sighs* explored a melodic, guitar-based path, redolent of

the late-period Jimi Hendrix, whom Robin was often criticized for merely aping. His lyrical technique, offset by Dewar's gritty delivery, nonetheless proved highly popular and the trio achieved considerable success in the USA. Although ex-Sly And Family Stone drummer Bill Lordan replaced Isidore in 1974, *For Earth Below* and *Long Misty Days* maintained the same musical balance. However, Trower's desire for a purer version of R&B resulted in his inviting black producer Don Davis to collaborate on *In City Dreams* and *Caravan To Midnight*. The new style alienated the guitarist's rock audience, while the rock-based *Victims Of The Fury* was bedevilled by weaker material. In 1981 he and Lordan formed BLT with bassist Jack Bruce, but within two years Trower had re-convened the Robin Trower Band with Dewar, David Bronze (bass), Alan Clarke and Bobby Clouter (both drums). *Back It Up* failed to repeat former glories and the artist was then dropped by longtime label, Chrysalis Records. The well-received *Passion*, released independently, engendered a new deal with Atlantic, for whom a new line-up of Trower, Bronze, Davey Pattison (vocals) and Pete Thompson (drums) completed *Take What You Need*.

Albums: *Twice Removed From Yesterday* (1973), *Bridge Of Sighs* (1974), *For Earth Below* (1975), *Robin Trower Live* (1976), *Long Misty Days* (1976), *In City Dreams* (1977), *Caravan To Midnight* (1978), *Victims Of The Fury* (1980), *Back It Up* (1983), *Beyond The Mist* (1985), *Passion* (1987), *Take What You Need* (1988). Compilation: *Portfolio* (1987).

Tubes

Never short of personnel, the Tubes comprised Rick Anderson (b. 1 August 1947, Saint Paul, Minnesota, USA; bass), Michael Cotten (b. 25 January 1950, Kansas City, Missouri, USA; keyboards), Prairie Prince (b. 7 May 1950, Charlotte, North Carolina, USA; drums), Bill Spooner (b. 16 April 1949, Phoenix, Arizona, USA; guitar). Roger Steen (b. 13 November 1949, Pipestone, Minnesota, USA; guitar), Re Styles b. 3 March 1950, USA; vocals), Fee Waybill (b. John Waldo, 17 September 1950, Omaha, Nebraska, USA; vocals) and Vince Welnick (b. 21 February 1951, Phoenix, Arizona, USA; keyboards). Founder members Anderson, Spooner and Welmick got together in Phoenix in the late 60s, but it was in San Francisco in 1972 that the Tubes were born. Fronted by Waybill, the band's stage act became wilder and crazier, a manic mixture of loud rock music, outrageous theatrics and burlesque. The videos were risque with scantily-clad women, a 'drugged-out superstar' Quay Lude and 'a crippled Nazi' Dr. Strangekiss. The group were signed to A&M Records in 1975 and their debut album, produced by Al Kooper, included the bombastic UK Top 30 hit 'White Punks On Dope'. Their alleged sexism was tempered somewhat during the late 70s. Their fourth album, *Remote Control*, was produced by Todd Rundgren, after which they left A&M for Capitol Records. *Completion Backward Principle* was regarded as a compromise, despite its flashes of humour. The group's satirical thrust declined due to over-familiarity but prior to their demise, they enjoyed their greatest commercial success with the US Top 10 hit 'She's A Beauty' in 1983.

Albums: *The Tubes* (1975), *Young And Rich* (1976), *Now* (1977), *What Do You Want From Your Life* (1978), *Remote Control* (1979), *Completion Backward Principle* (1981), *Outside Inside* (1983). Compilation: *T.R.A.S.H./Best Of The Tubes* (1981).

Tymes

Formed in Philadelphia during the 50s, George Williams, George Hilliard, Donald Banks, Albert Berry and Norman Burnett first came together in the Latineers. As the Tymes they secured a major hit with the evocative 'So Much In Love' (1962), a gorgeously simple performance which recalled the bygone doo-wop era while anticipating the sweet harmonies of 70s' Philly soul. Further less successful singles then followed as the group entered a somewhat lean patch before a version of 'People' restored them to the charts. The Tymes scored international hits with two 1974 releases, 'You Little Trustmaker' and 'Ms. Grace', (a UK number 1), which pitched the group's harmonies into a modern context. Although the original line-up stayed intact for several years, Hilliard, then Berry, eventually left the group, while two later additions, Terri Gonzalez and Melanie Moore, suggested yet a further shake-up of their image. Such changes, however, failed to sustain the Tymes' chart career beyond 1976.

Albums: *So Much In Love* (1963), *The Sound Of The Wonderful Tymes* (1963), *Somewhere* (1964), *People* (1968), *Trustmaker* (1974), *Tymes Up* (1976), *Turning Point* (1976), *Digging Their Roots* (1977).

Typically Tropical

This studio group was the creation of songwriters Jeffrey Calvert and Max West who set their sights firmly on the summer holiday market with the mock reggae 'Barbados'. With spurious Jamaican phrasing and an invitation to fly 'Coconut Airways' the song was novel enough to reach number 1 in the UK in August 1975. With no serious pretensions to extend their chart run, let alone perform, the duo soon became forgotten one-hit-wonders, although their legacy will always be the immortal holiday lyric 'Wo, I'm going to Barbados'.

U

UFO

The band formed in 1969, when drummer Andy Parker joined Phil Mogg (b. 1951, London, England; vocals), Pete Way (bass) and Mick Bolton (guitar) in Hocus Pocus. With a name change to UFO and a musical style that fused progressive space-rock and good-time boogie, they released three albums that were successful only in Germany and Japan. In 1974 Bolton quit, to be replaced by Larry Wallis (ex-Pink Fairies), followed by Bernie Marsden (later of Whitesnake) and finally Michael Schenker. Securing a deal with Chrysalis Records, they recorded *Phenomenon*, a stunning hard rock album that featured the all-time heavy metal classics 'Rock Bottom' and 'Doctor, Doctor'. Schenker's presence helped to forge their new sound, as he strangled the hard-edged metallic riffs out of his trusty Flying V. A series of excellent albums followed, and the band expanded to a five-piece in 1976, with the addition of a keyboardist, initially Danny Peyronel (ex-Heavy Metal Kids) and later Paul Raymond (formerly of Savoy Brown). *Lights Out* and *Strangers In The Night* consolidated the band's success, the latter a superb double live album recorded on their sell-out US tour of 1977. After long-running internal disagreements, Schenker quit in 1978 to rejoin the Scorpions and later form MSG. Paul Chapman (ex-Lone Star) was offered the guitarist's vacancy, having played with the band for short periods on two previous occasions. From this point on, the band never recaptured the level of success and recognition they had attained with Schenker. A string of uninspiring albums followed, that lacked both aggression and killer riffs. Paul Raymond joined MSG in 1980, with Neil Carter (ex-Wild Horses) taking his place. Pete Way split after the release of *Mechanix*, eventually forming Waysted and ex-Eddie And The Hot Rods/Damned bassist Paul Gray took over his position.

Making Contact represented the nadir of the band's creativity, being dated and devoid of the old energy. A farewell UK tour was undertaken in 1983, but it was a sad end for what was originally a fine band. Two years later Mogg resurrected the name with Raymond and Gray, plus ex-Magnum drummer Jim Simpson and the Japanese guitarist Atomic Tommy M. They recorded *Misdemeanor*,

which unsuccessfully attempted to rekindle the old flame, with up-front guitars and hard-line melodies. Success eluded them and they disbanded again. In 1991, UFO were re-born once more. This time the line-up featured the nucleus of Mogg and Way, plus guitarist Lawrence Archer (ex-Grand Slam) and drummer Clive Edwards (ex-Wild Horses). They have tried to recapture the halcyon days of 1974-78, with *High Stakes And Desperate Men*, but only time will tell, if they have the songs and ability to compete with the current market leaders in this field.

Albums: *UFO 1* (1971), *Flying* (1971), *UFO Lands In Tokyo - Live* (1971), *Phenomenon* (1974), *Force It* (1975), *No Heavy Pettin'* (1976), *Lights Out* (1977), *Obsession* (1978), *Strangers In The Night* (1979), *No Place To Run* (1980), *The Wild, The Willing And The Innocent* (1981), *Mechanix* (1982), *Making Contact* (1983), *Misdemeanor* (1985), *Ain't Misbehavin'* (1988), *High Stakes And Desperate Men* (1992). Compilations: *Classic Tracks 1970-73* (1981), *Headstone - The Best Of UFO* (1983).

Undisputed Truth

The Undisputed Truth were assembled by Motown producer Norman Whitfield in 1970, as a vehicle for the studio experimentation he had already begun on singles by the Temptations and Edwin Starr. Joe Harris, an ever-present member of the group, was originally teamed up with singers Billie Calvin and Brenda Evans, who had previously worked on the Four Tops' *Still Waters*. The group debuted with a stunning slice of psychedelic soul, 'Smiling Faces Sometimes', written by Whitfield with his regular lyricist, Barrett Strong. The song was an exercise in urban paranoia, widely interpreted as an oblique comment on President Richard Nixon's administration, and it allowed Whitfield room to preview new studio techniques which he hoped to use on Temptations' releases. It reached the USA Top 3, encouraging Whitfield to use the Undisputed Truth as a laboratory for testing his new material. The group enjoyed a small hit with Whitfield/Strong's 'Papa Was A Rolling Stone' several months before the Temptations' classic rendition reached the shops, and among their other hit songs were 'Ball Of Confusion', 'Friendship Train', and 'Just My Imagination' - all numbers which Whitfield had also recorded with other Motown acts. Whitfield continued to produce the group throughout the 70s, switching them in 1976 to his own Whitfield label, where they scored a US R&B hit with 'You + Me = Love'. By this time,

only Joe Harris remained of the original trio, accompanied by Tyrone Berkeley and Taka Boom, the sister of vocalist Chaka Khan. In the late 70s, their producer's attention was focused on the most successful act on his roster, Rose Royce, and the Undisputed Truth were among those who suffered from his lack of attention. The group eventually split in the early 80s after the collapse of Whitfield's label. In 1991 Joe Harris and Brenda Evans, together with ex-Brainstorm vocalist Belita Woods, recorded a new version of 'Law Of The Land' on Ian Levine's Motor City label
Albums: *The Undisputed Truth* (1971), *Face To Face With The Truth* (1972), *Law Of The Land* (1973), *Down To Earth* (1974), *Cosmic Truth* (1975), *Higher Than High* (1975), *Method To The Madness* (1977), *Smokin'* (1979). Compilation: *The Best Of The Undisputed Truth* (1977).

Uriah Heep

The critics have scoffed and generally poured derision on Uriah Heep but the band have sold millions of records and on five occasions placed albums above number 40 in the US charts. At worst, plagiarists (Led Zeppelin and Deep Purple most notably) and, at best, a technically brilliant heavy rock band, they deserve most credit for continuing despite almost 30 personnel changes and two deaths along the way! David Byron (b. 29 January 1947, Epping, Essex, England, d. 28 February 1985; vocals) formed the group with Mick Box (b. 8 June 1947, Walthamstow, London, England; lead guitar/vocals). The pair had teamed up in the Stalkers during the mid-60s and after the group split they assembled another called Spice. Spice evolved into Uriah Heep when the duo were joined by Ken Hensley (b. 24 August 1945, London, England; guitar/keyboards/vocals) and Paul Newton (b. 1946, Andover, England; bass). Hensley, a talented musician, had previously played guitar with Kit And The Saracens and the soul group, Jimmy Brown Sound. Before Uriah Heep were bonded under the experienced management of Gerry Bron, Hensley had played alongside Mick Taylor (later to become a member of the Rolling Stones) in the Gods. He had also played on an album by Toe Fat which included Cliff Bennett. The drummer's stool was very briefly taken by former Spice man Alex Napier, followed by Nigel Olsson (later with Elton John). Finding a permanent drummer was to remain one of the band's problems throughout their early years.
Their debut, *Very 'eavy, Very 'umble* in 1970 was a simplistic, bass-driven passage from electric folk to a direct, harder sound. They auditioned numerous drummers before offering the job to Keith Baker, who recorded *Salisbury* before deciding that the tour schedule was too rigorous for his liking. *Salisbury* was a drastic development from the debut, with many lengthy, meandering solos and a 16-minute title track embellished by a 26-piece orchestra. The group were near the forefront of a richly embossed, fastidious style of music later to become dubbed 'progressive rock'. During 1971 the line-up was altered again when Lee Kerslake, another former member of the Gods and Toe Fat, replaced Ian Clarke. An ex-member of the Downbeats and Colosseum, Mark Clarke, superseded Paul Newton on bass guitar but lasted just three months before Gary Thain (b. New Zealand; ex-Keef Hartley Band) took over. Gerry Bron had formed his Bronze Records by 1971 and *Look At Yourself* became the group's first entry into the UK charts when it reached number 39 in November. The stability of the new line-up enabled the band to enter their most successful period during the early 70s when the fantastical, eccentric nature of their lyrics was supported by a grandiose musical approach. The quintet recorded five albums, beginning with *Demons And Wizards*, their first to enter the US charts. The musical and lyrical themes continued on *Magician's Birthday*, the double set *Uriah Heep Live*, *Sweet Freedom*, *Wonderworld* (their last Top 40 entry in the US chart) and *Return To Fantasy* as the band revealed a rare thirst for tough recording and performance schedules. Gary Thain was asked to leave in February 1975 after becoming too unreliable. He died of a drug overdose the following year, 19 March 1976. John Wetton, formerly of King Crimson, Family and Roxy Music was expected to provide the impetus needed when he took over the bass guitar in March 1975. However, many observers considered that he had taken a retrogressive step in joining a group that was quickly becoming an anachronism. The union, celebrated on *Return To Fantasy*, failed on a creative level although it marked their first and last appearance in the UK Top 10. Wetton left after just over a year to back Bryan Ferry. Early in 1976, Uriah Heep were set to fold when internal arguments broke out and they found the previously winning formula had become archaic and undeniably staid. In Ken Hensley's own words, they were 'a bunch of machines plummeting to a death'. There had been an earlier, brooding row when Thain suffered a near-fatal electric shock in Dallas and said he had not been shown enough

regard for his injuries.

Hensley walked out during a tour of the USA in the summer of 1976 and in a subsequent power-struggle Byron was forced to leave. Byron soon afterwards joined Rough Diamond and after their brief lifespan released a series of solo albums before his own before his death in 1985. Hensley had already embarked upon a short, parallel solo career, releasing two albums in 1973 and 1975. John Lawton, previously the singer with Lucifer's Friend, debuted on *Firefly*. The new bassist was David Bowie's former backing musician, Trevor Bolder. The singer's position underwent further changes during the late 70s and early 80s as the group found themselves playing to a cult following that was ever decreasing. Ex-Lone Star singer John Sloman performed on *Conquest* after which Hensley left the group, leaving original member Mick Box to pick up the pieces. A brief hiatus resulted and a new Uriah Heep which included Box, Kerslake, John Sinclair (keyboards), Bob Daisley (bass) and Peter Goalby (vocals, ex-Trapeze) was formed. Daisley would later quit in 1983 and be replaced by the returning Bolder. Bronze Records collapsed in 1984 and the band signed with Portrait Records in the USA. Their earlier extensive touring allowed them to continue appearing at reasonably sized venues, especially across the USA, and in 1987 they had the distinction of becoming the first western heavy metal group to perform in Moscow. Inevitably, there were more personnel changes with the new additions of Bernie Shaw (vocals) and Phil Lanzon (keyboards), both formerly of Grand Prix. The band continues to please itself and its fans, relishing in its longevity, and proving wrong the American critic who once wrote of them: 'If this group makes it, I'll have to commit suicide'.

Albums: *Very 'eavy, Very 'umble* aka *Uriah Heep* (USA) (1970), *Salisbury* (1971), *Look At Yourself* (1971), *Demons And Wizards* (1972), *The Magician's Birthday* (1972), *Uriah Heep Live* (1973), *Sweet Freedom* (1973), *Wonderworld* (1974), *Return To Fantasy* (1975), *High And Mighty* (1976), *Firefly* (1977), *Innocent Victim* (1978), *Fallen Angel* (1978), *Conquest* (1980), *Abnominog* (1982), *Head First* (1983), *Equator* (1985), *Live In Moscow* (1988), *Raging Silence* (1989), *Still 'eavy, Still Proud* (1990), *Different World* (1991). Compilations: *The Best Of Uriah Heep* (1976), *Anthology* (1986), *The Uriah Heep Story* (1990), *Rarities* (1991).

V

Valli, Frankie

b Frank Castelluccio, 3 May 1937, Newark, New Jersey, USA. Originally a solo singer, he joined the Variatones in 1954. They made their first records as the Four Lovers but achieved lasting success when they became the Four Seasons in 1962. Although he was lead singer with the group, Valli also had a solo recording career, starting with '(You're Gonna) Hurt Yourself') in late 1965. He scored a million-seller in 1967 with 'Can't Take My Eyes Off You'. From the same album came further US hits, 'I Make A Fool Of Myself', and 'To Give (The Reason I Live)' while 'You're Ready Now' was a reissued success in Britain in 1971. Valli and producer Bob Gaudio now set up a dual career, with Valli recording for Private Stock and a new Four Seasons group for Warner Brothers. Valli had his first solo number 1 with the high-pitched vocals on 'My Eyes Adored You' in 1975, followed by 'Swearin' To God' and a revival of Ruby And The Romantics' 'Our Day Will Come'. In 1978 he sold two million copies of the Barry Gibb-composed theme song from *Grease*. The follow-ups, 'Fancy Dancer' and 'Where Did We Go Wrong' (a duet with Chris Forde) sold poorly and in 1980 Valli had a series of ear operations to cure his increasing deafness. He subsequently re-joined the Four Seasons and enjoyed further success when 'Big Girls Don't Cry' was included in the film *Dirty Dancing*.
Albums: *Solo* (1967), *Timeless* (1968), *Inside You* (1975), *Close Up* (1975), *Story* (1976), *Frankie Valli Is The Word* (1978), *Heaven Above Me* (1981). Compilation: *The Best Of Frankie Valli* (1980).

Van Day, David

This UK vocalist found success as a member of mid-70s singing group Guys And Dolls between 1974 and 1977. Along with co-member and girlfriend Thereze Bazar he broke away from the band and formed the duo Dollar. Between 1978 and 1982 they notched up 11 chart entries. The break-up of their relationship also marked a temporary halt to their recording career as a duo, and both embarked on solo careers. Van Day scored a minor hit with his first and only solo single 'Young Americans Talking'. He then turned his hand to artist management until he teamed up with Thereze again in 1986, and they picked up musically where they left off three years earlier.

Vangelis

b Evangalos Odyssey Papathanassiou, 29 March 1943, Valos, Greece. A child prodigy, Vangelis gave his first public performance on the piano at the age of six. In the early 60s he joined the pop group Formynx, later forming Aphrodite's Child with vocalist Demis Roussos and Lucas Sideras (drums). The group moved to Paris in the late 60s, recording the international hit 'Rain And Tears'. After it disbanded in 1972, Vangelis concentrated on electronic music, composing classical works as well as film scores for wildlife documentaries by Frederic Rossif. He next built a studio in London where he further developed his fusion of electronic and acoustic sound. *Heaven And Hell* was a Top 40 hit in the UK while the concept album *Albedo 0.39* included the voices of astronauts landing on the moon, as well as the dramatic favourite 'Pulstar'. Returning to Greece in 1978, Vangelis collaborated with actress Irene Papas on settings of Byzantine and Greek traditional song, before joining forces with Yes vocalist Jon Anderson who had previously sung on *Heaven And Hell*. As Jon And Vangelis they had international success with 'I Hear You Now' (1980) and 'I'll Find My Way Home' (1982). The following year, Vangelis resumed his activities as a film music composer with the award-winning *Chariots Of Fire*. The title track was a world-wide hit and prompted scores of imitation 'themes'. This was followed by scores for Kuruhara's *Antarctica*, Ridley Scott's *Bladerunner* and Costas-Gavras' *Missing* and Donaldson's *The Bounty*. In 1988, he signed to Arista Records, releasing *Direct,* the first in a series of improvised albums which he composed, arranged and recorded simultaneously.
Albums: *Dragon* (1971), *L'Apocalypse Des Animaux* (1973), *Earth* (1974), *Heaven And Hell* (1975), *Albedo 0.39* (1976), *Spiral* (1977), *Beaubourg* (1978), *Hypothesis* (1978), *Odes* (1978), *China* (1979), *See You Later* (1980), *Chariots Of Fire* (1981, film soundtrack), *Opera Sauvage* (1981), *To The Unknown Man* (1981), *Soil Festivities* (1984), *Ignacio* (1985), *Invisible Connections* (1985), *Mask* (1985), *Direct* (1988), *Antarctica* (1988, film soundtrack), *The City* (1990). Compilation: *The Best Of Vangelis* (1981), *Themes* (1989). As Jon And Vangelis: *Short Stories* (1980), *The Friends Of Mr Cairo* (1981), *Private Collection* (1983), *Page Of Life* (1991).

Village People

The Village People from New York City, USA, were a concept before they were a group. The brainchild of record producer Jacques Morali, the troupe was assembled in 1977 . His intention was to create a camp rock 'n' roll/dance act that would flaunt homosexual stereotypes yet appeal to gays. Before even constructing his dream group, Morali secured a recording deal with Casablanca Records, then riding high with a string of smash disco hits by Donna Summer. Morali's first recruit was Felipe Rose, a go-go dancer who was dressed in an American Indian costume when spotted by the entrepreneur. Morali then hired songwriters Phil Hurtt and Peter Whitehead to compose songs hinting at gay themes before filling out the group with Alexander Briley, Randy Jones, David Hodo, Glenn Hughes and Victor Willis (later replaced by Ray Simpson). Each member of the group was outfitted to cash in on the homosexual 'macho' stereotyping; in addition to the American Indian there was a cowboy, a policeman, a hard-hat construction worker, a biker and a soldier. The group first charted in the UK with the Top 50 single, 'San Francisco (You Got Me)' in 1977, but the group's first major US hit was the Top 30 'Macho Man' in 1978, followed by two international hits, 'Y.M.C.A.' (UK number 1/US number 2) and 'In The Navy' (UK number 3/US number 2). Although gays did embrace the group at first, they tired of it as the mainstream audience picked up on the Village People. In the UK their success continued with the Top 20 singles, 'Go West' (1979) and 'Can't Stop The Music' (1980). The latter was the theme-song to an ill-timed film excursion. With anti-disco fever prevalent in the USA, sales plummeted; the group's starring role in the universally panned film, *Can't Stop The Music*, virtually killed off their career. Attempts to resurface with new personnel and new styles (including a stint as Spandau Ballet-like 'New Romantics') did not aid their sagging fortunes. Miles Jaye, who had replaced Ray Simpson in the later years of the group, was signed to Teddy Pendergrass' Top Priority label as a solo artist, achieving some success in the US R&B singles chart. He subsequently signed to the Island outlet 4th & Broadway and released *Miles* (1987) and *Irresistible* (1989). Jacques Morali later died of an AIDS related-illness, aged 44 in December 1991.
Albums: *Village People* (1977), *Macho Man* (1978), *Cruisin'* (1978), *Go West* (1979), *Live And Sleazy* (1979), *Can't Stop The Music* (1980, film soundtrack), *Renaissance* (1981). Compilation: *Greatest Hits* (1988).

Vinegar Joe

This powerful, R&B-based group was formed in 1971 at the suggestion of Island Records boss, Chris Blackwell. The main core of the group comprised Elkie Brooks (b. 25 February 1948, Salford, Lancashire, England; vocals), Robert Palmer (b. 19 January 1949, Batley, Yorkshire, England; vocals) and Peter Gage (b. 31 August 1947, Lewisham, London, England; guitar/piano/pedal steel guitar). It evolved from the remnants of Dada (formed 1970), an ambitious 12-piece jazz-rock outfit. The three members had enjoyed limited success previously during the 60s: Brooks had recorded as a solo act, Palmer had sung with Alan Bown, while Gage was a former member of the Zephyrs and later with Geno Washington And The Ram Jam Band. Additionally the line-up comprised Steve York (b. 24 April 1948, London; bass), while early members Tim Hinckley and later John Hawken were supplanted in June 1972 by Mike Deacon (b. 30 April 1945, Surrey, England; keyboards), while Bob Tait and later John Woods were replaced in January 1973 by Pete Gavin (b. 9 August 1946, Lewisham, London, England; drums). Jim Mullen was an additional guitarist from September 1972 to April 1973. Renowned for a forthright, gutsy approach, Vinegar Joe was quickly established as a popular in-concert attraction, but despite recording three solid and respectable albums, the unit was unable to capture its live appeal on record and broke up late in 1973. Palmer and Brooks then embarked on contrasting, but highly successful, individual careers.
Albums: *Vinegar Joe* (1972), *Rock 'N' Roll Gypsies* (1972), *Six Star General* (1973).

Virgin Records

Founded in 1973 by entrepreneur Richard Branson, the Virgin label was the natural extension of his successful retail stores, and previously, mail-order organization. Its first release, Mike Oldfield's *Tubular Bells* had been turned down by most of Britain's major companies, but the album became a runaway smash, selling in excess of 5 million copies. It established Virgin's early reputation as a haven for experimental English rock as demonstrated by the early signing of Hatfield And The North, Robert Wyatt and Henry Cow. *Avant garde* continental acts, including Faust, Gong, Slapp Happy and Wigwam were also attracted by Virgin's enthusiasm for unconventional music,

Tony Visconti and May Pang

while the acquisition of America's Captain Beefheart, although later fraught by litigation, emphasized a desire to challenge. However, the advent of punk changed the label's perceived image to that of *passé* hippie and its catalogue was rendered old-fashioned almost overnight. This was rectified in 1977 with the signing of the Sex Pistols, and Virgin consolidated their new departure with releases by the Skids, the Ruts and XTC, the last-named of which has remained with the label to date.(The band's Andy Partridge stated that the reason Virgin have maintained XTC under contract for so long with only moderate sales is for 'tax-loss' purposes!) A steady promotion of reggae, punk's rebellious bedfellow, drew dividends through excellent albums by the Mighty Diamonds, Peter Tosh and U-Roy, issued on their Front Line subsidary. Yet it was not until the early 80s that Virgin established itself as a major outlet with international hits by the Human League, Heaven 17, Culture Club and Simple Minds. The success of Phil Collins, who came to the label through its acquisition of his former outlet, Charisma, established the artist as the company's one true household name, feted by royalty and a star of the magnitude of Elton John and Paul McCartney. Virgin's transition from idealism to pragmatism was reflected in its eclectic back catalogue, while the parent corporation boasted thriving recording facilities, an equally strong publishing arm and a series of flourishing subsidiaries, including Virgin America, the roster of which included Bob Mould and Lenny Kravitz. In a bid to concentrate more on the Virgin Atlantic airline, and future projects such as an independent British rail company, Branson sold his interests in Virgin Records to Thorn EMI in 1992, thereby bringing the story to a close.

Visconti, Tony

b. 24 April 1944, Brooklyn, New York, USA. Visconti came to Britain in the 60s and achieved his reputation as a crafted producer with his work for David Bowie. Their long relationship began with 'Space Oddity'-Visconti often contributed bass playing (an excellent example of his prowess can be heard on *The Man Who Sold The World*)- and continued throughout the 70s with such influential releases as *Heroes*. Visconti was also responsible for honing Marc Bolan's talent, transforming him from hippie minstrel to glam-rock, and successful pop star. At the same time the producer was also working with many artists such as Strawbs, Badfinger, Marsha Hunt, Mary Hopkins (who he married), Tom Paxton, Wings, Ralph McTell, Gentle Giant, Sparks, Iggy Pop, Thin Lizzy and Osibisa, a diversity which confirmed his talent. Unlike several contemporaries, Visconti was active during the punk/new wave movement, collaborating with Hazel O'Connor, the Boomtown Rats and the Stranglers. His undoubted skills remain constantly in demand.

Album: *Visconti's Inventory* (1977).

W

Wainwright, Loudon, III

b. 5 September 1946, Chapel Hill, North Carolina, USA. Loudon Wainwright I was in insurance while his son, Loudon Wainwright II, became a journalist for *Life* magazine. Wainwright's parents settled in Westchester Country, 60 miles outside of New York City although he went to a boarding school in Delaware ('School Days') and he was friends with an adolescent Liza Minnelli ('Liza'). He studied acting in Pittsburgh where singer George Gerdes encouraged his songwriting. By 1968, after a brief spell in an Oklahoma jail for a marijuana offence, Wainwright was playing folk clubs in New York and Boston and was signed to Atlantic Records. His first albums featured his high-pitched voice and guitar with few additions, and his intense, sardonic songs, described by him as 'reality with exaggeration', were about himself. He was hailed as the 'new Bob Dylan' for such songs as 'Glad To See You've Got Religion', 'Motel Blues' and 'Be Careful, There's A Baby In The House'. He later said: 'I wasn't the new anyone. Media people call you the new-something because it's the only way they know to describe what you do'. His UK debut, opening for the Everly Brothers, was disastrous as Teddy Boys barracked him, but he found his *métier* at the 1972 Cambridge Folk Festival.

Wainwright's third album, for Columbia Records, included a surprise US Top 20 pop hit in 'Dead Skunk'. 'I had run over a skunk that had been run over a few times already. It took 15 minutes to write. I remember being bowled over at how much people liked it when I had put so little into it. It's about a dead skunk but people thought it was about Nixon and that's all right by me.' Wainwright wrote 'A.M. World' about his success and, almost defiantly, he followed it with *Attempted Moustache*, that had indistinct vocals and was uncommercial even by his standards, although it did include the whimsical 'Swimming Song'. *Unrequited*, partly recorded live, was a return to form and included the hilarious, but controversial, 'Rufus Is A Tit Man' (which Wainwright described as 'a love song, not a dirty song'), one of many songs he was to record about his children ('Pretty Little Martha' and 'Five Years Old') His marriage to Kate McGarrigle (see Kate And Annie

McGarrigle) ended in 1977 and Loudon then had a child with Suzzy Roche of the Roches. His album, *A Live One*, actually recorded in 1976 demonstrates his wit but this gawky, lanky, square-jawed singer with enormous tongue, grimaces and contortions needs to be seen in person to be fully appreciated. Wainwright has appeared in a few episodes of the television series *M*A*S*H*, appeared on stage in *The Birthday Party* and *Pump Boys And Dinettes*, and he is most recently best known in the UK for his topical songs on the Jasper Carrott television series. His wit and neuroses surfaced in such songs as 'Fear Of Flying' and 'Watch Me Rock, I'm Over 30' (both from *T-Shirt*), but he reached top form on three albums for Demon - *Fame And Wealth*, *I'm Alright* and *More Love Songs*. The albums, sometimes co-produced with Richard Thompson, have included 'I Don't Think Your Wife Likes Me', 'Hard Day On The Planet' (written while watching Live Aid), 'Unhappy Anniversary', 'Not John' (a tribute to John Lennon) and 'This Song Don't Have A Video'. Many of his later compositions are about the music industry of which he later claimed, 'I wanna be in showbiz one way or another until I die, so it's a mixed blessing not to be a huge success. I've been successful on my own terms - by failing'.

Albums: *Loudon Wainwright III* (1969), *Album II* (1971), *Album III* (1972), *Attempted Moustache* (1974), *Unrequited* (1975), *T-Shirt* (1976), *Final Exam* (1978), *A Live One* (1979), *Fame And Wealth* (1983), *I'm Alright* (1984), *More Love Songs* (1986), *Therapy* (1989), *History* (1992).

Waits, Tom

b. 7 December 1949, Pomona, California, USA. A gifted lyricist, composer and raconteur, Tom Waits began performing in the late 60s, inspired by a spell working as a doorman in a San Diego nightclub. Here he saw a miscellany of acts - string bands, comedians, C&W singers - and by absorbing portions of an attendant down-market patois, developed his nascent songwriting talent. Having appeared at the Los Angeles' Troubador 'Amateur Hoot Nights', Waits was signed by manager Herb Cohen who in turn secured a recording deal with the emergent Asylum label. *Tom Waits* revealed a still-unfocused performer, as yet unable to draw together the folk, blues and singer/songwriter elements vying for prominence. It did contain 'Ol' 55', later covered by the Eagles, and 'Martha', a poignant melodrama of a now-middle-aged man telephoning his first love from 40 years previously. *The Heart Of Saturday Night* was an altogether more

Tom Waits

accomplished set in which the artist blended characterizations drawn from diners, truckers and waitresses, sung in a razor-edged, rasping voice, and infused with beatnik prepossessions. Waits's ability to paint blue-collar American life is encapsulated in its haunting, melodic title track. *Nighthawks At The Diner*, an in-concert set, and *Small Change*, closed the performer's first era, where the dividing line between life and art grew increasingly blurred as Waits inhabited the flophouse life he sang about. *Foreign Affairs* unveiled a widening perspective and while the influence of 'Beat' writers Jack Kerouac and Allen Ginsberg still inhabited his work - as celebrated in 'Jack And Neal/California Here I Come' - a duet with Bette Midler, 'I Never Talk To Strangers', provided the impetus for his film soundtrack to *One From The Heart*. *Blue Valentine* was marked by its balance between lyrical ballads and up-front R&B, a contrast maintained on *Heartattack And Vine*. A tough combo prevailed on half of its content.

Elsewhere, the composer's gift for emotive melody flourished on 'Jersey Girl', later covered by Bruce Springsteen. The album marked the end of Waits's term with both Cohen and Asylum; in 1983 he opted for Island Records and signalled a new musical direction with the radical *Swordfishtrombones*. Exotic instruments, sound textures and offbeat rhythms marked a content which owed more to Captain Beefheart and composer Harry Partch than dowdy motel rooms. Waits came close to having a hit single in 1983 with the evocative 'In The Neighbourhood', complete with a stunning sepia video. Waits also emphasized his interest in cinema with acting roles in *Rumble Fish*, *Down By Law* and *Ironweed*, in the process completing the exemplary *Rain Dogs*, which featured support from Keith Richard(s) on 'Big Black Mariah'. It also included 'Downtown Train', another in a series of romantic vignettes and later a hit for Rod Stewart. Waits' next release, *Frank's Wild Years*, comprised material drawn from a play written with his wife Kathleen Brennan and based on a song from *Swordfishtrombones*. *Big Time*, meanwhile, was the soundtrack to a concert film, since which the artist's recording career has been distinctly low-key. He continued his cinematic career with roles in *Candy Mountain* and *Cold Feet* and in 1989 Waits made his theatrical debut in *Demon Wine*.

Albums: *Small Change* (1973), *The Heart Of Saturday Night* (1974), *Nighthawks At The Diner* (1975), *Small Change* (1976), *Foreign Affairs* (1977), *Blue Valentine* (1978), *Heartattack And Vine* (1980), *Swordfishtrombones* (1983), *Rain Dogs* (1985), *Frank's Wild Years* (1987), *Night On Earth* (1992, film soundtrack), *Bone Machine* (1992). Compilations: *Bounced Checks* (1981), *Asylum Years* (1986), *The Early Years* (1991).

Further reading: *Small Change: A Life Of Tom Waits*, Patrick Humphries.

Wakeman, Rick

b. 18 May 1949, London, England. The spectacular extravaganzas undertaken in the mid-70s by the former Yes and Strawbs keyboardist, masked the talent of one of rock's premier musicians. In the early 70s he and Keith Emerson regularly battled it out in the annual music press reader's poll for the prestige of the world's top keyboard player. Wakeman made a series of conceptual classical rock albums that were overblown with ambition; *The Six Wives Of Henry VIII* and *Journey To The Centre Of The Earth* briefly made him a superstar. He took his success to extremes by staging *The Myths And Legends Of King Arthur And The Knights Of The Round Table* using a full orchestra and 50-strong choir at Wembley's Empire Pool, on ice! All three albums were hugely successful and Rick attempted more of the same, but he was hampered with a mild heart attack and a serious drink problem. In 1981 he contributed to Sky's Kevin Peeks' *Awakening*. That year he co-wrote a musical version of George Orwell's *1984* with Tim Rice, and followed with sensitive film scores for *Lisztomania*, *The Burning*, *G'Ole* and *Crimes Of Passion*. Having overcome his alcoholism he became a born-again Christian and offered his new faith in the shape of *The Gospels*. Wakeman has been a first class pianist for many years, and stripped of all the pomp and grandeur he demonstrates a superb style, perfectly shown on the new-age *Country Airs*. At the end of the 80s he was back with his former superstar friends as Yes re-formed for a new tour.

Albums: *The Six Wives Of Henry VIII* (1973), *Journey To The Centre Of The Earth* (1974), *The Myths And Legends Of King Arthur And The Knights Of The Round Table* (1975), *Lisztomania* (1975, film soundtrack), *No Earthly Connection* (1976), *White Rock* (1977, film soundtrack), *Rick Wakeman's Criminal Record* (1977), *Rhapsodies* (1979), *1984* (1981), *Rock 'N' Roll Prophet* (1982), *The Burning* (1982, film soundtrack), *G'Ole* (1983, film soundtrack), *Live At Hammersmith* (1985), *Silent Night* (1985), *Country Airs* (1986), *The Family Album* (1987), *The Cost Of Living* (1987), *Crimes Of*

Rick Wakeman

Passion (1987, film soundtrack), *The Gospels* (1987), *Suite Of Gods* (1988), *Time Machine* (1988), *Zodiaque* (1988), *Sea Airs* (1990). Compilation: *Best Known Works* (1978), *20th Anniversary Limited Edition* (1989).

Walsh, Joe

b. 20 November 1947, New Jersey, USA. Guitar hero Walsh started his long and varied career in 1965 with the G-Clefs. Following a spell with local band, the Measles, he found major success when he joined the James Gang in 1969. Walsh's growling, early heavy metal guitar technique was not unlike that of Jeff Beck's, and the Walsh sound had much to do with the achievements of the James Gang. He left in 1972 and formed Barnstorm with Joe Vitale (drums) and Kenny Passarelli (bass). The self-titled album promised much and made a respectable showing in the US charts. Despite the follow-up being credited to Joe Walsh, *The Smoker You Drink The Player You Get* was still Barnstorm, although the band broke up that same year. *Smoker* became his first gold album and featured some of his classic songs such as 'Meadows' and 'Rocky Mountain Way'. On the latter he featured the voice bag, from which his distorted voice emitted after being sung into a plastic tube. Walsh, along with Peter Frampton and Jeff Beck popularized this effect in the early 70s.

In 1974 he produced Dan Fogelberg's classic album *Souvenirs* and guested on albums by Stephen Stills, the Eagles and B.B. King. *So What* in 1975 was another gold album and featured the Walsh classic, 'Turn To Stone'. During the summer he performed at London's Wembley Stadium with the Beach Boys, Elton John and the Eagles. Five months later Walsh joined the Eagles when he replaced Bernie Leaden and became joint lead guitarist with Glen Frey. His distinctive tone contributed greatly to their milestone *Hotel California*; his solo on the title track is one of the highlights. Additionally he retained his autonomy by continuing his highly successful career and released further solo albums including the excellent *But Seriously Folks . . .* which featured the humorous autobiographical 'Life's Been Good'. The song dealt with his fortune and fame in a light-hearted manner, although there is a degree of smugness attached for example; 'I have a mansion, forget the price, ain't never been there, they tell me its nice'. Such was Walsh's confidence that at one point he announced he would stand for President at the next election. He was wise to have maintained his solo career, as the Eagles only made one further album. Walsh shrewdly kept his best work for his own albums. In 1980 Walsh contributed to the best-selling soundtrack *Urban Cowboy* and was rewarded with a US Top 20 hit 'All Night Long'. Both *There Goes The Neighborhood* and *You Bought It - You Name It* maintained his profile and although his 1987 album, *Got Any Gum?* was uninspiring, his career continues to prosper as a solo and session player. In 1992 he was playing with Ringo Starr on the latter's comeback tour.

Albums: *Barnstorm* (1972), *The Smoker You Drink, The Player You Get* (1973), *So What* (1975), *You Can't Argue With A Sick Mind* (1976), *But Seriously Folks . . .* (1978), *There Goes The Neighborhood* (1981), *You Bought It - You Name It* (1983), *The Confessor* (1985), *Got Any Gum?* (1987). Compilation: *The Best Of Joe Walsh* (1978).

War

Veterans of the Californian west coast circuit, the core of War's line-up - Leroy 'Lonnie' Jordan (b. 21 November 1948, San Diego, California, USA; keyboards), Howard Scott (b. 15 March 1946, San Pedro, California, USA; guitar), Charles Miller (b. 2 June 1939, Olathe, Kansas, USA; flute/saxophone), Morris 'B.B.' Dickerson (b. 3 August 1949, Torrence, California, USA; bass) and Harold Brown (b. 17 March 1946, Long Beach, California, USA; drums) - had made several records under different names including the Creators, the Romeos and Senor Soul. In 1969, the quintet was working as Nightshift, an instrumental group, when ex-Animal lead singer, Eric Burdon, adopted them as his backing band. Renamed War, the ensemble was completed by Lee Oskar (b. Oskar Levetin Hansen 24 March 1948, Copenhagen, Denmark; harmonica) and 'Papa' Dee Allen (b. 18 July 1931, Wilmington, Delaware, USA; percussion).

Their debut *Eric Burdon Declares War*, included the rhythmic 'Spill The Wine', but the group broke away from the UK vocalist, following a second collection. War's potent fusion of funk, R&B, rock and latin styles produced a progressive soul sound best heard on *All Day Music* and *The World Is A Ghetto*. They also enjoyed a significant success in the US singles charts with 'The Cisco Kid' (1973), 'Why Can't We Be Friends?' (1975) and 'Summer' (1976), each of which earned a gold disc, while in the UK they earned two Top 20 hits with 'Low Rider' (1976) and 'Galaxy' (1978). War's subsequent progress proved less fortunate. Despite an early promise, a move to MCA Records was

Joe Walsh

largely unproductive as the group's record sales dipped. Lee Oscar embarked on an intermittent solo career and further changes undermined their original fire and purpose. Two 1982 singles, 'You Got The Power' and 'Outlaw' suggested a renaissance but the band was later obliged to finance its own releases. However, a 1987 remake of 'Low Rider', a previous smash hit, did reach the minor places in the R&B chart.

Albums: as Eric Burdon And War, *Eric Burdon Declares War* (1970), *The Black Man's Burdon* (1970); as War, *War* (1971), *All Day Music* (1971), *The World Is A Ghetto* (1972), *Deliver The Word* (1973), *War Live!* (1974), *Why Can't We Be Friends?* (1975), *Galaxy* (1977), *Youngblood* (1978), *The Music Band* (1979), *The Music Band 2* (1979), *The Music Band-Live* (1980), *Outlaw* (1982), *The Music Band-Jazz* (1983), *Life (Is So Strange)* (1983), *Raw War* (1985). Compilations: *Love Is All Around* (1976, early recordings with Eric Burdon), *Greatest Hits* (1976), *Platinum Jazz* (1977).

Ward, Clifford T.

b. 10 February 1946, Kidderminster, Worcestershire, England. Ward typified the early 70s bedsitter singer/songwriter with a series of albums that were at best delightful and at worst mawkish. His debut album appeared on disc jockey John Peel's brave-but-doomed Dandelion label in 1972. *Home Thoughts* proved to be his finest work and gave him wider recognition. Schoolteacher Ward constructed each song as a complete story sometimes with great success. The beautiful 'Gaye' became a UK hit but surprisingly the stronger 'Home Thoughts From Abroad' and the infectious and lyrically excellent 'Wherewithal' failed to chart. *Mantlepieces* and *Escalator* contained a similar recipe of more harmless tales like the minor hit 'Scullery' with naïvely sexist lyrics like; 'You're my picture, my Picasso, you brighten up any scullery'. In later years although still recording the occasional album and still reluctant to perform live, Ward has received more kudos as a songwriter with his material being recorded by artists such as Cliff Richard and Justin Hayward. At the time of writing Ward was seriously ill after being struck down with multiple sclerosis. In 1992, friends and colleagues pieced together an album of out-takes and demos to give the ailing Ward some financial assistance.

Albums: *Singer Songwriter* (1972), *Home Thoughts* (1973), *Mantlepieces* (1973), *Escalator* (1975), *No More Rock And Roll* (1975), *Both Of Us* (1984), *Sometime Next Year* (1986), *Laugh It Off* (1992).

Compilation: *Gaye And Other Stories* (1987).

Weir, Bob

b. 16 October 1947, San Francisco, California, USA. Weir has enjoyed a lengthy career as rhythm guitarist and vocalist with the legendary west coast band the Grateful Dead. Like his colleagues, he has sporadically embarked on solo projects and has played with other bands. *Ace* in 1972 was a fine solo debut (albeit a Grateful Dead album in disguise). He joined up with Kingfish in 1976 which was an off-shoot from another Dead alumni, the New Riders Of The Purple Sage. In 1981 he performed with an aggregation called Bobby And The Midnites, which included jazz musicians Billy Cobham (drums), Alfonso Johnson (bass) and Grateful Dead colleague Brent Mydland (keyboards). This interesting combination tackled fusion, reggae and produced one self-titled album. Weir has an unusual, distinctive and underrated style, preferring to play chopping jazz chords in straightforward rock music structures. This can best be heard on the Grateful Dead's classic album *Live/Dead*.

Albums: Solo *Ace* (1972), *Heaven Help The Fool* (1978); with Kingfish *Kingfish* (1976), *Kingfish - Live And Kickin'* (1977); with Bobby And The Midnites *Bobby And The Midnites* (1981), *Where The Beat Meets The Street* (1984).

Wet Willie

Unusual among Southern boogie band of the 70s, Wet Willie included a strong R&B element in its music. The group was founded as Fox in 1970 in Mobile, Alabama by the Hall brothers, Jimmy (vocals, saxophone, harmonica) and Jack (bass). Other members were Ricky Hirsch (guitar), John Anthony (keyboards) and Lewis Ross (drums). Wet Willie was signed by Phil Walden to his Macon, Georgia-based Capricorn label, for whom it made seven albums before moving to Epic in 1978. The second album included Jimmy Hall's creditable version of Otis Redding's 'Shout Bamalama' but the first hit was the live recording *Drippin' Wet*, for which they added female singers Donna Hall and Ella Brown, who had made solo records for Capricorn. This was followed by a Top 10 hit with the title track of *Keep On Smilin'* which was produced by veteran Tom Dowd. The addition of keyboards player Michael Duke in 1976 brought another lead vocalist into the group, heard to advantage on the hard rocking 'Teaser' from *The Wetter The Better*. In 1978 Ross and Hirsch (who joined Gregg Allman's band) were replaced by guitarists Larry Bernwald and Marshall Smith plus Theophilus Lively (drums). With Gary Lyons producing, Wet Willie had Top 30 hits in 1978-9 with 'Street Corner Serenade' and 'Weekend'. The group split in 1980, with Jimmy Hall making two unsuccessful solo albums accompanied by his brother and Duke. Hall also recorded with the Allman Brothers Band in the 80s.

Albums: *Wet Willie* (1971), *II* (1972), *Drippin' Wet* (1973), *Keep On Smilin'* (1974), *Dixie Rock* (1975), *The Wetter The Better* (1976), *Left Coast Live* (1977), *Manorisms* (1978), *Which One's Willie* (1979).

White, Barry

b. 12 September 1944, Galveston, Texas, USA. Raised in Los Angeles, White immersed himself in the local music fraternity while still very young, playing piano on Jesse Belvin's hit, 'Goodnight My Love', at the age of 11. Barry made several records during the early 60s, under his own name, as 'Barry Lee', and as a member of the Upfronts, the Atlantics and the Majestics. However, he found a greater success as a backroom figure, guiding the careers of, amongst others, Felice Taylor and Viola Wills. In 1969 White put together Love Unlimited, a female vocal trio made up of Diana Taylor, Glodean James (his future wife) and her sister Linda. He also founded the Love Unlimited Orchestra, a 40-piece ensemble to accompany himself and the singing trio, for which he conducted, composed and arranged. Love Unlimited's success in 1972 with 'Walkin' In The Rain With The One I Love', featuring White's gravelly, passion-soaked voice on the telephone, rejuvenated Barry's own career, during which he scored major US hits with 'I'm Gonna Love You Just A Little More Baby', 'Never, Never Gonna Give Ya Up' (both 1973), 'Can't Get Enough Of Your Love, Babe' and 'You're The First, The Last, My Everything' (both 1974) all of which proved just as popular in the UK. With these, the artist established a well-wrought formula where catchy pop/soul melodies were fused to sweeping arrangements and the singer's husky growl. The style quickly verged on self-parody as the sexual content of the lyrics grew more explicit, but although his pop hits lessened towards the end of the 70s, he remained the idolatry subject of live performances. The singer's last major hit was in 1978 with Billy Joel's 'Just The Way You Are'. He later undertook several recordings with Glodean White before returning to the UK Top 20 in 1987 with 'Sho' You Right'. The subject of critical approbation, particularly with reference to his large

frame. White's achievements during the peak of his career, in securing gold and platinum discs for worldwide sales, should not be underestimated. Lisa Stansfield has often voiced her approval of White's work and in 1992, she and White re-recorded a version of Stansfield's hit, 'All Around The World' but it was not as successful as the original.

Albums: *I've Got So Much To Give* (1973), *Stone Gon'* (1973), *Can't Get Enough* (1974), *Just Another Way To Say I Love You* (1975), *Let The Music Play* (1976), *Is This Whatcha Wont?* (1976), *Barry White Sings For Someone You Love* (1977), *Barry White The Man* (1978), *The Message Is Love* (1979), *I Love To Sing The Songs I Sing* (1979), *Barry White's Sheet Music* (1980), *The Best Of Our Love* (1981), with Glodean James *Barry And Glodean* (1981), *Beware!* (1981), *Change* (1982), *Dedicated* (1983), *The Right Night And Barry White* (1987), *The Man Is Back!* (1989), *In Your Mix* (1991). Compilations: *Barry White's Greatest Hits* (1975), *Barry White's Greatest Hits Vol.2* (1977), *Heart And Soul* (1985), *Satin & Soul* (1987), *The Collection* (1988), *Satin & Soul Vol. 2* (1990).

White Plains

White Plains was one of several groups, drawn from a cache of British session singers that enjoyed hit singles during the early 70s. Tony Burrows, Robin Shaw and Pete Nelson were each ex-members of the Flowerpot Men, while the act's line-up was completed by songwriter Roger Greenaway, previously 'David' of David And Jonathan. The 'newcomer' co-wrote White Plains' debut hit, 'My Baby Loves Lovin'' (1970), with partner Roger Cook, and joined Burrows in the Brotherhood Of Man who enjoyed a contemporaneous UK Top 10 single, 'United We Stand'. Both vocalists then left White Plains to form the Pipkins, while Shaw and Nelson brought in replacement singers for studio and live work. Another Cook And Greenaway composition, 'I've Got You On My Mind', took the reshaped unit back into the Top 20, before their cover version of Bobby Sherman's US smash hit, 'Julie Do Ya Love Me?', reached number 8. The quartet enjoyed two further UK hits - 'When You Are A King' (1971), number 13 and 'Step Into A Dream' (1973, number 21) - but disbanded when early momentum proved unsustainable.

Albums: *White Plains* (1970), *When You Are A King* (1971).

Whittaker, Roger

b. 22 March 1936, Nairobi, Kenya. Born of English parents originally from Staffordshire, Whittaker spent his younger years living in Africa. It was here that he acquired his first musical instrument in the shape of a guitar made by an Italian prisoner-of-war. In 1956 he moved to South Africa to what was to be an ill-fated attempt at studying medicine in Cape Town. After a period of teaching, he arrived in Wales in 1959 to study marine biology and bio-chemistry. Until then, Whittaker had treated his musical career purely as a part-time occupation, entertaining small groups of friends and the occasional folk club date. By 1961, while still continuing his studies, he had played many cabaret slots and after recording an independently-funded single for charity, he secured a contract with Fontana Records. His second single, 'Steel Man' (as Rog Whittaker), reached the lower regions of the UK charts. Roger decided to eschew a promising career in science in favour of one in entertainment. His brand of romantic folk-ballads made him a favourite with audiences all around Britain, particularly in Northern Ireland, where he enjoyed a resident spot on the Ulster television show *This And That*.

His steady rise in popularity was bolstered by a successful appearance at the Knokke music festival in Belgium in 1967. Among his prize winning performances was the self-penned, 'Mexican Whistler', which was recorded in Paris soon after the festival and became a chart number 1 around the continent. Whittaker's easy-going, relaxed style made him a star performer on the European television and concert circuit. By learning the translation of his songs phonetically, he has taken the trouble to record especially for his German audience. This growing band of admirers spread in time to the Antipodes and Canada, yet he had still to crack the UK market. This was achieved in 1969 with 'The Leavin' (Durham Town)' and the follow-up, 'I Don't Believe In If Anymore'. Along with 'New World In The Morning', 'Why' (co-written with Joan Stanton) and 'The Last Farewell' (co-written with Ron Webster), these songs established Whittaker as a successful MOR performer and finally made him an star in his adopted home country, giving him his own BBC television series.

It was the 'Last Farewell' that eventually broke the singer in the USA, bringing him a Top 20 hit in 1975 and finally selling over 11,000,000 copies worldwide. During the ensuing round of coast-to-coast tours and talk shows, Roger launched a songwriting competition on behalf of UNESCO, earning him the B'nai B'rith Humanitarian Award. In 1986, after a gap of 11 years, Whittaker made a reappearance on the UK Top 10 singles chart with the standard 'The Skye Boat Song' in a duo performance with fellow light entertainer, Des O'Connor. He has never lost contact with his African roots and his concern for the diminishing numbers of rhinos in his native Kenya led to a campaign to fight the poachers, including the fund-raising song, 'Rescue The Rhinos'. As a prodigious recording and performing artist, Roger Whittaker's global record sales have reached in excess of 40,000,000, a glowing testimony of this singer's phenomenal success.

Albums: *Butterfly* (1965), *Dynamic* (1967), *Mexican Whistler* (1967), *This Is Roger Whittaker* (1968), *Settle Down With Roger Whittaker* (1969), *C'Est Ma Vie* (1969), *I Don't Believe In If Anymore* (1970), *New World In The Morning* (1971), *A Special Kind Of Man* (1971), *Whistling Round The World* (1971), *For My Friends* (1972), *Head On Down The Road* (1973), *The Last Farewell* (1974), *In Orbit* (1974), *Travelling With Roger Whittaker* (1974), *Live In Canada* (1975), *Ride A Country Road* (1975), *The Magical World Of Roger Whittaker* (1975), *Live - With Saffron* (1975), *Reflections Of Love* (1976), *Folk Songs Of Our Time* (1977), *Roger Whittaker Sings The Hits* (1978), *Imagine* (1978), *From The People To The People* (1979), *When I Need You* (1979), *Mirrors Of My Mind* (1979), *Wishes* (1979), *Mein Deutsches Album* (1979, German release), *Voyager* (1980), *With Love* (1980), *Changes* (1981), *The Roger Whittaker Album* (1981), *Live In Concert* (1981), *Roger Whittaker In Kenya* (1982), *The Wind Beneath My Wings* (1982), *Typisch* (1982, German release), *Roger's Canadian Favourites* (1983), *Take A Little, Give A Little* (1984), *Songs Of Love And Life* (1984), *Tidings Of Comfort And Joy* (1984), *The Country Feel* (1985), *The Romantic Side* (1985), *Singing The Hits* (1985), *The Songwriter* (1985), *Skye Boat Song And Other Great Songs* (1986), *Easy Riding* (1988), *Living And Loving* (1988), *Love Will Be Our Home* (1989), *Maritime Memories* (1989), *A Time For Peace* (1989), *Live From The Tivoli* (1989), *Home Lovin' Man* (1989), *World's Most Beautiful Christmas Songs* (1989), *I'd Fall In Love Tonight* (1989), *Nur Wir Zwei* (1990, German release), *The Country Collection* (1991), *You Deserve The Best* (1991, UK release), *Sincerely Yours* (1991), *Alle Wege Führen Zu Dir* (1990, German release), *You Deserve The Best* (1991, US release, different track listing from UK album), *Seine Grossten Erfolge* (1991, German release), *Mein Herz Schlagt Nur Fur Dich* (1991,

German release). Compilations: *The Very Best Of Roger Whittaker* (1974), *The Second Album Of The Very Best Of Roger Whittaker* (1976), *20 All Time Greats* (1978), *The Best Of Roger Whittaker* (1984), *His Finest Collection* (1987), *The Best Of Roger Whittaker* (1991).

Further reading: *So Far, So Good*, Roger and Natalie Whittaker.

Wild Cherry

Wild Cherry's claim to fame was the US number 1 and UK Top 10 single 'Play That Funky Music', in 1976 - the song, a funky dance number, has probably outlived the name of its creators in the minds of most fans. Wild Cherry was a white quintet formed that year in Steubenville, Ohio, USA. Its original membership consisted of Bob Parissi (guitar/vocals) and other musicians although they never recorded; Parissi re-formed the group with new recruits Bryan Bassett (guitar), Allen Wentz (bass), Mark Avsec (keyboards) and Ron Beitle (drums). The group took its name when Parissi, an accident victim laid-up in hospital, looked at a box of cherry-flavoured cough drops and liked what he saw. They recorded for a small label, Brown bag, owned by Grand Funk Railroad mastermind Terry Knight. The second line-up had the famous hit; signed to Epic Records, the group preferred hard rock but often played in discos where patrons would shout, 'Play that funky music, white boy'. Writing a song around that phrase, they took it to Cleveland record producer Carl Maduri and concert promoter Mike Belkin, who secured them a record deal. The group charted with four subsequent singles but never came close to repeating the success of their 'funky' hit although the famous chant was used by white rapper, Vanilla Ice for his hit follow-up to 'Ice Ice Baby'.

Albums: *Wild Cherry* (1976), *Electrified Funk* (1977), *I Love My Music* (1978), *Only The Wild Survive* (1979), *Don't Wait Too Long* (1979).

Williams, Paul

b 19 September 1940, Omaha, Nebraska, USA. A pop composer, Williams wrote some of the 70s most enduring melodies and had further successes as a singer and soundtrack composer. Short in stature, Williams entered show business as a stunt man and film actor, appearing as a child in *The Loved One* (1964) and *The Chase* (1965). He turned to script and songwriting, collaborating with Roger Nichols on two of the Carpenters' biggest hits, 'We've Only Just Begun' and 'Rainy Days And

Mondays'. The duo also provided material for Helen Reddy ('You And Me Against The World') and Three Dog Night ('Just An Old Fashioned Love Song'). Williams recorded his first solo album for Reprise in 1970 before moving to A&M Records the following year. None of these albums sold well but Williams developed a highly praised night-club act in the early 70s. His first film score was for *Phantom Of The Paradise*, Brian de Palma's update of the *Phantom Of The Opera* story, in which Williams starred. This was followed by songs for *A Star Is Born*, another modern version of an old movie which featured Kris Kristofferson and Barbra Streisand, but Williams' most impressive score was the 30s pastiche he provided for *Bugsy Malone*, the gangster spoof entirely acted by children. His later scores included *The End* (1977) and *The Muppet Movie* (1979) .

Albums: *Someday Man* (1970), *Just An Old Fashioned Love Song* (1971), *Life Goes On* (1972), *Here Comes Inspiration* (1974), *A Little Bit Of Love* (1974), *Phantom Of The Paradise* (1975, film soundtrack), *Ordinary Fool* (1975), *Bugsy Malone* (1975, film soundtrack). Compilation: *Classics* (1977).

Wilson, Meri

b. Japan. Meri Wilson was behind the 1977 US Top 20/UK Top 10 single 'Telephone Man', released on GRT/Pye Records. She was raised in Marietta, Georgia and began singing and playing piano and flute in her childhood. After attending college in Indiana, Wilson turned professional and worked as a jingle singer in the Dallas, Texas area. The innuendo-laden song 'Telephone Man' was her own composition and the recording was produced by Owen 'Boomer' Castleman and Jim Rutledge. Although Wilson recorded two subsequent singles and an album, she never again made the charts and her future endeavours remain a mystery.

Album: *Telephone Man* aka *First Take* (1977).

Wingfield, Pete

b. 7 May 1948, Kiphook, Hampshire, England. Wingfield was a pianist who previously led Pete's Disciples and played sessions with Top Topham, Graham Bond, and Memphis Slim. He was also an acknowledged soul music expert who started the *Soul Beat* fanzine in the late 60s, and in the 70s would write for *Let It Rock* magazine. While at Sussex University he met fellow students Paul Butler (guitar), John Best (bass), and local teacher Chris Waters (drums) and formed the band

Jellybread. With Wingfield doing most of the singing they made an album for their own Liphook label which they used as a demo and got themselves a deal with Blue Horizon Records. Although they gained some plaudits from the media they were generally unsuccessful and Wingfield left in the summer of 1971. He next played in Keef Hartley's band but that liaison ended when Hartley was invited to drum for John Mayall. Wingfield did further sessions for Freddie King, then joined Colin Blunstone's band, and also backed Van Morrison for a spell. With Joe Jammer, he became the core of the session band the Olympic Runners, who were the brainchild of Blue Horizon boss Mike Vernon. The Runners also included DeLisle Harper (bass) and Glen LeFleur (drums) who acted as the rhythm section on Wingfield's own 1975 album *Breakfast Special* which included the hit single '18 With A Bullet'. The Olympic Runners had some success in their own right late in the 70s. Wingfield still does sessions and various studio projects, putting out the occasional single. However, he is now better known for his production credits (like Dexys Midnight Runners' *Searching For The Young Soul Rebels*, plus Blue Rondo A La Turk and the Kane Gang).
Album: *Breakfast Special* (1975).

Winter, Edgar

b. 28 December 1946, Beaumont, Texas, USA. Although at times overshadowed by his brother, Johnny Winter, Edgar has enjoyed an intermittently successful career. The siblings began performing together as teenagers, and were members of several itinerant groups performing in southern-state clubs and bars. Edgar later forsook music for college, before accepting an offer to play saxophone in a local jazz band. He rejoined his brother in 1969, but the following year Edgar released *Entrance*. He then formed an R&B revue, Edgar Winter's White Trash, whose live set *Roadwork*, was an exciting testament to this talented ensemble. Winter then fronted a slimmer group – Dan Hartman (vocals), Ronnie Montrose (guitar) and Chuck Ruff (drums) – which appeared on the artist's only million-selling album, *They Only Come Out At Night*. This highly successful selection included the rousing instrumental, 'Frankenstein', which became a hit single in its own right. Guitarist Rick Derringer, who had produced Winter's previous two albums, replaced Montrose for *Shock Treatment*, but this and subsequent releases failed to maintain the singer's commercial

ascendancy. He rejoined his brother in 1976 for the *Together* album, since which Edgar Winter's professional profile has been considerably lean.
Albums: *Entrance* (1970), *Edgar Winter's White Trash* (1971), *Roadwork* (1972), *They Only Come Out At Night* (1972), *Shock Treatment* (1974), *Jasmine Nightdreams* (1975), *Edgar Winter Group With Rick Derringer* (1975), with Johnny Winter *Together* (1976), *Recycled* (1977), *The Edgar Winter Album* (1979), *Standing On The Rock* (1981). Compilation: *Rock Giants* (1982).

Wishbone Ash

In 1966 Steve Upton (b. 24 May 1946, Wrexham, Wales; drums) who had played with the Scimitars, joined Martin Turner (b. 1 October 1947, Torquay, Devon, England; bass/vocals) and Glen Turner (guitar) in the Torquay band the Empty Vessels. This trio moved to London where they took the name of Tanglewood. Glen Turner departed, and another man of the same surname, Ted Turner (b. David Alan Turner, 2 August 1950; guitar) joined the band. He had previously played in the Birmingham band, King Biscuit. Wishbone Ash was formed when Andy Powell (b. 8 February 1950; guitar) of the Sugarband joined Upton, Turner and Turner. Heavily influenced by the music of the Yardbirds and the Allman Brothers, Wishbone Ash's hallmark was the powerful sound of twin lead guitars. Their biggest commercial success was *Argus*, released in 1973. This was a prime example of the band's preoccupation with historical themes, complex instrumentals, and folk-rock. Ted Turner departed in 1974, and was replaced by Laurie Wisefield, formerly of Home. Wishbone Ash continued successfully, becoming tax exiles in the USA, returning to England in 1975 to play at the Reading Rock festival. In 1980 Martin Turner left Wishbone Ash, John Wetton, formerly of Uriah Heep and Roxy Music, serving as his replacement, and singer Claire Hammill joined the band, along with Trevor Bolder. This line-up released only one album before disbanding in 1982, and it was the recruitment of Mervyn Spence to replace Bolder that seemed to give some of its former vitality back to Wishbone Ash. It was in 1987 that the original quartet got back together again, recording *Nouveau Calls*. This project involved the renewal of Wishbone Ash's relationship with Miles Copeland, who was manager of the Police, and who had managed Wishbone Ash for a brief spell in the 60s. They continue to perform to a loyal and devoted following.

Edgar Winter

Wishbone Ash

Albums: *Wishbone Ash* (1970), *Pilgrimage* (1972), *Argus* (1973), *Wishbone 4* (1973), *Live Dates* (1974), *There's The Rub* (1974), *Locked In* (1976), *New England* (1977), *Frontpage News* (1977), *No Smoke Without Fire* (1978), *Live In Tokyo* (1978), *Just Testing* (1979), *Live Dates Vol. II* (1979), *Number The Brave* (1981), *Hot Ash* (1981), *Two Barrels Burning* (1982), *Raw To The Bone* (1985), *Nouveau Calls* (1987), *BBC Radio 1 Live In Concert* (1991, rec. 1972). Compilations: *Classic Ash* (1981), *The Best Of Wishbone Ash* (1982).

Withers, Bill

b. 4 July 1938, Slab Fork, West Virginia, USA. Having moved to California in 1967 after nine years in the US Navy, Withers began hawking his original songs around several west coast companies. He was eventually signed to Sussex Records in 1971 and secured an immediate hit with his debut single, 'Ain't No Sunshine'. Produced by Booker T. Jones, with Stephen Stills amongst the guest musicians, this sparse but compulsive performance was a million-seller, a feat emulated in 1972 by two more excellent releases, 'Lean On Me' and 'Use Me'. Withers light, folksy/soul continued to score further success with 'Make Love To Your Mind' (1975), the sublime 'Lovely Day' (1977), (a single revamped by a remix in 1988) and 'Just The Two Of Us' (1981), his exhilarating duet with saxophonist Grover Washington Jnr., which earned the two artists a grammy in 1982 for the Best R&B performance. 'Lovely Day' re-entered the UK pop charts in 1988 after exposure from a British television commercial, reaching the Top 5. A professional rather than charismatic performer, Withers remains a skilled songwriter.

Albums: *Just As I Am* (1971), *Still Bill* (1972), *Live At Carnegie Hall* (1973), *+'Justments* (1974), *Making Music* (1975), *Naked And Warm* (1976), *Menagerie* (1977), *'Bout Love* (1979), *Watching You Watching Me* (1985). Compilations: *The Best Of Bill Withers* (1975), *Bill Wither's Greatest Hits* (1981).

Wizzard

Having already achieved success with the Move and the Electric Light Orchestra, the ever-experimental Roy Wood put together Wizzard in 1972 with a line up comprising Rick Price (vocals/bass), Hugh McDowell (cello), Bill Hunt (keyboards), Mike Burney (saxophone), Nick Pentelow (saxophone), Keith Smart (drums) and Charlie Grima (drums). The octet made their debut at the 1972 Wembley Rock 'n' Roll Festival and hit the charts later that year with the chaotic but intriguing 'Ball Park Incident'. Wood was at his peak as a producer during this period and his Phil Spector-like 'wall of sound' pop experiments produced two memorable UK number 1 hits ('See My Baby Jive', 'Angel Fingers') and a perennial festive hit, 'I Wish It Could Be Christmas Every

Day'. There was even a playful stab at rivals ELO on the cheeky b-side 'Bend Over Beethoven'. Much of Wizzard's peculiar charm came from the complementary pop theatricalism of Roy Wood, who covered himself with war paint, painted stars on his forehead and sported an unruly mane of multi-coloured hair. Although less impressive on their album excursions, Wizzard's *Introducing Eddy And The Falcons* (a similar concept to Frank Zappa's *Cruising With Ruben And The Jets*) was a clever and affectionate rock 'n' roll pastiche with tributes to such greats as Del Shannon, Gene Vincent, Dion, Duane Eddy and Cliff Richard. By 1975, the group were making in-roads into the American market where manager Don Arden was increasingly involved with lucrative stadia rock. Wizzard failed to persuade the management to increase their financial input, however, and swiftly folded. Wood, Rick Price and Mike Burney abbreviated the group name for the short-lived Wizzo Band, whose unusual brand of jazz funk proved too esoteric for commercial tastes. After less than a year in operation, this offshoot group self-destructed in March 1978 following which, Wood concentrated on solo outings and production.

Albums: *Wizzard Brew* (1973), *Introducing Eddy And The Falcons* (1974), *Super Active Wizzo* (1977). Compilation: *See My Baby Jive* (1974).

Womack, Bobby

b. 4 March 1944, Cleveland, Ohio, USA. A founder member of the Valentinos, this accomplished musician also worked as a guitarist in Sam Cooke's touring band. He scandalized the music fraternity by marrying Barbara Campbell, Cooke's widow, barely three months after the ill-fated singer's death. Womack's early solo singles, 'Nothing You Can Do' and the superb 'I Found A True Love', were all but shunned and, with the Valentinos now in disarray, he reverted to session work. Womack became a fixture at Chips Moman's American Recording Studio, but although he appeared on many recordings, this period is best recalled for his work with Wilson Pickett. 'I'm In Love' and 'I'm A Midnight Mover' are two of the 17 Womack songs that particular artist would record. Bobby meanwhile resurrected his solo career with singles on Keymen and Atlantic Records. Signing with Minit, he began a string of R&B hits, including 'It's Gonna Rain', 'How I Miss You Baby' (both 1969) and 'More Than I Can Stand (1970). His authoritative early album, *The Womack Live*, then introduced the freer, more personal direction he would undertake in the 70s. The final catalyst for change was *There's A Riot Going On*, Sly Stone's 1971 collection on which Womack played guitar. Its influence was

Bobby Womack

most clearly heard on 'Communication', the title track to Womack's first album for United Artists.

Part of a prolific period, the follow-up album, *Understanding*, was equally strong, and both yielded impressive singles, which achieved high positions in the R&B charts. 'That's The Way I Feel About Cha' (number 2), 'Woman's Gotta Have It' (number 1) and 'Harry Hippie' (number 8), which confirmed his new-found status. Successive albums from *Facts Of Life*, *Looking For A Love Again* and *I Don't Know What The World Is Coming To*, consolidated the accustomed mixture of original songs, slow raps and cover versions. *BW Goes C&W* (1976), a self-explanatory experiment, closed his UA contract, but subsequent work for CBS and Arista was undistinguished. In 1981 Womack signed with Beverly Glen, a small Los Angeles independent, where he recorded *The Poet*. This powerful set re-established his career while a single, 'If You Think You're Lonely Now', reached number 3 on the R&B chart. *The Poet II* (1984) featured three duets with Patti LaBelle, one of which, 'Love Has Finally Come At Last', was another hit single. Womack moved to MCA Records in 1985, debuting with *So Many Rivers*. A longstanding friendship with the Rolling Stones was emphasized that year when he sang back-up on their version of 'Harlem Shuffle'. Bobby's more recent work proclaims himself 'the last soul singer'. An expressive, emotional singer, his best work stands among black music's finest moments.

Albums: *Fly Me To The Moon* (1968), *My Prescription* (1969), *The Womack Live* (1970), *Communication* (1971), *Understanding* (1972), *Across 110th Street* (1972, film soundtrack), *Facts Of Life* (1973), *Looking For A Love Again* (1974), *I Don't Know What The World Is Coming To* (1975), *Safety Zone* (1976), *BW Goes C&W* (1976), *Home Is Where The Heart Is* (1976), *Pieces* (1977), *Roads Of Life* (1979), *The Poet* (1981), *The Poet II* (1984), *Someday We'll All Be Free* (1985), *So Many Rivers* (1985), *Womagic* (1986), *The Last Soul Man* (1987). Compilations: *Bobby Womack's Greatest Hits* (1974), *Somebody Special* (1984), *Check It Out* (1986), *Womack Winners* (1989).

Wombles

The brainchild of producer, arranger and songwriter, Mike Batt, the anthropomorphic Wombles emerged from a children's television series to take the charts by storm in 1974. They enjoyed a series of hits based loosely on their Wimbledon Common lifestyle (an early attempt at ecological education for children, the Wombles recycled the rubbish found on the Common). 'The Wombling Song', 'Remember You're A Womble', 'Banana Rock' and 'Wombling Merry Christmas' were all Top 10 hits, making the group the most successful and consistent chart act of the year. By the end of 1975, however, the novelty had worn thin and Batt's solo outing 'Summertime City' was outselling his puppet counterparts.

Albums: *Wombling Songs* (1973), *Remember You're A Womble* (1974), *Christmas Package* (1974), *Superwombling* (1975), *Wombling Free* (1978, film soundtrack). Compilation: *20 Wombling Greats* (1977).

Wood, Roy

b. Ulysses Adrian Wood, 8 November 1946, Birmingham, England. Having been named after Homer's Greek mythological hero, Wood abandoned this eminently suitable pop star sobriquet in favour of the more prosaic Roy. As a teenager, he was a itinerant guitarist, moving steadily through a succession of minor Birmingham groups including the Falcons, the Lawmen, Gerry Levene and the Avengers and Mike Sheridan and the Nightriders. After a failed stab at art school, he pooled his talents with some of the best musicians on the Birmingham beat scene to form the Move. Under the guidance of Tony Secunda, they established themselves as one of the best pop groups of their time, with Wood emerging as their leading songwriter. By the time of 'Fire Brigade' (1967), Wood was instilled as lead singer and it was his fertile pop imagination which took the group through a plethora of musical styles, ranging from psychedelia to rock 'n' roll revivalism, classical rock and heavy metal. Never content to be bracketed to one musical area, Wood decided to supplement the Move's pop work by launching the grandly-named Electric Light Orchestra, whose aim was to produce more experimental albums-orientated rock with a classical influence. Wood survived as ELO's frontman for only one single and album before a personality clash with fellow member Jeff Lynne prompted his departure in June 1972. He returned soon after with Wizzard, one of the most inventive and appealing pop groups of the early 70s. During this period, he also enjoyed a parallel solo career and although his two albums were uneven, they revealed his surplus creative energies as a multi-instrumentalist, engineer, producer and even sleeve designer. Back in the singles chart, Wood the soloist scored several UK hits including the majestic 'Forever', an inspired and affectionate tribute to Neil Sedaka and the Beach Boys, with the composer playing the part of an English Phil Spector. Wood's eccentric ingenuity continued on various singles and b-sides, not least the confusing 'Bengal Jig', which fused bagpipes and sitar!

By the late 70s, Wood was ploughing less commercial ground with the Wizzo Band, Rock Brigade and the Helicopters, while his former group ELO produced million-selling albums. The chart absence of Wood since 1975 remains one of pop's great mysteries especially in view of his previous track record as producer, songwriter and brilliant manipulator of contrasting pop genres.

Albums: *Boulders* (1973), *Mustard* (1975), *On The Road Again* (1979), *Starting Up* (1987). Compilations: *The Roy Wood Story* (1976), *The Singles* (1982).

Woodward, Edward

b. 1 June 1930, Croydon, Surrey, England. This UK television actor had a brief musical career as a crooner in the early 70s. He trained at the Royal Academy of Dramatic Art in London and acted in numerous stage plays before achieving national recognition in the UK television series *Emergency Ward 10* (50s/60s), as the star of the crime series *Callan* (70s) and the transatlantic *Equalizer* (80s). His recording career began in 1969 when he transferred his 'English gentleman' persona onto record in a series of albums for DJM Records. Woodward's repertoire ranged from ballad standards of the 30s and 40s to contemporary easy-listening hits such as 'Send In The Clowns' and 'Windmills Of Your Mind'. *Edwardian Woodward* was a selection of music hall songs. His only minor hit single was a revival of Jerome Kern's 'The Way You Look Tonight' in 1971, though his second album reached the Top 20 the following year. In 1980 he released a single of the patriotic 'Soldiers Of The Queen' on the RK label.

Albums: *Grains Of Sand* (1969), *This Man Alone* (1970), *The Edward Woodward Album* (1972), *Edwardian Woodward* (1975), *The Way You Look Tonight* (1976) *Love Is The Key* (1976), *The Thought Of You* (1976), *Don't Get Around Much Anymore* (1977), *Woodward Again* (1981).

Wurzels

Originally Adge Cutler And The Wurzels, this English West Country group first scored a minor hit in 1967 with the comic 'Drink Up Thy Zider'. Following Cutler's tragic death in a car crash in 1974, Tommy Banner, Tony Baylis and Pete Budd soldiered on as the Wurzels. Producer Bob Barrett was impressed by their country yokel parodies of

Wurzels

well-known hits and persuaded them to provide comic lyrics to Melanie's 'Brand New Key', which emerged as 'Combine Harvester', a surprise UK number 1 in the summer of 1976. The trio almost repeated that feat with their reworking of the continental hit 'Uno Paloma Blanca' retitled ' I Am A Cider Drinker'. Although they only achieved one more success with 'Farmer Bill's Cowman' (based on Whistling Jack Smith's 'I Was Kaiser Bill's Batman') they continued to appear occasionally on British television shows and maintain their popularity on the UK club circuit.

Albums: *Adge Cutler And The Wurzels* (1967), *Adge Cutler's Family Album* (1967), *Cutler Of The West* (1968), *The Wurzels Are Scrumptious* (1975), *The Combine Harvester* (1976), *Golden Delicious* (1977), *Give Me England* (1977), *I'll Never Get A Scrumpy Here* (1978), *I'm A Cider Drinker* (1979). Compilation: *The Very Best Of Adge Cutler And The Wurzels* (1977), *Greatest Hits* (1979), *Wurzels* (1981).

Wyatt, Robert

b. 28 January 1945, Bristol, Avon, England. As the drummer, vocalist and guiding spirit of the original Soft Machine, Robert Wyatt established a style which merged the *avant garde* with English eccentricity. His first solo album, *The End Of An Ear*, presaged his departure from the above group, although its radical content resulted in a muted reception. Wyatt's next venture, the excellent Matching Mole, was bedevilled by internal dissent but a planned relaunch was forcibly abandoned following a tragic fall from a window, which left him paralyzed and confined to a wheelchair. *Rock Bottom*, the artist's next release, was composed while Wyatt lay in hospital. This heartfelt, deeply personal collection was marked by an aching vulnerability which successfully avoided any hint of self-pity. This exceptional album was succeeded by an unlikely hit single in the shape of an idiosyncratic reading of the Monkees hit, 'I'm A Believer'. *Ruth Is Stranger Than Richard*, released in 1975, was a more open collection, and balanced original pieces with outside material, including a spirited reading of jazz bassist Charlie Haden's 'Song For Che'. Although Wyatt, a committed Marxist, would make frequent guest appearances, his own career was shelved until 1980 when a single comprising of two South American songs of liberation became the first in a series of politically motivated releases undertaken for the Rough Trade label. These performances were subsequently compiled on *Nothing Can Stop Us*, which was then

enhanced by the addition of 'Shipbuilding', a haunting anti-Falkland War composition, specifically written for Wyatt by Elvis Costello which was a minor chart entry in 1983. Wyatt's fluctuating health has undermined his recording ambitions, but his commitment remains undiminished. He issued singles in aid of Namibia and the British Miners' Hardship Fund, and contributed a compassionate soundtrack to the harrowing 1982 *Animals* film. Wyatt's recent works *Old Rotten Hat* and *Dondestan* are as compelling as the rest of his impressive work. It is remarkable that an artist like Wyatt can come to terms with the tragic events of his accident and carry on with considerable enthusiasm, hope and creativity.

Albums: *The End Of An Ear* (1970), *Rock Bottom* (1974), *Ruth Is Stranger Than Richard* (1975), *Nothing Can Stop Us* (1982), *Animals* (1984), *Old Rotten Hat* (1985), *Dondestan* (1991).

Wyman, Bill

b. William Perks, 24 October 1936, London, England. Though his recruitment by the Rolling Stones may have saved him from a more mundane life, his frustrated artistic ambition - particularly as a composer - deserves a measure of sympathy. 1967's 'In Another Land' (b/w '2000 Light Years From Home') failed to reach the US Top 40, and only one other opus written solely by Wyman has ever been released by the group. Speculating in artist management and record production in the 60s, he was, nevertheless, able to foister some of his material onto the End, Bobbie Miller and other unsuccessful clients. By the mid-70s, his songs were heard by a much wider public when he issued his first solo record, *Monkey Grip*, on which he was accompanied mostly by Los Angeles session players. Amid hearsay that he was serving his notice with Mick Jagger and co., 1976's *Stone Alone* and its single - an overhaul of Gary 'US' Bonds' 'Quarter To Three' - employed renowned assistants like Van Morrison and Sly Stone as well as Stones associates Nicky Hopkins, Ron Wood and Al Kooper. Paradoxically, Wyman's resignation seemed less inevitable when 1982's witty '(Si, Si) Je Suis Un Rock Star' was the highest UK chart strike for any solo Stone. One of its follow-ups, 'A New Fashion' also sold well. Both were recorded when Wyman was labouring over the film score to *Green Ice*. His membership of the Stones guaranteed each single (and attendant album) some airplay but their chart placings testified to more intrinsic virtues in an industry where sales figures were arbiters of worth.

Among Wyman's numerous charitable works during the 80s was the shouldering of much of Ronnie Lane's load in organizing fund-raising galas for Action For Muscular Sclerosis. One such London event featuring his *ad hoc* 'Willie and the Poor Boys' was immortalized on video and included an appearance by Ringo Starr with whom Wyman invested in 'The Brasserie', an Atlanta restaurant. Its failure did not quell his appetite for catering as shown by the opening of *Sticky Fingers*, his London eaterie. Using the Stones' mobile studio, Wyman traversed the UK on a search for deserving unknown bands via Ambition Ideas Motivation and Success (AIMS), a project that fizzled out when the Pernod drink company withdrew its sponsorship. All these ventures were, however, less interesting to the tabloid press than his courtship and consequent troubled marriage to teenager Mandy Smith whom he allegedly seduced when she was 13 years-old. Wyman was further scrutinized by the press when a financial settlement was made following their divorce in 1992. Wyman published a tame autobiography in 1990. In January 1993 Wyman formally ended years of speculation by leaving the Rolling Stones.

Albums: *Monkey Grip* (1974), *Stone Alone* (1976), *Green Ice* (1981, film soundtrack), *Bill Wyman* (1982), with various artists *Willie And The Poor Boys* (1986).

Further reading: *Stone Alone*, Bill Wyman and Ray Coleman, .

X

X-Ray Spex

One of the most inventive, original and genuinely exciting groups to appear during the punk era, X-Ray Spex were the brainchild of the colourful Poly Styrene (Marion Elliot), whose exotic clothes and tooth brace, established her as an instant punk icon. With a line-up completed by Lora Logic, later replaced by Glyn Johns (saxophone), Jak Stafford (guitar), Paul Dean (bass) and B.P. Hurding (drums), the group began performing in 1977 and part of their second gig was captured for posterity on the seminal *Live At The Roxy WC2*. A series of extraordinary singles including 'Germ Free Adolescence', 'Oh Bondage Up Yours', 'The Day The World Turned Dayglo' and 'Identity' were not only rivetting examples of high energy punk, but contained provocative, thoughtful lyrics berating the urban synthetic fashions of the 70s and urging individual expression. Always ambivalent about her pop-star status, Poly dismantled the group in 1979 and joined the Krishna Consciousness Movement. X-Ray Spex's final single, 'Highly Inflammable' was coupled with the pulsating 'Warrior In Woolworths', a parting reminder of Poly's early days as a shop assistant. Although she reactivated her recording career with the album *Translucence* (1980) and a 1986 EP *Gods And Goddesses*, no further commercial success was forthcoming.
Album: *Germ Free Adolescents* (1978).

XTC

Formed during the punk boom of 1977 and originally known as the Helium Kidz, the band adopted the name XTC (ecstasy) and signed to Virgin Records. Except Andrews all members hailed from the Wiltshire town of Swindon; the band then comprised of Andy Partridge (b. 11 December 1953; guitar/vocals), Barry Andrews (b. 12 September, West Norwood, London, England), Colin Moulding (b. 17 August 1955) and Terry Chambers (b. 18 July 1955). The band's debut *White Music* lent more to pop than the energetic new wave sound, notwithstanding the album was a hit and critics marked their name for further attention. Shortly after the release of *Go2*, Barry Andrews departed, eventually to resurface in Shriekback. With Andrews replaced by Dave Gregory, both *Go2* and the following *Drums And Wires* were commercial successes and the quirky hit single 'Making Plans For Nigel' exposed them to an eagerly awaiting audience. Singles were regularly taken from their subsequent albums and they continued making the charts with quality pop songs including 'Sgt Rock (Is Going To Help Me)' and the magnificently constructed 'Senses Working Overtime', which reached the UK Top 10. The main songwriter, Partridge, was able to put his sharp observations to paper in a humorous and childish way that was totally palatable. The double set *English Settlement* was a bitter blow, as this critically applauded work struggled to nudge the charts. Partridge fell ill through exhaustion, and a stomach ulcer, and announced that XTC would continue only as recording artists (including promotional videos). Their subsequent albums have found only limited success, although their *alter ego* Dukes Of Stratosphear's, albums have reputedly sold more copies.

Their finest work to date, *Oranges And Lemons*, perceptively captured the feeling of the late 60s; this faultless album remains a perplexing commercial mystery. While it sold moderately well in in the USA, it barely made the UK Top 30. The highly commercial 'Mayor Of Simpleton' found similar fate, at a desultory number 46. In 1992 the credible *Nonsuch* entered the UK album charts and two weeks later promptly disappeared. Partridge was at work late in 1992 producing Blur's latest album. Quite what Andy Partridge, his colleagues in the band and Virgin Records feel they have to do remains uncertain. Partridge once joked that Virgin Records retain them only as a tax loss! XTC remain one of the most original pop bands of the era and Partridge's lyrics put him alonside Ray Davies as one of the UK's cleverest and most brilliantly eccentric writers.

Albums: *White Music* (1978), *Go2* (1978), *Drums And Wires* (1979), *Black Sea* (1980), *English Settlement* (1982), *Mummer* (1983), *The Big Express* (1984), *Skylarking* (1986), *Oranges And Lemons* (1989), *Nonsuch* (1992). Compilations: *Waxworks: Some Singles 1977-1982* (1982 - originally released with free compilation, *Beeswax*, a collection of b-sides), *The Compact XTC* (1986).

Y

Yamash' ta, Stomu

b. Tsutomu Yamashita, 15 March 1947, Kyoto, Japan. A percussionist and composer, Yamash' ta attempted to combine *avant garde* and rock music in the 70s. He studied at the Kyoto Academy of Music, making his concert debut as a soloist at the age of 16. From 1964-69 he studied and performed in the USA with both classical and jazz musicians. During the 70s, such modern composers as Hans Werne Henze and Peter Maxwell Davies created works for him which were recorded in 1972 for L' Oiseau-Lyre. From 1973, Yamash' ta created what he called 'floating music', a fusion of classical, rock and Eastern styles with his own European group, Come To The Edge. Among his shows were Red Buddha Theatre and The Man From The East, which included elements of Japanese kabuki theatre and were highly praised by British and French critics. He recorded six albums for Island with collaborators Steve Winwood, Klaus Schulze, Gary Boyle and Murray Head. *Go Too* was released by *Arista* with Dennis Mackay producing. During the 80s, Yamash' ta returned to the classical concert halls but also recorded instrumental works for new age company Celestial Harmonies.

Albums: *Contemporary* (1972), *Red Buddha* (1972), *Come To The Edge* (1973), *The Man From The East* (1973), *Freedom Is Frightening* (1974), *One By One* (1974), *Raindog* (1975), *Go* (1976), *Go Live From Paris* (1976), *Go Too* (1977), *Sea And Sky* (1987).

Yellow Dog

This 70s act revolved around the talents of Kenny Young and Herbie Armstrong. American-born Young was already an established songwriter, having penned 'Under The Boardwalk' for the Drifters and 'Captain Of Your Ship' for Reparta And The Delrons. The latter proved highly popular in the UK, inspiring the composer to move his base to London where he met his future partner. Guitarist Armstrong was a former member of the Wheels, a Belfast group contemporaneous with Them, before founding a duo with bassist Rod Demick. The duo met up when they both joined Fox and enjoyed a period of UK chart success. On the break-up of Fox in 1977, Yellow Dog was formed and their self-titled album was issued in 1977. However, its brand of sweet pop clashed with the year's endemic punk explosion. Andy Roberts (guitar, ex-Liverpool Scene and Plainsong), Gary Taylor (bass, ex-Herd) and Gerry Conway (drums, ex-Fairport Convention) augmented the duo on this promising debut, which spawned a UK Top 10 single in 'Just One More Night'. A second album, in part completed with the assistance of Demick and keyboard player Peter Bardens, proved less successful and the group's name was dropped soon afterwards.

Albums: *Yellow Dog* (1977), *Beware Of The Dog* (1978).

Yes

During the progressive music boom of the early 70s, Yes were rivalled only by Emerson Lake And Palmer and Genesis for their brand of classical-laced rock which was initially refreshing and innovative. They evolved into a huge stadium attraction and enjoyed phenomenal success until the new-wave came in 1977 and swept them aside. Yes were formed in 1968 by vocalist Jon Anderson (b. 25 October 1944, Accrington, Lancashire, England) and bassist Chris Squire (b. 4 March 1948, London, England). Both had been experienced with 60s' beat groups, notably the Warriors and the Syn, respectively. They were completed by Bill Bruford (b. 17 May 1948, London, England; drums), Pete Banks (b. 7 July 1947, Barnet, Hertfordshire, England) and Tony Kaye (b. 11 January 1946, Leicester, England). One of their early gigs was opening for Cream at their historic farewell concert at London's Royal Albert Hall, but it was pioneering disc jockey John Peel who gave them nationwide exposure, performing live on his BBC radio programme *Top Gear*. Their inventive version of Buffalo Springfield's 'Everydays' and the Beatles' 'Every Little Thing' combined with their own admirable debut 'Sweetness', made them club favourites. Banks was replaced in 1970 by guitar virtuoso Steve Howe (b. 8 April 1947, London, England; ex-Tomorrow) who added further complexity to their highly creative instrumental passages. Neither their debut *Yes* nor *Time And A Word* made much of an impression beyond their growing following.

It was with *The Yes Album* that the band created major interest and sales. Kaye then departed and was replaced by the highly accomplished keyboard wizard, Rick Wakeman (b. 18 May 1949, London, England; ex-Strawbs). Wakeman's improvisational skill, like Howe's, took the band into realms of classical influence, and their solos became longer, although often they sounded self-indulgent. *Fragile* was a major success and the band found considerable support from the UK music press, especially *Melody Maker*. *Fragile* was a landmark in that it began a series of Roger Dean's Tolkien-inspired fantasy covers, integrated with his custom-calligraphed Yes colophon. The album spawned a surprise US hit single 'Roundabout' which almost made the Top 10 in 1972. Shortly afterwards Bruford departed and was replaced by ex-Plastic Ono Band drummer Alan White. Later that year Yes released what now stands up as their finest work, *Close To The Edge*. Much of the four suites are instrumental, and allow the musicianship to dominate Anderson's often pretentiously abstract lyrics. Now a major band, they confidently issued a triple live album *Yessongs*, followed by a double, the overlong and indulgent *Tales From Topographic Oceans*. Both were huge successes, with the latter reaching number 1 in the UK.

Artistically, the band now started to decline, Wakeman left to pursue a triumphant solo career. His replacement was ex-Refugee Patrick Moraz, who maintained the classical influence that Wakeman had instigated. Following *Relayer* the band fragmented to undertake solo projects, although none emulated Wakeman, who was having greater success than Yes at this time. When the band reconvened, Wakeman rejoined in place of Moraz, and continued a dual career. *Going For The One* was a less 'cosmic' album and moved the band back into the realms of rock music. Another hit single, 'Wonderous Stories', made the UK Top 10 in 1977, at the height of the punk era. Yes were the type of band that was anathema to the new-wave, and while their vast following bought *Tormato*, their credibility plummeted. Internal problems were also rife, resulting in the second departure of Wakeman, immediately followed by Anderson. Astonishingly their replacements were Trevor Horn and Geoff Downes, who, as Buggles had topped the UK charts the previous year with 'Video Killed The Radio Star'. This bizarre marriage lasted a year before Yes finally said 'no' and broke-up in 1981. All members enjoyed successful solo careers and it came as a surprise in 1983 to find a reformed Yes topping the UK singles chart with the excellent Trevor Horn-produced 'Owner Of A Lonely Heart'. The subsequent *90125* showed a rejuvenated band with short contemporary dance/rock songs that fitted with 80s' fashion. No new Yes output came until four years later with *Big Generator*, and in 1989 *Anderson, Bruford, Wakeman And Howe* was released during a lengthy legal dispute. Yes could not use the name, so instead they resorted to the Affirmative; Anderson, Howe etc plays an 'Evening Of Yes Music' (cleverly using the famous logo). With the ownership problem solved, Yes announced a major tour in 1991, and were once again in the US Top 10 with *Union*. Over the years Yes have received more than their share of criticism for their sometimes naive attempts at serious music. They did however, represent, better than most, the way progressive music had moved in the early 70s and their intentions should be seen as entirely honourable and their contribution considerable.

Albums: *Yes* (1969), *Time And A Word* (1970), *The Yes Album* (1971), *Fragile* (1971), *Close To The Edge* (1972), *Yessongs* (1973), *Tales From The Topographic Oceans* (1973), *Relayer* (1974), *Going For The One* (1977), *Tormato* (1978), *Drama* (1980), *Yesshows* (1980), *90125* (1983), *90125 Live-The Solos* (1986), *The Big Generator* (1987), *Union* (1991). Compilations: *Yesterdays* (1975), *Classic Yes* (1981).

Young, Kenny

Young first drew attention in New York's song publishing fraternity as the co-author of 'Under The Boardwalk', a 1964 hit for the Drifters, later popularized by the Rolling Stones. His next major success was 'Captain Of Your Ship', recorded in 1968 by Reparata And The Delrons. Although unsuccessful in the USA, the song reached number 13 in the UK. In keeping with several contemporaries, including Carole King and Chip Taylor, Young subsequently began a recording career, but his engaging singer/songwriter releases were commercially unsuccessful. He moved to London during the 70s and later formed a partnership with Herbie Armstrong. The pair formed Fox, who scored a Top 5 hit with 'Only You Can' (1975), and Yellow Dog, which reached number 8 with 'Just One More Night' (1978). However, Young's unashamedly commercial style later fell from favour and he later withdrew from performing.

Albums: *Clever Dogs Chase The Sun* (1972), *Last Stage To Silverwood* (c.70s).

Z

Zappa, Frank

b. Frank Vincent Zappa, 21 December 1940, Baltimore, Maryland, USA. Zappa's parents were second-generation Sicilian Greeks; his father played 'strolling crooner' guitar. At the age of 12 Frank became interested in drums, learning orchestral percussion at summer school in Monterey. By 1956 he was playing drums in a local R&B band called the Ramblers. Early exposure to a record of *Ionisation* by *avant garde* classical composer Edgard Varese instilled an interest in advanced rhythmic experimentation that has never left him. The electric guitar also became a fascination, and he began collecting R&B records that featured guitar solos: Howlin' Wolf with Hubert Sumlin, Muddy Waters, Johnny 'Guitar' Watson and Clarence 'Gatemouth' Brown were special favourites. A school-friend, Don Van Vliet (later to become Captain Beefheart), shared his interest. In 1964 Zappa joined a local R&B outfit, the Soul Giants (Roy Collins - vocals, Roy Estrada - bass, Jimmy Carl Black - drums), and started writing songs for them. They changed their name to the Mothers ('Of Invention' was added at record company insistence). Produced by Tom Wilson in 1966 - the late black producer whose credits included Cecil Taylor, John Coltrane and Bob Dylan - *Freak Out!* was a stunning debut, a two-record set complete with a whole side of wild percussion, a vitriolic protest song, 'Trouble Every Day', and the kind of minute detail (sleevenotes, in-jokes, parodies) that generate instant cult appeal. They made great play of their hair and ugliness, becoming the perfect counter-cultural icon. Unlike the east coast band the Fugs, the Mothers were also musically skilled, a refined instrument for Zappa's eclectic and imaginative ideas. Tours and releases followed, including *We're Only In It For The Money*, (with its brilliant parody of the *Sgt Pepper* record cover) a scathing satire on hippiedom and the reactions to it in the USA, and a notable appearance at the Royal Albert Hall in London (documented in the compulsive *Uncle Meat*). *Cruising With Ruben & The Jets* was an excellent homage to the doo-wop era. British fans were particularly impressed with *Hot Rats*, a record that ditched the sociological commentary for barnstorming jazz-rock, blistering guitar solos, the

extravagant 'Peaches En Regalia' and a cameo appearance by Captain Beefheart on 'Willie The Pimp'. The original band broke up (subsequently to resurface as the Grandmothers). Both the previous two albums appeared on Zappa's own Bizarre record label and together with his other outlet Straight Records he released a number of highly regarded albums (although commercial flops), including those by the GTO's, Larry Wild Man Fischer, Alice Cooper, Tim Buckley and the indispensible Zappa-produced classic *Trout Mask Replica* by Captain Beefheart.

Eager to gain a 'heavier' image than the band that had brought them fame, the Turtles' singers Flo And Eddie joined up with Zappa for the film *200 Motels* and three further albums. *Fillmore East June '71* included some intentionally outrageous subject matter prompting inevitable criticism from conservative observers. 1971 was not a happy year: on 4 December fire destroyed the band's equipment while they were playing at Montreux (an event commemorated in Deep Purple's 'Smoke On The Water') and soon afterwards Zappa was pushed off-stage at London's Rainbow theatre, crushing his larynx (lowering his voice a third), damaging his spine and keeping him wheelchair-bound for the best part of a year. He spent 1972 developing an extraordinary new species of big band fusion (*Waka/Jawaka* and *The Grand Wazoo*), working with top west coast session musicians. However, he found these excellent players dull touring companions, and decided to dump the 'jazztette' for an electric band. 1973's *Overnite Sensation* announced fusion-chops, salacious lyrics and driving rhythms. The live band featured an extraordinary combination of jazz-based swing and a rich, sonorous rock that probably only Zappa (with his interest in modern classical music) could achieve. Percussion virtuoso Ruth Underwood, violinist Jean-Luc Ponty, featured in the *King Kong* project, and keyboardist George Duke shone in this context. *Apostrophe (')* showcased Zappa's talents as a story-teller in the Lord Buckley tradition, and also (in the title track) featured a jam with bassist Jack Bruce: it reached number 10 in the *Billboard* chart in June 1974. *Roxy & Elsewhere* caught the band live, negotiating diabolically hard musical notation - 'Echidna's Arf' and 'The Bebop Tango' - with infectious good humour. *One Size Fits All*, an under-acknowledged masterpiece, built up extraordinary multi-tracked textures. 'Andy' was a song about b-movie cowboys, while 'Florentine Pogen' and 'Inca Roads' were complex extended pieces.

Frank Zappa

In 1975 Captain Beefheart joined Zappa for a tour and despite an earlier rift, sang on *Bongo Fury*, both re-uniting in disgust over the USA's bicentennial complacency. *Zoot Allures* in 1976 was principally a collaboration between Zappa and drummer Terry Bozzio, with Zappa over-dubbing most of the instruments himself. He was experimenting with what he termed 'xenochronicity' (combining unrelated tracks to create a piece of non-synchronous music) and produced intriguing results on 'Friendly Little Finger'. The title track took the concept of sleaze guitar onto a new level (as did the orgasmic moaning of 'The Torture Never Stops'), while 'Black Napkins' was an incomparable vehicle for guitar. If *Zoot Allures* now reads like a response to punk, Zappa was not to forsake large-scale rock showbiz. A series of concerts in New York at Halloween in 1976 had a wildly excited crowd applauding tales of singles bars, devil encounters and stunning Brecker Brothers virtuosity (recorded as *Live In New York*). This album was part of the fall-out from Zappa's break-up with Warner Brothers, who put out three excellent instrumental albums with 'non-authorized covers' (adopted, strangely enough, by Zappa for his CD re-releases): *Studio Tan*, *Sleep Dirt* and *Orchestral Favourites*. The punk-obsessed rock press did not know what to make of music that parodied Miklos Rosza, crossed jazz with cartoon scores, guyed rock 'n' roll hysteria and stretched fusion into the 21st century. Undaunted by still being perceived as a hippie which he clearly was not (*We're Only In It For The Money* had said the last word on the Summer Of Love while it was happening!), Zappa continued to tour.

His guitar-playing seemed to expand into a new dimension: 'Yo' Mama' on *Sheik Yerbouti* (1979) was a taste of the extravaganzas to come. In Ike Willis, Zappa found a vocalist who understood his required combination of emotional detachment and intimacy, and featured him extensively on *Joe's Garage*. After the mid-70s interest in philosophical concepts and band in-jokes, the music became more political. *Tinseltown Rebellion* and *You Are What You Is* commented on the growth of the fundamentalist Right.

In 1982 Zappa had a hit with 'Valley Girl', with his daughter Moon Unit satirizing the accents of young moneyed Hollywood people. That same year saw him produce and introduce a New York concert of music by Edgar Varese. *Ship Arriving Too Late To Save A Drowning Witch* had a title track which indicated that Zappa's interest in extended composition was not waning; this was confirmed by the release of a serious orchestral album in 1983. In 1984 he was quite outrageously prolific: he unearthed an 18th century composer named Francesco Zappa and recorded his work on a synclavier; he released a rock album *Them Or Us*, which widened still further the impact of his scurrilously inventive guitar; and renowned French composer Pierre Boulez conducted Zappa's work on *The Perfect Stranger*. Two releases, *Shut Up 'N Play Yer Guitar* and *Guitar* proved that Zappa's guitar playing was unique; *Jazz From Hell* presented wordless compositions for synclavier that drew inspiration from Conlon Nancarrow; *Thing-Fish* was a 'Broadway musical' about Aids, homophobia and racism. The next big project materialized in 1988: a 12-piece band playing covers, instrumentals and a brace of new political songs (collected respectively as *The Best Band You Never Heard In Your Life*, *Make A Jazz Noise Here* and *Broadway The Hard Way*). They rehearsed for three months and the power and precision of the band were breathtaking, but they broke up during their first tour. As well as the retrospective series *You Can't Do That On Stage Anymore*, Zappa released eight of his most popular bootlegs in a 'beat the boots' campaign. In Czechoslovakia, where he had long been a hero of the cultural underground, he was appointed their Cultural Liaison Officer with the West and in 1991 he announced he would be standing as an independent candidate in the 1992 USA presidential election (almost immediately he received several death threats!). The man never ceases to astonish, both as a musician and composer: on the way he has produced a towering body of work that is probably rock music's closest equivalent to the legacy of Duke Ellington. In November 1991 his daughter confirmed reports that Zappa was suffering from cancer of the prostate; just what effect this illness will have on one of rock's most obsessive workaholics remains to be seen. Zappa's career in perspective shows a musical perfectionist using only the highest standards of musicianship and the finest recording quality. The reissued CD's highlight the extraordinary quality of the original master tapes and Zappa's idealism. Additionally, he is now rightly seen as one of *the* great guitar players of our time. Although much of his ouvre is easily dismissed as flippant, history will almost certainly recognize Zappa as a sophisticated, serious composer and a highly accomplished master of music. The additional fact that he does it all with a remarkable sense of humour should be seen as a positive bonus.

Albums: *Freak Out!* (1966), *Absolutely Free* (1967), *We're Only In It For The Money* (1967), *Lumpy Gravy* (1967), *Crusing With Ruben & The Jets* (1968), *Burnt Weeny Sandwich* (1969), *Uncle Meat* (1969), *Hot Rats* (1969), *Mothermania* (1969), with Jean-Luc Ponty *King Kong* (1970), *Weasels Ripped My Flesh* (1970), *Chunga's Revenge* (1970), *200 Motels* (1971), *Live At The Fillmore East June '71* (1971), *Just Another Band From LA* (1972), *Waka/Jawaka* (1972), *The Grand Wazoo* (1972), *Overnite Sensation* (1973), *Apostrophe (')* (1974), *Roxy & Elsewhere* (1974), *One Size Fits All* (1975), *Bongo Fury* (1975), *Zoot Allures* (1976), *Zappa In New York* (1977), *Studio Tan* (1978), *Sleep Dirt* (1979), *Orchestral Favourites* (1979), *Sheik Yerbouti* (1979), *Baby Snakes* (1979), *Joe's Garage Act 1* (1979), *Joe's Garage Acts 2 & 3* (1979), *Tinseltown Rebellion* (1981), *You Are What You Is* (1981), *Ship Arriving Too Late To Save A Drowning Witch* (1982), *Man From Utopia* (1983), *London Symphony Orchestra Vol I* (1983), *Francesco Zappa* (1984), *Does Humor Belong In Music?* (1984), *Them Or Us* (1984), *The Perfect Stranger* (1984), *Shut Up 'N Play Yer Guitar* (1984), *Guitar* (1984), *Jazz From Hell* (1984), *Thing-Fish* (1984), *Meets The Mothers Of Prevention* (1985), *London Symphony Orchestra Vol II* (1987), *Broadway The Hard Way* (1988), *The Best Band You Never Heard In Your Life* (1991), *Make A Jazz Noise Here* (1991). Beating The Bootleggers: (all released 'officially' in 1991) *'Tis The Season To Be Jelly* (1967), *The Ark* (1968), *Freaks And Motherfuckers* (1970), *Piquantique* (1973), *Unmitigated Audacity* (1974), *Saarbrucken 1978* (1978), *Any Way The Wind Blows* (1979), *As An Am Zappa* (1981). Compilations: *Rare Meat* (1962-63), *You Can't Do That On Stage Any More Vol 1* (1969-88), *You Can't Do That On Stage Any More Vol 2* (1974), *You Can't Do That On Stage Any More Vol 3* (1971-88), *You Can't Do That On Stage Any More Vol 4* (1969-88).

Further reading: *The Real Frank Zappa Book*, Frank Zappa with Peter Occhiogrosso.

Zavaroni, Lena

b. 4 November 1963, Rothesay, Scotland. This winsome singer came down from the Isle of Bute in Scotland during late 1973 to sing her way to victory over a season of ITV's *Opportunity Knocks* talent showcase. She was signed to manager Dorothy Solomon, partner of 60s' impresario Phil Solomon. Zavaroni gained a recording contract and reached the UK Top 10 almost immediately with a revival of the Johnny Otis Show's 'Ma He's Making Eyes At Me' - which was tied-in with a best-selling album. In 1974 too, her version of Lloyd Price's 'Personality' was a lesser hit. These chart strikes were a firm foundation for the exploitation of young Zavaroni as an all-round entertainer via a world tour, extensive television guest appearances, headlining at the London Palladium, a Royal Command Performance and her own BBC 1 series. However, her career had faded to virtual semi-retirement by the 80s, blighted as it was by anorexia nervosa - and the popular media's intrusive focus on unhappy Lena's incomplete success in regaining her health.

Selected albums: *Ma* (1974), *If My Friends Could See Me ...* (1976), *Presenting Lena Zavaroni* (1977), *Songs Are Such Good Things* (1978), *Lena Zavaroni And Her Music* (1979), *Hold Tight It's Lena* (1982).

Z.Z. Top

Formed in Houston, Texas, USA, in 1970, Z.Z. Top evolved out of the city's garage-band circuit and comprises Billy Gibbons (b. 12 December 1949, Houston, Texas, USA; guitar, ex-Moving Sidewalks) with Dusty Hill (b. Joe Hill, 1949, Dallas, Texas, USA; bass) and Frank Beard (b. 10 December 1949, Houston, Texas, USA; drums) both ex-American Blues. Z.Z. Top's original line-up; Gibbons, Lanier Greig (bass) and Dan Mitchell (drums), was also the final version of the Moving Sidewalks. This initial trio completed Z.Z. Top's debut single, 'Salt Lick', before Greig was fired. He was replaced by Bill Ethridge. Mitchell was then replaced by Frank Beard while Dusty Hill subsequently joined in place of Ethridge. Initially Z.Z. Top joined a growing swell of southern boogie bands. Their debut album, while betraying a healthy interest in blues, was firmly within this genre, but *Rio Grande Mud*, indicated a greater flexibility. It included the rousing 'Francine' which, although indebted to the Rolling Stones, gave the trio their first hit and introduced them to a much wider audience.

Their early career coalesced on *Tres Hombres*, a powerful, exciting set which drew from delta music and high energy rock. The group's natural ease was highly effective and Gibbons' startling guitar work was rarely bettered during these times. However successive releases failed to attain the same high standard and Z.Z. Top took an extended vacation following their expansive 1976-1977 tour. The reasons, however, were not solely artistic, as the group now wished to secure a more beneficial recording deal. They resumed their career in 1979 with the superb *Deguello*. Revitalized by their break, the trio offered a series

Lena Zavaroni

of pulsating original songs as well as inspired recreations of Sam And Dave's 'I Thank You' and Elmore James' 'Dust My Broom'. The transitional *El Loco* followed in 1981 and although it lacked the punch of its predecessor, preferring the surreal to the celebratory, the set introduced the growing love of technology which marked the group's subsequent release.

Eliminator deservedly became Z.Z. Top's best-selling album. Fuelled by a series of memorable, tongue-in-cheek sexist videos, it provided several international hit singles, including the million-selling 'Gimme All Your Lovin''. Additionally 'Sharp Dressed Man' and 'Legs' were gloriously simple yet enormously infectious songs. The group skilfully wedded computer-age technology to their barrelhouse R&B to create a truly memorable set which established them as one of the world's leading live attractions. The follow-up, *Afterburner*, was a comparative disappointment although it did feature some excellent individual moments in 'Sleeping Bag' and 'Rough Boy' and the cleverly titled 'Velcro Fly'. Aware of this dichotomy, Z.Z. Top undertook another lengthy break before returning with the impressive *Recycler*. One of rock's maverick attractions, Gibbons, Hill and Beard have retained their original inspirations, yet remain a contemporary force. Their eccentric, colourful image, dark glasses and stetson hats, complete with an almost casual musical dexterity have won over hardened cynics and carping critics. In addition to having produced a fine (but sparse) canon of work, they will stay in the record books as having the longest beards in musical history (although one member Frank Beard is clean-shaven!), and always destined to be the last entry in a popular music encyclopedia.

Albums: *First Album* (1971), *Rio Grande Mud* (1972), *Tres Hombres* (1973), *Fandango!* (1975), *Tejas* (1976), *Deguello* (1979), *El Loco* (1981), *Eliminator* (1983), *Afterburner* (1985), *Recycler* (1990). Compilations: *The Best Of Z.Z. Top* (1977), *Greatest Hits* (1992).

Zevon, Warren

b. 24 January 1947, Chicago, USA. After moving to the west coast, where he sought work as a songwriter in the mid-60s, Zevon wrote songs for the Turtles and Nino Tempo And April Stevens. He recorded several singles for the Turtles' label White Whale, including a version of Bob Dylan's 'If You Gotta Go', as Lyme And Cybelle. By the late 60s, he was signed to Imperial and recorded an inauspicious debut, *Zevon: Wanted Dead Or Alive*,

produced by Kim Fowley. One track from the album, 'She Quit Me', was featured in the movie *Midnight Cowboy*. When the album failed to sell, Zevon took a job on the road as musical director to the Everly Brothers. He subsequently appeared uncredited on their album *Stories We Could Tell* and also guested on Phil Everly's three solo albums. By the early 70s, Zevon was signed as a songwriter by entrepreneur David Geffen, and finally released his long-awaited second album in 1976. *Warren Zevon* was a highly accomplished work, which revealed its creator's songwriting power to an exceptional degree. Produced by Jackson Browne, the work featured the cream of LA's session musicians and included guest appearances from Lindsey Buckingham, Stevie Nicks and Bonnie Raitt. The material ranged from the piano-accompanied 'Frank And Jesse James' to the self-mocking singalong 'Poor Poor Pitiful Me', the bittersweet 'Carmelita' and the majestic sweep of 'Desperados Under The Eaves' with superb harmonies arranged by Carl Wilson. Linda Ronstadt's cover of 'Hasten Down The Wind' also brought Zevon to the attention of a wider audience.

The follow-up *Excitable Boy* was released two years later and revealed another astonishing leap in Zevon's musical development. The production was confident and accomplished and the range of material even more fascinating. Zevon tackled American politics and history on 'Roland The Thompson Gunner' and 'Veracruz', wrote one of his finest and most devastating love songs in 'Accidentally Like A Martyr' and employed his satiric thrust to the heart on 'Excitable Boy' and 'Werewolves Of London'. A superb trilogy of Zevon albums was completed with *Bad Luck Streak In Dancing School* which was most notable for its inventive use of orchestration. Again, it was the sheer diversity of material and mood that impressed. The classical overtones of the title track, 'Interlude No. 2' and 'Wild Age' were complemented by Zevon's biting satire which was by now unmatched by any American artist, bar Randy Newman. 'Gorilla You're A Desperado' was a humorous attack on LA consumerism, while 'Play It All Night Long' was an anti-romantic portrait of rural life that contrasted markedly with the prevailing idyllic country rock mentality. Zevon's vision was permeated with images of incest and disease: 'Daddy's doing sister Sally/Grandma's dying of cancer now/The cattle all have brucellosis/We'll get through somehow'. Zevon's ability to attract the interest and respect of his songwriting contemporaries was once more emphasized by the presence of Bruce Springsteen, with whom he co-wrote 'Jeannie Needs A Shooter'. Although Zevon seemed likely to establish himself as one of the prominent singer/songwriters of the 80s, personal problems would soon undo his progress. A promising live album was followed by the much neglected *The Envoy*. This concept album sold poorly and was the last major work from Zevon for five years. During the interim, he became an alcoholic and underwent counselling and therapy. He returned in 1987 with *Sentimental Hygeine*, a welcome return to top form, which featured a new array of guest stars including Neil Young, Michael Stipe and Peter Buck (from R.E.M.), Bob Dylan, Don Henley (formerly of the Eagles), Jennifer Warnes and Brian Setzer (ex-Stray Cats). Zevon also formed a band with Peter Buck, Mike Mills and Bill Berry under the name Hindu Love Gods, and issued an album in 1990 entitled *Hindu Love Gods*. Zevon's power was not lost among the star credits and shone through on a powerful set of songs, several of which brutally detailed his fight back from alcoholism. Never self-pitying, Zevon could afford a satiric glimpse at his own situation in 'Detox Mansion': 'Well it's tough to be somebody/And it's hard to fall apart/Up here on Rehab Mountain/We gonna learn these things by heart'. Zevon promoted the album extensively and has since built upon his reputation with the finely-produced *Transverse City* and well-received *Mr Bad Example*.

Albums: *Zevon: Wanted Dead Or Alive* (1969), *Warren Zevon* (1976), *Excitable Boy* (1978), *Bad Luck Streak In Dancing School* (1980), *Stand In The Fire* (1981), *The Envoy* (1982), *Sentimental Hygeine* (1987), *Transverse City* (1989), *Mr Bad Example* (1992). Compilation: *A Quiet Normal Life - The Best Of Warren Zevon* (1988).

The Guinness Encyclopedia of Popular Music

Compiled and Edited by Colin Larkin

' A landmark work. As much as the history of popular music deserves. ★★★★★' *Q Magazine*

'This is an absolutely invaluable addition to any musicologist's shelf.' *Vox*

The most comprehensive and authoritative guide to popular music that has ever been published, *The Guinness Encyclopedia of Popular Music* covers every important artist, band, genre, group, event, instrument, publisher, promoter, record company and musical style from the world of popular music in four 832-page volumes in a slipcase.

The product of over four years of intensive labour by an international group of more than 100 skilled writers, musicologists and advisors, its scope is truly global. Compiled in an A-Z format, it covers all forms of popular music from 1900 to 1992 and contains almost 10,000 entries varying in length from 100 to 5,000 words.

A bibliography of over 4,000 entries is included along with a full index of artists' names.

For further details of this essential reference work, please write to:
Section D,
The Marketing Department,
Guinness Publishing,
33 London Road,
Enfield,
Middlesex EN2 6DJ,
England.

Proposed Titles for Inclusion in the

'Guinness Who's Who of Popular Music Series'

The Guinness Who's Who of 50s Music
The Guinness Who's Who of 60s Music★
The Guinness Who's Who of 70s Music★
The Guinness Who's Who of 80s Music
The Guinness Who's Who of Indie and New Wave Music★
The Guinness Who's Who of Blues Music★
The Guinness Who's Who of Folk Music
The Guinness Who's Who of Reggae
The Guinness Who's Who of Soul Music
The Guinness Who's Who of Country Music★
The Guinness Who's Who of Jazz★
The Guinness Who's Who of Heavy Metal Music★
The Guinness Who's Who of Gospel Music
The Guinness Who's Who of UK Rock and Pop
The Guinness Who's Who of USA Rock and Pop
The Guinness Who's Who of Danceband Pop
The Guinness Who's Who of World Music
The Guinness Who's Who of Stage Musicals

★ Already published

For further information on any of these titles please write to:
Section D,
The Marketing Department,
Guinness Publishing,
33 London Road,
Enfield,
Middlesex EN2 6DJ,
England

The Guinness Who's Who of Jazz

General Editor: Colin Larkin

The history of jazz is a long and varied one, from its beginnings in the whorehouses and bars of the turn of the century, to the top concert halls of today. Encapsulating the embryonic forms of New Orleans, trad, boogie-woogie, and the ragtime of Louis Armstrong, Jelly Roll Morton, Scott Joplin and Fats Waller, The Guinness Who's Who of Jazz, follows the progress of jazz through the big bands and jive artists such as Paul Whitman, Bix Biederbeck, Duke Ellington, Count Basie, Glenn Miller, Cab Calloway and Louis Jordan on to the present day, via the innovative bop sounds of the 50s and 60s with Miles Davis, John Coltrane, Coleman Hawkins, Dave Brubeck, Dizzy Gillespie and the modern sounds of Andy Shepard, John Surman, Wynton Marsalis, Elton Dean and Courtney Pine. Special consideration is given to the talent of the past decade, making this book instantly more accessible than all its rivals.

The Guinness Who's Who of Jazz also contains entries on the various noted orchestra and band sidemen, the composers, arrangers and label owners. With hundreds of entries it will become an indispensable book for aficionados of the music and will act as an introduction to its many newcomers.

This book is available from all good bookshops and selected record stores. For information on this or on forthcoming titles in the series, please write to:

Section D,
The Marketing Department,
Guinness Publishing,
33 London Road,
Enfield,
Middlesex EN2 6DJ,
England

The Guinness Who's Who of Sixties Music

General Editor: Colin Larkin

From the publishers of *The Guinness Encyclopedia of Popular Music* comes the definitive guide to the groups and artists who created the music of the 60s. From the early years of Del Shannon, Bobby Darin, Ricky Nelson, and Cliff Richard; the Beach Boys, Jan and Dean and the Shangri-Las to the beat-boom with the Beatles and the Rolling Stones; the 'swinging London' era of the Who and the Kinks, and the explosion of sound from California's west coast with the Byrds, Doors, Jefferson Airplane and Grateful Dead. Folk protest, the blues boom, psychedelia, soul, jazz, ska, Merseybeat, pirate radio plus the impact on a whole generation by Bob Dylan - it's all told here with information on the musicians, songwriters and personalities.

From those who survived to those lost in the mists of time, everything you'd ever want to know is included in this complete and accurate record of the music and major artists of the decade. With hundreds of entries written by some of today's leading rock writers, this is the definative guide to the movers and shakers of 60s music.

This book is available from all good bookshops and from selected record stores. For information on this or on forthcoming titles in the series, please write to:

Section D,
The Marketing Department,
Guinnesss Publishing,
33 London Road,
Enfield,
Middlesex EN2 6DJ,
England

The Guinness Who's Who of Indie and New Wave Music

General Editor: Colin Larkin

From the publishers of *The Guinness Encyclopedia of Popular Music* comes the definitive guide to the groups and artists who have moulded the shape of popular music in the 70s 80s and 90s. From the beginnings of punk in the late-70s with the Sex Pistols, Clash, Damned, X-Ray Spex and the Buzzcocks in the UK, and Television, Talking Heads, Blondie and the Ramones in the US, modern popular music was shaken to its foundations. These bands paved the way in the ensuing years for many new and varied forms of exciting music including Siouxsie And The Banshees, Joy Division/New Order, the Cure, Smiths, Cocteau Twins, Birthday Party, Jesus And Mary Chain, Happy Mondays, Stone Roses, James and R.E.M.

This book contains entries on all these bands plus many others on groups and artists who are usually, and unjustifiably, ignored in lesser encyclopedias. In all, there are hundreds of entries including contributions by some of the leading pop and indie writers today plus an introduction by Johnny Rogan.

This book is available from all good bookshops and from selected record stores. For information on this or on forthcoming titles in the series, please write to:

Section D,
The Marketing Department,
Guinness Publishing,
33 London Road,
Enfield,
Middlesex,
EN2 6DJ,
England.

The Guinness Who's Who of Blues

General Editor: Colin Larkin

From the publishers of *The Guinness Encyclopedia of Popular Music* comes the definitive guide to the Blues. The return of Eric Clapton and Gary Moore to their blues roots has coincided with the rise of musicians such as Robert Cray and Jeff Healey. This, together with the phenominal revival of John Lee Hooker's career with *The Healer* and *Boom Boom* puts us in the midst of the biggest blues boom since the 60s. Collected in this volume are the artists who shaped the blues, which in turn greatly influenced the development of popular music in the 20th century. Included are, Elmore James, Robert Johnson, Muddy Waters, B.B. King, Lightnin' Hopkins, Leadbelly, Buddy Guy and Albert Collins; the great singers Bessie Smith, Victoria Spivey, Billie Holiday, Big Joe Turner and Koko Taylor and the legion of white musician's who have popularized the blues since the 60s, such as Alexis Korner, Paul Butterfield, Mike Bloomfield, Roy Buchanan, John Mayall, Johnny Winter, Peter Green and Stevie Ray Vaughan.

This book is available from all good bookshops and from selected record stores. For information on this or on forthcoming titles in the series, please write to:

Section D,
The Marketing Department,
Guinness Publishing,
33 London Road,
Enfield,
Middlesex,
EN2 6DJ,
England.